Writing for Television and Radio

Writing for

Television

and Radio

by

ROBERT L. HILLIARD

Third Edition, Revised & Enlarged

COMMUNICATION ARTS BOOKS

Hastings House, Publishers • New York 10016

Mary Ellen's book, with this

added dedication to Mark and Mara

First Edition, September 1962
Revised Edition, July 1967
Third Edition, Reset, Revised and Enlarged, January 1976

Library of Congress Cataloging in Publication Data
Hilliard, Robert L
    Writing for television and radio.
    (Communication arts books)
    Includes bibliographies and index.
    1. Television authorship. 2. Radio authorship.
I. Title.
PN1992.7.H5   808.2'2   75-15971
ISBN 0-8038-8048-0
ISBN 0-8038-8076-6 pbk.

Published simultaneously in Canada by
Saunders of Toronto, Ltd., Don Mills, Ontario
Designed by Al Lichtenberg
Printed in the United States of America

Contents

Preface

DURING A WORLD WAR II talk to the troops, Lieutenant General Brehan Somervell said that "we fight for free radio — for the right to listen to what we want and to turn off what we don't want." Freedom of communication is the keystone of a democratic society. The right to transmit and the right to receive. And the right not to transmit and the right not to receive. Communications, including radio and television, must be open to the marketplace of ideas. All people should have the privilege of communicating any and all ideas to all other people. All people should have the privilege of hearing those ideas or of turning them off. Only an informed, thinking society can remain free and be able to initiate and achieve individual and group self-realization and progress. An uninformed public or one with access to only one side of a controversial issue is easy prey for the subverter of individual and group freedoms.

A principal purpose of this book is to help you, as the writer of communications materials that influence people, to understand and implement the need to continuously make available all forms of information and all shades of opinion. This is true whether you write plays which, in their structure and orientation, are logical vehicles for a diversity of ideas or whether you write continuity which, by design, may ostensibly avoid significant ideas. A further purpose of this book is to present concrete approaches to and examples of the kinds of "bread and butter" writing being done professionally in all program types on television and radio. But its orientation is not solely "how-to." Its aim is to show, as well, what can be done in terms of the potentials of the media to affect humanistically the thinking and actions of people, to achieve high aesthetic standards in the media, to help you not only to write successfully the programs seen and heard today, but to improve that programming in the public interest.

You will find several program writing approaches in this book: those that have been tried frequently and successfully, including comments from practitioners in the field, particularly those who would hire you to write similar scripts; those that have only occasionally been tried, such as some of the approaches of an Edward R. Murrow; and others that have not yet been tried, but which you may be motivated to use as practicality and conscience permit and dictate.

Some of you will find degrees of disproportion in the book's coverage of certain types of writing, depending on your own special interests. In part this is due to the increasing costs of book publishing, which make a totally definitive volume priced beyond the means of many students. We set priorities. The areas of greatest potential employment for the broadcast writer are commercials, news and public affairs which, along with the play, comprise almost all of the writing being done for television and radio today.

All types of broadcast writing — the play, the documentary, the commercial, the news program, the children's program, the women's program, minority programs, talks programs, game shows, music programs, education and information programs, variety shows, special events and features, and others — are presented here with the understanding that you can't "teach" anyone through a book or in a classroom how to be a great writer. One can learn through these means the potentials of a medium and the approaches, forms and techniques of writing individual script-types. In the radio-television field this may well be sufficient to do a good job of writing the everyday kinds of programs that are considered professionally and commercially successful. I believe this book can help you do this. But becoming a great writer — or, to many people, even a competent writer — requires, in addition to technique, the kind of psychological/sociological/political/environmental/educational/aesthetic background that we sometimes refer to as "talent."

Picasso wrote some plays, but his principal talent was not in the field of writing. Working with this book will introduce you to the field of writing for television and radio. But it will not automatically make you a great writer. If you have the talent and you learn the techniques and you write, write, write until it comes out of your ears, then hopefully this book will have been of some help to you in achieving your goals. But don't bet on it. It may be that your time and efforts would have been better invested in buying an easel. Or a plumber's wrench.

There are many people to whom I am grateful for their help in completing this third edition of *Writing for Television and Radio:* Russ Neale, executive vice president of Hastings House, for his continued encouragement and calm, even in the face of many revisions and extended deadlines; his assistants, Jim Moore, Lee Tobin and Al Lichtenberg, for their dedication to what was a more than usually complicated job; Mary Ellen Verheyden-

Hilliard for her thorough editorial review of the second edition and her critique for changes and revisions; Barbara Allen for her detailed recommendations for updating, editing and new material; Yuri Tanaka for her graciousness in typing the manuscript in bits and pieces, frequently with short deadlines; and the many people in agencies, stations, networks, publications, production organizations and associations who went out of their way to provide scripts, quotes and other materials — if I tried to list all the names there are some who might inadvertantly be left out.

Russ Neale, publisher of the *Communication Arts Books* series, informs me that *Writing for Television and Radio* continues to be the leading work of its kind. I am grateful for its outreach and I hope that its humanistic as well as practical purpose may have had and may continue to have some effect on making television and radio — through your writing — more responsive to and more responsible for the advancement of the needs, desires and expectations of all people.

Washington, D.C.   Robert L. Hilliard
September, 1975

1

The Mass Media

THE TELEVISION AND radio writer aims at an audience that at one and the same time is very small and very large, that has much in common and almost nothing in common, that is a tightly knit group and a disunified mass.

Millions of people may be listening to or seeing the material developed by the writer. Yet, any one group within this vast audience is apt to be a small one — usually a family group, at home, in everyday surroundings. The distractions of everyday life are constantly at hand, continuously operative, and likely to pull the individual viewer or listener away from the program. Unlike the theatre or movie audience, the television and radio audience is not "captive." It has not paid a fee and, if it doesn't like what it sees or hears, it is under no compunction to stay. The theatre and film audience is, to varying degrees, selective; moreover, with the availability of newspaper reviews, it generally knows something about the play or film it is going to see. The television audience is less selective and frequently will tune in a program from force of habit or because it has nothing else to do at the time. The writer for television and radio, therefore, must capture the imaginations and interests of this undiscriminating audience as soon as possible. Each word, each picture must be purposeful, must gain attention and hold interest. Ideally, there should be no irrelevancies in the writing, no extraneous moments. (The concept of the television home audience is changing, however, and as cable systems with their monthly subscribers' fees continue to grow, and as "pay" television with its per-program fees enters more and more markets, the home television viewer may become more like the movie- and theatre-goer in terms of a monetary commitment to the program s/he has tuned in.)

Psychologists tell us that the smaller the group and the greater the physical distance between individual members of the audience, the better chance there is to appeal to the intellect. The physical groupings of the television and radio audience offer this opportunity to a greater extent than has been utilized thus far. On the other hand, because it is an audience that can remove itself quickly and easily with only the flick of a finger, emotional empathy must also be established. The use of universal emotional impressions is important because the audience largely is unknown to the writer and no immediate responses to determine the audience's reaction can be felt or measured.

Theatre audiences and, to some degree, film audiences — or at least those within any given movie house — may have common interests or backgrounds: a common geographical location, the same relative economic or social status within the residential area of the city where the movie house is located, or similar educational backgrounds or cultural interests which prompted their attendance. The television and radio audience, as a whole, watching or listening to any one given performance, is likely to have more diverse opinions, emotional prejudices, educational, social and political backgrounds and personal creeds than the theatre or movie audience. The audience of the mass media is as varied as is the population of the United States.

To make any single piece of material effective, the writer often tries to find a common denominator that will reach and hold as many as possible of the groups and individuals watching the more than 120 million television sets and listening to the more than 400 million radios in use in this country. The Federal Communications Commission's hearings and rule-making for diversity in program control — including the Multiple Ownership Rules (and the Duopoly Rule), the Prime-time Access Rule and the requirement for Ascertainment of Community Needs, plus the Department of Justice's concern with media cross-ownership — suggest that business rather than artistic or social considerations have controlled television and radio programming. The sponsor's primary aim frequently seems to be to present material that will not offend anyone. The sponsor and the producer thus far in the history of our mass media have searched for and often found the broadest common denominator, which frequently turns out to be the lowest. Rating organizations substantiate the advertising agency approach by measuring the percentages or numbers of people who allegedly watch any given program. Presuming that the ratings do have some validity — and many observers believe that the exceedingly small sample purportedly representing the entire American populace, as well as uncontrolled factors in interviewing techniques, nullify the claims of the rating systems — they do not usually measure accurately (although some of the ratings attempt to do so in part) the audience's reaction, its potential buying power, or the effectiveness of either the program or the commercial message.

In the late 1960s and early 1970s the concept of demographics began to play an important role in programming, particularly in radio. Stations began analyzing their markets and zeroing in on a target audience, specifically orienting program materials to reach one or more particular age, sex, professional, economic, educational and similar groups. Many stations carry their demographic breakdowns into which interest group might be listening in a particular place (home, work, car) at a particular time of day.

Generally, however, there is an acceptance of the lowest common denominator and a reliance upon a *quantitative* measurement. The cultural contributions of our mass media have become, for the most part, comparatively mediocre in quality and repetitive in nature. An outstanding casualty of this trend has been serious drama. In March, 1965, after a study of competition and responsibility in network television broadcasting, the FCC stated: "By and large, episodes of television series are produced on the basis of 'formulas' — approved in advance by the network corporation and often its mass advertisers — which 'set' the characters, 'freeze' theme and action and limit subject matter to 'tested' commercial patterns." As this is written, the pattern has with few exceptions remained the same.

In the early 1970s, spurred especially by Public Television's imports of several BBC drama series (such as those shown on PBS' "Masterpiece Theatre") and American-produced series such as "Hollywood Theatre" and, in part, by public pressures of several citizen groups, sporadic attempts were made by commercial television to bring non-"schlock" drama to the mass audience. Except for some individual productions such as Joe Papp's New York Shakespeare Festival TV presentations of "Much Ado About Nothing" and "Sticks and Bones," and specials such as "Miss Jane Pittman" and "The Execution of Private Slovik," no real revitalization occurred, and one of the artistically best commercial network series turned out to be an importation of BBC's "The Wives of Henry VIII."

RADIO AND THE MASS AUDIENCE

RADIO IS NOT limited by what can be presented visually. The writer can develop a mind picture which is bounded only by the extent of the audience's imagination. Sound effects, music, dialogue — even silence — are combined and integrated to provide the most effective presentation. However, the setting, physical characters, characterization, plot and all of the other elements of the dramatic or non-dramatic show must be conveyed through sound alone. This absence of sight may be a handicap as well as an advantage.

Radio does permit the writer complete freedom of time and place. There is no limitation on the setting or on movement in time or in space. The writer can create unlimited forms of physical action and can bypass in the twinkling of a musical bridge minutes or centuries of time. Orson Welles' radio adaptation of H. G. Wells' *War of the Worlds* is famous for its many provocative productions throughout the world. Television once attempted a similar adaptation. It was unsuccessful. Limiting the action to what one can present visually restricts the imaginative potentials of word and sound.

In listening to any given radio program, the audience is not selective. It does not pick out what it wants to, but hears only what the writer wants it to. In this way the writer controls the direction of the attention of the radio audience. Of course, different listeners may imagine the same sound stimulus in different ways because each person's psychological and experiential background is different. In the creation of a mind picture in the imagination, the audience does "see." The radio writer can create this mind picture more effectively than can the writer in any other medium. The audience "sees" places, characters and events just as the writer wants it to. The audience sometimes even experiences the emotions the writer wants it to. The subjectivity of the medium permits the writer to place the audience right alongside of or at any given distance from the character or participant in the radio show, providing the writer makes it quite clear exactly where that place is. Voice distances and relationships of the performers to the microphone determine the "view" the audience has of the characters and of the setting. For example, if the audience is listening to two characters in conversation and the writer has the first character "fade off" from the microphone, the audience, in its imagination, stays with the second character and sees the first character moving away.

Although a scene must be set in dialogue and sound rather than established through sight as in the other performing media, such orientation and exposition must not be done too obviously. Radio often uses a narrator or announcer to set the mood, establish character relationships, give information about the program participants, describe the scene, summarize previous action and even comment on the attitude the audience might be expected to have toward the program, the participants or the characters in the play. This background material may be given through dialogue, music, sound effects or, sometimes, even through silence.

Radio is, indeed, the art of the imagination. The radio writer is restricted only by the breadth and depth of the mind's eye of the audience. A vivid illustration of this and, appropriately, an example of good scriptwriting is Stan Freberg's award-winning spot, "Stretching the Imagination."

MAN:	Radio? Why should I advertise on radio? There's nothing to look at . . . no pictures.
GUY:	Listen, you can do things on radio you couldn't possibly do on TV.
MAN:	That'll be the day.
GUY:	Ah huh. All right, watch this. (AHEM) O.K. people, now I give you the cue, I want the 700-foot mountain of whipped cream to roll into Lake Michigan which has been drained and filled with hot chocolate. Then the Royal Canadian Air Force will fly overhead towing the 10-ton maraschino cherry which will be dropped into the whipped cream, to the cheering of 25,000 extras. All right . . . cue the mountain . . .

SOUND: GROANING AND CREAKING OF MOUNTAINS INTO BIG SPLASH!
GUY: Cue the air force!
SOUND: DRONE OF MANY PLANES.
GUY: Cue the maraschino cherry . . .
SOUND: WHISTLE OF BOMB INTO BLOOP! OF CHERRY HITTING WHIPPED CREAM.
GUY: Okay, twenty-five thousand cheering extras . . .
SOUND: ROAR OF MIGHTY CROWD. SOUND BUILDS UP AND CUTS OFF SHARP! Now . . . you wanta try that on television?
MAN: Well . . .
GUY: You see . . . radio is a very special medium, because it stretches the imagination.
MAN: Doesn't television stretch the imagination?
GUY: Up to 21 inches, yes.

Courtesy of Freberg, Ltd.

The *potentials* of radio as described above, however, are not necessarily reflected in radio of the 1970s. Except for commercials which, aside from the ethics involved in purpose and content, can be highly artistic, the "drama" aspects of radio are virtually dormant. In the early and mid-1970s there was a revival of "old-time" radio drama and some new dramatic series were tried out. But as this is written it is still too early to tell whether this is a reflection of the country's current "nostalgia kick" or whether there is a real trend toward the resurrection of radio drama. Many individual performers and producer/directors have experimented with the sound possibilities of radio, utilizing special effects and techniques in their own featured spots (distinguished here from the majority of disc jockeys, who primarily play records and tapes interspersed with some commentary). Radio in the late 1970s, however, is primarily music, news and commercials.

TELEVISION AND THE MASS AUDIENCE

TELEVISION MAKES USE of the same subjective potentials as does radio, but is more specific in directing the attention and feeling of the audience. Television utilizes many of the techniques of the theatre and of the film, and the audience is directed through sight as well as through hearing. With its use of mechanical and electronic devices, television has more flexibility than the theatre but, because of the limitation of sight as previously pointed out, not so much flexibility as has radio. Nevertheless, television can combine the sound and the audience-orientation of radio, the live continuous performance of theatre and the electronic techniques of the film. It is capable of fusing the best of all previous communications media.

On the other hand, television also has specific limitations. Although it can break the always flexible unities of time and place, it is greatly restricted in production by *physical* time and space. Time-wise, the writer cannot develop a script as fully as might be desirable. The Television Code of the National Association of Broadcasters (NAB) recommends a maximum of 16 commercial minutes per hour in non-prime time, 9½ minutes in prime time and 12 minutes for independent stations. The actual program length, therefore, after commercial and intro and outro credit time has been subtracted, runs from approximately 10- to 12-minutes for the quarter-hour program, 21- to 24-minutes for the half-hour program and 42- to 49-minutes for the hour program. (The recommendation for commercial minutes on both AM and FM radio, incidentally — which does not suggest the same considerations for the writer as do the TV times inasmuch as radio has very few cohesively scripted programs, as has TV — is 18-minutes.) This limitation is a particular hindrance in the writing of a dramatic program. Spacewise, the writer is hampered by the limitation of the camera view, the limitation of settings for live-type taped television (the term "live-type taped television," as used here, refers to the taped program which uses the continuous action, non-edited procedure of the live show; it is done as if it were a live show) and the comparatively small viewing area of the television receiver. The writer must orient the script toward small groups on the screen at any one time and make extended use of the close-up shot in studio-produced taped shows, as differentiated from TV films. Sets and outdoor effects are also obviously limited. These limitations prompted the intimate, subjective approach in dramatic writing and resulted, in television's so-called "golden age," in the probing, slice-of-life play.

Even studio-bound, taped television does have a reasonable freedom of movement, however. The camera serves, in a sense, as a moving proscenium arch. The writer may use detail sets, projections, electronic inserts, film clips and multiple sets to achieve a broadening or a variety of place. The application and gradual domination of film technique in television production, and the concomitant movement of television's production center from New York to Hollywood, has changed some of the writing approaches and has resulted in much TV being boxed-in versions of the motion picture.

Television combines both subjectivity and objectivity in relation to the audience, fusing two areas that are usually thought of as being mutually exclusive. Through use of the camera and electronic devices, the writer and director frequently may give the audience's attentions and emotions a subjective orientation by directing them to specific stimuli. The close-up, the split screen and similar devices are especially useful. The television audience cannot choose, as does the theatre audience, from the totality of presentation upon a stage. The television audience can be directed to a specific stimulus which most effectively achieves the purpose of the specific moment in the script. Attention can be directed to subtle reaction as well as to obvious action. At the same time, the television audience can be given an objective orientation in that the personality of the performer as a person can be brought more openly and directly to the viewer than can be done in the large auditorium of the theatre or movie-house. Although the purpose of most drama is to create illusion, the television narrator, master of ceremonies, announcer, actor or other performer can achieve excellent non-illusionary relationships with the audience. The small screen and the intimacy of the living-room create effects and require techniques quite different from those of the film being shown in the movie-theatre.

The basic exposition of a television program should be presented through the action, logically and quickly. In radio it is more difficult to reach the audience through the action, and a narrator or announcer frequently is necessary. Television may use a narrator or announcer, of course, but preferably as voice-over. Visual devices such as title cards, pantomime and other art work are effective, too. It must be remembered that radio is aural while television is essentially visual, and where a visual element in TV can achieve the desired effect, it should take precedence over sound — in many instances, dialogue even may be superfluous. There is the story told about the famous Broadway playwright, noted for his scintillating dialogue, who was asked to write a film script shortly after sound movies became practical and popular. He wrote a 30-page first act treatment in which a husband and wife, on vacation, went up to their hotel room. Through 30 minutes of witty and sparkling conversation it was revealed that the wife was becoming increasingly disturbed over her husband's attention to other women. An experienced movie director went over the script and thought it presented a good situation. He changed one thing. He substituted for the 30 pages of dialogue less than one page of visual directions in which the husband and wife enter the hotel, register and walk to the elevator perfunctorily, the husband looks appraisingly at the female elevator operator, and a look of great displeasure comes over the wife's face as the elevator doors close. Sound should be considered secondary in television production; the essential ingredient is visual action. This principle applies to most non-dramatic forms, as well as to the play.

SUBJECT MATTER

THE WRITER NOT only faces a problem with the quality level of the material, but faces concrete manifestations of this problem in the selection of specific subject matter. Television and radio writing is affected greatly by censorship. In commercial television and radio the control over the final script to be presented frequently rests in the hands of the advertising agencies representing the sponsor. In some cases, the person in charge of the television and/or radio division of the agency or of the individual account is an advertising executive, a businessperson with little or no knowledge of the artistic needs or potentials of the media. It has been alleged that three hostile postcards from a vacant lot will influence a sponsor or advertising agency to do almost anything. The sponsor, however, isn't the only potential censor. The originating station — or the continuity acceptance departments of the networks — may reject material it deems unsuitable.

By the early 1970s national spot advertising had grown to the extent that agency control over individual scripts gradually diminished and network control became predominant. At the same time, the gradual disappearance of network radio programming returned control over content to the individual radio station. Control may gradually move away from the networks and to the regional and local levels for television, too. The trend away from national advertising was underscored in 1974 by the Television Bureau of Advertising. In reorienting its goals "for the next 20 years," it changed its emphasis from selling national advertisers to developing local and regional television sponsorship.[1]

The increasing willingness of society to discuss issues and use language previously taboo was reflected in all media, and broadcasting — usually a follower, not a leader of public taste and thought, except in the area of news information — became more free in its presentation of the stuff of real life.

Censorable Material

Censorship falls into two major categories: material that is "censorable" and material that is "controversial."

Censorable material, as discussed here, is that which generally is considered not in good taste for the home television audience, although this same material might be perfectly acceptable in the legitimate theatre or in films. Profanity, the sanctity of marriage and the home, suicide, unduly provocative sex and other similar items are theoretically governed by censorship codes or, as sometimes called, standards of good conduct.

The broadcasting industry itself has set up codes of good standards, such as those developed by the National Association of Broadcasters (the NAB Television Code and Radio Code are in the Appendix). Virtually all of the major television and radio stations, most of the smaller ones and all of the networks belong to the NAB and subscribe to the Codes. On paper the Codes seem almost idyllic. Although considered by many to be too restrictive of realism and tending to reflect the attitudes of the "little old lady in tennis shoes," the Codes would, if adhered to, for the most part tend to raise the artistic and cultural levels of programming and of the public. Unfortunately, there is no effective enforcement of the Codes. The decision to follow Code procedures and the determination whether a given segment of material falls under a particular Code category is up to the individual director, producer, station, agency or network. In most situations "reviewers" — some would call them censors" — do check material for obvious breaches of the Code. Most particularly, however, they check for material which, even if it does fulfill the cultural or public service provisions of the Code, conflicts with the desires of the sponsor or the policy of the station. It is in these latter areas that the greatest dangers lie. Many of the items censored are not necessarily in bad taste. When they are not, any censorship constitutes not the censorship of *censorable* material, but the censorship of *controversial* material. The NAB has not generally been known to take forceful action against its members to enforce its Codes.

The Federal Communications Commission frequently acts as an arbiter of public taste. In addition to implementing the Communications Act of 1934, As Amended, which authorizes fines or license suspension for "communications containing profane or obscene words, language, or meaning . . . ." the FCC has by both suggestion and order acted, according to some people (particularly broadcasters), as a censoring body. Two prime examples: in 1971 the FCC issued an order requiring stations to review the lyrics of all records played to avoid any promotion, through such lyrics, of illegal drugs. In 1973 the FCC fined a station for its so-called "topless" radio format — a phone-in format in which women, particularly, were encouraged to discuss their sex attitudes and practices. Through thinly-veiled warnings to other stations the FCC successfully eliminated that short-lived but highly popular programming approach. The question of obscenity has been raised on a number of occasions and in some important cases — including a nominal fine of a non-commercial station which had aired a program containing profanity — the FCC sought a test case in the courts so that the Supreme Court ultimately would have to determine what constituted profanity and obscenity in broadcasting. But non-commercial and commercial stations alike "paid their money and went home."

What kind of language is or is not allowed is of critical importance to the writer. Language, whether explicit in words or implicit in visual action, is, after all, the essence of the writer's craft. The degree and kind of censorship of "censorable" material is a key to the degree and kind of artistic approach and script content permissible to the writer. Shortly after the FCC took a strong stand on obscenity and indecency over the air in the early 1970s, *BM/E* magazine published a summary of the FCC's approach and attitude: [2]

The question as to the scope of permissible language over-the-air has been the subject of heated debate in the courts, at the Commission, and a problem of great dimension to broadcasters. How does a broadcaster best balance the interests of a specialized audience's right to hear speech which is "like it is" with the general audience's right to be free from listening to language which offends their personal standards of decency? To what limits may a broadcaster allow an interviewed guest to come forth with spontaneous utterances of salty language? Will a broadcaster's restrictions on the type of language used inhibit or enhance the desired "robust and wide-open debate"[1] encouraged by the FCC?

1. *Red Lion Broadcasting Co.* v. *Federal Communications Commission,* 395 U.S. 367.

In a series of forthright opinions on free speech, U.S. Courts have proscribed certain well-defined and narrowly limited classes of speech, the prevention and punishment of which have never been thought to raise any constitutional problem. These include the lewd and obscene, the profane, the libelous, and the insulting or "fighting" words — those which by their very utterance inflict injury or tend to incite an immediate breach of the peace[2]. In all cases, the courts have set standards for proscribed speech which take into account the considerations which gave birth to the nomenclature — the nature of the speech and the circumstances under which it was uttered.

With both the constitutional imperative and historical case precedents in mind, Congress, in 1948, passed legislation which prohibited "obscene, indecent, or profane language by means of radio communication" and imposed a punishment of up to $10,000 fine or imprisonment of up to two years[3]. Its language was derived from Section 326 of the 1934 Federal Communications Act which expressed, to a substantial degree, that this prohibition was *not* to be construed as giving the Commission the power of censorship over programming.

The few opinions construing the U.S. Code 1464 prohibition have, when taken together, involved a mixing of principles which tend to obliterate any clear demarcation or distinction. Like the "freedom of speech" cases before them, the FCC and the courts have imposed no semantic straightjacket in defining a standard for "obscene, indecent, or profane language." *Per contra,* in the few pertinent cases, they have attempted to balance a number of considerations, including the following:[4]

1) Whether to the average person, applying contemporary community standards, the dominant theme of the language taken as a whole appealed to prurient interests;[5] 2) the subject matter of the program, the context in which the utterance was made, and the value or relevance of the utterance to the segment of listeners to which it was directed; 3) whether the questionable language was essential to the integrity or reality of the presentation; 4) the time of the broadcast, the likelihood that children might be in the audience, and the mitigating fact of cautionary announcements; 5) whether the broadcaster had an opportunity to control the content of the speech, whether the utterance was spontaneous, and whether the program presented was live or filmed.

Like the criterion established in the general "obscenity cases" *(Roth, Jacobellis, Memoirs, Ginsburg),* the prevailing limits of permissible language over-the-air is, at best, confusing. An attempt to cite the perimeters of free speech, in order to give broadcasters some boundaries for judging their own problems in this area, follows.

Marginal or objectionable language, which falls into the category of "obscene, indecent, or profane," often occurs over-the-air during the "talk show" or "personal interview." Such language usually appears in the form of the curse expletive ("hell," "damn," "God damn it!") or the sexual expletive ("f . . .," "m.f.," "s . . ."). In the *WUHY-FM* case, the FCC found the personal interview

---

2. See *Chaplinsky* v. *New Hampshire,* 315 U.S. 568, 572 (1942), 86 L.Ed. 1031, 1035, 62 S.Ct. 766, opinion by J. Murphy.
3. 18 U.S.C. §1464.
4. See *In re WUHY-FM,* 24 FCC 2d 408 at 410.
5. *Roth* v. *U. S.,* 354 U.S. 476, at 479, 77 S.Ct. 1304, at 1311 (1957).

comments of Jerry Garcia of the rock music group, "The Grateful Dead," to fall within the 1464 prohibition. Garcia's use of sexual expletives interspersed with his comments were found objectionable to the FCC because of the following:

a) Although such language is commonly used in the average person's everyday personal life, it is not commonly used in public (e.g., on an elevator, when testifying in court).

b) Such language has no redeeming social value, is patently offensive, and conveys no extension of thought or meaning to the interviewee's comments.

c) The use of such language has very serious consequences to the "public interest in the larger and more effective use of (broadcast media)."[6]

The Commission distinguished between "obscene" and "indecent" in finding Garcia's language objectionable. Finding that his use of sexual expletives had no "dominant appeal to prurience or sexual matters," and, hence, was not obscene, the Commission found such language "indecent." By this, it meant the "vulgar, coarse and offensive use of sexual terminology in a manner far exceeding the bounds of common decency."[7] Hence, the broadcaster must be cautious in permitting guest interviewees who tend to use such language to appear lest he be faced with (a) a law suit or (b) the loss of part of his viewing audience.

In another recent case, the courts found the spontaneous use of curse expletives by an interviewed guest not prohibited by 1464.[8] Here, the words "God damn it" uttered in a moment of anger were held not to be "obscene, indecent or profane." Determinative factors in *Gagliardo* were:

a) The words were delivered in the heat of debate and were not a matter of course.

b) The interviewee's intent to use the words uttered could not be proved.

Thus, a distinction emerged which appears to permit the spontaneous utterance by an interviewed guest, but not the voluntary expression — for voluntariness implies the power of choice. It is the duty of the broadcaster to control the language content of his programs. Analysis of the foregoing cases reflects the following general guidelines:

a) If a broadcaster has an interview containing objectionable language on tape or film, he'd be wise to refrain from broadcasting same. That the interviewee has spoken spontaneously no longer prevails as the issue; the *broadcaster* has had time to consider the interview's contents and, unlike the interviewee, can choose not to air it.

b) It is not so much the words used as the manner and context in which they are utilized which is determinative. If used spontaneously and without warning to the broadcaster, he is not charged with the burden of control.

c) The broadcaster will be held accountable for objectionable language by interviewed guests unless he can show that such language was essential to the integrity or reality of the presentation. In this case, the broadcaster is usually

---

6. Section 303(g).
7. The Commission relied heavily on *U. S.* v. *Limehouse,* 285 U.S. 424, 52 S.Ct. 412, 76 L.Ed. 843 (1932) which held that the word "filthy" included language that was "course, vulgar, disgusting and indecent and plainly related to sexual matters."
8. *Gagliardo* v. *U. S.,* 366 F.2d 720 (1966).

protected if the presentation is limited to readings from classics or descriptions of works of art.

Obviously, the Commission possesses great latitude in proceeding in this area under the "public interest" standard. Heretofore, it has yielded free speech a "preferred position" and given nearly all language full protection of the guarantees. It would prefer not to be responsible for interpreting and applying 1464 at all. Relying on the principle in *Burstyn*,[9] the Commission regards the interpretation of 1464 as "a matter of first impression which can only be definitively settled by the courts."[10] With the boundaries of permissible language inconstant and the value varieties utilized by the Commission and the courts for determining language that is "obscene, indecent, or profane" so ephemeral, the broadcaster would be wise to seek the advice of counsel whenever a 1464 problem arises.

Public attitudes on censorship changed in the 1960s, with a growing realization that the facts of life do not disappear by banning them from public discussion or observation and pretending that they do not exist. Following the lead of some European countries the United States has gradually come to realize that open discussion and evaluation of all aspects of human conduct make them easier to understand, and for people, particularly youngsters, ultimately to make intelligent choices about, as to their own personal attitudes and behavior.

The advent of the Broadway plays "Hair" and "Oh, Calcutta" and some Court decisions have removed most of the arbitrary censorship of plays and films, as well as printed matter, in most states. The lessening of censorship for radio and television, however, has not nearly begun to approach that of other media. On occasion a film is shown on television (at a late hour) that only a few years ago would have been considered out of the question. Yet, such films are heavily censored and at least in one instance the producer of a film shown on television disassociated himself from it because television censorship had so changed the film that its philosophic purpose and content came out almost diametrically opposite to what the producer had originally intended.

Sex innuendos of the titillating kind are common on television. "Laugh-In" broke fresh ground in this direction. Even the college-type of broad sex humor has made it to television. The "Dean Martin Show" was a good example. Uninhibited, unmarried love is acknowledged, sometimes without smug condemnation, on drama programs. "Hell" and "damn" are frequently heard over the air, even in situation comedies, and there is even an occasional "bastard" and "bitch" found in the context of a dramatic story. Talk and interview shows have frequently dealt frankly with such subjects as prostitution and homosexuality. By and large, however, the content of television remains relatively prophylactic.

---

9. *Burstyn* v. *Wilson*, 343 U.S. 495, 502-503 (1951).
10. *In re WUHY-FM, supra,* at 342.

Erik Barnouw, discussing censorship in the movies in his *Mass Communication,* indicates an approach which just as readily may be applied to television and radio. Barnouw writes: "Banning evil example . . . does not ban it from life. It may not strengthen our power to cope with it. It may have the opposite effect. Code rules multiply, but they do not produce morality. They do not stop vulgarity. Trying to banish forbidden impulses, censors may only change the disguises in which they appear. They ban passionate love-making, and excessive violence takes its place."[3]

Although Barnouw's comments no longer generally apply to the movies (which do not stint on either love-making or violence), they are perfectly applicable to the "new" medium, television, which has taken on the content coloration that movies once had. Violence has become a staple of television. Murder and mayhem are apparently considered more desirable for the American public than is making love. A true "Alice-in-Wonderland" attitude, when one stops to think about it!

Professor Barnouw's example proved to be more than theoretic analogy. Public concern with violence on television became so great that a federal Commission on Television and Social Behavior was formed to study the matter, issuing in 1972 what became known as the Surgeon General's Report on television and violence: "Television and Growing Up: The Impact of Televised Violence." After an initial flurry of activity designed to 1) reduce violence on television or 2) reduce the public's concern with violence on television — depending on whether the source was the broadcasting industry or Congress and consumer groups — the continuing existence of the problem led in 1974 to hearings on televised violence by the Senate Commerce Committee's Subcommittee on Communications.

Controversial Material

Censorship of controversial material is of concern to the writer. Controversial material refers to subject matter which in the broadest sense might disturb any viewer. Such material might relate to any area of public thinking, including certain aspects of political, social, economic, religious and psychological problems. "When a story editor says, 'We can't use anything controversial,' and says it with a tone of conscious virtue, then there is danger," observes Erik Barnouw.[4]

There is a great danger to freedom of expression and the democratic exchange of ideas in American television and radio because many of the media executives fear controversy. On the grounds of service to the sponsor and on the basis of high ratings for non-controversial but mediocre entertainment, anything controversial has been avoided in too many cases. Many companies will refuse to sponsor a program with controversial material if they feel it will in any way alienate any potential customer anywhere. It can be said that if a sponsor permits a product to be identified with a controversial issue that may offend even small groups of citizens, there may be damage to the company's prestige. It can also be said, on the other hand, that anyone using the public airwaves has a responsibility not only to a private company, but to the public as a whole. Censorship of controversial material is particularly prevalent in dramatic programs. Reginald Rose, one of the great writers of television's golden age, who had some plays censored because they contained alleged controversial material, believes that such controversial productions help more than harm advertisers; that people are made more aware of the program and of the product, as opposed to their barely noting the sponsorship of innocuous shows. [5]

As far back as the early 1960s the Federal Communications Commission held hearings on television programming and, with few exceptions, heard almost all of the leading industries in this country state that the television programs they advertise on must be oriented toward their sales policies and must reflect their corporate images. Retired *New York Times* critic, Jack Gould, summed up the attitude of the television sponsor: "As a business man governed by concern for his customers and stockholders, the advertiser wants to avoid displeasing any substantial segment of the public, wants to establish a pleasant environment for his product, wants to make sure the private life of a performer is not embarrassing to his company, and wants to skirt any possibility of being accused of taking one side in a situation where there are two sides." [6]

Some sponsors do not succumb to pressure and they maintain the integrity of the programs they pay for. The Bell & Howell Corporation told the FCC that despite threats of boycott as a result of its sponsorship of controversial programs on the "Closeup" series, it would not abandon either the "conviction and faith that most Americans are fair-minded people who realize they must know more if our society is to survive," or "the principle that has served this country so well — the idea that the press should be free of advertising influence." [7]

The 1970s saw more and more network coverage of controversial issues — with or without sponsors. The gradual move of program control away from the agencies to the networks provided more freedom; the networks were no longer dependent upon full sponsorship, but relied more and more upon national spots. This did not, of course, mean public access and public control; the networks simply replaced the advertisers as the principal arbiters of thought and taste in broadcasting. For example, although networks provided honest and stark coverage of the war in Vietnam (such factual news coverage was considered controversial by some people), the networks did not reveal the full extent of the overwhelming opposition of the American people to the Vietnam war, particularly in their degree and kind of coverage of the many anti-war marches on Washington and similar rallies all over the country. News and documentaries, interviews and discussions delved into prison reform, such as the study of the Attica massacre; into citizen massacres such as Kent State and Jackson State Universities, including a powerful analogy on the former in the dramatic series, "The Bold Ones"; into previously forbidden subjects such as homosexuality; into coverage that let America's dirty linen hang out, such as the Watergate hearings; into the 1974 impeachment proceedings; into many social, political, environmental, educational, economic, sexual problems that were critical and controversial. Not enough for some people; too much for others.

But a start was made. There was plenty of backsliding, to be true, and plenty of censorship to avoid any real impact on the establishment's status quo. Joe Papp's contract with CBS-TV called for a number of plays produced by the New York Shakespeare Festival, including Ellis Rebman's "Sticks and Bones," a powerful, cynical play that placed the blame for war at the psyches of every family that gave lip service to the platitudes that engendered war through its own attitudes toward people. It was not a pretty play and got to the heart of some of the sickness in people, and just before it was scheduled the network cancelled its showing. When it was aired some months later exactly half of the CBS affiliates did not carry it — a record for affiliate rejections.

The overall picture in the 1970s was considerably better than that in the 1960s. In the 1960s frequently anything that was even vaguely controversial was censored: a talk by a clergyman on interdenominational friction was cancelled by a network; a play about homesteading in the west was cancelled because the sponsor didn't want anything presented which touched on the government giving economic help to farmers; the writer of a play about discrimination against a Black family, based on headline newspaper stories, was forced to change the protagonist to an ex-convict; one ironic example was the cancellation of a play about a network censoring a commentator, even after the script had been put into production and publicity about it had been released — the network that cancelled the play had not long before censured one of its own top commentators.

Some censorship takes place not because of feared public reaction or even because of the sponsor's vested interest, but because of direct prejudice. One program, the true story of the owner of a large concern who was Jewish and who gave his entire fortune to fight cancer was stopped by the sponsor because the play allegedly would give "Jewish department store owners" an unfair advantage over other department store owners.

Censorship which eliminates any material that might possibly put the sponsor's product in a poor light or which might, even obliquely, suggest a competing product, is responsible for a number of classic situations that we have all heard about and which are true: among others, the program dealing with the German atrocities of the 1930s and 1940s from which the sponsoring gas company eliminated all references to "gas chambers," and the deletion of a reference to President Lincoln in another program because it is also the name of an automobile produced by a competitor of the sponsor.

We've come a long way — at least sometimes — from these classic examples of censorship. Consider the language and references of "All in the Family," the real-life situations, such as abortion, on "Maude," the sophisticated and unsubtle sexual references on "Laugh-In," and the political realities presented on the late 1960s "Smothers Brothers Show" (the latter was cancelled by the network).

In 1972 television writers representing the Writers Guild of America, West, testified at hearings on press freedom held by the Senate Judiciary Committee's Constitutional Rights Subcommittee and chaired by Senator Sam Ervin. The writers said that scripts on controversial subjects are heavily censored by broadcast executives. David W. Rintels, head of the Guild's censorship committee, said that broadcast executives "allow laughter but not tears, fantasy but not reality, escapism but not truth . . . 75 million people are nightly being fed programs deliberately designed to have no resemblance at all to reality, nonsense whose only purpose is to sell snake-oil and laxatives and underarm deodorants. . . . Writers by the dozens report that they have written characters who are black and have seen them changed to white. They have written Jews and seen them converted to gentiles. They have proposed shows about South African apartheid, Vietnam, old folks, mental disease, politics, business, labor, students and minorities; and they have been chased out of studios. . . . These instances are symptomatic of the rigorous and final institutionalization of censorship and thought control on television." Rintels further stated that a poll of Guild members showed that 86% had experienced censorship of their work and that 81% believe that television is presenting a distorted picture of what is happening in America. He added that television drama fostered a "mythology which states that a punch in the mouth solves all problems and doesn't really hurt anyone."[8]

At the same hearings, Norman Lear, producer of "All in the Family," had praise for the CBS network for permitting his program to deal with subjects that were once taboo, such as racial and religious bias and impotence. But he made clear that this was an exception and that "this country is ready for a lot more truth than it's getting."[9]

The attitudes of most broadcast executives are, of course, somewhat different. Their greatest concern is that the broadcasters should and do have the right to determine the content of programming and that any government interference — such as the enforcement of the Fairness Doctrine by the Federal Communications Commission — is tantamount to government censorship. The Nebraska Broadcasters Association has stated that "Fairness Doctrine interpretations by the FCC, the FTC, and the courts, have attacked the very foundation of freedom of speech and free enterprise."[10] Julian Goodman, then president of the National Broadcasting

Company, said that broadcasters "have always adhered to the journalistic standard of fairness. We simply feel that we do not require additional exterior regulatory reasons to enforce that. We feel that the judgment of broadcasters can be trusted."[11]

Broadcasters themselves rarely answer the charges of censorship of the kind brought by David Rintels. The broadcast press, however, sometimes has something to say about the network and station prerogatives and responsibilities. An editorial by *Television/Radio Age* publisher S. J. Paul put it this way:

> In network entertainment programming, there is a behind-the-scenes battle that goes on — and has been going on for years — between writers and producers on one hand, and the establishment, i.e. the networks, on the other. The writers are seeking that so-called complete freedom to ply their craft. The networks, of necessity, must establish the guidelines within the canons of good taste. Establishing the criteria is a responsibility that the networks cannot duck. Anyone who has viewed the programs in this new season would have to conclude that all three networks have lowered their standards, particularly in the over-emphasis on violence and sex.
>
> The arguments in favor of this kind of permissiveness have been recited many, many times — that we are now in a period of transition, that public tastes are changing along with moral standards, and that to muzzle creativity is to block progress and stifle the libido.
>
> Actually, it requires more imagination to present entertainment in good taste than it does to present a dramatic series where this kind of sensationalism serves no end except questionable vicariousness, and, believe me, the writers know exactly what they are doing when they introduce these extraneous elements into a plot. . . .
>
> There are certain types of entertainment fare that belong in the theatre or motion pictures that are not applicable to television.
>
> It has been said many times, television is the mass medium of family entertainment. It is an invited guest in the home. If it loses sight of this basic precept, it will further compound its many problems.[12]

Many television and radio writers have found that censorship covers a far wider range than that specified in the NAB production codes and by individual stations and networks. Each sponsor has a special list of unacceptable subjects or ideas. For example, on one program sponsored by an automobile manufacturer no one ever had an auto accident, nor was one ever referred to by any character. One can find similar examples for almost every sponsored show on the air, and these are restrictions the writer who would write for that show must face. Although the most dramatic examples of censorship, as noted in this chapter, occur in plays, censorship applies as well to other forms of television and radio writing.

It does not have to be a question of either-or, however, In French television, for example, when material is presented which generally is deemed acceptable for a mature and intelligent audience but which may not be entirely acceptable to every family audience at home, an announcement before the program begins asks the viewers to watch the program with indulgence and to put the children to bed. On British Broadcasting Corporation programs there is virtually no dialogue code. Although good taste is a general guide for writers, in a dramatic show, for example, a character can make any reference that is necessary to the play.

Sydney W. Head, a leading teacher and writer in the communications field, has written that ". . . television, as a medium appears to be highly responsive to the conventional conservative values," and that a danger to society from television is that it, television, will not likely lend its support to the unorthodox, but that "it will add tremendously to cultural inertia."[13] Former Federal Communications Commission Chairman Newton N. Minow characterized television programming as a "vast wasteland," and former Chairman E. William Henry called it an "electronic Appalachia."

Censorship is the rule rather than the exception in American broadcasting. The great impact of the media and the ability of television and radio to so strongly affect the minds and emotions of people are clearly recognized by the censors, who represent the status quo of established business, industry, social and political thought — those who control the media have achieved success which has placed them squarely into the leadership of established society. The impact of the media is clearly reflected in the success and importance of Madison Avenue. Commercials *do* sell products and services. The impact of media has enabled news and public affairs programs, even in their frequently limited and sometimes biased coverage of controversial issues, to become significant factors in changing much of our political and social policies and beliefs. Television is credited with bringing to much of the American population an understanding of the violence and prejudice practiced against Blacks, with its coverage of the civil rights movement in the south in the early 1960s; watching hate in the street with the rest of the mob is one thing, watching it in your living room is another, and it was television which motivated many people to demand Congressional action to guarantee all Americans civil rights. Although selective and limited in its coverage and hardly objective in its evaluation of the breadth and depth of the "peace marches" in Washington during the Vietnam war, the media nevertheless brought to people in their homes some of the horrors of Vietnam and some of the actions of millions of Americans in actively opposing the war. The result was nationwide citizen pressure that caused one president to end his political career and another president to ultimately wind down and end most of American war participation in southeast Asia. In the early 1970s the live coverage of the Watergate hearings and the Nixon impeachment proceedings brought sharply to the American people information, ideas, feelings and, in many cases, motivated action that would not have otherwise come.

Frank Stanton, former president of the Columbia Broadcasting System, has said: "But the effect of broadcasting upon the democratic experience has gone far beyond elections. The monumental events of this century — depression, wars, uneasy peace, the birth of more new nations in two decades than had occurred before in two centuries, undreamed of scientific breakthroughs, profound social revolution — all these were made immediate intimate realities to Americans through, first, the ears of radio and, later, the eyes of television. No longer were the decisions of the American people made in an information vacuum, as they witnessed the towering events of their time that were bound to have incisive political repercussions."[14]

The writers who prepare continuity and background material for programs dealing with such issues and events can have the satisfaction of knowing that they are contributing to human progress and thought and are directly participating in changing society and solving problems of humanity. There are not too many professions in which one can accomplish this on such a broad and grand scale!

Theoretically, the writer can help to fulfill the responsibility of the mass media to serve the best interests of the public as a whole, can raise and energize the cultural and educational standards of the people and thus strengthen the country. Realistically, the most well-intentioned writer is still under the control of the network and advertiser whose first loyalties seem to be directed toward their own interests and not necessarily toward those of the public. Occasionally, these interests coincide. The writer who wishes to keep a job in the mass media is pressured to serve the interests of the employer. It is hoped that conscience will also enable the writer to serve the needs of the public.[15]

NOTES TO CHAPTER 1

[1] *Broadcasting,* June 10, 1974, pp. 22-23.
[2] "Boundaries of 'Obscene or Indecent' Language Over-the-Air," *BM/E,* December, 1971, pp. 12, 14.
[3] Erik Barnouw, *Mass Communication* (New York: Holt, Rinehart and Winston, Inc., 1956), pp. 148; 267-268.
[4] *Ibid.*
[5] Reginald Rose, *Six Television Plays* (New York: Simon and Schuster, 1956), pp. 249-251.
[6] *The New York Times,* October 8, 1961.

[7] *The New York Times,* September 28, 1961 and *New York Herald Tribune,* September 28, 1961.

[8] For the complete testimony of Mr. Rintels, Norman Lear and Liam O'Brien representing the Writers Guild of America and containing many examples of censorship, see "Freedom of the Press," Hearing before the Subcommittee on the Judiciary, United States Senate, Ninety-second Congress, September 28, 29, 30, October 12, 13, 14, 19 and 20, 1971 and February 1, 2, 8, 16 and 17, 1972. Washington, D.C.: U.S. Government Printing Office, 1972, pp. 515-547.

[9] *Ibid.*

[10] *Ibid.,* p. 172.

[11] *Ibid.,* p. 152. See Mr. Goodman's complete testimony, pp. 145-152.

[12] *Television/Radio Age,* November 12, 1973, p. 14.

[13] *Sydney W. Head,* "Content Analysis of Television Drama Programs," *Quarterly of Film, Radio and Television,* 1X (Winter, 1954), pp. 192-193.

[14] "Freedom of the Press," Hearings before the Subcommittee on the Judiciary, United States Senate, *op. cit.,* pp. 786-789; a speech to the National Association of Broadcasters, April 11, 1972.

[15] For a tragi-comedy account of the writer's problems, the reader is referred to the book by Merle Miller and Evan Rhodes, *Only You, Dick Daring* (New York: William Sloane Associates, 1964).

REFERENCE BOOKS

ON AESTHETICS, GROWTH AND REGULATION

Publications on the history, growth, regulation and aesthetics of television and radio are too numerous to list in a chapter bibliography. A selected number — from which an even more select group should be chosen according to your individual needs — are listed below. Among the bibliographies on broadcasting, which will provide you with a wider selection, are:

Blum, Eleanor. *Basic Books in the Mass Media.* Urbana: University of Illinois Press, 1972.

Broadcasting Yearbook. Washington, D.C. (Usually in Section E.)

Lichty, Lawrence W. *World and International Broadcasting: A Bibliography.* Washington, D.C.: Broadcast Education Association, 1971.

Rivers, William L. and William T. Slater. *Aspen Handbook on the Media: Research. Publications. Organizations.* Palo Alto: Aspen Program on Communication and Society, 1973.

Sparks, Kenneth, comp. *A Bibliography of Doctoral Dissertations in Television and Radio.* 3rd ed. Syracuse: School of Journalism, 1971.

Weiss, Frederic A. *Sources on Information on World and International Radio and Television.* Bloomington, Ind.: Indiana University, 1970.

Other works on broadcasting which may be of help to the writer are:

Barnouw, Erik. *A Tower in Babel,* Vol. I: To 1933. (1966); *The Golden Web.* Vol. II: 1933-1953. (1968); *The Image Empire.* Vol. III: From 1953. (1970). New York: Oxford University Press. The most comprehensive work on the history and development of broadcasting.

Bogart, Leo. *The Age of Television.* New York: Frederick Ungar, 1972. Includes relationship of TV and radio to other media.

Bower, Robert T. *Television and the Public.* New York: Holt, Rinehart & Winston, 1973. Updating of the 1963 Steiner audience study.

Broadcasting Yearbook. Statistics, information on all phases of television and radio.

Brown, Les. *Television: The Business Behind the Box.* New York: Harcourt, Brace, Javanovich, 1971. Revealing analysis of network programming and management.

Buxton, Frank and Bill Owen. *The Big Broadcast: 1920-1950.* New York: Viking Press, 1972. Listings of network programs, including some script samples.

Chester, Giraud, Garnet R. Garrison, and Edgar E. Willis. *Television and Radio.* 4th ed. New York: Appleton-Century-Crofts, 1971. Comprehensive view of structure, programming and techniques.

Devol, Kenneth S., ed. *Mass Media and the Supreme Court.* New York: Hastings House, 1971. Anthology of cases related to First Amendment issues.

Diamant, Lincoln. *The Broadcast Communications Dictionary.* New York: Hastings House, 1974.

Dizard, Wilson P. *Television: A World View.* Syracuse: Syracuse University Press, 1966. History and trends, including role of U.S.

Drinan, Robert E. *Democracy, Dissent and Disorder/The Issues and the Law.* New York: Seabury Press, 1970. Includes mass media.

Emery, Walter B. *Broadcasting and Government: Responsibilities and Regulations.* 2nd ed. East Lansing: Michigan State University Press, 1971. Rules and policies of federal agencies.

————. *National and International Systems of Broadcasting: Their History, Operation and Control.* East Lansing: Michigan State University Press, 1969. Factual material includes U.S.

Federal Communications Commission Rules and Regulations. Washington, D.C.: U.S. Government Printing Office. Periodically Updated.

Head, Sydney W. *Broadcasting in America: A Survey of Television and Radio.* 2nd rev. ed. Boston: Houghton Mifflin, 1972. Comprehensive and factual view on history, regulation, inter-media relationships, advertising and effects on society.

International Television Almanac. Ed., Charles S. Aaronson. New York: Quigley Publications, annually. Data on all phases of TV, principally in U.S.

Jennings, Ralph M. *Guide to Understanding Broadcast License Applications and Other FCC Forms.* New York: United Church of Christ, 1974. Simplifies public participation in licensing process.

Johnson, Nicholas. *How to Talk Back to Your Television Set.* Boston: Little, Brown, 1969. By former FCC Commissioner. The public owns the airwaves and how they can do something about it.

Kahn, Frank J., Jr., ed. *Documents of American Broadcasting.* Rev. Ed. New York: Appleton-Century-Crofts, 1973. Primary reference sources.

Le Duc, Don F., ed. *Issues in Broadcast Regulation.* Washington, D.C.: Broadcast Education Association/National Association of Broadcasters, 1974.

Lichty, Lawrence, W. and Malachi C. Topping. *American Broadcasting: A Source Book on the History of Radio and Television.* New York: Hastings House, 1975. Some 90 selections covering the major areas of broadcasting history.

Mayer, Martin. *About Television.* New York: Harper & Row, 1972. Sympathetic survey of problems in the field.

McLuhan, Marshall with Quentin Fiore. *The Medium Is The Message.* New York: Bantam Books. The "classic" in paperback.

Pennypacker, John H., and Waldo W. Braden, eds. *Broadcasting and the Public Image.* New York: Random House, 1969. Position papers principally on programming, FCC.

Price, Monroe and John Wicklein. *Cable Television.* Philadelphia: Pilgrim Press, 1972. Its future and service to the public.

Public Television: A Program for Action. New York: Harper & Row, 1967. Report and recommendations of the Carnegie Commission on Educational Television.

Quaal, Ward L. and James A. Brown. *Broadcast Management,* 2nd ed. rev. and enl. New York: Hastings House, 1976. All aspects of Radio/TV station management.

Shaheen, Jack G. *The Survival of Public Broadcasting.* Edwardsville: Southern Illinois University Division of Mass Communications, 1974.

Shayon, Robert Lewis. *The Crowd Catchers.* New York: Saturday Review Press, 1973. Introductory overview to television, including aesthetic criticism.

Siepmann, Charles A. *Radio, Television and Society.* New York: Oxford University Press, 1950. Still a classic.

Skornia, Harry, and Jack Kitson, eds. *Problems and Controversies in Television and Radio: Basic Readings.* Palo Alto: Pacific Books, 1968. Various viewpoints on corporate and public responsibility.

Smith, Ralph Lee. *The Wired Nation: The Electronic Communication Highway.* New York: Harper Colophon Books, 1972. Definition, background and role.

Stanley, Robert H., ed. *The Broadcast Industry: An Examination of Major Issues.* New York: Hastings House, 1975. A report on the IRTS Fourth Faculty/Industry Seminar.

Steinberg, Charles S., ed. *Mass Media and Communication,* 2nd ed. rev. New York: Hastings House, 1972. Impact of mass media on society.

———. *The Communicative Arts.* New York: Hastings House, 1970. An introduction to mass media against background of their social and cultural significance.

————, ed. *Broadcasting: The Critical Challenges.* New York: Hastings House, 1974. Cogent discussions from the recent IRTS Faculty/Industry Seminar on the current problems of radio and television.

Television and Growing Up: The Impact of Televised Violence. Washington, D.C.: U.S. Government Printing Office, 1972. Report of the Surgeon General's scientific advisory committee on television and social behavior.

Leading periodicals in the field include:

Billboard, BM/E (Broadcast Management Engineering), Broadcasting Magazine, Educational and Industrial Television, Journal of Broadcasting, Public Telecommunications Review, Television Digest, Television Quarterly, Television/Radio Age, and *Variety.*

2

Basic Elements
of Production

BEFORE THE ADVENT of videotape, television was a "live" medium. Kine-scope recordings had very poor "air" quality. When the television industry began to move to the west coast it adopted the so-called Hollywood ap-proach — the use of film and the style and technique of writing that go with it. Drama was no longer live, but pre-recorded on film. News and public affairs, when done in the field, had of necessity always been on film. Although stations developed remote facilities for live coverage of on-the-spot happenings, stories were filmed and rushed to the studio for processing and airing on the regular news shows. Although commercials were live in the early days — yes, Betty Furness did open that refrigerator door, live, on camera — it was soon easier and more efficient to prepare commercials as film inserts, even for otherwise live productions. Film soon became the production means for virtually all programs that by necessity or special design were not presented live.

When videotape came along in the 1950s many people looked for a revolution. Magnetic tape did replace film in many areas of TV production, but film remained dominant in entertainment programs, particularly drama, and in news and commercials. With the refinement of videotape equipment and techniques, some inroads were made, but it wasn't until the early 1970s that something along the lines of a real revolution — or, perhaps, instant evolution — began to be seen.

In the mid-1970s a number of stations, and even major production studios, concluded that the advantages of videotape in many ways surpass those of the film and were switching to tape. It will probably take a decade to determine if videotape will, indeed, replace film or if the industry will by and large come around to combining the advantages of both in any given production situation.

BM/E magazine analyzed some of the reasons for the movement toward tape:

> Instant replay — it saves big hunks of time and money — if the first take is wrong, the director knows right away and can reshoot without leaving the set.
>
> Totally quiet cameras that accommodate a wider range of light values and color temperatures than film cameras.
>
> The current high-band VTRs — these lifted recording quality to the level the movie-makers wanted.
>
> Ability of the current video cameras to use a range of lenses similar to that of film cameras.
>
> The TV monitor as a large, well-lighted, easily multiplied viewfinder, which sees exactly what the camera sees.
>
> Recent advances in editing technology which makes editing videotape easier and cheaper than the old standard film editing methods.
>
> Recent developments in small van-mounted video production units, with two or three cameras feeding control equipment and recorders in the van. Set up time is usually much faster with this equipment than with portable movie units (for example, the camera can be warmed up on the way to the shooting site).
>
> Capping it all is electronic processing of the program: color, aperture, gamma correction; picture enhancement of various kinds; dissolves, wipes, all the bag of special effects that the TV broadcaster today expects to come out of a smallish box when he punches the button.[1]

Even in the Hollywood stronghold of filmed drama, videotape is making its mark. Filmmakers are becoming aware of the fluidity and flexibility of early live, continuous action television that the single-sequence film technique never reached. In television the writer can write a sequence in which the action can be seen simultaneously from as many viewpoints, both physical and attitudinal, as there are cameras in the studio. Producer Bob Markell has moved into a "mixed-media" approach, shooting on tape, transferring to film for editing, and then transferring back to tape. "At that point," states Markell, "I know, to the frame, exactly what I want on that final tape." Markell cites the economic advantages: "It's very expensive to edit on tape. It means I might settle for a first cut. Editing on film I can change my mind often, if necessary, so that creatively and artistically I can do a better show. . . . I believe if we're free of any major technical problems, we can just about cut production time in half."[2] Director Alex March states that "We can shoot more quickly, more efficiently and with less lighting. It's something I've been preaching for years. I think its definitely the wave of the future. . . . Those scenes we shot on Fifth Avenue, for instance, with all those thousands of people around; we were able to capture it all so easily on tape. Had it been film, it would have been much more difficult. It would have required so much more equipment, for one thing . . ."[3] Producer Bruce Basset adds: "One of the main advantages is that you see it at the moment you do it. We can shoot two block away with people hardly realizing it."[4]

For the writer the significant thing is that the live, studio type approach is·returning, adding to it the special advantages of the editing of film. As will be noted particularly in Chapter 12 on writing the play, the modern television writer must adapt for television the most appropriate techniques of the theatre, creating a moving proscenium, and of the movies, expanding the physical place and time. As March and Bassett clearly indicate, even that area of studio television most criticized — its limited space — no longer holds true when the videotape approach is applied to outdoor scenes.

Another mainstay of film use in television has been commercials production. In the first few years of the 1970s, however, the use of tape for the production of commercials rose geometrically — about 50%, for example, from 1971 to 1972 — and by 1974 it was estimated that more than one-third of the commercials produced were on tape. Advertising agency head Bill Mosely has stated: "I used to have a good feel that an ad was a tape ad or a film ad, but today we are getting material from videotape that I can't tell from film material, and I know the game has changed. The video camera has grown up."[5]

From the writer's standpoint the production technique, on the surface, does not make that much difference. It is the persuasive approach, content and type of commercial that matter, as described in Chapter 3. However, being aware of whether a single film camera or a battery of video cameras is being used can help the writer decide on some of the artistic effects and fluidity possible.

For coverage of live news events, particularly where there is action and the cameraperson needs to get right into the crowd, the film camera, such as the small, lightweight 16mm, surpasses the video camera. Video still requires more equipment than does film. Yet, there are many instances where the "instant replay" quality of videotape, as differentiated from the need to process film, makes videotape critically advantageous for news coverage. For example, in one special news conference held by Henry Kissinger in which he revealed dramatic progress in peace talks he was negotiating, WTOP-TV in Washington, D.C. was able to get the story immediately on the air because it had covered it with a remote video camera and recorder, while its competitors were left behind because of the time it took them to process their film coverage of the event. Although the writer is usually not involved in preparation — except perhaps on occasion for Intro, Outro and background material — for on-the-spot events, the writer does prepare the studio news report which incorporates such material, and should be aware of what technique is being used.

Most of the other types of programs — excluding such forms as the documentary, of course — are "studio-type" programs, and the writer usually applies video rather than film techniques, even when the program might be filmed rather than taped for subsequent presentation. Included are such programs as game shows, studio interviews, panel discussions.

We have dealt exclusively with television thus far in this chapter. This was not done to slight radio; it is because television is still emerging in terms of its techniques and approaches, whereas radio some time ago had pretty thoroughly explored its basic potentials. Multiplexing and quadruplexing and the electronic synthesizer have presented new opportunities for experimentation by the radio writer, producer and director, but television is still making determinations of technique on a comparatively much younger growing-up level.

Although, in the mid-1970s, there are as yet relatively few jobs in cable television, the anticipated growth of cable suggests that it will need many writers on the local level, as well as writers preparing material for syndication on regional and national levels. Aside from the probable limitations on equipment in many local cable origination studios (compared to broadcast station equipment), and an emphasis on materials in many instances more highly localized than at wider-ranging broadcast stations, the writing techniques — at least until cable develops unique aesthetic and audience needs of its own — will be largely the same as those for broadcast television. The basic techniques, considering many cable systems' needs for "live" programming to provide continuing local services, have been and will probably continue to be closer to the basic, classic "live" television writing approaches than to the "film" type approach that grew to dominate network TV.

This book does not propose to present a comprehensive analysis and how-to of film and videotape techniques. That would take another volume. What this chapter does is to present an overview, an introduction to some of the basic and, in some instances, classic elements of production so that you may have a working knowledge of terms and the critical and elemental information to enable you to write the scripts without necessarily equipping you to produce or direct them. We strongly recommend that you complement this book with other works on production and, for that, we refer you to the bibliography at the end of this chapter.

It is necessary to know the elements of television and radio that affect writing technique. The writer must learn what the camera can and cannot do, what sound or visual effects are possible in the control room, what terminology is used in furnishing directions, descriptions, and transitions, and what other technical and production aspects of the media are essential for effective writing.

RADIO

THE PRIMARY TECHNICAL and production potentials the radio writer should be aware of and should be able to indicate in the script, when necessary, pertain to microphone use, sound effects, and music. The writer should understand how the studio and control room can or cannot implement the purposes of the script.

The Microphone

The basic element of radio broadcasting is the microphone. The number of microphones used in a show usually is limited. For the standard program — a deejay or news program — only one is needed. Even in a dramatic show there may be only one or two for the announcer and the cast. Another may be used if there are any live sound effects. A musical group may require still another. A panel, discussion or interview program may have a mike for each person or for every two people. Not all microphones are the same. The audio engineer selects certain types of microphones in terms of their sensitivity and uses for specific effects. The writer has only one important responsibility in this area: to indicate the relationship of the performer to the microphone. It is this physical relationship which determines the orientation of the listener. For example, the audience may be with a character riding in a car. The car approaches the edge of a cliff. The writer must decide whether to put the sound of the character's scream and the noise of the car as it hurtles down the side of the cliff "on mike," thus keeping the audience with the car, or to fade these sounds into the distance, orienting the audience to a vantage point at the top of the cliff, watching the character and car going downward.

There are five basic microphone positions. The writer should indicate every position except "on mike," which is taken for granted when no position is designated next to the line of dialogue. Where the performer has been in another position and suddenly speaks from an "on mike" position, then "on mike" should be written in.

On mike.   The performer speaks from a position right at the microphone. The listener is oriented to the imaginary setting in the same physical spot as the performer.

Off mike.   The performer is some distance away from the microphone. This conveys to the audience the impression that the sound or voice is at a proportionate distance away from the physical orientation point of the listener, which is usually at the center of the scene. The writer may vary this listener orientation and, by removing the performer's voice but through the dialogue indicating that the performer has remained in the same physical place, it is the listener and not the performer who has been removed from the central point of action.

Fading on. The performer slowly moves toward the microphone. In the mind's eye of the listener, the performer is approaching the physical center of the action.

Fading off. The performer moves away from the microphone while speaking, thus moving away from the central orientation point.

Behind obstructions. The performer sounds as if there were a barrier between him or her and the focal point of the audience's orientation. The writer would indicate that the performer were behind a door, outside a window, or perhaps under the bandstand.

The writer may indicate the need for special microphones. One is the filter mike, which creates the impression that the voice or sound is coming over a telephone. The voice at the focal point of the audience's orientation, even though speaking over the telephone, too, would be on mike. Another is the echo chamber, which creates various degrees of an echo sound, ranging from an indication that a person is locked in a closet to the impression of a voice in a boundless cavern.

Note the use of the five positions in the following sample material*:

---

* The radio or television script is usually typed with double-spacing between speeches, sound effects, music directions and (for television) video directions. However, in the interests of a more compact typographic arrangement, single spacing has been used within most scripts in this book.

COMMENTARY	AUDIO
1. There is no mention of position. The character is assumed to be on mike.	GEORGE: I'm bushed, Myra. Another day like the one today, and I'll just . . . (THE DOORBELL RINGS) MYRA: Stay where you are, George. I'll answer the door. GEORGE: Thanks, hon. (DOORBELL RINGS AGAIN)
2. The orientation of the audience stays with George as Myra leaves the focal point of the action.	MYRA: (RECEDING FOOSTEPS, FADING) I'm coming . . . I'm coming. I wonder who it could be at this hour.
3. George must give the impression of projecting across the room to Myra who is now at the front door.	GEORGE: (CALLING) See who it is before you open the door. MYRA: (OFF) All right, George. (ON MIKE) Who is it?
4. Myra's physical position is now clear to the audience through the distance of her voice. Then as soon as we hear her ON MIKE, the audience's physical position arbitrarily is oriented to that of Myra at the front door.	
5. This is an example of the "behind an obstruction" position.	MESSENGER: (BEHIND DOOR) Telegram for Mr. George Groo.
6. The physical orientation of the audience stays with Myra. George is now OFF MIKE.	MYRA: Just a minute. (CALLING) George, telegram for you.

GEORGE: (OFF) Sign for me, will you Myra?

MYRA: Yes. (SOUND OF DOOR OPENING) I'll sign for it. (SOUND OF PAPER BEING HANDED OVER AND THE SCRATCH OF PENCIL ON PAPER)

MESSENGER: Thank you, Ma'am. (SOUND OF DOOR BEING CLOSED)

MYRA: (SOUND OF TELEGRAM BEING OPENED) I'll open it and . . . (SILENCE FOR A MOMENT)

GEORGE: (OFF) Well, Myra, what is it? (STILL SILENCE)

GEORGE: (FADING ON) Myra, in heaven's name, what happened? What does the telegram says? (ON MIKE) Myra, let me see that telegram!

7. Note the complete shift of audience orientation. After Myra goes to the door the audience stays with her, hears George from the other end of the room, finally knows that George, who is coming on or fading on, is approaching the spot where the audience and Myra are. Finally, George is at that spot. Note the use of the term ON MIKE at the end, when the character comes to that position from another position.

The Studio

The physical limitations of a radio studio sometimes may affect the writer's purposes, so, if possible, the size of the studio should be checked to see if it is large enough. In addition, though most professional studios are satisfactorily equipped acoustically, some smaller stations are not, and the writer should attempt to determine whether it is possible to achieve the sensitivity of sound planned for the script.

The Control Room

The control room is the focal point of operation in which all of the sound, music, effects and broadcast silence are coordinated — carefully mixed by the engineer at the control board, and sent out to the listener. The control room usually contains the turntables on which transcriptions and recordings can be incorporated with the live action in the studio. The control room also contains recording and taping equipment which permit the capture of the program either for rebroadcast or for initial public broadcast at a later time.

The control board regulates the volume of output of all microphones, turntables and tapes, and can fade or blend the sound of any one or combination of these elements.

Sound Effects

There are two major categories of sound effects: those that are recorded, and those that are made manually or live. Virtually any sound effect desired may be found on records. Examples range from various types of airplane motors to the crying of a baby. For split-second incorporation of sound into the live action of the program, however, manual or live effects are more effective. Manual effects would include such sounds as the opening and closing of a door (coming from a miniature door located near the microphone of the sound effects operator) or the rattling of cellophane to simulate the sound of fire. Under this category fall natural effects — those emanating from their natural sources, such as the sound of walking feet in which the microphone might be held near the feet of a sound effects person marking time. In some instances entirely new combinations of sounds may be necessary, including an amalgamation of recorded, manual and natural effects.

Inexperienced writers occasionally have a tendency to overdo the use of sound. Sound effects should be used only when necessary, and then only in relation to the psychological principles which determine the orientation of the listener. Reflect on your own orientation to sound when listening to the radio. For example, a high pitch or high volume or rising pitch usually suggests a climax or some disturbing element, while a low pitch or low volume or descending pitch usually suggests something soothing and calm. However, combinations of these sounds and the relationship of the specific sound to the specific situation can alter these generalizations. For instance, a low pitch in the proper place can indicate something foreboding rather than calm; or the combination of a low pitch and a high volume, as in thunder and an explosion, can create anything but a soothing effect.

Sound can be used for many purposes and effects, as follows:

Establish the locale or setting. For example, the sound of marching feet, the clanging of metal doors and the blowing of a whistle will suggest the locale or setting of a prison. The soft sounds of violin music, the occasional clatter of dishes and silverware, the clinking of glasses and the whispered sounds of talking would suggest not only a restaurant, but perhaps an old world Hungarian, Russian or Gypsy restaurant.

Direct the audience attention and emotion by emphasis on a particular sound. The sudden banging of a gavel in a courtroom scene will immediately direct the mind's-eye view of the audience toward the judge's bench. In a sequence in which the audience is aware that a person alone at home is an intended murder victim, the sound of steps on a walk and the sound of knocking on a door, or the more subtle sound of the turning of a doorknob, will direct the audience attention toward the front door and orient the audience's emotions toward the suspenseful terror of inevitable and perhaps immediate violence.

Establish time.   The clock striking the hour or the crowing of the cock are obvious, oft-used but nevertheless effective devices. The echo of footsteps along a pavement, with no other sounds heard, would indicate a quiet street very late at night or very early in the morning. If an element referred to in the program, such as an airplane or the rumbling of a subway train, has been established as indicating a certain time, then the moment the sound effect signifying that element is used, the audience will know the time.

Establish mood.   Anyone who has heard a dramatization of a Sherlock Holmes story is familiar with the mood created by the echo of a baying hound followed by the muffled strokes of a clock striking twelve. The sounds of laughter, loud music and much tinkling of glasses would establish a much different mood for a party than would subdued whispers and the soft music of a string quartet. Sound may be used effectively as counterpoint in setting off an individual character's mood. The attitudes and emotions of someone who is worried, sullen, morose and fretful may be heightened by placing the character in the midst of sounds indicating a wild, loud party.

Signify entrances and exits.   The sound of footsteps fading off and the opening and closing of a door, or the reverse, the opening and closing of a door and the sound of footsteps coming on, are unmistakable in indicating an exit or entrance. Transportation sounds and human and non-human sounds may be used to signify a character's coming to or leaving a place. The departure of a soldier from an enemy-held jungle island after a secret reconnaissance mission could be indicated by the sound of boat paddles, the whine of bullets and the chatter of jungle birds and animals. If the bullet, bird and animal sounds remain at a steady level and the paddling of the boat fades off, the audience remains on the island and sees the soldier leave. The audience may leave with the soldier if the paddling remains at an on-mike level and the island sounds fade off.

Serve as a transition between program segments or between changes of time or place in a dramatic program.   For example, if the transition is to cover a change of place, the sound used may be the means of transportation. The young graduate is about to leave home to travel to the big city to make good. Tender farewells are said. The farewells cross-fade into the sounds of a train, with appropriate whistles. The train sounds cross-fade into the sounds of the hustle and bustle of the big city. These sounds in turn cross-fade into the live sequence in which the protagonist makes arrangements for the renting of a room in the big-city rooming-house. The change of place has been achieved with sound providing an effective transition.

If the transition is to cover a lapse of time, the sound may be that of a timing device, such as a clock striking three, the tick of the clock fading out, fading in again, and the clock then striking six.

The sound indicating the transition may not relate necessarily to the specific cause of the transition. It may be of a general nature, such as a montage of war sounds to cover a change of place or lapse of time when the action relates to a war. Sometimes a montage, or blending of a number of sounds, can be particularly effective when no single sound fits the specific situation.

In a non-dramatic program, sounds relating to the content of the next segment may be used for transition. In some situations the sounds may have a relationship to the program as a whole rather than to a specific circumstance, such as the use of a ticker or telegraph key sound as a transition device for a news program. On comedy shows sounds completely irrelevant to the material may be used for transitional purposes, serving at the same time, because of their irrelevance, as comedy material.

Create unrealistic effects. Note Norman Corwin's description in "The Plot to Overthrow Christmas"[6] of the audience's journey to Hades, "To the regions where legions of the damnéd go."

> (CLANG ON CHINESE GONG. TWO THUNDER PEALS. OSCILLATOR IN AT HIGH PITCH BEFORE THUNDER IS ENTIRELY OUT. BRING PITCH DOWN GRADUALLY AND FADE IN ECHO CHAMBER WHILE HEAVY STATIC FADES IN, THEN OUT TO LEAVE NOTHING BUT OSCILLATOR AT A LOW OMINOUS PITCH; THEN RAISE OSCILLATOR PITCH SLOWLY. HOLD FOR A FEW SECONDS.)

Combinations of sound and music may be used to create almost any unrealistic effect demanded, from the simplest to the most complicated.

Sound also may be used to achieve not only one, but a combination of the various purposes already noted. One of the classic sound effects sequences — to many people the best and most famous sequence of all, along with Fibber McGee's closet — is that which accompanied Jack Benny's periodic visits to his private vault. Younger people who have listened to the revivals of "old-time radio" programs in the 1970s have probably heard it, too. The sounds used establish setting, orient the audience's emotions and direct its attention, establish mood, signify entrances and exits, serve as transitions between places and indicate lapses of time, and create unrealistic effects.

SOUND: FOOTSTEPS . . . DOOR OPENS . . . FOOTSTEPS GOING DOWN . . . TAKING ON HOLLOW SOUND . . . HEAVY IRON DOOR HANDLE TURNING . . . CHAINS CLANKING . . . DOOR CREAKS OPEN . . . . SIX MORE HOLLOW FOOTSTEPS . . . SECOND CLANKING OF CHAINS . . . HANDLE TURNS . . . HEAVY IRON DOOR OPENS CREAKING . . . TWO MORE FOOTSTEPS (DIALOGUE BETWEEN THE GUARD AND JACK) . . . LIGHT TURNING SOUND OF VAULT COMBINATION . . . LIGHT TURNING SOUND . . . LIGHT TURNING SOUND . . . LIGHT TURNING SOUND . . . HANDLE TURNS . . . USUAL ALARMS WITH BELLS, AUTO HORNS, WHISTLES, THINGS FALLING . . . ENDING WITH B.O. FOG-HORN . . .

Courtesy of J & M Productions, Inc.

The writer must keep in mind that many sounds, no matter how well or accurately done, sometimes are not immediately identifiable to the audi-

ence, and often may be confused with similar sounds. It may be necessary
for the writer to identify the sound through the dialogue. For example, since
the rattling of paper may sound like fire, and the opening and closing of a
desk drawer may sound like the opening and closing of almost anything else,
note the need for identifying dialogue in the following sequence and the
attempt to make the designation of the sound logical and a natural part of
the dialogue.

DICK: (RUFFLING THE PAGES OF A MANUSCRIPT) Just about the worst piece of
             junk I've ever done in my life.
ANNE: Well, even if you don't like it, I think it can become a best seller.
DICK: (RUFFLING PAGES AGAIN) Three hundred and forty-two pages of pure
             unadulterated mediocrity. Listen to them. They even sound off-key. (SOUND
             OF A DESK DRAWER OPENING) There. That's where it belongs. (SOUND
             OF MANUSCRIPT BEING THROWN INTO THE DRAWER)
ANNE: Don't lock it up in your desk. I think it's good.
DICK   Nope! That drawer is the place where all bad, dead manuscripts belong.
             (SOUND OF DESK DRAWER CLOSING) Amen!

Music

Music is an important part of all radio programming. The writer
should understand its several uses, including the following:

As the content for a musical program.   Live music, in the form of an
orchestra or a musical performer, has virtually disappeared from radio. Recorded or transcribed music is the primary content of radio today, as exemplified in the popular disc jockey type of program.

As the theme for a dramatic or non-dramatic program.   Those of us
over 40 remember that the first few bars of "Love in Bloom" meant that
Jack Benny was about to make his entrance. Those over 30 know that "A
Hard Day's Night" meant that The Beatles were about to appear. Although
the "theme" identification with a person or group is not as strong as it was
when radio required a sound theme to serve what today might be a visual
cue, it still exists under certain circumstances and those over 20, for example, know that "Everybody Loves Somebody Sometime" is the cue for
Dean Martin. Music may be used not only as a theme for a program as a
whole, but for a specific event or a particular character. The action or character is immediately identifiable when the theme music is heard. This may
be true in the dramatic program or with the personality on the non-dramatic
program. Theme music is used in dramatic shows, too. It is similar here to
its use as a bridge, described next, except that it is not applied during the
action but only for the opening, closing and sometimes during the commercial breaks. Note the use of music as a theme in the following excerpts from
the beginning and end of one program of a dramatic series entitled "The
Delaware Story."

ANNOUNCER:	WDEL presents "The Delaware Story."
MUSIC:	THEME IN, UP, AND UNDER.
NARRATOR:	When we think of lawless robber barons and land pirates, our thoughts turn to the early wild and unsettled west. Yet, in the late seventeenth century . . . if it had not been for the interference of the King of England, the State of Delaware, through the unscrupulous efforts of one man, might have become annexed to Maryland and never became a separate state at all.
MUSIC:	THEME UP AND OUT.
ANNOUNCER:	COMMERCIAL And now, back to today's "Delaware Story," "The Man Who Almost Stole A State."
MUSIC:	THEME IN, UP AND OUT.
NARRATOR:	In 1681 Charles II of England granted to William Penn a charter . . .

The narrator introduces the live dramatic action. Following the dramatic sequences, the narrator again resumes, completing the story.

NARRATOR:	. . . but Talbot did not succeed in stealing a state, and he remains, fortunately, a not too successful chapter in "The Delaware Story."
MUSIC:	THEME IN, UP AND OUT.

After the final commercial and program credits, the theme is again brought in, up and out to close the show.

For the bridging of divisions in the non-dramatic program, or for a change of time or place in the dramatic program. The musical bridge is the most commonly used device for transitions. Music lasting only a few notes or a few bars or, in some cases, of longer duration may be used to indicate the break between segments of the non-dramatic presentation. For example, in the variety show the writer would indicate a music bridge following the completion of an act, before the master of ceremonies introduced the next act. Sometimes the bridge may also serve as a short musical introduction or finale. The musical bridge also may be used to demark the commercial insert from the rest of the program.

In the dramatic program the musical bridge frequently is used to indicate a change of place or a lapse of time. Care must be taken that the bridge is representative of the mood and content of the play at that particular moment. The musical bridge usually is only a few seconds long.

Note the use of the bridge separating dramatic sequences and narration in the following condensed excerpt, again from one of "The Delaware Story" series.

LORD BALTIMORE:	Go to Philadelphia and speak with William Penn. Ask him to withdraw. If he does not, then we can consider other methods.
MUSIC:	BRIDGE.
TALBOT:	(FADING IN) . . . and if you choose to remain, we are left with only one recourse. I need not amplify, my dear Mr. Penn, need I?
PENN:	You have had my answer, Talbot. If you think you can frighten me from land legally deeded to me, then your presumptuousness is exceeded only by your stupidity.
MUSIC:	SNEAK IN SHORT BRIDGE.
NARRATOR:	Talbot returned to Maryland and immediately began his campaign to regain the land he believed rightfully belonged to Lord Baltimore . . .
SOUND:	CROWD OF MEN'S VOICES, ANGRY, UNDER.

TALBOT:	We must fight for the right. I've called you together because we shall and must fight like vigilantes. Our first line of defense will be Beacon Hill. The firing of three shots means danger . . . the blowing of horns will mean we assemble to ride. Are you with me?
ALL:	(SHOUTING) Aye! Aye!
MUSIC:	SNEAK IN SHORT BRIDGE.
NARRATOR:	And ride they did. Talbot now assumed dictatorial powers . . .

As a sound effect. For example, brass and percussion instruments often may be very effective in conveying the sound of a storm or in heightening the feeling of a storm presented through sound effects alone. Some effects cannot be presented potently except through music. How better could one convey on radio the sound of a person falling from the top of a tall building than through music moving in a spiral rhythm from a high to a low pitch and ending in a crash?

For background or mood. Music can heighten the content and mood of a sequence, especially in a dramatic presentation. Background music is an extremely important part of film making, and is used effectively in nonmusical TV plays. The music must serve as a subtle aid, however, and must not be obvious or, in some instances, even evident. The listener who is aware of a lovely piece of background music during a dramatic moment has been distracted from the primary purpose of the production. The music should have its effect without the audience consciously realizing it. Background and mood music should not be overdone or used excessively in the manner of the piano player accompanying a silent film. Well known compositions should be avoided, to prevent the audience from being distracted from the dialogue by too great a familiarity with the music.

Sound and Music Techniques and Terms

Several important terms are used by the writer to designate the techniques used in manipulating sound and music. These techniques are applied at the control board.

Segue (pronounced *Seg-way*). The smooth movement from one sound into the next. This is particularly applicable to the transitions between musical numbers, in which one number is faded out and the next is faded in. Technically, it is used in the dramatic program as well as in the music show, but in the dramatic program the overlapping of sounds makes the technique a cross-fade, rather than a segue.

An example in the music program:

ANNOUNCER:	Our program continues with excerpts from famous musical compositions dealing with the Romeo and Juliet theme. First we hear from Tchaikowsky's "Romeo and Juliet" overture, followed by Prokofieff's "Romeo and Juliet" ballet, and finally Gounod's opera, "Romeo et Juliette."
MUSIC:	TCHAIKOWSKY'S "ROMEO AND JULIET" SEGUE TO PROKOFIEFF'S "ROMEO AND JULIET" SEGUE TO GOUNOD'S "ROMEO ET JULIETTE"
ANNOUNCER:	You have heard . . .

An example in the dramatic program:

ANNOUNCER: And now, to today's mystery drama.
MUSIC: THEME IN AND UP, HOLD FOR FIVE SECONDS AND OUT,
SEGUE INTO
SOUND: TINKLING OF GLASSES, VOICES IN BACKGROUND IN ANGRY
CONVERSATION, JUKEBOX PLAYING.

Cross-fade. The dissolving from one sound into another. The term cross-fade sometimes is used interchangeably with the term segue. The cross-fade is, however, the crossing of sounds as one fades in and the other fades out, while the segue is simply the immediate following of one sound by another. In the following example

MUSIC: THEME IN AND UP, HOLD FOR FIVE SECONDS, CROSS-FADE
INTO THE RINGING OF A TELEPHONE.

the telephone ringing becomes blended for a second or two with the theme before the theme is entirely out and then only the telephone ringing remains.

An example in a dramatic program:

CLARA: I don't know where Harry is, but if he's with some blonde in some
bar . . .
MUSIC: STAB IN BRIDGE, HOLD FOR THREE SECONDS, CROSS-FADE
INTO SOUND OF PIANO IN A BAR PLAYING A BLUES NUMBER.

Blending. Two or more different sounds combined and going out over the air at the same time. These may include combinations of dialogue and music, dialogue and sound effects, sound effects and music or a combination of all three. The earlier example of the combination of tinkling glasses, angry voices in the background, and the playing of a jukebox is illustrative of blending dialogue, sound effects and music. The blending of sounds may be used effectively to create unrealistic effects.

Cutting or Switching. The sudden cutting off of one sound and the immediate intrusion of another. It is a jarring break and sometimes is used for special effect purposes. It may simply designate the switching sharply from one microphone to another microphone or sound source. It also may be used for remotes:

ANNOUNCER: We now switch you to Times Square where Tom Rogers is ready with his
"Probing Microphone."
CUT TO REMOTE, ROGERS AT TIMES SQUARE
ROGERS: Good afternoon. For our first interview, we have over here . . .

Fade In and Fade Out. Bringing up the volume or turning it down. This is a relatively simple operation. It frequently is used to fade the music under dialogue, as well as to bring it into the program and out of the program. The writer indicates that the music should be "faded in," "up," "under," or "out."

The following example illustrates the use of the fade in and fade out on the disc jockey show.

MUSIC: THEME, "You Rocked My Rocker With A Rock," IN, UP AND UNDER.
ANNOUNCER: Good evening, cats, and welcome to the Rockin' Rollo Rock Repertory.
MUSIC: THEME UP, HOLD FOR FIVE SECONDS, THEN UNDER AND OUT.
ANNOUNCER: This is Rockin' Rollo ready to bring you the next full hour right from the
              top of the charts. And starting with number one on the rack, it's The
              Kitchen Sink and their new hit . . .
MUSIC: SNEAK IN AND HOLD UNDER, "Clip Joint."
ANNOUNCER: That's right, you guessed it, The Kitchen Sink is smokin' away with
              "Clip Joint."
MUSIC: UP FAST, HOLD TO FINISH, AND OUT.

TELEVISION

As NOTED EARLIER, although the mid-1970s saw a trend toward video-taping and the New York style television show, most programs still followed the Hollywood style. The terms and techniques of the film will be used more frequently by the writer of the drama program, including the situation comedy-private eye-western-medical and whatever-else-is-popular-this-year type of show, than will the techniques of live television. But the medium is still television, and though techniques and script form may differ, basic grounding in television skills — many of which are, of course, similar to film skills — will not only provide the most practical preparation, but will permit the writer to move more easily and flexibly into whatever mode is being most used when he or she breaks into the field. In many instances, when the writing is done as a staff person, rather than freelance, the writer uses one technique for one type of program and another for another type.

Although the television writer does not have to know the various co-ordinate elements of theatrical production as does the writer of the stage play, it is important to know how to use and integrate settings, lights, costumes, makeup and the visual movement of performers into the script, dramatic or non-dramatic. The television writer, like the radio writer, can use all the elements of sound. In addition, the television writer must achieve at least a basic understanding of the special mechanical and electronic devices of the television medium. There are six major areas pertaining to television production that the writer should be aware of: the studio, the camera, the control room, special video effects, editing, and sound. Familiarization with books on production, as listed in the bibliography to this chapter, and/or a course in television production would be of value to the beginning writer.

The TV Studio

Studios vary greatly in size and equipment. Network studios, where drama series and specials are usually produced, have not only all the technical advantages of a television studio, but the size and equipment, as well, of a movie sound stage. Some individual stations have excellent facilities, others are small and cramped. A large regional station may have one or two relatively small studios, limiting production to news and panel shows, while a nearby school system may have an instructional television studio that would be the envy of any commercial station. The writer should be aware of studio limitations before writing the script, especially where the show may be videotaped or produced live, and it is necessary to avoid too many sets or large sets. Except in the largest studios or in the filmed production that has a budget to do location shooting, exterior sets and large nature effects are usually not possible.

The Camera

Whether the show is being recorded by a film camera or by a television camera on videotape, the basic movements of the camera are the same. Even the terminology is the same. The principal difference is the style: short, individual takes for the film approach; longer action sequences and continuous filming for the television approach. With many television directors having moved to films and film directors to television over the past decade, and with videotape editing becoming easier, the two approaches have tended to move toward each other, combining elements of both.

In either case, the writer should consider the camera as a moving and adjustable proscenium through which the attention of the audience is directed just as the writer and director wish. There are three major areas of audience attention that may be changed via the camera: the distance between the audience and the subject, which includes the amount of the subject the audience sees; the position of the audience in relation to the subject; and the angle at which the viewer sees the subject. Various uses of the camera, including camera movement, lens openings and types of shots, may be made to effect all of these approaches in varying degrees.

Camera movement may change the position, angle, distance and amount of subject matter seen. There are five specific movements the writer must be aware of and be prepared to designate, when necessary, in the script.

Dolly in and dolly out/zoom in and zoom out. The camera is on a dolly stand which permits smooth forward or backward movement. This movement to or away from the subject permits a change of orientation to the subject while keeping the camera on the air and retaining a continuity of action. The zoom lens accomplishes the same thing without moving the camera. Some writers believe that psychologically the dolly is more effective, moving the audience closer to or further from the subject, while the zoom gives the feeling of moving the subject closer to or further from the audience.

Tilt up and tilt down. This consists of pointing the camera up or down, thus changing the view from the same position to a higher or lower part of subject area. The tilt also is called panning up and panning down.

Pan right and pan left. The camera moves right or left on its axis. This movement may be used to follow a character or some particular action or to direct the audience attention to a particular subject.

Follow right and follow left. This is also called the "travel" shot or the "truck" shot. It is used when the camera is set at a right angle to the subject and either moves with it, following alongside it or, as in the case of a stationary subject such as an advertising display, follows down the line of the display. The audience's eyes, through the camera lens pointed sharply to the right or left, pick up the subjects in the display. This shot is not used as frequently as are the previous ones.

Boom shot. Originally familiar equipment for Hollywood filmmaking, the camera boom became more and more part of standard television production practices. Equipment, usually attached to the moving dolly, enables the camera to "boom" from its basic position in or out, up or down, at various angles — usually high up — to the subject.

Note the use of the basic camera movements in the following scripts. In the first, using the standard television format, the writer would not ordinarily include so many camera directions, but would leave their determination to the director. They are included here to indicate to the beginning writer a variety of camera and shot possibilities. The left hand column, as shown here, would be written in on the mimeographed script almost entirely by the director.

VIDEO	AUDIO
	DETECTIVE BYRON
ESTABLISHING SHOT.	(AT DESK, IN FRONT OF HIM, ON CHAIRS IN A ROW, ARE SEVERAL YOUNG MEN IN DUNGAREES, LEATHER JACKETS AND MOTORCYCLES CAPS) All right. So a store was robbed. So all of you were seen in the store at the time of the robbery. So there was no one else in the store except the clerk. So none of you know anything about the robbery.
DOLLY IN FOR CLOSE-UP OF BYRON.	(GETTING ANGRY) You may be young punks but you're still punks, and you can stand trial whether you're seventeen or seventy. And if you're not going to cooperate now, I'll see that you get the stiffest sentence possible.

VIDEO	AUDIO
DOLLY OUT FOR LONG SHOT OF ENTIRE GROUP. CUT TO CU. PAN RIGHT ACROSS BOYS' FACES, FROM ONE TO THE OTHER, AS BYRON TALKS. FOLLOW SHOT ALONG LINE OF CHAIRS IN FRONT OF BOYS, GETTING FACIAL REACTIONS OF EACH ONE AS THEY RESPOND.	Now, I'm going to ask you again, each one of you. And this is your last chance. If you talk, only the guilty one will be charged with larceny. The others will have only a petty theft charge on them, and I'll see they get a suspended sentence. Otherwise, I'll send you all up for five to ten. (OFF CAMERA) Joey? <center>JOEY</center>(STARES STRAIGHT AHEAD, NOT ANSWERING.) <center>BYRON</center>(OFF CAMERA) Al? <center>AL</center>I got nothin' to say. <center>BYRON</center>(OFF CAMERA) Bill? <center>BILL</center>Me, too. I don't know nothin'. <center>BYRON</center>(OFF CAMERA) O.K., Johnny. It's up to you. <center>JOHNNY</center>
TILT DOWN TO JOHNNY'S BOOT AS HE REACHES FOR HANDLE OF KNIFE. TILT UP WITH HAND AS IT MOVES AWAY FROM THE BOOT, INTO AN INSIDE POCKET OF HIS JACKET. CUT TO MEDIUM SHOT ON BOOM CAMERA OF JOHNNY WITHDRAWING HAND FROM POCKET. BOOM INTO CLOSE-UP OF OBJECT IN JOHNNY'S HAND. (ORDINARILY, A BOOM SHOT WOULD NOT BE USED HERE. A ZOOM LENS WOULD BE EASIER TO USE AND AT LEAST AS EFFECTIVE.)	(THERE IS NO ANSWER. THEN JOHNNY SLOWLY SHAKES HIS HEAD. UNPERCEPTIBLY, BYRON NOT NOTICING, HE REACHES DOWN TO HIS MOTORCYCLE BOOT FOR THE HANDLE OF A KNIFE. SUDDENLY THE HAND STOPS AND MOVES UP TO THE INSIDE POCKET OF HIS JACKET. JOHNNY TAKES AN OBJECT FROM HIS POCKET, SLOWLY OPENS HIS HAND.)

Although the format in the following, a film script, is different, note that the terminology and the visual results are virtually the same. The numbers in the left-hand column refer to each "shot" or "sequence," with film scripts usually shot out of sequence, all scenes in a particular setting done with the cast at that location. The numbers make it possible to easily designate which sequences will be filmed at a given time or on a given day, such as "Barn Set — sequences 42, 45, 46, 78, 79, 81."

FADE IN
1. EXT. BEACH — SUNRISE — EXTREME LONG SHOT
2. PAN ALONG SHORE LINE AS WAVES BREAK ON SAND
3. EXT. BEACH — LONG SHOT
   Two figures are seen in the distance, alone with the vastness of sand and water surrounding them.
4. ZOOM SLOWLY IN UNTIL WE ESTABLISH THAT FIGURES ARE A MAN AND A WOMAN.

5. MEDIUM LONG SHOT
   The man and woman are standing by the water's edge, holding hands, staring toward the sea. They are about 50, but their brightness of look and posture make them seem much younger.
6. MEDIUM SHOT — ANOTHER ANGLE ON THEM
   They slowly turn their faces toward each other and kiss.
7. CLOSE SHOT
8. MEDIUM CLOSE SHOT
   Their heads and faces are close, still almost touching.
   >GLADYS:
   >I did not feel so beautiful when I was 20.
9. CLOSE SHOT — REGINALD
   as he grins
   >REGINALD:
   >Me neither. But we weren't in love like this when we were 20.
   CUT TO
10. INT. BEACH HOUSE — ENTRANCE HALL — MORNING
    The door opens and Gladys and Reginald walk in, hand-in-hand, laughing.

As you study the scripts in the chapters dealing with specific program forms, you will note that the film script format usually is used only for the play. Virtually all other program types use the television script format, including those plays that are videotaped.

Lenses

Although it is the director who must know what the camera lenses can do so that he or she may most effectively interpret the writer's intent, it would not hurt for the writer to obtain a working knowledge of what the camera can do focally. The following, from *BM/E* magazine, is a good introductory guide:

In the beginning, the user was confined to four lenses on a turret. This made framing a shot difficult as well as time consuming. With the old turreted camera there were only four focal lengths readily available, which necessitated a good deal of dollying with the resultant time loss and undesirable framing of a shot due to the limited number of focal lengths. Then along came the zoom lens with its great number of focal lengths immediately available. The director could now get the exact framing he wanted quickly. Now that it is here, can one zoom do everything? Of course not! The correct lens for your application may not be applicable to someone else's needs. A good studio lens is not a good remote lens although it may cover some remote applications. The remote lens works quite often at long focal lengths under low light levels requiring f stops of f/3 at 500mm or f/6 at 1000mm, or better. The average studio lens can attain 500mm with range extenders but it needs over 3 times more light at that focal length due to its limited aperture. The remote lens cannot fulfill all of the requirements in a studio because its close focusing distance is 10 ft. and its wide angle is about 30° less than a studio lens (a cumbersome retro zoom will, however, help measurably). If your studio is small, you will need a lens with a wide angle so that it isn't necessary to dolly back to one side of the studio to get an overall shot of a set on the other side. Close focusing is necessary so that magnification is possible as well as interesting special effect shots. It should be noted here that two lenses with the *same* long focal length and different close focusing capability will magnify an object to a different degree, the greater magnification going with the closer focusing of the two. If commercial production is contemplated, then more capability will be demanded of the lens because agency people, as well as clients, want the dramatic eye-catching shot that will make the product memorable.

Taping time must be held to a minimum to earn more money for the station and less added cost to the advertiser. The lens can be of great help here. If a lens can, in fast sequence, go from an extreme close-up to a wide overall shot and back to a close-up then taping time will be lessened because there will be no need to stop the tape for different shot sequences.

However, if all that is done is news and weather, the simple good quality wide angle 10 to 1 lens may be all that is needed. [7]

Types of Shots

Among those directions most frequently written in by the writer are the shots designating how much of the subject is to be seen, as illustrated in the script examples a few pages back. Ordinarily, the determination is left up to the director, but in many instances the writer needs to capture a specific subject for the logical continuity of the script or for the proper psychological effect of that moment upon the audience. When the specific shot required might not be obvious to the director, the writer has the prerogative of inserting it into the script. Shot designations range from the close-up to the medium shot to the long shot. Within these categories there are gradations, such as the medium long shot and the extreme close-up. The writer indicates the kind of shot and the specific subject to be encompassed by that shot. The use of the terms and their meanings apply to both the film and the television format. Here are the most commonly used shots:

Close-up. This may be designated by the letters CU. The writer states in the script: "CU Harry," or "CU Harry's fingers as he twists the dials of the safe," or "CU Harry's feet on the pedals of the piano." The close-up of the immediate person of a human subject will usually consist of just the face and may include some of the upper part of the body, with emphasis on the face, unless specifically designated otherwise. The letters XCU or ECU stand for extreme close-up and designate the face alone. The term shoulder shot indicates an area encompassing the shoulders to the top of the head. Other designations are bust shot, waist shot, hip shot and knee shot.

Medium Shot.   This may be designated by the letters **MS**. The camera picks up a good part of the individual or group subject, the subject usually filling the screen, but usually not in its entirety, and without too much of the physical environment shown.

Long Shot.   The writer may state this as LS. The long shot is used primarily for establishing shots in which the entire setting, or as much of it as necessary to orient the audience properly, is shown. From the long shot, the camera may move to the medium shot and then to the close-up, creating a dramatic movement from an over-all view to the impact of the essence or selective aspect of the situation. Conversely, the camera may move from the intriguing suspense of the extreme close-up to the clarifying broadness of the extreme long shot.

Full Shot.   This is stated as FS. The subject is put on the screen in its entirety. For example, "FS Harry" means that the audience sees Harry from head to toe. "FS family at dinner table" means that the family seated around the dinner table is seen completely.

The writer should be aware of any necessity to change lenses, focus the lenses or dolly the camera for a new shot. Depending on the number of cameras used in the show, if it is live or live-style videotaped, the writer should leave enough time between shots for the cameraperson to properly perform these functions.

Note the use of different types of shots in the following hypothetical script example. The video directions are necessary at the beginning of this script because the writer is dealing solely with pictures. Subsequent video directions may be left out by the writer, except, as at the end, where necessary to convey the meaning and action. You will note that in many of the actual scripts used in this book, the writer provides very few video directions.

VIDEO	AUDIO
FADE IN ON LONG SHOT OF OUTSIDE OF BAR. ESTABLISH STREET FRONT AND OUTSIDE OF BAR. DOLLY IN TO MEDIUM SHOT, THEN TO CLOSE-UP OF SIGN ON THE WINDOW: "HARRY SMITH, PROP." CUT TO INSIDE OF BAR, CLOSE-UP OF MAN'S HAND DRAWING A GLASS OF BEER FROM THE TAP. FOLLOW MAN'S HAND WITH GLASS TO TOP OF BAR WHERE HE PUTS DOWN GLASS. DOLLY OUT SLOWLY TO MEDIUM SHOT OF HARRY, SERVING THE BEER, AND MAC, SITTING AT BAR. CONTINUE DOLLYING OUT TO LONG SHOT, ESTABLISHING ENTIRE INSIDE OF BAR, SEVERAL PEOPLE ON	

VIDEO	AUDIO
STOOLS, AND SMALL TABLE AT RIGHT OF BAR WITH THREE MEN SEATED, PLAYING CARDS.	**JOE** (AT TABLE) Harry. Bring us another deck. This one's getting too dirty for honest card players.
	HARRY Okay. (HE REACHES UNDER THE BAR, GETS A DECK OF CARDS, GOES TO THE TABLE.)
TIGHT 2-S HARRY AND JOE	**JOE** (TAKING THE CARDS, WHISPERS TO HARRY.) Who's the guy at the bar? He looks familiar.
	HARRY Name of Mac. From Jersey someplace.
CUT TO CU JOE	**JOE** Keep him there. Looks like somebody we got business with. (LOOKS AROUND
CUT TO FS TABLE	TABLE) Right, boys? (THE MEN AT THE TABLE NOD KNOWINGLY TO HARRY.)
	HARRY Okay if I go back to the bar?
	JOE Go ahead.
PAN WITH HARRY TO BAR. DOLLY IN TO BAR, MS HARRY AND MAC AS HARRY POURS HIM ANOTHER DRINK. MCU HARRY AS HE WRITES. CUT TO CU OF WORDS ON PIECE OF PAPER.	**HARRY** (WALKS BACK TO BAR, POURS DRINK FOR MAC. SCRIBBLES SOMETHING ON PIECE OF PAPER, PUTS IT ON BAR IN FRONT OF MAC.)

Control Room Techniques and Editing

The technicians in the control room have various electronic devices for modifying the picture and moving from one picture to another — thus giving television its ability to direct the attention and control the view of the audience and to bypass the unities of time and place effectively. The technicians in the film editing room have the same capabilities, except that the modifications are done during the editing process, while in live-type videotaped television the modifications are done during the recording of the program. Further modifications can take place when editing the videotape. The writer should be familiar with the terminology and function of control room techniques and their similar function in film editing in order to know what the potentials of the medium are and to be able to indicate, if necessary, special picture modifications or special changes in time and/or place. The terms used have the same meaning in television and film. A look at some of the books on TV production and film editing listed in the bibliography at the end of this chapter is recommended.

The Fade. The fade-in consists of bringing in the picture from a black (or blank) screen. (You've often heard the term, "Fade to Black.")

The fade-out is the taking out of a picture until a black level is reached. The fade is used primarily to indicate a passage of time, and in this function serves much like the curtain or blackout on the legitimate stage. Depending on the sequence of action, a fast fade-in or fade-out or slow fade-out or fade-in may be indicated. The fade-in is used at the beginning of a sequence, the fade-out at the end. The fade sometimes also is used to indicate a change of place. The writer always indicates the fade-in or fade-out in the script.

The Dissolve. The dissolve is similar to the cross-fade of radio. While one picture is being reduced to black level, the other picture is being brought in from black level, one picture smoothly dissolving into the next. The dissolve is used primarily to indicate a change of place, but is used sometimes to indicate a change of time. There are various modifications of the dissolve. An important one is the matched dissolve, in which two similar or identical subjects are placed one over the other and the fading out of one and the fading in of the other shows a metamorphosis taking place. The dissolving from a newly lit candle into a candle burned down would be a use of the matched dissolve. The dissolve may vary in time, and may be designated as a fast dissolve — almost a split-second movement — or as a slow dissolve — anywhere up to five seconds. The writer always indicates the use of the dissolve in the script.

The Cut. The cut is the technique most commonly used. It consists simply of switching instantaneously from one picture to another. Care must be taken to avoid too much cutting, and to make certain that the cutting is consistent with the mood, rhythm, pace and psychological approach of the program as a whole. The writer ordinarily is not concerned with the planning or designation of cuts in the TV script, but leaves it up to the director. In the film script, particularly when the transition from one sequence to the next is a sharp, instantaneous effect rather than a dissolve or fade, the writer may indicate "CUT TO . . ."

The Superimposition. The "super," as it is sometimes called, means the placing of one image over another, thus creating a fantasy kind of picture. This sometimes is used in the stream-of-consciousness technique when the thing being recalled to memory is pictured on the screen. The superimposition may be used for non-dramatic effects very effectively, such as the superimposition of titles over a picture or the superimposition of commercial names or products over the picture. To obtain necessary contrast in the superimposition, when the two pictures are placed on the screen together one picture must be of a higher light intensity than the other. The writer usually indicates the use of the superimposition.

The Wipe. This is accomplished by one picture literally wiping another picture off the screen in the manner of a window shade being pulled down over a window. The wipe may be from any direction: horizontal, vertical, or diagonal. The wipe may also blossom out a picture from the center of a black level or, in reverse, envelop the picture by encompassing it from all its sides. The wipe can be used to designate a change of place or time.

The Split Screen. In the split screen the picture on the air is actually divided, with the shots from two or more cameras occupying adjoining places on the screen. A common use is for phone conversations, showing the persons speaking on separate halves of the screen. The screen may be split in many parts and in many shapes, as is sometimes done when news correspondents report from different parts of the nation. One segment of the screen of virtually any size may be split off from the rest, as often is done in sports broadcasts; for example, one corner of the screen may show the runner taking a lead off first base while the rest of the screen encompasses the main action of the ball game.

Film and Slides. For live-type television production, such as newscasts and in many college and university training studios which may not have sophisticated film or videotape equipment, film clips (short-lengths of 16-millimeter motion picture film) and slides are important. Films and slides provide visual information not available in the studio for news, sports, feature and documentary programs. In news and sports programs particularly, videotape rather than film may be used to serve the same function. The film clip may also be used in live-type videotaped drama to provide background shots necessary to the production which could not be achieved in the limited settings of the studio. Exterior scenes and nature effects may be captured on film. The split-second electronic adjustments make it possible to integrate the film or slides with "live" action, as in chroma key, front screen and rear screen uses.

In the "old, old" days of television, when drama production was "live," film frequently was used as "cover" material — that is, as a means of continuing the action while the character or characters involved in the next scene changed costume, altered makeup or got to another set. Voice-over prerecorded material was another "cover" device. Other "cover" techniques used by the writer included concentration on some action or on a close-up of another performer, giving the impression that the first performer is present but involved in the action off-screen; cutting to other characters in another set or substituting a similarly dressed performer, showing only the back of the head or an incomplete image, thus creating the impression that the original character is still there. Although the writer is never or rarely ever likely to need such "cover" material in professional television production at its present (and future) stage of development, it is mentioned here not only for its historical interest but because in many college and university studios, by design or because of lack of equipment, the "live" approach is used and "cover" techniques may come in handy for the beginning writer.

Note the use of different control room techniques for modifying the picture and moving from one picture to another in the following hypothetical script example:

COMMENTARY	VIDEO	AUDIO
1. The fade-in is used for the beginning of the sequence.	FADE IN ON SHERIFF'S OFFICE. SHERIFF FEARLESS AND DEPUTY FEARFUL ARE SEATED AT THE DESK IN THE CENTER OF THE ROOM.	FEARLESS I wonder what Bad Bart is up to. He's been in town since yesterday. I've got to figure out his plan if I'm to prevent bloodshed. FEARFUL I've got faith in you, Fearless. I heard that he's been with Miss Susie in her room. FEARLESS Good. We can trust her. She'll find out for us. FEARFUL But I'm worried about her safety. FEARLESS Yup. I wonder how she is making out. That Bad Bart is a mean one.
2. The dissolve is used here for a change of place without passage of time. This scene takes place simultaneously, or immediately following the one in the sheriff's office.	DISSOLVE TO MISS SUSIE'S HOTEL ROOM. BART IS SEATED IN AN EASY CHAIR. SUSIE IS IN A STRAIGHT CHAIR AT THE OTHER END OF THE ROOM.	BART I ain't really a killer, Miss Susie. It's only my reputation that's hurting me. Only because of one youthful indiscretion. SUSIE What was that, Mr. Bart?
3. The superimposition is used here for a memory recall device.	SUPERIMPOSE, OVER CU BART, FACE OF MAN HE KILLED AS HE DESCRIBES SCENE.	BART I can remember as well as yesterday. I was only a kid then. I thought he drew a gun on me. Maybe he did and maybe he didn't. But I shot him. And I'll remember his face as sure as I'll live — always. SUSIE I guess you aren't really all bad, Mr. Bart. BART You've convinced me, Susie. I've never had a fine woman speak to me so nice before. I'm going to turn over a new leaf.
4. The cut would be used without indication from the writer throughout this script.	PAN WITH BART TO THE HALL DOOR. CUT TO HALL AS HE ENTERS IT.	(WALKS INTO THE HALL.

COMMENTARY	VIDEO	AUDIO
Here, the cut specifically indicates a different view of the character in the same continuous time sequence.		AN EARLY MODEL TELE-PHONE IS ON THE WALL.) I'm going to call the Sheriff. Operator, get me the Sheriff's office.
		FEARLESS
5. The wipe here moves from left to right or right to left. It designates a change of place. The use of the split screen indicates the putting of two different places before the audience at the same time.	HORIZONTAL WIPE INTO SPLIT SCREEN. BART IN ONE HALF, SHERIFF PICKING UP TELEPHONE IN OTHER HALF.	Sheriff's office.
		BART
		Sheriff. This is Bad Bart. I'm going to give myself up and confess all my crimes. I've turned over a new leaf.
		FEARLESS
		You expect me to believe that, Bart?
		BART
		No, I don't. But all I'm asking is a chance to prove it.
		FEARLESS
		How do you propose to do that?
	WIPE OFF SHERIFF OFFICE SCENE. CU BART'S FACE AS HE MAKES HIS DECISION.	BART
		I'm coming over to your office. And I'm not going to be wearing my guns.
6. The fade here indicates the passage of time. If this next scene were in the Sheriff's office, the fade would have indicated a passage of time and change of place.	FADE OUT. FADE IN ON MISS SUSIE SEATED ON HER BED.	SUSIE
		That's all there was to it, Fearless. The more I talked to him, the more I could see that underneath it all he had a good heart.
7. The sustained opening on Susie is necessary, for live-type, continuous action television, to provide time for Bart to get off the set and for Fearless to get on. The 15 or 20 seconds at the opening of this scene, in which we do not yet see Fearless, though Susie's dialogue indicates he is there, should be sufficient "cover" time.		(SHE WALKS TO THE SMALL TABLE AT THE FOOT OF THE BED, TAKES A GLASS AND BOTTLE, THEN WALKS OVER TO THE EASY CHAIR. WE SEE SHERIFF FEARLESS IN THE EASY CHAIR.) Here, Fearless, have a Sarsa-parilla. You deserve one after what you've done today.
		FEARLESS
		No, Susie. It was you who really did the work. And you deserve the drink. (AFTER A MOMENT) You know, there's only one thing I'm sorry for.
		SUSIE
		What's that?
		FEARLESS
		That Bart turned out to be good, deep down inside, and gave himself up.
		SUSIE
		Why?

COMMENTARY	VIDEO	AUDIO
		FEARLESS Well, there's this new gun I received this morning from the East that I haven't yet had a chance to use!
8. Fade is used to signify the end of a sequence, and, note the next scene, a passage of time and change of place.	THEME MUSIC IN AND UP STRONG. SLOW FADE OUT.	
9. Since this is a videotaped studio show, the film clip is necessary for the exterior scene, not reproduceable in a studio. Such film clip inserts could be used at any time during the play itself. For example, there might have been a short chase on horses between Fearless and Bart, the pre-filmed chase sequences integrated into the studio-taped action.	FADE IN FILM CLIP FEARLESS AND SUSIE ON THEIR HORSES ON THE TRAIL WAVING GOODBYE TO BART, WHO RIDES OFF INTO THE DISTANCE.	
10. "Super" refers to superimposition. "Telop" refers to the opaque projection transmission into a camera and to a monitor, titles, credits and other written, drawn, printed and similar material. The superimposition is used here for credits.	SUPER TELOP WITH CREDITS OVER THE SCENE AS FEARLESS AND SUSIE CONTINUE TO WAVE.	

Special Video Effects

Titles. Although the writer is not responsible for the kind of titling done, he should be aware of the various types of titling devices — such as title cards, title drum, book titles, slides, superimpositions and others.

Nature Effects. Though it is difficult to achieve realistic nature effects in some studios, it is possible to obtain some through special effects. These include snow, rain, smoke and flame.

Miniatures. In lieu of film or live exteriors, a miniature of a setting that cannot be duplicated in full in the studio may serve very well for establishing shots. For example, a miniature of a castle may be used for an opening shot. The camera dollies toward the front gate of the miniature. Then a cut is made to the live set which may consist of the courtyard or an interior room.

Detail sets. Detail sets serve to augment the close-ups of television.

Where the camera might find it difficult to pick up the precise movements of the fingers turning the dial of the safe on the regular set, another camera may cut to a detail set of the safe and capture the actor's fingers in every precise action. Detail sets are used frequently in instructional TV.

Puppets, Marionettes and Animation. These devices are particularly effective in commercial presentation and may be easily integrated into "live action" sequences. Animation is a staple and frequently the most creative approach in the production of commercials.

Rear, Front and Overhead Projection. As noted under *Film and Slides,* scenes or effects may be electronically projected from the front or the rear onto the background. Use of overhead projectors for special effects in titling and in graphic presentations became an important part of educational television production.

Remotes. One or more cameras may be set up at a place remote from the studio and send back material for incorporation into the program, live, as with a newscast, or taped, as with a play or documentary. An entire program may be done remote, such as a football game.

Additional Film Considerations. Although the basic approach to writing still is that of the live-type taped television show, some of the special requirements of the film should be kept in mind. While the initial shooting script for the film may seem disjointed and is frequently produced and directed in such a manner, the opportunity to have a number of takes of any given sequence and to put together the whole into what might even seem an entirely new and different script in the editing room provides much more flexibility in transitions for the writer than does the TV script. Even when videotaped, the TV production follows a more-or-less continuous action line, and the writer must clearly link the continuity of action through the transitions from sequence to sequence. Although film stresses different angles of the same subject, even from the same distance on the same set (usually difficult and sometimes impossible in live-type television), don't overdo it. Extreme angles, particularly with frequency, can be unduly disturbing. With transition of some of the fine TV directors, such as Sidney Lumet, to the motion pictures, film technique has shown more and more use of TV technique, including the TV approach of longer shots, of not being afraid to stay on one camera and have the action, rather than the camera, move.

Sound

Basically, sound is used in television in the same way as in radio, as analyzed earlier in this chapter. There are, however, some obvious modifications. Sound in television does not convey movement and does not physically orient the audience as it does in radio. The microphone in the television play usually is not stationary, but is on a boom and a dolly to follow the moving performers. In the single-action shot of the film, it may be stationary if the actors do not move. Chest mikes, table mikes and cordless mikes are also used, usually for the non-dramatic studio program, such as the interview and panel, but also occasionally for the drama, in pre-set situations and positions. The dialogue and sound on the set emanate from and must be coordinated with the visual action. Off-screen sound effects may be used, but they clearly must appear to be coming from off-screen unless they represent an action taking place on-camera. Sound may be pre-recorded or, as in filmed productions, added after the action has been shot. Television may use narration, as radio does. In television the voice-over may be a narrator, an announcer or the pre-recorded thoughts of the character. Television uses music as program content, as background and as theme. If a performer in television purportedly plays an instrument, the impression must be given that the person involved is really playing the instrument. Other uses of sound and music in radio may be adapted to television, as long as the writer remembers that in television the sound or music does not replace visual action, but complements or heightens it.

NOTES TO CHAPTER 2

[1] "Is Videotape Taking Over? Can Film Hang In There?," *BM/E,* January, 1973, pp. 24-25.

[2] "Network Taping Too," *Television/Radio Age,* March 6, 1972, p. 39.

[3] *Ibid.*

[4] *Ibid.*

[5] "Is Videotape Taking Over? Can Film Hang In There?," *op. cit.,* p. 25.

[6] Corwin, Norman, *Thirteen By Corwin* (New York: Holt, Rinehart and Winston, Inc., 1942), p. 90.

[7] Rice, Ken, "What a Broadcaster Should Know About Zoom Lenses," *BM/E,* June, 1974, pp. 31-32.

REFERENCE BOOKS

ON RADIO AND TELEVISION PRODUCTION

This chapter is necessarily only a brief summary of the basic production elements. The writer is advised to consult books such as the following for detailed, illustrated explanations of production techniques that may be useful to know when preparing a script. For a more comprehensive list, please consult the works noted at the beginning of the bibliography to Chapter 1.

BIBLIOGRAPHY

Bluem, A. William and Roger Manvell, eds. *Television: The Creative Experience.* New York: Hastings House, 1967. Includes aesthetics and the writer's viewpoint.

Burder, John. *The Technique of Editing 16mm Films.* Rev. Ed. New York: Hastings House, 1971.

Gottesman, Ronald and Harry Geduld. *Guidebook to Film: An Eleven-in-One Reference.* New York: Holt, Rinehart & Winston, 1972. Includes bibliography on writing.

Halas, John and Manvell, Roger. *The Technique of Film Animation,* 3rd ed. New York: Hastings House, 1971. Includes storyboard and writing techniques for commercials, instructional, other forms.

Happé, Bernard. *Basic Motion Picture Technology,* Rev. Ed. New York: Hastings House, 1975. Application of film fundamentals to television.

Hilliard, Robert L., ed. *Radio Broadcasting,* 2nd ed., rev. New York: Hastings House, 1974. Introduction to all phases, including writing.

————, ed. *Understanding Television.* New York: Hastings House, 1964. Introduction to all phases, including writing.

Levitan, Eli L. *An Alphabetical Guide to Motion Pictures, Television and Video Tape Production.* New York: McGraw-Hill, 1970. Comprehensive source of practical information.

Lewis, Colby. *The TV Director/Interpreter.* New York: Hastings House, 1968.

Manvell, Roger and Lewis Jacobs, eds. *The International Encyclopedia of Film.* New York: Crown, 1972.

Millerson, Gerald. *The Technique of Television Production.* 9th rev. ed. New York: Hastings House, 1972. All phases including imagery and composition.

Nisbett, Alec. *The Technique of the Sound Studio.* 3rd rev. ed. New York: Hastings House, 1972. Comprehensive treatment for radio, television, film.

————. *The Use of Microphones.* New York: Hastings House, 1974.

Oringel, Robert S. *Audio Control Handbook,* 4th edition. New York: Hastings House, 1972. For television and radio both, including program formats.

Reisz, Karel and Gavin Millar. *The Technique of Film Editing,* Rev. and Enlarged Ed. New York: Hastings House, 1968. A classic in its field.

Spottiswoode, Raymond, ed. *The Focal Encyclopedia of Film and Television: Techniques.* New York: Hastings House, 1969. Comprehensive and cross-referenced.

Stone, Vernon and Bruce Hinson. *Television Newsfilm Techniques.* New York: Hastings House, 1974. A project of the Radio Television News Directors Association, giving latest information on this important aspect of news reporting.

Zettl, Herbert. *Sight, Sound, Motion: Applied Media Aesthetics.* Belmont, Calif.: Wadsworth, 1973. Aesthetic and artistic considerations.

FOR APPLICATION AND REVIEW

RADIO
1. Write a short sequence in which you use all five microphone positions.
2. Write one or more short sequences in which you use sound effects to: establish locale or setting; direct the audience attention by emphasis on a particular sound; establish time; establish mood; signify entrances or exits; create transitions between program segments; create unrealistic effects. More than one of the above uses may be indicated in a single sequence.
3. Write one or more short sequences in which you use music: as a bridge; as a sound effect; to establish background or mood.
4. Write a short script in which you use the following techniques: segue; cross-fade; blending; cutting or switching; fade in or fade out.

TELEVISION
1. Write a short sequence in the New York "TV-style" script form in which you use the following camera movements: the dolly-in and dolly-out; the tilt; the pan; the follow shot.
2. Write a short sequence in the Hollywood "film-style" script form in which you use the following camera movements: zoom; pan; boom; change of camera angle.
3. Write a short sequence in "TV-style script" in which you, the writer must indicate the following shots: CU, M2S, LS, FS, XLS, XCU. Do the same thing using the "film-style script."
4. Write a short sequence in "TV-style script" in which you, the writer, must designate the following effects: fade-in and fade-out; dissolve; superimposition; wipe; split-screen; film insert; rear projection.
5. Write a short sequence in "film-style script" in which you, the writer, must designate the following effects: fade-in and fade-out; cut; dissolve.
6. Watch several television programs and analyze the use of camera movements, types of shots and control board or editing effects. Can you determine the writer's contributions in relation to the use of these techniques as differentiated from the director's work?

3

Announcements and Commercials

CHARLES "CHUCK" BARCLAY, director of Creative Services for the Radio Advertising Bureau, has said: "Even the worst commercial, repeated often enough, sometimes produces results."

John Crosby, when he gave up television criticism for the *New York Herald-Tribune,* wrote: "I don't mind the commercials. It's just the programs I can't stand."

S. J. Paul, publisher of *Television/Radio Age,* has written: "The commercial-makers are themselves the stars of the radio-television structure. For in the short time frame of 20, 30, or 60 seconds a mood is created — a message is transmitted — and a sales point is made. This finished product is the result of many talents. In some cases, as it has often been remarked, the commercials are better than the programs."[1]

Some commercials are awful because they insult our aesthetic sensibilities. Some are awful because they insult our logic and intelligence. Some are awful because they play on the emotions of those least able to cope with the incitements to buy — such as children.

Some commercials are good because they are, indeed, more aesthetically pleasing than the programs they surround. Some are good because they are educational and do provide the viewer with informational guidelines on goods and services.

All commercials are, however, designed to sell something — a product or service or idea. It is the existence of these commercials that provide the economic base for the American broadcasting system as it is now constituted.

Except for the further development of public television and public radio, which rely on federal, state and local governmental funding, citizen donations, foundations, industries and other institutional support which do not require commercial advertising — which is barred, anyway, from non-commercial stations by the FCC Rules and Regulations — the American system of broadcasting is likely to remain dependent on commercials for a long time.

In early radio and television there were few commercials, and what there were were usually gratis. In radio, for example, many of the first stations were operated by newspapers in order to promote the newspapers. Many others were operated principally to sell the receiving equipment manufactured by the stations' owners. It wasn't until two years after regular broadcasting began that station WEAF, New York City, in late 1922 carried the first sponsored program. When the sponsoring real estate firm's two advertised buildings were sold through the radio ads, commercial radio was born. In television the first stations, needing material, were happy to present films dealing with "electronics for progress" and showing "how rubber is made" — films which just happened to carry the clearly indicated brand name of the rubber company and the electronic appliance manufacturer and the other firms which supplied the films. The total expenditures by advertisers on television in 1974 amounted to $4.35 billion. Of this sum, advertisers spent $2.01 billion on network commercials, $1.24 billion on spot announcements and $1.01 billion on local station commercials. Of the total of $1.7 billion spent by advertisers on radio, $61 million was for network commercials, $384 million for spot announcements and $1.29 billion for commercials on local stations. It is significant that in 1974 over half of the income of members of the Screen Actors Guild came from commercials, with the remainder coming from other television work and/or from regular Hollywood films. Almost all of the writing of commercials is done in advertising agencies. In a few cases an advertiser, particularly on the local level, may prepare commercials in-house — sometimes not very well. Most often local commercials are prepared locally, frequently by someone connected with the station.

This puts the writer squarely in the middle. On one hand, the writer has a responsibility to the agency and advertiser, creating not only the most attractive message possible, but one which convinces/sells. On the other hand, the power of the commercial (yes, many people believe that Madison Avenue can sell/convince anybody of anything!) charges the writer with the responsibility of being certain that the commercial has a positive and not a negative effect on public ethics and actions.

SOME ETHICAL CONSIDERATIONS

MORE AND MORE the pressures of audiences, civic and citizen organizations, some professions and the federal government itself are changing the approaches to commercial writing and presentation. At one time some commercials were blatantly racist. Since the Civil Rights movement of the

1960s racism in the media, including commercials, gradually lessened. But even as anti-Black stereotypes waned, an organization called the Mexican-American Anti-Defamation Committee was formed to combat media racism against Chicanos. BEST (Black Efforts for Soul in Television) was developed to keep a watchful eye on media portrayals and to try to effect positive changes. The writer who has been at all sensitive to the public events of the past 20 years is not likely to get caught in any intentional racism in commercials writing — although there is enough indication to show that many writers should check even a seemingly innocuous reference to or portrayal of a Black, Spanish-surnamed, Oriental, American Indian or other minority with a qualified spokesperson from that group for unintentional and inadvertent racism.

Most advertisers and agencies have recognized the need not only to avoid stereotyped portrayals of minorities, but, particularly for Blacks, to include minorities as non-stereotyped characters in commercials. Some of the cynical among us might suggest that economics plays at least as large a part as ethics. At the beginning of the 1970s decade Blacks constituted some 12% of the population with a buying power of some $40 billion. Over 500 stations had some sort of programming for Blacks, with some 125 programming totally for Blacks. The latter did about $40 million in commercial accounts, of which some $10 million was in national spots. We hope it won't be necessary for writers and producers and agencies to look at the buying power of Spanish-surnamed, American Indians, Orientals and others before making representatives of those groups a regular and positive part of commercial messages.

Prejudicial portrayals have not been limited to race. Negative ethnic references, particularly those related to national origins — Italy, Poland, for example — have also needed pointing out and correction.

Perhaps one of the most flagrant areas of prejudice, still existing in the mid-1970s, has been that regarding women. If Blacks, for example, were portrayed in commercials the way women are today, there would be a national scandal. But the women's movement, giving historical guidelines for action to Blacks in the early 1960s, learned in turn from the Blacks in the early 1970s and, particularly through the efforts of NOW (National Organization for Women), began forceful action against insulting media stereotypes, including the stereotyping of women in subservient roles in society. A study of commercials by NOW in the early 1970s showed that in 42.6% of the commercials women were doing household work; in 37.5% their role was to provide help or service to men; and in 16.7% their main purpose was for male sex needs. In only 0.3% of the commercials were women shown as independent individuals. From the "Fly Me" sex object to the "My wife, I think I'll keep her" household object, women have been presented, by and large, as vacuous, usable *things*. It is not surprising that a *Good Housekeeping* survey in 1971 found that one-third of the women have at one time or another turned off commercials because they found them offensive.

The public image created of a person or a race or an ethnic group or of women affects the acceptance of that individual or group into the mainstream of economic endeavor — specifically the job market and other opportunities which relate to the job market. Given the current situation where male-dominated business and industry generally keep women's pay lower and deny women equal opportunity to compete with men for top-paying jobs, some people believe that there is a "hidden agenda" behind the commercials and other representations of women in the media. That is not to say that the commercial writers, producers and ad agency representatives consciously and with overt deliberation are conspiring to keep women in a certain economic — and hence socio-political-sexual — place; but the role of their subconscious or unconscious might be examined in light of the product they turn out.

Ethical considerations relate not only to portrayals of people, but to representations of products as well. In 1970 ACT (Action for Children's Television) petitioned the FCC to, among other things, eliminate all commercials from children's programming, citing content and approaches which ACT believed were harmful to children. Following a study by an FCC task force, pressure from citizen groups, and overt concern expressed by the FCC, the NAB (National Association of Broadcasters), in 1974, voluntarily amended the TV Code to reduce the commercial minutes in children's programs from 12 minutes per hour to 10 minutes in 1975 and to 9¼ minutes in 1976 on Saturday and Sunday mornings — children's prime time — and from 16 minutes per hour to 14 minutes in 1975 and to 12 minutes in 1976 in the Monday-Friday schedule. In addition, the Code introduced content restrictions: a ban on all "non-prescription medications" and "supplemental vitamin" products; all "products advertised to children must conform to established safety rules and regulations"; program content and advertising messages must be clearly separated from each other by an "appropriate device"; additional costs for toys, such as the need to purchase batteries must be disclosed. Pressures still continue from citizen and consumer groups (at this writing), including proposals to especially ban advertising of products that may be considered harmful to children — such as cereals and other foods containing principally sugars. Very strongly resisted by the broadcasting industry is the proposal of the Federal Trade Commission to ban all advertising of premiums for children on children's programs. In late 1974 an FCC Policy Statement on Children's Television did not adopt ACT's proposals concerning advertising, but did include reiteration of the principal commercial restrictions adopted by the NAB.

When we think of the country's tradition about motherhood and children being sacred, we wonder why the writer (and the producer) had to have restrictions imposed, and where the hypocrisy really lies!

When pushed hard enough the broadcasting industry does take action, not only in relation to children but in relation to specific product areas. Let's note some recent examples. The drug-mania of the early 1970s caused fears in many quarters — some reasonable, some unreasonable. Perhaps the greatest pusher of drugs was broadcasting, daily and nightly exhorting the audience to buy this or that patent medicine to cure almost anything and everything. Congress began to fear that broadcast advertising was contributing to the growing drug culture, and in response to indications that governmental action would soon be necessary, the industry — those who subscribed to the NAB Code — adopted its own guidelines. As an example of the kinds of the ethical product marketing approaches the writer should be aware of, here are the NAB Code guidelines on drug advertising: [2]

Claims of product effectiveness must be substantiated by clinical evidence.

Ads should include reference to need to read and follow product labeling, directions.

Portrayal of immediate relief should be avoided unless accurately substantiated.

Avoid audio/visual approaches commonly associated with the "drug culture" or which imply a casual attitude towards the use of drugs.

Use of children is not permitted in presentations made to adults.

Products shall be presented for occasional use only.

Avoid depicting reliance on non-prescription medications in dealing with everyday problems.

References to non-prescription medications as "non-habit forming" is not permitted.

Celebrity product endorsements and on-camera pill-taking not permitted.

Product identification by over-emphasis on color should be avoided.

Ads for non-prescription medications shall not be scheduled in or adjacent to children's programs.

Aside from ethical consideration of the effect of advertising on the public, the industry occasionally resolves internecine fights on approaches to advertising. For a while in the late 1960s and early 1970s Brand "X" took a beating. "Comparative" ads, as they are called, not only stated that a certain electric shaver was better than the competition, but also showed the viewer a demonstration between the advertised product and the competitors' products in order to emphasize the point, running down the competition in the process. This and similar commercials in which Brand "X" — clearly named — was knocked around, resulted in strong concern and action in the industry and in comparative commercials guidelines by the 4As (American Association of Advertising Agencies — AAAA), the advertising counterpart to the NAB:[3]

The intent and connotation of the ad should be to inform and never to discredit or unfairly attack competitors, competing products or services.

When a competitive product is named, it should be one that exists in the marketplace as significant competition.

The competition should be fairly and properly identified but never in a manner or tone of voice that degrades the competitive product or service.

The advertising should compare related or similar properties or ingredients of the product, dimension to dimension, feature to feature.

The identification should be for honest comparison purposes and not simply to upgrade by association.

If a competitive test is conducted it should be done by an objective testing source, preferably an independent one, so that there will be no doubt as to the veracity of the test.

In all cases the test should be supportive of all claims made in the advertising that are based on the test.

The advertising should never use partial results or stress insignificant differences to cause the consumer to draw an improper conclusion.

The property being compared should be significant in terms of value or usefulness of the product to the consumer.

Comparatives delivered through the use of testimonials should not imply that the testimonial is more than one individual's thought unless that individual represents a sample of the majority viewpoint.

Some writers may find guidelines restrictive; others may find them stimulating toward more responsible writing. All writers will find they require awareness of what may and what may not specifically go into a commercial, in form, purpose and content. All, hopefully, will also identify with the commercials-creator who believes that "Accounting to a set of practical, working rules allows a good balance of involvement with the industry and accountability to the consumer public. It's hard to try and dupe, or con the viewer when you feel 'we are they' . . . and realize that you are only cheating yourself."[4]

SOME PRODUCTION CONSIDERATIONS

As POINTED OUT in Chapter 2, the 1970s saw a swing toward the use of video tape instead of film in making TV commercials. At first this was true principally in studio production, but with the increased use of tape in sports and news events, and the refinement of lightweight, portable TV cameras, tape also grew in location-produced commercials. Part of the reason for location shooting, providing a different milieu and different form considerations for the writer, was the onset of galloping inflation in the 1970s. The costs of materials and constructing sets went up so high that producers found location shooting less expensive than building studio settings. Many directors found this a desirable as well as necessary move, preferring the new look of "reality." However, while moving the commercial location to an outdoor environment, inflation also restricted the scope of commercials — as well as that of other forms of TV production. As long as money remains tight, writers have to come up with smaller casts and, even outdoors, simpler action and settings. The latter is particularly true for studio work. The aesthetic considerations for the writer in producing on tape rather than film are noted in Chapter 2.

Radio commercials also moved into new production trends in the 1970s. Donald Frey, a leader in sound production recording, states that "Until the latter part of the mid-1960's, the radio campaign was prepared first. TV was the ancillary, with radio spots routinely being sent to some 1,700 stations for a given campaign. From about 1967 we all became very video conscious, so radio production took a back seat. Now we've gone back to creating spots specially for radio."[5]

Writers are required to be more creative than ever with radio ads, harkening back to the basic concept that radio spots can create mind-images far superior to the eye-images of television spots. Scripts and equipment and production techniques are becoming more sophisticated, reflecting the greater personalization and individuality of the radio commercials. Writing and producing staffs, acting talent, sound and special effects personnel and equipment have been given new and greater attention and support.

Good commercials production is a team job. Bill Duryea, executive producer at Young & Rubicam, describes Y & R's creative process: "The producer here gets not only first hand knowledge about filmmaking, he is totally immersed in the experience. The creative group at Y & R involves an art director, a copywriter, and a filmmaker — which is how we choose to refer to the agency producer. We don't have the art director and copywriter create the concept, do the boards and then tell the filmmaker to arrange for the shooting. We involve the filmmaker in the process so intensely, they learn it almost through osmosis."[6]

LENGTHS OF ANNOUNCEMENTS AND COMMERCIALS

ANNOUNCEMENTS AND COMMERCIALS differ mainly in that most of the former promote not-for profit ideas, products and services — which may include ideological participation through personal time, energy or money contributions — while the latter sell, for profit, products and services. Some announcements are clearly commercial in nature, though not directly paid for by some advertiser or agency — such as a cross-plug by the station for one of its upcoming programs. Another difference is in the length; commercials are usually 20- 30- or 60-seconds (sometimes 10-) while announcements frequently are 10-seconds in length and sometimes less than that, filling with the station ID a 10-second station break. The techniques of persuasion used in announcements, including the public service kind, and commercials are identical. On occasion, the forms differ and, of course, content is different.

Many copywriters, in writing announcements and commercials for radio, use a word count scale to determine the number of words that will go into a given time segment of a radio announcement or commercial, but, at best, such word counts are approximate. The length of individual words, the complexity of the ideas, the need for emphasis through pause and variation in rate, and the personality of the performer delivering the announcement are some of the factors which may affect the number of words that may be spoken effectively in a given length of time. Some generalizations may be made, however. The 10-second ID will contain about 25 words; the 20-second announcement, about 45 words; the 30-second announcement, about 65 words; the 45-second announcement, about 100 words; the one-minute announcement, about 125 words; the minute and one-half announcement, about 190 words; and the two-minute announcement, about 250 words. These word counts cannot be applied to television, except in the instance of a continuous spoken announcement, because the visual action in television may be expected to take up a portion of the time without dialogue or verbal narration.

For years the FCC has been concerned with the problem of program-length commercials — some 5-minutes, some 15-minutes, others as much as an hour or more. What constitutes a program-length commercial depends on a number of variables, including placement, substance, location, intent. Although the FCC has not taken action regarding 5-minute segments consisting entirely of commercial matter, it has stated that "the broadcast of 15-minute program-length commercials [is] inconsistent with the public interest." The FCC has also held that the "program-length commercial policies pertain only to programs which promote the sale of commercial goods and services and, therefore, do not apply to programs sponsored by non-profit organizations to raise funds for their non-profit activities." The public service announcements of the kind discussed in this section, therefore, would be exempt. In terms of continuous length, although the FCC has not found 5-minute commercial spans to be "program-length," it has frowned on periods over 5 minutes. For a clarification of program-length definitions and policies, see the FCC Public Notice "Program-Length Commercials: Applicability of Commission Policies."

Spot announcements may be commercial or non-commercial. The non-commercial kind are called public service spots or announcements. Commercial spots may be inserted either within the course of a program or during the station break. Until the late 1960s the NAB recommended maximum station-break times, but has since substituted three other approaches relating to announcements on television: no more than four consecutive announcements within the body of a program; no more than three consecutive announcements during station breaks, with limited waivers for stations under certain circumstances; and a recommended maximum of two in-program breaks in prime time and four in non-prime time. The nature of radio programming has prompted the NAB to avoid any such recommendations for that medium. NAB recommendations for overall announcement time is 18-minutes per hour for radio at all times, 16-minutes for television in non-prime time, and 9½-minutes for network affiliates and 12-minutes for independent stations in prime time.

Spot announcements may be, therefore, of varying lengths. The overwhelming number of spots are 30-seconds long, although, when the economy is up, there is a marked increase in 60-second spots. Some advertisers have occasionally attempted the "split 30" commercial — that is, combining two 15-second commercials for two of its products into one 30-second spot. Agencies have generally opposed this, however, believing that most products or services need more than 15-seconds to be effectively presented and sold. Spots frequently are found in 20-, 40-, and 50-second lengths, particularly in radio.

Announcements may be also of varying forms and kinds. The station-break announcement will include a station identification, and accompanying or following it may be a public service announcement, a news flash, a service announcement, a "cross-plug" for one of the station's other programs or, of course, a commercial message. Sometimes commercial messages are tied to service announcements, such as a brief "weather report brought to you by . . . ." or the latest "news flash brought to you by . . . ." Spot announcements of the same type are sometimes bunched together into a particular break in a given program (if not enough commercial time has been sold, they may all be public service announcements). First, the *non*-commercial announcement.

The ID

The purpose of the station break is for the station identification, or ID. The ID is usually 10 seconds long. If accompanied by a commercial announcement, it may be a brief 2 seconds long, followed by an 8-second commercial. The ID consists of the call letters of the station, the city in which the station is located and, sometimes, the operating frequency of the station. Occasionally, the station will attempt to find an identifying phrase to go with the ID.

A simple, direct ID would be: "You are listening to NBC, six-sixty, WNBC, New York."

A special identification for radio would be: "America's number one fine music station, WQXR and WQXR-FM, New York."

CBS-TV has used the following audio-video slogan as a special identification:

VIDEO	AUDIO
SLIDE: Channel 2's "Eye"	Keep your eye on Channel 2. CBS, New York

Some radio stations use singing commercials for ID's as promotion material. A frequently used break is the video picture of the identifying seal of the NAB, with the voice-over announcing that "This seal of good practice identifies this station as a subscriber to the code of the National Association of Broadcasters," followed by the name of the station, its channel and city.

In writing an ID, the writer must remember that an ID is a public relations trademark for the station and must be identifying and distinctive at the same time.

PUBLIC SERVICE ANNOUNCEMENTS (PSA)

ANNOUNCEMENTS IN THE "public service" frequently are given as part of the ID, and may be of any length. The local station usually receives such announcements in a form already prepared by the writer for the distributing organization. The following is an example of the station ID and the PSA presented together:

> This is _____, your election station. If you've been listening
> to the important campaign issues on _____, you'll want to vote
> on Election Day. Register today so you can.

Many organizations issue radio and television kits containing various forms and lengths of announcements. One of the 10-second PSAs of the American Foundation for the Blind, designed for broadcast during a station break, reads:

> There is a book without pages. For the latest information about the
> Talking Book for the blind contact the Library of Congress or the
> American Foundation for the Blind, 15 West 16 St., New York City.

Here's the same idea expanded into 40 seconds:

ANNOUNCER: Besides being visually or physically handicapped so that they can't read ordinary books, Talking Book readers come in: black, yellow, white, Spanish, French, German, mystery addicts, sports nuts, philosophers, psychologists, child, adult, and teenage. . . .

And so do Talking Books.

No matter what your age, race, or interest, if physical limitations prevent you from reading ordinary books, your Library will mail you as many records as you can read.

You can register with the Talking Book Division of the

_____,   _____,
(library or agency)   (street address)

_____, and start reading some
(city, state, zip)
good records.

Reprinted with the permission of the American Foundation for the Blind, Inc.

The American Heritage Foundation's non-partisan "Register, Inform Yourself, and Vote" program issued public service announcements of 10-seconds, 20-seconds, 30-seconds and 60-seconds in length. The following examples illustrate the form the public service announcement may take.

● *Analyze each of the following announcements. Determine the kind of writing approach in each and the kind of material added with each subsequent time extension.*

10-SECOND ANNOUNCEMENT

ANNOUNCER

You can't vote if you're not registered. Protect your right to vote. Register now at

_____,   _____,   _____.
(place)   (dates)   (hours)

20-SECOND ANNOUNCEMENT

ANNOUNCER

The right to vote is a great right. It helps you run your government. But you can't vote unless you're registered. Register now so you can vote on Election Day. Register now at

_____,   _____,   _____.
(place)   (dates)   (hours)
Register now.

30-SECOND ANNOUNCEMENT

ANNOUNCER

It's not much bigger than a phone booth. But it's the place where your town gets its schools built and its streets paved. What is it? It's your precinct voting booth. And you'll be locked out of this year's important election on _____ — if your
                                                                    (date)
name's not in the book . . . the voter's registration book. So get your name in the book. Go to _____, _____, _____.
                    (place)   (dates)   (hours)
Register before the deadline _____. Register now.
                                                (date)

60-SECOND ANNOUNCEMENT

ANNOUNCER

It's not much bigger than a telephone booth. And it's open only a couple of days a year. But it's the place where your schools are built, roads are paved, streets are lighted. What is it? It's the voting booth in your precinct. And you'll want to be there on Election Day, along with your friends and neighbors, helping to make the decisions that make your town a better place to live in. But — is your name in the book? Because if it isn't — if you haven't registered — you'll never see the inside of that voting booth. So be sure you aren't left out. Registration closes _____. Go now to _____,
                                              (date)   (place)
_____ and get your name in the book. And then, on Election Day, we'll see you
        (hours)
at the polls.

Courtesy of American Heritage Foundation

PSA Types

Service groups, government agencies and other organizations devoted to activity related to the public welfare, such as Public Health Departments, educational associations, societies aiding the handicapped and ecology groups, among others, have devoted more and more time in recent years to special television and radio workshops for their regular personnel and volunteer assistants. The foregoing public service announcements on voting, presented by such an organization, are general spots and illustrate form only. Public service announcements are written specifically, too, for special program types and in terms of special occasions. They are written to fit into disc jockey, news, women's, sports and other programs. They may be prepared for delivery with a weather bulletin or with a time signal. They can relate to a given national or local holiday. The following examples illustrate how the "organization" writer may go beyond the general spot announcement.

WASHINGTON'S BIRTHDAY SPOT (20 SECONDS, RADIO)

This is station _____ reminding you that a holiday like Washington's Birthday brings a sort of break into the routine of daily living. This applies also to America's estimated 400,000 legally blind people — or had you thought of them as a group apart? They certainly aren't. For information about blindness contact your nearest agency for the blind or the American Foundation for the Blind, 15 West 16th Street, New York City.

TIME SIGNAL (20 SECONDS, RADIO)

ANNOUNCER

It's _____ . . . and right now an emotionally disturbed child in _____
(time)   (town or area)
needs your help and understanding. This is National Child Guidance Week. Observe it . . . and attend the special program on emotionally disturbed children in _____
(town or area)
presented by the _____ PTA, on _____ at
(date)

_____.
(place)

DISC JOCKEY PROGRAM (30 SECONDS, RADIO)

(AFTER MILLION-RECORD SELLER)

DISC JOCKEY

_____ . . . a record that sold a million copies.
(title and artist)
Easy listening, too. But here's a figure that's not easy to listen to: Over 1,000,000 American children are seriously emotionally ill. During National Child Guidance Week, the _____ PTA, in cooperation with the American Child Guidance Foundation, is holding a special meeting to acquaint you with the problems faced by children in _____. It's to your benefit to attend. Be there . . .
(town or area)
_____ . . . learn what you can do to help.
(date and address)

WOMEN'S PROGRAM (30 SECONDS, RADIO)

WOMAN

Women are traditionally the moving spirits behind community efforts concerning children. And now comes a problem so close to us, as women, that I can't stress its importance enough. I'm speaking about the many emotionally disturbed children in _____.
(town or area)
Your help is needed . . . and you can start by attending the _____ PTA meetings during child Guidance Week on _____ at _____.
(date)   (place)
Attend this meeting . . . learn about the nature and extent of emotional illness affecting our children. And learn how you can help.

LOCAL WEATHER FORECAST (20 SECONDS, RADIO)

ANNOUNCER

That's the weather forecast for _____, but the outlook for chil-
                                    (town or area)
dren with emotional illness is always gloomy. This is National Child Guidance Week, and
you can help by learning the facts about the problem in _____.
                                                          (town or area)
Attend the _____ PTA meeting on _____ at
                                                          (date)

_____.
      (place)

• *The preceding announcements on child guidance specify the
time, date, place and sponsor of a meeting. What if there is no
meeting scheduled? Reread the previous announcement written
for the disc jockey show and then read the following announcement, written for the same show, but without the information on a
specific meeting. Note how the specifics are transferred smoothly
into generalities — and vice versa.*

DISC JOCKEY PROGRAM (30 SECONDS, RADIO)

(AFTER MILLION-RECORD SELLER)

DISC JOCKEY

_____ . . . a record that sold a million copies.
      (Title and Artist)
Easy listening, too. But here's a figure that's not easy to: Over 1,000,000 American children
are seriously emotionally ill. During National Child Guidance Week, many PTA groups, in
cooperation with the American Child Guidance Foundation, are holding special meetings
concerning these problems faced by children. Find out when your meeting will be . . . and
attend . . . Learn what you can do to help.

*Prepared for American Child Guidance Foundation, Inc.
by its agents, Batten, Barton, Durstine & Osborn, Inc.*

The good PSA is like the good commercial: it puts the product or
service in the setting, using the strongest attention-getting, attention-keeping
and persuasive elements, including personalities, drama and other special
needs. Before you get to the analyses of good announcement writing in the
remaining part of this chapter, what persuasive devices do you find in the
following American Foundation for the Blind PSAs, in addition to their
illustration of the elements noted above?

CLORIS LEACHMAN (60 SECONDS, RADIO)

I'm Cloris Leachman. Sometime actress . . . ah . . . speaking about blindness . . . thinking about blindness. I'm suddenly blind for this few moments . . . I've closed my eyes. I've shut out any light with my hands and I'm struggling to contend with it. Am I suddenly gifted with musical genius . . . because I'm blind . . . ? No. Am I hard of hearing? Hardly. I'm thinking about these things because I've had occasion. Sometimes as an actress, to ah . . . think about it and . . . and now, this day for the American Foundation for the Blind. But it's something for us all to think about — if you want to find out more about it you can write to FACTS, F-A-C-T-S FACTS, Box one-eleven, New York one-double-oh-eleven.

VIDEO (PICTURE) 30 SECOND SPOT, TV	AUDIO (SOUND)
LONG SHOT OF MAN AND DAUGHTER. HE IS ABOUT TO SHAVE. FILLS HAND WITH LATHER, AND PROCEEDS TO SHAVE. DAUGHTER READS FROM BOOKLET. LOGO: Teaching Guide, American Foundation for the Blind, Box 111, New York 10011	When a man becomes blind he must learn to do everyday things — like shaving — all over again. His daughter is helping him to learn with the aid of a brand-new teaching guide available right now in both braille and printed editions. For information write: Teaching Guide, The American Foundation for the Blind, Box one eleven, New York one double oh eleven.

(30 SECONDS, RADIO)

If you're physically or visually handicapped, you still have the right to vote. It's protected by law. Here, in California, the law is the Election Code, Section 14423. It says, in general, that if you're physically or visually handicapped, you may be helped at the polls by no more than two persons you designate. So, don't let a visual or physical handicap keep you from the polls this election year. This message was brought to you as a public service by the American Foundation for the Blind and this station.

(A similar spot to the one above, incidentally, is prepared for every State in the union.)

COMMERCIALS

WRITING THE COMMERCIAL is not just technique, talent and an inspiration at 3 A.M. that turns out to be the Clio Award* storyboard. It is attitude, basic preparation, tested procedure and, in some instances, guts and/or a hard head. Two consistent award-winners, Roy Grace and John Noble, creators of the Volkswagen ads, state that the best ad may end up in a back drawer unless the creators believe in it strongly enough to sell it to the account executive. Grace says that "50% is doing the work, and 50% is fighting for it. . . . Too many young people are willing to do the work, but at the first No they surrender. You can be the greatest talent in the world, the greatest team doing the greatest work, but if you're not willing to defend

---

* The Clio Awards (represented by a statuette somewhat similar to the "Oscar" of the movies) are jury-selected and presented annually at the American TV and Radio Commercials Festival.

it, it'll never see the light of day." Noble warns that "there are account men who can talk young creative people out of a concept very easily. But if it's been approved by the Creative Department, that means it ain't a bad ad when it goes up there. There may be certain problems, but for creative people to come back immediately after seeing an account man and say 'We can't do this because so-and-so says we can't do this' is wrong. There should be a battle."[7]

Clearly, the commercials field is not for the writer who wishes to hide behind the typewriter in a secluded place and not be bothered with the outside world except to pass along the sheets of genius to the outstretched hands of a benevolent and understanding producer.

Robert Levenson, creative director of the Doyle Dane Bernbach advertising agency, suggests some guidelines for judging what is a good commercial. He starts out with two basic assumptions:

1). We are looking at a storyboard of a commercial or at a comp. of an ad. The advertising hasn't run yet, so we have zero hindsight. 2.) We have agreement on a strategy or a position or a copy platform or something, so when we decide whether the advertising is good or not, it's the advertising that we're talking about and nothing else. O.K. What do we look for?. . . There is only one first right answer in my opinion: The commercial should be on the product. . . . If the commercial is on the product, the only right second question is: is it clear? I think if we stopped right there, we might upgrade half the commercials on the air because half the commercials I see leave me not knowing what product they're talking about or what they're saying about whatever they're talking about. So, if the commercial we're looking at is clearly on the product, we're half way home.

In other words, the discipline of keeping your eye on what you're selling and how clearly you're selling it is half the battle. . . . What I left out is that, even though a commercial is on the product and is clear, it's not necessarily good. What I left out, of course, are all the skills, the talents, the instincts, the hard work that the best creative people bring to their jobs. The best creative people understand discipline and they understand direction and they understand soundness. They also understand that those things aren't enough. But they also understand that you can't make good advertising without them.

The discipline comes first. Then we get to . . . attention-getting, warm, human, life-like, funny and all the rest. . . . Sometimes, with some products, you don't have to go too far past the discipline. That was true years ago with Polaroid. All we did was have Garry Moore and Steve Allen stand up there — live — and take a Polaroid picture. A minute of copy later, there it was. The audience applauded like crazy, people went out and bought Polaroid cameras by the tens of millions.... And what did we do? We let the product be the star of the commercials.

Here's the test: If you look at a commercial and fall in love with the brilliance of it, try taking the product out of it. If you still love the commercial, it's no good.... Don't make your commercials interesting; make your products interesting."[8]

Barbara Allen, copywriter and teacher of television and radio writing, sets forth five preliminary steps in putting commercials together: 1.) know the product or service; 2.) pick the central selling idea; 3.) choose the basic appeal; 4.) select the format; and 5.) start writing.

Techniques of Writing Commercials

Emotional Appeals. The appeal of the commercial is an emotional one. By emotional we do not mean the evoking of laughter or tears. Emotional appeal means, here, the appeal to the non-intellectual, non-logical aspects of the prospective customer's personality. It is an appeal to the audience's basic needs or wants. For example, one of the basic wants in our society is prestige. Look at the next commercial you see for an automobile. Does it appeal to logical, to intellectual needs? Does it recommend that you buy the car because it is shorter than the other makes, thus enabling the driver to find a parking space more easily? Does it emphasize lower horsepower as one of the car's major advantages, enabling the owner to save on gasoline consumption and at the same time still achieve the maximum miles-per-hour permissible on our highways without risking a speeding ticket or, more importantly, one's life? Sometimes, in a buyer's market, yes. Sometimes, in a real or manufactured "gas shortage," yes. But most of the time the appeal is to prestige, to our emotional needs, not to logic. The commercial stresses the longer length of the car, longer than that of the competing make. The commercial emphasizes greater horsepower for umpteen miles-per-hour speeds, faster than the other make. Have the longest, fastest car in the neighborhood!

The development of commercials for the compact car is a good case in point. "Big car room" became an important ingredient in selling small cars. The compact must be bigger than the competing compact. One couldn't own a small car; one had to own a king-sized small car! And how many automobile commercials show the driver climbing into the car to be seated next to a pretty girl looking as much as possible like Raquel Welch! The emotional implication is, of course, that men who drive this make of automobile have sitting with them women who look like movie stars. This is the prestige factor again. Or, so goes the implication, if the prospective customer does not have such women immediately available, the very presence of the automobile in his driveway will attract them. This would be an appeal to power, in this instance the power to draw women — a strong emotional appeal.

There are a number of basic emotional appeals that have been particularly successful and upon which the writer of commercials may draw as the motivating factor within any individual commercial. The appeal to self-preservation is perhaps the strongest of all. Drug commercials, among others, make good use of this appeal. Another strong appeal is love of family. Note the next commercial presented by an insurance company. Other widely used emotional appeals include patriotism, good taste, reputation, religion, loyalty to a group and conformity to public opinion. And, of course, "Fly Me" and "We'll really move our tail for you" are clear and, according to sales reports, effective examples of the appeal to sexual power and adventure. *Time* magazine reported that the ad makers reportedly told the stewardesses who perform in the commercials to say the words "like you're standing there stark naked." (The responsibility of the writer in preparing sexual appeal ads which are sexist is discussed earlier under *Ethical Considerations.*)

The following commercial illustrates, primarily, the effective use of the appeal to prestige. The implications are that if one does not serve Libby's foods, one does not have *good taste,* is not a *smart shopper* and, by further implication, would not have the prestige of sophistication and intelligence of those who do serve Libby's. The use of emotional appeals does not mean, of course, that the implications may not be valid.

> • *As you read the commercial see if you can find an additional emotional appeal and a sample of what we shall call logical appeal.*

VIDEO	AUDIO
1. MCU ANNOUNCER BESIDE LIBBY'S DISPLAY.	ANNOUNCER: LIBBY's presents a word quiz. What is the meaning of the word "epicure?" Well, according to our dictionary the word means a person who shows good taste in selection of food. And that's a perfect description of the homemaker who makes a habit of serving . . .
2. INDICATES DISPLAY.	LIBBY'S famous foods. Yes, everyone in every family goes for
3. INDICATES EACH PRODUCT IN SYNC (IF POSSIBLE CUT TO CU LIBBY'S PEACHES . . . THEN PAN IN SYNC).	LIBBY'S Peaches . . . Fruit Cocktail . . . LIBBY'S Pineapple—chunks, Crushed or Sliced . . . Pineapple Juice . . . LIBBY'S Peas . . . Beets . . . Corn—Whole Kernel or Cream Styled . . . LIBBY'S Tomato Juice . . . Corned Beef Hash . . . and LIBBY'S Beef Stew. AND right now, smart shoppers are stocking up on LIBBY'S famous

4. HOLDS UP LIBBY'S COUPONS (IF POSSIBLE CUT TO CU LIBBY'S COUPONS).

5. MOVE IN FOR CU LIBBY'S DISPLAY.

foods . . . because there's still time to cash in those LIBBY'S dollar-saving coupons you received. You can save a whole dollar on this week's food bill. So stock up now on LIBBY's famous foods . . . and cash in your LIBBY'S coupons and save! Always make LIBBY'S a "regular" on your shopping list!

Courtesy of Libby's Famous Foods

You may have noted the appeal to love of family in the statement that "everyone in every family goes for. . . ." The logical appeal was the emphasis, at the end of the commercial, on the saving of money through the use of Libby coupons. (Should this commercial have stressed "nutritious" food as another logical appeal?) Logical appeals are those which strike the intellect, the logical, analytical thinking processes. An example of a logical appeal would be that which, with accurate information, emphasizes that the electronic structure of the television set being advertised has certain elements that make it longer lasting or which provide a clearer picture than other makes. This kind of logical appeal may be contrasted with the emotional appeal which ignores the organic functioning of the television set but emphasizes the shape, color or styling of the cabinet, items which have nothing to do with the logical purpose for using a television set.

Commercials frequently use logical appeals in combination with emotional appeals, as in the following example:

(MUSIC UP THEN UNDER)

MORRIS: When you go looking for a new car, what do you really look for . . . ?

(MUSIC UP THEN UNDER)

MORRIS: Do you look for style? Do you look for things you can't see . . . ?

(MUSIC UP THEN UNDER)

MORRIS: Things like electronic ignition for less maintenance — and dependable starting. Torsion bar suspension for handling. Electronic voltage regulator to help give you longer battery life. Unibody construction for protection from every direction. These are just a few of the standard things you get when you buy any 1973 Chrysler Corporation car built in this country.

(MUSIC UP THEN UNDER)

MORRIS: If style is your bag, then take a good look at our cars. They're designed in style to make you look good. In a Chrysler Corporation car, what you don't see is what you get, and what you see is out of sight.

SINGERS: EXTRA CARE IN ENGINEERING . . . MAKES A DIFFERENCE . . .

MORRIS: The difference is there in every 1973 Dodge, Chrysler or Plymouth. Check one out in style today.

Courtesy of Ross Roy, Inc., Detroit

Commercials often only *seem* to use logical appeals; closer examination of many commercials reveals that the appeals are really emotional in content. Emotional appeals are far more effective in commercial advertising than are logical appeals.

Audience Analysis. Before choosing and applying the specific emotional or logical appeals, the writer must know, as fully as possible, the nature of the audience to whom the message is directed. In the mass media of television and radio it is often impossible to determine many specifics about a given audience at a given air time. The audence is a disunified mass of many attitudes and interests, economic, social, political and religious levels, spread out over a broad geographical area — particularly in television. When advertisers sponsored entire programs and were, indeed, identified with particular programs and personalities, the writer could make some judgment on the kinds of people who watched that particular show. Since the spot ad began to replace the full-sponsor program, it has been harder for the writer to make such an analysis.

Although audience analysis has been with us a long time, demographics — the science of analyzing the audience makeup as a base for specific commercial content and technique and, in radio, for a particular station format and "sound" — is relatively recent. In the early 1970s demographics began to become critically essential to ad agency operations. In 1972 the Radio Advertising Bureau analyzed the frequency of occurence of elements in 100 Clio Award commercial entries. RAB notes that no definitive conclusions can be drawn from its analysis, that a larger sample needs to be used, that there is no indication whether the commercials were liked by the listeners or not, or that the writers were correct in their choices of creative elements.

The following chart, however, does provide an indication of which elements writers *thought* would be effective and which ones they put into radio commercials in terms of their analyses of the sex and age of the audience.

Commercial Elements — Frequency of Occurrence

ELEMENTS	TOTAL SAMPLE	ADULT MEN	ADULT WOMEN	ADULT WOMEN & MEN	TEENS
Singing	45%	45%	23%	47%	75%
Instrumental music only	18	10	27	17	15
Announcer/primary role	47	50	37	50	55
Announcer/secondary role	32	15	40	37	30
Celebrity announcer	5	5	10	3	0
Humor	46	35	70	47	20
Dialogue/interview	39	40	53	37	20
Sound effects	33	45	33	37	15
Base	100	20	30	30	20

There are some basic elements of audience analysis that the writer may apply in both television and radio. These are: age, sex, size, economic level, political orientation, primary interests, occupation, fixed attitudes or beliefs, educational level, ethnic background, geographical concentration, and knowledge of the product. The writer should try to include appeals to all the major groups expected to watch the given program — and commercial. Be careful, however, not to spread the message too thin. Here are several award-winning commercials that appeal to a large audience segment, but at the same time contain some specific appeals that relate to a few particular characteristics of the audience. As you analyze each of these commercials for the specific audience appeals, determine what kind of audience each might be particularly aimed toward.

VIDEO	AUDIO
FRONT OF HOUSE. DAD WASHING CAR. WE HEAR PHONE INSIDE HOUSE. KID STICKS HIS HEAD OUT OF SECOND-STORY WINDOW.	(MUSIC EST. AND UNDER) KID: Hey, Dad! It's a long-distance telephone call from Chicago! DAD: (PANIC) Illinois?! KID: Yeah! Come on, hurry up!
DAD STRUGGLES WITH NOZZLE TO TURN OFF HOSE. IT RESISTS. WORKS HIS WAY AROUND CAR.	ANNCR(VO): Remember when a long-distance call was really a big thing.
MOM RUNS OUT ONTO PORCH. DOG COMES OUT ALSO AND STARTS TO BARK.	
MOM IS ACCIDENTALLY SPRAYED. DAD IS TRYING TO FREE HOSE FROM BENEATH WHEEL.	DAD: Oh, I'm sorry. MOM: It's long distance!
MOM RUNS BACK INTO HOUSE, COLLIDES WITH KID WHO'S RUNNING OUT.	ANNCR(VO): Long distance isn't a special event anymore. It's a natural, casual part of everyday life. And it costs so little.
MOM OPENS WINDOW AND THRUSTS PHONE OUTSIDE. DAD GRABS IT. THEY ALL GET QUIET.	MOM: He'll be right with you.
	ANNCR(VO): So why get uptight about something as simple as long distance.
FREEZE FRAME.	DAD: Hello!
TRANSITION TO MICHIGAN BELL LOGO. "Dial Direct and Save" HOLD ON LOGO	SFX: (TOUCH-TONE RANDOM NOTES) ANNCR(VO): Relax and let it happen!

Courtesy of Ross Roy, Inc., Detroit

1. WOMAN: I got restless.

2. Things like uh ... security ... dependability ...

3. I don't know. They ... they just weren't enough anymore.

4. So I left.

5. For looks.

6. (CYNICAL LAUGH)

7. I found out pretty quickly how much looks are worth.

8. So now I'm back.

9. For good.

10. ANNCR: (VO) Another person who found out that inner goodness

11. is far more important than outward appearance.

*Doyle Dane Bernbach Inc.
for Volkswagen of America*

VIDEO	AUDIO
CUT TO BICYCLIST RIDING DOWN STREET.	May a little bitey bite of sunshine come your way
AERIAL VIEW OF BICYCLIST RIDING DOWN STREET.	come your way
SIDE VIEW OF BICYCLIST RIDING PAST WATER FOUNTAIN.	(MU)
CUT TO BICYCLIST RIDING ON HIGHWAY.	a little bite of love and happiness
CUT TO SIDE VIEW OF BICYCLIST ON HIGH BRIDGE SURROUNDED BY TREES.	everyday, everyday I wish you
CUT TO SIDE VIEW OF BICYCLIST ON HIGHWAY.	no good-byes
CUT TO PAN ACROSS OF CU OF BICYCLISTS.	but a new friend every morning
CUT TO BICYCLIST RIDING IN COUNTRY NEAR FIELDS.	clear blue skies are the simple things in
CUT TO BICYCLIST RIDING ON HIGHWAY IN COUNTRY IN THE RAIN.	life that are good and true that's the world I wish for you
CUT TO CU OF COCA-COLA CAP ON BOTTLE BEING OPENED.	It's the real thing
CUT TO SIDE VIEW OF BICYCLIST DRINKING COKE.	may you always have someone
CUT TO BICYCLISTS FIXING THEIR BIKES AND DRINKING COKE.	to share all your happy moments through
CUT TO PAN UP OF COKE BEING POURED INTO GLASS.	somebody who will sit
CUT TO CU OF BICYCLIST DRINKING COKE.	and laugh and share some Coke
CUT TO GIRL AND BOY ON BLANKET IN GRASS DRINKING COKE.	with you
CUT TO BICYCLIST RIDING IN TUNNEL.	because they're the real things
CUT TO BICYCLIST RIDING IN SMALL COUNTRY TOWN.	and I'd like to fill your life with
CUT TO CYCLIST RIDING PAST HOUSES WITH TWO ELDERLY LADIES STANDING IN FRONT.	real thing

Courtesy of The Coca-Cola Company. McCann-Erickson, Inc.

VIDEO	AUDIO
FADE IN:	NARRATOR:
SC 1 MCU Black Couple side by side. Woman puts cigarette in mouth. Man takes cigarette away and gives her a kiss.	Next time she wants a cigarette give her a kiss instead.
DISSOLVE TO:	
SC 2 TITLE	
"For tips on quitting call us American Cancer Society" (sword)	For tips on quitting call the American Cancer Society.
FADE OUT	

The research done by the creative agency team goes beyond preliminary audience analysis. Even after the commercial is created, it is not finalized until it is tested, evaluated, rewritten and reproduced in terms of audience-reaction research. The concept of advertising agency research has grown over the past two decades. Indeed, when intensive television advertising began in the early 1950s, "creative" research hardly existed at all. David Ogilvy, chairman of Ogilvy & Mather International advertising agency, thinks that "research has helped us create more effective advertising. But all this research is creating a serious problem. Instead of creating *one* campaign for each product, we are now called upon to create half a dozen, for testing. Nobody can do that for very long without running out of ideas."[9]

Familiarization with Product.   Earlier in this chapter we noted Robert Levenson's stress on the product itself as the key to a good commercial. Before the writer can apply audience analysis or choose emotional appeals, it is essential that he or she become thoroughly familiar with the product. This does not mean that the male writer needs to use a particular girdle before preparing an ad for it or that the female writer must test a particular shaving cream before writing the commercial for it — and this is not meant facetiously because in both cases testing the product on a personal basis is clearly possible. In addition to personal observation or use of the product, the writer should get as much information as possible about it from those closely connected with it. A good source of information is the research department of the company. From the information obtained about the product and from the personal feeling developed about it (woe for the writer who develops an antipathy toward the product!), the writer can then coordinate the audience analysis with emotional and logical appeals and hopefully develop a unique or novel way of presenting the product most effectively to the audience.

The writer should either have or develop flexible and receptive tastes when it comes to particular products. The ad agency may be fortunate enough to land an account for a product with built-in excitement: a new, revolutionary camera like Polaroid or a low-cost, high gas-mileage, long-lasting engine, small car with large seating capacity and storage space like

Volkswagen — successful commercials for both of which are included in this chapter. On the other hand, the writer may have to deal with a seemingly prosaic product like a pill for indigestion and still have to be able to open up his or her imagination to create an ad that will have an entire country saying "Try It, You'll Like It!"

The six leading advertising categories on television in 1973, in order of total dollars spent, were 1.) food and food products; 2.) toiletries and toilet goods; 3.) automotive; 4.) proprietary medicines; 5.) soaps, cleansers and polishers; and 6.) household equipment and supplies.

Organization of the Commercial. Inasmuch as the commercial's primary purpose is to persuade, the writer should be aware of the five basic steps in persuasive technique. First, the commercial should get the attention of the audience. This may be accomplished by many means, including humor, a startling statement or picture, a rhetorical question, vivid description, a novel situation or suspenseful conflict. Sound, specifically the use of pings, chords and other effects, effectively attracts attention, too.

Second, after attention is obtained, the audience's interest must be held. Following up the initial element with effective examples, testimonials, anecdotes, statistics and other devices, visual or aural, should retain the audience's interest.

Third, the commercial should create an impression that a problem of some sort exists, related vaguely to the function of the product advertised. After such an impression has been made, then, fourth, the commercial should plant the idea in the audience's mind that the problem can be solved by use of the particular product. It is at this point that the product itself might even first be introduced. (See the Bank of America and Choice Morsels commercials on the following pages). Finally, the commercial must finish with a strong emotional and/or logical appeal, one which achieves the fifth step in persuasion — getting action. This final step prompts the audience to go out and buy the product.

All of the award-winning commercials below illustrate the five steps of persuasion, some of them in clear sequence, others not so obviously, but nevertheless effectively.

In the following storyboard for "Charlotte," a commercial for Choice Morsels, attention is achieved by a combination of melodramatic humor (the takeoff on the "Gone With the Wind" type movie), and exaggerated dramatization. Interest is held by obviously pointed suspense: someone — in terms of movie lore undoubtedly a southern belle — is starving herself to death in a locked room. Who can it be? The not eating, of course, sets up the relationship of the problem to the product. Attention and interest are further heightened by the *macho*-male approach — "I'm coming in; I'm giving you your choice." At that point the fourth and fifth steps are quickly presented and it is only at this point that the product is actually first introduced.

60-SECONDS

1. (MUSIC)

2. MAN: Charlotte! I'm home, Charlotte!

3. You hear me, Charlotte?

4. WOMAN: It's about time you got back!

5. MAN: Magnolia, where's Charlotte? Where is she?

6. WOMAN: She's been in there, for days.

7. MAN: Is that true, Charlotte?

8. WOMAN: She won't come out. She won't eat.

9. MAN: I'm coming in.

10. Charlotte.

11. I'm giving you your choice.

12. (SFX: CAT MEOWS)

13. ANNCR: (VO) Introducing Choice Morsels, a delicious new recipe that only Purina has.

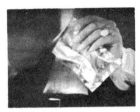

14. This easy to serve,

15. it's a full nutritious meal,

16. and it comes in six varieties.

17. It's moist, and different. For cats with discriminating tastes.

18. New Choice Morsels from Purina. It's the cat's choice.

19. MAN: Charlotte my pet. (SFX: CAT MEOWS)

Doyle Dane Bernbach Inc.
for Ralston Purina Co.

• *See if you can find the steps of persuasion in the following announcements, three of them award-winning commercials and one a PSA. The Alka-Seltzer spot is now a classic and a direct, clear statement on a product solving a problem. How do these commercials differ from the previous one not only in the use of the five steps of persuasion, but in the approaches used within each step? You should conclude that the five steps of persuasion are a guide, not a mandate, in the structure of a commercial, although, overall, the commercial should achieve the purpose of the five steps.*

60 SECONDS

ANNCR:	1	Hi audience.
AUDIENCE:	2	Hi Bill.
ANNCR:	3	Welcome to "Win or Lose," and now here's our contestant, Frank Mather.
FRANK:	4	Hi, Bill.
ANNCR:	5	Your question, Frank, is (DRUM ROLL) figure out your bank checking
	6	statement.
FRANK:	7	Oh . . .
	8	(TICKING OFF TIME BEHIND FRANK)
	9	Let's see . . . Thirty-two dollars . . . that was my gasoline bill. I think.
	10	Twelve dollars and eight cents . . . that was . . . can I use my check stubs?
ANNCR:	11	Go right ahead, Frank.
FRANK:	12	Let's see. That amount must be my car payment . . . No . . . Yes!
ANNCR:	13	Time's running out, Frank.
FRANK:	14.	Well all these amounts all over my statement . . . how can anybody figure
	15	it out?
ANNCR:	16	(BUZZER SOUNDS) Oh, sorry, Frank. You lost.
ANNCR 2:	17	Figuring out a checking statement can be a problem. So Bank of America
	18	has done something about it. We've introduced the Timesaver Statement.
	19	We put your check numbers on it and list them in numerical order. We
	20	indicate any checks still outstanding. A glance down the column tells you
	21	which checks haven't come in yet. It's that simple and there's no charge
	22	to customers using our scenic checks. Drop by and ask for our
	23	Timesaver Statement. Bank of America. Member F.D.I.C.

Courtesy of Grey Advertising, Inc.

60-SECONDS

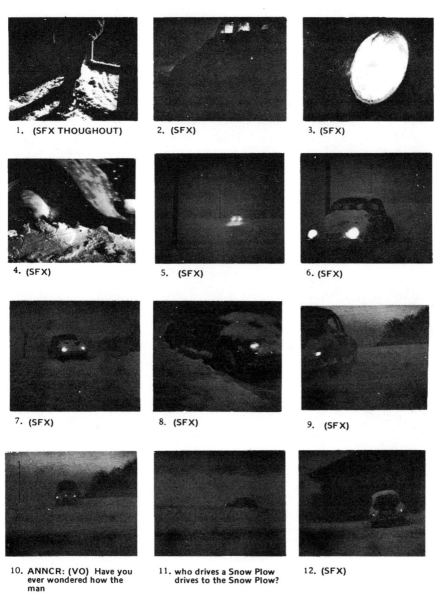

1. (SFX THOUGHOUT)

2. (SFX)

3. (SFX)

4. (SFX)

5. (SFX)

6. (SFX)

7. (SFX)

8. (SFX)

9. (SFX)

10. ANNCR: (VO) Have you ever wondered how the man

11. who drives a Snow Plow drives to the Snow Plow?

12. (SFX)

continued on page 94

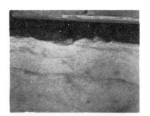

13. **This one drives a Volkswagen.**   14. **(SFX)**   15. **So you can stop wondering.**

16. **(SFX)**   17. **(SFX)**   18. **(SFX)**

19. **(SFX)**

Doyle Dane Bernbach Inc.
for Volkswagen of America

60-SECOND TV SPOT

VIDEO	AUDIO

OPEN ON RUGGED LOOKING MAN AT COCKTAIL PARTY SMOKING CIGARETTE AND TALKING.

RUGGED MAN: (OC) (Speaking sympathetically)
Hey, Harry, you look like you haven't seen the sun for a month. You ought to get out more.

CUT TO REVEAL AN ANEMIC LOOKING MAN.
CUT TO RUGGED LOOKING MAN.

HARRY: (OC)
I go out. What do you mean go out?
RUGGED LOOKING MAN:
You'd feel better if you got out in the great outdoors . . .

RUGGED LOOKING MAN STRETCHES EXPANSIVELY, ATTEMPTING TO CONVEY THE JOY OF THE OUTDOORS.
CUT TO HARRY, THE ANEMIC-LOOKING MAN. HE REACTS AGGRESSIVELY, AS THOUGH HE HAS BEEN PERSONALLY ATTACKED BY THE RUGGED LOOKING OUT-DOORS MAN.
CONTINUE WITH HARRY'S DIATRIBE. HE PUFFS ON A CIGARETTE.

. . . stretched your muscles . . . got your lungs full of fresh air.

HARRY: (Angrily . . . feeling he has been personally attacked.)
What fresh air? You call the air around here fresh air? .

HARRY:
It's like living in a coal mine, it's so polluted around here.

CONTINUE WITH HARRY, SMOKING AS HE TALKS.

HARRY:
You know what you see on your windowsill in the morning? Soot! This thick. (He gestures with fingers).

OTHERS GATHER AROUND HARRY, ALL OF THEM SMOKING.

HARRY'S VOICE CONTINUES:
And in traffic — in your car — carbon monoxide.

PAN ACROSS CIGARETTES OF ON-LOOKERS.
ECU CIGARETTES.

HARRY'S VOICE CONTINUES:
Every day it's killing you.
HARRY CONTINUES:
You want me to get more fresh air . . .

ECU CIGARETTES.

HARRY:
. . . then start doing something about the air pollution in this town.
HARRY:
Tear down the smoke stacks. . . .

PAN UPWARD FROM ON-LOOKERS TO SMOKE RISING TO CEILING.
SCREEN FULL OF SMOKE.

HARRY:
Get rid of that big incinerator out on the flats. . . .

FREEZE FRAME ON HARRY'S FACE, SEEN DIMLY THROUGH SMOKE.

ANNOUNCER: (VO)
If you'd like to do something about air pollution, we suggest you start with your own lungs.

Courtesy of American Cancer Society

30 SECONDS

VIDEO	AUDIO
OPEN MCU MAN SEATED AT TABLE IN RESTAURANT. BEHIND HIM YOU SEE OTHER CUSTOMERS AND WAITER WHO IMITATES THE MAN'S GESTURES.	SFX: Restaurant noises. Low murmur, clatter of dishes, knives and forks. MAN: Came to this little place. Waiter says, "Try this, you'll like it." "What's this?" "Try it, you'll like it." "But what is . . . ?" "Try it, you'll like it." So I tried it. Thought I was going to die. Took two Alka Seltzer.
CUT TO TWO ALKA SELTZER DROPPING IN GLASS OF WATER. PAN ACROSS ASPIRIN BOTTLE AND TWO ASPIRINS. CONTINUE PAN ACROSS ROLL OF ANTACIDS AND TWO ANTACIDS. CONTINUE PAN TO FOIL PACK OF ALKA SELTZER.	ANNCR VO: For headache and upset stomach, no aspirin or antacid alone relieves you in as many ways as Alka Seltzer. For headache and upset stomach.
CUT BACK TO CU MAN IN RESTAURANT.	MAN: Alka Seltzer works. Try it, you'll like it!

Courtesy of Miles Laboratories and Wells, Rich, Greene, Inc.

Writing styles. The writer constantly must be aware of the necessity for keeping the commercial in good taste. Although there have been commercials from time to time which have been repugnant to individuals or groups, the sponsor tries not to alienate a single potential customer. The style should be direct and simple. If the commercial is to seem sincere, the performer presenting it must have material of a conversational, informal nature that permits him or her to present it so that the audience really believes what it hears or sees. This does not mean that the writer uses ultra-colloquial or slang words. The vocabulary should be dignified, though not obtuse; it must be attention-getting, but not trite. Usually, the writer will avoid slang and colloquialisms entirely unless these forms have specific purposes in specific places in the commercial.

The writer should be certain that the writing is grammatically correct. Action verbs are extremely effective, as are concrete, specific words and ideas. If an important point is to be emphasized, the writer must be certain to repeat that point in the commercial, although in different words or in different forms. One exception would be the presentation of a slogan or trade mark which the sponsor wishes the audience to remember; in this case word for word repetition is important. Keep in mind that for television the visual rather than the aural picture is frequently the key. For some commercials on TV the writer can make it virtually all visual, as with the VW "Snow Plow" spot a few pages back.

The writer should avoid, if possible, the use of superlatives, false claims, phony testimonials and other elements of obvious exaggeration.

Even for the writer whose ethical standards are nonexistent, such writing is a mistake, for it might antagonize a large part of the audience, even if particularly effective in deceiving another part. Network commercials are sometimes more honest than those on independent stations. Frequently, the commercial on the small station is not only presented, but written by the disc jockey or announcer who may have sold the show or the air time in the first place. Extravagant claims sometimes are made in order to keep the account.

The Television Storyboard

Commercial continuity is basically the same for both radio and television. However, it must be remembered that while the radio commercial must convey everything through sound, the television commercial is essentially visual. The television announcement should be able to hold the viewer with the picture. It seems that some producers lack confidence in the visual effectiveness of their own spots. Listen to the sound on your television set the next time there is a commercial break in the program. Chances are you will be able to hear it all the way to the refrigerator, or even, depending on your acuity and tastes, all the way to the wine cellar. The visual continuity in the commercial should be such that the technician does not have to turn up the sound for every advertising message. Well-written commercials don't need to rely on a high volume of sound. The video should not be treated merely as an adjunct to the audio. In fact, commercial producers (and account people, sponsors) like to see as fully as possible the visual contents for a prospective commercial in its early stages. For this purpose a "storyboard" is used. The storyboard usually is a series of rough drawings showing the sequence of picture action, optical effects, settings and camera angles, and it contains captions indicating the dialogue, sound and music to be heard. A good example is the award-winning Eastern Airlines "River Raft" storyboard on pages 98-99. There are frequently many refinements from the storyboard that sells the commercial to the advertiser to the finished film or tape that sells the product to the viewer.

Some producers work from storyboards alone. Others want scripts, either in the Hollywood or New York style, containing the visual and audio directions and dialogue. The non-commercial commercial — a highway safety PSA by the U.S. Department of Transportation — on pages 100-102 provides a comparison between the storyboard and the TV script.

60 SECONDS

1. (MUSIC)

2. (MUSIC)

3. (MUSIC)

4. (MUSIC)

5. WELLES: Away from it all in the Caribbean, . . .

6. there's more for father and son to share than just scenery. (PAUSE)

7. (MUSIC)

8. (MUSIC)

9. (MUSIC)

10. (MUSIC)

11. There's a true family vacation of learning and sharing memories together.

12. Of living the kinds of experiences you don't find at home. (PAUSE)

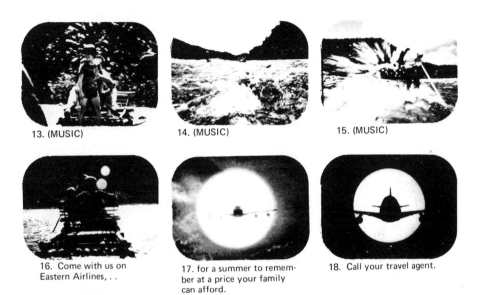

13. (MUSIC)

14. (MUSIC)

15. (MUSIC)

16. Come with us on Eastern Airlines, . .

17. for a summer to remember at a price your family can afford.

18. Call your travel agent.

19. Or Eastern. The Wings of Man.

Created by Young & Rubicam International for Eastern Airlines

60 SECONDS

C-1 I want to watch the sun come up another fifty years.

C-2 I want to write a novel that will bring the world to tears.

C-3 And I want to see Venice.

C-4 I want to see my kids have kids. I want to see them free.

C-5 I want to live my only life. I want the most of me.

C-6 I want to dance. I want to love. I want to breathe.

C-7 Janie died. On an endless road in America.

C-8 Because a lonely man was driving drunk out of his mind.

C-9 Problem drinkers who drive are responsible for more than 40 deaths every day. Get the problem drinker off the road.

C-10 I want to know what's out there beyond the furthest star.

C-11 I even want to go there if we ever get that far. And I want to see Venice.

C-12 Help. Do something about the problem drinker. For his sake. And yours.

(60 SECONDS)

VIDEO	AUDIO
FADE UP ON MLS OF WIFE, HUSBAND AND CHILD IN LARGE HAMMOCK. MOVE IN TO MCU OF MOTHER AND CHILD. DISSOLVE TO LEFT SIDE MCU SHOT OF ALL THREE. DISSOLVE TO MCU OF FRONT SHOT OF MOTHER AND CHILD.	JANIE SONG: I want to watch the sun come up another fifty years I want to write a novel that will bring the world to tears And I want to see Venice
DISSOLVE TO CU OF CHILD. DISSOLVE TO CU LEFT SIDE SHOT OF MOTHER AND CHILD.	I want to see my kids have kids I want to see them free
DISSOLVE TO MLS OF ALL THREE — MOVE IN TO MS. DISSOLVE TO LEFT SIDE MS OF MOTHER AND CHILD.	I want to live my only life I want the most of me I want to dance
DISSOLVE TO MS OF RIGHT SIDE OF MOTHER AND CHILD.	I want to love
DISSOLVE TO CU LEFT SIDE OF MOTHER AND CHILD.	I want to breathe
FREEZE FRAME AND DISSOLVE TO B & W.	ANNCR VO: Janie died On an endless road in America
PULL BACK FROM B & W PHOTO IN A PICTURE FRAME AND DOLLY PAST EMPTY BED	Because a lonely man was driving drunk out of his mind
	Problem drinkers who drive are responsible for more than 40 deaths every day Get the problem drinker off the road. JANIE SONG: I want to know what's out there beyond the furthest star I even want to go there if we ever get that far
TITLE: "GET THE PROBLEM DRINKER OFF THE ROAD." FADE TO BLACK.	And I want to see Venice.

- *Go back over the two storyboards and analyze them in terms of product emphasis (does the product stand alone?) and organization (the five steps of persuasion).*

Placement of Commercials

As noted earlier, there is a variety of commercial lengths. Length is frequently dependent on placement. Knowing whether the spot is to be a station break, a hitchhiker, a participating announcement on radio or a program announcement on television can help the writer analyze the audience, particularly as to their psychological attitude or physical behavior at the time they hear or see the spot. Here are the major areas of placement.

IDs and Service Announcements. The station identification, as already stated, is usually a 10-second break. Attached to the ID may be an

8-second commercial, for television, or a longer one (for a longer break) for radio. A service announcement accompanying an ID may be from 5-to 10-seconds long, consisting of a commercial message accompanying public service information, such as a time signal or weather report. For example:

It's _____ PM, Soporific Watch Time. See the Soporific Wrist
Alarm — date and calendar — 21 jewels.

Chain Breaks.   The chain is another name for the network. The time available between the network station identification and the local station identification is sold to advertisers either on a network or local basis. This is an especially good source of revenue for local stations. Television advertisers on the chain break usually fill the time with 20-second commercial films. Radio advertisers use an announcement of about 50 to 60 words in length.

30- and 60-Second Announcements.   As noted at the beginning of this chapter, programs do not end at the 30-minute or 60-minute mark. Time is allowed for the ID and one or more commercials. In some instances, a sponsored program following another sponsored program will start late to permit more time for the ID and announcements. Sometimes the network affiliate will fade out a program early or fade in a program late to permit more time for commercials in the time break. 20-second, 30-second and full-minute commercials are most often the lengths used for both television and radio.

Participating Announcements.   When a show is unable or unwilling to get just a single sponsor, it may get a number of participating advertisers. The various advertisers jointly share the cost of the entire program, and the length and frequency of their commercials vary in proportion to the share of the program cost they have contributed. Disc jockey shows on radio, with their frequent commercial announcements, and films on television, with their sometimes constant interruptions for commercials, are examples of the participating announcement program. As noted earlier, tight money in the early 1970s accelerated the trend to participating rather than single sponsors on television; radio had, since the disappearance of the feature program, become a participating sponsor medium.

Program Announcements.   When a single sponsor has purchased the entire show, either as a one-shot arrangement or a series, all the commercials on that program will come from that sponsor. The commercials are called program announcements. The sponsor may space the commercials into short announcements, or may lump the commercial time for one long announcement.

The program announcements for the longer programs, those which are half-hour, hour, or 90-minute shows, follow a fairly standard transitional form, each one building upon the previous one, but nevertheless containing enough variety so that the audience does not become bored through repetition. The average show usually has three program announcements: at the beginning, in the middle and at the end. Occasionally there are four commercials, divided into short opening and closing "billboards," and two insertions within the program itself.

Cowcatcher and Hitchhiker. Prior to the actual start of a scheduled program, but after the station break and in the time segment of the program, a commercial announcement may be inserted. This is the "cowcatcher." When such an announcement is inserted following a program, but prior to the station break, it is called a "hitchhiker." These usually are short announcements, but they may vary from 6 seconds to more than a minute. The term "piggyback" is applied to these announcements when they advertise an additional product distributed by the sponsor of the major product constituting the program announcements on the show.

Co-op announcements. These are the commercials of several sponsors who have purchased a particular network show. They differ from participating announcements in that the co-op sponsors are in different cities, and instead of their announcements being consecutively on the same show, they are given simultaneously. The network leaves fixed commercial time in the program for the local station to fill in with the message from the co-op sponsor in that locality.

Commercial Formats

There are five major format types for commercials: straight sell, testimonial, humorous, musical and dramatization. Any single commercial may consist of a combination of two or more of these techniques. In the mid-1970s humor and music had become the most popular forms. The straight sell is, of course, the basic commercial approach.

Straight Sell. This should be a clear, simple statement about the product. Be careful about involving the announcer or station too closely with the product. Do not say "our product" or "my store." Only if a personality is presenting the commercial, the combination of testimonial and straight sell techniques may permit such personal involvement.

The straight sell may hit hard, but not over the head and not so hard that it may antagonize the potential customer. The straight sell is straightforward, and although the statement about the product is basically simple and clear, the writing technique sometimes stresses a "gimmick," usually emphasizing something special about the product, real or implied, that makes it different or extra or better than the competing product. A slogan frequently characterizes this special attribute. The following is a good example of the straight sell with a gimmick. Sometimes the straight sell is built around a slogan, which accompanies the product in every commercial. The following 50-second award-winning radio commercial is an example of the straight sell that features both a personality and a slogan.

SFX:	CLOCK GONGING. HORSE AND CARRIAGE.
ORSON WELLES:	It's 3 A.M. in the French Quarter of New Orleans. How'd you like the best cup of coffee in town? And a beignet. That's a square donut without a hole.
SFX:	PEOPLE TALKING, DOORS OPENING AND CLOSING, PLATES RATTLING.
ORSON WELLES:	This is the place. Morning Call. Find a stool at one of the elbow-worn marble counters and while you're waiting for your order, take a look around.
MUSIC:	EASTERN THEME FADE UP AND THROUGHOUT.
ORSON WELLES:	The place hasn't changed much in the past 100 years. Same counters, same foot rail. Same mirrors where you can watch and be watched sipping coffee and sprinkling powdered sugar on hot beignets, that still cost a nickel. Only in New Orleans . . . one of the places that make Eastern what it is . . . the second largest passenger carrier of all the airlines in the free world . . . the Wings of Man.

Created by Young and Rubicam International for Eastern Airlines

Sometimes the straight sell is a simple presentation of the product within an attention-getting visual or sound device. The 30-second TV spot on page 106 entitled "Zoo" is an example.

The Testimonial. The testimonial commercial is very effective when properly used. When the testimonial is given by a celebrity — whose social and economic status is likely to be quite a bit higher than that of the average viewer — the emotional appeals of prestige, power and good taste are primary. What simpler way to reach the status of the celebrity, if only in one respect, than by using the same product he or she uses? The writer must make certain that the script fits the personality of the person giving the endorsement.

A winner of many awards in the 1970s and a coup in celebrity advertising by featuring one of the most prestigious artists of the century, is the following commercial for Polaroid with Sir Laurence Olivier.

60 SECONDS

VIDEO	AUDIO
LS OLIVIER, CAMERA IN HAND, APPROACHING VASE OF FLOWERS FROM OUT OF DARK BACKGROUND.	FOOTSTEPS
MLS OLIVIER, HOLDING UP AND POINTING TO CAMERA, FLOWERS IN FOREGROUND.	OLIVIER: Polaroid's new SX-70.
MS OLIVIER PREPARING CAMERA TO TAKE PICTURE.	
MS OLIVIER POINTING TO BUTTON ON CAMERA.	OLIVIER: Just touch the button . . .
MCU OLIVIER TAKING PICTURE OF FLOWERS.	
CU OLIVIER TAKING PICTURE OF FLOWERS, ONE PICTURE OUT OF CAMERA.	OLIVIER: Now, these pictures,

(continued on page 107)

1. (SFX)

2. (SFX)

3. (SFX)

4. (SFX)

5. ANNCR: (VO) Minutes hang like hours

6. when someone's waiting for you.

7. If you only had an Accutron watch,

8. you'd have the right time to within one minute a month.

9. And you wouldn't get growled at so often.

10. (SFX)

Doyle Dane Bernbach Inc. for Bulova Watch Co.

VIDEO	AUDIO
CU OLIVIER TAKING PICTURE OF FLOWERS, TWO PICTURES OUT OF CAMERA.	OLIVIER: developing themselves, outside the camera,
CU OLIVIER TAKING PICTURE OF FLOWERS, THREE PICTURES OUT OF CAMERA.	OLIVIER: are hard and dry.
MCU THREE PICTURES STILL ALMOST BLANK.	MUSIC
CU THREE PICTURES, FLOWERS BARELY BEGINNING TO SHOW.	OLIVIER: There's nothing to peel,
CU THREE PICTURES, FLOWERS SHOWING A LITTLE MORE.	OLIVIER: nothing even to throw away,
CU THREE PICTURES, FLOWERS EMERGING MORE.	OLIVIER: nothing to time.
CU THREE PICTURES, FLOWERS CONTINUE TO EMERGE.	MUSIC
CU THREE PICTURES, FLOWERS BECOMING CLEARER.	MUSIC
CU THREE PICTURES, FLOWERS MORE CLEAR.	OLIVIER: In minutes, you will have a finished photograph of such dazzling beauty.
CU THREE PICTURES, FULLY PRINTED.	OLIVIER: that you will feel you are looking at the world for the first time.
XC FINISHED SINGLE PICTURE.	MUSIC
MCU OLIVIER HOLDING CAMERA OPENED.	OLIVIER: The new SX-70 Land Camera.
MCU OLIVIER HOLDING UP CAMERA CLOSED.	OLIVIER: From Polaroid.

Doyle Dane Bernbach Inc. for Polaroid Corporation

An alternative to the traditional celebrity testimonial is the testimonial from the average man or woman — the worker, the homemaker, the man- or woman-in-the-street with whom the viewer at home can more easily identify. Through such identification the viewer may more easily accept the existence of a common problem in a physical, economic or vocational setting of common experience and, concomitantly, may more readily accept the solution adopted by the person in the commercial — using the sponsor's product. You see this form frequently with laundry products and cosmetic comparisons. The following is an example which has an interesting variation: not using the actual subject referred to.

1. (MUSIC THROUGHOUT)
   ANNCR: (VO) Robert
   Ammon...

2. Michigan.

3. Mrs. James Simonds...
   New Hampshire.

4. Mrs. Frank O'Brien...

5. Alabama.

6. Mrs. Travis Wiginton...
   California.

7. Robert Geroy...

8. North Carolina.

9. James Edelstein...
   Wisconsin.

10. Mrs. D. M. Olson...
    Minnesota.

11. Ask them whether an
    American Tourister
    is a great suitcase to have...

12. when you hit the road.

Doyle Dane Bernbach Inc. for American Tourister

Sometimes, when emotional appeals are dominant, an "everyman" or "everywoman" approach is used, as in the following:

60 SECONDS, RADIO

Hello, I'd like to tell you something about myself.
I used to be a drunk, and a chronic drunk driver. In the ten years between my first arrest and having my license revoked I racked up 19 major traffic violations, I caused 6 serious accidents, injured 3 people besides myself and had my license suspended twice.
I was still driving and drinking.
Then one night I was driving home after work and I had a few and I hit this kid on a bicycle. He died before they could get him any help. He was just 11 and a little younger than my oldest boy. I'm living with that now.
I was too drunk to see him then, but, I can see him now . . . and I remember.

ANNCR: This message was brought to you by The General Motors Corporation.

General Motors Corporation "Safer Driver Radio" series
Created by Robert Dunning, N. W. Ayer & Son, Inc., New York

The above announcement does not promote a product, but, instead, a public service idea. It is, therefore, educational in nature and is what is termed an "institutional" commercial — one which does not sell a product but which is designed to create good will for the sponsor.

The writer should be careful in the use of testimonials in programs aimed at children. Children are particularly susceptible to the exhortations of hero and heroine figures, including the live performers who may appear on a particular program. In 1975 strong pressures by citizen groups and other public interest sources resulted in many broadcasters removing such testimonials from the commercial content on children's shows. The 1974 FCC Policy Statement on Children's Television suggested the avoidance of "host selling and other sales techniques that blur the distinctions between programing and advertising."

Humor. Just as public attitudes toward humor change over the years, so do the humorous approaches in commercials. Always an effective attention-getter, humor in commercials, to be succsesful, must reflect the humorous trends of the time. The use of humor in commercials grew rapidly in the early 1970s and then, suddenly, as inflation, Watergate, industry rip-offs, pollution, impeachment, depression and other grim problems overtook the public, some things weren't very funny any more. A number of advertisers who had used humor heavily began to move away from it, playing it safe with the straight sell, frequently with a personality endorsement.

At one time the "gag," the "one-liner," was the staple of commercial humor. That has largely been replaced by more gentle humor, by parody, by subtle satire (never of the audience, of course). In a sense, this approach is a return to the past, when Bob and Ray as "Harry and Bert Piel" provided some of the finest humor in broadcasting, commercials and programs both. Henry Morgan did it on radio even before there was television, with

30 SECONDS

1. MAN: I'm insecure about some things but not my new Volkswagen.

2. Because it comes with an Owner's Security Blanket.

3. I'm covered for 12 months or 20,000 miles, whichever comes first.

4. (Or roughly 10,000 trips to mother's house).

5. If I have trouble with any part,

6. in normal use and service,

7. they'll fix it free except for tires and filters.

8. And they do a lot of other things for me too.

9. I haven't felt this secure since my Mommy tucked me in at night. (LAUGHS)

For 12 months or 20,000 miles
we'll fix any factory defective part,
except tires and filters,
on any properly maintained 74 VW.
Overnight loan-a-bug by appointment.
3 Computer Check-ups free.

10. (SILENT)

Doyle Dane Bernbach Inc. for Volkswagen of America

parody so sharp that he lost sponsors — even while the satire of the sponsors was selling their products and making them money. In more recent years Stan Freberg has been one of the more prolific practitioners of the parody. Some advertisers and agency people believe that one of the problems with the really top-notch humorous commercials was that the audience got so involved in the humor that they didn't pay enough attention to the product. The fate of the Piel's commercials — winners of numerous awards but apparent losers in selling the product — seems to bear that out.

Commercials in this genre tend to stress mood and feeling, to involve the audience not only in the action, but in the inside comment, in sometimes knowing something that the character in the commercial seemingly has yet to find out. Rather than information, such commercials convey a feeling — the kind of emotional motivation that is usually much more effective than logical information. When gentle parody and information can be combined, we have an award-winning commercial as shown on the opposite page.

Some humorous commercials use what seems to be a juxtaposition of seemingly incongruous elements — but the topicality makes the point clear, as in the following example:

10 SECONDS

1. (SILENT)

2. ANNCR: (VO) If gas pains persist ...

3. (SFX)

4. Try Volkswagen.

Doyle Dane Bernbach Inc. for Volkswagen of America

Some top commercial producers, like Chuck Blore, feel that parodies have been overdone, that any satire in commercials has got to be fresh, innovative and unique.[10] The parody should be so good that the public will want to hear it over and over again. The most effective parodies have been those which have a story line, even a limited one, in which the situation is dominant. Within the situation are the references to the product. The following example is a classic of this type:

30 SECONDS

VIDEO	AUDIO
OPEN ON HUSBAND SITS UP IN BED IN SLIGHT TRANCE, OBVIOUSLY UNABLE TO SLEEP. WIFE IS IN BED BESIDE HIM.	HUSBAND: I can't believe I ate that whole thing. WIFE: You ate it Ralph. HUSBAND: I can't believe I ate that whole thing. WIFE: No Ralph, I ate it! HUSBAND: I can't believe I ate that whole thing. WIFE: Take two Alka-Seltzer.
CUT TO TWO ALKA-SELTZER DROPPING IN GLASS OF WATER. PAN ACROSS ASPIRIN BOTTLE AND TWO ASPIRINS. CONTINUE PAN ACROSS ROLL OF ANTACIDS AND TWO ANTACIDS. CONTINUE PAN TO FOIL PACK OF ALKA-SELTZER.	ANNCR. V.O.: For headache and upset stomach, no aspirin or antacid alone relieves you in as many ways as Alka-Seltzer. For headache and upset stomach.
CUT TO CLOSE UP OF HUSBAND.	WIFE: Did you drink your Alka-Seltzer? HUSBAND: The whole thing.

Courtesy of Miles Laboratories and Wells, Rich, Greene, Inc.

Music. The musical commercial has always been one of the most effective for having an audience remember the product. How many times have you listened to a song on radio or television, been caught up in its cadence, and then suddenly realized it was a commercial and not the latest popular hit tune? I remember when, more than 20 years ago, the landlord sent a painter to do the legally required triannual paint job on my apartment in New York. For three days, to amuse himself as he worked, the painter sang over and over again in varying tempos, volume and pitch, "Be Happy, Go Lucky, Be Happy, Go Lucky Strike." A major difference in the musical commercials today, however, is that they are no longer jingles, but full-fledged songs.

Producer Susan Hamilton states that "music is still basically an emotional thing. And the reason we are producing commercials that sound like records is to try and grab the listeners. We're always told that when a commercial comes on the radio kids immediately turn the dial. But when you make your spots sound like songs, there's a chance you may be able to reach those kids before they reach those dials."[11] In fact, some commercials, such as Pepsi-Cola's "The Girl Watchers Theme," Alka-Seltzer's "No Matter What Shape" and Coca-Cola's "I'd Like to Teach the World to Sing," did become hit songs.

In the mid-1970s musical commercials accounted for about 65% of all radio spots. Because it has to be singable the musical commercial usually follows the contemporary trend — the hit pattern of the particular year. There are exceptions, of course. Acid rock and progressive jazz, for example, have not usually proven appropriate for effective commercials. Producer Sid Woloshin believes that "commercials music is at its best when it leads rather than follows."[12]

With the increased emphasis on musical commercials, more sophisticated techniques of production developed, requiring higher costs. The electronic synthesizer, properly used, can be very effective, and the multi-track recording came over from the record industry.

Music has been so effective in writing commercials that many of us have come to identify and remember Coca-Cola, McDonald's and United Air Lines, among others, first with their theme music and only secondarily with a particular sales message. One of the most effective examples, now a classic, is the following:

60 SECONDS

VIDEO	AUDIO
	Song:
CUT TO CU OF GIRL'S FACE AND SINGING.	I'd like to buy the world a home and furnish it with love. Grow apple trees
PB TO REVEAL GIRL SINGING WITH BOY AND GIRL WITH COKE BOTTLE ALSO SINGING.	and snow white turtles doves
DISS TO PAN ACROSS OF BOYS AND GIRLS IN NATIVE DRESS WITH COKE BOTTLES IN HAND AND SINGING.	I'd like to teach the world to sing (sing with me) in perfect harmony (perfect harmony) and I'd like to buy the world a coke and keep it company. It's the real thing.
DISS TO SIDE VIEW OF ROWS OF BOYS AND GIRLS IN NATIVE DRESS AND SINGING.	I'd like to teach the world to sing (what the world wants today)
DISS TO PAN ACROSS OF ROWS OF BOYS AND GIRLS IN NATIVE DRESS SINGING.	In perfect harmony (perfectly) I'd like to buy the world a Coke.
DISS TO PAN ACROSS OF COKE BOTTLES IN HANDS OF BOYS AND GIRLS.	and keep it company
DISS TO CU OF GIRL'S FACE AND SINGING.	It's the real thing. (Coke is)
DOUBLE EXPOSE CU GIRL'S FACE SINGING OVER CROWD SHOT TO PB TO REVEAL CROWDS OF BOYS AND GIRLS OF ALL NATIONS ON HILL WITH CRAWLING TITLE AND MATTE:	What the world wants today Coca-Cola . It's the real thing. What the world wants today Coke is. Coca-Cola.

VIDEO   AUDIO

SUPER: ON A HILLTOP IN ITALY WE
ASSEMBLED YOUNG PEOPLE
FROM ALL OVER THE WORLD
TO BRING YOU THIS MESSAGE
FROM COCA-COLA BOTTLERS
ALL OVER THE WORLD. IT'S THE
REAL THING. COKE.

*Courtesy of The Coca-Cola Company. Words and music by Roger Cook,
Roger Greenaway, William Becker and Billy Davis. McCann-Erickson, Inc.*

Dramatizations.   A dramatization is, in effect, a short play — a happening that creates suspense and reaches a climax. The climax is, of course, the revelation of the attributes of the product. In the classic structure of the play form, the resolution is the members of the audience all rushing out of their homes to buy the particular product. Dramatizations frequently combine elements of the other major commercial forms, particularly music, testimonials and humor. Here are several award-winning commercials in the dramatization form.

> • *As you study them, 1.) determine which forms, in addition to drama, they contain, and 2.) analyze their use of the five steps of persuasion, including their use of emotional appeals.*

60 SECONDS

VISUAL	AUDIO
1. COUNSELOR WALKING DOWN STEPS OF ROW HOUSE.	Song: "Hey, look at you lookin' at the sunrise . . .
2. CU OF COUNSELOR TALKING TO BOY.	"There's such a brighter . . .
3. BOY BEING PULLED UP.	"look in your . . .
4. COUNSELOR AND BOY WALKING DOWN SIDEWALK, TALKING.	"eyes.
5. COUNSELOR AND BOY CROSSING STREET.	"Now that I know you've felt the wind . . .
6. COUNSELOR AND THREE KIDS WALKING DOWN SIDEWALK.	"that's blowing, reaching out . . .
7. PAN OF COUNSELOR AND KIDS.	"and wanting life's good things.
8. LONG SHOT OF PLAYGROUND GATE OPENING AND KIDS WAITING.	"Now that you're seein' . . .
9. OPEN GATE AND KIDS RUSHING IN.	"All things grow.
10. CU OF COUNSELOR TURNING AROUND.	(MUSIC UP)
11. COUNSELOR PASSING BALL TO BOY.	
12. COUNSELOR JOGGING TO BOY BEHIND FENCE.	"There is more love in . . .
13. CU OF JOSÉ.	"you than anyone . . .
14. COUNSELOR ASKING BOY TO FOLLOW.	"I know.

VIDEO	AUDIO
15. COUNSELOR WITH ARM AROUND JOSÉ, INTRODUCING HIM TO KIDS.	"You take time for friends . . .
16. COUNSELOR PLAYING CHECKERS WITH KIDS, GIRL DRINKING COKE.	"and simple talking . . .
17. CU OF COUNSELOR DRINKING COKE.	"Sippin' Coke . . .
18. LS OF COUNSELOR SWINGING BOY AROUND.	"enjoyin' life's . . .
19. PAN OF KIDS DRINKING COKE AGAINST FENCE.	"good things. It's the Real Thing.
20. CU OF PRODUCT AGAINST FENCE.	"Oh . . . Coca-Cola.
21. PAN OF KIDS AGAINST FENCE.	"It's the Real Thing.
22. PRODUCT AGAINST FENCE.	"Oh . . . Coca-Cola.
23. COUNSELOR GIVING JOSÉ A COKE.	"It's the Real Thing.
24. PRODUCT AGAINST FENCE WITH SUPER: "It's the real thing. Coke."	"Oh . . . Coca-Cola.
25. COUNSELOR WITH JOSÉ ARM IN ARM. SUPER: "It's the real thing. Coke."	"It's the Real Thing."

Courtesy of The Coca-Cola Company. McCann-Erickson, Inc.

30 SECONDS

VIDEO	AUDIO
OPEN ON STEWARDESS IN APARTMENT. EARLY MORNING. SHE'S GETTING READY TO LEAVE. BUTTONING JACKET, PUTTING ON HAT, PACKING AIRLINE BAG, ETC.	GIRL: I love to go places . . . with me it's a "thing," you know? I get to thinking about friends, the family. Why shouldn't we get together as often as possible? So I don't wait for "special occasions."
PICKS UP PHONE ON VANITY TABLE.	I visit when I *want* to visit. (BIG SMILE) Spontaneous Communication —wow! And visiting these days . . . it's so inexpensive, so easy, you know? Long distance . . .
SHE DIALS A NUMBER QUICKLY AND EASILY.	
SMILES AND PUTS RECEIVER TO EAR. LOOKS AT CAMERA. FREEZE FRAME ON HER SMILE.	Oh, go on . . . take a phone trip now!
TRANSITION TO MICHIGAN BELL LOGO. "Dial direct and Save" HOLD ON LOGO.	SFX: (TOUCH-TONE RANDOM NOTES) GIRL: What a nice ride!

Courtesy of Ross Roy, Inc., Detroit

60 SECONDS

1. ANNCR: (VO) This is a dramatization of a true story.

2. On November 28th, 1970,

3. a storm developed in the Sierra Nevada Mountains

4. that was termed "the worst ever".

5. Six months later,

6. when emergency crews were finally able to clear the roads,

7. something strange happened.

8. (SFX)

9. (SFX)

10. (SFX)

11. A car was found ...

12. a Volkswagen buried beneath tons of snow and ice.

13. But even stranger than that,

14. when the crew's supervisor turned the ignition key,

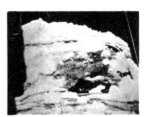

15. (SFX)

16. (SFX: CAR STARTING)

17. (SFX)

18. (SFX)

19. ANNCR: (VO) The 1974 Volkswagen. Covered by VW Owner's Security Blanket.

Doyle Dane Bernbach Inc.
for Volkswagen of America

60-SECOND SPOT — "POKER GAME"

VIDEO	AUDIO
LS A FRIDAY NIGHT POKER GAME.	HOWARD COSSELL: The Friday night game at Carl's and someone's playing with marked cards.
CU OF DEALER.	DEALER: Five card draw, gentlemen, jacks or better to open.
CU 1ST PLAYER.	1ST PLAYER: I open for two.
CU 2ND PLAYER.	2ND PLAYER: I'll see you.
CU 3RD PLAYER	3RD PLAYER: I never win at this game. By me.
LS OF GAME.	HOWARD COSSELL: All these men know who's playing with the marked cards but they don't mind.
	DEALER: Cards.
	1ST PLAYER: I'll take two.
	2ND PLAYER: Let me have three.
CU OF 2ND PLAYER.	HOWARD COSSELL: He's the one, he's blind and the cards are marked in braille. They're made available by the American Foundation for the Blind. Brailled cards are just one of the hundreds of aids and appli-
SUPER ADDRESS.	ances made and adapted for blind people. If you want a catalog, write BLIND AIDS, Box 111, New York 10011.
	1ST PLAYER: I've got three Queens.

Courtesy of the American Foundation for the Blind

Other Commercial Forms. Two of the most effective appeals involve family and children. The viewer identifies strongly and is left with a good feeling toward the product, service or idea. Here are two award-winning examples:

60 SECONDS

VIDEO	AUDIO
LONG SHOT OF CAB ON COUNTRY ROAD.	"I was raised on country sunshine
CU OF GIRL IN CAB.	
LS OF KIDS ON SWING.	Green grass beneath my feet
LS OF CAB.	
KIDS ON HORSE.	Runnin' thru fields of daisies
KIDS ON TREE FISHING.	Wadin' thru the creek
LS OF FATHER ON TRACTOR.	
PAN OF CAR WITH GIRL.	You love me and it's invitin'
SHOT OF HAY LOFT.	To go where life is
MOTHER ON PORCH.	More excitin'
LONG SHOT OF CAB.	But I was raised
CU OF FATHER REACTING TO CAB.	On country sunshine
CU OF CAB.	
CU OF GIRL ON SWING REACTING TO CAB.	I was raised

VIDEO	AUDIO
CU OF BOY IN HAY LOFT.	On country
BOY JUMPS OUT OF HAY LOFT.	sunshine. I'm a happy
MOTHER ON PORCH REACTING TO GIRL.	With the simple
LONG SHOT OF CAB ARRIVING AT HOUSE.	Things — a Saturday night dance
PRODUCT SHOT.	A bottle of Coke
GIRL GREETS FAMILY.	The joy that the Bluebird brings
	I love you please believe me
CU OF GREETING.	And don't you ever leave me
CU OF FAMILY ON PORCH.	Cause I was raised on country sunshine
CU OF KIDS DRINKING COKE.	It's the real thing
PRODUCT SHOT.	Like Coke is
GUY GETTING OUT OF TRUCK.	That you're hoping to find
GIRL AND GUY EMBRACE.	Like country sunshine, it's the real thing
COUPLE ON SWING.	Coca-Cola."
SUPER: "It's the Real Thing."	

Courtesy of The Coca-Cola Company. McCann-Erickson, Inc.

60 SECONDS

Montage of Children

I love you, Daddy.
He brung me to the circus once.
I love my daddy more than everything.
My daddy is sweet.
My daddy is regular.
My daddy is skinny.
Sometimes when I'm riding in the car with him
    he goes so fast I'm sort a scared.
Slow down daddy.
He might skid and drive the car off the road.
When Daddy drives I worry because
    he has lots a crashes.
A policeman can come right around the
    corner and my Dad might get arreseted.
I wish he would come back.
He didn't come home yet.
I want him to come back.
I'm scared.
I would feel worried about him.
I get scared because he goes so fast.

ANNCR: If you don't care about your own safety, remember that those who love you do.
Please slow down.
This message was brought to you by the General Motors Corporation.

General Motors Corporation "Safer Driver Radio" series
Created by Robert Dunning, N. W. Ayer & Son, Inc., New York

Psychologists tell us that one of the appeals to people's emotions and motivations is the new experience, the prospect or even the thought of adventure. The "Walter Mitty" syndrome doesn't have to be a parody; it can be something simple and realistic that every viewer can easily do, as in the commercial shown on the next two pages.

60 SECONDS

1. (MUSIC UNDER THROUGHOUT) ANNCR: (VO) Perhaps once or twice in a lifetime,

2. there comes an invention so radically new,

3. it actually changes the way we live our lives.

4. Television was one.

5. Now Polaroid invents the SX-70.

6. (SFX)

7. Less than two seconds after you touch the red electric button,

8. (SFX) the camera hands you the picture.

9. (MUSIC)

10. It's nothing to peel,

11. nothing even to throw away.

12. nothing to time.

13. The image blooms before your eyes,

14. and in minutes,

15. you have a finished photograph, seemingly as real as life itself.

16. (MUSIC)

17. (MUSIC)

18. The new SX-70 Land Camera, from Polaroid.

19. (SFX) It can reveal the world to you as you have never seen it before.

Doyle Dane Bernbach Inc.
for Polaroid Corporation

The non-commercial commercial (see the highway safety PSA earlier in this chapter under *The Television Storyboard*) and the anti-commercial commercial were phenomena of the 1970s. Even after cigarette advertising went off the air, stations continued to carry anti-smoking spots.

> • *What writing techniques (i.e. steps of persuasion, emotional appeals) does the following use to unsell a product? Do its writing techniques differ from those of the "commercial" commercial?*

JOHN AND EVIE (60 SECONDS)

MUSIC:	SMOKE GETS IN YOUR EYES
GIRL:	(NORMAL) John . . .
BOY:	(NORMAL) Evie . . .
GIRL:	(BIT ROMANTIC) John . . .
BOY:	(BIT ROMANTIC) Evie . . .
GIRL:	(GIGGLY) John . . .
BOY:	(GIGGLY) Evie . . .
GIRL:	(MORE ROMANTIC) John . . .
BOY:	(MORE ROMANTIC) Evie . . .
SOUND:	Lighting cigarette . . . and Puffing
GIRL:	John . . .
BOY:	Evie . . .
GIRL:	(UPSET) John!
BOY:	(PERSISTING) Evie!
SOUND:	KISS
GIRL:	(BLOWING AWAY ANNOYING SMOKE) John . . .
BOY:	(BLOWING AWAY SMOKE) Evie . . .
GIRL:	(SLIGHT COUGH) John . . .
BOY:	(SLIGHT COUGH) Evie . . .
GIRL:	(LOOKING FOR JOHN) John???
BOY:	(LOOKING FOR EVIE) EVIE???
GIRL:	(INCREASED COUGHING) John . . .
BOY:	(INCREASED COUGHING) Evie . . .
GIRL:	(FRANTIC COUGHING AND CALL FOR HELP) Johnnnnn!!!
BOY:	(FRANTIC COUGHING AND CALL FOR HELP) Evieeee!!!
MUSIC:	COUGHING AND MUSIC FADE OUT
ANNCR:	The American Cancer Society reminds you that smoking cigarettes is a drag and you'd better believe it.

One of the classic statements on radio commercials came from Maurice B. Mitchell in 1949 as director of broadcast advertising for the National Association of Broadcasters. The continuing validity of the five points presented by Mr. Mitchell, since 1967 Chancellor of the University of Denver, was emphasized by *Broadcasting* magazine on September 10, 1973, when it reprinted Mr. Mitchell's 1949 statement under the headline: "Second time around: words about radio still ring true." Although Mr. Mitchell's comments related to radio advertising in general, they are in some instances specifically and in other instances by implication oriented toward the job of the commercial continuity writer. Mr. Mitchell stated, in part:

"How can you use radio more effectively? What are things you can do to get greater results from radio? I would tell you five simple things — the five points into which all our study and all our research can be boiled down.

"No. 1. Before you can use radio for maximum effectiveness, you have got to understand your objectives. Before an advertiser, before a retailer sets up his radio advertising budget or buys any time, he should know what he expects to advertise and to whom he expects to address his advertising message. What do you want from radio and whom do you want to talk to? It's just that simple. . . .

"No. 2. The retailer should take advantage of a technique we have found to be overwhelmingly successful — the beamed program technique. If you know what you want to say and you know whom you want to say it to, you can buy a vehicle that will, without waste, talk directly to the people you want to address. It's a rifle shot at a target, not a buck-shot at a barn door. . . .

"No. 3. We think the retailer who wants maximum success from advertising should advertise his strong departments and his strong lines, advertise his in-demand merchandise and advertise it on the radio regularly. . . .

"No. 4. You've got to have the kind of copy that will do the selling job right. Not just 'copy' — not just the stuff you poke out with one finger on the typewriter for your newspaper *and* your radio advertising . . . sometimes. One of the things we've never been able to understand is why an advertiser will put phrases in his advertising copy that people would never say aloud. Did you ever hear of a woman who called her husband on the phone and said to him, 'Would you mind stopping in at Jones's Department Store today and buying me a pair of slippers because, there, quality and variety go hand in hand?' A lot of advertisers are saying that sort of thing every single day of the week. Don't you think perhaps she might actually say, 'I wish you'd buy me a pair of slippers at Jones' because their sale ends today and I can't get downtown?' She is telling her husband specifically what she wants, specifically why she wants it, and she makes a decision to buy for a specific reason.

"One of the best examples I've seen is the copy of an advertiser who used the radio recently to advertise purses. In his early advertising, he was using this kind of copy: 'Stop in here for a purse because we have purses that will help complete a smart costume ensemble at budget prices.' Now, nobody buys 'a smart costume ensemble at budget prices.' But when he later began to say, 'Here's where the working girl will always find a purse at $8.98,' or 'Here's where you'll find plastic bags that wash as easily as your face,' or 'Here's where you'll find plastic bags and purses in bright colors that will go with your dark suit,' he was talking to people in the terms in which they thought of his merchandise. He was talking specifically to the listeners about the specific things his merchandise could do for them, and he wasn't being vague and saying, 'This merchandise which we have to sell has this attribute.' He was saying '*You* ought to buy this because this will do this for *you*.'

"We also think the kind of copy that produces the maximum results for a retailer is truthful, believable copy. If you will sit down and take the trouble to find out those things that you can say about your goods that are truthful and that are believable, then you have taken a step towards greater success in radio. That kind of copy sticks in a person's mind for a long time. It doesn't always produce results *today*, but continual repetition will cause people to remember the store that uses that kind of advertising. Joske's (of San Antonio) continual repetition of 'the largest store in the largest state,' and similar slogans used by other great stores, stay in the minds of many people who aren't planning a purchase the first time they hear it. The fact that when they do get around to buying they'll remember that here's where they've wanted to shop — that's the real effect of that kind of copy. Truthful copy, like truthful clerks, is a lot more convincing. Very few retailers would instruct their clerks to deliberately lie to a potential buyer. Yet many retailers don't deliberately lie but — let me say — deviate somewhat from the bare facts in their advertising.

"Most important of all, invite your customer to take direct action. Don't say: 'You should buy a pair of slippers because they're wonderful,' but say: 'Come on down to our store tomorrow morning at 10 o'clock and go into the entrance just off Main Street. You don't even have to go upstairs — the slippers are right near the door. You can buy them and be out in five minutes.' You've given a direct invitation to take direct action.

"I've heard some taxi-cab advertising recently that impressed me. Typical was a line of taxi cabs that said, 'Here's where you can have dependable, clean, efficient taxi service.' Now I don't particularly care if the taxi cab company is run efficiently. If it isn't, I assume they'll go bankrupt and somebody else will come around when I call. Dependability is certainly not the key customer advantage for a taxi-cab company to promote as a basic reason for calling a cab. On the other hand, I have heard another taxi company say, 'It's raining out today! Don't get wet! Call a taxi. Call this number. Be sure you call this number if you need a taxi. And if you need a taxi, call this number.' They're talking to me about a service I'm liable to need right then in terms of why I might need it and they make sure I can find it if I do.

"One of the things I get a big kick out of, and I'm sure many other advertising men do, is the Christmas approach — 'Be sure you bring something home to your wife that will put the lovelight in her eyes.' I can put the lovelight in my wife's eyes without the help of any advertising. But there are some other reasons why I might buy her a Christmas present. Some pretty good, sound selling reasons. 'Put the old lovelight in your wife's eyes' looks wonderful on a typewriter, but it sounds silly in advertising and doesn't persuade anybody. The direct-action copy approach, talking to people in terms that they understand, in the terms in which they think of the use of the merchandise themselves, will sell.

"No. 5. Coordinate your advertising. . . . How do you coordinate your advertising? It's very simple. You display radio-advertised merchandise at the place where you said it could be bought. . . . Make sure you promote your radio programs in all of your other advertising media. . . . Conversely, use radio to make your other media work better. . . . Let radio give emphasis and increased publicity to all of your other advertising purchases."

NOTES TO CHAPTER 3

[1] Paul, S. J., "Publisher's Letter," *Television/Radio Age*, May 27, 1974, p. 14.

[2] *Television/Radio Age*, November 26, 1973, p. 41.

[3] *Television/Radio Age*, April 29, 1974, p. 30.

[4] *Television/Radio Age*, November 26, 1973, p. 95.

[5] *Television/Radio Age*, December 14, 1970, p. 37.

[6] *Television/Radio Age*, May 27, 1974, p. 35.

[7] "Grace and Noble on Chemistry, Honesty and Controversy," DDB (Doyle Dane Bernbach) *News*, February, 1970.

[8] "Levenson's Acid Test for Knowing What Good Is," *DDB News*, October, 1971.

[9] *Television/Radio Age*, July 8, 1974, p. 65.

[10] *Television/Radio Age*, May 27, 1974, p. 94.

[11] *Broadcasting*, July 10, 1972, p. 26.

[12] *Television/Radio Age*, December 14, 1970, p. 72.

REFERENCE BOOKS

ON WRITING ANNOUNCEMENTS AND COMMERCIALS

Cary, Norman D., *The Television Commercial: Creativity and Craftsmanship.* New York: Decker, 1971. Overview from selling to production.

Diamant, Lincoln, *The Broadcast Communications Dictionary.* New York: Hastings House, 1974. Some 2,000 terms in current usage covering all phases of broadcasting.

————, *Television's Classic Commercials: The "Golden Years" 1948-1958.* New York: Hastings House, 1971. Assesses sales impact, marketing and sociological impact.

————, ed., *The Anatomy of a Television Commercial.* New York: Hastings House, 1970. Creation and production of Kodak's multi-award winning "Yesterdays."

Gordon, George N., *Persuasion: The Theory and Practice of Manipulative Communications.* New York: Hastings House, 1971. Basic concepts are applicable to commercial persuasion.

Lavidge, Arthur W., *A Common Sense Guide to Professional Advertising.* Blue Ridge Summit, Penna.: Tab Books, 1973. A study of agency's total functions, including work of the copywriter.

Peck, William A., *The Anatomy of Local Radio-TV Copy.* Blue Ridge Summit, Penna.: Tab Books, 1968.

Terrell, Neil, *The Power Technique for Radio-TV Copywriting.* Blue Ridge Summit, Penna.: Tab Books, 1971.

Wainwright, Charles Anthony, *Television Commercials: How to Create Successful TV Advertising,* Revised Edition. New York: Hastings House, 1970.

In addition to the periodicals listed in the bibliography to Chapter 1, the following are of special value for the writer of announcements and commercials: *Advertising Age: The National Newspaper of Marketing* — weekly; *Marketing/Communications.*

FOR APPLICATION AND REVIEW

1. For both television and radio, choose a product, a program and a station. Develop a commercial for each, in terms of the following considerations: audience analysis; logical and emotional appeals; familiarization with the product and its basic place in the commercial; the five steps of persuasion: attention, interest, impression of a problem, solving of a problem, getting action.

2. Using the same considerations, write a PSA for television and a PSA for radio.

3. Write a television and a radio ID for your local stations.

4. Watch and listen to several commercials and analyze the specific emotional appeals used. Write television and radio commercials in terms of the analysis of the audience in your locality, using one or more of the following emotional appeals in each commercial: prestige, power, good taste, self-preservation.

5. Watch and listen to television and radio commercials until you are certain you can identify each of the following formats: straight sell, testimonial, humorous, musical, dramatization. Write short television and radio commercials which illustrate each of these forms.

4

News
and Sports

NEWS

ANY REAL HAPPENING that may have an interest for or effect upon people is news. The television and radio reporter has a limitless field. Anything from a cat up a tree to the outbreak of a war may be worthy of transmission to the mass media audience. The gathering of news, however, is not our primary concern here. The writing of news broadcasts is.

Sources of News

Two major agencies, the Associated Press and United Press International, which serve as news sources for the newspapers, also service television and radio stations. The same information given to newspapers is made available for broadcasting. For broadcast purposes, however, the style of writing of the news should be changed so that the stories become shorter and more pointed, oriented toward the needs of television and radio transmission. In television, in addition, the news stories are not used alone, but are coordinated with visual elements such as films, slides, photographs and wirephotos. A number of organizations provide special news material, particularly pictorial matter, for television. Special newsreel and photo companies operate in almost every city containing a major television station. The larger networks have their own news gathering and reporting organizations. The Columbia Broadcasting System, for example, operates a most effective newsfilm division which supplies material to various stations throughout the country.

All television and radio stations of any consequence, even small local stations, subscribe to at least one wire service. The small station also may use more immediate sources for local news, such as telephoned reports from city agencies or even private citizens, special information from the local newspapers, word of mouth communications, and sometimes special reporters of their own. The local news story must be written from scratch and, for television, written to fit in with the available visual material.

In the large station, the news usually is prepared by writers in a special news department. Most small stations do not have separate news departments, so news broadcasts are prepared by available personnel. The continuity department, if there is one, prepares the special local reports. Generally, the job will fall to the program director or to the individual announcer. The news received through teletype, as well as from local sources, is edited in the large station by the producer or director of the news program or by the individual commentator. The commentator on the small station does this job. The announcer has to make certain that the news reports he or she reads on the air fit his or her personality, vocabulary and, often, station policy. More important, the amount of news prepared must fit the time limit of the show and the organization of the news must adhere to the format of the program. A writer preparing news for a particular program and for a particular announcer will edit it so that it conforms to the above requirements as the specific case demands. For example, Steve Steinberg, chief writer for ABC news reporter and commentator Howard K. Smith, matches "his style to the speaking habits and story preferences of Smith. For example, you will not hear Smith say the word 'particularly' on the air. Steinberg doesn't use it because Smith can't pronounce it. And Smith likes to set up stories with historical backgrounds . . . 'If it was up to Howard, everything in the show would begin: 'On July 4, 1776 . . .' "[1]

Special Considerations

Local News. One of the spurs to radio and television news in the early 1970s was the FCC's prime-time rule, requiring return to local stations by the networks of one-half hour of time during the prime viewing hours for local originations. The most common pattern for use of the additional local programming time was to increase the half-hour news show to one hour. This included not only straight news and commentary, but public affairs programming of a feature and mini-documentary type.[2] In major markets local news programs began to become viable competition with network news broadcasts,[3] in many instances even strong competition for even the most popular entertainment programs. One of the reasons for the surge in the 1970s of local news was the development of the mini-camera, which permits immediacy in local news gathering. This, in turn, affected the form of local news; it became more people-oriented, more informal in nature. Stations began to develop local "magazine" approaches, including not only the traditional feature material, but adding new concepts such as consumer advocate reports, investigative reporting and special reports on vital and frequently controversial issues[4] such as educational practices, racial discrimination, child abuse and feminist concerns.

The FCC requirement for ascertainment of community needs played a significant role in the reorientation of local news content in the 1970s. More and more local stations began to deal more and more with the gut concerns in their communities. Instead of simply reporting on what happened, stations became oriented toward the problems of their towns and cities, as specified in the FCC Ascertainment Primer, and sought solutions to these problems. The approach is basically the same, whether the local station is in a large city or a small one. Robert E. Shay, director of broadcasting at WCBS-TV in New York City, has stated: "We're not issue-oriented. The entire station is geared to people. We basically want to show them how to cope. If we discuss housing, we talk to the people with the problems and not so much with the experts. The same is true when we cover things like the energy crisis."[5] Dick Dudley, president of the Forward Communications Group, discussed the news approach of WSAU-TV, Wasau, Wisconsin: "In a small market such as ours, the interest of the audience is quite often vastly different from that of a major metropolitan market. Thus we have to develop a more acute news sense of our community and area. The network news covers most major stories with a broad brush. We have to utilize a finer news approach to fulfill our commitments to our community."[6]

TV News Special Status. The attitude of the people of the United States toward television news places the writer (and producer) in a position of great influence and ethical responsibility. Surveys continue to show that television is considered by most Americans to be the most believable of all mass media and the major source of their news information. One of the questions asked in the yearly surveys is which of the media should be given more credibility in instances where news reports conflict; about half the public chooses television, about a quarter picks newspapers and the remainder is divided between magazines and radio. About twice as many people say they get most of their news from TV as from newspapers.[7] In light of the power they have to affect the minds and emotions of people, what personal restraints and commitments are there or should there be on television newswriters and producers? What, if any, outside guidance or controls — such as regulation by the federal government — should there be?

Fairness and Equal Time. Broadcast news also has a special status in that it is affected more than any other type of programming by the FCC's two most controversial regulations: the Fairness Doctrine and the Equal Time rule (see Chapter 1). Any presentation of an issue of controversy in a given community must contain all the major sides of that controversy. As with editorializing, if a station is proven to the satisfaction of the FCC not to have presented the controversial issues "fairly," it may be required to provide comparable broadcast time for those sides considered to have been omitted. The Equal Time rule applies to political affairs only and requires a station to provide equal time on the air to all bona fide candidates for a given office, preventing the station, in effect, from providing one candidate with an advantage in reaching the public. Although it is generally accepted that broadcasters are against the Fairness Doctrine and that citizen groups are for it, a survey of stations by *Television/Radio Age*[8] found a substantial minority of program directors and station managers in favor of it. William Sheehan, president of ABC News, stated: "I don't think the Fairness Doctrine is a problem. It doesn't inhibit enterprising broadcast journalism at all. During all this time we've been operating under it, ABC has continued to present news and documentary programming in a frank and hard-hitting manner and no subject has been taboo."[9] On the other hand, Thomas Frawley, as president of the Radio and Television News Director's Association, advocated abolishment of the Fairness Doctrine: "What it all boils down to is that the Fairness Doctrine is as strong or as weak as the sitting Commission decides it will be. Which strongly suggests that there's nothing really consistent about it .... The Commission has been saying all along that it isn't judging news content, just balance. But the mere fact that the Doctrine is there at all, whether it is administered strictly or not, inhibits broadcasters from doing a lot of the courageous things in news that they want to do."[10] Many broadcasters believe that the Fairness Doctrine is in violation of the First Amendment, while some broadcasters and virtually all public-interest groups representing the viewing public believe that the Fairness Doctrine prevents those in control of the broadcast media from unduly influencing public thought and belief by slanting the news.

Those who oppose equal time — and that includes almost all broadcast executives — believe that it limits the amount of political coverage stations provide because it requires equal time for minority as well as majority candidates. Those who favor the Equal Time rule believe that it prevents the broadcast media, particularly in small markets with a limited number of stations, from eliminating minority or dissenting political opinions or giving unfair advantage to one major party candidate over another.

As long as the Fairness Doctrine and Equal Time rule are on the books, however, the news writer must be constantly alert to their provisions and be certain that any given script — even a segment of a news broadcast or news feature — is not a violation of federal regulations. One way in which writers can do this is to do thorough research on a given subject and to obtain as many varying opinions as possible on a controversial issue before preparing it for broadcast. Although this means more work, it also should guarantee a much more valid and in-depth news story.

Format

In some instances the writer may do little more than prepare the transitional continuity for a particular program, leaving out the news content itself. It is then up to the individual commentator to edit the news to fit his or her own announcing abilities, personality, and the program approach. In many cases the writer prepares only the opening and closing for a program, the broadcaster or a special writer filling in the news portions with wire service reports and other materials. The basic radio news format has changed little over the years, except that the 15-minute news program has on many stations become 5-minutes. A still valid format, retained here from an earlier edition of this book for nostalgia as well as illustrative purposes, and in respect for one of the country's greatest journalists, is the following prepared format for an Edward R. Murrow 15-minute news broadcast.

EDWARD R. MURROW — FORMAT

BRYAN: The FORD ROAD SHOW presents EDWARD R. MURROW with the news . . . This is George Bryan speaking for Ford, whose new Interceptor V-8 engine brings you gas-saving Precision Fuel Induction.
(One minute commercial) — Now, Edward R. Murrow.

MURROW: (11 minutes of news) . . . . . I'll be back in a moment with the word for today. Now, a word from George Bryan.

BRYAN: (1-minute 30-second commercial) Now here is Mr. Murrow with his word for the day.

MURROW: Word for the day.

BRYAN: The FORD ROAD SHOW has presented Edward R. Murrow with the news. This is George Bryan speaking for Ford, whose new Interceptor V-8 engine brings you gas-saving Precision Fuel Induction. Listen through the week for the other FORD ROAD SHOWS with Bing Crosby, Rosemary Clooney, Arthur Godfrey, and the morning World News Roundup.

CBS Radio Broadcast

The Murrow format is for a network program. The following format is for a local news broadcast, but on a network's pilot station in a large market. Not only the format sheet, but the accompanying materials are included here.

WNBC NEWSCAST FORMAT

TIME: 1:05 P.M.   DATE: 9-20-73

OPEN: (tease lead story or run very brief actuality clip)
Rockefeller said to be against PATH fare hike

IT'S ___72___ DEGREES AND ___SUNNY___ AT ___1:05___ .
　　　　(temp.)　　　　　　　　　(weather)　　　　　　(time)

I'M _____Jack Welby_____ , WNBC NEWS.
　　　　　　　(name)

LIST TAPE CUTS

1. Carl Ash Union county NJ prosecutor on Ann Logan death. _____

2. Ted Maynard on Lower Manhattan Bldg. Collapse. _____

3. _____.

CLOSE: THIS IS _____ Jack Welby _____ , WNBC NEWS.
                              (name)

*****follow format exactly unless you receive a direct intro from program host.
        In such cases, adjust accordingly.

The Port Authority has filed a request with the Interstate Commerce
Commission for permission to boost Port Authority Trans Hudson
fares from 30 to 50 cents. But Governor Rockefeller reportedly
does not like the idea. Sources close to the Governor report
he would accept a five cent increase, to 35 cents a ride. The
Governors appeal is intended to gain wide support for the proposed
three and a half billion dollar transportation bond issue he initiated
earlier in the year. Public hearings on the proposed PATH fare
hike, will begin next Monday, in Jersey City.

Buildings Commissioner Theodore Kharageuzoff says a Manhattan
garage, that collapsed yesterday, at 249 West 28th Street,
was operated in violation of the law, since cars were parked on
the buildings roof. The three-story garage had recently had
extensive renovation. A fire official said the building collapse
was caused by structural weakness. Three people were injured and
100 cars were damaged in the collapse.

A six-story building, under demolition in lower Manhattan,
collapsed a short while ago, and WNBC newsman Ted Maynard is
on the scene, and files this report.

opens . . . switch

runs . . . 30 seconds

closes . . . near the Bowery

19-year-old Ann Logan of Elizabeth left her job at a Garwood,
New Jersey supermarket Tuesday nite at 11:15, and that was the
last time she was seen alive. The girl's battered body was found
the next morning in nearby Roselle. Union County prosecutor,
Carl Ash, has asked the public for help in finding the girl's killer.

opens . . . switch

runs . . . 23 seconds

closes . . . such a heinous attack

Police say they have no leads in the case.

Courtesy of WNBC, New York

Some local, independent stations use the wire services almost exclusively for their news programs. Even when that is done, a format must be prepared containing an opening, a closing and transitional lead-ins for the specific organizational parts of the newscast, including the commercials. Here is such a format:

FIVE MINUTE NEWS FORMAT — SUSTAINING

OPEN:	Good (morning) (afternoon) (evening). The time is _____. In the news _____. (Note: use 4 stories . . . mixing national, world and local by order of importance).*
ANNCR:	More news in just a moment.
TAPE:	COMMERCIAL (if logged)
ANNCR:	In other news _____.
	(NOTE: use 2 stories . . . national, world and/or local).
ANNCR:	WGAY weather for the Washington area _____.
	(NOTE: use complete forecast, including temperature, humidity and winds).
CLOSE:	That's news and weather . . . I'm (anncr. name)

*Total local news content: 3 stories in entire newscast.

Courtesy of WGAY, FM & AM, Washington and Silver Spring

Although not prepared as a format by the station, yet able to serve as one within the station's TV news program format, is the rundown of the network film feed to affiliates. News departments frequently use several of these each day. Included here are examples of two of the stories.

NEWS PROGRAM SERVICE FOR SUNDAY, FEB. 3, 1974 — FINAL

WE HAVE 13 STORIES INCLUDING 3 SPORT STORIES

1. (SECAUCUS, N.J.) TOUGHER RULES FOR AUTO POLLUTION LIMITS SET BACK TWO MONTHS IN NEW JERSEY (POLLUTION) PKG SOF 1.29
2. (SAIGON) INTERNATIONAL CEASE FIRE COMMISSION MAKING LITTLE HEADWAY IN VIETNAM (VIETNAM) PKG SOF 1.02
3. (PHNOM PENH) U.S. OFFICIALS THINK GOVERNMENT TROOPS WILL BE ABLE TO HOLD CAMBODIAN CAPITAL (CAMBODIA) PKG SOF .42
4. (BRISBANE, AUSTRALIA) THIRTEEN DEAD IN AUSTRALIA'S SEVEREST FLOOD IN LIVING MEMORY (FLOOD) ACT SIL .42
5. (NEW YORK) FIRST BLACK EPISCOPAL BISHOP IN 189 YEAR HISTORY OF N.Y. DIOCESE IS CONSECRATED (RELIGION) PKG SOF 1.24
6. (PHILA.) FIRST QUADRAPLEGIC PRIEST IS ORDAINED IN PHILADELPHIA (PRIEST) ACT SOF TO CUM
7. (FOREST PARK, S.C.) HIGH SCHOOLERS WORK AS PARA-MEDICS TO FILL GAP IN EMERGENCY SERVICE PERSONNEL (RESCUE) PKG SOF 1.47
THE NPS SPORTS REPORT BEGINS WITH:
8. (NEW YORK) JAMES "FLY" WILLIAMS NUMBER THREE SCORER IS BACK IN ACTION WITH AUSTIN PEAY UNIV. (BASKETBALL) ACT SOF 1.45
9. (YUGOSLAVIA) JAN HOFFMAN OF EAST GERMANY WINS EUROPEAN MEN'S FIGURE SKATING TITLE (SKATING) ACT SOF .50
10. (N.Y.) DUANE BOBBIC OLYMPIC HEAVYWEIGHT HAS SCORED 16 KAYOS IN AS MANY PRO FIGHTS (BOXING) PKG SOF

11. (N.Y.) START YOUR OWN BUSINESS SHOW OFFERS IDEAS TO HOPEFUL
    TYCOONS (BUSINESS) PKG SOF 1.24
12. (GREAT NECK, N.Y.) HIGH SCHOOL STUDENTS PUT ON DAILY CLOSED CIRCUIT
    TV NEWS SHOW FOR FELLOW STUDENTS
    (TELEVISION) PKG SOF 1.59
13. (N.Y.) INTERPRETIVE DANCE TROUPE USES RIBBONS AND LIGHTS TO CREATE
    UNIQUE EFFECTS (ENTERTAINMENT) PKG SOF 1.16

PRIEST   COL SOT 1.33
ON CAMERA   WILLIAM ATKINSON A FORMER FOOTBALL PLAYER HAS JUST
BEEN ORDAINED A PRIEST. THAT IN ITSELF IS NOT AT ALL UNUSUAL.
WHAT IS EXTRAORDINARY IS THE FACT THAT ATKINSON — A STUDENT AT
VILLANOVA — IS A QUADRIPLEGIC — THE FIRST EVER TO ACHIEVE THE
PRIESTHOOD. AN ACCIDENT WHILE TOBAGGANING NEARLY 9 YEARS AGO
PARALYZED ATKINSON'S ARMS AND LEGS BUT HE STUCK TO HIS GOAL TO MAKE
THE CHURCH HIS LIFE WORK. AND THE VALIANT UPHILL BATTLE WAS
TAPE IN (4 SECONDS SIL)
(VOICE OVER)
      CULMINATED YESTERDAY WITH THE ORDINATION OF THE REVEREND
WILLIAM ATKINSON IN UPPER DARBY, PENNSYLVANIA.
SOF STARTS WHEN YOU FOUND THE EXTENT . . .
TAPE ENDS . . . GOD WILLING HE DID.

TELEVISION COL SOT 1.59
ON CAMERA   IN GREAT NECK, NEW YORK, A COURSE IS BEING GIVEN IN THE
PRODUCTION OF TELEVISION NEWS — AND IT IS THE REAL THING FOR THE
STUDENTS TAKING THE COURSE AS THEY PUT ON NEWS PROGRAMS THAT ARE
SEEN AND HEARD VIA A CLOSED CIRCUIT IN CLASSROOMS THROUGHOUT THE
SCHOOL. KEN ALVORD NBC NEWS REPORTS.
TAPE IN   IT WAS SORT OF LIKE . . .
TAPE ENDS . . . GET INTERVIEWED OURSELVES.

TODAY'S NPS STORIES RAN IN FOLLOWING ORDER.
1. VIETNAM 2. FLOOD 3. POLLUTION 4. CAMBODIA 5. RELIGION 6. PRIEST
7. RESCUE 8. BASKETBALL 9. SKATING 10. BOXING 11. BUSINESS
12. TELEVISION 13. ENTERTAINMENT.
THIS ENDS NPS FEED FOR TODAY
THANKS
      NPS/NY

Styles of Writing

The writer of the news broadcast is, first of all, a reporter whose primary duty is conveying the news. The traditional "5 W's" of news reporting must apply. In the condensed space of a few sentences, comparable to the lead paragraph of the newspaper story, the television or radio report must contain information as to What, Where, When, Who, and, if possible, Why. In addition, the television and radio news writer must include as many of the details as possible within the limited time devoted to the story. The key word is *condensation*.

The writer must be aware of the organization of the broadcast in order to provide the proper transitions, which should be clear and smooth between each story. The writer should indicate to the audience the different divisions of the broadcast. For example, note the introduction: "Now here is Mr. Murrow with his word for the day," in the format on page 130. Similar divisions might be: "And now the local news," or "Now, the feature story for the day," or "Now, the editor's notebook."

The writer must be aware of the content approach, whether it is straight news, analysis or personal opinion, so as not to confuse editorializing with news. It is wise not to try to fool the audience, at least not too often, although some of our popular commentators have been doing so for years. Distortion of stories or the presentation of only one side of the picture can change a news story into an opinion comment. Incomplete statements and the excessive use of color words can do the same thing. Avoid unnecessary sensationalism. Remember that the newscaster is coming into the home as a guest, and is generally accepted as a personal visitor. The approach should be informal, friendly and — hopefully — honest.

Inasmuch as the announcer tries to establish an informal and friendly relationship with the audience, avoid unnecessarily antagonizing or shocking stories, particularly at the very beginning of the broadcast. Consider the time of the day the broadcast is being presented — whether the audience is at the dinner table, seated comfortably in the living room, or rushing madly to get to work on time. The writer should think of the news as dramatic action. The story with an obvious conflict (the war, the gang fight, the divorce case, the baseball pennant race) attracts immediate attention. Because action is important, write the stories with verbs. The immediacy of television and radio, as opposed to the relatively greater time lapse between the occurrence and reporting of the incident in print journalism, permits the use of the present tense in stories about events which happened within a few hours preceding the newscast. The television and radio writer should be cautious in the use of questions as opposed to direct statements as the opening element of a story. Although the rhetorical question is an excellent attention-getting device in speech making, the nature of objective broadcasting makes its use in radio and television dubious. Rather than beginning with a question such as: "What will happen to the Mars space capsule . . .?," it is more dramatic to say: "The question in all the capitals of the world tonight is: What will happen to the Mars space capsule?" Negative approaches to the news should be avoided. It is better to give whatever details are available without comment than to say: "This is an incomplete story, but . . ."

The writer should begin the news story with precise, clear information. The opening sentence should be, if possible, a summary of the story as a whole. Be wary of including too many details. Remember that the audience hears the news only once and, unlike the newspaper reader, cannot go back to clarify particular points in the story. The audience must grasp the entire story the first time it hears it. The writing, therefore, must be simple and understandable and, without talking down to the audience, colloquial in form. This does not imply the use of slang or illiterate expressions, but suggests informality and understandability. Repetition must be avoided, and abstract expressions and words with double meanings should not be used. The information should be accurate and there should be no possibility of a misunderstanding of any news item. Make certain that the terminology used is correct. For example, don't refer to a figure in a story as a "car thief" if the person has not been convicted and is, in actuality, an "alleged car thief."

The writer must help the announcer to convey numbers accurately and to pronounce words correctly. The writer should not put long numbers in figures, but should write them out in words. It is sometimes helpful to place the numerical figures in parentheses. The writer should avoid using long, difficult words or tongue-twisters. After foreign words and difficult names the writer should place in parentheses a simplified sound spelling of the word. Note the following newswire excerpts and pronunciation guide.

HERE IS THE LATEST NEWS FROM THE ASSOCIATED PRESS:

SOUTH VIETNAMESE PREMIER KY AND THE LEADER OF REBELLIOUS GOVERN-
MENT TROOPS, LIEUTENANT-GENERAL NGUYEN CHANH THI (NWEN CAHN TEE),
MET SECRETLY TODAY AT THE U-S MARINE BASE AT CHU LAI (CHOO LY). RESULTS
OF THE MEETING WERE NOT REVEALED BUT THERE WAS SPECULATION THAT THE
PREMIER IS MOVING TOWARD A SHOWDOWN WITH HIS BUDDHIST AND MILITARY
OPPONENTS IN HUE (HWAY).

IN HUE (HWAY), WHERE STUDENT MOBS SET FIRE TO THE U-S INFORMATION
SERVICE BUILDING YESTERDAY, THE U-S HAS EVACUATED MANY AMERICAN AND
OTHER CIVILIANS TO SAIGON. AMERICAN CONSULATE EMPLOYEES STILL IN HUE
HAVE MOVED FROM THEIR HOMES TO THE U-S MILITARY ASSISTANCE COMMAND
COMPOUND, WELL PROTECTED BY U-S SOLDIERS.

AN OFFICIAL OF THE MALAYSIAN FOREIGN OFFICE SAYS THE VISIT BY AN INDO-
NESIAN MILITARY DELEGATION TO MALAYSIA PROMISES AN END TO THE THREE-
YEAR-OLD UNDECLARED WAR BETWEEN THE TWO COUNTRIES. THE INDONESIANS
ARRIVED IN KUALA LUMPUR (KWAH'-LAH LOOM'-POOR) TODAY TO COMPLETE PREP-
ARATIONS FOR PEACE TALKS SCHEDULED TO START IN BANGKOK, THAILAND, NEXT
MONDAY.

RELIABLE SOURCES IN SANTO DOMINGO SAY NEGOTIATIONS ARE UNDER WAY
FOR THE WITHDRAWAL OF WILLIAM BONNELLY FROM NEXT WEEK'S DOMINICAN
PRESIDENTIAL ELECTION SO THAT HIS FOLLOWERS CAN SUPPORT DR. JOAQUIN
BALAGUER (WAH-KEEN BAH-LAH-GHEHR'). AN ANNOUNCEMENT ON THE RESULT OF
TALKS BETWEEN THE PARTIES CONCERNED IS EXPECTED WITHIN THE NEXT TWO
DAYS. THE NEGOTIATIONS STARTED THREE DAYS AGO. SUPPORTERS OF JUAN
BOSCH (WAHN BOHSH) ARE CONFIDENT HE CAN DEFEAT BALAGUER, EVEN IF
BALAGUER GETS THE SUPPORT OF BONNELLY'S FOLLOWERS.

PARTS OF WESTERN TEXAS SUFFERED HEAVY FLOOD AND FIRE DAMAGE TODAY
IN THE WAKE OF CLOUDBURSTS AND VIOLENT THUNDERSTORMS. WATER WAS SIX
FEET DEEP IN THE STREETS OF ANDREWS, WHERE ALMOST THREE INCHES OF RAIN
FELL IN HALF AN HOUR. ANOTHER THREE INCHES FELL IN MIDLAND, TURNING
STREETS INTO SMALL RIVERS. FIRES STARTED BY LIGHTNING DESTROYED A
COTTON WAREHOUSE AT PYOTE (PY-OHT') AND DAMAGED AT LEAST TWO HOUSES
IN MIDLAND.

- PROUNCIATION GUIDE -
    BRIGADIER-GENERAL PHAM XUAN NHUAN, COMMANDER OF VIETNAMESE FIRST
DIVISION — FAHM ZWAHN NWASHN.
    GUYANA, NEW NAME OF FORMER BRITISH COLONY OF GUIANA AFTER DECLARA-
TION OF INDEPENDENCE — GHEE-AH'-NAH.
    MILTON OBOTE, UGANDA OFFICIAL IS CENTER OF POLITICAL TURMOIL — OH-
BOH'-TAY.
    TUY HOA, SCENE OF BUDDHIST DEMONSTRATIONS IN VIET NAM — TWEE HWAH.
    GROTON, CONNECTICUT, SCENE OF SEA TRIALS OF NUCLEAR SUBMARINE
"FLASHER" — GRAT'-UN.

United Press Broadcast Wire

Approach

Putting a news broadcast together involves many people. The writer
is only one, but in a way the central figure, tying together into a script
everything that is to go over the air. The writer may be many people —
producer, reporter, cameraperson, announcer, editor — contributing to a
script. Or the writer may be one person doing many different jobs — including writing the script.

A description of the operation of "Action News," the 6 P.M. news
program of television station WPVI, Philadelphia, provides an insight into
many factors that affect and result in a script for the show.

> "Life at Action News starts early in the morning. By 8:30 A.M.
> film crews have come to the brightly lighted, compact newsroom on
> the fourth floor of the WVPI Building to pick up their morning's as-
> signments. A photographer who shoots only silent film is already in
> the suburbs, getting film to use in that evening's 'wrap,' a segment of
> five-to-ten second news stories about events in outlying areas that
> would normally never make it to the air."

The news director, assignments editor and executive producer
"gather around a blackboard and chalk in the day's stories. Then they
decide which reporters and camera crews will cover them. There's
never a shortage of stories — most of them are either gleaned from
the hundreds of press releases that flood the newsroom each day or
are submitted by the staff of TV reporters. A few of them are assigned
to beats (e.g. City Hall, police headquarters, education). By knowing
what's scheduled in their area of expertise, they can advise where it
might be advantageous to send a camera."

". . . the biggest cross TV news has to bear is the charge of super-
ficiality. With 31 stories in 16 minutes, how can anything be in depth?
'TV news *is* strictly surface,' admits news director Mel Kampmann.
'We're the headline, the first paragraph. If you took all the words we
used in a 30-minute show, you wouldn't fill more than half the front
page of the *Bulletin*. But that copy is all of the topgoing news you'd

need that day. Anyone who wants to know total background involvement of a news story should go to a newspaper or news magazine and get it. TV news does not have time to dwell.' Anchorman Larry Kane knows the limitations of his medium. 'It's just a basic summary. Our achievement is getting a fast-paced, well-mixed diet of the day's events into a fresh, interesting format.' 'You can't equate an in-depth story with time on the air,' says executive producer Howard Glassroth in defense of TV. Visual impact is worth a lot of words. A 30-second film of a fistfight is just as good as a three-page description of it. Better. And a 90-second clip plus narration is often the distillation of several hours of reporting. Each reporter has to know how to use the tools of TV journalism — the camera and microphone — to slice a story crosswise properly and get a true segment of what's going on."

". . . By 4 P.M. the early edition Action News starts taking shape. . . . By now, every reporter is back and filmed reports have been edited or are in the process of being edited. . . . 'We have some very definite guidelines on what we put on the air, and how we do it,' says Kampmann. 'We always want to be able to *show* the viewer instead of *tell* him. If there's a story about the new airport tax, we'll show planes taking off at the airport rather than some guy talking at City Council. If the milk board has changed some prices, we'll show an interior shot of a supermarket. People can hear with their ears. They don't have to watch someone reading them the news. They should be able to see something while they're listening. If we don't have film, our artist works up an illustration to superimpose . . . .' "

" 'In addition to straight news, a TV news program must also include sports and weather,' Kampmann explains . . . 'people don't want to hear about cold fronts and occluded fronts. Nobody knows what they are, anyway . . . Weather reporter Jim O'Brien will be telling people how to dress their kids for school tomorrow, whether to carry an umbrella, and what to wear if they are going out at night. It will be a service told in a way that people use the weather.' "

Anchorman Kane, following the show, "likes to be back at his desk by 7:30, to start updating and rewriting the 6 P.M. show for the 11 o'clock offering. The shows usually have a different lead story and sound."[11]

Although specific orientations and logistic approaches differ, the basic cohesion of many elements from many sources into a final script is the same at all stations. The person responsible for the script, whether designated a writer at a network or performing the duties of an announcer and/or producer and/or editor and/or writer at a medium-sized or small station, must consider all of the policy, personality and procedural aspects, as in the process followed for "Action News."

Relatively new to news is a demographic breakdown of potential audiences. As noted under styles of writing and under organization of the news program elsewhere in this chapter, stories are chosen and placed in terms of the probable attitude and makeup of the audience being reached at the hour of broadcast. The overall approach of a station's news presentations are beginning to approximate the planning for a music station's image, as described in the discussion on demographics in Chapter 7. The profile of the audience of a given station has an effect on the news approach, just as the news approach attracts a certain kind of audience. The following tables show the nationwide demographic breakdown of network news audiences:

Network evening news audiences by key demographic categories
Source: Market Section Audience report, NTI, February 1974

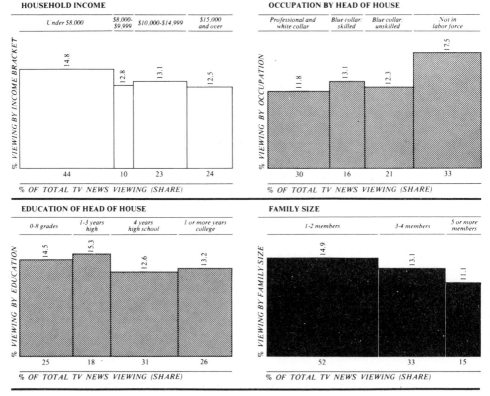

All data above are based on household viewing measurements. Height of bars shows per cent of households within each group which viewed network news. Width of bars shows share of *each group's viewing to total viewing. For example, in household income chart, data show that 14.8 per cent of all households with incomes under $8,000 viewed average network* *evening news show during period studied. These viewers accounted for 44 per cent of all viewing of network evening news programs by U.S. tv households.*

• *Assume that these demographic breakdowns are accurate for the city in which you are living. Plan a news approach and format for a local radio station which will attract the largest possible audience. Would the same approach and format apply for a local television station?*

Types of Broadcasts

The most common type of television and radio news broadcast is the straight news presentation, on radio usually in 5- or 15-minute segments and on television usually in 15-minute and half-hour periods. There are also commentator-personalities who present news analysis and/or personal opinions on the news. Sometimes these are included in the straight news show. In recent years news analysis in depth, stressing feature stories and dramatic aspects of the news, has become more common. Networks and staions frequently have "specials" which probe the news. Many of these programs utilize serious research and present their findings in documentary or semi-documentary form, following the approaches so effectively developed for the media by Edward R. Murrow and Fred W. Friendly with their "Hear It Now" and "See It Now" programs. Although usually under the direction of the news department, the documentary and feature are covered here in a separate chapter. Other news-show types such as the panel and interview are also covered in a separate chapter, on "Talks" programs.

In addition to the general news program, there may be straight news shows devoted to specific topics, such as the international scene, financial reports, garden news, consumer affairs, educational or campus news, and so forth. The approaches within these categories may vary, of course, such as stressing the public service aspect or the human interest elements.

Most news programs are a combination of the live announcer or announcers, film and videotape for TV and audiotape for radio of the recorded events, other visuals for TV, and in some cases where a story is breaking at that moment, live remotes. There can be, as well, multiple pickups from various studios, involving reporters closer to the scenes of the events. Networks frequently present news roundups from various parts of the country and, on radio and through satellite on TV, from various parts of the world. There are also frequent — though, perhaps, not frequent enough — on-the-spot news broadcasts which show or narrate the event actually taking place. The live remote is one of the most important contributions television can make and deserves fuller utilization.

Organization of the News Program

There are specific kinds of news programs, as indicated above, including those emphasizing a special topic or a special approach. In the straight news program the writer should look for a clear and logical organization, no matter what the topic or approach. One such organization is for the placement of stories to follow a topical order; that is, the grouping of similar stories into sections, although the order of the sections themselves may be an arbitrary one. A geographical grouping and order is another organizational form. For example, the news coverage may move from North America to Europe to Asia to South America to Africa to the rest of the world. Another frequently used grouping organizes the material into international, national and local news categories. The order of presentation often moves, within these categories, from the largest (international) to the smallest (local). Probably the most common approach is to place the most important story first in order to get and hold the audience's attention, much as does the lead story in the newspaper.

The organization is determined, in part, by the audience being reached. In the mid-morning newscast, for example, stories are frequently chosen and placed to appeal primarily to women, the bulk of the listening group at that time. In the early evening the organization usually is one that will reach most effectively the male listener or viewer who has just returned from work. The news broadcast just before prime-time on TV frequently seeks to reach a family group watching together. The time of day is also important in relation to what the audience already knows of the news. In the early morning newscast it is desirable to review the previous day's important late stories. In the late evening broadcasts the current day's news should be reviewed and the audience should be prepared for the next day's possible happenings.

The physical format of the news show may vary. It may begin with an announcer giving the headlines, then a commercial, and then the commentator coming in with the details. It may start with the commentator beginning directly with the news. It may be a roundup of different reporters in different geographical areas.

> • *In the following pages, purposely presented in haphazard order, is a 5-minute Associated Press news report.**
> *1) How would you rearrange this material to develop a news broadcast oriented around a clear, effective organization? Organize the newscast along geographical lines; organize it according to international, national and local news; organize it along topical lines, grouping similar types of stories; organize it according to the importance of the stories.*
> *2) After you have practiced organizing the material, analyze the writing itself to determine whether: the five W's are clearly included; the principle of conflict is utilized; clarity, simplicity and the direct statement are evident; informality is present.*

---

* From *Television/Radio News Workbook* by Irving E. Fang, Pages 61-64, 1974, published by Hastings House, New York.

3) *What kind of news broadcast is this? Straight news? Commentary? Documentary? Rewrite this news broadcast into at least one form other than its present orientation.*

(WASHINGTON) — THE DIRECTOR OF THE GOVERNMENT'S NEW OFFICE OF PROFESSIONAL STANDARDS REVIEW CHARGED TODAY THAT THE DEPARTMENT OF HEALTH, EDUCATION AND WELFARE HAS NOT GIVEN HIM ADEQUATE BACKING AND RESOURCES. DR. WILLIAM BAUER LEVELED HIS CRITICISM AS HE RESIGNED HIS POST.

(BALTIMORE) — PUBLISHED REPORTS SAY THAT FOR SEVERAL YEARS VICE PRESIDENT AGNEW HAS RECEIVED REGULARLY FREE GROCERIES FROM JOSEPH RASH, A BALTIMORE EXECUTIVE OF THE FOOD FAIR SUPERMARKET CHAIN. AND OTHER REPORTS SAY HE HAS RECEIVED GIFTS OF FOOD, WINE, LIQUOR, AND CASH FROM FRIENDS SINCE HIS RISE TO PROMINENCE. AGNEW'S AIDES SAY THE ALLEGATIONS ARE BEING PUBLISHED BECAUSE OF A FEDERAL PROBE OF AGNEW IN CONNECTION WITH ALLEGED POLITICAL CORRUPTION IN MARYLAND.

THE ONLY PERSON INDICTED SO FAR BY A MARYLAND GRAND JURY INVESTIGATING CORRUPTION, DALE ANDERSON, PLEADED INNOCENT AT HIS ARRAIGNMENT TODAY. THE BALTIMORE COUNTY EXECUTIVE — WHO SUCCEEDED AGNEW IN THAT POST — IS CHARGED WITH BRIBERY, EXTORTION AND CONSPIRACY.

A TENTATIVE TRIAL DATE HAS BEEN SET FOR JANUARY SEVENTH.

(WASHINGTON) — SECRETARY OF STATE-DESIGNATE HENRY KISSINGER WAS CRITICIZED TODAY AS A WAR CRIMINAL AND RACIST. WITNESSES OPPOSED TO HIS NOMINATION TESTIFIED BEFORE THE SENATE FOREIGN RELATIONS COMMITTEE. TEN OPPONENTS CRITICIZED MAINLY THE NIXON ADMINISTRATION'S VIETNAM WAR POLICIES.

THE COMMITTEE IS EXPECTED TO VOTE TUESDAY TO RECOMMEND CONFIRMATION OF KISSINGER.

(WASHINGTON) — PRESIDENT NIXON HAS GONE TO CAMP DAVID IN THE MARYLAND MOUNTAINS FOR THE WEEKEND. RAINY WEATHER FORCED HIM TO TRAVEL BY CAR RATHER THAN BY HELICOPTER AS HE USUALLY DOES.

THE PRESIDENT WAS ACCOMPANIED BY HIS WIFE, DAUGHTER JULIE AND FLORIDA FRIEND C. G. REBOZO.

WHITE HOUSE SOURCES SAY IT NOW SEEMS UNLIKELY THAT PRESIDENT NIXON WILL TRAVEL TO TEXAS A WEEK FROM TOMORROW FOR THE DEDICATION OF THE HUGE NEW FORT WORTH-DALLAS AIRPORT. WHILE THERE NEVER WAS AN ACTUAL ANNOUNCEMENT OF A PRESIDENTIAL TRIP, THERE HAD BEEN INDICATIONS NIXON WOULD ATTEND THE AIRPORT OPENING.

(WASHINGTON) — THE AFL-CIO URGED CONGRESS TODAY TO DIRECT THE FEDERAL RESERVE SYSTEM TO ALLOCATE AT LEAST SOME BANK CREDIT TO PRIORITY AREAS SUCH AS HOUSING. UNION LEGISLATIVE DIRECTOR ANDREW BIEMILLER TOLD THE HOUSE BANKING COMMITTEE THE ONLY WAY TO GET BANKING MONEY INTO HOUSING IS TO MAKE IT MANDATORY.

CONSUMER ADVOCATE RALPH NADER EARLIER MADE A SIMILAR PROPOSAL.

(MORE)

(ALBANY, NEW YORK) — A DREAM 66-YEARS IN THE MAKING WILL COME TRUE MONDAY FOR JOHN KALINYAK OF ALBANY, NEW YORK. HE WILL BECOME A CITIZEN OF THE UNITED STATES. THE 86-YEAR-OLD NATIVE OF AUSTRIA-HUNGARY FIRST CAME TO THIS COUNTRY IN 1907.

(WASHINGTON) — THE WHITE HOUSE SAID TODAY THAT THERE IS NO GREAT DISAGREEMENT BETWEEN TREASURY SECRETARY SHULTZ AND PRESIDENTIAL AIDE MELVIN LAIRD OVER TAX POLICY. BUT SPOKESMAN GERALD WARREN CONCEDED THERE COULD BE SOME MISUNDERSTANDING BETWEEN THEM.

SHULTZ CHASTISED LAIRD TODAY FOR THE WHITE HOUSE DOMESTIC AIDE'S
ANNOUNCEMENT YESTERDAY THAT PRESIDENT NIXON WAS CONSIDERING A TEN
PER CENT INCOME TAX SURCHARGE TO FIGHT INFLATION. SHULTZ SAID LAIRD
SHOULD KEEP HANDS OFF ECONOMIC POLICY. LAIRD HAS NOT BEEN AVAILABLE
FOR COMMENT.

(WASHINGTON) — PRESIDENT NIXON SIGNED WITHOUT FANFARE TODAY A BILL
THAT WOULD BAN TELEVISION BLACK-OUTS OF AT-HOME PROFESSIONAL FOOTBALL
GAMES SOLD OUT THREE DAYS IN ADVANCE. THE MEASURE WILL PERMIT HOME
TELECASTS OF A NUMBER OF NATIONAL FOOTBALL LEAGUE OPENING GAMES
SUNDAY.

(WASHINGTON) — THE U-S APPEALED TODAY FOR OTHER NATIONS TO ABIDE BY
THE POLITICAL AGREEMENT SIGNED BY THE LAOTIAN GOVERNMENT AND THE
COMMUNIST PATHET LAO. THE PACT SETS A COALITION GOVERNMENT WITH
PREMIER SOUVANNA PHOUMA AS ITS HEAD.

(DETROIT) — BARGAINING BETWEEN CHRYSLER AND THE UNITED AUTO
WORKERS HAS ENTERED THE FINAL HOURS BEFORE A MIDNIGHT STRIKE DEAD-
LINE. AND THE OVERTIME ISSUE APPEARS TO BE THE KEY BOTTLENECK TO A
SETTLEMENT.
THE UNION WANTS OVERTIME TO BE VOLUNTARY. CHRYSLER IS STANDING BY
THE PRESENT ARRANGEMENT WHICH CALLS FOR MANDATORY OVERTIME.
AT LUNCHTIME TODAY, WORKERS WALKED OFF THEIR JOBS IN AN OVERTIME
DISPUTE AT CHRYSLER'S WARREN AND HAMTRAMCK, MICHIGAN PLANTS FORCING
THE PLANTS TO SHUT DOWN.

(WASHINGTON) — WITNESSES TOLD A SENATE COMMITTEE TODAY THAT INADE-
QUATE FEDERAL CONTROLS ALLOW THE SALE AND USE OF INOPERATIVE OR
INEFFECTIVE MEDICAL DEVICES, INCLUDING HEART PACEMAKERS AND RESPIRATORS.
THE HEAD OF HEALTH RESEARCH GROUP, DR. SIDNEY WOLF, SAID THE WASHING-
TON BASED CONSUMER GROUP HAS UNCOVERED FOUR DEATHS SINCE FEBRUARY
IN WHICH FAILURES OF A STRUCTURAL ELEMENT IN ONE COMPANY'S HEART
VALVES WERE INVOLVED.
BILLS TO REQUIRE PRE-MARKET TESTING OF SUCH DEVICES ARE BEFORE THE
SENATE.

Another organizational approach frequently used is to concentrate on
one major news story, with the orientation of all other news around that
story. For example:

"Here is today's news:

President Ford said at a news conference today that he pardoned
former President Nixon because of his concern for Mr. Nixon's health and
because he felt that attention to Watergate was distracting the country from
more important needs."

*(The announcer then went on to give the background of the news con-
ference and the major emphasis of the questions.)*

"President Ford stated that there was absolutely no deal made between him and Mr. Nixon for a pardon as a part of Mr. Nixon's decision
to resign.

The first question put to Mr. Ford was:"

*(The taped excerpt, audio for radio, video for TV, was inserted here,
with similar introductory material and appropriate tape inserts following.)*

Following the report on the news conference, which dealt almost entirely with President Ford's pardon of former Persident Nixon, the program reported on Congressional attitudes and action concerning the appropriation of funds for a staff and other transitional services for Mr. Nixon, dealt with some Congressional charges concerning White House briefings being flown to Mr. Nixon in California, the latest developments in the Watergate trials, and news and commentary on the relationship of President Ford's pardon for Mr. Nixon with pardon or amnesty for those who refused to fight in Vietnam.

On this particular news day, the most important continuing stories happened to be interelated and happened to deal with national affairs. Following this coverage, the news broadcast went into the other news of the day, including international events.

News vs. Opinion

As noted earlier, most news broadcasts are straight news, and these usually are presented without comment or coloration. Other broadcasts interpret the news, through objective analysis and sometimes with the comment of experts representing at least the two major sides of the issues being discussed. Some news broadcasts take a clearly philosophical approach, coloring the story with selection or placement of information and sometimes with clearly-stated subjective personal opinion. We have all heard certain news broadcasters and commentators labelled "liberal" or "conservative," and CBS radio news has had a regular news commentary with Carl Rowan designated the "liberal" and James Kilpatrick the "conservative."

Sometimes, in times of stress, even objective commentary will be labelled subjective by some people — if only because it goes into a news area that some people would rather not have publicly aired at all. This was true of the extensive coverage given the Watergate affair, trials, the impeachment proceedings, the Nixon resignation and the subsequent pardon of Mr. Nixon by President Ford. Some of the commentary on these issues was attacked as biased by the pro-Nixon people; other commentary was attacked as being too apologetic and not candid enough. An example of news commentary which was criticized by some as being biased against Nixon (its inclusion of material principally implying guilt), and at the same time was criticized by others as waffling (implying that public opinion was sharply and, therefore, perhaps equally divided, and equating Watergate conspirators with Vietnam dissenters) is the following.

> • *Your own evaluation of this script will indicate how difficult it is to present a news commentary acceptable in every way to anybody or acceptable in any way to everybody.*

This is Roger Mudd reporting, with news and commentary, on the CBS network. If our long national nightmare is over, as President Ford says, the unresolved status of his predecessor continues to hover over the nation. A look in a moment.

PLOUGH :60

Will former President Nixon be indicted for his role in the Watergate coverup? Should he be subject to possible indictment? Or instead, should he be exempted from prosecution?

Here's the situation at present. Constitutionally, Mr. Nixon could be indicted, in an ordinary criminal proceeding, since he's no longer President. There may be new grounds for indicting him in the three tapes he released just nine days ago — specifically, his recorded instructions to H. R. Haldeman, on using the C.I.A. to obstruct the F.B.I.'s investigation of the Watergate burglary. There are persistent reports of further damaging evidence in tapes not yet made public — the tapes surrendered only on orders from the U.S. Supreme Court. There also are reports that the Watergate grand jury which named Mr. Nixon an unindicted co-conspirator while he still was President wishes to amend its work and indict him now that he's no longer protected by the presidential office.

President Ford could excuse Mr. Nixon personally from federal prosecution — but Mr. Ford once said the public wouldn't stand for such an act — and he now shows no signs of changing his mind. Attorney-General Saxbe says the decision on whether or not to prosecute rests entirely with Watergate Prosecutor Jaworski. Jaworski seems in no hurry to make up his mind. He has said he made no deals with Mr. Nixon on this matter before the resignation. It's constitutionally dubious that Congress could seek to protect Mr. Nixon individually from prosecution. And anyway, Congress doesn't even seem inclined to try, since Mr. Nixon balks at specifying the exact degree of his responsibility for the coverup.

Public opinion seems sharply divided. On one hand, there are those who think the humiliation of being the first President forced to resign is punishment enough. Besides, they say, it would further upset and divide the nation if an ex-President is treated like a common criminal. But others say the nation would be equally upset — and respect for law would be diminished — if one man gets off while others pay the penalty, merely because of his former, high office. Then there are Mr. Nixon's own (well-known) views on excusing possible malefactors from the legal process. Speaking about Vietnam draft evaders and deserters, he once said, "We have all made mistakes. But also, it is a rule of life, we all have to pay for our mistakes. . . ." The price, he went on, "is a criminal penalty for disobeying the laws of the United States." Surely, it is unlikely for a man admittedly devoted to lofty principles, like Mr. Nixon, to change his views on amnesty merely because he might now be receiving it, instead of giving it.

The parallels with the fugitive Vietnam dissidents are on the minds of many including former U.S. Supreme Court Justice Arthur Goldberg. He said today he would not recommend giving Mr. Nixon immunity from prosecution. But, he adds, if such immunity is to be granted, that immunity should be extended. — Extended from the former President to former assistants who acted illegally under him — provided they didn't act for personal gain. — And such immunity should be extended as well — Goldberg feels — to those Vietnam dissenters whom Mr. Nixon would not forgive when he still had the power to do so. In a sense, Goldberg feels, the draft dodgers and the Watergate conspirators were victims of the same national mania. If the offenses of one class are to be forgotten, the offenses of the other should be, too.

Such an amnesty at least offers the possibility of putting a lot of bad feeling behind us — and starting anew. — If everyone also can forget that Mr. Nixon would be excused by a means he himself rejected in the past, for others.

BODY ALL :30
TRAVEL LODGE :30

This is Roger Mudd reporting, for CBS NEWS.

Courtesy of CBS News

We have all heard "dramatic" commentators who attempt to disguise news analysis and personal opinion as straight news. For some broadcasters this has become a trademark. What is straight news and what is opinion should clearly be designated as such. The FCC Fairness Doctrine has in some cases rectified and in countless cases prevented misleading of the public in the presentation of opinion or the biased selection of material as objective news.

Rewriting

One of the newswriter's duties, particularly on the local level, is *re-writing*. A smaller station without a newsgathering staff is sometimes almost totally dependent on the newswire. The announcer, given sufficient time and energy, edits those stories that can be appropriately adapted to include a local angle, evaluating their impact on the community. In effect, the announcer *re*writes the news. As noted above, news broadcasts are organized into homogenous groupings. Finding a unifying thread that means something special to the listener in that community frequently requires rewriting. For example, segments in a topical grouping of stories dealing with the economy might be rewritten to reflect their relationship to the local unemployment figures.

Perhaps the most common form of rewriting is updating. An important story doesn't disappear after it is used once. Yet, to use exactly the same story in subsequent newscasts throughout the day is likely to turn off those listeners who hear it more than once and conclude that the station is carrying stale news. Updating is an important function of the network newswriter. There are several major areas to look for in updating news stories. First, the writer determines if there is any further hard news, factual information to add to the story. Second, if the story is important enough it is likely that investigative reporting will have dug up some additional background information not available when the story was first broadcast. Third, depending on the happening's impact on society, it will have been commented upon after its initial release by any number of people from VIPs to ordinary citizens. In addition, a story may by its very nature relate to other events of the day, that relationship being made clear in the rewriting.

Note the final paragraph in the material earlier in this chapter on WPVI's "Action News." Television stations with their own news staffs try to rewrite the news from one newscast to the next, not only updating it, but reorienting it toward a different audience. How many times have you been disappointed or even angry when the 11 P.M. news coverage was virtually the same as the 6 P.M. newscast, especially when there was an important happening that you were eagerly awaiting further information about?

Remotes

One of the most exciting aspects of media news writing and reporting — and viewing and listening — is the "remote." On both radio and television the remote brings the audience directly to the scene of the event, as it is happening, live. Some remotes are reports following the event, equivalent to the reporter phoning in the story to the newspaper the moment after it has happened. The remote is usually handled by someone who is a combination writer-reporter, insofar as the material must be gathered, written and reported on by the same person. Louis Alexander of Houston, Texas is a writer who is a reporter, handling remotes for networks and stations throughout the country. He is also a professor of journalism at the University of Houston who teaches that news reporting is a partnership between reporter and editor, one knowing best what has happened and the other knowing best how and what to fit into the overall picture. Alexander describes the duties and procedures of handling the remote broadcast, from his vantage point as a writer as well as a reporter. Although his description specifically relates to a radio remote, the basic concepts as they apply to the writer are equally true for television.

Remote feeds enable the radio reporter to beat the other media with the news. The sound of the voice coming over the phone, broadcast by the station, adds to the listeners' excitement by reminding them that they are hearing it from the very scene of the action — political convention, freeway accident, sports arena or close by the launching pad. Some experienced reporters arrange a continuous feed, live, during the event. Most remote feeds, however, must fit into scheduled newscasts. Most stations can connect a studio recorder to the incoming telephone line and record it directly; and some stations have special high-fidelity telephone lines that preserve most of the voice quality.

A remote feed from the scene of action — live — is a continuous report of what is going on. You need a good knowledge of events and the people involved in them, and quick articulation and recognition of what's going on. Several days in advance, or longer, order a telephone line from the phone company in that local area. For an extra charge you may have them install a line with higher voice quality. Make arrangements in advance with the local authorities or their public relations representative for a spot with good visibility and good access to whatever information services will be provided locally.

First the reporter gathers information and records statements by the participants or observers, then reads the notes and decides what is most important to pass on to the radio audience. This enables the reporter, while listening to the actualities, to decide which statements are the most significant as well as good quality sound. Do your homework: gather background information, write a few short pieces to fill in during quiet, inactive moments, and learn to identify as many as possible of the main personages by their faces and their voices. Arrange with your news director the schedule of times to be on the air and the cues that switch the broadcast between studio and remote site. Come on the air before the main action starts and set the stage for the listener: provide the background needed to understand and appreciate what is about to happen. Then provide continuing word pictures of events, conditions, attitudes. Be sure to switch to the studio, or to a colleague, on cue; also switch whenever you are on the verge of running out of worthwhile things to report. Before you sign off from the remote site, be sure to acknowledge local assistants and summarize what has happened, unless the studio newscaster plans to do that.

The process for the remote feed which is not live is slightly different. The reporter writes the story, holding it to whatever length is desirable or required — 40 seconds, one minute, two minutes or more. If the story includes an actuality, the reporter writes an intro, times the actuality to fit into the overall time allotted for the story, and inserts a transition phrase after the outcue, to pick up the thread of the text. The reporter then cues the tape to the beginning of the actuality.

Feeding the story over the telephone is technically easy. It is simplest when the reporter is feeding without an actuality: telephone the station's news room, advise you are ready to feed, wait for the studio personnel to connect a recorder onto the receiving line, count '3-2-1' to allow time for the recording to roll, read the story to the end, with a signoff that indicates you are on the scene: 'This is John Smith, at the Johnson Space Center in Houston.' The ordinary telephone transmits most levels of the human voice with good quality, and many stations have at least one telephone line which the phone company has upgraded to high-fidelity reproduction. The recorded story comes onto the tape in the studio with good sound quality — with just enough of a 'remote tone' to remind the listener that the voice is coming from the scene of the action.

When the reporter is feeding an actuality the process has additional technical requirements: a tape recorder which has the appropriate circuitry — a few of the better quality models have it; and a line that plugs into the recorder's output and has two alligator clips on the other end. The reporter unscrews the telephone mouthpiece and removes it (although some telephone company regulations forbid this, the practice is nevertheless generally accepted) and connects the alligator clips to the two terminals within the telephone mouthpiece. The reporter connects the microphone to the tape recorder, providing a circuit that can feed into the telephone, alternately, the recording or the reporter's voice. The reporter speaks through the microphone and listens through the telephone receiver. With the actuality cued on the tape recorder, the reporter feeds the story through the microphone, switches on the actuality at the proper point, and switches back to the microphone for the ending.

Some reporters like to record the entire story, even when there is no actuality included. Then they feed it from the recorded version to the radio station. This has the advantage of enabling the reporter to send the best version the first time, eliminating fluffs and repeats, and may also hold down the telephone charge for long distance time.

The following is a script prepared and used by Alexander for the kind of remote described above (the underlined words are reminders for vocal emphasis):

National Public Radio

Friday, Sept. 21 (1973)

TENNIS

The largest crowd ever to watch a tennis match saw Ms. Billie Jean King upset Bobby Riggs last night in three straight sets.

The exhibition was a $100,000 — winner take all — answer to the question, "Can a good woman player beat a good man player?"

Ms. King, at 29, is the world's number one woman player. Riggs at 55 has won 40 national and world championships.

Ms. King won by outplaying Riggs — catching him out of position with passing shots and cross-court shots — never letting Riggs set up the lobs and trick shots for which he is famous. The scores were 6-4, 6-3, 6-3.

Riggs said afterwards that Ms. King played well within her game, but he couldn't get his own game started. "She made better shots off my best shots," Riggs said.

In the Astrodome the crowd of 30,000 mostly expected Riggs to win — yet they cheered more loudly for Ms. King. An estimated 40 million people watched over television throughout the United States and 35 other countries.

Today Ms. King is back in the Virginia Slims women's tournament in Houston. She has a third round match to play, and she said she has to fight against a letdown after last night.

For National Public Radio, this is Louis Alexander in Houston.

Some TV Considerations

The types, styles, organization and approaches are essentially the same for the television and the radio news broadcast. The combinations of studio, recorded and live remote materials apply to both media. The most important difference is the obvious one: television is visual. The reporter, feeding a remote or in the studio, must have a visual personality. In the past two decades the television news personality — the Murrows, Huntleys and Brinkleys, Cronkites — have become the stars of television. (This was true of radio as well, when it was *the* medium for broadcast news, with its Gabriel Heatters, Lowell Thomases, Fulton Lewis, Jrs., Elmer Davises and H.V. Kaltenborns.) The physical setting should be interesting and attractive, consistent with the concept of informational and exciting news. Even the presentation of content that in itself may be undramatic should be visually stimulating. For example, watch the techniques and "gimmicks" introduced by weather reporters in the nightly weather segment of the news program. Television news should stress the visual and may use videotape, film, slides, photographs, inanimate objects and, where necessary for emphasis or exploration in depth, even guests in the studio. Except for relatively extensive use of an anchorperson to keep together the physical continuity of the program or, through that person's special personality, to instill confidence or, as a star, to motivate viewing by the audience, the TV news program should *show* the news, not *tell* about it. We have all seen TV news programs where a reporter merely read the news to us and we felt that we might as well have heard it on radio and not taken time to sit down in a living room to watch. Even when insufficient time or great distance or geography makes it impossible to show a film or tape of the event or carry it as a live remote, a blow-up photo or a slide of the scene or of the persons involved may be used as a background to the reporter's narration.

Writing the script that appears over the air is only the final stage of a long, arduous and frequently complicated process. Planning and development begin early in the day, even for a program such as "CBS Evening News with Walter Cronkite" which may not go on until early evening. Susan Leavitt of CBS News lists the many preliminary materials preceding finalization of an actual script: 1) CBS Program Log is distributed on the morning of the show, showing all the film pieces used on the Morning News, Midday News, Evening News and even on the other network news programs from the previous day; 2) written about 6 or 7 A.M. and distributed around 8:30 A.M. is a "CBS News Insights" sheet, with logs, which shows who is assigned to what coverage, what the planned assignments are for the day, and with a domestic and foreign "Who's Where" so that any member of the staff is reachable at all times; 3) about 11 A.M. a "Who Does What" rundown is distributed, showing which associate producers and which reporters are doing what and where; 4) about 11:15 A.M. a "Morning Line" is issued, with more information on the big stories and who is assigned to them; 5) about 12:30 or 1 P.M. a "Pre-Lineup" is completed, providing a list of the stories expected to be used on the program; 6) about 3:30 P.M. or shortly thereafter the "Line-up" comes out, listing the stories that will be on, their page numbers and times; 7) about 5 P.M. there is an "Editorial Line-up" with more exact information on what each page will be; 8) up until show time there are "Line-up Revisions," incorporating any changes warranted following the time the first line-up was prepared; 9) the final script itself.

The following are selected examples of this material, to give the writer an indication of some of the preparation that goes into the final product. Here, all pertaining to the same broadcast, are 1) the "Morning Line," 2) the "Pre-Lineup," 3) a first revision of the "Lineup," and 4) the first portion of the final complete script.

As you study these materials note that the "line-up" (or, as it is also called and as used in this book, "rundown" sheet) lists not only the subject, but the source, whether live or recorded, and the timing for each segment. The numbers at the far left of the rundown sheet have corresponding segment numbers on the script. The script also has information for the director on transitions and where visuals are to be used, including film, tape and stills. Note, too, the combinations of visual techniques.

CBS EVENING NEWS W/WALTER CRONKITE *FRIDAY JULY 12, 1974*, THE MORNING LINE

1 — SEVAREID: Is *not* working today.

2 — WATERGATE
   a — Fielding burglary jury hears judge's charge, then begins deliberations; Graham, artist will be covering in the trial's new quarters.
   b — House Judiciary hears Henry Peterson, closed session; Morton.

3 — HOSTAGES
   We have live and film units outside U.S. District Courthouse, Stahl inside; Peterson Bradley outside, and arrangements to pick up the action should it move into the streets, towards an airport, etc.

4 — BALTIMORE STRIKE
   McNamara, producer Ganzer, and one crew, soon to be two, are in position for us; overnight, police began joining the garbage strikers but so far, city appers calm with enough police still on duty. This story will probably come to New York for air.

5 — WASHINGTON VARIOUS
   a — Democratic state chairmen meet for second day, hearing from Sens. Kennedy & Jackson; NBenton is there.
   b — Roy Ash economic briefing at the White House; Kalb/Schieffer cover.
   c — President Signs Congressional Budget Bill, designed to make Congress more savvy and more responsible in fiscal affairs; Schieffer.
   d — Earl Warren funeral; President will appear. Strawser.

6 — DOMESTIC VARIOUS
   a — Stock market has surged in early minutes; if rally continues impressive; MKrauss will be there to tell us why.
   b — In Detroit, Plante covers murder trial in which star eyewitness is 12-year-old deaf-mute daughter of victim. She will tell her story in hand language.
   c — Cesar Chavez is announcing a new lettuce boycott; DDow covers, switchable KPIX.
   d — NY state hearings into difficulties of getting mortgages; Krauss.

7 — FOREIGN VARIOUS
   a — Natanson's material for completing the torture story, in hand; Burrough cutting, early line is around 4:00.
   b — Quint's African Drought update, in hand, available tonight.
   c — Overnight troubles of Belfast, including one bomb-blast and aftermath of others, *birdable*; London to advise.
   d — Simon's report on Israeli efforts to foil terrorists, arrives midafternoon, cut long at 4:20. Center track.

8 — POOR LAGNIAPPE
   Kuralt's Singing Orderly 2:30
   Kuralt's Craft Olympics 3:35
   Kuralt's Bullfighter, new, ready tonight.

PRE-LINEUP   FRI., JULY 12, 1974

1. HOSTAGES/STAHL	WASH	
2. PLUMBERS JURY OUT/GRAHAM	WASH	
3. PETERSEN-JUDICIARY/MORTON	WASH	
4. BALTIMORE POLICE STRIKE/MC NAMARA	NY	
5. DEAF MUTE CHILD TESTIFIES/PLANTE	DETROIT	
6. WARREN FUNERAL/STRAWSER	WASH	

POSSIBLES:

1. STOCKS SOAR/KRAUSS	NY
2. SINGING ORDERLY/KURALT	NY
3. CHAVEZ/D. DOW	SAN FRAN
4. WHITE HOUSE RESPONSE/SCHIEFFER	WASH
5. IF TERRORISTS COME/SIMON	NY
6. TORTURE/NATANSON	NY
7. AFRICAN DROUGHT/QUINT	NY
8. DEMOCRATS MEET/BENTON	WASH
9. ERVIN-BAKER PRESS CONFERENCE/SCHORR	WASH

1st Revision   1st Revision
— CBS EVENING NEWS WITH WALTER CRONKITE — FRIDAY — JULY 12, 1974 —

1.	OPEN (ANNOUNCE)	SP/9 VT/13	:25
2.	Cronkite	live	
3.	PLUMBERS GUILTY/GRAHAM	WASH	3:00
4. 5. 6.	Cronkite	live	
7.	1st CMCL (Clear Eyes/Breakfast Squares)	VTR/12	1:05
8.	Cronkite	live	
9.	HOSTAGES/BRADLEY	WASH	1:30
10.	Cronkite	live	
11.	WATERGATE WRAPUP/SCHORR	WASH	1:30
12.	Cronkite	live	
13.	2nd CMCL (Hid. Valley Salad Dressing/ DAP Paint Product)	VTR/2	1:05
14.	Cronkite	live	
15.	COPS STRIKE/McNAMARA	VTR/9	2:00 N.Y.
16.	Cronkite	live	
17.	DEAF CHILD/PLANTE	VTR/12	1:15 Detroit
18.	Cronkite	live	
19.	3rd CMCL (Alka Seltzer/Ralley Wax)	VTR/2	1:05 (Reg./SE)
20.	Cronkite	live	
21.	WARREN FUNERAL/STRAWSER	WASH	1:15
22.	Cronkite	live	
23.	ISRAELI & TERRORISTS/SIMON	VTR/9 STBY/14	3:00 N.Y.
24.	Cronkite	live·	
25.	4th CMCL (Ocusol/D-Con)	VTR/2	1:05
26.	Cronkite	live	
27.	SINGING ORDERLY/KURALT	VTR/12	2:30 N.Y.
28.	Cronkite goodnight	live	
29.	5th CMCL (Subaru/Mentholatum)	VTR/2	
30.	CLOSE (ANNOUNCE)	SP/9 VT/13	1:05
31.	CTN	SL/3	

Final   Final
FROM CBS NEWS HEADQUARTERS IN NEW YORK
THIS IS THE CBS EVENING NEWS WITH
WALTER CRONKITE . . .
AND . . .
IN WASHINGTON:
FRED GRAHAM
BRUCE MORTON
ED BRADLEY
DANIEL SCHORR
BOB MCNAMARA IN BALTIMORE
BILL PLANTE IN DETROIT
AND BOB SIMON IN HANITA, ISRAEL

2. CRONKITE   Good evening:
                       John Ehrlichman, for four years a powerful associate of
                       President's Nixon's at the White House, was convicted today of
                       conspiracy and perjury.— The verdict for his role in the break-in
                       at the office of Daniel Ellsberg's psychiatrist during the
                       Pentgon Papers controversy.
                       Also convicted:
                       Ehrlichman and 3 co-defendants — G. Gordon Liddy, Bernard
                       Barker and Eugenio Martinez.
                       Fred Graham reports from Washington.

3. Graham VTR   TRACK UP

FRED GRAHAM: After only 3 hours of deliberation, the jury found all 4 defendants guilty of
conspiring to violate the civil rights of Daniel Ellsberg's psychiatrist. Ehrlichman was also
found guilty of 1 count of lying to the FBI and 2 counts of lying to a grand jury. He was
found not guilty of another count of lying to the grand jury.

JOHN EHRLICHMAN [convicted conspirator]: We've just come from a meeting with our
attorneys to review the matter, and I have instructed them to prepare to file an appeal in
our behalf. As I think you know, we've been concerned from the very beginning about our
ability to secure a fair trial in this district and certainly one of the grounds of our appeal
will go to that question. It was also a matter of concern to us that a great deal of the
substance in the background of this entire case was excluded from the evidence by rulings
of the court and obviously that would be another question to be raised on appeal in this
matter.
    I have, and have for many years had, an abiding confidence in the American judicial
system. Nothing that happened today has in any way shaken that confidence, and we look
forward to an eventual complete exoneration as this matter moves through that process.

QUESTION: Do you feel you were betrayed by those at the White House who asked you to
do this?

EUGENIO MARTINEZ [convicted plumbers burglar]: I do not want to use the word
"betray", but it looks like the one that gave the order. — At the time of the trial, everyone
tried to run away. Everyone lost their memory. Everyone — [laughs] No one knew what's
going on. And, really, it looks [MARTINEZ] like the only one who knew were us. And the
little assignment that we had was for certainly — is as our attorney said. I'm sure that the
case didn't have to start in Miami.

QUESTION: You think you got stuck holding the bag?

MARTINEZ: Well, I believed you say it.

GRAHAM: The defendants will remain free without bond until they are sentenced on July
the 31st. Ehrlichman could get a maximum of 25 years in prison; the others, up to 10 years
in prison.

Fred Graham, CBS News, at the D.C. Court of Appeals.

4. Cronkite   On the question of impeachment of the president, a key matter
                       now being examined by the house judiciary committee is
                       whether he illegally received and passed on Watergate grand
                       jury information. And a key figure in that matter is assistant
                       attorney general Henry Peterson who was in charge of that
                       investigation. He was before the committee today.
                       Bruce Morton reports.

Folo 4. MORTON VTR   TRACK UP

VO Peterson silent	Members said Peterson told them it was proper for him to pass information about the grand jury to the President, and for the President to use it. Hogan of Maryland said Peterson said he really only gave the President information about what the prosecutors were doing, not the grand jury. But in at least one case, the President promised not to pass on what Peterson told him . . . and yet the information did get to the President's men.
White House transcripts	The edited White House transcript of a President to Peterson phone call, the evening of April 16, 1973 . . .
Nixon	President: I just want to know if there are any developments . . . anything you tell me, as I think I told you earlier, will not be passed on. Because I know the rules of the grand jury.
Peterson still	Peterson: You asked about Colson. Colson and Dean were together with Erlichman when Erlichman advised Hunt to get out of town . . . so he is going to be in the grand jury.
Nixon	The President repeats, making sure the grand jury will call Colson.
Erlichman	Early next morning. Erlichman called Colson. "My grapevine tells me you are going to be summoned over there today . . . They're going to ask you about a meeting in my office."
on camera	Erlichman reminds Colson of the meeting. Colson says he wasn't there, but is sure he never heard any order to Hunt to leave town and will so swear. A few minutes later, just before ten ayem, the White House transcripts show Haldeman telling the
Haldeman	President: "Colson flatly says there was never anything where he was where there was a discussion of Hunt getting out of the country . . . Erlichman has checked out everyone who was at that meeting and nobody recalls that being said except Dean."
on camera	So Peterson's information was apparently used by the President's men. Peterson testified today he saw nothing improper in that; one Democrat called him "a good soldier," bm, cbs n, wash
4A. Cronkite	Presidential lawyer James St. Clair and White House news spokesman Gerald Warren issued conflicting statements today about whether Mr. Nixon expects the House Judiciary Committee to vote for his impeachment. Warren said the President expects a committee vote for impeachment, but also believes the full House will vote in the President's favor. St. Clair said he spoke to Mr. Nixon just this morning and didn't hear any such view expressed. Later, Warren took the blame for all the confusion and said that actually the President thinks it would be inappropriate to make predictions.
No 5 or 6	
7. Cmcl	CMCL

COML # 1   :60VT

Clear Eyes/Breakfast Squares

FALSE OUT AT :30

OUT CUE: "There's Breakfast Squares"

| 8. CRONKITE | Two prison convicts are still holding 7 hostages at gunpoint in the basement cellblock of the U.S. District Court House in Washington.
Ed Bradley has that story. |

| 9. BRADLEY | TRACK UP |

ED BRADLEY: The district court in downtown Washington has been effectively cut off from the rest of the city. Though just 2 blocks from the Capitol, it's a cordoned-off area, the center of the long wait between the 2 prisoners inside with their hostages and the hundreds of heavily-armed police outside and in the rest of the building. One hostage, a U.S. Marshal, was released last night, but 6 men and 5 woman are still being held. And the 2 prisoners are demanding a plane for a so-called "freedom flight", to Africa, Algeria, or Cuba.

Frank Gorham is the leader. He's been serving a prison sentence of 73-years-to-life on a variety of charges. In 1972, Gorham was one of the ring-leaders, along with Robert Jones, of the escape attempt from the Washington jail.

Last night, Jones spoke by telephone to a Washington radio station.

ROBERT JONES [voice only]: . . . stand in front of a firing squad and die alone. We're going to take somebody with us, since we're going. So what we want you to understand is that if we killed the harmless, we're going to kill these other people.

BRADLEY: Gorham's mother, a local evangelist, has been at the court for most of the day.

MRS. VELMA JONES [prisoner's mother]: From 1-year-old to 20-years-old, this man never had a police record. He never even was — was arrested for no reason. You see what I'm saying? I hope I'm not getting loud but I want you all to know that this boy is not just something born around and from the ghetto. I raised this boy.

BRADLEY: Gorham and Jones rejected a plan to fly them to a federal prison in Oklahoma. Now, at the insistence of the 2 prisoners, officials here are trying to arrange a meeting with the families of the hostages and the families of the prisoners with someone from the Justice Department. Gorham and Jones feel that possibly this pressure will force the government to let them go.

Ed Bradley, CBS News, Washington.

| 10. CRONKITE | The Senate Watergate Committee has put together a final report of its findings, based on months of hearings and investigation of the 1973 presidential campaign.
Daniel Schorr reports. |

| 11. Schorr | TRACK UP |

SCHORR: A year ago, when it was all on live television, the seven senators seldom missed a session.

Today there was a bare quorum — without Senators Baker, Talmadge and Gurney — as they met one last time to discuss their final report.

The report itself — three volumes, result of a $2 million 17-month investigation — is under wraps until tomorrow night. But not the senatorial rhetoric, stressing how the committee turned the country around.

SOF:WEICKER: I think the result of what was wrought here is going to have its impact for many years to come. At least I hope so because the ball is no longer in this particular court, specifically the senate caucus room, rather really with the American people.

SCHORR: In the era of impeachment and trials, the report avoids conclusions about presidential responsibility, and everything else.

SOF:ERVIN: You know, you want to prove that a horse is a horse. There's two ways to do it. You draw a picture of the horse, which is a great likeness of the horse, and the other is to do that and then write under it, this is a horse. We just drew the picture . . . [laughter]

SCHORR/CLOSE: It's a far cry from a year ago when the hearings in this caucus room dominated the living rooms and cocktail lounges of the nation. The Watergate Committee ended — bypassed by action in the courts and action in the impeachment investigation — action that it helped to generate.

Daniel Schorr . . CBS News . . . in the Senate Caucus Room, Washington.

Courtesy of CBS News

Special Events — News

As a result of public interest group and citizen pressures, rulings of the FCC and, in circular fashion, media-induced increased interest in public affairs by young people, the special event became increasingly significant in broadcasting during the past decade. The dramatic nature of media-covered special events in the United States, such as the moon-landings, the Vietnam protest marches, the Watergate hearings and the impeachment proceedings stimulated interest in this aspect of broadcasting as never before.

The special event is usually under the direction of the news department and is essentially something that is taking place live and is of interest — critical or passing — to the community. It is usually a remote, on-the-spot broadcast. Special events usually originate independently and include such happenings as parades, dedications, banquets, awards and the openings of new films and supermarkets. More significant kinds of special events, perhaps, are political conventions and astronaut launchings. The assassinations of John F. Kennedy, Martin Luther King, Jr. and Robert F. Kennedy were fully covered by the media although, of course, unanticipated. The first human landing on the moon, the Watergate hearings and the impeachment proceedings in the House of Representatives were also fully covered, but as planned events with time for preparation in depth.

Sometimes special events are merely introduced, presented without comment, and — occasionally — summarized or critiqued when over. Sometimes they are narrated on radio and are accompanied by commentary on television. The opening and closing material and, frequently, transition and filler material are provided by the writer. The latter two are sometimes handled directly by the broadcaster who is assigned to the event and who presumably is an expert on the subject being covered.

Most special events are more effective on television than on radio. If the event is for presentation within a regular news program, it is frequently pre-recorded (see the section on "Remotes" earlier in this chapter). The picture captures the action and the commentary provides background and clarifying information. Films or tapes of special events usually are edited and sometimes carefully prepared beforehand in terms of format, transitions, introductions and additional material to be recorded. Sometimes they are so fully prepared that they take on the characteristics of the special feature rather than the special event. There is often only a fine line between the special event and the feature and any given program might be either one or a combination of the two. The feature and its ultimate refinement, the documentary, are discussed in the next chapter. Suffice to note now, in terms of difference between the two forms, that the special event is a broadcast which covers an actual happening that is part of the current mainstream of life, while the feature may or may not be part of current events and is usually devised, developed and executed by the broadcaster or other producing organization.

Techniques. For events other than those which require only a short intro and outro, the writer should collect as much material as possible. News stories, maps, press releases, historical documents, books, photographs, locales and similar sources can be pertinent and helpful in preparing continuity. Copy should be prepared for all emergencies as well as for opening, closing, transition and filler uses. Material should include information on the personalities involved, the background of the event and even on probable or possible happenings during the event.

Coverage in depth of a special event requires considerable preliminary work. Russ Tornabene, Vice President and General Manager of the NBC Radio Network, states: "Extensive research goes into the preparation of material to be used as background for broadcasting special events. For example, the research document prepared for the 1972 Olympics ran to about 500 pages. For the 1972 primaries and political conventions there were several books prepared, each with several hundred pages. They were even tabbed for quick reference, with color-coded sections, for various categories such as candidates, issues, etc. The job of the writer, therefore, in preparing background material for special events is an important one. In addition, the correspondents doing the broadcasts add to the basic book with research, interviews and materials of their own."

Because the form of the special event is extemporaneous, the material, though prepared as fully as possible, should be simple, straightforward and informal, and should sound as though it were ad-libbed.

Types. As previously noted, some special events are simply coverage of the event taking place. They do not require commentary and the writer needs to prepare only an appropriate opening and closing. The following illustrates continuity that may be used for a continuing special event that is broadcast more than once:

PRGM: FCC HEARINGS

DATE:

TIME:

- -

ANN: Good morning.
    Good afternoon.
    In just a few moments, your city station will bring you the _____ day of the
    Federal Communications Commission hearings on network television policies
    and practices.
      The hearings are taking place in the Interstate Commerce Building in
    Washington, D.C., before the entire Federal Communications Commission.

    We take you now to Washington, D.C.

* * *

      That concludes this (morning's) (afternoon's) session of the FCC hearings on
    network television policies and practices. Your city station is bringing you these
    important broadcasts direct from Washington, D.C., in their entirety, through the
    week of February 5th. We are interested in your reaction to these broadcasts.
    Write, FCC Hearings, WNYC, New York 7. And join us again (at 1:45) (tomorrow
    morning at 10) for the next session.

Courtesy of the Municipal Broadcasting System —
Stations WNYC, WNYC-FM, WNYC-TV — New York City

Other types of special events permit and require the development of
transition and background material during the event. The best example of
this kind of special event is the broadcast of the live sports event — which
is discussed later in this chapter under "Sports."

A further type, which falls close to a feature but is largely extemporaneous, is the commentary or analysis on what went on during the special
event. In this instance, only a prepared opening, although sometimes a
lengthy and explanatory one, is necessary. Here are two examples, the first
following the Watergate hearings on October 4, 1973 and broadcast from
12:04 A.M. to 12:34 A.M., and the second following the impeachment
hearings on July 11, 1974 and broadcast from 11:30 P.M. to 12 midnight.

(Watergate)	The activities Chairman Sam Ervin asked witness Martin Douglas Kelly about were Political Dirty tricks, the subject of today's session of the Senate Watergate hearings.
	I'm George Herman, CBS News, Washington, with my colleague Nelson Benton. And, in just a moment, today's budget of ditry tricks.
	Courtesy of CBS News
(Impeachment)	Good Evening:
	Washington has been inundated by another massive set of Watergate transcripts.
	This stack of documents was distributed by the House Judiciary Committee yesterday to the news media for dissemination this evening.
	These 8 volumes contain what the Committee has been hearing and reading and leaking from behind its closed doors since the 9th of May.

In a moment, 5 reporters from the Washington Bureau of CBS
News will tell you what IS and what is NOT in these 8 volumes.

ANN & COMMERCIAL

Courtesy of CBS News

One type of special event virtually indistinguishable from a feature is that which has been carefully pre-planned and developed and is a special event only because it is being presented in front of an audience. Productions of the arts fall into this category — though who could say that such an event is not a feature or vice versa. When the station participates in the preparation for the event, the writer can provide special input as to its actual development and perhaps its outcome. When the station does not participate in the actual action of the event — such as a concert or recital — the writer's job is somewhat different. There may be a need to prepare only the opening and closing, as in the following example. (Note the detailed video directions — SC refers to "studio card" or card bearing the indicated information.)

VIDEO	AUDIO
OPENING:	
Cover shot of Choral Group	Channel five presents . . .
Super Slide: L-20	the INTERCOLLEGIATE CHORAL FESTIVAL . . .
	The festival, which was held last evening at William Neal Reynolds Coliseum, included choral groups from ten colleges throughout North Carolina . . . and a massed chorus of over 450 voices.
Super SC: Dr. Knud Anderson	The director is Dr. Knud Anderson of the New Orleans Opera House.
Super SC: Willa Fay Batts	Piano Solist is Willa Fay Batts;
Super SC: Beatrice Donley	Alto Soloist, Beatrice Donley; and
Super SC: Mary Ida Hodge	Accompanist, Mary Ida Hodge. And now . . . the Premiere INTERCOLLEGIATE CHORAL FESTIVAL OF NORTH CAROLINA:
CLOSING	
Super Slide: L-20	Channel Five has presented The Premiere of THE INTERCOLLEGIATE CHORAL FESTIVAL OF North Carolina, directed by
Super SC: Dr. Knud Anderson	Dr. Knud Anderson.

Courtesy of WRAL-TV, Raleigh, N.C.

SPORTS

AT ONE TIME the sports department of a station or network was an offshoot of the news department. But the phenomenal growth of live sports event coverage has given sports new status in broadcasting and more and more sports divisions are separate, independent functions from the news division. The smaller the station, of course, the greater the likelihood that sports will be a function of the news department, rather than a separate entity. The writing of sports is similar to the writing of news. If anything, the style for sports broadcasts must be even more precise and more direct than for news broadcasts. The language is more colloquial and though technical terms are to be avoided so as not to confuse the general audience, the writer of sports may use many more expressions relating to a specialized area than can the writer of news.

Types of Sports Programs

The straight sportscast concentrates on recapitulation of the results of sports events and on news relating to sports in general. Some sportscasts are oriented solely to summaries of results. These summaries may come from wire service reports or from other sources of the station. Material which is rewritten from newspaper accounts or which is taken from the wires should be adapted to fit the purpose of the particular program and the personality of the broadcaster.

The sports feature program may include live or recorded interviews with sports personalities, anecdotes or dramatizations of events in sports, human interest or background stories on personalities or events, or remotes relating to sports but not in themselves an actual athletic event.

A sports show may amalgamate several approaches or, as in the case of the after-event critique or summary, may concentrate on one type alone. Many sports news shows are combinations of the straight report and the feature.

The most popular sports broadcast is, of course, the live athletic contest while it is taking place. In some instances economic or legal factors prevent the direct broadcast of the event, and it is recorded and broadcast at a scheduled time after the event has taken place.

Organization of Sports News

Formats for the sports news broadcast parallel those of the regular news broadcast. The most common approach is to take the top sport of the particular season, give all the results and news of that sport, and work toward the least important sport. In such an organization the most important story of the most important sport is given first unless a special item from another sport overrides it. Within each sport the general pattern in this organization includes the results first, the general news (such as trades, injuries and so forth) next and future events last. If the trade or injury is of a star player or the future event is more than routine, such as the signing for a heavyweight championship fight, then it will become the lead story. The local sports scene is usually coordinated with the national sports news, fitting into the national reporting breakdowns. The local result or story, however, will usually be the lead within the given sports category and sometimes the local sports scene will precede all other sports news. Formats vary, of course.

An example of sports news without results of contests is the following script of Sports Director Dave Brandt at WGAL-TV, Lancaster, Pennsylvania. A veteran of some 25 years in broadcasting, Brandt does not write a standard opening and closing for his show. Note that this particular script consists of a feature-commentary on the most important "local" sports event — the Philadelphia Eagles football game of the day before — and news of several important upcoming events. Note that as a local sports show more slides than tape are used and that the format is not the usual two-column video-audio setup.

SPORTS FINAL MONDAY

DAVE: 2 x 2 #6982 IN B G (McCORMACK)

Our tip of the hat tonight goes to Mike McCormack, the honest, levelling coach of the Philadelphia Eagles, who refused to blame yesterday's loss to New Orleans on the officials or the crowd. McCormack, after looking over game films, said he thought the Birds did not play with much intelligence, and he does not understand some of the Eagles' mental mistakes.

Punch to 2 x 2 #6771 EAGLES IN B G

The crowd undoubtedly affected the game, cutting into the Eagles' momentum, and the officials were afraid to rouse the rooters more by applying the penalty cure. But the Eagles blew the game in the final stages and just weren't high — as contenders have to be — in this game against a lightly-held opponent.

Punch to 2 x 2 #6921 FOREMAN IN B G

Heavyweight champion George Foreman is an 11-5 choice to retain his title in tomorrow nite's bout with Muhammed Ali in Africa. Philadelphian Zach Clayton is expected to be the third man in the ring. Ex-champ Joe Frazier arrived for the bout. He hopes to meet the survivor — and he told the press he believes that would be Foreman, altho' he isn't counting out the veteran Ali.

COMMERCIAL

SPORTS FINAL (2) —

DAVE: 2 x 2 #7035 FB IN B G

The New England-Buffalo game coming up next Sunday shapes up as one of the best of the year — Buffalo took advantage of Chicago mistakes to trample the Bears yesterday.

TAPE FOR TODAY. 6-second cue: 12:20. SOT. Runs 1:10. Out cue: Johnny Morris, NBC news.

2 x 2 HORSE RACING IN B G

Desert Vixen, the leading U-S filly, has been entered in the Nov. 9 Washington D-C International at Laurel as a challenger for Dahlia, which won the Canadian International at Woodbine and is the favorite to win the Laurel classic for the second straight year.

CLOSING

Courtesy of Dave Brandt, WGAL-TV, Lancester, Pa.

Sports Special Events

The live on-the-spot coverage of an athletic contest is the most exciting and most popular sports program. The newspaper and magazine cartoons showing a viewer glued to a television set for seven nights of baseball in the summer or seven nights of football, basketball and hockey in the winter are no longer exaggerations.

The sports special event can be other than a contest, however. Coverage of an awards ceremony, of an old-timer's day, of a Cooperstown Hall of Fame induction, of a retirement ceremony are all special events that are not live contests on the playing field or court.

The contest. Although the jobs of television and radio broadcasters differ, those of the continuity writers are essentially the same. In television the broadcasters are announcers and not narrators, as they are in radio. Even if they wanted to, the television broadcasters would find it difficult to keep up with the action as seen by the audience, except in slow games such as baseball. Since sports are visual to begin with, the less description by the television broadcaster the better. The television announcer is primarily an encyclopedia of background information. The radio announcer needs background information, too, but sometimes is too busy with narration to use very much of it.

The sports broadcaster must have filler material; that is, information relating to pre-event action and color, statistics, form charts, information on the site of the event, on the history of the event, about the participants, human interest stories and similar materials which either heighten the audience's interest or help clarify the action to the audience. This material must be written up and must be available to the broadcaster to be used when needed, specifically during lulls in the action, and in pre-game and post-game opening and closing segments. At one time staff writers prepared this material. More recently, sports broadcasters have been expected to be experts in their field and to know and to provide their own filler material.

Former sports stars have been hired to do "color" at live events, providing first-hand technical and human interest information not usually known to the non-player. Because of indications that too many sportscasters were not objective, but were "homers" who might falsify, distort or suppress facts to aid the attendance and public relations of the home team, the FCC in 1974 required that the sports broadcast must disclose "clearly, publicly, and prominently" during each athletic event whether the announcers are being paid, chosen or otherwise controlled by anyone other than the station.

The primary function of the writer for the live contest is that of a researcher and outliner. The script may be little more than an outline and/ or a series of statistics, individual unrelated sentences or short paragraphs with the required background and transition continuity. The following outline is more complete than most. Note that the material contains not only the opening and closing format, but includes the commercial format so that the announcer knows when to break, and also has the lead-in script material for the commercial. Each page of the opening and closing formats are set up so that after the first page the announcements of network sponsors or local sponsors may be inserted without disrupting the continuity.

PROFESSIONAL HOCKEY — OPENING BILLBOARD

VIDEO	AUDIO
Up from black	Sneak theme
FILM	
PROFESSIONAL HOCKEY (Super)	ANNCR: Coming your way now is PROFESSIONAL HOCKEY, the fastest game in the world . . .
SUPER (NAME OF TEAMS)	and BIG match it is — the _____ against · the _____. (Theme up and under)
CBS SPORTS (Super)	ANNCR: This is the _____ in a series of exciting matches that will be brought to you every Saturday afternoon during the season . . .
BEST IN SPORTS (Super)	As part of the continuing effort of CBS SPORTS to present the BEST IN SPORTS all the year around. (Theme up and under)
NATIONAL LEAGUE HOCKEY (Super)	ANNCR: This is an important regular season contest in the National Hockey League . . . hockey's MAJOR league . . .

NAME OF STADIUM
(Super)

being brought to you direct from famed
_____ in _____.

(Theme up and under)

NAME OF TEAM

ANNCR: So now get ready to watch the
match between the _____
and the _____ . . .

NAMES OF SPORTCASTERS
(Super)

with description by _____
and _____.

Now let's go to (Name of Stadium)
_____.

(Theme up and hold)

CLOSING BILLBOARD

VIDEO	AUDIO
PROFESSIONAL HOCKEY	You have just seen a presentation of fast-moving PROFESSIONAL HOCKEY . . .
NATIONAL LEAGUE HOCKEY	one of the big regular season matches of the NATIONAL HOCKEY LEAGUE . . . the MAJOR league of hockey.
	(Theme up and under)
NAME OF TEAMS	Today's exciting contest was between the _____ and the _____.
NAME OF STADIUM	Played on the _____ home ice, the famed _____ in _____.
	(Theme up and under)
NEXT SATURDAY	We invite you to join us again NEXT Saturday afternoon for another big Professional Hockey Match . . .
NAME OF TEAMS	Next week's televised contest will bring together the (Name of Team) _____ and the (Name of Team) _____ at the (Name of Stadium) _____.
	(Theme up and under)
NAMES OF SPORTSCASTERS	The description of today's match has been provided by _____ and _____.
PROFESSIONAL HOCKEY is a CBS TELEVISION NETWORK Presentation PRODUCED BY CBS SPORTS	This presentation of PROFESSIONAL HOCKEY has been produced by CBS SPORTS.
	(Theme up and hold)

HOCKEY COMMERCIAL FORMAT

Before Opening Face-Off — "Very shortly play will be starting here at (name or arena) and we will have action for you."
(1 minute commercial)

First Period — During 1st period of play three 20 second commercials are to be inserted at the discretion of each co-op station. Audio Cut: "There's a whistle on the ice and the score is _____ & _____."

1st pause during play-by-play.	.20 seconds
2nd pause during play-by-play.	.20 seconds
3rd pause during play-by-play.	.20 seconds

End of First Period — "That is the end of the first period and the score is _____ & _____."
(1 minute commercial)

Middle First Intermission — "In just a moment, we are going to have more entertainment for you during this intermission."

Before Second Period Face-Off — "Very shortly, play will be starting in the second period at (name of arena) and we will have more action for you."
(1 minute commercial)

Second Period — During 2nd period of play three 20 second commercials are to be inserted at the discretion of each co-op station. Audio Cue: "There's a whistle on the ice and the score is _____ & _____."

1st pause during play-by-play.	.20 seconds
2nd pause during play-by-play.	.20 seconds
3rd pause during play-by-play.	.20 seconds

End of Second Period — "That's the end of the second period and the score is _____ & _____."
(1 minute commercial)

Middle Second Intermission — "In just a moment we are going to have more entertainment for you during this intermission."

Before Third Period Face-Off — "Very shortly play will be starting in the third period here at (name of arena) and we will have more action for you."
(1 minute commercial)

Third Period — During third period of play three 20 second commercials are to be inserted at the discretion of each co-op station. Audio Cue: "There's a whistle on the ice and the score is _____ & _____."

1st pause during play-by-play.	.20 seconds
2nd pause during play-by-play.	.20 seconds
3rd pause during play-by-play.	.20 seconds

End of Third Period — "That is the end of the game and the score is _____ & _____."
(1 minute commercial)

Statistical Wrap-up

Before Closing Billboard — "This wraps up another National Hockey League telecast. Final score _____ & _____."

By permission of CBS Television Sports

In the preceding format the writer prepared a fair amount of actual script continuity. In the following football format there is less dialogue prepared but considerably more directions provided for the actual telecasting process. The planning is more precise, with time segments and total elapsed time after each segment.

NFL TODAY, PART 1 — PRE GAME

00:00	Open and Tease the Day	2:30
02:30	Commercial 1	1:02
03:32	Football Segment 1	7:30
	(includes 2-minute field report supplied by NFL Films)	
11:02	Commerical 2	1:32
12:34	Sports News Segment	5:00
	(probably include 1½- to 2-minute non-football feature supplied by NFL Films)	
17:34	Commercial 3	1:32
19:06	Football Segment 2	7:25
	(includes 2-minute feature supplied by NFL Films)	
26:31	Commercial 4	1:02
27:33	Close	1:02
28:35	Game Opening Billboard	1:00
29:35	System	

CUE: WE'LL BE READY FOR THE START OF TODAY'S NATIONAL FOOTBALL LEAGUE GAME AFTER THIS WORD FROM YOUR LOCAL STATION. (Pause) THIS IS CBS.

Note: 72-Second Station Break

NFL TODAY, PART II — GAME

01:00	Announcers set scene	1:10

LEAD TO COMMERCIAL 1

CUE: WE'LL BE READY FOR THE START OF TODAY'S GAME IN JUST A MOMENT.

02:10	Commercial 1	1:32
	(On doubleheaders this will be a 2-minute position)	
03:42	Announcers set starting lineups, cover coin toss ceremony if going on at time	1:18
05:00	Kickoff — First Quarter	

Commercials 2, 3 and 4

CUE: During Action — WITH (time) REMAINING IN THE (_____) QUARTER, THERE'S A TIME OUT WITH THE SCORE (team & score) AND (team & score).

Note: If there's a problem with the clock, we'll use: IN THE (_____) QUARTER, THERE'S A TIME OUT WITH THE SCORE (team & score) AND (team & score).

Unless there are regional commercial positions, we will not employ these cues except at the end of the quarters; countdown cues will be used.

End of First Quarter

Commercial 5 and NFL PSA 1:45

CUE: THAT'S THE END OF THE FIRST QUARTER WITH THE SCORE _____

Second Quarter

Commercials 6, 7, 8 & 9

Note: Network promos will be in fixed positions following commercials
7 & 16. In the vast majority of cases we hope that these will be
12-second videotape announcement that can be included in the
commercial reel. If, for any reason, they are straight copy, the
announcements should still be held to 12 seconds.

CUES WILL BE THE SAME AS THOSE LISTED FOR FIRST QUARTER.
End of First Half

NFL TODAY, PART II — HALFTIME

00:00	CUE: THAT'S THE END OF THE FIRST HALF WITH THE SCORE _____	:10
00:10	Commercial 10 (90 secs.) Note: On the second games of doubleheaders this will be a 60-second position. If there are first game sponsors involved in the second game, one 30-sec. commercial will shift to position 1	1:32
	STATION BREAK CUE: WE'LL JOIN JACK WHITAKER IN CBS CONTROL AFTER THIS WORD FROM YOUR LOCAL STATION.	
01:42	System (from Coord)	:10
01:52	Station Break (62 seconds)	1:05
02:57	(a) Sports News Segment	5:20
	(includes 1-minute commercial as part of total time) Note: This segment will include 2:30 feature supplied by NFL Films.	
08:17	(b) Football Scores & Hilites	5:00
13:17	CUE TO BILLBOAD: WE'RE ALMOST READY TO BEGIN THE SECOND HALF WITH (team) KICKING TO (team)	:10
13:27	Middle Billboard	:31
	Title Slide — National Football League — :05	
	Copy: "Today's National Football League game is being sponsored by _____."	
	Sponsor A — :05	
	Sponsor B — :05	
	Sponsor C — :05	
	Sponsor D — :05	
	Copy: "Today's game will continue in just a minute."	
13:58	Commercial 11	1:02
15:00	Second Half Kickoff — Third Quarter	

Commercials 12, 13 & 14
CUES WILL BE THE SAME AS THOSE LISTED FOR FIRST QUARTER.
End of Third Quarter
CUE: THAT'S THE END OF THE THIRD QUARTER WITH THE
       SCORE _____. WE NOW PAUSE FOR A WORD
       FROM YOUR LOCAL STATION. (SYSTEM)
Note: If the station break does not fall at the end of the third quarter
       (see Station Break Summary), the cue will be as follows: WE'LL
       RETURN TO (stadium) AFTER THIS WORD FROM YOUR
       LOCAL STATION. (SYSTEM)

Station Break (62 seconds) and NFL PSA	1:45

Fourth Quarter
Commercials 15, 16 & 17 (see note following commercials 6, 7, 8, & 9)
CUES WILL BE THE SAME AS THOSE LISTED FOR THE
FIRST QUARTER.
End of Game

Commercial 18	1:02

Note: In all games this commercial will be scheduled in fourth quarter
       action should sufficient commercial opportunities occur.
CUE: THAT'S THE END OF THE GAME AND THE FINAL SCORE
       IS _____. WE'LL BE BACK AT (_____)
       STADIUM IN JUST A MOMENT.

Play-by-play announcers will fill as required (Note: Should be maximum
of 4 minutes) and then cue to Pro Football Report.

CUE: NOW WE TAKE YOU TO (Announcer) IN CBS CONTROL FOR
PRO FOOTBALL REPORT.

Note: On doubleheader dates we will cue directly to station identification.

CUE: STAY TUNED FOR (team vs. team) GAME IMMEDIATELY
FOLLOWING THIS WORD FROM YOUR LOCAL STATION.
(Pause) . . . THIS IS CBS.

Blackout markets carrying a first game will have to cover the second game
with a STAY TUNED FOR PRO FOOTBALL REPORT.

NFL TODAY, PART III — POST GAME

00:00	Program Segment 1	4:00
	(Scores of 4 games, VTR hilites on 2 of 4)	
04:00	Commercial 1	1:02
05:02	Program Segment 2	4:00
	(Scores of 4 games, VTR hilites on 2 of 4)	
09:02	Commercial 2	1:02
10:04	Program Segment 3	4:00
	(Scores of 4 games, VTR hilites on 2 of 4)	
14:06	Commercial 3	1:02
15:08	"Goodbye" and Closing Billboard	1:00

Note: This will have to be pre-taped and racked on separate machine so
that it can follow any commercial position. . . . System should be
included on tape.

Station Note: There will be no fill procedures. The Post Game Show on
first games will run 16:08 regardless of the end time of the game. See
Doubleheader Procedures for instructions on second game sign-offs.

The _____ Show was produced by CBS Television Sports

• *What significant differences, if any, are there in the preparation
of the rundown sheet for a network sports event and for the following local sports event?*

VIDEO	AUDIO
OPENING: LONG SHOT OF SPORTLAND:	(BOOTH ANNCR.) NOW LIVE FROM BEAUTIFUL SPORTLAND ON U.S. 1 NORTH OF RALEIGH — WRAL-TV PRESENTS . . .
CUE THE MUSIC — SUPER L-317-s	BOWLING FROM SPORTLAND . . . THE EXCITING NEW BOWLING SHOW WHERE
PAN SLOW RIGHT	EACH WEEK YOU'LL SEE THE TOP BOWLERS IN THIS AREA COMPETE FOR
CUT TO CU OF BOWLER	PRIZES AND THE TITLE OF KING OF THE HILL — PLUS A CHANCE TO WIN $10,000
ZOOM BACK SLOWLY	SHOULD THEY BOWL A PERFECT 300 GAME. NOW HERE'S YOUR BOWLING HOST, JIM HEAVNER.
DROP SUPER AND ZOOM IN ON JIM HEAVNER, FADING OUT THE MUSIC	(JIM) HELLO, LADIES AND GENTLEMEN, I'M JIM HEAVNER AND I'LL BE YOUR HOST . . . (DOES WARM-UP) (INTRODUCES BOWLERS) (DOES THE INTERVIEW) (THEN RIGHT BEFORE THE START OF THE FIRST GAME) WE'LL START OUR FIRST GAME RIGHT AFTER THIS IMPORTANT MESSAGE.

CUT TO STUDIO FOR BREAK ONE:	(SIXTY SECONDS)
BACK LIVE:	(STARTS FIRST GAME) (AFTER FIRST GAME, WE WILL HAVE INTERVIEWS ONLY IF WE ARE INSIDE OF 0:15) (CUT TO SECOND BREAK WITH CUE — WE'LL START OUR SECOND GAME RIGHT AFTER THIS IMPORTANT MESSAGE)
CUT TO STUDIO FOR BREAK TWO:	(SIXTY SECONDS)
BACK LIVE:	(START SECOND GAME) (WE SHOULD HAVE FINISHED SECOND GAME PRIOR TO 0:38) (IF WE'RE RUNNING NEAR OR OVER THIS KILL BREAK THREE) (TIME PERMITTING CUT TO THIRD BREAK WITH CUE — WE'LL START OUR THIRD GAME RIGHT AFTER THIS IMPORTANT MESSAGE)
CUT TO STUDIO FOR BREAK THREE:	(SIXTY SECONDS)
BACK LIVE: PAN LEFT	(STARTS THIRD GAME) (AFTER GAME, TIME PERMITTING, HE INTERVIEWS WINNER AND LOSER HANDING THEM THEIR ENVELOPES) (IF WE NEED A PAD, HEAVNER BRINGS OUT CHARLIE BOSWELL FOR THE BOWLING TIP OF THE WEEK) (IF FURTHER PAD IS NEEDED USE FOURTH PROMO CUTAWAY) (CLOSE IS REVERSE OF THE OPENING — HEAVNER BOWS OUT)
CUT TO LONG SHOT OF SPORTLAND WITH MUSIC SUPER SLIDE: L-317-s AND CUE MUSIC SUPER SLIDE: L-207-s	(BOOTH ANNCR.) LIVE FROM BEAUTIFUL SPORTLAND ON U.S. 1 NORTH OF RALEIGH WRAL-TV HAS PRESENTED BOWLING FROM SPORTLAND . . . BE WITH US AGAIN NEXT WEEK WHEN TOP BOWLERS IN THIS AREA AGAIN COMPETE FOR PRIZES AND THE TITLE OF KING OF THE HILL — PLUS A CHANCE TO WIN $10,000 ON BOWLING FROM SPORT-LAND — BOWLING FROM SPORTLAND WAS DIRECTED BY ROSS SHAHEEN.
SUPER SLIDE: L-307-s	
SUPER SLIDE: L-317-s: MUSIC UP AND OUT:	
BLACK:	

By permission of Sportland, Inc.

The Non-contest. The principal difference between this special event and the live contest is that this one can be more completely prepared for and, in some instances, even can be outlined in terms of anticipated sequences. Although it should come over as extemporaneous, the writer can, through pre-interviewing and working with the producer and director in setting up certain actions, write an outline that contains specific happenings rather than non-content transition phrases. The following detailed rundown was adapted from a network presentation.

RUNDOWN SHEET ON STADIUM REMOTE, FOOTBALL COACH TRIBUTE

Approx. 2:15 P.M.: Panoramic view of Stadium. Super card: "Football Coach's Last Game." Announcer voice over.

Approx. 2:55 P.M.: Panoramic view of half-time ceremonies at Stadium. Super card: "Football Coach's Last Game." Announcer voice over.

Approx. 4:50 P.M.: Announcer introduction to closing minutes of football game. Feature scoreboard clock running out. Super card over action on field as gun sounds ending game. Interviewer describes closing moments of game.

1. Interviewer stations Football Coach on the field facing the field camera. Bands of the competing universities line up behind Football Coach and Interviewer.
2. Band music concludes and Interviewer thanks the bands on behalf of Football Coach. (Interviewer's mike should be fed into stadium public address system for any narration while on field.)
3. Football Coach and Interviewer walk up ramp to field house followed by special guests. At entrance to field house they are picked up by camera on dolly and led down the hall of the University dressing room. The University squad and the opposing team's captain follow closely.
4. Interviewer introduces some friends and former players of Football Coach, with brief comments from the guests and from Football Coach. It is hoped that the Presidents of both Universities can be present, and that the President of Football Coach's University can quote from letters written to Football Coach by prominent persons in government and in other fields. At some point during the proceedings an outstanding national football coach will talk to Football Coach from station studio via split screen.
5. At conclusion of program Interviewer presents Football Coach with award from Network.
6. Brief comment from Football Coach to his University alumni throughout the country.

NOTES TO CHAPTER 4

[1] Hilts, Philip J., "Howard K. Smith and the Rise of ABC News," *The Washington Post/Potomac*, August 11, 1974, p. 12.

[2] *Television/Radio Age*, August 9, 1971, pp. 23-28.

[3] *Television/Radio Age*, October 30, 1972, p. 28.

[4] *Broadcasting*, August 19, 1974, pp. 41-42.

[5] *Television/Radio Age*, October 14, 1974, p. 26.

[6] *Ibid.*

[7] Television Information Office press release, March 28, 1973.

[8] Bradshaw, Tom, "Time for Hand-holding with Gov't and Camera," *Television/Radio Age*, October 14, 1974, pp. 23-25, 66, 74, 80, 82.

[9] *Ibid.*

[10] *Ibid.*

[11] Mandel, William K., "Manufacturing the News at Channel 6," *Philadelphia Magazine*, July, 1972, pp. 64-69, 132-40.

[12] *Television/Radio Age*, October 14, 1974, p. 32.

REFERENCE BOOKS

ON WRITING NEWS AND SPORTS

Barron, Jerome A., *Freedom of the Press for Whom?* Bloomington: Indiana University Press, 1973. Subtitle: The Right of Access to Mass Media.

Bender, James F., comp., *NBC Handbook of Pronounciation.* New York: Thomas Y. Crowell (current edition). The correct way to pronounce thousands of words and names frequently mispronounced.

Blanchard, Robert O., ed., *Congress and the News Media.* New York: Hastings House, 1974. How Congress and the news media interact in the legislative and public policy-making processes.

Bliss, Edward, Jr. and John M. Patterson, *Writing News for Broadcast.* New York: Columbia University Press, 1971. Various approaches to writing radio and television news, with good descriptive examples including comparison of same evening newscasts of the three major networks.

Brucker, Herbert, *Communication is Power: Unchanging Values in a Changing Journalism.* New York: Oxford University Press, 1973.

Chester, Edward W., *Radio, Television and American Politics.* New York: Sheed & Ward, 1971. History of broadcasting's influence on local and national politics.

Dary, David, *How to Write News for Broadcast and Print Media.* Blue Ridge Summit, Pa.: TAB Books, 1973.

————, *Radio News Handbook.* Blue Ridge Summit, Pa.: TAB Books, 1970. How to put together the radio news program for the small station.

————, *Television News Handbook.* Blue Ridge Summit, Pa.: TAB Books, 1971. How to put together the television news program for the small station.

Dennis, Everette E. and William L. Rivers, *Other Voices: The New Journalism in America.* San Francisco: Canfield Press, 1973.

Effron, Edith. *The News Twisters.* New York: Manor Books, 1973.

Epstein, Edward J., *News from Nowhere: Television and the News.* New York: Random House, 1973.

Fang, Irving, *Television News,* 2nd Ed., Rev. New York: Hastings House, 1972. Deals with principal problems in writing and reporting news on TV, including editorials, fairness doctrine, libel, election coverage, access, equal time and privacy. Includes a chapter on radio.

Gilbert, Robert E., *Television and Presidential Politics.* Quincy, Mass.: Christopher Publishing House, 1972. The role and influence of TV in presidential nominations, campaigns and elections.

Hall, Mark W., *Broadcast Journalism: An Introduction to News Writing.* New York: Hastings House, 1971. A basic introduction to radio-TV newswriting, including style, techniques, sources and types of stories covered.

Hohenberg, John, *Free Press, Free People: The Best Cause.* New York: Free Press, 1973. A history of freedom of the press.

Krieghbaum, Hillier, *Pressures on the Press.* New York: Thomas Y. Crowell, 1972. Government, business, lobbies, citizen group criticism and the question of news management.

Lawhorne, Clifton O., *Defamation and Public Officials: The Evolving Law of Libel.* Carbondale: Southern Illinois University Press, 1971. Court case histories for journalists who deal with public affairs.

McNaughton, Harry H., *Proofreading and Copyediting.* New York: Hastings House, 1973. Subtitle: A Practical Guide to Style.

Merrill, John C., *The Imperative of Freedom.* New York: Hastings House, 1974. Subtitle: A Philosophy of Journalistic Autonomy. Threats to press freedom and a growing conformity require a renaissance of journalistic commitment and self determination, author states.

——— and Ralph D. Barney (eds.), *Ethics and the Press: Readings in Mass Media Morality.* New York: Hastings House, 1975. A provocative collection of 35 timely articles on press ethics and problems.

Meyer, Philip, *Precision Journalism: A Reporter's Introduction to Social Science Methods.* Bloomington: Indiana University Press, 1973.

Mickelson, Sig, *The Electric Mirror: Politics in an Age of Television.* New York: Dodd, Mead, 1972. TV's key problems in politics.

Phelps, Robert H. and E. Douglas Hamilton, *Libel: Rights, Risks, Responsibilities.* New York: Macmillan, 1966.

Schuneman, R. Smith, ed., *Photographic Communication: Principles, Problems and Challenges of Photojournalism.* New York: Hastings House, 1972. Philosophies and process of top practitioners.

Siller, Robert C., *Guide to Professional Radio and TV Newscasting.* Blue Ridge Summit, Pa.: TAB Books, 1972. Includes equipment, preparation, writing, marking and timing, use of tape.

Skornia, Harry J. *Television and the News.* Palo Alto: Pacific Books, 1974.

Small, William, *To Kill A Messenger: Television News and the Real World.* New York: Hastings House, 1970. The day-to-day decision processes of selecting, analyzing and presenting news, from his viewpoint as Vice President and Washington Bureau Manager, CBS News.

Statistical Abstract of the United States. Washington, D.C.: U.S. Government Printing Office. Annual summary prepared by Bureau of Census on social, economic and political organizations of the United States, including communications.

Stone, Vernon and Bruce Hinson, *Television Newsfilm Techniques*. New York: Hastings House, 1974. A project of the RTNDA, this is a manual of practices and trends at TV stations.

Tyrrell, R. W., *The Work of the Television Journalist*. New York: Hastings House, 1972. A primer describing every job from writer and producer to camera operator, recordist, film editor, newscaster. Compares British and American television news.

United States Government Organization Manual. Washington: D.C.: U.S. Government Printing Office. Annual directory prepared by General Services Administration of legislative, judicial and executive branches.

Weber, Ronald, ed., *The Reporter As Artist*. New York: Hastings House, 1974. A collection of materials on the pros and cons of the "New Journalism" controversy.

FOR APPLICATION AND REVIEW

1. Clip out the front page stories from your daily newspaper and organize them for a radio news broadcast according to each of the following approaches: topical; geographical; international, national, local; from most to least important, regardless of category. Write the script for a 15-minute straight news broadcast for radio, using one of the organizations developed above.

2. Rewrite the radio broadcast you have developed in the exercise above for a television news program, utilizing photos, film, tape, slides and other visuals.

3. Prepare the opening and closing continuity and the filler material for a live local broadcast — for television and radio both — of the next athletic event in your community. Rewrite your material as though the same event were to be broadcast over a national network.

4. Find out what special event worthy of news coverage, other than an athletic contest, will take place in your community in the near future. Prepare the opening and closing, transition and filler material for radio. Include, if possible, an interview with one or more personalities taking part in the event. Revise for television the material you prepared for radio.

For those who are especially interested in newswriting, the following workbook is recommended for practice materials: Fang, Irving E., *Television/Radio News Workbook*. New York: Hastings House, 1974.

5

Features and Documentaries

FEATURES AND DOCUMENTARIES are usually under the direction of the news department of the television or radio station or network. They deal with news and information and, frequently, opinion, sometimes pertinent to current events, sometimes of an historical nature, and sometimes academic, cultural or abstract without necessarily relating to an immediate or major issue of the day.

FEATURES

THE FEATURE OR, as it sometimes called, the special feature, falls somewhere in between the special event and the documentary. While the special event is coverage of an immediate newsworthy happening, sometimes unanticipated, the special feature is pre-planned and carefully prepared. There are special events, of course, such as sports events, which are pre-planned. The difference is that in the special event the producer is covering a happening as it unveils and does not know what the outcome is going to be. In the feature the outcome is known and, indeed, the program may have been well-rehearsed and is usually pre-recorded. The broadcaster usually has more control over the sequence of events in the feature than in the special event. The special event usually is live, while the feature usually is filmed, taped or, if live, produced from a script or at least a routine sheet or detailed rundown sheet. Special events usually are public presentations that television and radio arrange to cover. Features usually are prepared solely for television and radio presentation and generally are not presented before an in-person audience. The special event is part of the stream of life while the feature is designed by a producing organization.

Features usually are short — 2- to 5- or 15-to 30-minutes in length; the former for fillers and the latter for full programs of a public service nature. The subject matter for the feature varies. Some sample types: the presentation of the work of a special service group in the community, a story on the operation of the local fire department, an examination of the problems of the school board, a how-to-do-it broadcast, a behind-the-scenes story on any subject — from raising chickens to electing public officials. The feature offers the writer the opportunity to create a program of high artistic quality closely approaching the documentary.

Writing Approach

Because it does come so close to the documentary, the feature requires careful research, analysis and evaluation of material, and writing based on detail and depth. That does not mean that it requires a full and complete script. Because the feature is composed, frequently, of a number of diverse program types — such as the documentary, the interview, the panel discussion and the speech — it may be written in routine sheet or rundown form. Some features have combinations of script, rundown sheet and routine sheet.

Because the feature is usually a public service presentation it often contains informational and educational content. But it doesn't have to be purely factual or academic in nature. It can even take the form of a variety show or a drama — or certainly have elements of these forms within the program as a whole. The feature is an eclectic form and can be oriented around a person, an organization, a thing, a situation, a problem or an idea. The following example is principally oriented toward an organization (the Red Cross) but also includes a problem (disaster work) and a situation (a specific disaster in the Harrisburg area and a specific technique, artificial respiration). Note that this feature was produced by a local commercial station as part of a regular public service series and is a live-type program with film inserts.

HOW RED CROSS DOES IT

VIDEO	AUDIO
SLIDE #1 TRI-STATE STORY	MUSIC: RECORD "RED CROSS SONG" IN AND OUT BEHIND STATION ANNOUNCER:
SLIDE #2 RED CROSS EMBLEM	As a public service, WEHT presents TRI-STATE STORY — a half hour prepared through the cooperation of the Springfield Chapter of the American Red Cross. Here to introduce our guests for this evening is Mr. John Smith, Director of Public Relations for the Springfield Red Cross. Mr. Smith:

CAMERA ON SMITH	(MR. SMITH THANKS ANNOUNCER AND INTRODUCES TWO GUESTS, MR. HARVEY AND MR. JONES. THEN ASKS MR. HARVEY TO SPEAK.)
CAMERA ON HARVEY CLOSEUP OF PHOTOS ON EASEL	(MR. HARVEY TELLS OF RECENT DISASTER WORK IN HARRISBURG AREA, SHOWING PHOTOGRAPHS OF SERVICE WORKERS. HE WILL RISE AND WALK TO THE EASEL.)
CAMERA ON SMITH AND JONES	(MR. SMITH INTRODUCES MR. JONES. THEY DISCUSS SUMMER SAFETY SCHOOL FOR SWIMMERS. JONES LEADS INTO FILM WITH FOLLOWING CUE):
	"Now I'd like our viewers to see a film that was made at Lake Roundwood during last year's Summer Safety School."
SPECIAL FILM	(8:35) (SILENT — JONES LIVE VOICE-OVER)
CAMERA ON JONES	(JONES INTRODUCES ARTIFICIAL RES-PIRATION DEMONSTRATION.)
CAMERA ON TWO BOYS	(JONES DESCRIBES METHODS OFF CAMERA.)
CAMERA ON SMITH	(SMITH THANKS JONES AND HARVEY AND GIVES CONCLUDING REMARKS.)
SLIDE #3 TRI-STATE STORY	MUSIC: THEME IN AND UNDER STATION ANNOUNCER: Tri-State Story, a WEHT Public Service Presentation, is on the air each week at this time. Today's program was prepared through the cooperation of the Springfield Chapter of the American Red Cross.

By permission of American National Red Cross

"Day By Day" is an award-winning feature series on a public television station. As with the Red Cross feature, note how the basic introduction of the main idea (in "Day By Day," the world of the deaf) leads into the building of an understanding of the subject through background, discussion and demonstration. It is, in dramatic terms, a rising action, moving the audience along to greater interest and empathy. This is a desired technique in writing the feature. Without expensive technical requirements, such as location filming, and using only one set and a demonstration area, the writer-researcher of "Day By Day" was able to obtain variety and excitement.

> • *What are the different program forms and techniques used in this rundown sheet? Without increasing the budget, is there any*

additional or different material or approaches you, as writer, would have used?

Vol. — 3   December 12, 1973
Tol. No. — 346   Wednesday
Yr. No. —55

DAY BY DAY
1973
WUCM-TV
DELTA COLLEGE
UNIVERSITY CENTER, MICHIGAN

3:00 P.M. (Live) & 7:30 P.M. (Repeat)

Partial Script

Host/Prod. — A. Rapp   Direct. — M. Baldwin
Anncr. — L. Scott   Vid. Eng. — H. Conley
Vol. Prog. Coord. — J. Arvoy   Writer/Resch. — K. Semion
                                        Series Sec. — B. Meyers

Guests — 8
Segments — 2 (Same Topic)

VIDEO	AUDIO
BLACK VT OPEN (SLIDE MONTAGE)	TAPE THEME ("DAY BY DAY") ANNCR. (STAND OPEN) THE FOLLOWING PROGRAM IS PRO- DUCED IN THE STUDIOS OF WUCM-TV FROM DELTA COLLEGE AT UNIVERSITY CENTER, MICHIGAN. THIS IS DAY BY DAY. (PAUSE) LIVE AT 3 REPEATED ON VIDEO TAPE AT 7:30 P.M. YOUR HOST IS ANDY RAPP AND I'M LAMARR SCOTT.
MS OF ANNCR.	ANNCR. (SPEC. OPEN): IMAGINE, IF YOU CAN, A WORLD OF UTTER SILENCE. (PAUSE) IMAGINE THAT YOU COULD CLOSE YOUR EARS AS YOU CAN CLOSE YOUR EYES, AND THERE WOULD BE NO FOOT- STEPS, NO WHISTLING WIND. IMAGINE THE WORLD OF THE DEAF. TODAY, WEDNESDAY, DECEMBER 12, WE'LL EXPLORE THE WORLD THAT HAS INCLUDED SUCH GREAT PERSONS AS THOMAS EDISON AND JOHANN SEBASTIAN BACH. AND NOW, HERE'S ANDY. APPROX. 1 MIN.
WS OF SET	HOST & ANNCR. (AD LIB CHAT): — NATIONAL "DING-A-LING" DAY

SHOW PHONE NOS.

— ASK FOR TELEPHONE CALLS
APPROX. 2 MIN.

SEGMENT #1
4 GUESTS WALK ON SET AND SIT

SEGMENT #1
ANNCR. (GUEST INTRO.): IT'S EASY TO
THINK NEGATIVELY WHEN YOU THINK
OF DEAFNESS, AND THAT'S WHY
TEACHING DEAF PERSONS TO DEVELOP
POSITIVE SELF IMAGES IS AN IMPOR-
TANT GOAL OF OUR GUESTS.
BERT POOS (PAHZ) IS SUPERINTENDENT
AND DEAN OF STUDENTS FOR THE
DEAF IN FLINT. HIS WIFE, EDIE POOS
(PAHZ), IS COORDINATOR OF THE
HEARING IMPAIRED PROGRAM AT MOTT
COMMUNITY COLLEGE IN FLINT. EARL
JONES IS AN INSTRUCTOR AT THE
MICHIGAN SCHOOL FOR THE DEAF AND
DIRECTOR OF THE MOTT ADULT
EDUCATION PROGRAM FOR THE DEAF.
AND MARIE ERICKSON IS AN INTER-
PRETER FOR THE MOTT COLLEGE
PROGRAM.

(DISCUSSION AREA)
VID. SPOT EFFECT SIGN READER

HOST (INTERVIEW) #1: FOUR GUESTS.
TOPIC: "THE PROBLEMS OF BEING
DEAF OR HARD OF HEARING."
APPROX. 10 MIN.

SEGMENT #2
(DEMONSTRATION AREA)
DEAF STUDENTS PERFORM
PANTOMIME SKIT

SEGMENT #2
HOST (INTERVIEW) #2: FOUR GUESTS
DEMO.
NARRATED BY GUEST ON DISCUSSION
SET.
GUEST INTROS STUDENTS.
APPROX. 10 MIN.
ANNCR. (SPEC. CLOSE): THIS POEM,
CALLED THE WORLD OF SILENCE, WAS
WRITTEN BY A DEAF PERSON:
"THE RING OF BELLS — WHAT IS IT?
THE RUSTLE OF LEAVES, CAN YOU
HEAR IT?
CAN YOU HEAR THE CLOCK TICK TOCK.
A BABBLING BROOK, A FRIEND'S HELLO,
THE BARK OF A DOG, THE TELEPHONE'S
RING?
TO ME, THESE SHOULD NOT MEAN
A THING,
BUT I CARE — I CARE.
I FEEL THE SOUNDS I CANNOT HEAR."

FOR ANDY RAPP, THIS IS LAMARR
SCOTT, WISHING YOU A GOOD EVENING.

RANDOM SHOTS OF GUESTS
BLACK

TAPE THEME ("DAY BY DAY")
APPROX. 30 MIN.
EXACT: 28:30 MIN.

Day By Day, 1973-74 Season, WUCM-TV, Delta College,
University Center, Michigan; Andersen Rapp, Executive Producer

The following is from a regular feature series on NBC radio entitled "Emphasis."

> • *As you analyze it, note 1) in what ways, if any, as a network program, it differs from the previous two non-network feature examples; 2) what special writing approaches and techniques mark it as a radio, rather than a television, presentation. Rewrite it as a network television feature.*

Even if you go to Washington with a closed mind, keep your eyes open. Bill Cullen, At Ease. More after this for Best Western Motels.

Just about anybody who gets to Washington sees the Lincoln Memorial . . . most get to the Smithsonian Institution . . . and some even manage to find Ford's Theater . . . where Lincoln was shot.

But there are hundreds of monuments in the nation's capital that hardly any visitor notices . . . and that most Washingtonians themselves know little about. For instance, there are thirty statues of men on horseback . . . which may be one or two too many. Some of the riders . . . like Ulysses S. Grant . . . you may have heard of . . . but there are a lot of other generals there that no one now remembers. In the middle of DuPont Circle there is an elegant marble fountain held up by some partly draped ladies. The fountain honors a Union admiral in the Civil War named DuPont. The man who designed the fountain was Daniel Chester French . . . one of this country's great sculptors. French also did a lovely statue of a deaf girl learning sign language. It's at Florida Avenue and Seventh Street.

If your taste runs more to nostalgia, there are relief sculptures of 1926 automobiles on the Capital Garage . . . and, for modernists, a lot of strictly abstract sculpture will go on display at the new Hirshhorn Museum next year.

When somebody wants to put in a piece of decoration or sculpture, Washington is where they want to do it . . . and you can spend weeks there just looking around.

Bill Cullen, Emphasis, At Ease.

Now a word for Best Western.

Courtesy of NBC News

Procedure

If we consider the feature a mini-documentary — and in many instances it is exactly that — the procedure for its preparation is similar to that of the documentary. After a topic is chosen, a preliminary outline is developed and research is done. As with the "Day By Day" series, the writer and researcher are frequently the same person. Following completion of the research a rundown sheet or, as it is sometimes called, a working script, is prepared. From this working script the feature or mini-documentary is made. Usually much more material is obtained than called for, and the working script provides a base for editing, both as to organization and content of the program and as to time. Ideally, the final working script and the transcript of the program as aired would be identical, except that the transcript would contain the complete program material, the "actualities" of interviews and other non-announcer input. Some producers prepare their scripts in rundown or working script form, without the actualities. Others include the complete actualities.

The following are the working script and the transcript with the actualities for the same program from CBS Radio's "The American Challenge" series. They illustrate the form the writer uses *after* he or she has completed the research and, in this instance, after the producer has put together the necessary material. A preliminary working script would not usually contain the timing and the precise quote of the interviewee, but would indicate the name of the person to be interviewed and the gist of the material sought. A final working script, however, for final editing, would contain the fuller information.

"THE AMERICAN CHALLENGE"

pgm 10   ward   to live free

MUSIC THEME   up 3 seconds then under for
    CRONKITE: The American Challenge. Thirty Special Reports this weekend brought to you by _____.

THEME UP TO END AT :13
    CRONKITE: This is Walter Cronkite, CBS News, reporting on the CBS Radio Network. In a time when the relationship between Great Britain and the colonists in America was steadily growing worse, Thomas Jefferson wrote: "The God who gave us life gave us liberty at the same time; the hand of force may destroy, but cannot disjoin them."
    That's not true anymore. Drugs, electrical stimulation of the brain, the techniques of behavioral psychology can leave life, while taking liberty. An American Challenge, after this. (COMMERCIAL INSERT)
    Defining freedom is probably a job better left to philosophy students and the people who put dictionaries together. Historian Blanche Cook, a teacher at New York's John Jay College of Criminal Justice believes it is easier to say what freedom is not.
        In: You start looking at what . . .
        Runs: :30
        Out: . . . and stops this man.
    Behavioral psychologist B. F. Skinner believes that a concern for freedom has outlived its time.
        In: I think you can show . . .
        Runs: :36
        Out: . . . then the behavior will change.
    Our very survival, says Dr. Skinner, depends upon controlling people. And the techniques for maintaining that control are available.
        In: I think we have that . . .
        Runs: :16
        Out: . . . to use it.
    For historian Cook, the problem is quite different.
        In: We're using this really splendid . . .
        Runs: ·25
        Out: . . . which could free us, really.
    To find freedom and the limits of freedom. A matter for debate and an American Challenge; to make liberty more than a word stamped on our coins.
    This is Walter Cronkite, CBS News.

#10 — TO LIVE FREE

(MUSIC)

WALTER CRONKITE: THE AMERICAN CHALLENGE. Thirty special broadcasts this weekend. This is Walter Cronkite reporting on the CBS Radio Network.

In a time when the relationship between Great Britain and the colonists was steadily growing worse, Thomas Jefferson wrote, "The God who gave us life, gave us liberty at the same time. The hand of force may destroy, but cannot disjoin them."

That's not true anymore. Drugs, electrical stimulation of the brain, the techniques of behavioral psychology can leave life, while taking liberty. An American challenge, after this.

*   *   *

CRONKITE: Defining freedom is probably a job better left to philosophy students and the people who put dictionaries together. Historian Blanche Cook, a teacher at New York's John Jay College of Criminal Justice, believes it is easier to say what freedom is not.

BLANCHE COOK: You start looking at what the various police departments, for instance, have done with the technology that came out of Vietnam. The most bizarre thing of all is a fancy program: plant an electrode into somebody's brain who steals a lot, let's say, and gets arrested all the time. And he's going downtown to the supermarket, let's say, and all of a sudden the computer picks up that his adrenalin is going fast, and his heartbeat is going fast, and they figure out, well, he's going to steal something. The computer programs a shock, and stops this man.

CRONKITE: Behavioral psychologist B. F. Skinner believes that a concern for freedom has outlived its time.

B. F. SKINNER: I think you can show that we are misguided in our insistence on the right of the individual, for example, to breed as he wants, or to consume more than a reasonable share of the resources of the world, to pollute the environment. There are not real freedoms, they are the products of our present culture. And if we can change that culture, then the behavior will change.

CRONKITE: Our very survival, says Doctor Skinner, depends upon controlling people, and the techniques for maintaining that control are available.

SKINNER: I think we have that. We have the rudiments of it. And we have to change our culture in such a way that we will be permitted to use it.

CRONKITE: For historian Cook, the problem is quite different.

COOK: We're using this really splendid technology, which could be used to feed people, you know, to really make our lives very comfortable, we're using it to control people. I think that's the really big challenge: how do we use the technology that we have, which could free us, really.

CRONKITE: To find freedom, and the limits of freedom, a matter for debate, and an American challenge, to make liberty more than a word stamped on our coins.

This is Walter Cronkite, CBS News.

Courtesy of CBS News

THE DOCUMENTARY

IT IS SOMETIMES said that next to the drama the documentary is the highest form of televion and radio art. Many broadcast news personnel say that the documentary, combining as it does news, special events, features, music and drama, *is* the highest form. At its best the documentary not only synthesizes the creative arts of the broadcast media, but it also makes a signal contribution to public understanding by interpreting the past, analyzing the present or anticipating the future. Sometimes it does all these in a single program, in highly dramatic form, combining intellectual and emotional meaning.

Types

Robert Flaherty is considered the seminal figure in the development of the modern documentary. His "Nanook of the North," completed in

1922, set a pattern for a special type of documentary film: that which went beneath the exterior of life and carefully selected those elements which dramatized people's relationships to the outer and inner factors of their world. Flaherty started with an attitude toward people: he eulogized their strength and nobility in a hostile or, at the very least, difficult environment.

Pare Lorentz, noted for his productions of "The Plow That Broke the Plains" and "The River" under Franklin D. Roosevelt's administration in the 1930's, forwarded another type of documentary: the presentation of a problem affecting a large number of people and the ways in which that problem could be solved. Lorentz's type of documentary called for positive action on the part of the viewer to remedy an unfortunate or ugly situation. A third type of documentary is exemplified in the British film, "Night Mail," produced by innovator John Grierson. The details of ordinary, everyday existence — in this instance the delivery in Britain of the night mail — are presented in a dramatic, but non-sensational manner. In this type we see people and/or things as they really are; we receive factual information without a special attitude or point of view expressed or stimulated.

These types (the student of documentary writing is urged to view the films noted above) provide the bases for writing the television and radio documentary. The documentary for the mass media may use one of the three approaches or — and this frequently is the case — combine two or more of the types in varying degrees.

Form

Although the documentary is dramatic, it is not a drama in the sense of the fictional play. It is more or less a faithful representation of a true story. This is not to say, however, that all documentaries are unimpeachably true. Editing and narration can make any series of sequences seem other than what they really are. The documentary form is flexible. The semi-documentary or fictional documentary has achieved a certain degree of popularity. Based on reality, it is not necessarily factual. It may take authentic characters but fictionalize the events of their lives; it may present the events accurately but fictionalize the characters; it may take real people and/or real events and speculate, as authentically as possible, in order to fill in documentary gaps; it may take several situations and characters from life and create a semi-true composite picture. Some of Norman Corwin's semi-documentaries, such as "On A Note of Triumph," raised radio to its highest creative levels.

Although the documentary deals with issues, people and events of the news, it is not a news story. It is an exploration behind and beneath the obvious. It goes much more in depth than does a news story, exploring not only what happened but, as far as possible, the reasons for what happened, the attitudes and feelings of the people involved, the interpretations of experts, the reactions of other citizens who might be affected, and the implications and significance of the subject not only for some individuals, but for the whole of society.

The difference between the news story and the documentary may sometimes not relate so much to content as it does to approach. Where the news report is oriented toward objectivity, the documentary is oriented toward interpretation and often presents a distinct point of view. For example, a news program on a murder in New York City may present fully all the known factual material. A documentary on the same subject — such as the classic "Who Killed Michael Farmer?" on page 189 — covers considerably more in background and character exploration and provides an understanding and an impact that otherwise would be missing.

Ordinarily, the documentary is filmed or taped out in the field. The fact that a program may be done outside the studio, however, does not guarantee that it will be a good one or a better one than that done only in the studio. Sometimes small stations can't send out a crew for the time it takes to prepare the program effectively. In that case the documentary may have to be done in the studio with already existing materials and good transitional narration. However, actualities — the people and events live on tape — always make for a better documentary, all other factors being equal.

Procedure

Essentially, the documentary contains the real words of real persons (or their writings, published and unpublished, including letters if they are not living or cannot possibly be reached and there is no record of their voices), the moving pictures of their actions (or photos and drawings if film or video tape is unavailable or they lived before motion pictures) and, concomitantly, the sounds and visuals of real events. These materials, sometimes seemingly unrelated, must be put together into a dramatic, cohesive whole and edited according to an outline and then a script. A good documentary script cannot be created in the isolation of one's bedroom, no matter how much inspiration one may find there.

First, the writer must have an idea. What subject of public interest is worthy of documentary treatment? The idea for the program frequently comes not from the writer, but from the producer. Increasing hunger and starvation in the world? Murder and violence by a given government to supress political enemies? Political and economic discrimination against minorities? Corruption in a country's leadership? Economic crises and unemployment? People's protests against a war? What about something on the scenic pleasures of southern California? Or the experience of riding a train across Siberia? Or the life and times of Leonardo Da Vinci?

A documentary does not have to be controversial, but can be more a feature of the how-it-works or how-it-was or how-to type. The very use of live people and live events, however, does make most documentaries pertinent to ongoing life and, therefore, to a greater or lesser degree, controversial.

In the 1970s the investigative documentary came into focus — possibly because such events as Watergate, impeachment, the Pentagon Papers and other national and international actions offered so much to investigate.

All documentaries should have a point of view. The writer and/or producer may suggest; the network and/or sponsor have the final word. What is the *purpose* of the particular documentary? To present an objective many-sided view of a community's traditions or problems? By lack of criticism, to justify violence as a means of international political gain? To show the courage of a minority group in a hostile social environment? To present the attitudes and motivations of dissident and nonconforming college students as well as their overt actions? To show that the only way to find true rejuvenation of body and spirit is to spend all one's vacation time in encounter groups — or health clubs or dude ranches — in northern California? To what degree will the writer's personal beliefs (or those of the producer or network or agency or sponsor) determine program content (see Chapter 1 for comments on censorship)?

When the subject and the point of view are determined, the real work starts: from thorough research in libraries, to personal visits to people and places, to investigations of what video and audio materials on the subject are already available. When the research is completed, the writer can prepare a more definitive outline.

Until the material is accumulated and editing begins, and work on a final script is started, the writer's work may seem temporarily in abeyance. Not so! As a writer, you may be involved intricately in the production process. You may suggest the specific materials to be obtained, sometimes recommend the orientation these materials should take, and even help gather them. In terms of getting actualities on tape, you may write transition material, including lead-ins and lead-outs and, in some cases, the questions and even some of the answers for interviews. You may prepare preliminary narration to tie the materials together as a final script begins to take shape in your mind. As the materials come in you will be constantly revising your outline, making it more and more complete, and you may begin juxtaposing narration with the filmed or taped material.

After all the materials have been gathered and have been heard, usually many, many times by the writer, the development of a final script can begin in earnest. The final script is used for the selection and organization of the specific materials to be used in the final editing and taping of the program. It is significant, in terms of the high degree of coordination and cooperation needed to complete a good documentary, that in a great many instances the writer also serves as the producer and even as the director and editor.

Sometimes an entire documentary may come from just a few minutes of audio tape or from a short piece of film which carries material available to no other reporter or station. The writer may decide that this material would make a good beginning or a good ending, and plan the rest of the program around it. For example, a network may have an exclusive film of a minute's duration of a secret meeting between the heads of two major world powers. From this short film, with the aid of newsreels, interviews and further filming not necessarily related directly to the event, a documentary program can be created.

Technique

Human interest is the key to good documentary writing. Even if you want to present only facts, even if the facts seem stilted and dry, make them dramatic. Develop them in terms of the people they represent. Even if the subject is inanimate — such as a new mechanical invention — endow it with live attributes; and, indeed, we have all known machines that seem more alive then some people we have known! The documentary script should be developed in dramatic terms: the exploration of character, the introduction of a conflict (the problem which creates the happening that requires documentary treatment), and the development of this conflict through the revelation of the complications involved until a crisis is reached. Although the big things create the action, the little things, the human interest elements, are important in creating and holding interest.

The documentary utilizes many elements of the drama, including background music, special settings in television, exotic non-realistic and visually unproducable settings in radio, narration, special effects and, in the semi- or fictionalized documentary, actors portraying real persons, living or dead. A narrator is almost always used in the documentary. Use the narrator judiciously. A narrator who plays too great a role may distract from the "live" material. Avoid the possibility that the program will sound or look like a series of taped interviews or lectures. Make the points clear and concise. Sometimes relatively important material must be deleted — for legal or time reasons — from the presentations of actual persons. A narrator frequently can summarize on-the-spot materials that cannot be presented as actualities.

Application: Radio

Process. A radio documentary may be produced with virtually no budget and little equipment save two or three tape recorders and some tapes. One such documentary, produced as a college course project and the recipient of a national award for public service reporting, illustrates how simple and direct the documentary-making process can be.

• *If you are studying this chapter as a member of a class or other writing group, plan to write and produce, with your colleagues, a similar documentary based on a problem in your community.*

First, the class decided on a subject: the problems of the small farmer in the Piedmont region of North Carolina (where the University is located) and the possible relationships of these problems to politics.

The three major documentary types were combined in the purpose of the documentary: to present information in a straightforward, unbiased manner; to show by implication that there was a problem that had to be solved and to indicate several possible solutions; and to present the farmer as a persevering person in a difficult economic environment. It was decided that not only farmers, but experts from the university should be interviewed and their tapes edited in a sort of counterpoint fashion.

Research was the next step, with as much material as could be found on the problem gathered from an examination of all available literature and from preliminary talks with farmers and persons familiar with the farm problem. The subject and purpose were clarified further and, on the basis of the projected findings of the documentary, specific interviewees were chosen — farmers in terms of size, location and crop of the farm, and experts in terms of their academic department and special area of study.

A careful distillation of material already gathered led to the formation of a series of pertinent and inter-related questions to be asked the farmers and the experts. After the interviews were completed, a script containing the narration and a description of the taped material to be inserted was developed from all the material available, including tapes, library research and personal interviews. An analysis of the script indicated places that were weak, some because of the lack of material and others because of the superfluity of material. Further field work and the addition and pruning of material resulted in a final script, ready for the editing process.

The following are excerpts from a composite of the script and a verbatim transcription of the program. The final script is shown in capitals; the material in parentheses is that actually recorded and incorporated into the program with the narration. Note here the use of numbers indicating the tape and cut to be used, with notations of the first and last words of each cut to help the editor.

• *One criticism of this script may be that it tries to cover too many subjects. Another may be that it is not sufficiently dramatic. If you find any validity to these criticisms, take the material contained in the script, plus other material that you can get through your personal research, and rewrite this documentary in outline form, improving on it as you think necessary.*

THE PIEDMONT, NORTH CAROLINA FARMER AND POLITICS

OPEN COLD: TAPE #1, CUT 1, DUPREE SMITH: "I WOULD LIKE VERY MUCH . . .
               BEST PLACE TO WORK."
               (I would like very much to spend my entire life here on the farm
               because I feel like being near the land and being near the soil and
               seeing the operation of God on this earth is the best place to live and
               the best place to work.)

MUSIC: IN, UP, AND UNDER

NARRATOR: THIS IS THE SMALL FARMER IN THE PIEDMONT OF NORTH
               CAROLINA.

MUSIC: UP AND OUT

NARRATOR: YOU ARE LISTENING TO "THE PIEDMONT, NORTH CAROLINA
               FARMER AND POLITICS." THE VOICE YOU JUST HEARD WAS
               THAT OF DUPREE SMITH, A FARMER IN PIEDMONT, NORTH
               CAROLINA. IN RURAL AMERICA A CENTURY AGO THE FARM
               PROBLEM WAS AN INDIVIDUAL ONE OF DIGGING A LIVING OUT
               OF THE LAND. EACH FARMER SOLVED HIS OWN INDIVIDUAL
               PROBLEMS WITHOUT GOVERNMENT AID. NEARLY EVERYONE
               FARMED. TODAY, BECAUSE OF INCREASING COST OF MAIN-
               TAINING CROPS, LARGER SURPLUSES, HEAVIER STORAGE COSTS
               AND LOWER FARM INCOME, THE SMALL FARMER IN NORTH
               CAROLINA, AS WELL AS ACROSS THE NATION, HAS BEEN
               UNABLE TO DEPEND ON HIS LAND FOR A LIVING. PRODUCTION
               CONTINUED TO GROW. SURPLUSES MOUNTED. FARM INCOMES
               FELL AND THE GOVERNMENT SUBSIDIES NECESSARILY GREW.

PROFESSOR
KOVENOCK: TAPE #2, CUT 1: "THE COMMON PROBLEMS . . . ARE THESE."
               (The common problems shared by almost all national farmers today
               and, at the same time, most North Carolina farmers, are these.)

NARRATOR: YOU ARE LISTENING TO PROFESSOR DAVID KOVENOCK OF THE
               POLITICAL SCIENCE DEPARTMENT OF THE UNIVERSITY OF
               NORTH CAROLINA.

KOVENOCK: TAPE #2, CUT 2: "FIRST OF ALL . . . SHELTER FOR HIS FAMILY."
               (First of all, a decline in the income going to the farmer — a problem
               of — this is particularly for, let us say, the marginal farmer, the farmer
               with a small operation in North Carolina and the rest of the country —
               the problem of obtaining employment off the farm, that is, some rela-
               tively attractive alternative to continuing an operation on the farm that
               is becoming insufficient for feeding, clothing, and buying shelter for
               his family.)

NARRATOR: THIS IS DUPREE SMITH'S PROBLEM.

SMITH: TAPE #1, CUT 2: "YES, THAT WAS MY DESIRE . . . PART TIME
               AND WORKING."
               (Yes, that was my desire after returning from service, was to go back
               to nature and live and raise a family where I felt that I would enjoy
               living to the fullest. For several years, on this same amount of land, I
               was able to support my family and myself adequately. For the last year
               or two, this has been on the decrease. The decline has been to such
               extent, that I've had to go into other fields — my wife helping part time
               and working.)

NARRATOR: WHAT SPECIFICALLY ARE DUPREE SMITH'S PROBLEMS?

KOVENOCK: TAPE #2, CUT 3: "THE COMMON PROBLEM . . . OCCUPATIONAL PURSUIT?"
(The common problem shared by the North Carolina farmer and by the national farmer would be, first of all, the condition of agriculture, the relationship of the supply of agricultural commodities to the demand and, of course, consequently, the price that the farmer receives which, of course, now is somewhat depressed. The second major problem is the condition of the rest of the economy as a whole — that is, is it sufficiently good so that the farmer has some alternatives to continuing his, currently, rather unsatisfactory occupational pursuit?)

NARRATOR: FARMERS ARE MARKETING MORE, BUT ARE RECEIVING LOWER PRICES FOR THEIR CROPS AND PRODUCE. DR. PHILLIPS RUSSELL, A FORMER COLLEGE PROFESSOR AND RETIRED FARMER, HAS THIS TO SAY:

PHILLIPS
RUSSELL: TAPE #3, CUT 1: "THE FARMER HAS BEEN LOSING . . . IN AN UNPROTECTED MARKET."
(The farmer has been losing out everywhere, because he has to buy the things that he needs in a protected market and he has to sell in an unprotected market.)

NARRATOR: WHAT IS THE FARMER'S ANSWER TO THIS PROBLEM? FARMING HAS BECOME A BUSINESS INSTEAD OF A WAY OF LIFE. THE FARMER IS FORCED TO CURTAIL HIS ACTIVITIES ON THE FARM IN ORDER TO SUPPORT HIS FAMILY. DR. RUSSELL SAYS:

RUSSELL: TAPE #3, CUT 2: "THAT'S THE ONLY WAY . . . 24-HOUR FARMER."
(That's the only way that a man can continue in farming — is to make some extra money in town to spend it out in the country because he's losing everywhere as a 24-hour farmer.)

NARRATOR: FARMER HARRY WOODS COMMENTS:

HARRY
WOODS: TAPE #4, CUT 1: "I WOULD HATE . . . AT THIS TIME."
(I would hate to have to try — let's put it that way — right at this time.)

INTERVIEWER: TAPE #1, CUT 1 (CONT.): "WOULD YOU LIKE . . . IT FULL TIME?"
(Would you like to be able to work it full time?)

WOODS: TAPE #4, CUT 1 (CONT.): "WELL, I ENJOY . . . IT'S PRETTY ROUGH."
(Well, I enjoy farming. I enjoy it, but as far as actually making a living out of it, I would hate to think that I had to do it, because it's pretty rough.)

NARRATOR: MANY BELIEVE THAT THE BASIS FOR SOLVING THE PROBLEM LIES AT THE FEDERAL GOVERNMENT LEVEL. HARDEST HIT IS THE FARMER WHO CAN LEAST AFFORD IT, THE SMALL COMMER-CIAL FARMERS WORKING INFERIOR LAND. THEY LACK ADEQUATE CAPITAL TO IMPROVE THEIR HOMES. MUCH OF THEIR EFFORT GOES INTO PRODUCING THEIR OWN FOOD. OFTEN THEY DON'T HAVE THE MECHANICAL AIDS TO MAKE THEM MORE EFFICIENT. THEY ALSO GET LITTLE BENEFIT FROM THE SUBSIDIES AND HIGH SUPPORTS BECAUSE THEIR YIELD IS LOW AND THEY CAN'T AFFORD TO STORE UNTIL THE GOVERNMENT MAKES PAYMENT.

RUSSELL: TAPE #3, CUT 3: "IF FARMING . . . THAT'D BE FATAL."
                  (If farming is to be continued, and the country still has to rely on the
                  farms for three very important things: food, feed, and fiber, and if
                  the farming system collapses, we won't have enough fiber, and in case
                  of war, that'd be fatal.)
                                          *   *   *

NARRATOR: BESIDES PRICE SUPPORTS, STORAGE AND SOIL BANKS, THE
                  GOVERNMENT SPENDS SOME TWO AND A HALF BILLION DOLLARS
                  TO OPERATE ITS OTHER FUNCTIONS FOR THE IMPROVEMENT OF
                  FARMING. THERE IS LITTLE AGREEMENT AS TO JUST WHAT
                  ROLE GOVERNMENT SHOULD PLAY IN ASSISTING THE FARMER.
                  FARMER HARRY WOODS HAD THIS TO SAY:

WOODS: TAPE #4, CUT 2: "THE FARM PROBLEM . . . TO HAVE THEM."
                  (The farm problem has been with us ever since I've known anything
                  about the farm, and there have been both sides in, and it's never been
                  solved yet. Until they really get down to business and want to solve it,
                  why, it never will be. Now, you said something about politics, why, you
                  know, and I think that everybody else realizes that there is politics in
                  the farm program as they are administered. By the time that they go
                  into the Congress and come out, you know what happens, and, it's
                  difficult to ever work out something that, well, that is workable. But, as
                  far as Republicans or Democrats, why, we've had farm problems under
                  both parties, and I think we'll continue to have them.)

KOVENOCK: TAPE #2, CUT 4: "THERE'S COMMON AGREEMENT . . . THIRTY-
                  EIGHT CENTS."
                  (There's common agreement, common ground for agreement, that
                  during the last seven or eight years that farm income has gone down
                  roughly twenty-five per cent. The farm purchasing power is at the
                  lowest point since sometime during the 1930's. Further, we have rela-
                  tively great social dislocations among farmers and non-farmers in rural
                  America due to the relative decline of the position of the farmer in the
                  economic sphere. We now have more employees in the Department of
                  Agriculture than we've ever had before, and, of course, they are serving
                  fewer farmers. The size of the surplus is, of course, grounds for
                  common agreement. It's multiplied six or seven times; it's now worth,
                  roughly, seven billion dollars. And, of course, the farmer's share of the
                  dollars that we spend in the grocery store has declined now to a low
                  point of thirty-eight cents.)
                                          *   *   *

MUSIC: IN AND UNDER

NARRATOR: THESE ARE THE PROBLEMS.

MUSIC: FADE OUT

NARRATOR: THE ANSWERS ARE NOT APPARENT. THE FARM INCOME
                  DILEMMA SPELLS TROUBLE, NOT ONLY FOR THE FARMERS, BUT
                  FOR THE PEOPLE WHO DO BUSINESS WITH THEM, POLITICIANS,
                  GOVERNMENT OFFICIALS AND TAX PAYERS ALIKE. WHAT DOES
                  THE FARMER, AS A MEMBER OF THE AMERICAN SOCIETY,
                  DESERVE? PROFESSOR S. H. HOBBS OF THE SOCIOLOGY
                  DEPARTMENT OF THE UNIVERSITY OF NORTH CAROLINA HAD
                  THIS TO SAY:

HOBBS: TAPE #5, CUT 1: "ONE IS THE PROBLEM . . . ECONOMIC
                  SYSTEM."
                  (One is the problem of maintaining income adequate to maintain a

level of living comparable with other groups. This does not mean that farmers deserve an income equal to that of any other group, but he does deserve to have an income that enables him to live comfortably in the American economic system.)

NARRATOR: IN A REGULATED, PROTECTED, AND PARTIALLY SUBSIDIZED ECONOMY SUCH AS OURS, THE FARMER REQUIRES CONSIDERABLE PROTECTION. THE TASK IS TO DEVISE NEW METHODS WHICH WILL PROVIDE HIM WITH AN ADEQUATE INCOME FOR THE VITAL FOOD WHICH HE PRODUCES.

SMITH: TAPE #1, CUT 1: "I WOULD LIKE . . . PLACE TO WORK."
(I would like very much to spend my entire life here on the farm because I feel like being near the land and being near the soil and seeing the operation of God on this earth is the best place to live and the best place to work.)

MUSIC: IN, UP, HOLD, UNDER.

NARRATOR: YOU HAVE BEEN LISTENING TO "THE PIEDMONT, NORTH CAROLINA, FARMER AND POLITICS." THIS PROGRAM WAS A STUDENT PRODUCTION OF THE RADIO PRODUCTION CLASS IN THE DEPARTMENT OF RADIO, TELEVISION AND MOTION PICTURES OF THE UNIVERSITY OF NORTH CAROLINA. ASSOCIATED WITH THE PRODUCTION WERE: BUD CARTER, YOSHI CHINEN, JIM CLARK, WILLIAM GAY, ROGER KOONCE, JOHN MOORE, ANITA ROSEFIELD, ALEX WARREN, ANNE WILLIAMS, STEVE SILVERSTEIN AS ENGINEER, AND WAYNE UPCHURCH, YOUR ANNOUNCER.

MUSIC: UP AND OUT.

Structure. One of the broadcasting's finest documentaries was CBS' "Who Killed Michael Farmer?", an exploration in depth of a murder, the murderers and their environment. It is not only a classic, but remains an excellent example today of how to write documentaries. Part of the documentary is presented here, with underlined comments analyzing the structure of the script and some of the writing techniques used.

"WHO KILLED MICHAEL FARMER?"

<u>OPENS COLD:</u>

MURROW: This is Ed Murrow. Here is how a mother and a father remember their son — Michael Farmer.

ET: <u>MR. AND MRS. FARMER:</u>

MRS. FARMER: Michael was tall and very good looking. He had blond hair and blue eyes. Maybe I'm prejudiced as a mother, but I thought he had a saintly face.

MR. FARMER: He was always laughing and joking. He was a very courageous and spirited boy. He was athletic, even though he walked with a limp from an attack of polio when he was ten years old. He was an excellent student who had great plans for his future. It's a hard thing to realize that there is no future any longer.

MURROW: Michael Farmer died on the night of July 30, 1957. He was fifteen years old. He was stabbed and beaten to death in a New York City park. Boys in a teenage street gang were arrested for this crime. Ten gang members — under fifteen years of age — were convicted of juvenile delinquency and committed to state training schools. Seven other boys — fifteen to eighteen — stood trial for first degree murder . . . were defended by twenty-seven court-appointed lawyers. Their trial lasted ninety-three days; ended last Tuesday. This was the verdict of an all male, blue ribbon jury.

ET: JUROR:

We found Louis Alvarez and Charles Horton guilty of murder in the second degree, and we also found Lencio de Leon and Leroy Birch guilty of manslaughter in the second degree. We found Richard Hills and George Melendez not guilty because we believe these boys were forced to go along with the gang the night of the murder. We also found John McCarthy not guilty because we were convinced, beyond a reasonable doubt, that this boy was mentally sick and didn't know what was going on at any time.

MURROW: It would seem that this case now is closed. All that remains is for a judge to pass sentence. Under the law, the gang alone is guilty of the murder of Michael Farmer. But there is more to be said. More is involved here, than one act of violence, committed on one summer night. The roots of this crime go back a long ways. In the next hour — you will hear the voices of boys and adults involved in the case. This is <u>not</u> a dramatization.

The tragedy first became news on the night of July 30, 1957. At 6:30 on this steaming summer evening in New York City, the Egyptian Kings and Dragons gang began to assemble. They met outside a neighborhood hangout — a candy story at 152nd Street and Broadway, in Manhattan's upper West Side. They came from a twenty-block area . . . from teeming tenements, rooming houses and housing projects. One of their leaders remembers the number of boys present this night.

    A standard method of effectively opening a radio documentary is to select carefully cut of the mass of taped material several short statements by persons involved and present them immediately in order to get the audience attention and interest as well as to tell, sharply and concretely, what the program is about. This is especially effective here in the opening statements of Mr. and Mrs. Farmer. The stark nature of the beginning of the program — it opens cold, no introduction, no music — lends force to the opening. Short opening quotes are not usually sufficient, however, to provide enough background information. The narrator condenses and states in terse terms the necessary additional material. The type of documentary is suggested close to the beginning. The statement: "But there is more to be said. More is involved here . . . the roots of crime go back a long ways" indicates the line of development: not only will the event and the people involved be explored in depth, but a problem will be presented and solutions will be sought.

ET: GANG MEMBER:

We had a lot o' little kids, big kids, we had at least seventy-five — then a lot of 'em had to go home before nine o'clock; we was supposed to leave at nine o'clock but then we changed our plans to ten o'clock, you know. So I told a lot o' little kids I don't wanna see them get into trouble, you know, nice guys, so I told them they could go home. So they went home. That left us with around twenty-one kids.

MORROW: People sitting on the stoops and garbage cans along this street watched them . . . grouped together, talking excitedly. They called each other by their nicknames: Magician, Big Man, Little King, Boppo. No one bothered to ask what they were talking about. This boy remembers.

ET: GANG MEMBER:

                  They were talking about what they were going to do and everything.
                  They were going to fight and everything. But they'd never planned
                  nothing. They just said we were gonna go to the fight and we were
                  just gonna get some guys for revenge. They said we ain't gonna let
                  these Jesters beat up any of our guys no more.

MURROW: The Jesters are a street gang in an adjoining neighborhood —
                  Washington Heights, where Michael Farmer lived. The two gangs
                  were feuding. Boys on both sides had been beaten and stabbed.
                  There is evidence that this night the gang planned to surprise and
                  attack any Jesters they could find. They came prepared for a fight.

ET: GANG MEMBER:

                  Some picked a stick and some had got some knives and chains out of
                  their houses and everything. One had a bayonette. No, a machete.

MURROW: Holding these weapons they lingered on the corner of a brightly
                  lit street in the heart of a great city. A police station was one block
                  away. One gang leader went to a candy store . . . telephoned the
                  President of a brother gang . . . requested guns and cars for the
                  night's activity . . . was told: "We can't join you. We have troubles
                  of our own tonight." Shortly after nine PM, the gang walked to a
                  nearby park . . . was followed there by some girl friends. A gang
                  member, 14 years old, continues the story.

ET: GANG MEMBER:

                  We went down to the park and sat around for a while. Then we started
                  drinking and we drank whiskey and wine and we was drunk. Then we
                  started talkin' about girls. We started sayin' to the girls that if
                  they get us to bring us some roses an' all that — that if we get
                  caught to write to us and all this.

MURROW: In one hour, Michael Farmer would be dead. The gang prepared to
                  move out. Some had doubts.

Suspense is an important ingredient of the documentary. But it is not the suspense
of finding out what is going to happen. The documentary is based on fact: we already
know. The suspense is in learning the motivations, the inner feelings, the attitudes of
the persons involved even as the actual event is retold. This is implied in the narrator's
previous speech.

ET: GANG MEMBER:

                  I didn't wanna go at first, but they said come on. So then all the big
                  guys forced me to go. I was scared. I was worried. I realized like
                  what I was doing I'd probably get in trouble.

MURROW: They left the park and headed for trouble at about ten PM. They
                  walked uptown toward the neighborhood of the rival gang — the
                  Jesters. They walked in two's and three's to avoid attention. Along
                  the way, they met, by chance, this boy.

ET: GANG MEMBER:

                  I was walkin' uptown with a couple of friends and we ran into Magician
                  and them there. They asked us if we wanted to go to a fight, and we
                  said yes. When they asked me if I wanted to go to a fight, I couldn't
                  say no. I mean I could say no, but for old-times sake, I said yes.

MURROW: He was a former member of the gang—just went along this night,
                  "For Old-times Sake." Next stop: Highbridge Park . . . within the

territory of the Jesters. Michael Farmer lived one block from the park. In the summer, the Egyptian Kings and Dragons fought the Jesters at the park swimming pool. This pool is closed at ten PM but not drained. Boys in the neighborhood frequently slip through a breach in the gate to swim here late at night. The Egyptian Kings and Dragons regrouped near the pool. Two gang members continue the story.

ET: GANG MEMBERS:

FIRST BOY: We were waiting over there, in the grass. Then two guys went down to see if there were a lot of the Jesters down there. To check. I was kind of nervous; felt kind of cold inside.

SECOND BOY: They sent three guys around the block. We walked around the block to see how strong the club was we was gonna fight. To see if they had lots of guys and what-not. What we saw, they had lots of big guys. I'd say about nineteen, twenty or eighteen, like that. And we figured it out so we kept on walking around the block.

MURROW: While their scouts prowled the neighborhood, Michael Farmer and his friend, sixteen year old Roger McShane, were in Mike Farmer's apartment . . . listening to rock 'n' roll records. This is Mrs. Farmer.

We can see the use here of D. W. Griffith's technique of dynamic cutting: switching back and forth between two or more settings and two or more persons or groups of people who are following a parallel course in time and in action. The actions of the gang have been presented in chronological order. Now time is moved back and the actions of Michael Farmer and Roger McShane will catch up in time and place.

ET: MRS. FARMER:

They stayed in his room playin' these new records that they had bought and Michael came out to the kitchen, just as I asked my husband what time it was, to set the clock. It was then five after ten. He asked for a glass of milk and as he walked from the kitchen, he asked, "I'm going to walk Roger home." And that was the last time I saw him.

MURROW: Both boys had been warned by their parents to stay out of Highbridge Park at night. But, as they walked along the street on this steaming July evening, they decided to sneak a swim in the park pool. At this pool, the Egyptian Kings and Dragons were waiting for their scouts to return. Here is what happened next; first in the words of Roger McShane; then in words of the gang members.

ET: McSHANE AND EGYPTIAN KINGS:

McSHANE: It was ten-thirty when we entered the park; we saw couples on the benches, in the back of the pool, and they all stared at us, and I guess they must 'ave saw the gang there — I don't think they were fifty or sixty feet away. When we reached the front of the stairs, we looked up and there was two of their gang members on top of the stairs. They were two smaller ones, and they had garrison belts wrapped around their hands. They didn't say nothin' to us, they looked kind of scared.

FIRST BOY: I was scared. I knew they were gonna jump them, an' everythin' and I was scared. When they were comin' up, they all were separatin' and everything like that.

McSHANE: I saw the main body of the gang slowly walk out of the bushes, on my right. I turned around fast, to see what Michael was going to do, and this kid came runnin' at me with the belts. Then I ran, myself, and told Michael to run.

SECOND BOY: He couldn't run anyway, cause we were all around him. So then I said, "You're a Jester," and he said "Yeah," and I punched him in the face. And then somebody hit him with a bat over the head. And then I kept punchin' him. Some of them were too scared to do anything. They were just standin' there, lookin'.

THIRD BOY: I was watchin' him. I didn't wanna hit him, at first. Then I kicked him twice. He was layin' on the ground, lookin' up at us. I kicked him on the jaw, or some place; then I kicked him in the stomach. That was the least I could do, was kick 'im.

FOURTH BOY: I was aimin' to hit him, but I didn't get a chance to hit him. There was so many guys on him — I got scared when I saw the knife go into the guy, and I ran right there. After everybody ran, this guy stayed, and started hittin' him with a machete.

MURROW: The rest of the gang pursued Roger McShane.

ET: McSHANE:

I ran down the hill and there was three more of the gang members down at the bottom of the hill, in the baseball field; and the kids chased me down hill, yelling to them to get me.

MURROW: Members of the gang remember.

ET: EGYPTIAN KINGS AND McSHANE:

FIRST BOY: Somebody yelled out, "Grab him. He's a Jester." So then they grabbed him. Mission grabbed him, he turned around and stabbed him in the back. I was . . . I was stunned. I couldn't do nuthin'. And then Mission — he went like that and he pulled : . . he had a switch blade and he said, "you're gonna hit him with the bat or I'll stab you." So I just hit him lightly with the bat.

SECOND BOY: Mission stabbed him and the guy he . . . like hunched over. He's standin' up and I knock him down. Then he was down on the ground, everybody was kickin' him, stompin' him, punchin' him, stabbin' him so he tried to get back up and I knock him down again. Then the guy stabbed him in the back with a bread knife.

THIRD BOY: I just went like that, and I stabbed him with the bread knife. You know, I was drunk so I just stabbed him. (LAUGHS) He was screamin' like a dog. He was screamin' there. And then I took the knife out and I told the other guys to run. So I ran and then the rest of the guys ran with me. They wanted to stay there and keep on doin' it, so I said, "No, come on. Don't kill the guy." And we ran.

ET: FOURTH BOY: The guy that stabbed him in the back with the bread knife, he told me that when he took the knife out o' his back, he said, "Thank you."

McSHANE: They got up fast right after they stabbed me. And I just lay there on my stomach and there was five of them as they walked away. And as they walked away they . . . this other big kid came down with a machete or some large knife of some sort, and he wanted to stab me too with it. And they told him, "No, come on. We got him. We messed him up already. Come on." And they took off up the hill and they all walked up the hill and right after that they all of 'em turned their heads and looked back at me. I got up and staggered into the street to get a cab. And I got in a taxi and I asked him to take me to the Medical Center and get my friend and I blacked out.

MURROW: The gang scattered and fled from the park. This boy believes he is the last gang member who saw Michael Farmer this night.

194

ET: GANG MEMBER:

While I was runnin' up the footpath, I saw somebody staggering in the
bushes and I just looked and turned around, looked up and kept on
runnin'. I think that was the Farmer boy, he was staggerin' in the
bushes.

The suspense has been built and a climax reached. The selection and editing of taped
materials to tell the story of the assault and murder are done magnificently. Excerpts from
the taped interviews were selected to follow a chronological pattern and to present the
actions, feelings and attitudes of the gang members in terms of increasing tempo and
violence. Various physical and emotional viewpoints are presented, all relating to one
another and building the suspense into an ultimate explosion. The documentary should be
dramatic. Is there any doubt about the existence of drama in the preceding sequence?
The audience is put into the center of the action, feeling it perhaps even more strongly than
if the incident were fictionalized and presented, as such incidents frequently are, on a
"private-eye" series. Could any line of a play be more dramatic than, in context, "That
was the least I could do, was kick 'im," or "(LAUGHS) He was screamin' like a dog," or
"The guy that stabbed him in the back with the bread knife, he told me that when he took
the knife out o' his back, he said 'Thank you'."?

MURROW: He left behind a boy nearly dead . . . continued home . . . had a glass
of milk . . . went to bed. But then.

ET: GANG MEMBER:

I couldn't sleep that night or nuthin' cause I used to fall asleep for about
half an hour. Wake up again during the middle of the night. My
mother said, "What was the matter with you? Looks like something
is wrong." I said, "Nothin'."

MURROW: That boy used a baseball bat in the attack. This boy used a bread
knife.

ET: GANG MEMBER:

First I went to the river to throw my knife away and then I went home.
An' then I couldn't sleep. I was in bed. My mother kept on askin' me
where was I and I . . . I told her, you know, that I was in the movies.
I was worried about them two boys. If they would die . . . I knew I
was gonna get caught.

MURROW: At Presbyterian Medical Center, Roger McShane was on the critical
list. Before undergoing major surgery that saved his life, he told
about the attack in Highbridge Park. The official police record reveals what happened next. The speaker: New York City's Deputy
Police Commissioner, Walter Arm.

ET: COMMISSIONER ARM:

A member of the hospital staff notified the police and patrolmen of the
34th precinct arrived at the hospital a few minutes afterwards and
learned from the McShane boy that his friend Michael Farmer was
still in the part, under attack. The patrolmen rushed to the park,
where they found the Farmer boy just before eleven PM. He was lying
on the ground off the footpath and moaning in pain. The policemen
were soon joined by detectives and young Farmer told them, "The
Egyptian Kings got me." The Farmer boy made this comment as he
was being rushed to the hospital at 11:05 PM. The parents of the boy
were notified.

MURROW: Mr. and Mrs. Farmer continue the story.

ET: MR. AND MRS. FARMER:

MR. FARMER: The Sergeant from the 34th Precinct called us, and asked who I was, and was I the father of Michael Farmer. I said I was, and he said, "Well, your boy is in Mother Cabrini Hospital, in serious condition." I identified myself further, as a fireman in this area, and he said, "Oh, I'll come right down and give you a lift down to the hospital." So this sergeant drove us down to the hospital; as we walked in, the officer who was on duty there called the sergeant, and he said the boy had died fifteen minutes earlier.

MRS. FARMER: And the sister there in the hospital, took us downstairs to identify the body. He had an expression as though he was just calling for help.

MR. FARMER: Well, it was real bad . . . he was my number one boy.

MURROW: This boy had never been in trouble with the police. Several Egyptian Kings and Dragons claim they often saw him with the Jesters; assumed he was a member. The Jesters say neither Farmer nor McShane belonged to their gang . . . and according to police, there is no evidence to the contrary. From the Jesters, police learned which boys might have been involved in the assault at Highbridge Park. At 6:30 AM, this gang member heard somebody knocking at the door of his apartment in a housing project.

ET: GANG MEMBER:

I hear this knockin' on the door. I didn't think it was the police, you know. 'Cause, you know, I thought I wasn't gonna get caught, so I was layin' in bed and told my mother, "Mommie, I think that's the milkman knockin' on the door or somebody." She said, "Why don't you answer it," and I said, "No, I'm in my underwear." So she says, "OK, I'll go." She opened the door and my mother comes over, "You get in any trouble last night?" And I says, "No, Mommie, I didn't get in no trouble last night." And then she says, "Well, there's a policeman over here, wants to see you." And I says, "What for," and he says, "Somethin' that happened last night," and I says, "OK," then, I started thinkin' of trying, you know, runnin' away from the house, so I put on my clothes and acted innocent, you know. He said to me, "You know what happened last night?" I say, "No, No. I don't know a thing that happened last night. I was in the car from ten on." He says, "Oh, if that's the truth, you have nothin' to worry about. You like to come down to the police station with us?" And I said, "OK."

MURROW: Another gang member spent the morning in Children's Court, pleading innocent to a robbery committed two weeks earlier. He was released, pending a hearing. When he returned home, police were waiting to question him about the murder of Michael Farmer. This is the boy who used a bread knife in the assault at Highbridge park.

ET: GANG MEMBER:

Well, when we was goin' to the . . . to the paddy wagon, the detective, he kept wipin' his feet on my suit. So I told him to cut it out, and he still won't cut it out. So then, then the Sergeant says, "Cut it out," so then he said, "Why don't you mind your business," and he kept on doin' it. He kept on wipin' his feet on my suit, and I just got the suit out of the cleaners, that's all. I told him, "I just got the suit out of the cleaners," and he says to me, "That's just too bad. That suit belongs in the garbage can." So he kept on wipin' his feet on my suit, and he kept on sayin', "You murderer" and all this. They kept on sayin', "You're gonna get the electric chair, you're gonna get the electric chair." He kept on sayin' that to me; he made me mad. If I had a gun, I would have shot them all.

MURROW: He told us, "I hate cops." The police say his story of what happened in that paddy wagon is fantasy. They also deny threatening another gang member who explains why he wanted to be caught.

ET: GANG MEMBER:

I was crackin' up 'cause I wanted them to hurry up and come and get me and get it over with, so when I got picked up, I felt safe then. We went in the car and then they threatened me. I mean, not exactly a threat, but they told me what was goin' to happen: I'd get beat up if I didn't talk. So I told them, "Tell me, who was the guy that squealed?" They told me, "Who do you think you are, Dillinger or somebody — ya gonna get even with the guy?" I said, "No, I just wanted to know." They said, "No." So they took me to the Precinct; it made me laugh to see all the guys sitting there in the . . . in the . . . when I walked in, everybody said, "Ha ha, " and started laughin' so I felt all right with the fellas then. My girl was sitting there anyway, and she . . . she had the knives.

MURROW: Police found two hunting knives hidden in the bureau drawer of a fifteen-year-old girl-friend of the gang. Two gang members admitted that they gave these knives to the girl after the assault at Highbridge Park. The police record continues.

ET: COMMISSIONER ARM:

The search of the gang during their interrogation yielded five knives, several garrison belts and a heavy length of chain. All of the young men arrested made full admissions to police officers and to representatives from the staff of District Attorney Hogan. At 8:00 PM the following day, seven of the boys were charged with homicide, two others were charged with attempted homicide, and ten others were charged with juvenile delinquency.

MURROW: Police said, "This is the largest group of boys ever arrested for a New York City killing." Statistically, they were among 58 youths in the city arrested in 1957 for murder and non-negligent manslaughter . . . among more than three thousand youths under twenty-one arrested in the nation last year for crimes of major violence . . . and among an estimated one million youths arrested for crimes of all kinds. The father of Michael Farmer attended the preliminary court hearing of the gang members later indicted for the murder of his son. As he watched them arraigned before a judge, he made a judgment of his own.

ET: MR. FARMER:

They are monsters — in my mind I classify them as savage animals. That's all. I don't think that they have any civilization in them. I think they're just two-legged animals. They haven't any concept of living with other people, outside of to show that they can do something worse than the other or to claim any sort of notoriety. These boys didn't even hang their heads, most of them, when they came to court. They stood erect and looked around the court for their relatives. And so forth. One of them had a small smirk when they looked in our direction. They should be put away, and kept away. Or if the penalty is death, to be executed. Certainly they set themselves up in the form of a judge, jury and execution squad in the case of my son. All in the matter of minutes. This is pure jungle activity.

Thus far the script has told what happened. In the material dealing with actions and attitudes after the crime was committed, the script begins to imply that there is more to the story than what happened, that the persons involved are not the two dimensional characters of the television fiction series. Yet, the act was so grievous and wanton that it is not too difficult to come to the same conclusion as Mr. Farmer. This speech indicates a division in the script. Can we simply leave the story there—this is a jungle and the only solution is to destroy the animals therein? The script begins to explore motivation, begins to get behind the problem.

MURROW: Two detectives told the judge at the gang's arraignment, "These boys showed no remorse and gave us little cooperation." At their murder trial, some of the boys testified that police beat and frightened them into making confessions. The police officers accused, denied this under oath. First reports on this crime suggested that at least one gang member had stabbed for thrills. Police said the fourteen-year-old boy who used a bread knife in the attack told them, "I always wanted to know what it would feel like to stick a knife through human bone." This same boy denied to us that he said that; gave us three other reasons for his crime. First.

ET: GANG MEMBER:

I told you I didn't know what I was doing, I was drunk. I went out, you know, I . . . you know, I was drunk, I just went like that, and I stabbed him.

MURROW: We asked him, "Did you know the boy you stabbed?" Answer: "No, but I thought he was a Jester." Question: "Had the Jesters ever done anything to you?" Answer:

ET: GANG MEMBER:

They kept on callin' me a Spick. They kept on saying, "You dirty Spick, get out of this block." Every time I go in the pool, they said to me the same thing. I don't bother them, 'cause, you know, I don't want to get into no trouble with them, but one day they beat me up. You know, there was about five of them, and they wouldn't leave me alone. They beat me up, and I had to take a chance to get the boys so we could beat them up.

MURROW: He said his third reason for stabbing a boy he did not know involved his fear of gang discipline.

ET: GANG MEMBER:

See, because we say before, if anybody don't beat up somebody, when we get back, he's gonna get beat up. So I say, "OK." They got special guys, you know, to keep their eyes on the boys. Anyone who don't swing out is gonna get it when we come back. They got to pass through a line; they got about fifteen boys over here, and fifteen boys over there, and you know, in a straight line, like that. They got to pass through there and they all got belts in their hand.

MURROW: So far, we have heard that a boy was killed because other boys — most of them under fifteen —got drunk, wanted revenge, feared gang discipline. Only one boy charged with murder pleaded not guilty on grounds of insanity. He was declared legally sane. But a psychiatrist testified in court that this boy was epileptic and "incapable of premeditating and deliberating." Court-appointed defense council did not request psychiatric examination of the other six boys on trial for their lives. The jury that convicted some of them heard very little about their mental and emotional make-up. Our reporter tried to get psychiatric reports on the other gang members too young to be tried for murder. He questioned Marion Cohen, head of the treatment service, New York City Youth House. She told him.

ET: MISS COHEN AND REPORTER:

COHEN: We see our function as holding boys remanded temporarily by Children's Court until disposition of their case is made by a judge. While the boy is here, we try to study and diagnose his problem.

REPORTER: Well, now, the younger members of the gang that killed Michael Farmer were brought here. Did you study the individual boys; make reports on them for the judge who was going to try them?

COHEN: No, we did not.

REPORTER: Why not?

COHEN: Because the judge did not request it.

REPORTER: Is this usual practice?

COHEN: No, in most cases, judges are interested in finding out as much as they can about the individual boy's problems, in order to differentiate his needs.

REPORTER: But in this case, nothing was found out about the mental make-up or the individual needs of these boys. Is that right?

COHEN: Yes.

REPORTER: Do you usually wait for the court to request such studies?

COHEN: No, when we are fully staffed, we do a study on every boy who is here for more than a week.

REPORTER: Why didn't you study these boys then?

COHEN: Because we are two-thirds under-staffed. We have only four case-workers for three-hundred boys.

MURROW: The New York City Youth House is a brand-new five-million-dollar building. It has a swimming pool, self-service elevators — the most modern equipment. But there are only four case-workers for three-hundred boys. Reason: low pay and a shortage of trained personnel. Our reporter continues his conversation with Marion Cohen.

ET: MISS COHEN AND REPORTER:

REPORTER: Can you make any generalizations about the gang members you have studied?

COHEN: Yes, these are kids who essentially feel in themselves weak and inadequate . . . and have to present a tough facade to others. Of course, most adolescents feel insecure. But these boys have a distorted idea of what real adequacy is. They become easy prey for leaders whose sole drive is aggressive. They are egged on by their peers to establish a tough reputation . . . each kid daring the other to go one step farther. They have to compete on a level of violence.

MURROW: It would seem that members of the Egyptian Kings and Dragons gang fit the pattern. Consider the statement of this fourteen-year-old gang member who participated in the assault at Highbridge Park.

The interviews with the experts may be considered transition material. It is established that there is a problem. Some of the reasons for the problem are tentatively suggested. The audience now is ready for exploration of the problem and a clarification of the reasons.

ET: GANG MEMBER:

I didn't want to be like . . . you know, different from the other guys. Like they hit him, I hit him. In other words, I didn't want to show myself as a punk. You know, ya always talkin', "Oh man, when I catch a guy, I'll beat him up," and all of that, you know. So after you go out and you catch a guy, and you don't do nothin', they say, "Oh man, he can't belong to no gang, because he ain't gonna do nothin'."

MURROW: Are we to believe that a boy is dead — murdered — because those who killed him fear being called "punks"? Another gang member says he acted to protect his reputation. He calls it "rep."

ET: GANG MEMBER:

Momentarily, I started to thinking about it inside: did I have my mind made up I'm not going to be in no gang. Then I go on inside. Something comes up den here come all my friends coming to me. Like I said before, I'm intelligent and so forth. They be coming to me — then they talk to me about what they gonna do. Like, "Man, we'll go out here and kill this guy." I say, "Yeah." They kept on talkin' and talkin'. I said, "Man, I just gotta go with you." Myself, I don't want to go, but when they start talkin' about what they gonna do, I say, "So, he isn't gonna take over my rep. I ain't gonna let him be known more than me." And I go ahead just for selfishness. I go ahead, and get caught or something; sometimes I get caught, sometimes I don't. I'm in some trouble there.

MURROW: That boy admits that he kicked and punched Roger McShane during the attack at Highbridge Park . . . didn't stab him because he didn't have a knife. We asked, "Suppose you had a knife; would you have used it? Answer:

ET: GANG MEMBER:

If I would of got the knife, I would have stabbed him. That would have gave me more of a build-up. People would have respected me for what I've done and things like that. They would say, "There goes a cold killer."

MURROW: He wants people to say, "There goes a cold killer." He is only fourteen years old — the same age as the boy who used a bread knife in the Highbridge Park attack . . . and who told us why he too wants to be known as a "cold killer."

ET: GANG MEMBER:

It makes you feel like a big shot. You know some guys think they're big shots and all that. They think, you know, they got the power to do everything they feel like doing. They say, like, "I wanna stab a guy." and then the other guy say, "Oh, I wouldn't dare to do that." You know, he thinks I'm acting like a big shot. That's the way he feels. He probably thinks in his mind, "Oh, he probably won't do that." Then, when we go to a fight, you know, he finds out what I do.

MURROW: Some gang members told police that they bragged to each other about beating and stabbing Farmer and McShane . . . wanted to make certain they would be known as "tough guys." According to the official police record, this was the reaction of their parents.

ET: COMMISSIONER ARM:

During the hours that the boys were rounded up and brought to the police station, many of their parents came to the scene. They expressed shock and bewilderment and disbelief over the fact that their boys were being questioned by police and might have had a part in this hideous crime. When they finally realized that this was true, they still couldn't believe it.

MURROW: One mother told our reporter.

ET: MOTHER OF GANG MEMBER AND REPORTER:

MOTHER: I had absolutely no problems with him. Everyone in the neighborhood can vouch for that. When I walked out there this morning, all my store-keepers and everythin' just can't believe that my son is mixed up in anything like this. (SIGH) I have no idea

what I can do for him right now. I doubt if there is anything we can
do for him right now.

REPORTER: Do you plan to go over to see him?

MOTHER: Of course I have to go to see my child.
(SOBBING) I can't let him down now. Even though he was wrong, I
still can't just turn my back on him. (SOBBING)

MURROW: Parents went to see their sons in jail; and how did they react when they
saw them? One boy said:

ET: GANG MEMBER:

My mother said she was ashamed of me, and everything, and I told
her that it wasn't my fault and I couldn't help it. My father wanted to
kill me at first, and after I explained to him what happened he was
still. . . he was still like . . . felt bad about it, ashamed to walk the
streets after somethin' like that, but then you know, he wouldn't touch
me then, after I told him what happened.

MURROW: The statement of another gang member.

ET: GANG MEMBER:

My father understood. He didn't actually understand, but you know,
he didn't take it as hard as my mother. My mother . . . it came out
in the newspapers, she had a heart attack. It's a lucky thing she's
alive today.

MURROW: One mother talked to her son in the presence of the other boys arrested. Here is what she said, according to this gang member present.

ET: GANG MEMBER:

When she sees him she says to him, "How did it feel when you did
that to Farmer? It was good, eh?" You know, jokin' around with the
kid. So we told her, "You know what your son did?" I says, "He
stabbed him in the back." She says, she just went like that, shrugged
her, you know, shoulders. Then we didn't pay any attention to her,
because ya know, you don't like to see a mother actin' like that with
a kid ya know.

MURROW: What is known about the mental and emotional make-up of parents
whose children commit crimes? Dr. Marjorie Rittwagen, staff
psychiatrist for New York Children's Courts, gave us some statistics.

ET: DR. RITTWAGEN:

We find that some seventy-five to eighty per cent of parents of
children who are brought into this court are emotionally ill or have
severe personality or character disorders. They include sociopathic
personality disorders, alcoholics and the like. And about ten per cent
of this seventy-five to eighty per cent are commitably psychotic — in
fact, some parents go completely berserk in Court, threaten judges
and are sent to psychiatric wards for observation. Most of these
parents are so overwhelmed with their own problems, that they ignore
their children. Kids feel not so much rejected as nonentities. Usually,
in these homes, there are no fathers.

MURROW: There are no fathers in the homes of five of the seven gang members
tried for the murder of Michael Farmer. Four of these boys live with
their mothers; one with his grandparents. His mother told our reporter why she left her son.

ET: MOTHER OF GANG MEMBER AND REPORTER:

MOTHER: He has lived with my mother all his life from birth. (SOBS) I lived there up to two, three years ago. It seems like since I left my child everything has happened. (SOBS) Not that I just walked out on him, but when I planned to get married I spoke to him. He said, "Well, go ahead, you have to have some happiness; you can't just stay with me all the time." So I said, "Will you be willing to come with me?" He said, "No, I don't want to leave my grandparents." (SOB)

REPORTER: Do you think that it would have been important if he had stayed with you?

MOTHER: I think it would have been important had I stayed with him and not leave him at the age of fifteen. I wouldn't advise that to anyone who has a boy, or any other child. (SOBS)

MURROW: Eleven of the eighteen boys arrested in the Farmer case come from homes broken by desertion, divorce or death. Children's Court psychiatrist Marjorie Rittwagen says this is the pattern.

ET: DR. RITTWAGEN:

Some seventy to eighty per cent of our children come from homes broken by desertion or divorce. Most of the children stay with their mothers. At critical times in their lives they are left in a fatherless home. They're almost afraid to relate too closely to their mothers, and are often driven into the streets to seek companionship with a gang. They find the superficial group relationship more comfortable than individual ones. In fact, difficulty in relating to people is one of their big handicaps. They don't talk out their problems, they act them out.

MURROW: Example: this thirteen year old boy. He lives with a mother married and divorced three times. She works to support him . . . cannot spend much time with him. Her son has plenty of problems, but she doesn't know about them.

ET: GANG MEMBER:

I never tell her about my problems. One reason is that if I tell her my problems, like some guys were beating me up, she would keep me in the house . . . and wouldn't let me go out. Or if I tell her I'm doing badly in school, she'll probably hit me. Or if I tell her I had an argument with a teacher, or something like that, she'd probably hit me. She don't give me a chance to explain, you know. She just comes out, and pow, she hits me. I don't tell her anything.

MURROW: He doesn't talk out his problems; he acts them out — sometimes by firing a beebee gun at adults.

ET: GANG MEMBER:

Tell you the truth, I used to shoot people myself. Sometimes I would shoot the people I don't like too much, you know. (LAUGHS) I would be up on the roof and they would be walkin' by with packages or something — and Pow, I would shoot them.

MURROW: Violence is all around him, he says.

ET: GANG MEMBER:

Usually I go for horror pictures like "Frankenstein and the Mummy" or things like that. I like it when he goes and kills the guy or rips a guy in half or something like that. (LAUGHS) Or when he throws somebody off a cliff. You know, all them exciting things.

MURROW: Next: the gang member who used a bread knife in the Highbridge Park attack. He lived with his mother and step-father; told us he often quarreled with his mother; wanted his step-father to spend more time with him.

ET: GANG MEMBER:

I'll ask him to take me boat-riding, fishing, or some place like that,
ball game. He'll say, "No." He don't go no place. The only place
where he goes, he goes to the bar. And from the bar, he goes home.
Sleep, that's about all he do. I don't talk to my parents a lot of times.
I don't hardly talk to them — there's nothing to talk about. There's
nothing to discuss about. They can't help me.

MURROW: They can't help me! What he wants, he says, is to be like his
                       favorite comic book hero.

ET: GANG MEMBER:

Mighty Mouse — he's a mouse — he's dressed up like Superman.
He's got little pants — they're red. The shirt is yellow. You know,
and then he helps out the mouse. Everytime the cats try to get the
mouse, Mighty Mouse comes and helps the mouse, just like Superman.
He's stronger than the cats. Nothing can hurt him.

MURROW: Another boy told us: "My father doesn't want to hear my troubles.
                       They make him mad." Reason:

ET: GANG MEMBER:

He wants me to be better than my other brother. That's why every
time he comes to me and say, "You see, you gonna be like your
brother. The one that's in the Tombs. If you keep on doing wrong,
you gonna be like him." He kept on telling me that, so I said, "Well,
if he wants me to be like him, I'm gonna be like him." So I started
doing wrong things. And then he says to me, "I don't wanna catch you
in trouble." Well, in one way he should have got me in trouble before,
because he found a gun that I had . . . you know, I had a home-made.
And he found it, and he didn't say nothin', he just broke it up and
threw it away and kept me in the house for one day. He should have
took it to the police or somethin', and told them that I had it. Maybe
I would have been sent to the Youth House or someplace, before, and
I wouldn't have gotten into so much trouble, and I would have learned
my lesson.

MURROW: This was his first arrest. But ten of the eighteen boys involved in the
                       Farmer case had previous records as juvenile offenders; some for
                       such minor offenses as trespassing or chalking names on buildings;
                       others for serious crimes, including assault, burglary and attempted
                       grand larceny. Three gang members were under the supervision of
                       probation officers. But how much supervision does a boy on probation
                       get, in New York City? Clarence Leeds is Chief Probation Officer at
                       Children's Court.

   The script is now fully into the problem as it concerns the characters of the story.
The transitions, through selecting and editing, are excellent, moving logically, yet not
obviously, from the boys to the parents. The statements of the boys and the parents all
follow a pattern, validating the diagnosis of the sociologist and the psychiatrist. Now the
documentary can attempt an investigation of the solutions to the problem, those attempted
and those still to come.

ET: CLARENCE LEEDS:

Our probation officers have minimum case loads of between sixty and
seventy delinquent boys apiece. This means that at best they can talk
to each boy perhaps once a month. And you can't give a child the
guidance and help he needs by seeing him that infrequently. We are
doing just about double the number of case loads and investigations
that we're equipped to handle and possibly as a consequence of this,
about thirty per cent of the boys on probation commit new offenses
which will bring them to the attention of the court once again.

MURROW: Three Egyptian Dragons on probation participated in the murder of Michael Farmer. Another member of this gang had served one year in a state training school for juvenile delinquents . . . was diagnosed as a "dangerous psychopath" . . . but received no psychotherapy. Reason: there are 500 boys in this institution; only one psychiatrist and one psychologist to treat them. Five months after this "dangerous psychopath" was released from the institution, he stabbed Roger McShane at Highbridge Park. Who is to blame? John Warren Hill, Chief Justice of New York's Children's Court, told us why many very disturbed children are released quickly by state institutions.

ET: JUDGE HILL:

It is a shocking fact that children committed to state institutions by this court often are discharged from these institutions within four to six months without having received any real treatment or help. Why? Because our state facilities for the long term care of delinquent children are so shockingly inadequate that our state institutions must make these discharges quickly in order to make room for new court commitments. For while the rate of delinquency has increased in New York City, since 1951 through 1956, by 83 per cent, as revealed by our own court statistics, there's not been a single additional bed provided in our state institutions for delinquent children, aside from some few which the city made available for use by the state. But that was a bare nothing compared to the great need which has developed increasingly in this area.

MURROW: Children released from New York institutions are put on parole. The Egyptian Dragon diagnosed as a "dangerous psychopath" was assigned to a youth parole worker . . . was under the supervision of this worker at the time of the Farmer murder. But how closely was he watched? Joseph Linda is in charge of youth parole workers, New York City area.

ET: JOSEPH LINDA:

Each of our youth parole workers supervises about 80 boys, and in some cases, about 100 boys, because of staff shortage. This means that they may see these boys as infrequently as once every two months.

MURROW: Youth parole and probation agencies are non-existent in half the counties of this nation. In most of the other counties, they are under-staffed, according to a survey by the National Probation and Parole Association. Some responsibility for supervising problem children often is shifted to the schools by the courts. This happened in the case of several Egyptian Kings and Dragons brought to court prior to the murder of Michael Farmer. The speaker, Murray Sachs, court liaison officer, Board of Education, New York City.

ET: MURRAY SACHS:

The courts had made a number of requests in the helping of these youngsters. The unfortunate thing about these children was this: they would refuse to come to school. Not coming to school, they wouldn't be doing the things that we think are constructive and helpful. Those, we know, have such deep-rooted behavior problems must be dealt with on that basis by specialists who are equipped to handle it, and, for heaven's sake, our community, our citizens should not expect the school to do that. It seems that the only one that might help them would be the institution where they might be placed, and given individualized and controlled assistance, of one kind or another. Again we're faced with the serious problem of there's just no place for them.

MURROW: In the richest state of the nation, long-term institutional care is not available for eighty per cent of delinquent children under twelve years of age. No state institution for these children exists. The few private institutions are jammed. One gang member involved in the Farmer case committed five offenses before he was twelve years old. Within a week or two after each arrest, he was set free in the community. At twelve, children are eligible for state training schools. But even then it is difficult to place them because of overcrowding. John Warren Hill, Chief Justice of New York's Children's Court, sums up the result.

ET: JUDGE HILL:

In a great number of cases of very disturbed children, children who should be removed from the community, this court has been unable to find any placement for the child and our only alternative has been to place these children on probation, which, of course, means their return to the community.

MURROW: They are sent back to the streets — unhelped, unsupervised. Set free in the community, what do they do with their time? Listen to one boy describe a typical summer day in his neighborhood of brick tenements in Manhattan's upper west side.

ET: GANG MEMBER:

I usually get up at 11 or 12 o'clock, you know, I sleep late. And then I will go out and see the guys, sitting on the stoop, you know, doing nothin'. I would sit there with them, and sometimes they will say, "Let's split and go to a movie," so I would go to the movie with them. Or sometimes we would try and get a game of stickball or somethin' like that. Our block is crowded, we didn't hardly have a chance to play because the busses kept going back and forth, back and forth. We couldn't do nothin'. So that we just sit, then when it got to night-time, well, you know, we would go around, and say, "Come on, man, let's go break windows for some excitement" or "Come on man, let's go boppin'." Then we would go and look for guys, to beat 'em up. Then we would come back. And then, (LAUGHS) we would sit on the stoop, man, and we'd hear a cop car outside and we would all fly up to the roof, or somethin' like that. Then, we just come down and start talkin' and talkin'.

MURROW: Consider the day of another boy, sixteen years old. He makes the rounds of schools, pool halls, and candy store hangouts. He works for a syndicate . . . sells marijuana cigarettes to other children and smokes them himself.

ET: GANG MEMBER:

I'd get the dough by sellin' it. I'd take about four or five a day. It keeps me goin'. All depends . . . when I get up in the morning I take one or two; three hours later take another one. If I ain't got nothin' to do, I just feel like goofin', crackin' up and everythin'. I just take another one. Go to a dance, take two or three. If you don't get it easy, you try all kinds of — not violence, but you see an easy dollar to rob, you rob it. You see somethin' to pawn, you pawn it.

MURROW: Boys troubled and adrift in the community formed the gang that killed Michael Farmer. Sociologists call gangs of this breed "anti-social groups" or "fighting gangs." They exist in most of our large cities. According to police estimates there are 134 of these gangs in Los Angeles County; 24 in Miami; 110 in New York, including the Egyptian Kings and Dragons.

You have read about two-thirds of the documentary script. The voices and sounds of realism have been presented. The thoughts and feelings of as many different and varied persons as might be found in a Shakespearean tragedy have been explored. "What" happened moved into "why" it happened into the evolution of a problem that demands a solution. Much as do the films of Pare Lorentz, "Who killed Michael Farmer?" then examines the possible solutions to the problem. The final few pages of the documentary script sum up:

ET: GREENHILL REPORT:

Residents trace the origin of juvenile crime to parents' inability to
control their children, racial issues, newcomers in the area, lack of
police protection, intimidation of teachers and policemen by youth
gangs, and a lack of restrictive measures in Highbridge Park. Persons interviewed reported 16 major incidents leading to death or
hospitalization in the last three years. Ten of them in the last two
weeks. Most of the incidents had not been reported to police for fear
of gang retaliation. Among the population in general, there were attitudes of hopelessness and fear. A large number of people expect
gang retaliation after the present crisis has quieted down. They are
cynical and see no way of preventing retaliation for it has always
occurred in the past. About 40 per cent of children between the ages
of 3 and 16 reacted immediately with a variety of physical and
emotional symptoms. For the first time, some children began to
carry knives for their own protection.

MURROW: One boy in the neighborhood who fears for his life is Michael Farmer's
friend, Roger McShane — a State's witness at the murder trial of the
Egyptian Kings and Dragons. During the trial, McShane received two
death threats in the mail. One letter said: "You are alive. But if
them guys get the chair, we will kill you." That threat possibly came
from a crank. But no one can be sure — least of all Roger McShane.

ET: Mc SHANE:

There's nothing you can do except protect yourself. It's just gonna
get wilder and wilder. I mean, it's just gonna get worse. You can't
have a policeman walking around with every boy or girl that leaves
his house at night. And follow him to the store if he has to go to the
store or follow him up to the show or you can't have a policeman
follow each individual all around the neighborhood just so they can be
protected.

MURROW: The parents of Michael Farmer.

ET: MR. AND MRS. FARMER:

MR. FARMER: I'm very much afraid for my son Rayme.
Rayme's 14. Who knows the rest of these Egyptian Kings won't come
up looking for him, or trying to extend their activities; make themselves a little bit more infamous. You can't reason with the type of
minds that they have. You don't know what they'll come up with next.

MRS. FARMER: I'm worried about all of us. There was a time
when I'd run down at night for milk, or to mail a letter, now I
wouldn't go down the street after nine o'clock. I just have that terrible
feeling that something is lurking there in the dark.

MURROW: Fear remains in this community. A new summer approaches . . . and
according to one volunteer youth worker in the area already there are
danger signals.

ET: YOUTH WORKER:

The situation is beginning to look critical once again. We find that one
of the Egyptian Kings apparently not involved in the Michael Farmer
killing is now trying to reorganize a gang and is recruiting in the
area. Unless something is done very quickly with this particular gang,
we are definitely going to run into the same situation in a very short
time. You can't say whether that will be six months or a year from
now, but if this gang is allowed to reorganize again, there may be
more killings and something had better be done, fast, if we are
interested in saving other children from the fate of Michael Farmer.

MURROW: What has been solved by the verdict of a jury and the commitment of
                 15 boys to institutions which are ill-equipped to re-habilitate them;
                 and because of overcrowding, may soon return them to the com-
                 munity? The problem of juvenile crime continues. The experts may
                 list all sorts of causes. But they agree on one answer to why these
                 conditions continue to exist: We permit them to. This is Ed Murrow.
                 Good Night.

Approach. The most common approach to the documentary, in both
radio and television, is that which relies principally on interviews and statements, including those already on the record, combining new and old information and opinions from persons involved in a particular problem or topic.
These documentaries build on ideas, rather than on a dramatic structure.
Selection and editing become more important than the actual writing. Issues
of the day and important people of the day provide ready-made material.
The beginning of one of NBC's award-winning "Second Sunday" programs
illustrates this approach:

MAN: The accepted use of executive power compelled the Congress and the
United States to re-examine itself and its role ...

MAN: ... The dislocations and the frictions between the Congress and the
White House has been exaggerated ...

MAN: ... Nineteen seventy-six will either be 200 years of the glorious
republic, or else it's going to be the year two or three of the Executive
Monarchy in the United States ...

MAN: ... To the extent that Congress hasn't exercised the full scope of its
authority in the past, it really doesn't have the President to blame; it has
itself to blame ...

JACOB JAVITS: ... Who made the bargains? The Congress and the President.
One cannot undo the bargain ...

GERALD FORD: The American people are on the side of the President.

(MUSIC)

ANNOUNCER: Second Sunday, the award - winning documentary series presented
each month by NBC News. Our subject for March: Congress and the President --
A Constitutional Crisis. Here is NBC News Correspondent, Paul Duke.

PAUL DUKE: We're going to examine what may be the most serious confrontation
between two branches of Government this century. It's a clash which may have a
major impact on the American system, and perhaps, even affect the future of
representative democracy. It's a clash of strong opinions, and strong wills.
And it's producing a crescendo of comment and criticism across the country.

But most of all, as voiced by Washington satirist Mark Russell on Capitol
Hill.

(PIANO MUSIC)

MARK RUSSELL: You know, we go to the trouble in our country of electing Senators and Congressman. Then we send them out in the cold, to Washington. It's a lonely place, and it's a lonely place for the bills they pass, too. Because they're passed, and they see the light of day, and then they're cut off. Yes, Washington is a lonely town, for our Congressmen and our Senators sometimes sing: Nixon doesn't love us anymore.

DUKE: If love means doing what Congress wants, then President Nixon is a rejecting suitor. Mr. Nixon is doing what he wants, and what he believes is best for the country. He is making the White House more of a center for Federal power, and policy making. In the process Congressional power is being eroded and diminished. The irony is that the President's declared goal is to reduce the authority of the Federal Government, including his own authority. He struck the central theme in his inaugural address in January.

PRESIDENT RICHARD NIXON: We have lived too long with the consequence of attempting to gather all power and responsibility in Washington. Abroad and at home, the time has come to turn away from the condescending policies of paternalism; of Washington knows best. In trusting too much in government, we have asked of it more than it can deliver. This leads only to inflated expectation, to reduced individual effort, and to a disappointment and frustration that erode confidence both in what government can do, and in what people can do.

DUKE: It's not the President's goal, but the President's tactics which have precipitated the gathering fury on Capitol Hill. Mr. Nixon has refused to spend money appropriated by Congress. In some instances, after Presidential vetoes were overridden. He has moved to close out Federal programs without Congressional consent. He has named three super-secretaries of the Cabinet, without Congressional confirmation. He has drawn a cloak of executive privilege around his top aides, to prevent them from testifying before major committees on issues of war and peace. In all of this, Democratic leaders believe the President has gone too far, exceeding his authority under the Constitution, and the result, as House Speaker Carl Albert sees it, is a crisis that goes to the heart of the American system.

CARL ALBERT: The issue here is where do we draw Constitutional lines, and do we believe what we say when we say that we will support and defend the Constitution of the United States. That's the overriding issue.

DUKE: Senate Democratic leader Mike Mansfield is concerned, not just by the erosion in Congressional authority, but that a fundamental alteration may be taking place in the checks and balances built into the Constitution by the Founding Fathers.

MIKE MANSFIELD: If that document is ever undermined, and one of the three branches of the government becomes too subordinate, as we are on the way to becoming at the present time, then all I can say is, "God help the Republic" because the foundations will have been broken, and perhaps broken down at least in part.

DUKE: To some extent, President Nixon is only accelerating a trend which began when Franklin Roosevelt came to office during the Great Depression of the 1930's. Since then, power has steadily flowed down Pennsylvania Avenue from the Capitol to the White House. Accordingly, as Democratic Representative Morris Udall of Arizona observes, the country has grown accustomed to Presidents exercising strong commands.

MORRIS UDALL: I credit this to two unusual coincidental incidents in the life of our nation. One was the Depression. All of a sudden the whole free enterprise system has failed, and a third of the people out of work, and anything the President wanted, he set up a bill in the morning and the Congress

would pass it that afternoon. Or let the President fill in the details. We
were just recovering from that and Congress, you will recall, in the late
thirties, was beginning to assert itself again, and saying "Hold on, now, we
make the policy in the Congress," when along came World War II-- the whole free
world threatened with extinction by two powerful dictators. And we said to the
President, whatever he wants --bombers, ships, selective service-- turn it over to
the President. And so we've developed a whole generation of leaders in the
Congress who are sort of conditioned to stand back and let the President make
decisions.

DUKE: The country's growth, and the emergence of the United States as a
great world power has established the President as a pre-eminent world leader.
The people have come to look to the President as the country's principal
protector. Speaker Albert believes the wars of the Twentieth Century made it
inevitable that the White House would gain added stature, with Congress less
involved.

ALBERT: I think that the tendency is for the President to be strengthened in
time of crisis, because faster action is required. I think the Congress --
the Congress enjoyed its greatest period of prestige between the War of 1812 and
the Civil War, and that was the longest peace-time period we ever had. And that's
when the giants who overshadowed the President appeared on the scene: like
Craig, Webster, Calhoun, and Haines and others.

DUKE: But some critics, such as Democratic Congressman John Conyers of
Detroit, believe the President has seized upon the dangers of the Atomic Age
as justification for seizing more power than is warranted.

JOHN CONYERS: The use of nuclear weapons required that we vest unprecedented
power in the executive office, along with the decision-making right that goes
along with it. This was the natural base for the executive to balloon in this
power far beyond anything conceived by the framing of the Constitution. Now, in
many instances, it was perfectly rational and logical. But the whole question of
these powers being not only taken by the executive, but then being used as a base
to go even further afield. And then we move of course into the questions of
impoundment, the right of the executive to legislate after we have, in effect;
on the questions of executive secrecy, in which the White House now literally
instructs anyone that is invited to testify before Congressional Committees that
their testimony may in some way disclose the secrets of the executive branch
that are not ready for public disclosures that this point, which all now goes far
beyond the historical reasons that the executive began to gain power over the
Congress and at the expense of Congress.

DUKE: If there was any catalyst that stirred Congress to ponder the
trend toward Presidential government, it was the Viet Nam War. As the nation
was torn over the American policy, so was Congress torn. But more than that,
the critics began to question the President's power to commit U.S. forces to
faraway places. Thus, today's outcry is directed at the expansion of the Presidential power both at home and abroad. The man who is leading the Congressional
counterattack is Senator Sam Ervin of North Carolina. For 18 years, Ervin has
been the principal Congressional custodian of the Constitution. The 76-year-old
Democrat's stubborn convictions about the Constitution have led him into many
lonely and unpopular battles. But now, quite suddenly, he is the man of the
moment. Ervin has long believed the greatest threat to the country's freedoms
comes from the government, and the men who run the government.

SAM ERVIN: I think that most public officials, including the President and
including some of us, and including Congress, have an insatiable thirst for
power. And I think the reason the Constitution was written was to keep them from
being able to indulge their insatiable thirst for power. And this kind of conflict has gone on throughout the history of the Republic to a more or less extent;
but it's been very much accentuated of late by the wholesale impoundments,
and I think the conflict will go on more or less forever. I think it was
Justice Brandeis who said that Our Constitution wasn't written to make the

most efficient government; was written to insure liberty and also to put in
its place the forces of friction; as to keep one department of government
from trespassing upon the domain of another. And that was the same idea
George Washington expressed in his farewell address.

DUKE: Nothing has aroused Congress so much as the President's refusal
to spend money appropriated by Congress. Senator Ervin and other critics contend
that the President's impoundment of 12 billion dollars in funds for Government
programs presents a theft of legislative power. President Nixon has defended
the action by claiming an absolutely clear Constitutional right to hold up the
funds. But Senator Ervin contends the Constition does not give the President
so much as a syllable of such power.

At a Senate hearing, Deputy Attorney General Joseph Snead argued the
administration's case in a confrontation with Ervin, who insisted the
President's Constitutional responsibility is limited to executing the laws.

ERVIN: Now, this word execute has several meanings. For example, the law
used to say a person shall be executed for certain crimes. They have had laws
like that. The word execute does not mean that his life will be exterminated.
Now, with this provision of the Constitution, the President shall take care that
the laws be faithfully executed does not contemplate that the President should
kill those laws.

JOSEPH SNEAD: Senator, I don't think the word executed as used in the
Constitution, Article II, Section III, is used in the same sense as it is used
in phrasing of sanctions for penal purposes.

ERVIN: Doesn't it mean that he shall take care to see that the laws that
are in force are carried out, and made effective, according to their terms?

SNEAD: Senator, he has the responsibility, under the Constitution, as we have
said, and as you have indicated, to see that the laws be faithfully executed. He
has, however, at all times, to consider all the laws. And it has been our
position, as my statement indicated, that he is confronted, and was confronted in
the '73 budget issue, with laws consisting of appropriatioh acts; laws consisting
of the 1946 full employment act; laws consisting of the debt ceiling; and laws
consisting of the Economic Stabilization Act. And above and beyond that, he was
looked to in part by Congress and certainly by the public, as one having a very
profound responsibility for price stability. But when we put all that together,
the problem is how best to faithfully execute the laws.

ERVIN: Well, now, the President doesn't have the responsibility in a
governmental sense, for anything except the things that the Constition and the
laws force on him. Isn't that true?

SNEAD: Yes, sir.

ERVIN: And the fact that the people look to him to do something doesn't
give him either Constitutional effect or authority to do it, does it?

SNEAD: No. I'm merely injecting the political realities...

ERVIN: Yes, but the political realities are supposed to bow to a
Constitutional government.

SNEAD: Indeed they do.

ERVIN: Yes.

Courtesy of NBC News

Application: Television

The basic approaches and techniques are essentially the same for the television and radio documentary. The most important difference, obviously, is the use of visuals in television. Where the radio documentary gathers words and sounds, the television documentary adds film, tape, photos and graphics. Where the radio program must use dialogue and/or narration to describe something, the television program needs only the picture itself. Television has the advantage of the motion picture's "visual writing," the ability to tell a story more concisely and sometimes more meaningfully through showing instead of telling.

The picture may be the primary element in any given sequence in the television documentary, with the narration and taped dialogue secondary. The people and their actions may be actually seen and thus understood, rather than being imagined through verbal descriptions of what they did and saw. On the other hand, the words of the people and the narrator may be the prime movers, with the pictures merely filling in visually what is being described in words.

Approach. As with radio, the most popular approach to the television documentary is that which concentrates on narration and interviews and does not attempt dramatic technique. The visuals may be little more than graphics relating to the subject, plus actualities with interviewees. Such a documentary is the CBS News Special Report, "What's Going On Here? — The Troubled American Economy." Note the simple format: John Hart, anchorperson, introduces through narration different aspects of the troubled economy and then switches to a correspondent who conducts the actualities for that segment. Excerpts from the first part of the program follow, illustrating the organization as well as the approach.

HART:	Good evening. As it turns out, six weeks ago were the good old days. When our brand new President told us our political nightmare was over. And now we were going to work on our economic one.
FORD: VTR:	My first priority is to work with you to bring inflation under control. Inflation is domestic enemy number one.
HART:	He called for an economic summit meeting where the best brains from labor, industry and agriculture would help him plan the attack. That meeting begins this Friday in Washington. In the six weeks we have been waiting for — and the brains have been preparing for — the summit, these things have happened. The stock market slid to its lowest value in 12 years. Homebuilding to its lowest point in 4 years. Wholesale prices made their biggest jump in one year. Tonight we are going to look at our economy and the summit and what to expect from both of them.
ANNOUNCER:	This is a CBS News Special Report . . . WHAT'S GOING ON HERE? . . . THE TROUBLED AMERICAN ECONOMY . . . With CBS News Correspondent John Hart.

lst Commercial

ANNOUNCER: Here is John Hart.

HART: What is going on here is more than one thing in more than one place. We have a mixture of troubles. We have inflation. It is everywhere. We have stagnation, in a number of places where things just aren't moving much, forward or backward. We have recession in places where things have been going backward for sometime. We have depression in places where things are going straight down. We even have some strengths left, here and there. It is not ALL bad. Just mostly. There are a number of what the economists call indicators — trends they look at at to see where the economy is weak and where it is strong and how much.

RP LIST: We are going to look at 12 indicators, of what has been going on since the first of the year.

CONSUMER PRICES: The obvious indicator is prices. They have been going up on an average of one per cent a month. 12 per cent a year. This is a weakness in our economy. A clear minus.

POP ON
WHOLESALE
PRICES: Wholesale prices are another indicator of inflation. They have gone up more than two per cent a month on the average, or 27 per cent per year. Another weakness.

POP ON MINUS: Another minus.

RETAIL SALES: Retail sales indicate how people are reacting to prices. Dollar volume has gone up every month this year, except in June.

POP ON PLUS.   In one way that is a strength, in that it helps keep business in business.

POP ON MINUS: But in another way these retail sales dollars hide weakness. In many cases we are buying fewer things and simply paying more for what we buy, as with cars.

PROFITS: The profits picture is a plus. Corporate profits after taxes grew at an annual rate of 55 per cent over 1973, keeping well ahead of inflation.

WAGES: Wages went up at an annual rate of 4.4 per cent, but did NOT keep up with inflation.

POP ON PLUS: Real income went down for the millions of people living on wages but ironically, a plus for the economy as a whole, in that wages are not giving a big push to inflation.
                        *   *   *
                The reasons are that the three things we cannot do without — food, shelter and fuel — are things this economy is rationing by inflation. Bernard Kalb reports on food.

VTR

KALB: You can't do without it, it should be a pleasure. But what you're eating is costing you more, and more, and more. The bad news on food prices from Secretary of Agriculture Earl Butz.

BUTZ: Our estimate is that the average of 1974 will be approximately 15 to

16 per cent over the average of 1973. It would be approximately a 30 per cent jump in two years. It's been severe, there's no question about that.

KALB: No question either about the shock among consumers. A trip to the supermarket these days can be a little like walking through a mine field . . . new prices exploding everywhere. All this has made a mockery of earlier official forecasts that food prices during this period would remain steady . . . and even decline slightly; once again, a case of governmental optimism outrunning reality.

Ellen Zawel, President of the National Consumer Congress on the mood of consumers.

ZAWEL: Most people are depressed. They just don't know what to do. It becomes scary and you don't know where you gonna cut down next. Everybody feels they're being shafted. Somebody's taking advantage and they're not sure who.

BUTZ: I think we're all inclined to zero in on the farmer and say, look out there . . . that guy . . . he's the guy that's running up the price of food. He gets 39 cents on the average today of the consumer's food dollar. Somebody else gets 61 cents.

KALB: That "somebody else" is the middleman, or rather, middlemen — the various companies that pick up the raw commodities, process them, transport them around the country, and sell them. For some items, the middleman gets most of the consumer's dollar. For a one pound loaf of bread, the farmer gets 7 cents; the midlleman, 28 cents. For a can of tomatoes, 3 cents to the farmer, 26 cents to the middleman. A can of peaches: the farmer, 9 cents; the middleman, 41 cents. A head of lettuce: 16 cents for the farmer, 34 cents for the middleman. The middleman's cut of the dollar has made the middleman contro-versial.

The case for the middleman — George W. Koch, President of the Grocery Manufacturers of America.

KOCH: The middleman adds a lot. First of all, he adds a tremendous amount of jobs, to take that raw commodity of wheat, of flour, of rice and turn it into a sum . . . what some call, who visit from overseas, the modern American miracle. We enabled the housewife to be liberated, to get out of the kitchen, go to work, come home and in seven minutes feed her children.

KALB: What have you done to the pocketbook?

KOCH: What do you want? Eight thousand to ten thousand items and you can adjust your budget. You can buy raw commodities, you can make it yourself or we will give you peas in a bag with onions mixed in.

KALB: For his contribution, the middleman has been repaid with a whole new set of attractive statistics. One analysis shows that among major food retailers, profits were more than 200 million dollars in the first six month reporting period of 1974, an increase of 50 per cent compared with the same period last year.

* * *

The trouble in our economy is made worse these days, by the fact that an old ally against inflation has gone over and joined the other side. Recession used to cure inflation, but now they work side by side. The clearest example of this is in housing as David Culhane reports.

TRACK

CULHANE: Unemployment in the housing construction industry stands at 11.1 per cent — about twice the jobless rate for the labor force in general. The national median price for a one-family house since 1970 has jumped a stunning 50 per cent — to 35,500 dollars. Mortgage interest rates for home buyers are at the highest levels in decades — the national average for conventional home loans without government backing is about 9 per cent. Because of the dizzy climb of costs and mortgage rates, 431,000 houses stand unsold. New housing construction has plummeted — the rate of decline for new house starts over the last two years has been nearly 50 per cent. In short, while the rest of the economy simply talks fearfully about depression, the housing construction industry is in a state of depression — they say the worst since 1930.

BLUMENAUER: This is certainly true and from what I read many many builders now are bankrupt because they can't sell what they've produced and there's no money for them to start new projects.

KETTLER: By year end our unemployment rate in the building industry will probably be in excess of 20 per cent. Now, 10 per cent by many people is depression standards.

CULHANE: In many ways, Joseph Abbatiello, of Long Island, New York, is typical of the small builders around the country who are now in trouble. He is suffering a 65 per cent drop in sales and he is simply cutting back the number of houses he builds.

ABBATIELLO: I would say in 1970 we did about 68, I believe. '71 we did 60 '72 we did about 40. '73 we did about 40. And this year we're going to do 26 the way it looks.

CULHANE: In just two years for Joseph Abbatiello the cost of a box of nails went from seven dollars twenty-five cents, to seventeen dollars fifty cents. Shingles, concrete, insulation, asphalt for roads — everything went up. In one year plumbing for one house increased by six hundred dollars. And all these costs are passed on to the buyer.

* * *

Courtesy of NBC News
Leslie Midgley, Executive Producer; Hal Haley and Bernard Birnbaum, Producers

The documentary continues with the same format. John Hart introduces succeeding segments and special correspondents dealing with critical aspects of the economy. Each segment combines narration and interviews. "George Herman reports on the energy industry." . . . "Inflation around the world is so strong that last week the International Monetary Fund said it can do serious and prolonged damage to the world economy if it isn't stopped. John Sheahan reports." . . . "On Wall Street there is increasing talk that 1929 has already returned to the American Stock Market. Mitchell Krauss reports." The documentary ends with Hart summing up the material presented, suggesting options for the country and the economy, and stating what future actions are likely to have an effect on the problem.

Process.   As with radio, you don't need a major network in order to produce a first-rate television documentary. It does take more than a few audio tape recorders, but with careful planning and imagination local stations can produce dramatic and pertinent documentaries. Though not usually controversial, the subject of libraries is a significant one in most communities, and Barbara Allen of WGAL, Lancaster, Pennsylvania, decided that it was pertinent to viewers in the many cities within her station's signal. Her approach was to take an ostensibly inanimate thing and humanize it. In doing so she captured many of the aspects of libraries that relate to human drama — in this case those of a worrisome nature that require action on the part of the viewers. Her approach was to dramatize the problem, but in the form of a factual statement, not a semi-documentary.

> • *As you study the script, note the combination of approaches used: narration, interviews, on-site events. Note, too, the combination of visuals used. Make a list of all of the visual techniques you can find. What are some of the interest-catching techniques used in the writing?*

LIBRARIES: BRUISED, BATTERED AND BOUND

VIDEO	AUDIO
CU OF INITIALS CARVED IN TABLES, WALLS, ETC., FOR EACH LOCATION	MUSIC UNDER — LOVE THEME FROM "ROMEO AND JULIET"
	BARB: This is a love story with an unhappy ending. In Harrisburg, R.P. loves B.L. In Lebanon, A.M. loves P.S. In York, it's M.O. and S.T. In Reading, C.K. loves P.R. and in Lancaster, Brenda loves Bill. START TO FADE MUSIC
COVER SHOT OF TABLE TOP	But love is a very private relationship and these intials are written in very public places. MUSIC OUT
SUPER TITLE SLIDE OVER TABLETOP	They are your public libraries and they are Bruised, Battered and Bound.
DISSOLVE TO COVER OF BARB AND LIBRARIANS AT TABLE	Hello, I'm Barbara Allen. With me around this bruised and battered library table are five librarians from the Channel 8 area.
ZOOM IN TO BARB	They're not here to tell you about what your local library has to offer. They're here to talk about larceny, decay, suffocation and rape. These things are happening in your library right now. If you don't stop them, the next time you visit your library, you may be greeted by this.

:05 FILM PERSON PUTTING CLOSED
SIGN IN WINDOW

BARB, THEN MR. DOHERTY

(INTRODUCE MR. DOHERTY, CHAT WITH
HIM ABOUT CLOSED SIGN AT READING
PUBLIC LIBRARY AND ASK HIM ABOUT
THE PROBLEMS AT THE READING
LIBRARY THAT YOU CAN SEE)

1:15 FILM SHOWING EXTERIOR OF
LIBRARY AND VISUAL PROBLEMS INSIDE

MR. DOHERTY VOICE OVER FILM

MR. DOHERTY

(CHAT WITH BARB ABOUT ONE
PROBLEM YOU CAN'T SEE)

BARB, THEN MISS YEAGLEY

(ASK ABOUT PROBLEMS YOU CAN SEE
AT MARTIN MEMORIAL LIBRARY, YORK)

1:15 FILM SHOWING EXTERIOR OF
LIBRARY AND VISUAL PROBLEMS INSIDE

MISS YEAGLEY VOICE OVER FILM

MISS YEAGLEY

(CHAT WITH BARB ABOUT ONE
PROBLEM YOU CAN'T SEE)

BARB INTRODUCES MR. GROSS

(ASK ABOUT PROBLEMS YOU CAN SEE
AT THE HARRISBURG PUBLIC LIBRARY)

1:15 FILM SHOWING EXTERIOR OF
HARRISBURG LIBRARY AND VISUAL
PROBLEMS INSIDE

MR. GROSS VOICE OVER FILM

MR. GROSS

(CHAT WITH BARB ABOUT ONE
PROBLEM YOU CAN'T SEE)

BARB INTRODUCES MR. MARKS

(ASK ABOUT PROBLEMS YOU CAN SEE
AT LEBANON COMMUNITY LIBRARY)

1:15 FILM SHOWING EXTERIOR OF
LEBANON LIBRARY AND VISUAL
PROBLEMS INSIDE

MR. MARKS VOICE OVER FILM

MR. MARKS

(CHAT WITH BARB ABOUT ONE
PROBLEM YOU CAN'T SEE)

BARB INTRODUCES MR. JENKINS

(ASK ABOUT PROBLEMS YOU CAN SEE
AT THE LANCASTER COUNTY LIBRARY)

1:15 FILM SHOWING EXTERIOR OF
LANCASTER LIBRARY AND VISUAL
PROBLEMS INSIDE

MR. JENKINS VOICE OVER FILM

MR. JENKINS

(CHAT WITH BARB ABOUT ONE
PROBLEM YOU CAN'T SEE . . . COSTS
OF WHICH THE PUBLIC IS UNAWARE . . .)

:20 FILM SHOWING ONE PILE OF
BOOKS, THEN ANOTHER

(NUMBER OF BOOKS $50 BOUGHT TEN
YEARS AGO AND WHAT IT WILL BUY
NOW)

:45 FILM SHOWING SIX OR SEVEN
STEPS IN PROCESSING

(NUMBER OF PEOPLE IT TAKES TO
SELECT AND PROCESS ONE BOOK)

BARB, THEN LIBRARIANS

(WHAT LIBRARIES ARE DOING TO HELP THEMSELVES. GENERAL CONVERSATION . . . THEN ASK MR. JENKINS ABOUT USE OF VOLUNTEERS AT LANCASTER LIBRARY)

:30 FILM SHOWING VOLUNTEERS DOING THREE DIFFERENT THINGS

MR. JENKINS VOICE OVER

BARB: How do you think the public would react if the libraries were closed?

LIBRARIANS

(GENERAL ANSWERS)
BARB: We asked some of the users of public libraries that question, and some others. This is how they replied.

2:00 SOF, MAN ON STREET INTERVIEWED IN FRONT OF LANCASTER LIBRARY. ANNOUNCER TALKING TO PEOPLE AS THEY COME OUT

SOF

BARB AND LIBRARIANS

Do any of these replies surprise you?
(GENERAL ANSWERS)
BARB: What can the public do or stop doing to help?

LIBRARIANS

(GENERAL ANSWERS)
(FILL TILL 1:00 CUE)

CLOSING
BARB: We've been talking about larceny, decay, suffocation and rape . . . things that are happening in your library right now. You may prefer to call them petty theft, deterioration, shortage of funds and malicious mischief but they are leaving your library bruised, battered and bound . . . suffering slow strangulation. If you don't stop these things from happening, the next time you visit your library, you may be greeted by this.

DISSOLVE TO :30 FILM STARTING WITH CU OF CLOSED SIGN BEING PLACED IN WINDOW AND ZOOM OUT TO LONG SHOT OF LIBRARY AND WINDOW

SUPER TITLE AND CREDIT SLIDES OVER ABOVE

DISSOLVE TO BLUE

Courtesy of Barbara Allen and WGAL-TV, Lancaster, Penna.

Writing the script alone is not the limit of the writer's contribution. As pointed out earlier, the writer and producer are frequently the same person. In the case of the "Libraries" documentary the producer required herself, as writer, to prepare other materials needed in the production of the program. In addition to "Questions for Man-on-the-Street Interviews" and "Film Footage Needed — Chronologically According to Script," both of which follow as examples of such preparation, Allen also prepared "Film Footage Needed — Geographically According to Location," "Additional Film Footage Needed for Promos," and "Official List of Names of Libraries and Librarians and Addresses." Further, each participant in the program was sent a letter describing the format and procedure in taping the show. This letter, reproduced here, is a good guide for the researcher-writer-producer in preparing any participants who will appear in the documentary.

January 27, 1971

Dear

Since we will not have much time to chat prior to the videotaping of Libraries: Bruised, Battered and Bound on Thursday, February 4 at 1:30 PM, I want to let you know how the program will proceed.

After introducing the subject, I will ask you to briefly describe the problems you can see in your library. We will use the film footage here showing the exterior of the library and allowing approximately ten seconds for each problem.

Then I will ask you about one problem that is not visible, which you can describe in one minute. Mr. Jenkins will be talking about the high cost of books and the number of people and steps it takes to select and process one book. I would suggest that you think of several possibilities; the more startling, the better. Then, when you arrive at the station you can compare notes with the other librarians to make sure each of you mentions a different problem.

I will also be asking you what the library is doing to help itself and how the public could help.

There will be a brief filmed "man-on-the-street" interview concerning libraries and I will ask for your reactions.

I know that there could be a whole series of programs on this subject, but since we are limited to thirty minutes it would be best to keep answers fairly brief and yet revealing for it is obvious that the public has no conception of the depth of the library crisis. It's up to us to create an impact.

Librarians participating are: Dean C. Gross (Harrisburg Public Library), Louisa Yeagley (Martin Memorial Library), Robert Marks (Lebanon Community Library), Edward Doherty (Reading Public Library) and Harold R. Jenkins (Lancaster County Library).

Would appreciate any advance promotion you can give the program in or out of the library. Air date and time is February 8 at 7 PM.

Thank you for your cooperation.

Sincerely yours,

Barbara Allen

QUESTIONS FOR MAN-ON-STREET INTERVIEWS

LIBRARIES: BRUISED, BATTERED AND BOUND
(to be asked by reporter outside front and back doors of Lancaster Library of people who are coming out of Library)

1. How would you feel if lack of money caused the library to close indefinitely?
2. What does the library mean to you?
3. How do you think libraries could meet rising costs?

FILM FOOTAGE NEEDED FOR LIBRARIES: BRUISED, BATTERED AND BOUND

CHRONOLOGICALLY (according to script):

:05	CU initials carved in Harrisburg Library
:05	CU initials carved in Lebanon Library
:05	CU initials carved in York Library
:05	CU initials carved in Reading Library
:05	CU initials carved in Lancaster Library
:15	COVER SHOT top of Lancaster Library table with carvings
:05	Person putting CLOSED sign in Reading Library window

:10	Showing exterior of Reading Library
*1:00	Close-ups of visual problems inside Reading Library

:10	Showing exterior of York Library
*1:00	Close-up of visual problems inside York Library

:10	Showing exterior of Harrisburg Library
*1:00	Close-ups of visual problems inside Harrisburg Library

:10	Showing exterior of Reading Library
*1:00	Close-ups of visual problems inside Reading Library

:10	Showing exterior of Lancaster Library
*1:00	Close-ups of visual problems inside Lancaster Library

:20	Close-up of hands piling books that could be bought for $50 ten years ago, then pan to hands piling books that can be bought for $50 today
:45	Pan six or seven sets of hands showing the people and steps necessary to select and process one book at Lancaster Library

:30	Cover shots of three different volunteers doing three different things at Lancaster Library
2:00	SOF interview outside Lancaster Library . . . some at front door, some at rear
:30	Start with close-up of CLOSED sign in Reading Library window and zoom out to cover on library and window

* — see geographical sheets for explanation

{ — consecutive footage

REFERENCE BOOKS
ON FEATURES AND DOCUMENTARIES

Baddeley, W. Hugh, *The Technique of Documentary Film Production.* New York: Hastings House, 4th ed., 1975. A guidebook covering all the steps in producing a documentary film, including initial idea and written treatment.

Bluem, A. William, *Documentary in American Television.* New York: Hastings House, 1965. Creative approach to form, function and method.

Elliott, Philip, *The Making of a Television Series.* New York: Hastings House, 1972. Examines the making of a seven-part controversial documentary series, including conceptual work, gathering of materials, preparing outlines and scripts.

Friendly, Alfred W. *Due to Circumstances Beyond Our Control.* New York: Random House, 1967.

MacCann, Richard Dyer, *The People's Films.* New York: Hastings House, 1973. A political history of U.S. government documentary films.

Murrow, Edward R. *In Search of Light.* Edited by Edward J. Bliss, Jr. New York: Avon, 1974. The broadcasts of Edward R. Murrow, 1938-1961.

Rotha, Paul, S. Road and R. Griffith, *Documentary Film.* New York: Hastings House, 3rd ed., 1952. The standard work on the world documentary film movement to the 1950s.

Strasser, Alex, *The Work of the Science Film Maker.* New York: Hastings House, 1972. The science and technology films studied are of a genre frequently used as features on television.

Yellin, David G., *Special: Fred Freed and the Television Documentary.* New York: Macmillan, 1973. A biography which shows how the news documentary developed and its relationship to current events.

FOR APPLICATION AND REVIEW

1. Write a routine sheet for a how-to-do-it *radio* feature. The subject should be one of importance to a professional or vocational group in your community.

2. Write a script for a behind-the-scenes human interest *television* feature. The purpose should be to persuade as well as to inform. Try a public health or social welfare subject.

3. Write a documentary script for television *or* radio, using one or a combination of the basic documentary types. The subject should be one that is vital to the welfare and continued existence of humanity, and that is of some controversy in your community as well as nationally.

4. Write a documentary script for the medium not used above. The subject should be one which is relatively unimportant and which is not of vital interest to humanity. Can you, even so, incorporate a point of view which makes the documentary pertinent in your community?

6

Talks Programs and Game Shows

"TALKS PROGRAM" IS used sometimes as an all-inclusive term, encompassing virtually all program types that are not news, documentaries, drama, music or commercials. Included in "talks programs" are interviews, discussions, speeches and, in many instances, quiz, audience participation and celebrity panel shows. With their increasing popularity in the 1970s, game shows have been put by many stations and production firms in separate, independent categories. For purposes of compactness, Game Shows are included in this book in the same chapter as Talks Programs, although in a separate section.

TALKS PROGRAMS

SPEECHES ARE, OF course, fully prepared — or, at least, ought to be. Interview and discussion programs are outlined, either in rundown or routine sheet form. A principal reason they cannot be prepared in complete script form is that the very nature of an interplay of ideas and, sometimes, feelings among people requires extemporaneity. Another reason is that the participants, excluding the interviewer or moderator, usually are non-professionals and cannot memorize or "read" a prepared script without seeming strained and stilted.

Nevertheless, the writer should prepare as much of the script as necessary — whether a detailed routine sheet or a simple outline — for the best possible show. Why take a chance with an unprepared question or sequence when the chances of success are better with prepared material? The rundown sheet is the key for most talks programs. As noted in earlier chapters, the rundown sheet is a detailed listing of all the sequences in a given program, frequently with the elapsed time, if known, for each item. Because broadcasting operates on a split-second schedule, the final version of the rundown sheet must be adhered to in the taping or live broadcast of the program. Some talks shows use the more detailed routine sheet, which includes as much of the actual dialogue and action as can be prepared. Rundown and routine sheets sometimes include alternate endings of different lengths so that the extemporaneous nature of the program can be maintained and still end on time through the choice of the proper-length sequence for the final item in the program.

THE INTERVIEW

THE INTERVIEW ON radio or television may be prepared completely, with a finished script for interviewer and interviewee; it may be oriented around an outline, where the general line of questioning and answering is prepared, but the exact words to be used are extemporaneous; it may be completely unprepared, or ad-lib. Very rarely are interviews either completely ad-lib or completely scripted. The unprepared interview is too risky, with the interviewee likely to be too garrulous, embarrassing or embarrassed, or just plain dull, and the interviewer likely to be faced with the almost impossible task of organizing, preparing and thinking of appropriate questions on the spot. The prepared script usually results in a stilted, monotonous presentation except when both the interviewer and interviewee are skilled performers who can make a written line sound extemporaneous, a situation not often likely to occur.

Approach

Most interviews are set up in outline form. A broad outline of the purpose and form of questioning is prepared by the interviewer and staff and, on the basis of knowledge or research concerning the interviewee, a number of questions are prepared. In order to be ready to ask questions in a logical order, the interviewer must have an idea of the possible answers to the major questions already developed. For this purpose a preliminary conference or pre-interview, if possible, is held with the interviewee who is briefed, sometimes lightly, sometimes fully, on the questions to be asked. The interviewee indicates the general line of answering. On the basis of this conference the interviewer is able to develop follow-up and probing questions and arrange the general line of questioning in its most effective order.

The written material for the extemporaneous interview is the rundown and/or routine sheet, a step-by-step outline of the program which includes a list of questions and content of answers as determined in the pre-interview session. Sometimes, of course, the interviewee will not be available for a conference before the show, and the interviewer and staff must guess at the probable answers to their questions — based on thorough research of the interviewee, whose answers to certain questions, if consistent, can fairly accurately be anticipated. Sometimes the interviewee can be persuaded to appear at the studio a substantial time before the program, and a rehearsal will serve, in part, as a pre-interview session. On some occasions the interviewee is not only available for a pre-interview conference but also comes to a rehearsal, thus solidifying the show while retaining its extemporaneous quality.

In all interviews — prepared, extemporaneous, ad-lib — the writer, ideally, prepares at least the opening and closing continuity, introductory material about the interviewee and for each section of the program, lead-ins and -outs for commercial breaks and an outline of the questions and, if possible, answers. The closing continuity should be of different lengths in case the program runs shorter or longer than expected. The writer should be certain that the background of the guest is clearly presented. Except where the interviewee is very well known, it is sometimes helpful to begin with questions of a human interest nature so that the audience gets to know something about the personality of the guest before the interview is too far along. Even with a well-known guest this sometimes is advisable. In the strictly informational, newstype interview this approach could be distractive, although even in such programs the interviewer frequently asks "personality" questions.

Types

There are three major interview types: the opinion interview, the information interview and the personality interview. Any given interview can combine elements of all three.

The Opinion Interview. Any interview that concentrates on the beliefs of an individual may be an opinion interview. However, inasmuch as many of the interviews of this nature are with prominent people, usually experts in their fields, such interviews are not only opinion but, to a great extent, information and even personality types. Even in the completely ad-lib "street" interview, the interviewer should have an introduction, a question, and follow-up questions developed in the light of possible answers. Prospective interviewees may be briefed before the program is taped or goes on the air.

The Information Interview. The information interview usually is of the public service type. The information may be delivered by a relatively unknown figure or by a prominent person in the field. Since the main object is the communication of information, sometimes a complete script may be prepared. The interviewee may provide direct factual material, may deliver information oriented toward a cause or purpose or may combine information with personal belief. If a script is written, the personality of the speaker should be kept in mind. If the interviewee is not likely to be a performer, that is, a good "reader," then it is better to prepare a detailed outline and rehearse the program as an extemporaneous presentation.

A news interview such as "Face The Nation" (see page 224) falls into the category of the information interview. When important personalities are the subjects, the information frequently is mixed with opinion — although what might be called opinion by some is called fact by others.

The Personality Interview. This is the human interest, feature story kind of interview. The format of the program may be oriented toward one purpose — to probe or to embarrass or to flatter — or it may be flexible, combining and interweaving these various facets. The most successful personality interview programs of recent years seem to be oriented toward a combination of probing for personal attitudes and revelation of personal beliefs and actions. To prepare pertinent questions for the personality interview, full background information on the interviewee must be obtained. The questions must be outlined and the interviewee must be talked with before the program in order to prepare the depth questions and the logical order of questioning.

Television Considerations

We usually think of the interview as static: two or more people talking at each other. However, even in the simplest question-and-answer process, some visual interest can be injected. The visual movement may be of a subjective nature, with the camera probing the facial expressions and bodily gestures of the interviewee. The visual approach may be broader and more objective, with film clips or photographs of places, events or personalities referred to by the interviewee. For example, an interview with a college professor may have a film clip of the institution where he or she teaches; an interview with a scientist may include visual material concerning his or her experiments. Shots of the interviewee's home town are sometimes effective. Because television is visual, the interviewer (and writer-producer-director) must be cautioned about misleading the audience, even unintentionally. One classic story is about the television interviewer who made much in pre-program publicity of a forthcoming interview with a famous stripper. Although the audience should have known better, many viewers were quite disappointed that she didn't do what she obviously couldn't do on television.

Technique

Format is paramount. Each interview program has its own organization and the writer must write for that particular format. Some interview shows open with an introduction of the program, introduce the guest and then go into the actual interview. Others open cold, with the interview already under way, in order to immediately grab and hold the audience's attention, with a subsequent cut-in for the standard introductory material. The following scripts for "Face The Nation" illustrate the latter approach. Note the use of the term "tease" for this kind of opening. Note, too, the alternate closings prepared for edited and non-edited versions of the radio broadcast. Do you find any distinctive differences between the radio and television scripts? Should there be any special, different techniques used for each respective medium?

CBS RADIO — "FACE THE NATION"

12:30:00 - 12:58:55 P.M.	June 9, 1974
2:30:00 - 2:53:30 P.M.	(Date)
(Edited Version)	

OPENING: Radio takes TV audio (Herman asks tease question, guest(s) answer(s). Before TV announcer comes in, Radio cutaway as follows:

SOUND: RADIO "PUBLIC AFFAIRS SOUNDER"

ANNOUNCER: "From CBS News, Washington . . . Face the Nation . . . on the CBS Radio Network . . . a spontaneous and unrehearsed news interview with _____Senator Henry Jackson (Democrat of Washington)_____

_____Senator Jackson_____ will be questioned by CBS News Diplomatic Correspondent Marvin Kalb, David S. Broder, National Political Correspondent for the Washington Post and by CBS News Correspondent George Herman. We shall resume the interview in a moment. But first, here is George Herman.

(2:00 Herman Tape)

ANNOUNCER: "And now, we continue with Face the Nation."

INTERVIEW

CLOSING: Radio cuts away from TV audio on Herman's cue:
                  (. . . "Thank you very much for being here to Face the Nation, a word about next week's guest in a moment.")

(PAUSE: :02 PROMO: _____)

ANNOUNCER: "Today on Face the Nation, _____Senator Henry Jackson (Democrat of Washington)_____ was interviewed by CBS Diplomatic Correspondent Marvin Kalb, David S. Broder, National Political Correspondent for the Washington Post, and CBS News Correspondent George Herman.

                  Next week, _____(another prominent figure in the news)_____

                  (_____)

                  will "Face the Nation".

12:30 feed   Today's broadcast was recorded earlier today in Washington and was produced by Sylvia Westerman and Mary O. Yates. Robert Vitarelli is the director. Face the Nation is a production of CBS News.

(CLOSING PUBLIC AFFAIRS SOUNDER)　　(CRN CUE)

2:30 feed

　　Today's broadcast was recorded earlier today in Washington and was edited to conform to time requirements. It was produced by Sylvia Westerman and Mary O. Yates. Robert Vitarelli is the director. Face the Nation is a production of CBS News.

(CLOSING PUBLIC AFFAIRS SOUNDER)　　(CRN CUE)

Courtesy of CBS News

　　　CBS TELEVISION — "FACE THE NATION"

HERMAN TEASE QUESTION _____

SEN. JACKSON ANSWERS _____

(ANNCR: V.O.)

FROM CBS NEWS WASHINGTON . . . A SPONTANEOUS AND UNREHEARSED NEWS INTERVIEW ON "FACE THE NATION", WITH SENATOR HENRY JACKSON, DEMOCRAT OF WASHINGTON. SENATOR JACKSON WILL BE QUESTIONED BY CBS NEWS DIPLOMATIC CORRESPONDENT MARVIN KALB, DAVID S. BRODER, NATIONAL POLITICAL CORRESPONDENT FOR THE WASHINGTON POST AND CBS NEWS CORRESPONDENT GEORGE HERMAN. "FACE THE NATION" IS PRODUCED BY CBS NEWS, WHICH IS SOLELY RESPONSIBLE FOR THE SELECTION OF TODAY'S GUEST AND PANEL.

BILLBOARD _____ 10 sec. _____
　　(IMBB　　1801)　　　　　　　　　　(VTR)

COMMERCIAL _____ 1:40 _____
　　(SRA MATH　　IMSR　　5112)　　　　(VTR)

(HERMAN CLOSING)

I'M SORRY GENTLEMEN, BUT OUR TIME IS UP. THANK YOU VERY MUCH FOR BEING HERE TO "FACE THE NATION".

COMMERCIAL _____ :36½ _____
　　(THIRTY SECONDS　　IMCO　　3312FN)

(ANNCR: V.O.)

TODAY ON "FACE THE NATION", SENATOR HENRY JACKSON, DEMOCRAT OF WASHINGTON, WAS INTERVIEWED BY CBS NEWS DIPLOMATIC CORRESPONDENT MARVIN KALB, DAVID S. BRODER, NATIONAL POLITICAL CORRESPONDENT FOR THE WASHINGTON POST AND CBS NEWS CORRESPONDENT GEORGE HERMAN.

(BILLBOARD　　IMBB　　4806　　6 sec.)

"FACE THE NATION" HAS BEEN SPONSORED BY IBM.

(ANNCR: V.O.)

NEXT WEEK, ANOTHER PROMINENT FIGURE IN THE NEWS WILL "FACE THE NATION". THIS BROADCAST WAS PRODUCED BY CBS NEWS.

(ANNCR: V.O.   CREDITS)

VISIT SAUDIA ARABIA — ONE OF THE STOPS ON PRESIDENT
NIXON'S UPCOMING TRIP TO THE MIDDLE EAST — AND MEET THE
KING WHO SITS ON TOP OF ONE THIRD OF THE WORLD'S OIL,
ON 60 MINUTES LATER TODAY.

(ANNCR: V.O.)

"FACE THE NATION" ORIGINATED FROM WASHINGTON, D.C.

Courtesy of CBS News

In *Approach,* above, we noted what the writer "ideally" prepares. The interviewer's technique, configuration of the program itself, and the producer's and director's styles modify what is ideal. The script preparation becomes what is necessary and effective. For example, Duncan MacDonald was her own writer, producer and interviewer for the program she conducted on WQXR, New York. After a while she did not need written-out opening, closing and continuity preparation. Her concentration was on the content. One of her keys was to be certain that under each major question there were enough follow-up or probe questions, so that she was not faced with the possibility of getting single-phrase answers and running out of questions and topics in a few minutes. The following is the rundown outline used for one of her 30-minute programs.

Today is the anniversary of the signing of the United Nations Charter in San Francisco. In observance of this anniversary our guest today is Dr. Rodolphe L. Coigney, Director of the World Health Organization liaison office with the UN in New York City.

Dr. Coigney was born and educated in Paris. His career in international health began in 1944. In 1947 he became director of health for the International Refugee Organization. In his present post at the UN he represents WHO — the World Health Organization — at Economic and Social Council meetings, the Committee of the UN General Assembly, and other bodies of the UN.

1) Dr. Coigney, as one of the 10 specialized agencies of the UN, what is WHO's specific function?
   a) Is it included in the Charter of the UN?
   b) Active/passive purpose?
   c) Is WHO affected by various crises within UN?
      Financial/political? Your own crises in health?
   d) Do you have specific long term goals, or do you respond only to crises in health?
      Earthquakes/Floods/Epidemics?

2) How does the work of WHO tie in with other UN organizations?
   UNICEF/ILO/Food and Agriculture/UNESCO/International Civil Aviation/
   International Bank/Reconstruction and Development/International Monetary Fund/
   Universal Postal/International Communications/World Meteorological.

3) Background of WHO.
   a) How started? Switzerland?
   b) Headquarters for all international organizations?

4) How much would the work of WHO differ in a country medically advanced, such as Sweden, as opposed to developing countries: Africa, Far East?
   a) Religious or social taboos?
   b) Witch doctors?
   c) Birth Control?

5) Can you give an example of a decision made at Headquarters and then carried out in some remote area of the world?

6) What do you consider WHO's greatest success story in fighting a specific disease: malaria, yaws?
   a) Ramifications of disease? Economic/Disability for work?

7) Your secretary mentioned on the phone that you were going to Latin America. What specifically takes you there now?

8) How does a country get WHO assistance?
   a) Invited?
   b) Matching funds?

9) We are aware of the shortage of doctors and nurses in the United States. What is the situation world-wide?
   a) Do you think Public Health is an important career for young people? Now? For the future?

Courtesy of Duncan MacDonald

Some interview shows do not prepare rundown or routine sheets, but attempt to develop spontaneous exploration between interviewer and interviewee. This does not mean, of course, that there is no preparation. A highly successful "guest" TV program on WTTG, Washington, D.C., "Panorama," does not have a written format, intro or outro, but does prepare extensive research material for use during the show.

Within a tested process for development of each program, all staff members make suggestions and present materials relating to possible topics and guests, achieving a flexible framework of operations described by "Panorama" producer Jane Caper as a "give and take, working back and forth, pulling information and ideas" among researcher, producer, interviewer and guest. At weekly staff meetings staff members with topic and/or guest suggestions have already done preliminary research, validating as fully as possible their recommendations. If a suggestion is adopted — with producer Caper having final say — arrangements are made for the guest to appear and further research, in depth, is done. Before the program a pre-interview session is held with the guest, on the basis of which further research may be done, depending on the special areas of interest or expertise brought out in the pre-interview. At this point all the information is consolidated for the interviewer into a research or information sheet. The following is an example of the "info sheet" prepared for a "Panorama" program:

Art Linkletter co-hosts — BIO material on desk, plus book to be promoted.

Guests:　　Mildred Berl, Educational Director, Agnes Bruce Greig School, teaches and supervises kids from different environments — inner city, urban, suburban —is bringing three of school's students with her (Christopher Coleman lives in far N.E.; Ben Goldstein lives in Gaithersburg; Toni Mallory lives on Farragut, N.W. — they range in age from 13-15).

　　　　　　Dr. Robert Williams, Social Psychologist, Head, Department of Psychology, D.C. Teachers College, former crime consultant working with adolescents.

　　　　　　Dr. Harry Wachs (you remember him from before, co-authored book "Thinking Goes to School" — demonstrated thinking games with children) —educational consultant — applies Piaget theory to actual practice in classroom — promotes thinking through problem solving — bringing children from Parkmont Junior High, whom he has worked witih (Carl Fogel, black, 13, lives in N.E.; rest from suburbs — Chris Swann, 12; Mary Duffy, 14; Sally Nicolson, 12).

We want to go into strengths and weaknesses of kids growing up in inner-city and suburban environments — how different stimuli and experiences result in growth and in problems emotionally, physically, socially, educationally.

Inner City	Suburban
Often have physical problems that go undetected due to poor medical care, no money — e.g. hearing, vision loss; sickle cell anemia; malnutrition.	Usually escape undetected illnesses due to frequent checkups, good doctors.
Families often more cohesive, because more people living in close quarters —also greater reliance on all family members — need to pull together — often more emotional support, more physical intimacy without guilt, more courage and ability in handling situations "out in the world" because their environment forces them to.	Often see their parents as successful people, but inaccessible — mom and dad are too busy gaining fame and fortune to help kid with his problems — can develop rebellious attitude to get parent's attention — also take for granted luxuries they have — develop "world owes me a living" attitude.
Kids often see their parents as victims of society, as inadequate — this poor image of parents can lead kids to go after power — "the man isn't gonna screw me like he did my parents".	Often want same prestige and success as parents, but have been given no encouragement in developing own talents and in working out practical ways to achieve goals — or can revolt entirely against materialism of parents.

Mrs. Berl can give many examples of kids' problems stemming from what goes on at home, from her own observations and talk with kids.

Dr. Williams can, besides contrasting inner-city and suburban environmental effects on kids, illustrate how blacks make the mistake of trying to copy the wrong things in white society, e.g. emphasis on amassing money, possessions; putting pressure on kids to conform, inhibiting emotional expression — also, having been a crime consultant, he can talk about problems kids get into — such as, shoplifting, drugs, unwanted pregnancies — how suburban and ghetto kids get into same kinds of trouble for different reasons, and how parents may react differently to these situations.

Dr. Wachs can relate learning ability and achievement to environment — e.g. inner-city kids are often better at movement thinking, they are exposed to the street early, have more mobility, less protection, but not as much opportunity to develop graphic thinking (transferring thoughts to paper) or auditory thinking (verbalizing, and transferring sound into thought. Also inner-city parents are less likely to want to expose their kids to new forms of learning — stress basic skills — learn to read and write and get a job. He also emphasizes that any environment can challenge thinking, but perhaps different types of thinking, being able to excel at different types of activities. An important aspect of Wachs' teaching is that students do not work for approval, but for self-fulfillment.

Courtesy of WTTG, Washington, D.C.

Even after the "Panorama" info sheet has been absorbed by the interviewer, the program remains flexible and the material may be changed up to the very last minute.

Producer Caper believes that talk shows as we've known them for the past 20 years are on the way out. "People are interested in more substantive things. Instead of trivia they want to know what's going on in the world. The one-on-one interview is also on the way out. For example, some of those programs bring in only one person, such as a politician, and present only one point of view. Interview shows should present various points of view." Caper believes that interview shows should not be promotional vehicles for "schlock" and hopes that television itself will change its image and reputation in this regard and concomitantly upgrade the understanding and appreciation of the average TV viewer.

DISCUSSION PROGRAMS

DISCUSSION PROGRAMS ARE aimed toward an exchange of opinions and information and, to some degree, toward the arriving at solutions, actual or implied, on important questions or problems. They should not be confused with the interview, in which the purpose is to elicit, not to exchange.

Approach

The writer of the discussion program has to walk a thin line between too much and not enough preparation. It is not possible to write a complete script, partially because the participants can't know specifically in advance what their precise attitude or comment might be on any given issue or statement brought up in the discussion. On the other hand, a complete lack of preparation would likely result in a program in which the participants would ramble; it would present the moderator with the impossible task of getting everybody someplace without knowing where they were going. To achieve spontaneity, it is better to plan only an outline, indicating the general form and organization of the discussion. This is, of course, in addition to whatever standard opening, closing and transitions are used in the program. This might include opening and closing statements for the moderator, introductions of the participants, and general summaries to be used by the moderator in various places throughout the program.

The discussion outline should be distributed to all participants in advance of the program so that they may plan their own contributions in accordance with the general format. It will give them time to do necessary research and prepare specific information for use during the discussion. The writer should indicate in the format the issues to be discussed, the order in which the discussion will take place, and, where feasible, the time allotted for each point or each participant. If possible, the participants, in consultation with the writer (and/or producer and/or director) should prepare brief statements of their general views so that there can be a pre-program exchange of ideas and a coordination of all participants' contributions toward a smooth, well-integrated program. Just as too much preparation can result in a dull program, too little preparation may result in the participants being unable to cope with the needs of a spontaneous program. In addition, without pre-planning with the participants, there may be an unnecessary duplication of material. A program in which everyone agrees on everything can become quite boring; pre-planning should assure, for incorporation in the rundown or routine sheet, that all points of view on the given issue receive adequate representation — unless, of course, the program is deliberately oriented toward a particular, non-objective viewpoint.

A decision should be made in the early stages of planning whether to use a controversial topic, certainly a good way to achieve vitality and excitement in the program, and whether to promote or avoid disagreement among the participants. The topics should be presented as questions, thus provoking investigation and thought. In addition, the topics should be broadly oriented, preferably in terms of general policy, and should not be so narrow that they can be answered with a yes or no response or with obvious statements of fact.

In the extemporaneous discussion program the same principles apply as in the interview. Opening and closing remarks and introductions should be written out. If possible, general summaries should be prepared for the moderator or master of ceremonies. In some instances, depending, as in the interview program, on format and approach, a brief outline or routine sheet consisting of a summary of the action of the program and a listing of the topics to be covered, or a rundown sheet, may be sufficient.

In television visual elements should be incorporated. The setting should, if possible, relate to the topic. Although the visual element may be relatively simple, it should help to convey a feeling of excitement and challenge in terms of the topic under consideration.

Types

There are several major types of discussion programs: the panel, the symposium, the group discussion and the debate.

Panel.   The panel discussion — not to be confused with the quiz-type or interview-type panel — is the most often used and the most flexible. It presents a number of people in a round-table type of situation exchanging ideas on some topic of interest. There is no set pattern or time limit on individual contributions and sometimes not even a limitation on the matters to be discussed. The participants usually do not have prepared statements and have done whatever background preparation each one individually has deemed necessary. Usually the participants are experts in the particular area of discussion and, therefore, frequently discuss the problem "off the tops of their heads." A moderator, who usually does not participate in the discussion, attempts to guide it and to see that it does not get out of hand or too far from the topic. The approach is informal, with the participants offering personal comments and evaluations at will. On occasion the discussion may become heated between two or more participants. The moderator tries to see that the discussion is not dominated by just one or two persons. No solution to the problem being discussed is necessarily reached, although the moderator frequently summarizes in order to pull the discussion together and to clarify for the audience — and the participants — the point at which the panelists have arrived. A routine sheet usually consists of the moderator's opening remarks, introduction of the panel members, statement of the problem, flexible outline of subtopics to be discussed under the main topic (the outline should be given to each panel member sometime prior to the program, preferably in time for them to prepare materials, if they wish), and the closing.

As you read the following beginning and end of a script-routine sheet prepared for a panel discussion program, note the careful and liberal insertion of subtopics. The complete script repeats the principal question-subtopics organization four times for a one-hour show.

> • *Apply to this script the following questions — which you should apply to any discussion script that you may subsequently write. Do you feel that the phrasing of the subtopics provide the essentials for a good discussion? Is the development of the topic too limited or is there opportunity for the clear presentation of varied opinions, attitudes and information? Does the organization of the program seem to move logically toward a climax? Does there seem to be a logical interrelationship between the various parts of the discussion? Are the participants properly introduced? Does the structure permit periodic summarizing?*

WUNC "CAROLINA ROUNDTABLE"

"The Berlin Crisis"

Thursday, 7-8 P.M.

MODERATOR (GEORGE HALL): (OPEN COLD) West Berlin — to be or not to be? This question has been reiterated thousands of times by the peoples of the world. With the erection of physical barricades between the Eastern and Western zones of Berlin, conflict between the East and West German regimes has become one on which may very well hang the future of the entire world.

This is your Moderator, George Hall, welcoming you to another "Carolina Roundtable."

All of us are by now fearfully aware of the critical importance of West Berlin. Most of us recognize that the East Berlin limitations on inter-city travel and the West Berlin opposition to negotiation with and recognition of the East have created an impasse that demands a response from both sides. What is that response to be — not only that of the West and of the United States, but that of the Communist East and of the Soviet Union? How will the choice of a course of action determine not only the fate of both Berlins, but of mankind? Are there any areas of compromise that would be satisfactory to all parties?

This evening, with the aid of our guests, we will attempt to seek answers to these questions.

Dr. Charles B. Robson is a professor of Political Science at the University of North Carolina and an authority on Germany. Dr. Robson teaches in the fields of German government and in modern political theory. He recently spent a year in Germany studying that country's political affairs. Good evening, Dr. Robson.

ROBSON: (RESPONSE)

MODERATOR: Dr. Leopold B. Koziebrodzki is an associate professor of Economics and History at the University of North Carolina. His special field is Russian foreign relations in the twentieth century, and he has observed first-hand government policies of eastern European countries in relation to the Soviet Union. Good evening, Dr. Koziebrodzki.

KOZIEBRODZKI: (RESPONSE)

MODERATOR: Dr. Samuel Shepard Jones is Burton Craige Professor of Political Science at the University of North Carolina. His area of specialization is United States foreign policy and international politics. He has served as cultural attache with the U.S. State Department, and has lectured before the National War College. Good evening, Dr. Jones.

JONES: (RESPONSE)

MODERATOR: I'd like to remind our participants and our listeners that questions are encouraged from our listening audience. Any one having a question for any or all of our panel members is invited to phone the WUNC studios at 942-3172. Your question will be taped and played back for our panel to answer at the first opportunity. That's 942-3172.

With the East German government having seized the political offensive, it seems as if the next step is up to the West. In view of the growing power and influence of the small and uncommitted countries in the United Nations, what concessions, if any, should the West be prepared to make in the interest of peace in Berlin? Dr. Jones, would you start the discussion on this matter?

(BRING IN OTHER PANELISTS ON THIS QUESTION. THROUGH PRE-DISCUSSION, DETERMINE TENTATIVE AGREEMENT ON SOME AREAS, AS BELOW.)

(SUB-TOPICS, AS NEEDED)

1. Berlin to be a free city under U.N. jurisdiction, as proposed by Soviet Union?
2. Recognition of East German government?
3. Demilitarization with foreign troops withdrawn?
4. Admission and roles of West and East Germany in U.N.?

MODERATOR: (REMINDER TO AUDIENCE ON PHONE CALLS)

* * *

MODERATOR: (IF ABOVE TOPICS NOT CONCLUDED BY 8 MINUTES BEFORE THE END OF THE PROGRAM, SKIP TO FOLLOWING): Of all the possibilities discussed on the program, which, if any, do you think have the most chance of acceptance?

(IF FEW OR NONE, ASK ABOUT ALTERNATIVES AND POSSIBILITIES OF WAR.)

MODERATOR: (SUMMARY AT 3-MINUTE MARK)

1. Possible concessions by West.
2. Attitudes and actions of East Germany and the East.
3. Attitudes and actions of West Germany.
4. Future of Berlin.
5. Chances of war.

MODERATOR: (AT 1-MINUTE MARK) Dr. Charles Robson, Dr. Leopold Koziebrodzki, and Dr. Shepard Jones of the University of North Carolina, we thank you for being our guests this evening on this "Carolina Roundtable" discussion of the possible solutions to the Berlin problem.

GUESTS: (MASS RESPONSE OF GOOD NIGHT, ETC.)

MODERATOR: We thank you all for listening and invite you to join us next week at this same time when "Carolina Roundtable's" guests, _____, _____, and _____ will discuss _____.

This has been a presentation of WUNC, the FM radio station of the Department of Radio, Television and Motion Pictures, in the Communication Center of the University of North Carolina. Continuity was written by Gilbert File, and the program was directed by Reno Bailey. Your moderator has been George Hall.

Symposium. The symposium presents several persons who have prepared individual solutions to a given problem. Each of the participants is given an equal period of time in which to present his or her ideas. First, each participant presents, with the same time limit for each, a prepared statement on the question. The question should be one which has at least two distinct sides, such as "Should the Twenty-first Amendment to the Constitution Be Repealed?" After the participants have presented their prepared talks, members of the audience may direct questions to any or all members of the symposium. During this question period the participants sometimes cross-question each other and exchange ideas. After a specified time period, the questions from the audience are ended and each participant is permitted an equal amount of time for summing up his or her viewpoint. "America's Town Meeting of the Air," on radio for many years, was an outstanding example of the symposium. The typical routine sheet or outline contains the moderator's opening remarks, the introduction of the participants, set time limits for the prepared statements, audience question period and summaries, and the closing for the program.

Group Discussion. Group discussion is a form of problem-solving that has been used very effectively in industry and in some professional situations. Although rarely used in radio or television, it has the potential for arriving at objective information and action for mutually beneficial purposes, not only among the participants, but for the audience as well. Group discussion differs from most other forms of discussion in that it attempts to solve a problem by employing the objective, cooperative thinking and research of all the participants. The participants do not attempt to impose their own viewpoints and do not take opposing positions, but attempt to examine all materials in an unbiased manner and, in common investigation and unanimous decision, reach a solution acceptable to and best for the entire group. A moderator, who does not participate, guides the discussion and sees that it remains objective, that all group members participate and that none dominates, and that the discussion does not go off the track. A basic organizational approach for a group discussion would be a definition and limitation of the problem, a determination of the causes of the problem through objective research, and a determination of solutions based on the causes. Ideally, each participant is prepared with an outline containing facts pertinent to each step in the discussion process. The question itself should be a broad one, not answerable by a "yes" or a "no," such as "Should Legal Penalties For Marijuana Use Be Abolished?," but necessitating analysis, such as "What Should be Done About Legal Penalties For Marijuana Use?" The prepared material need be only an outline containing the opening, the introduction of the participants, some basic factual information under each step of the process, and the closing.

Debate. Another form of discussion rarely seen on television or heard on radio is the formal debate, except for a public broadcasting network series in the early 1970s, occasional network specials and series on individual local stations. Yet, by the very nature of its form of dramatic conflict, the debate is a natural for broadcasting. A debate consists of two distinctly opposite sides of a question, one side taking the affirmative, the other side the negative. In the debate the participants devote all of their energies to disputing each other, to building up their own arguments and destroying those of the opponent. The debaters may be individuals or may be in teams of two or more on a side. The debate itself has a number of distinct forms of organization. In all forms, however, there are just two sides, and each side is given a specified time for presentation of an initial argument, for rebuttal of the opponent's argument, and for summary. Some forms utilize direct confrontation and cross-examination. The prepared continuity need be only the opening, introduction of participants, introduction and time limits for each phase of the debate, explanations and interviews, if desired, and closing.

SPEECHES

MOST SPEECHES ARE prepared outside the station and the staff writer usually has no concern with them except to write the opening and closing material for the station announcer, which may include introductory comments on the speaker, depending on how well known the latter is. It is improper to go beyond: "Ladies and gentlemen, The President of the United States." However, if The President is speaking at a special occasion or for a special public purpose, pre-speech commentary would describe the occasion and/or purpose, with appropriate background material. Commentary and analysis may also follow a speech.

If the speaker is not well known — for example, a spokesperson responding to a station's editorial — information about that person's position and qualifications as a spokesperson on the issue should be presented, as well as a statement on the reason for his or her appearance. A good rule to remember is that the better known the speaker is, the less introduction is needed.

In some instances, usually on the local level, speakers unfamiliar with radio and television's time requirements may have to be advised how and where to trim their speeches so they are not cut off before they finish. Speakers unfamiliar with television and radio techniques frequently do not realize the necessity for split-second scheduling and their speeches may not only run long, but, sometimes, too short, leaving unfilled program time. In other instances it may be necessary to remind (or even help) the speaker to rewrite in terms of legal, FCC or station policy concerning statements made over the air, including libel, obscenity, personal attack and fairness doctrine considerations.

If a speech is prepared by the writer in the station, it must, of course, be done in collaboration with the speaker. First, the format should be determined. Will it be a straight speech? Will there be a panel or interviewer present? Will there be questions from an audience? Will the speech be read from a desk or lectern, be memorized, or be put on cue cards? At all times the speech style should fit the personality of the speaker.

Occasionally, the speech on television may be developed into more than a simple verbal presentation and may include film clips, tape, photos and other visual material. Such speeches are, however, essentially illustrated talk or lectures and would more likely be prepared as features.

A simple, basic format, containing "intro," "outro" and transitions, is the following, used for speeches during a political campaign.

ANNCR: In order to better acquaint Virginia voters with the candidates and issues in the upcoming general election . . . the WGAY Public Affairs Department presents . . . "Platform '73"

Now . . . here is _____
_____.

(play cart)

You've just heard _____
_____.

Now . . . here is _____

_____.

(play cart)

You've just heard _____

_____.

In the public interest, WGAY has presented "Platform '73" . . . a look at Virginia general election candidates and issues. The opinions expressed are those of the candidates and do not necessarily reflect the feelings of WGAY or its sponsors. Stay tuned for other candidates and their views throughout the campaign.   (PAUSE)

From atop the World Building . . . WGAY FM & AM, Washington & Silver Spring. (WGAY-FM in Washington)

GAME SHOWS

THE MID-1970's SAW the Game Show become a staple of commercial television, starting early in the morning and filling program schedules through the afternoon and into prime time. The formats for the game show are many, ranging from the quiz of a contestant or an entire panel, to the performance of an audience member, to the participation of a celebrity. In all formats the participant is put into competition with another person or persons or with a time or question barrier. In each case someone is expected to solve some problem in order to achieve the specific goal of the game — that is, win money or goods. The problem may be to stump a panel of experts, guess what someone else is thinking, answer extremely complicated or extremely elementary questions about some subject, or hit one's spouse in the face three out of five times with a custard pie.

Most of the TV game shows fit into one of five major formats: celebrity participation, word games, variations on gambling, straight question-and-answer games and non-game games. The variations are virtually endless. "Match Game" is mostly celebrity entertainment with a quiz involving the contestants, who are asked to complete phrases stated by the host and who win when their answers match that of a celebrity. Much of the appeal of the show comes from the questions, which are designed for sexual *double-entendre*. "Password" and "The $10,000 Pyramid" involve pairs of contestants who give each other clues while trying to get each other to say certain words. "Dealer's Choice" and "High Rollers" use huge dice; "Gambit" uses huge playing cards; "The Joker's Wild" uses a huge slot machine. "Jeopardy," one of the longest running game shows, follows the straight question-and-answer format, except that the contestants are given the answers and must guess the questions. "The New Treasure Hunt" is an example of the non-game game show; contestants take their pick of gift-wrapped boxes piled on the stage, some of which contain valuable prizes and some of which are virtually worthless.[1] Invent your own game!

Game Shows are invariably spontaneous — or made to look that way. Because the participants are in part or totally non-professionals in the acting field, it is not possible to write out a complete script. The "readings" would come out stilted. Yet, as with any well-prepared program, as much of the continuity as possible is written out, and the routine or rundown sheets for many game shows are quite detailed.

Opening and closing continuity, introductions, ad-lib jokes, questions, commentary introducing and ending sequences and similar material are written out. The material should be flexible and adaptable to the spontaneity of the participants. The prepared material should be designed to fit the personality of the person hosting the show and should be developed in consultation with him or her. In some audience participation shows virtually all of the dialogue, except that which will be given by the non-professional participants, is scripted. In many instances even the participants' supposedly ad-lib dialogue is prepared, even if only in outline form. Sequences — including routines, stunts, matches or whatever the particular game show calls for — should be timed accurately beforehand so that the basic script fits into the required time length. Extra material of different time lengths may be prepared in case the show begins to run too long or too short.

It is essential to grab the audience interest immediately. The conflict-contest aspect of the show should be put into immediate focus so that the audience doesn't want to leave until it finds out who won — or lost — what. If there are a series of participants or sequences in the show it is necessary to develop a line of continuity and suspense — equivalent to the rising action of the drama — so that the audience doesn't lose interest and switch to another channel and a different game show in the middle of the program. The prepared material should set the tone and mood of the show — a fast-paced suspenseful conflict. Some game shows use celebrities who not only provide human-interest images but also supply comedy. Gag writers are needed, although the comedy-personality will usually use his or her own.

The visual elements of the particular game should be stressed. Charts, pyramids, curtains, models, all bigger than life, are some of the set pieces for game shows. As the years progress they and the games seem to become more and more complicated. Yet, a game show can be simple. For example, one of the most effective formats in the entire history of game shows was that of an individual grimacing and sweating in the confines of a glamorized telephone booth with tens of thousands of dollars seemingly hanging on his or her answer to a question.

One of the longest-running game shows, stressing the audience participation approach, is "Truth or Consequences." Producer Ed Bailey states that this show is based on a "spontaneous, ad-libbed format, and thus the script merely outlines the stunt or consequence. Our Master of Ceremonies, Bob Barker, is very quick-witted and glib, and on the basis of the script outline of the consequence, improvises the entire show." As you examine the routine sheet note that most of the participation sequence is designated by only one item, number 10, and that the actual continuity is of an introductory and transitional nature.

"TRUTH OR CONSEQUENCES"

BOB BARKER

1. Bring on contestants.

2. Interview and question.

3. Now, I know it probably never happens in your family, but every once in a while you hear about some member of a family putting a little money away for a rainy day, so to speak . . . and the interesting thing about some of these deposits is that only the person who put the money away knows where it is.

4. Tell me, Mrs. _____, do you think your husband has a few bills tucked away that you know nothing about?
(HEH HEH)
And, Mr. _____, do you think that Mrs. _____ might have a dollar or two hidden in a teapot that you know nothing about?
(ANSWER)

5. In any event, when such a thing does happen the money is put in a secret place known only to the one who put it there. Now, today we want to conduct a little experiment.

6. Reveal table and props.
(WE NEED ONLY THREE PROPS . . . A COOKIE JAR . . . A PIGGY BANK, AND A COPY OF PLAYBOY FOR THE COFFEE TABLE)

7. I want you to notice that we have on display a cookie jar . . . a piggy bank . . . and there on the table, a man's type magazine.

8. Now, here's what's going to happen. Mrs. _____, I want you to take these bills.
You'll note there is a one dollar bill . . . a five dollar bill, and a one hundred dollar bill.

9. Now, Mrs. _____, I want you to hide one of these bills in the cookie

jar . . . one in the piggy bank, and one
in the magazine. We'll close the curtains
so not even the studio audience will
know where you put the money. The
first one Mr. _____ picks
is the bill you take home.

10. Play act.

11. Award winnings and consolation, if
necessary.

Courtesy of Ralph Edwards Productions

The most successful game show in syndication in the mid-1970s is
"Hollywood Squares." It is a celebrity game in which nine well-known personalities are seated at the different levels of a three-story stage set, something like a human ticktacktoe board, equipped with flashing lights. While
telling jokes, the celebrities try to help two contestants answer enough questions to fill in the Xs and Os in a winning pattern.[2] Harry Friedman, associate producer of the show, says that once the formula is set, the writer's
work is largely done, and it is then primarily necessary to keep in mind the
guidelines of the program when preparing continuity. Friedman stresses two
principal writing techniques: good research to be certain that information
used on the program in the questions and answers is reliable and accurate,
and a journalistic style. He compares the writing of a game show to writing
a good newspaper article: "it must be interesting, fast-moving, concise and
brought to a logical conclusion." He cautions writers of game shows not to
use extraneous information or material not absolutely necessary to the piece.

> • *As you examine the following routine sheet for "Hollywood
> Squares" remember that one of the important aspects of the game
> show is to involve the viewing audience in the conflict and sus-
> pense. How does "Hollywood Squares" do this? Although contain-
> ing a combination of formats and a relatively large participant
> group, what elements make the program move quickly, simply and
> smoothly to a "logical conclusion"?*

FADE UP ON GAME BOARD WIDE   OPENING

ANNOUNCER:
Today . . . one of these stars is sitting in   ELEC.:
the SECRET SQUARE, and the contestant   SET X'S & O'S FROM YESTERDAY'S
who picks it first could win _____.   SHOW WITH FRAME LIGHTS ON ALL
Which star is it: SQUARES.

CUE MUSIC

ANNOUNCER:

(1) _____	EACH SQUARE LIGHTS (STARS' NAMES IN ORDER OF INTRODUCTION)
(2) _____	
(3) _____	
(4) _____	1 2 3
(5) _____	8 9 4
(6) _____	
(7) _____	7 6 5
(8) _____ OR	
(9) _____	ALL SQUARES FLASH

ALL in THE HOLLYWOOD SQUARES.

APPLAUSE
And here is the Master of THE HOLLY-
WOOD SQUARES . . . Peter Marshall.

PETER:
Thank you very much. Hello STARS
("HELLO PETER.") And Hello _____
and _____.

BRIEF INTERVIEWS

PETER:
Your object is to get THREE stars in a row
. . . either ACROSS . . . UP AND DOWN
. . . or DIAGONALLY.

ELEC.:
PLAY FRAME LIGHTS IN PATTERNS
WITH PETER: (X's & O's STILL UP FROM
TOP OF SHOW)

It's up to you to figure out if a star is giving
a correct answer or making one up.

VIDEO:
CAMERAS STAY ON BOARD FOR 5 TO
10 SECONDS.
(ELEC.: TAKE OUT FRAME LIGHTS ON
BOARD FOR ALL SQUARES WITH X's
& O's.)

That's how you get the squares. A game is
worth $200. We'll play a two out of three
match, so you're playing for $400.

(FOR 2 NEW CONTESTANTS ONLY)
_____ you won the toss
backstage so you go first.

(OR — IF GAME IS CONTINUED.)
This was the game as we left it last time
. . . Study it . . .

(NO MENTION OF WHO HAS WHAT.)

And it was _____ turn. So
which star are you going to pick?
(PRECEDING FIRST NEW GAME)

PETER:
This game is for the SECRET SQUARE.

PETER:
If either of you pick the SECRET SQUARE
. . . and win it . . . this is what you get.

KENNY:
PRIZE COPY. (Adding carryovers as well.)

PETER:
And now . . . let's show our home audience
the SECRET SQUARE.

NOW SECRET SQUARE GAME IS PLAYED.
WHEN SECRET SQUARE IS CHOSEN.
SOUND EFFECT: .... SPECIAL EFFECT FOR SECRET SQUARE.
SHOW SECRET SQUARE.
ALL STAGE MONITORS OUT.

COMMERCIAL THREE
MIDDLE BREAK:

PETER:
If either one of our contestants wins five
matches and $2,000.00, he or she will win
the his and her cars plus an additional
$3,000.00.

KENNY:
ANNOUNCE: CAR PLUG AND GREEN
STAMPS

PETER:
We'll be right back after this short
announcement.

COMMERCIAL FOUR

PETER:
Congratulations. You've won _____.
Tomorrow we'll have another SECRET
SQUARE for another special prize.

IF NOT WON . . .

PETER:
The SECRET SQUARE wasn't won. So, in
addition to what we had today, we'll add
something new on our next show.

PETER:
Time is up. We'll continue the game from
exactly this point on our next show. (TO
CONTESTANTS) Thank you _____
and _____.
And thank you Stars. Good-bye.

STARS:
Good-bye Peter.

KENNY:
(Merchandise to loser.)

NOTES TO CHAPTER 7

[1] Funt, Peter, "Game Shows Now Dominate Daytime TV," *The New York Times,*
    July 14, 1974, Sec. II, pp. 15-16.
[2] *Ibid.,* p. 16.

REFERENCE BOOKS

ON TALKS PROGRAMS AND GAME SHOWS

Cavett, Dick and Christopher Porterfield. *Cavett.* New York: Harcourt Brace
    Jovanovich, 1974.
Fishman, Ed. *How to Strike It Rich on TV Game Shows.* Los Angeles: Price,
    Stern, Sloan, 1972.
MacNeil, Robert. *People Machine: The Influence of Television on American
    Politics.* New York: Harper and Row, 1968.
McGuiniss, Joe. *Selling of the President.* New York: Trident Press, 1969.
Minow, Newton, John B. Martin and Lee Mitchell. *Presidential Television.* New
    York: Basic Books, 1973. A Twentieth Century Fund report.
Routt, Ed. *Dimensions of Broadcast Editorializing.* Blue Ridge Summit, Penna.:
    TAB Books, 1974.

FOR APPLICATION AND REVIEW

1. Prepare an outline, rundown and routine sheet for: an opinion
   interview; a personality interview; an information interview.
   Each interview should be with a *different person* of local importance.
2. Do the same exercise, using the *same person* as the subject for
   all three interview types.
3. Prepare an outline, rundown and routine sheet for a panel discussion program on a highly controversial subject, first for radio,
   then for television.
4. Invent a TV Game Show and prepare the routine sheet for one
   program.

7

Music and
Variety Programs

EXCEPT FOR A relatively few all-talk and all-news stations, radio programming today is music programming. Independent stations rely primarily on recorded music for program content and network affiliates insert principally news and feature feeds into what is otherwise an all-music format. Since the 1930s, when Martin Block made famous the concept of a radio announcer playing records separated by comment and commercials, the disc jockey and the record show have become national institutions. Before television drew so much of the live talent away from radio, live studio musical programs featured symphony orchestras, popular singers, jazz bands, opera stars and other musical soloists and groups. Virtually all such programs gradually disappeared from radio, although some of the quality shows such as the Texaco Opera series and the Telephone and Firestone programs continued on radio a long time in the age of television. Some radio shows made a transition to television, particularly the comedy-variety programs. One musical program that lasted ten years on television after several decades on radio was "Your Hit Parade" — revived, briefly, in the mid-1970s in virtually the same format to try to capture that decade's interest in nostalgia.

Television has not utilized the musical program to the same degree that radio did. There have been some successful series of musical personalities and orchestras, such as Liberace and Lawrence Welk, and occasional attempts at adapting the radio disc jockey program — in effect, on the-air discotheques with youngsters in the community dancing to the TV deejay's records and commentary. Dick Clark's success with this format in Philadelphia and then nationally led to similar shows in many cities. Popular entertainers who are primarily singers, such as Carol Burnett and Dean Martin, have been successful with TV variety, rather than with strictly musical shows. With the phenomenal overnight popularity of rock groups, large audiences have watched TV specials featuring some of the better known groups. Continuing series of music programs of special quality have occasionally proven popular, such as Leonard Bernstein's children's concerts and Arthur Fiedler's Boston Pops concerts on public television.

The job for the scriptwriter in the area of music and variety is principally in preparing continuity for the TV variety show, the radio magazine — which combines music, variety, news and talks — and the classical music deejay program. The variety program, however, depends greatly on humor, and you will notice that the credit crawls at the end of such programs frequently contain long lists of names of comedy writers. That kind of writing is a craft in itself and, according to most producers and writers in the field, can't really be taught. Like singing, there has to be some natural and early developed talent and attitude, which then can be improved by practice. This book does not go into the area of comedy writing.

It does, however, provide an introduction to the format of the variety program for the staff writer who may also be an associate producer, or for the associate producer who at the same time may prepare the basic continuity.

MUSIC PROGRAMS ON RADIO

A MUSICAL PROGRAM must have organic continuity. That is, there should be a central program idea, a focal point around which all the material is organized and from which the program grows and develops. That is not to say that all disc jockey programs have scripts. Very few have. Yet, very few disc jockeys are clever enough to grab a batch of records at the last minute and spontaneously organize them into a good program. Although virtually all disc jockeys are spontaneous with their continuity, almost all of their programs are planned and organized in terms of musical content.

The format preparation for each program reflects the format preparation for the station as a whole. The concept of specialization in radio took hold in the late 1960s and within a few years became the cardinal principle of station programming and image. Most stations have a particular type of format, such as beautiful music or rock or contemporary or MOR (middle-of-the-road, combining popular and standard music). Some stations combine several types of programming and a recent American Research Bureau (ARB) survey showed that stations in the top 50 markets which had the highest quarter-hour audience shares for the longest time were those which combined two or more types of music and included news, talks and features. These so-called "full-service" stations have dominated their markets for many years. As the size of the market grows smaller, however, the music stations become the leaders. Next to the full-service stations in popularity in the largest markets are contemporary, or "top-40" stations, and

MOR stations. In the early days of FM, most listeners equated FM with "good" music, especially classical music. FM stations have programmed more and more for the young listener, however, and in the early 1970s progressive rock, for example, was the fastest growing FM format type.

Definitions of music are constantly changing and formats change accordingly. MOR, for example, has a different connotation today than it had ten years ago. Contemporary music means the music of living composers to some programmers, but is limited to current hit songs for others. Music both reflects culture and builds it. It is the dialogue of youth, providing a sense of psychological freedom for the listener and a sense of artistic freedom for the performer. Pop music is a sociological phenomenon, partly because it reflects the flexibility, growth and change of society, particularly young society. The Beatles changed not only the face of popular music but also the attitudes and behavior of youth. The Beatles motivated an escape from the traditional formulas, and their music was not music alone of bodily rhythm, but music of ideas, the communicating of unspoken and spoken meanings that were vital and forceful to the young people who eagerly pursued them. The basic concept was not new. The blues of the '30s, the soul music of the '50s all had meaning. But the Beatles put it all together, combining and adding as all true innovators do to create what feels fresh and new. Combined with the inexpensive availability of the transistor radio receiver, the new music made radio the link between creative artistry and creative reception as never before.

Record companies and radio stations believe that radio-record music is a democratizing tool, serving the desires of the public. Occasionally the question may arise, of course, as to whether wants are the same as needs and whether the "democratic denominator" may be a euphemism for "lowest common denominator." In any event, record companies and radio stations have found that "democratic" and/or "lcd" are broad in scope and that one cannot be all things to all listeners. Thus, the trend toward specialization and development of a number of major formats, with individual stations in individual communities tending more and more to exclusivity within any given type.

Format Types

In the late 1940s radio needed a new approach. Post-war growth in the number of stations was almost completely local and local revenues began to exceed those of the networks. Music programs on local stations had affinity blocks — that is, 15-minute or half-hour segments devoted to a particular band or vocalist. Format was what was decided on each day by the program director, deejay or music librarian; the latter frequently prepared actual continuity. In many local stations the disc jockey would sign on in the morning with piles of records already waiting, prepared for each show for that day by the music librarian the night before, and the deejay might not even know what the music for each show was before it was played. Then came Top-40, an attempt to reflect and appeal to the tastes of the listeners by choosing records based on popularity as judged by sales charts, juke box surveys and record store reports. Top-40, at its beginning, was eclectic, with stations playing the same 40 most popular selections and the deejay's personality providing the principal differences between station images. Soon, however, many stations began to seek specialized audiences and concentrated on certain types of Top-40 music, such as country and western, rock and roll, soul and other forms. By the late 1960s many Top-40 stations had become almost mechanical, with virtually no disc jockey patter, a play list of only the most popular records and quick segues from record to record. Recently, Top-40 stations have been rejuvenating by bringing back emphasis on the disc jockey and on continuity, providing "warmth" between the playing of records and more flexibility in format. Personality is important again and some disc jockeys are spending more time on continuity.

MOR, middle-of-the-road music, is probably still the most popular "sound." It is essentially "adult" music, programming without extremes in volume, rhythm, timing or technique. Of course, the meaning of MOR changes. To one generation it is Frank Sinatra, Peggy Lee and Nat King Cole. To another it is The Beatles and The Fifth Dimension. And to still another it is The Kitchen Sink and The Electric Grater. Adult tastes are different because adults are different and, to some degree, even contemporary rock can be considered MOR. MOR is personality-oriented and announcer-deejays are likely to become local and even regional celebrities.

MOR is probably the least specialized of the specialized formats and includes one approach that is sometimes a complete station format or image in itself: "Golden Oldies." These are MOR records usually limited to popular music of some 15 to 30 years vintage. Its popularity is probably attributable to the same reason for all shifts to nostalgia: discontent of the people with the events of their time. Some Golden Oldies formats mix oldies with more current MOR, alternating, for example, an Elvis Presley hit of the mid-1950s with a Sammy Davis, Jr. recording of just a few years ago.

Beautiful Music sometimes is also called semi-classical or dinner music. This is the music of Mantovani, Percy Faith, Andre Kostelanetz, Ray Coniff and Broadway shows. It is chosen carefully to fit different moods and tempos of different times of the day. Some 20 to 25% of the radio audience listens to beautiful music. The format is usually standardized into quarter-hour segments, each segment cohesive and providing a consistent mood in itself.

Rock was easy to categorize when it was new. Hard rock, underground rock and acid rock began to require flexibility and reorientation of rock formats. The socio-political nature of some rock lyrics, for example, required a "soft" sound, as opposed to the emphasis on tempo and sound alone some years back. Jazz and folk rock have led many artists into combinations of country music and rock.

Country Music became one of radio's major formats in only a few short years in the 1970s. Country music represents three principal types: modern or "soft" country, standard country and western or "hard" country, and the popular "Nashville sound." A growing number of sophisticated professionals, such as bankers and lawyers and scientists, boast about their conversion to country music, perhaps seeking escape from the ever-increasing stresses of their everyday urban world. Country music stations vary in format: some emphasize one of the three major types; others cross types but, as do some MOR stations, concentrate on the oldies mixed with traditional-sounding new songs; some find excellent audience reaction to a combination of one country and one pop or to mixing country with soft rock.

These are only the major station music formats in radio today, a few of the many which include, as well, religious, soul, jazz, ethnic and rhythm and blues. Even within each of these types there are endless variations and adaptations to the individual station's market and listening audience.

Theme

Some music programs, in addition to cohesiveness through a type of music, are developed around a central theme: a personality, an event, a locality — anything that can give it unity. The writer — that is, the person who prepares the script or rundown sheet continuity — can find ideas for central themes in many places: special days, national holidays, the anniversary of a composer's birth, a new film by a popular singing star, a national or international event that suggests a certain theme such as love, war, the jungle, adventure, corruption, drugs and so forth. The musical selections themselves should have a clear relationship to each other, and the non-musical transitions should indicate this relationship.

The following program, one of a series sent to RCA Victor subscriber stations, is illustrative of continuity for the classical recorded music program built around a theme. Note that a listing of records according to catalogue number and according to playing time precedes the script, thus providing a simple rundown sheet.

MUSIC YOU WANT

LM-6026	Catalani: LORELEI: DANCE OF THE WATER NYMPHS NBC Symphony Orchestra, Arturo Toscanini, conductor	
SIDE 3:	Band 4	6:23
LM-1913	Delibes: COPPELIA: EXCERPTS Boston Symphony Orchestra, Pierre Monteux, conductor	

SIDE 2:   Entire   25:31

LM-2150   Stravinsky: SONG OF THE NIGHTINGALE
               Chicago Symphony Orchestra, Fritz Reiner, conductor

SIDE 2:   Entire   22:13

G07L-0783   AIR FOR G STRING (fading after 20 seconds)

ANNCR: (Sponsor or) His Master's Voice is on the air with THE MUSIC YOU
               WANT WHEN YOU WANT IT, a program of RCA Victor High Fidelity Red
               Seal records.

G07L-0783   AIR FOR G STRING (Up 5 seconds and fade out)

ANNCR: Today's program is devoted to musical works that deal with the super-
               natural. One of the three selections is from an opera, one is a suite from
               a ballet, and the third — from a new RCA Victor album — is a symphonic
               poem, later used for a ballet.
               The supernatural has always had a strong hold on the imagination of man.
               The unknown and the unusual, with the laws of nature in a distorted or
               suspended state, has occupied story-tellers from their earliest days. It
               is only natural that this strong impulse, throughout time and all races,
               should attract composers as suitable subject matter. Our three works today
               deal with three separate types of the supernatural: mythological creatures
               who are portents of evil for mankind — a mechanical doll with complete but
               superficial resemblance to living beings — and animals with human
               characteristics and traits.
               We open with a selection from Catalani's opera Lorelei. The opera deals
               with maidens who inhabit a rock in the middle of the Rhine River and lure
               sailors to destruction. We hear the Dance of the Water Nymphs, in a
               performance by Arturo Toscanini and the NBC Symphony Orchestra.

LM-6026
SIDE 3:
Band 4   Catalani: LORELEI: DANCE OF THE WATER NYMPHS   8:05

ANNCR: We have opened today's program with the Dance of the Water Nymphs from
               the opera, Lorelei, by Catalani. Arturo Toscanini led the NBC Symphony
               Orchestra in our performance.
               Our second selection devoted to the supernatural in music is the suite from
               the ballet, Coppelia (Coe-pay-lyah), or the Girl with the Enamel Eyes, by
               Leo Delibes (Lay-oh Duh-leeb). Coppelia, one of the most popular of all
               evening-length ballets, had its first performance at the Paris Opera in
               May, 1870. The dominant figure in the story is Coppelia, an almost human
               mechanical doll. The youth Frantz falls in love with her, much to the
               chagrin of his lively fiancee Swanhilde. But all ends happily, and in the
               final act the betrothal of Frantz and Swanhilde is celebrated.
               The selections we are to hear from Coppelia are as follows: Prelude —
               Swanhilde's Scene and Waltz — Czardas — The Doll's Scene and Waltz —
               Ballade — and Slavic theme and variations. We hear Coppelia in a
               performance by members of the Boston Symphony Orchestra under the
               direction of the veteran French composer, Pierre Monteux. Selections from
               the ballet, Coppelia, by Leo Dilebes.

LM-1913
SIDE 2:
Entire   Delibes: COPPELIA   34:52

ANNCR: Members of the Boston Symphony Orchestra under the direction of Pierre Monteux have just been heard in selections from the ballet Coppelia by Leo Delibes.

Animals with human traits and emotions are at least as old as Aesop. Igor Stravinsky, before composing his ballet, The Firebird, wrote the first act of an opera, The Nightingale, which — for a number of years — remained unfinished. The opera was to deal with a nightingale who, moved by pity, returns to save the life of a man who previously rejected it. Stravinsky was prevailed upon to finish his score after the composition of his revolutionary Le Sacre du Printemps. Naturally, he was a different composer at that time, disparities of musical style resulted, and Stravinsky remained dissatisfied with the opera. He took the later sections of The Nightingale and turned them into a symphonic poem, changing the title to The Song of the Nightingale. Like most of his works, this symphonic poem became the basis for a ballet.

The Song of the Nightingale concerns the Emperor of China who shifts his affection from a live nightingale to a mechanical one, a present from the Emperor of Japan. He falls ill and is on his deathbed. The real nightingale, contrite at having deserted the Emperor after his change-of-heart, returns to sing to him and restores him to health.

The Song of the Nightingale, a symphonic poem by Igor Stravinsky, in a new RCA Victor recording by Fritz Reiner and the Chicago Symphony Orchestra.

LM-2150
SIDE 2:
Entire   Stravinsky: THE SONG OF THE NIGHTINGALE   58:33

ANNCR: Fritz Reiner and the Chicago Symphony Orchestra have just played Stravinsky's Song of the Nightingale, a new RCA Victor recording. The other side of this album, Prokofieff's Lieutenant Kije (Kee-gee), will be played at a later date.

STANDARD CLOSE
Next Program (Premiere): — Monteux interprets Tchaikovsky's Sleeping Beauty Ballet.

G07L-0783   THEME UP TO END OF BROADCAST PERIOD.

Examples of further types of central themes are evident in the following excerpts:

ANNCR: The three greatest masters of the Viennese classical school are Ludwig von Beethoven, Wolfgang Amadeus Mozart and Franz Joseph Hayden. Today we will hear works by each of these three masters.

ANNCR: Our program today offers Russian music of the 19th century. We open with Borodin's atmospheric orchestral sketch, "On the Steppes of Central Asia." Leopold Stokowski leads his orchestra in this performance.

Reprinted by permission of Radio Corporation of America (RCA Victor Record Division)

Organization and Technique

It is important to get variety into any musical program, notwithstanding the impression that the teenage audiences of disc jockey shows sometimes seem to appreciate only the same repetitious sound and incomprehensible lyrics. The musical program should reflect the elements of any good entertainment program. It should open with something that gets the attention of the audience. Then it may relax a bit — not so as to fall to mediocrity, but by presenting something that may not be on so exciting a plane as the initial number. The building to a climax should be neither boring nor repetitious. Offer the listener a change of pace throughout; after each high point give the audience a rest and then move on to a higher point.

The deejay-producer-writer must analyze the potential audience — similar to the way writers of commercials make a demographic analysis, as described in Chapter 3. Though the audience is given the music that interests it — the station format and image are created for a particular audience — the program should not play down to the audience, should not pander to a low level of taste. The deejay-producer-writer, in great degree, molds and determines the tastes in popular music. No matter what type of music is used, the best of that type should be presented.

The purpose of the program should be adhered to. Never forget that the audience tunes in to that program because it likes that particular musical format. Its reasons for listening may differ: for relaxation, for thinking, for education, for dancing, for background while working, for reinforcement while playing, or for many other purposes. This suggests an adherence to a single type of music. Although there are exceptions, the mixing of "Beethoven" with "bop" or of rock with string quartets is not likely the most effective way to reach and hold an audience. At the same time, the program organization and continuity should fit the personalities of the performers, whether an orchestra, a vocalist or a disc jockey.

Continuity always seems to be limited to orchestras which "render," and singers who give "vocal renditions of," or pianists who always have "impromptu meanderings" and are always playing "on the eighty-eight," and to songs which are "cool," "ever-popular" or "scintillating." The trite joke or play-on-words for transitions and lead-ins has become an over-used device. Phrases such as "For our next number," "Our next record," and "Next on the turntable" have long ceased to serve a worthwhile purpose. Perhaps that doesn't leave much choice? If it is impossible to think of something new and fresh and not trite, the best approach is to keep it simple.

The timing of the show has to be exact, with the combination of musical selections, continuity and commercials coming out to the length of the program. You do this by outlining all these elements on a rundown sheet. Each record or tape cut has a specific time length indicated. Each commercial is written for a specified time. Don't forget to leave time in between for transitions and lead-ins. Rundown sheets such as the following are frequently used:

THE JIM LOWE SHOW, AUGUST 28, 10:10-10:30 A.M.

1. S'WONDERFUL   SHIRLEY BASSEY   MGM
            LIVE: COMMERCIAL (60)

```
2. PUT AWAY YOUR TEARDROPS    STEVE LAWRENCE    COL
        LIVE: COMMERCIAL (30)
3. VOLARE    ELLA FITZGERALD                    VERVE
        LIVE: PROMO, NEWS (15)
4. THE JOLLY PEDDLER    HARRY SOSNICK          MERCURY
        ET: COMMERCIAL (60)
5. I LOVE PARIS    ANDY WILLIAMS               CADENCE
6. COMIN' HOME BABY    JACK LAFORGE            REGINA
        OFFTIME: 29:55
```

Courtesy of WNBC-AM/FM, New York

Rundown or format sheets such as the following may be prepared for an entire evening's schedule, containing the timing for each musical piece and the listing of non-musical program segments.

```
9:00      yes we can can/pointer sisters  6:00
          half moon/janis joplin  3:50
          water song/hot tuna  5:17
news      #21 roller coaster/bs&t  3:25
          brandy/looking glass  3:07
          sylvia/focus  3:32
9:30      something so right/paul simon  4:34
          let's get together/youngbloods  4:39
          so what/monty alexander  10:29  (FADE)
*news     #14 too high/stevie wonder  4:35
          out in the country/three dog night  3:08
10:00     hollywood/chicago  3:53
          ooh la la/faces  3:35
          jessica/allman brothers band  7:00
news      #2 angie/stones  4:30
          dolly/nicky hopkins  4:42
10:30     brandenburg/walter carlos  5:05
          aquarius/ronnie dyson & company  2:55
          aubrey/grover washington, jr.  3:40
          lady honey/pan  4:07
**news    #9 all i know/art garfunkel  3:50
          super strut/deodato  8:55

*BACKGROUND REPORT #1
**EDITORIAL
```

Courtesy at WMAL-FM, Washington, D.C.

The Popular Music Program. Although very few popular music deejay shows have written continuity, it doesn't mean that preparation similar to that for writing a script is not done. There may be personalities somewhere who can recall, organize, interrelate and present ideas correlated with musical numbers with speed and fluency. Unfortunately, too many deejays who can't, think they can. Ad-libbing off the top of the head usually becomes boring and repetitious or just plain silly. Successful deejays rarely take a chance with complete ad-libbing. Why be half-safe when you can be more sure with some preparation?

Harold Green, General Manager of WMAL, Washington, D.C., details the kind of preparation required for his music programs, including the gathering and development of material to be used as continuity:

The day of the "limited" announcer is about over. Just a beautiful voice, or just a snappy, witty or attractive personality is not enough for today's successful radio station. All the tricks, gimmicks, formats, points of view have been tried in one form or another. Some are quite successful in a limited way. The danger that the individual suffers is the strong possibility that he will remain submerged or anonymous. This is particularly true in a station that depends strongly on a particular "format." We feel that the stations that matter in the community don't limit themselves to a format or other gimmick. The key is community involvement — information with a purpose — and a continuity of sound (in music and personality) that will continually serve, and please, the audience that particular station has cultivated.

Our announcers go on the air each day with a thick folder of clippings, personal observations, letters from listeners, and tears from all the news and sports wires. By the time a man actually goes on the air each day, he is fully briefed on all that is happening that is significant in the news, in sports, special events in the community, special broadcasts of more than routine interest scheduled for that day and week, or anything else that amounts to information *with a purpose*. He has spent a minimum of two hours in the music library. Generally, each day's music preparation time amounts to approximately 50% of air time. A 4-hour program requires about two hours to prepare musically. This is for one who is thoroughly familiar with the library. Otherwise it becomes a 1:1 ratio, or even longer. This is because the music list must reflect variety and balance: up-tempo music, boy vocal, lush orchestral, girl vocal, combo or variety, group vocal, and back around again. Specialty, novelty, or other types that break the pattern must be showcased by the D.J. There must be a reason for playing these "extras," and it must be explained.

It is safe to say that when a man does a smooth, informative, professional 4-hour show — and one that teased the imagination and piqued the curiosity — he did an equal four hours of preparation. If he doesn't, he'll know it in about an hour, I'll know it in about an hour and a half, and the listener will know it before noon the next day. Without preparation, background, genuine interest in the world around him, and diligent attention to getting informed and staying informed, a broadcaster sinks instantly into mediocrity. He is then relying on tricks . . . he is ordinary . . . he is short-changing his audience.

He won't last long.

The music library is of great importance. Know its content. Records, when received, should be auditioned, timed and catalogued. Cross-indexing is desirable, with separate indices for theme, performer, composer and any other area which may be a determinant in the organization of a program.

Be conscious of the changing fads and fancies in popular music. An Elvis Presley style may become a Beatles style which may become a Bob Dylan style which may become a Rod McKuen style which may become a Jackson Five style in a matter of months.

.Do not assume that because popular music is not considered in the same intellectual league with classical music that it is not serious music to many of the listeners. In certain pop music forms, such as acid rock and jazz, the deejay is expected to be highly knowledgeable. The serious innovative approach to music by The Beatles educated an entire generation to the intricacies of some types of modern music.

The Classical Music Program. As noted earlier, very few radio music programs have prepared scripts, and these are usually limited to classical shows. Continuity for the classical music program must be, in general, more "expert" than continuity for the pop music program. The educational and intellectual levels of the listener of the classical music show are likely to be above those of the average listener of the pop music show, and our classical music audience is likely to be more critical of the written material presented. The audience expects more than a cursory introduction, and more continuity is needed than in the pop program. The listener likely already knows something about the music to be presented and expects intelligent and informational background material and, frequently, aesthetic comment and interpretation. The "expert" analysis must be presented thoroughly. It is not sufficient to say "This is the finest example of chamber music written in the twentieth century." The writer should give the reasons why.

Classical music continuity may be oriented toward special areas. There may be a concentration on symphonies, or on chamber music, or on operatic excerpts and so forth. Note how the program on pages 247-249 dealing with the "supernatural" is able to combine, within its central theme, opera, symphony and ballet.

Examine the following scripts for examples of continuity in another classical music area, the complete opera. Note that each program is an hour in length, the continuity for each program overshadowed by the length of the opera itself. Had there been more program time, the continuity could have been more detailed.

• *Determine the degree to which the continuity presents "expert" information, as well as serves the other requirements of the good musical program.*

MUSIC YOU WANT

LM-6025   Beethoven: FIDELIO: ACT ONE
                 Bampton, Steber, sops.; Laderoute, ten.; NBC Symphony Orchestra,
                 Arturo Toscanini, conductor

SIDES 1
and 2:   Entire   58:09

G07L-0783   AIR FOR G STRING (fading after 20 seconds)

ANNCR: (Sponsor or) His Master's Voice is on the air with THE MUSIC YOU WANT
                 WHEN YOU WANT IT, a program of RCA Victor High Fidelity Red Seal
                 records.

G07L-0783   AIR FOR G STRING (Up 5 seconds and fade out)

ANNCR: We are to hear today and tomorrow Beethoven's opera Fidelio, interpreted
                 by Arturo Toscanini. The story of Act One, which we hear today, concerns
                 Florestan, a political prisoner unjustly imprisoned by his enemy Pizarro,
                 governor of the state prison. Florestan's wife, Leonora, disguises herself as
                 a boy and — using the name of Fidelio — becomes assistant to the jailer
                 Rocco. Pizarro decides to kill Florestan upon learning that the Prime
                 Minister is to visit the prison, and bids Rocco dig a grave. Rocco balks,
                 however, at murder and Pizarro decides personally to kill Florestan. Rocco
                 allows the prisoners access to the courtyard, but Leonora, scanning the
                 faces, is unable to find Florestan. She rejoices when she finds she is to
                 accompany Rocco to the dungeon.
                 Arturo Toscanini conducts the NBC Symphony and the following soloists:
                 Rose Bampton — Leonora; Herbert Janssen — Pizarro; Sidor Belarsky —
                 Rocco; Eleanor Steber — Rocco's daughter; and Joseph Laderoute —
                 Rocco's assistant. The Overture and Act I of Beethoven's Fidelio.
LM-6025
SIDES 1
and 2:
Entire   Beethoven: FIDELIO: ACT ONE   59:38

ANNCR: You have just heard Act I of Beethoven's Fidelio, in a rendition conducted by
                 Toscanini. Listen tomorrow at this same time for the conclusion of Fidelio.
                 STANDARD CLOSE

MUSIC YOU WANT

LM-6025   Beethoven: FIDELIO: ACT TWO
                 Bampton, Steber, sops.; Laderoute, ten.; NBC Symphony Orchestra,
                 Arturo Toscanini, conductor
SIDES 3
and 4:   Entire   53:54

G07L-0783   AIR FOR G STRING (fading after 20 seconds)

ANNCR: (Sponsor or) His Master's Voice is on the air with THE MUSIC YOU WANT
                 WHEN YOU WANT IT, a program of RCA Victor High Fidelity Red Seal
                 records.

G07L-0783   AIR FOR G STRING (Up 5 seconds and fade out)

ANNCR: Yesterday we brought you the Overture and Act One of Fidelio, an opera by
                Ludwig van Beethoven. We conclude our playing today of this RCA Victor
                complete opera recording, an album taken from Arturo Toscanini's NBC
                Symphony broadcasts for December 10th and 17th, 1944. Our artists include
                Jan Peerce, Rose Bampton, Nicola Moscona, Eleanor Steber and Herbert
                Janssen.

                Beethoven had long wanted to write an opera because — more than any
                other musical medium — opera was an art of and for the people. He also
                knew it was lucrative — a consideration one should never rule out in
                Beethoven's case. He searched for a suitable libretto for many years. Finally
                he decided on an old French story and hired a German versifier to make a
                libretto of it. The original title was "Leonora, or Conjugal Love."

                The German composer's efforts on his opera were titanic, even for him. His
                sketch-books reveal no fewer than eighteen different beginnings for
                Florestan's second act aria, and ten for the final triumphant chorus.

                Similar uncountable revisions figure throughout the score. Perhaps the
                quintessence of this desire for perfection is illustrated by the four overtures
                Beethoven wrote in his obsession to find just the proper mood with which to
                begin his opera. Because the opera was originally entitled Leonora, the first
                three overtures retain that title. The lighter, less heroic Fidelio Overture was
                finally chosen by Beethoven as being more in keeping with the emotional
                mood of the opera's opening scene.

                The premiere of Fidelio took place in 1805. It was a failure. Beethoven,
                prevailed upon by friends, compressed the opera into two acts and cut three
                whole numbers from the opening parts of the score. The second production
                was on its way to becoming a success when Beethoven, in one of his
                typical, unreasonable rages, withdrew Fidelio from the boards. The opera's
                third production, in May of 1814, was the last during Beethoven's lifetime.

                The story of the second — and last — act of Fidelio is as follows: Florestan,
                the husband of Leonora (now disguised in man's attire as Fidelio, the jailer's
                assistant), is chained to a wall in the prison dungeon. He sings of his
                miserable plight. Leonora and Rocco, the jailer, appear. Upon seeing her
                husband, whom she recognizes with difficulty, she says nothing and assists
                Rocco to dig the grave, intended for Florestan and ordered by Pizarro,
                governor of the state prison. Pizarro appears and tries to stab the defense-
                less prisoner. Leonora rushes to shield Florestan. "Kill his wife first," she
                cries out. Enraged, Pizarro attempts to kill them both; Leonora defends
                herself and Florestan with a concealed pistol. At this point the long awaited
                Prime Minister arrives and releases all the political prisoners unjustly held
                by Pizarro, who is arrested and led away.

                The cast includes Jan Peerce as Florestan — Rose Bampton as Leonora —
                Nicola Moscona as Don Fernando, the Prime Minister — Herbert Janssen
                as Pizarro — Sidor Belarsky as Rocco, chief jailer — Eleanor Steber as
                Marcellina, Rocco's daughter — and Joseph Laderoute as Jacquino, Rocco's
                assistant, in love with Marcellina. The choral director is Peter Wilhousky and
                Arturo Toscanini conducts the NBC Symphony Orchestra. Act Two of
                Beethoven's opera, Fidelio.

LM-6025
SIDES 3
and 4:
Entire   Beethoven: FIDELIO: ACT TWO   57:35

ANNCR: We have just brought you the second act of Beethoven's opera, Fidelio, as
              recorded from Arturo Toscanini's NBC broadcasts for December 10th and
              17th, 1944. Yesterday we brought you Act One of this score, Beethoven's
              only opera. Included in our cast were Rose Bampton as Leonora — Jan
              Peerce, Florestan — Nicola Moscona, the Prime Minister — Herbert Janssen,
              Pizarro — Sidor Belarsky, Rocco — Eleanor Steber, Marcellina — and
              Joseph Lauderoute, Jacquino.
              STANDARD CLOSE
                        Next Program (premiere): Presenting Tozzi (TOT-see), a program of
                                                 nine bass arias by Mozart and Verdi by
                                                 Giorgio Tozzi, the sensational American
                                                 basso of the Metropolitan Opera.

G07L-0783   THEME UP TO END OF BROADCAST PERIOD

              Reprinted by permission of Radio Corporation of America (RCA Victor Record Division)

MUSIC PROGRAMS ON TELEVISION

ONE OF THE REASONS that musical programs have not been especially
popular or successful on television is that music, obviously enough, is not a
visual art form. Attempts to make visual action the focal point of musical
programs on television often have defeated the purposes of musical presentation and have resulted in unfulfilled goals, both aurally and visually.
The action must remain secondary to the sound. Yet, the action must be
of sufficient interest to make worthwhile the audience's full attention and
time to the television screen. Otherwise, the listener might just as well hear
the music on radio or on a phonograph.

The success of the "rock" specials on television illustrate the importance of the visual action. It is not the music that the audience looks for
as much as the gyrations of the personalities, some of them demi-gods and-
goddesses to the younger viewers. For the first time, they can get extreme
close-ups of their heroes and heroines, who heretofore they worshipped
from the cavernous recesses of a stadium.

The first thing the writer must ask is: "What will the picture add to
the sound?" Avoid gimmicks, strange angles and bizarre shots which may
be exciting in themselves, but which have no integral relationship to the
music. If you first develop a central theme, such as a relationship to a locale,
an interpretation or representation of a situation, or the conveying of a
mood, it will be easier to find the specific visual elements for the program.

The most common approach, and in its simplicity perhaps the most
effective, is the direct presentation of the performers on camera. This is the
principal form of the disc jockey show on television, where the disc jockey,
the guest performer, or a studio audience of youngsters dancing to the
music is the usual visual ingredient. As stated above, the emphasis on the
performer is the key to the contemporary music program on television.

Different sections or members of the orchestra, band or other musical
group may be the focal points. This permits a visual concentration on and

an examination of the different aspects of the performance, such as the brass section, the first violinist, the drummer or the conductor. The same approach may be used with vocalists. Elements of the variety show may be incorporated with this visual emphasis on the performers. For example, the antics of a hillbilly band in costume may provide effective visual action.

Abstract representations also may be used effectively. These abstractions, or visual symbols conveying the meaning and mood of the music, may be drawings or paintings, free forms, architectural compositions, or a kaleidoscope of any of the elements of the plastic arts. Color combinations can be used to great advantage.

Other art forms, specifically pantomime and dance, may provide interpretive visualizations of the music. Inanimate objects and forms, such as photographs, paintings, slides and film, can also illustrate realistic and nonrealistic interpretations. Landscapes, people, places, actions and events may be shown, indicating various environmental and psychological meanings and moods of the music.

> • *The following is the script for one of the Arthur Fiedler-Boston Pops "Evening At Pops" programs on public television. The educational and aesthetic-interest level of the audience is likely to be fairly high. What techniques would you add to make the program visually informative as well as entertaining? Note how this program emphasizes both the music and the personalities, the latter consisting not only of the singer, but the conductor, too.*

EVENING AT POPS
Soloist: MISS PEGGY LEE
Show No.: 4

VIDEO	AUDIO
	WELCOME TO SYMPHONY HALL IN BOSTON FOR AN EVENING AT POPS WITH ARTHUR FIEDLER AND THE BOSTON POPS ORCHESTRA . . . TONIGHT'S GUEST ARTIST, MISS PEGGY LEE.
	EVER SINCE PEGGY LEE AND ARTHUR FIEDLER PERFORMED TOGETHER ON A NETWORK TELEVISION SHOW HONORING RICHARD RODGERS, IT HAS BEEN MR. FIEDLER'S WISH TO INVITE THIS GREAT, POPULAR SINGER TO PERFORM IN BOSTON AT A POPS CONCERT. AND, TONIGHT, YOU'LL HEAR HER WITH THE POPS SINGING SONGS BY SUCH GREATS AS RICHARD RODGERS, GEORGE GERSHWIN, AND IRVING BERLIN.
	ALSO ON TONIGHT'S EVENING AT POPS, ARTHUR FIEDLER HAS CHOSEN MUSIC BY SUPPÉ, STRAUSS, AND A MEDLEY OF POPULAR TUNES ARRANGED BY JACK MASON. AND NOW TO GET THINGS STARTED, HERE IS ARTHUR FIEDLER TO OPEN THIS EVENING AT POPS WITH ALLA MARCIA FROM THE KARELIA SUITE BY SIBELIUS. THE BOSTON POPS ORCHESTRA. NOW, OVERTURE TO THE BEAUTIFUL GALATEA BY SUPPÉ.

EDIT (total time here 12 sec.)
GALATEA
CUE: :06 OVERTURE TO THE BEAUTIFUL GALATEA BY
SUPPÉ. ARTHUR FIEDLER AND THE BOSTON POPS.
(roll thru)
CUE: :18 NEXT, ACCELERATIONS, WALTZES BY STRAUSS.
EDIT
ACCELERATIONS
CUE: :05 ACCELERATIONS, WALTZES BY STRAUSS . . .
ARTHUR FIEDLER AND THE BOSTON POPS ORCHESTRA.
(roll thru)
CUE: :27 IN JUST A MOMENT ARTHUR FIEDLER AND MISS
PEGGY LEE WILL BE ON STAGE TO CONTINUE THIS EVENING
AT POPS WITH A SELECTION OF HER POPULAR TUNES.
EDIT
CUE: :02 ACCOMPANYING MISS LEE ARE GEORGE GAFFNEY,
PIANO; DICK BORDEN, DRUMS; TODD CLARK, BASS; AND LEE
RITENOUR, GUITAR. TO START, HERE IS MISS PEGGY LEE,
ARTHUR FIEDLER AND THE BOSTON POPS FOR LOVE SONG
BY DUNCAN.
LOVE SONG
CLOUDS
MISS PEGGY LEE WITH ARTHUR FIEDLER AND THE BOSTON
POPS ORCHESTRA . . . NOW MISS LEE'S RENDITION OF
IRVING BERLIN'S ALWAYS.
ALWAYS
ALWAYS BY IRVING BERLIN. NOW PEGGY LEE IS JOINED BY
THE POPS FOR A MEDLEY, WAIT 'TIL YOU SEE HIM AND I'VE
GOT A CRUSH ON YOU.
MEDLEY
A RICHARD RODGERS/GEORGE GERSHWIN MEDLEY WAIT 'TIL
YOU SEE HIM AND I'VE GOT A CRUSH ON YOU . . . MISS
PEGGY LEE WITH ARTHUR FIEDLER AND THE BOSTON POPS
ORCHESTRA. NEXT, WHEN I FOUND YOU BY RANDALL.
WHEN I FOUND YOU
CUE: :10 WHEN I FOUND YOU BY RANDALL . . . MISS PEGGY
LEE WITH ARTHUR FIEDLER AND THE BOSTON POPS
ORCHESTRA. NOW A MEDLEY . . . THE MORE I SEE YOU AND
I'LL BE SEEING YOU.
THE MORE I SEE YOU
I'LL BE SEEING YOU
CUE: :03 TONIGHT'S GUEST ON EVENING AT POPS, MISS
PEGGY LEE
EDIT
CUE: :03 WITH MISS PEGGY LEE WERE GEORGE GAFFNEY,
PIANO; DICK BORDEN, DRUMS; TODD CLARK, BASS; AND
LEE RITENOUR, GUITAR.
CUE: :25 NOW TO CONCLUDE THIS EVENING AT POPS,
ARTHUR FIEDLER AND THE ORCHESTRA WITH JACK MASON'S
ARRANGEMENT, MANY HAPPY RETURNS.
MANY HAPPY RETURNS
CUE: :05 MANY HAPPY RETURNS, A BOSTON POPS
ARRANGEMENT BY JACK MASON. THIS CONCLUDES TONIGHT'S
EVENING AT POPS WITH ARTHUR FIEDLER, THE BOSTON
POPS ORCHESTRA, AND SPECIAL GUEST MISS PEGGY LEE.
NEXT WEEK ARTHUR FIEDLER HAS INVITED THE AMAZING
BROTHER-SISTER TEAM, THE CARPENTERS. YOU WILL HEAR
THEIR POPULAR TUNES, AND RICHARD CARPENTER MAKES
HIS DEBUT AS PIANO SOLOIST FOR THE WARSAW CONCERTO

VARIETY PROGRAMS

READING A CHAPTER of a book or reading a dozen books will not give a
writer the craft of comedy of a Goodman Ace or a Carl Reiner or a
Norman Lear. This book does not provide techniques for comedy writing.
It does, however, provide some basic approaches to the organization of
the variety program, which includes elements of comedy, situation, suspense,
and music.

Program Types

The term, variety, implies a combination of two or more elements of
entertainment and art: a singer, a dancer, a stand-up comic, a comedy skit,
a Shakespearean actor, a puppeteer, a ventriloquist, a pianist, a rock group.
Depending on the personality who is the principal figure in the program
(e.g. Carol Burnett, Flip Wilson, The Smothers Brothers), several of these
elements would be incorporated in a manner that shows off the star to the
best advantage.

The basic variety show types are the vaudeville show, the music hall
variety, the revue, the comic-dominated show, the personality (usually
singer or dancer) program with guests, the musical comedy approach and
the solo performance. Although all of these forms have been on television
from time to time over the years, they vary according to audience reception
and interest, and in the mid-1970s one saw principally the personality program and the solo presentation. The variety show is not a haphazard con-
glomeration of different acts. Even the vaudeville show — exemplified in
television history by the long-running "Ed Sullivan Show" — carefully
integrates and relates its various acts and frequently is oriented around a
clear central theme. Vaudeville and music hall variety are basically the
same, oriented around specialty acts of different kinds. The revue is organized primarily in terms of music and dance, however, with comedians
frequently providing the continuity and transitions between musical numbers.

The comic-dominated show may consist of a comedian as the central
performer, with various guests and/or standard acts, as in a Bill Cosby or
Bob Hope "special" or a Flip Wilson continuing series.

A personality such as Carol Burnett may mix her own songs and
participation in comic skits with contributions from guests, creating what
is in essence a revue centered around one performer. When such shows
have a thread of continuity, no matter how thin, they become musical
revues. The thread may be any kind of theme: the songs of a particular

composer, a national holiday, an historical happening, the biography of a famous entertainer, a locale — almost anything can serve.

When more than a thread, but a plot line (even a meager one) is used, we have the makings of a musical comedy. A notable example of television musical comedy is Rodgers and Hammerstein's "Cinderella," which has been repeated over the years on TV. Some musical comedies on television pretend to that category in name only, however, and may be little more than thinly connected series of songs and dances by popular entertainers.

An adaptation of the vaudeville variety show has been highly successful on American television, substituting a host or hostess who rarely participates in the overt performing and who introduces and interviews various guest entertainers. Because most of the program is banter between host and guest (and in these segments the host or hostess is a principal entertainer) these are frequently called talk shows and in recent years have been most exemplified by NBC's "The Tonight Show" with Johnny Carson, ABC's "Dick Cavett Show" and Metromedia's "Merv Griffin Show." The content ranges from the innocuous and frivolous to the relevant and searching — although the latter approach apparently didn't get the attention of enough viewers to keep Dick Cavett regularly on the air.

The solo performance became a significant "special" on television in the mid-1970s, with emphasis on the "star" performer such as Barbra Streisand, Marlene Dietrich and Liza Minnelli.

There may, of course, be combinations of various types of performances and variety forms in any given program.

Approach and Organization

The most important thing for the writer of the variety show to remember is that there must be a peg on which to hang a show. You must develop a clear, central theme, capable of being organized into a sound structure, with a unity that holds all the parts of the program together. Otherwise, each number will be a number in itself, and unless the audience knows what the next act is and especially wants to watch it, it would feel free at any time to tune in another station at the end of an act. The theme could be a distinct one or the continuity factor could simply be the personality of the master of ceremonies or comedian. The exception to the need for strong continuity is the vaudeville-music hall type of presentation. In these shows the audience is held by frequent reminders of the special acts still to come.

Within each separate type of variety show there are distinct orientations that must be determined by the writer. Will the musical portions stress popular or novelty numbers? Will the dances be classical in style? Modern? Presentational? Representational? Interpretive? The comedy must be written to fit the personality of the comic, and it must contain a sufficient amount of ad-lib material to forward the public concept of the comic's spontaneous talents. What kind of comedy will be emphasized? Simple good humor? Wit? Satire? Slapstick? Will it combine elements of several types? Will it go into special areas of farce, of sophisticated humor, of irrelevancy, or irreverance? Does the comedian's style require material oriented toward broad, physical gags? Toward sophisticated wit? The intellectual approach? The irreverant type of satire? A seminal prototype of the "complete comedy" program was "Laugh-In," which used a basic concept of satire, but overlaid it with all of the other specific forms of comedy to fit the personalities of the particular performers.

When planning a variety show consider the intrinsic meaning of the term "variety." There must be a differentiation between each successive number and among the various segments of the program. Contrast is important — not too great a contrast to disturb the viewers, but enough so that there can be no feeling of sameness, a feeling too easily transferred into boredom. Musical number should not follow musical number, comedy routine should not follow comedy routine — except for the special formats of a purely musical program, as with a solo singer, or of a total comedy program, as with the "Laugh-In" type of show. The suspense created by a juggler who balances an unbelievable number of fiery hoops on the end of his nose should not be directly followed by the similar suspense of a group of acrobats balancing one another on each other's noses. The effect upon the audience of these acts is too much the same.

In programs that use outside acts — that is, those that cannot be scripted and timed exactly, as with vaudeville or with late-night talk/ variety programs, the final number or act should have two versions, a short one and a long one, so that the proper one can be called for depending on the time remaining when that act is about to begin.

• *Compare and contrast the following rundown sheets for two of the leading TV "variety" shows of the 1970s — "The Carol Burnett Show" and "The Tonight Show."*
• *1.) How would you classify each of these shows in terms of variety show "form"? 2. Are the acts or sequences so arranged that there is enough variety in each succeeding one? 3.) Is there a preponderance, either in number or appearances or in allotted time, of any one type of act? If so, is it helpful or harmful to the particular program? 4.) Are the commercials well-placed? Considering the exigencies of commercial television, could or should they have been placed any differently? 5.) What are the major similarities as well as the major differences between the two programs?*

THE CAROL BURNETT SHOW

PRODUCTION #717	TAPE:	FRIDAY, JANUARY 18, 1974
AIR SEQUENCE #19	AIR	SATURDAY, FEBRUARY 2, 1974

RUNDOWN (a/o 1/16/74)　　　　　　GUESTS:　　TIM CONWAY, STEVE LAWRENCE

1.	QUESTIONS & ANSWERS (Carol)	(1)
2.	SHOW FILM (Lyle V.O.)	(1)
3.	THE OLD DRESSER (Harvey, Tim)	(2)
4.	OPENING COMMERCIAL BB (FIRST HALF) (Lyle V.O.)	(11)
5.	COMMERCIAL #1	(12)
6.	INTRO & "HERE'S THAT RAINY DAY"/"RAINY DAYS AND MONDAYS" (Steve, Carol [V.O.])	(13)
7.	COMMERCIAL #2	(15)
8.	BACHELOR PARTY (Carol, Steve, Lyle, Boy Dancers)	(16)
9.	COMMERCIAL #3	(22)
10.	INTRO & THE AD MEN (Carol)	(33)
11.	CLOSING COMMERCIAL BB (FIRST HALF) & INTRO STATION BREAK (Lyle V.O.)	(34)
12.	STATION BREAK	34)
13.	OUT OF STATION BREAK (Lyle V.O.)	(34)
14.	COMMERCIAL #4	(35)
15.	DAY SHIFT - NIGHT SHIFT (Carol, Tim)	(36)
16.	COMMERCIAL #5	(40)
17.	KITCHEN COMMERCIALS (Carol, Harvey, Vicki, Lyle, Steve, Tim, Dancers)	(41)

18. COMMERCIAL #6   (50)

19. FINALE: GERSHWIN SALUTE   (51)
     (Carol, Steve, Vicki,
     Harvey, Dancers)

20. GUEST BB & GOODNIGHT   (67)
     SONG
     (All)

21. CLOSING CREDITS   (68)

22. PROMO FOR PROD. #717 —   (71)
     AIR SEQ. #19

Courtesy of CBS Television

THE TONIGHT SHOW
TAPED: THURSDAY, MAY 9, 1974
AIRED: FRIDAY, MAY 10, 1974

6:00:00   (12:00:00)

9.   STARRING SL

GUESTS: JACK PALANCE (PAPUSH)
          JOANNA CASSIDY (SAM)   9A. ANNOUNCE UPCOMING GUESTS
          JOSE MOLINA (DOLCE)
          ORSON BEAN (DOLCE)   10. ORSON BEAN

HOST: JOHNNY CARSON
ANNCR: ED McMAHON   11. COMML: SUNBEAM/ROCKWELL —
                                           LCI
                                           (FM/VT) — MTC SL)

NOTES: 12. JOANNA CASSIDY

                                      13. COMML: WAMSUTTA/SIMMONS — LCI
                                           (VT/FM — MTC SL)

                                      14. JOANNA CASSIDY

                                      15. COMML: SEARS — LCI
                                           (FM — MTC SL)

                                      16. STATION BREAK
          5:30:00   (11:30:00)   6:30:00   (12:30:00)

1.   THEME AND OPENING TAPE   17. STARRING SL

2.   JOHNNY MONOLOGUE   18. JACK PALANCE

3.   COMML: DUPONT/CLOROX — LCI   19. COMML: WINTHROP/GLENBROOK —
     (VT/RM — MTC SL)   LCI
                                           (VT/VT — MTC SL)

4.   MATERIAL   20. JACK PALANCE

5. COMML: VICK/SIMMONS — LCI (VT/FM — MTC SL)	21. COMML: KENTUCKY FRIED CHICKEN — LCI (CHICKEN BUCKET) (VT — MTC SL)
6. ORSON BEAN	22. JOSE MOLINA (Dance to Panel)
7. COMML: NO. AMERICAN SYSTEMS/ J & J — LCI (VT/FM — MTC SL)	23. MTC VT & NET FILL & LOGO SL
7A. CONTINENTAL SL	24. PANEL
	25. DISC SLS & LOGO SL / STATION BREAK
8. STATION BREAK	

Courtesy of NBC Television Network

THE RADIO MAGAZINE

ONE OF THE interesting experiments of post-television radio has been the magazine format, in which a continuous stream of different kinds of materials — music, news, interviews, discussions, human interest, features, sports, special events, skits, and a voluminously interspersed series of commercials — is presented over a given, extended time period. This format seems oriented toward the person on-the-go, the listener who may be occupied primarily in other things and who will listen with one ear most of the time and with both ears some of the time and who can be held with a well-produced, interesting variety of short program segments. (Although the radio magazine goes beyond the "music and variety" format, as do the late night "talk" shows, it, too, seems to be more oriented toward the formats of this chapter than to any of the others and is therefore included here.)

The writer's job is two-fold: research and organization. The writer must prepare a routine sheet which clearly delineates the time length for each presentation and which accurately schedules the commercial announcements. Accurate background material must be provided for introductions to the differing sections of the program and sometimes complete script materials are written for a prepared and rehearsed segment. Much scripting is done by local people in the "field," for most of the material on the program is usually "remote." Perhaps the most difficult job is total arrangement of the program over many hours to provide continuity and variety in subject matter and length at the same time.

The most successful of such programs has been the National Broadcasting Company's *Monitor*. Examine the following excerpt from one of its routine sheets (more akin to the "rundown" sheet described earlier) and the accompanying script for the same time period. The opening of each hour of *Monitor* is a five-minute "news package." Note that the final script substitutes a sports feature for the "Movie Critic" scheduled for 9:12:45.

BUD DRAKE		MONITOR ROUTINE SHEET		PAGE
CHARLES GARMENT				DATE
MELANIE TURNER		HOST: BILL CULLEN		TIME

9:00:00	BEEPER		
	BILL:	INTRO	
	CART	RCIA COMMERCIAL	(1:00)
	CART	LYSOL COMMERCIAL	(0:30)
9:05:25	BEEPER		
9:05:30	DISC/BILL:	SOUL MAKOSSA MANU DIBANGO RUNS 3:00 PLAY TOP & FADE ON CUE	
9:07:40	BEEPER		
9:07	CART:	THEME #5F	(0:11) FADE AT :111
9:07:55	BILL:	BB & ID	(0:30)
9:08:25	DISC/BILL:	LOVES ME LIKE A ROCK PAUL SIMON RUNS 2:55 SNEAK :08 — ID OVER	(2:55)
9:11:20	CART/BILL:	SOUNDER & TIP	(0:15)
9:11:35	CART:	DUTCH BOY COMMERCIAL	(1:00)
9:12:35	BILL:	INTRO	(0:10)
9:12:45	TAPE:	MOVIE CRITIC	(2:00) APX.
9:14:45	BILL:	OUTRO	(0:10)
9:14:55	CART:	ARMOUR COMMERCIAL	(0:30)
9:15:25		BEACON CUE	(0:05)

	BEEPER		
9:15:30	CART:	"B" — CUT #1	(1:10)
NEWS PACKAGE			
BEEPER			
DISC:		SOUL MAKOSSA (ESTAB AND UNDER ON CUE FOR ID)	
BILL (OVER):		You take a heaping helping of "soul . . . add a measure of "makossa" . . . get Manu Dibango to stir it all up . . . and what have you got?	

I don't know what you've got . . . but Monitor has a couple of minutes of "Soul Makossa" . . . that's wot.

DISC: UP AND TO FADE ON CUE

CART: THEME #5F
                      (UNDER AFTER :11)

BILL: Yes . . . Bill Cullen and Monitor 73 are back . . . and I trust we're a bit more welcome than something else that's back again . . . namely . . . talk about raising the income tax . . . which is what the President's counselor, Melvin Laird, brought up a couple of days ago. However . . . Congressional reaction seems to be negative . . . so we can now proceed into our weekend with a positive, cheerful attitude . . . and music to match.

DISC: LOVES ME LIKE A ROCK
                      (ESTAB FOR :04 UNDER UNTIL :08)

BILL (OVER):   This is Paul Simon's big hit . . . "Loves Me Like A Rock:

DISC: UP AND TO END

CART: TIP SOUNDER

BILL: A Monitor Household Tip: Material leftover from making slipcovers can be cut into strips and sewed onto the tapes on Venetian blinds to add a decorative note to the window treatment.
                      Now something else for the home-maker:

CART: DUTCH BOY COMM   (:60)

BILL: Now . . . a Monitor Sports Feature.
                      The bill ending the professional football TV blackout of home games went into effect yesterday. Doing some "Saturday-morning quarter-backing" on the reasons and effects of this legislation are the Commissioner of football, Pete Rozelle, and Monitor Sports Editor Len Dillon.

TAPE: PETE ROZELLE
                      O: COMMISSIONER PETE ROZELLE
                      C: FOR MONITOR SPORTS   (1:56)

BILL: I would imagine that among the other avenues to be explored . . . which the Commissioner did not mention . . . would be pay TV. But that's getting way ahead of the game. How about some football type food now?

CART: ARMOUR COMM   (:30)

BILL: Dom De Luise . . . a very funny fella . . . who got rave reviews for his brand new NBC show . . . "Lotsa Luck" . . . will prove that it wasn't luck . . . by being funny here, too . . . in a couple of minutes as a guest on the Monitor beacon.

BEEPER

CART: CUTAWAY

Material provided by the NBC Radio Division

REFERENCE BOOKS

ON MUSIC AND VARIETY PROGRAMS

Bogue, Donald L. *The Radio Audience for Classical Music*. Chicago: University of Chicago, 1973. The case of station WEFM, Chicago.

Galanoy, Terry. *Tonight*. New York: Warner Paperback Library, 1974. About "The Tonight Show."

Passman, Arnold, *The Deejays*. New York: Macmillan, 1971. A comprehensive account of music and radio from its beginning. Includes personal knowledge of personalities.

Sanger, Elliott M., *Rebel in Radio*. New York, Hasting House, 1973. The story of WQXR, New York, the "good music" station.

Shelton, Robert and Burt Goldblatt, *The Country Music Story*. New Rochelle, N.Y.: Arlington House, 1971. Illustrating the development of one type of pop music on radio and television.

Taylor, Sherril W., *Radio Programming in Action*. New York: Hastings House, 1967. Analyses by prominent broadcasters include music shows.

The principal periodical relating to music and variety programs on radio and television is *Billboard*. Others that contain background material useful to the writer are *BM/E, Broadcasting, Record World, Television/Radio Age* and *Variety*.

FOR APPLICATION AND REVIEW

1. Prepare rundown sheets for three different local disc jockey pop music radio shows, each with a different music format.
2. Write the complete script for a half-hour radio classical music record show, to be distributed on a national basis to local stations.
3. A. Watch a television variety show. Analyze and evaluate the following: theme, if any; organization of the acts; general approach to the material (kinds of dances, comedy, music); freshness of writing; special use of visual techniques.

   B. With other members of a writing team (i.e. other members of your class), write a half-hour variety show for television, each member of the team concentrating on a special part of the program and all cooperating in the over-all planning of the show. State your central theme for the show; the special organization of the material; the reasons for the placement of each act; the reasons for the approaches used in the dance, music and comedy sequences.
4. With the same or another writing team, prepare the rundown sheet and script for a half-hour segment of a radio magazine show.

8

Children's Programs

THE FACE OF children's programs on television changed greatly in the 1970s. One significant influence was the development of the Children's Theatre Workshop, producers of "Sesame Street" and "The Electric Company." Another was the establishment of Action for Children's Television (ACT), which petitioned the Federal Communications Commission to require an upgrading of children's programming on commercial television and to ban all commercials from children's shows. As described in Chapter 3, commercial broadcasting in the mid-1970s began to drastically revise its approaches to the type and frequency of commercials aimed at children.

Another strong influence on commercial TV children's programming was the 1972 Report of the Surgeon General on Television and Social Behavior, which stated that

> . . . the possibility that behavior can be acquired observationally and retained, without necessarily being performed immediately, has important implications for our understanding of the effects of television. . . . If a child has learned some new behavior, then he clearly possesses the potential to produce it if (or when) he finds himself in a situation in which such a performance appears to be desirable, useful or likely to serve his own purpose.

Following much public pressure and implied regulatory action from the Federal Communications Commission and the Federal Trade Commission, in late 1974 and early 1975 the commercial television networks began to introduce programs with live human beings in place of some of the previously dominant cartoon characters, began to eliminate some of the physical violence which dominated children's shows, to inject what the networks called "pro-social values" into a number of programs, and to clearly separate the program materials from the commercials so as not to confuse or mislead the child-viewer. The inane violence in almost all the cartoon programming began to give way to greater realism and to consideration of the impact of television upon children's minds and emotions.

Before the ACT petition was resolved by the FCC, the National Association of Broadcasters and the Association of Independent Television Stations voluntarily, in 1974, set advertising limitations and more responsible content guidelines for children's programming. The subsequent FCC action later that year rejected ACT's proposals to ban all advertising from children's programs, to require specific amounts of children's programming daily and at certain time periods, and to eliminate mention of brand names on children's shows. Rathern than rule-making, the FCC adopted a policy statement which clarified broadcasters' responsibilities in programming and advertising aimed at children:

Television stations must provide a reasonable amount of programming for children and a significant portion of this programming must be educational or informational in nature.

Children's programming should make some provisions for the special needs of the pre-school child.

This programming should not be confined solely to weekends.

The level of advertising should be reduced in general accordance with reforms instituted by the broadcasting industry.

Host selling and other sales techniques that blur the distinctions between programming and advertising should be avoided.

A clear separation between program and advertising content should be made.

In 1975, following increasing public complaints and a specific request from Congress, the FCC issued a report on violence and obscenity on television. In relation to what is appropriate for viewing by children, the FCC concluded that "self-regulation by the broadcast industry was preferable to the adoption of rigid Federal standards." It stated that the adoption of a "family viewing period" by the three major networks and the NAB Television Code Board was "commendable" and was a long step toward protecting children from "violent and sexually-oriented materials." The FCC said that any rules limiting such material would be difficult to institute, requiring "an appropriate balance between the need to protect children from harmful material and the adult audience's interest in diverse programming."

Whether efforts toward program responsibility to children will blossom into full recognition of the child's welfare and needs remains to be seen. Some areas continue to be largely ignored — sexism, for example. In testifying before the Senate Commerce Committee's Subcommittee on Communications hearings on children's television programming in 1974, Mary Ellen Verheyden-Hilliard, National Director of the Education Task Force of the National Organization for Women (NOW) stated:

> Television, the most influential of all media, serves as the modern child's window to the world; and it betrays its responsibility by offering our children a grossly distorted and limited view of the role women and girls play in our society . . . because the child assumes the presentation is valid, her or his attempts at socialization will conform to the roles and reactions she or he has seen on television. . . . Studies carried out by the National Organization for Women and others show that females are simply not seen as often in children's programming as are males; and when females are shown, they are disproportionately the victims of violence and are portrayed in a limited range of roles performing stereotypical tasks.

Ms. Verheyden-Hilliard pointed out that although females represented 51% of the population, only 27% of the characters in children's dramatic and live-action shows were females, with the percentage in cartoons even lower. She noted that, in a study she conducted in 1973, females made up only from 17% to 25% of characters with speaking parts in network television children's programs, and that 38% of all children's shows on the three networks had either only one female speaking role or no female characters at all, while every show on all networks had more than one male character. She further stated that:

> The message conveyed to little girls is that females play only a marginal role in American society. Those few women and girls who are shown in children's programming are portrayed in limited and stereotypical roles. They are most often supportive, subservient and submissive characters. Girls are shown unable to perform semi-complicated tasks, receiving assistance from males, or supporting males in their tasks . . . male characters in children's cartoons instigated more than 75% of the action. Females, on the other hand, were overwhelmingly the recipients and victims of the action.

The concept of the writer developing a good action program to keep the kids at home on the edge of their seats, glued to the violence and, not incidentally, the hard-sell commercials is, hopefully, a thing of the past. The writer of children's programs must, first and foremost, keep in mind the effect of the programs on the vulnerable minds and emotions of the child-viewers. The writer must be socially aware and, hopefully, have a social conscience. Even unintended violence, prejudice or sexism is inexcusable.

If the writer comes up with a good program idea, it would be well to test it out with child experts and child advocaters in many different areas before proceeding to write a treatment or script that may be harmful to the child.

APPROACH

IMAGINATION IS THE KEY WORD in the preparation and writing of programs for children. The imaginations of children are broad, exciting, stimulating. It is only when we approach adulthood that we begin to conform, to restrict our minds and thoughts, to dry up that most precious of creative potentials.

A young friend of mine, when three years old, one day placed strips of transparent tape across the dials of his family's television set, stepped back to look at what he had done, and then seriously observed, "Now I control the world."

And in a sense, he was right. For it is through television that much of the world first makes itself known to the small child. Writing for children offers an excellent opportunity for creativity, for children are open and willing to receive what the world has to offer. At the same time, because what comes to them through the TV set has such meaning and importance, they are not willing to accept commercial television's usual narcotizing program content as easily as are most of their parents.

Some advertisers, producers and writers think that children will believe anything. Yet, because their imaginations are so sharp, they are sometimes more critical than adults. They can release themselves to be led into almost any fantasy, *provided there has been a valid, believable base to begin with.* In this manner, the children's program approximates the approach to writing the adult farce-comedy. As long as characters, situation and environment are initially believable, and as long as what has been established is developed logically and in terms of the characters' motivations, the subsequent actions and events will be accepted within the context of the play.

Many so-called children's shows attempt to capture the interest of parents and other assorted adults. This is fine, if it is not done for an ulterior reason. Indeed, in some cases the term "children's program" is a misnomer because many of these supposedly bi-oriented shows really are aimed at adults almost exclusively. In some instances the parents are brought in because it is the parent, after all, who will decide on whether or not a product is to be purchased.

The writer must be consistent in the format and execution of the program idea. The writer should assume the place and attitude of the viewing adult — a task of some proportion for some writers, judging by some of the programs on television and radio. If an adult watching a children's program finds it dull and tasteless and not worth the time, then quite likely that program is not going to enrich the child's day, develop taste or be worth the time. One must differentiate between audience ratings and value to the child. The child may "love" the program. But that is not the only criterion of its value, entertainment-wise or otherwise. The child may "love" candy, too, but a responsible parent — and writer — will not allow the child to subsist on it during all the waking hours. The child may release some aggressiveness by throwing mud pies in the park, but the responsible parent — and writer — will not permit the child to be exposed to continuous participation in or observation of aggressive violence.

Grace Stanistreet, one of the country's leading teachers of creative arts and drama for children, has written about some of the responsibilities of children's theatre that may be applied just as validly to children's television:

> In judging plays that are good for children, adults too often remain spectators. Actors and adult audience accept the fact that the play may not jar the adult out of the spectator role. If you accept the statement that any play should create life on stage and stimulate the audience to play its role than we have discovered one standard by which to judge what is good for children. Many people with the responsibility of selecting programs for the young, watch the child at the children's play and take his or her reaction to it as the best recommendation. Would they take a child's word about what to include in the week's menus? Or what the family should wear, or when they should go to the dentist? But these things are fundamental for good living they may protest. Is theatre different? Isn't exposure to cultural experience fundamental to good living?

> A child has no definitive standards for judgment and evaluation. He or she is in the process of acquiring good habits, appetites, taste, standards, by association, example, influence. The wise parent knows the part he or she must play in developing these in the child. The parent must select the exposures, the images, the experiences out of a greater knowledge of the child's needs and what will serve these needs. The parent does not impose his or her will, desires, purpose, taste but refers and defers at times to the child's purpose, desires and abilities. The parent makes decisions based on both, not solely on one or the other.

CONTENT

IN CHAPTER 3 WE NOTED some recent changes in the National Association of Broadcasters' standards governing commercials on children's programs. The content of the programs has been one of the broadcasting industry's most vulnerable areas of neglect, more by commission than by omission. The NAB Television Code (children's programming has virtually disappeared from radio) presents some good, hopeful general approaches in the section entitled "Responsibility Toward Children."

Broadcasters have a special responsibility to children. Programs designed primarily for children should take into account the range of interests and needs of children, and should contribute to the sound, balanced development of children.

In the course of a child's development, numerous social factors and forces, including television, affect the ability of the child to make the transition to adult society.

The child's training and experience during the formative years should include positive sets of values which will allow the child to become a responsible adult, capable of coping with the challenges of maturity.

Children should also be exposed, at the appropriate times, to a reasonable range of the realities which exist in the world sufficient to help them make the transition to adulthood.

Because children are allowed to watch programs designed primarily for adults, broadcasters should take this practice into account in the presentation of material in such programs when children may constitute a substantial segment of the audience.

All the standards set forth in this section apply to both program and commercial material designed and intended for viewing by children.

The interpretations by networks, stations and producers vary widely, however, and prior to the pressures and changes noted at the beginning of this chapter, the viewer would have been hard-pressed to find many programs either ostensibly for children or watched by children that did not violate the principles in the Code. Acts of violence were and still are commonplace, and are often presented as heroic deeds. Even murder is commonplace and, if performed by the "good guy," frequently is justified as ethical. The Saturday morning children's block of cartoon programs traditionally stressed violence and various forms of prejudice. As this is written, the mid-1970s' change in children's programming has not been in effect long enough to judge the extent or permanence of the change or whether, indeed, the changes are merely surface sops with the basic effects of the programs on children essentially the same.

The NAB Codes have frequently been criticized as too vague. Perhaps they require specific definitions of terms and clarifications relating to positive approaches to programming? The Codes are not enforced; there is no industry authority (or compunction) that requires producers and writers to present material of a beneficial or, at least, non-harmful nature to our children. Without strong and unequivocal industry enforcement of positive approaches toward touching children's minds and personalities, ethical program content depends entirely on the integrity of the individual sponsor, producer and writer. By not policing itself, the broadcasting industry has invited public pressure and federal regulation.

FORMAT

OVER A DECADE AGO, at the Federal Communications Commission's hearings on television, Melvin Helitzer, the advertising director of a toy manufacturer that spends 90% of its advertising budget on television, gave some advice that most television producers, unfortunately, paid no attention to. He stated that one of the reasons for the failure of some shows written for children was that "the intelligence level of the writing was below that of the children." He said that "children are more intelligent than most adults believe" and that a program produced by people "who have no respect for children" was doomed to failure. Although it took more than a decade to remove some of the unintelligent violence that permeated Saturday morning cartoons on the air, time and citizen pressure ultimately proved Mr. Helitzer right.

The best format is, indeed, of a level of intelligence that respects the child who is watching. Traditionally, in theatre as well as in the mass media, we have found that certain age levels do respond best to certain kinds of content forms. Age levels have been used as a primary determinant in the approach to individual programs for children. Given programs of intellectual and emotional stimulation on a high plane, children of certain age levels will respond in a positive manner to certain approaches.

In the first edition of this book in 1962, for example, we wrote: "For the pre-school child the activity program featuring some elements of fantasy, such as Mother Goose rhymes, as well as the use of things familiar to the child's world, is common." That such a format works is shown in the most successful application of this concept since that was written, in examples of both fantasy and familiar: Big Bird and a street called Sesame.

The child in the first few grades of elementary school is able to relate to material containing beginning elements of logical thinking. Sketches with simple plots and fairy tales are usually successfully appealing. Activities with which the child can get involved, if not too sophisticated or complicated, are effective. Note the combination of activities in the "Sundown's Treehouse" routine sheet later in this chapter: using invisible ink, dancing, learning foreign words, visiting a hospital.

The child over eight or nine years of age is able to respond readily to the activities and accounts of the outside world; again, note the "Sundown's Treehouse" approaches and some of the materials in the "Sesame Street" script. At this age drama begins to be very effective, particularly stories of adventure and individual action, where the child can identify with the heroine or hero.

The mid- and upper-grade elementary school child is ready for elements of reality, through drama, discussion, documentary, and participatory and observational activity. These children have begun to read many parts of their daily newspapers and have watched news and documentary programs on television. The reality may relate to political and social events of the world about them or it may deal with scientific and environmental history and happenings. The writer should be careful, however, to avoid sensationalism and to ensure that the elements of reality used are not disturbing or exciting out of context for a full understanding of what is being presented.

The best children's program is not that which is written exclusively for a certain age level. Though the specific format of the program may appeal more to one age level than another, the good program should be meaningful to and be enjoyed by all ages on different levels. For example, an atomic science program may be too advanced for the pre-schooler; the pre-schooler's program must be on a different plane. However, if the pre-schooler's program seems silly to the elementary school child and vulgar to the adult, it is not because it is below their level of understanding. It probably is because it *is* silly and vulgar. A dramatization of *Winnie the Pooh,* for example, can be seen by the pre-schooler, the elementary school child, the teen-ager and the adult, and if it is a well-done program it will appeal to all these groups, although on different levels.

One of the more successful and positive-experience formats in the 1960s and 1970s, in fact, has been the adaptation of book characters to TV, such as Pooh and, well-remembered by college-age people, the Dr. Seuss books and Charlie Brown and Snoopy.

SPECIFIC WRITING TECHNIQUES

THE CHILD SHOULD BE REACHED in a direct manner. The presentational approach is most effective, with the narrator or character relating to the viewer candidly. The children must be able to understand the ideas presented. Be simple and be clear. This does not imply that children should be talked down to. On the contrary, avoid patronizing children; they are only too aware when this is happening. Too much dialogue is not advisable, either in a dramatic or non-dramatic program. Action and vivid, colorful presentation of ideas are most effective. This implies an adherence to a simplified plot in the dramatic story. Too much shouldn't be presented at one time and the story should not be drawn out; children have neither the practice of holding too many ideas at once nor the sitting patience of adults. Material of a light nature should be featured on children's programs or, if the material is serious in content, it should not be morbid and it should not contain the sometimes disturbing psychological probing often found in the better adult programs. This is especially true of programs oriented primarily for younger children. The resolutions should not be ambiguous and the characters, though not necessarily real, should be believable.

The child identifies to an extraordinary degree with those dramatic elements that are within his or her own realm of experience and understanding. The zeal of the Marshall or the Detective — or their writers — to beat up or shoot as many "bad guys" as possible in the course of a half-hour or hour may stimulate latent tendencies toward violence and sadism in some children, but the story and the characters may have little or no lasting effect on the well-adjusted child (although any residue of violence as a way of life is unacceptable, of course). "Lassie," however, may have a continuing impact because she is, to so many children, the "dog-next-door"!

If you wish to present a program of an educational nature, avoid the simple repetition of material that children viewing the program may have gotten in school. Known material may be used in the educational program, but it should be used to stimulate the child to participate in the program through thinking and applying the knowledge already learned, and to learn more. Some programs go beyond the schools in quality and teach what most schools never taught but which capable parents always taught — self-esteem and self-ego and a relationship of self to the social, political and environmental ideas and happenings of the real world.

The writer should not pad the children's program. Determine the purpose of the program and stick to it. Don't try to fool or confuse the child, hoping that s/he won't be aware of a bad piece of writing. If a moral is to be presented, make it definite and clear, at the same time stimulating the child to think more about it.

Several techniques have been especially successful in the story or drama for the child audience. First, there must be suspense. Children, like adults, should be caught up in a conflict, no matter how simplified, and should want to know what is going to happen. Children should be let in on a secret that certain characters in the play do not know. And, finally, children always love a good "chase" no less than the adults who assiduously followed the "Keystone Cops" in silent films and who follow the westerns and mysteries on television today. Keep in mind, however, that there must be a believable base and that slapstick for slapstick's sake usually ends up as low-level violence, as evidenced in too many of the Saturday morning cartoon programs over too many years!

Television Techniques

The visual element of television can be used very effectively in children's programs. On any show, in any format, the writer can use actors, special set pieces, puppets and marionettes, film clips, interesting makeup and costumes, attention-getting camera angles and movements and, particularly enjoyable for children, special electronic devices and effects.

The presentational approach, mentioned earlier, is important. On television the performer can play directly to the camera and to the child-viewer. Care must be taken not to overdo this because children know when the performer is fawning or condescending.

Television is particularly good in illustrating visual elements and experiences in society and in involving children in some kind of activity. Pre-school programs frequently use this approach, emphasizing painting, construction, dancing, cooking, and other arts and crafts and visual-action games. Television also can introduce ideas and sights beyond the games and art activities through such things as visits to museums, demonstrations by artists, an inside view of a fire station, backstage at a theatre, in the dressing room or on the playing field at an athletic event, on the assembly line at a factory, in a courtroom — the possibilities are unlimited.

Drama, however, continues to dominate the children's market. Much of it — many of the cartoons and animated programs, some of the old movies, some of the lowest-common-denominator made-for-adults situation comedies, for example — is not suitable to a child's intellectual and emotional growth. Some of it does provide visual experiences and relationships to reality that would not be possible if the same drama were to be seen on the stage or heard over radio. It should be noted, however, that radio's greater freedom and stimulation of the imagination permits a child's own psyche to provide bases for interpretation that sometimes is too explicitly and inflexibly spelled out on television, bounded by the literalness of the TV picture. It is sometimes more difficult for the child to screen out undesirable elements from the television drama than from the radio or theatre presentation.

Radio Techniques

With their orientation to the visual element of television and the need to bring almost nothing to much of the entertainment they receive, children who have grown up in the second half of the twentieth century have not exercised the disciplines of imagination or concentration developed by those a bit older who grew up with radio. The radio writer today must consider this lack of concentration and short attention span, and at the same time should be aware of the need — and opportunity — to rejuvenate the creative imaginations of our children. How many children did you know at the beginning of the 1970s (were you a child then?) who were fascinated by the revival of "old-time" radio drama and who surreptitiously stayed up extra late to hear the CBS Radio Mystery Theatre? So many children suddenly discovered something "new" that, as they said, excited their imaginations more than did any television dramas.

THE MANUSCRIPT

MANY CHILDREN'S SHOWS are written out completely. That is, the complete dialogue and directions are presented, as in the "Sesame Street" script later in this chapter. In many situations, particularly for non-dramatic programs that use a "live-type" production approach, it is difficult to prepare complete scripts. Usually, detailed outlines or routine sheets are written, from which the performers are able to develop extemporaneously the informal content. The following excerpts are from the combination script and routine sheet of "Captain Kangaroo," television's long-running, high-quality children's show.

> • *As you examine this script, analyze it in terms of the principles for good children's program writing. Discuss the following, evaluating the reasons for your answers.*
> 1) *Is the action simple and clear?*
> 2) *Is there sufficient action?*
> 3) *Art there elements of comedy? Of a chase?*
> 4) *Is the presentational approach used effectively?*
> 5) *Does the show build, with suspense for individual sequences as well as for the program as a whole?*
> 6) *Are there educational values in the script?*
> 7) *Does the production make use of special visual elements?*
> 8) *Does the program attempt to raise the viewers' standards of artistic and cultural appreciation?*

CAPTAIN KANGAROO — February 12

ITEM	PROPS AND MUSIC
1. OPENING "CK" Telop.	gobo
2. OPERA BIT (TBA) Bob dances off the gobo and turns off theme at the desk. Greeting. He asks the boys and girls if they would like to hear a story. "There are many ways to tell a story, this is one way (takes book from pocket). Ballet is a story told in dance. Opera is a story told in song. This morning Mr. GJ, Mr. Moose and I are going to tell a story in song, we're going to present an Opera. The name of our Opera is, 'The Happy Magic of Mr. Moose', and it's all about a King who learns that everyone in his Kingdom is happy all day long. The King is delighted that his people are so happy but he can't help wondering what has made them so. He thinks perhaps his Court Jester has gone thru the streets making everyone happy and gay, and as the Opera begins the King is in his castle waiting for his Court Jester. Mr. GJ plays the Jester, Mr. Moose plays himself and I play the King." DISSOLVE TO CURTAIN TELOP, "TBA" CLASSICAL UNDER. DISSOLVE FROM TELOP to Bob wearing crown and robe, he is pacing the floor in deep thought. "TBA"-OUT. Bob paces, stops and sings: "This news is grand!" (He paces then stops) "Throughout my land!" (He paces then stops) "Everyone is happy and gay But what has made them that way? — " (He paces floor).	Book, cue cards for lyrics, Moose flower cart COSTUME: King's crown and robe (Bob), Court Jester costume (GJ), Robin Hood hat (Moose) MISC: curtain telop "the end" telop

(GJ enters wearing Court Jester costume. Bob goes to him and sings:)

BOB: (TUNE: "THE MUFFIN MAN")

"Oh have you heard the latest news
The latest news, the latest news
Oh have you heard the latest news
Thank you Jester mine"

GJ:
"Oh yes I heard the latest news
The latest news, the latest news
Oh yes I heard the latest news
But thank good Mister Moose"

(Bob delivers an "aside" to camera: "A Moose? Did he say a Moose?")

BOB:
"Oh did you say thank Mister Moose
Thank Mister Moose, thank Mister Moose
Oh did you say thank Mister Moose
For this our Happy Land?"

The song continues for several verses.

(Bob and GJ join hands and dance in circle as they sing:)

"Yes yes we found the Magic Moose
Yes yes we found the Magic Moose
Yes yes we found the Magic Moose
Hurry with us if you care"

(Bob and GJ tiptoe to garden where GJ points out the flower cart)

(Bob tiptoes to the cart and inspects it carefully before giving this aside:
"My Jester has done his job well for the Magic Moose lives here
And perhaps the Moose will tell us the secret of spreading good cheer")

(The Moose pops up CUT TIGHT on him as he says:
"Magic? . . . Me a Magic Moose?
I spread good cheer without magic I fear
But lend an ear and my secret you'll hear")

MOOSE: (TUNE: "LONDON BRIDGE)

"Be-ing nice to every-one, every-one, every-one
Be-ing nice to every-one is my secret

Be-ing kind to every-one, every-one, every-one
Be-ing kind to every-one is my secret

Be-ing good to every-one, every-one, every-one
Be-ing good to every-one is my secret (Moose Call)."

(Bob gives this aside:
"Here is a lesson we must learn well
Join in the singing, the whole world we'll tell!")

Verse is repeated.

DISSOLVE TO TELOP: "THE END," "TBA" MUSIC UP AND UNDER

3. TAG OPERA BIT (LEADS CARTOON)
   DISSOLVE TO BOB AT DESK sans costume. Bob: "And
   so the 'Happy Magic of Mr. Moose' was nothing more
   than being nice to everyone and only those who have
   tried this magic know how well it really works." Bob
   leads cartoon per content.

4. CARTOON

5. POCKETS (LEADS "BLING BLING")   3 mechanical toys
   Bob empties pockets at desk. As he finishes playing the
   last pocket prop (SE: AXE CHOPPING WOOD).   SOUND:
   Bob: "That's Mr. GJ, he's splitting some logs to make a   axe chopping wood
   new fence, in the old days that's the way they used to
   make houses. They'd split the logs and then pile them on
   top of one another until they had a log cabin. Do you
   know a log splitter who later became the President of the
   United States? . . . Abe Lincoln, that's right. Did you
   know that today is his birthday? Mr. GJ and I are going
   to talk about President Lincoln in just a little while but
   right now let's pretend we've split a whole pile of logs
   and we're going to build a log cabin." HIT RECORD

6. RECORD: "BLING BLANG BUILD A HOUSE FOR BABY"   Lincoln logs sprayed
   Bob panto's while a log cabin, in three sections, is matted with UV
   from limbo (GUS). Lincoln logs are sprayed with UV.

7. LINCOLN EXHIBIT   covered wagon (oxdrawn
   On hand RESEARCH gives short incidents covering Abe's   if possible), log cabin,
   kindness, his home, his education, his honesty and his   one room school house,
   first law book. Extended RESEARCH to cover dates of   1/2 lb. of tea, 6 pennies,
   office, birth, death, etc. As "Bling Blang" tags GJ enters law book (Blackstone's
   with a picture of Lincoln and puts it on Goat. Bob invites "Commentaries" if possi-
   the boys and girls to the Goat where the exhibit is set.   ble), a picture of Lincoln,
   They follow his life from cabin to President.   model Capital building

8. and 9.:
Lead in and Record, "Swinging on a Star."

10. PLAYTIME   shirt cardboard,
    Bob makes a log cabin from shirt cardboard. Cut strip   scissors, pencil, tape
    of shirt cardboard approx. 4 inches wide, fold three times
    to shape of house and tape. Add cardboard roof. Draw
    on logs.

11. CLOCK "KNOCK KNOCK" BIT
The sequence involves the studio audience and the viewers.

12. DRUM BIT (LEADS "NOISY FAMILY")   large bass drum (straps)
    GJ comes in with bass drum strapped to his back. Grange   and drumsticks
    Hall Parade next week. Bob asks if the drum is easier
    to play with it strapped on the back. GJ: "You know I was SOUND:
    wondering about that Captain, I only put it there so I   police whistle
    could see where I'm going." Bob suggests GJ try to hit
    the drum with the drumsticks. GJ tries but can't. Bob tries COSTUME:
    to loosen the strap but it won't come off. "That's a shame 2 Shako hats
    Mr. GJ, I thought maybe we could march around the T.H.

and play the drum." GJ suggests that Bob take the drumsticks and follow him around. Bob agrees and panto's blowing whistle (SE: POLICE WHISTLE). Bob: "Fooowarrd maaarrch!" HIT RECORD.

13. RECORD: "THE NOISY FAMILY"
Bob and GJ march around the T.H. Relief shots in limbo of the various musical instruments are supered into drum.

small bass drum, toy snare drum, cymbals, triangle, and striker

14. BAND BIT — TBA
At tag of record GJ still cannot remove drum from his back.
The sequence involves playing of record.

2 tablespoons,
2 whisk brooms,
toy piano

15. LEAD IN TO CARTOON
Per content.

17. HIDE AND SEE BIT
Sequence in which Bob tries unsuccessfully to find Bunny Rabbit.

two dinner bells,
two carrots,

18. LEAD IN TO "WINTER WONDERLAND"
Bob comes to sandbox where model houses, trees and cars are set. Bob "asks" the boys and girls about the placement of buildings, etc., as he makes a village. GO TIGHT on village when it is finished. Bob drops snow on it saying, "Now if we drop some "Wonder Snow" on our town what will we have? . . . That's right, a Winter Wonderland." HIT RECORD, DISSOLVE TO LIMBO.

houses, cars, trees,
large box of "snow"

19. RECORD: "WINTER WONDERLAND"
Limbo. Entire table is set as a snow covered village (end to end). Table is covered with snow and has snowmen and candy canes strewn about. Snow crawl.

entire plasticville town,
2 small snowmen,
6 candy canes, large box of "snow"

MISC:
snow crawl

20. CLOSING CREDITS

21. SONGTIME: "MARY HAD A LITTLE LAMB"
Bob does songtime to allow GJ time for costume change. Bob at desk tells the boys and girls the song he is going to sing and calls BR "so he can act as the lamb." BR is not to be found. The Moose pops up at door and Bob asks him to play the part. Moose agrees. HIT RECORD. Moose keeps giving his call instead of Lamb imitation. At tag Bob explains and demonstrates lamb's "Baaa" to Moose. Moose catches on. Bob: "Now say goodbye to the boys and girls." Moose: "Baaa baaoys aan girls, basa you tomorrow."

22. SIGN OFF

Although it has been frequently criticized on many grounds — including that of being oriented toward rote learning and of using materials more familiar to the backgrounds of white middle class children rather than economically deprived minority children, for whom it was supposed to be aimed (special committees of the British Broadcasting Company examined and evaluated it and found it seriously wanting) — "Sesame Street" has nevertheless become the most acclaimed children's program in the United States.

Setting aside the relevance of its content and its impact on children's creativity, it has been highly successful in helping children learn information and skills more effectively and quicker. It has also been helpful in shaping positive humanistic attitudes in relation to children of different backgrounds and conditions. In part, "Sesame Street" is an entertainment program which includes cultural materials. Its highly innovative use of the television medium employs techniques which motivate and hold the audience's interest. Principally, it is an instructional program and, along with "The Electric Company," is watched not only at home, but as part of school curricula. (We are not dealing with "Sesame Street" here as an instructional program, however; writing the formal instructional program is discussed in Chapter 11.)

As you examine the following script excerpts of "Sesame Street," note that it doesn't "talk down" to children. The writing presents the material in non-condescending terms, using varied forms of audience persuasion and motivation. For example, some segments are in variety-show form; others are in audience-participation show form; still others use the dramatization or skit. Comedy, ranging from gentle satire to farce, is also used. Drawing on the persuasive impact of commercials writing, "Sesame Street" frequently captures and holds its audience's attention by adapting the form of the commercial.

Another effective writing approach used is the continuing segment and the continuing characters, not only providing in some instances the suspense that causes an audience to tune in from day-to-day, but in this case providing familiar approaches that do not require the child to readjust every day to a new format and permit the child to more easily react to the learning stimuli; it provides the child with character identification or empathy that also motivates watching and facilitates comfortable and friendly openness to the materials presented by those characters.

"Sesame Street" is outstanding in its use of the kinds of television techniques noted earlier: its combination of various elements such as puppets, settings and actors, its presentational approach, its expert use of electronic effects — its total "visualness." It is an excellent example of how children can more effectively learn print — that is, how to read — through the proper use of the visual medium rather than the print medium.

> • As you examine the script, list the different types of television program formats used, and analyze each one as to its potential effectiveness on a child audience.

- *List, as well, the various production techniques used, such as animation, puppets, etc. Do you find any that seem to be more effective than others?*

SHOW #494

CHILDREN'S TELEVISION WORKSHOP

S E S A M E   S T R E E T

AIR: MARCH 15, 1973   VTR: DECEMBER 7, 1972
Final Air Version

1. Film: Show Identification   :15

2. Film: Opening Sesame Street Theme   :50

3. DAVID IS STUDYING (SOCIAL ATTITUDES)   2:02

HOOPER DRESSED IN DAY OFF OUTFIT ENTERS NEAR FIXIT SHOP. HE GREETS AND THEN GOES INTO STORE. DAVID IS BEHIND COUNTER. HE IS READING A BOOK AND TAKING NOTES.
HOOPER: Hello David.
DAVID: Oh hi Mr. Hooper. What are you doing here? This is your day off.
HOOPER: I know but I just happened to be in the neighborhood and I thought I'd drop by. (NOTICES DAVID WAS READING) Reading huh?
DAVID: Uh . . . yeah I was.
HOOPER: (LOOKS MIFFED) Reading on the job?
DAVID: Hey wait a minute. I know this looks bad . . . but there were no customers in the store and I just . . .
HOOPER: (CUTS HIM OFF) Yes I know . . . but the floors could use a sweeping . . . and the shelves could be straightened. I don't know . . . in my day when I was young like you . . . when I worked . . . I worked.
DAVID: (A LITTLE MIFFED) Listen Mr. Hooper. I know I shouldn't be reading when you're paying me to work, but I wasn't just reading. I was studying.
HOOPER: Studying?
DAVID: Yeah, I have a big law school test tonight.
HOOPER: A test? Why didn't you say so? Studying is very important. It's a good thing I came by. You shouldn't be here in the first place. (STARTS USHERING DAVID OUT OF THE BACK INTO THE ARBOR) Come on come on. You gotta study. I'll work today.
THEY GET TO ARBOR . . .
DAVID: Wait, Mr. Hooper, That's not fair to you. It's your day off.
HOOPER: So you'll work on your day off and make it up. You want to be a big lawyer some day no?
DAVID: O.K. If you say so. Thanks a lot, Mr. Hooper, I appreciate it. (SITS AND STARTS TO READ, AT TABLE)
HOOPER: My pleasure, Mr. Lawyer, my pleasure.

SCENIC: Street, Arbor, Store
TALENT: David, Hooper
PROPS: Constitutional Law Book, note book, pencil
COSTUMES: Hooper in regular clothes

4. VTR: BEAT THE TIME-TRAIN (GUY, CM, AM) (446) (33a)   3:03

5. BB STUDIES WITH DAVID   3:03

BB ENTERS ARBOR AREA CARRYING A SCHOOL BAG. DAVID IS STUDYING.
THERE IS A STOOL AT TABLE OPPOSITE DAVID.
BB: Hi David. Do you mind if I study with you?
DAVID: What are you gonna study BB?
BB: (REACHES INTO SCHOOL BAG AND TAKES OUT LETTER "U" AND PUTS
IT ON TABLE) The letter "U." It takes a lot of study you know.
DAVID: O.K. BB go ahead. (GOES BACK TO READING)
BB: (GETS CLOSE TO LETTER) U . . . U . . .
DAVID: (LOOKS UP) BB quietly.
BB: Oh sorry David. (TAKES A UKULELE OUT OF SCHOOL BAG, PUTS IT
NOISILY ON TABLE THEN DOES THE SAME WITH AN UMBRELLA.
DAVID: BB what now?
BB: Oh these are just some things that begin with the letter "U." A ukulele and
an umbrella. See it makes it easier to learn a letter if you know a word that begins
with that letter.
DAVID: I know . . . I know. But listen BB. You can't be putting all kinds of things
on the table. It bothers me.
BB: Oh sorry Dave. Well then how about if I do something that begins with the
letter "U"?
DAVID: (WILLING TO AGREE TO ANYTHING BY NOW) O.K. Sure. As long as
you're quiet.
BB: I'll be quiet.
DAVID GOES BACK TO READING
BB: (GETS UP AND TIPTOES TO SIDE OF TABLE . . . BENDS OVER AND
PUTS HIS HEAD UNDER THE TABLE AND TRIES TO GO UNDER IT . . .
POSSIBLY KNOCKING IT OVER)
DAVID: BB what now?
BB: I was going under the table. Under starts with the letter "U."
DAVID: BB you're driving me crazy.
BB: Gee it's not my fault the letter "U" is a noisy letter to study. Well anyway
I'm finished studying it.
DAVID: Good.
BB: Are you finished studying your law book?
DAVID: No.
BB: Well don't feel bad. Not everybody is as fast a learner as me. (STARTS
GATHERING HIS STUFF TOGETHER)
DAVID: (BURN)

SCENIC: Arbor
TALENT: BB, DAVID
PROPS: BB school bag, letter "U", a ukulele, umbrella

6.   FILM: U IS FOR UP   :34

7.   FILM: DOLL HOUSE #2   1:32

8.   FILM: U CAPITAL   :46

9.   BB AND SNUFFY STUDY WITH DAVID   2:57

BB AND SNUFF NEAR 123. BB HAS A #2.
BB: O.K., Mr. Snuffleupagus, are you all set to go study with David?
SNUFF: Sure Bird. I'm ready. What are we gonna to study?
BB: The number two. (HOLDS UP NUMBER)
SNUFF: Oh goody. Let's go.
BB: O.K., but be very quiet. Don't make a sound. We mustn't bother David.
SNUFF: O.K. Bird. I won't even say a word.
THEY GO TO ARBOR . . . SNUFF SITS IN BACK OF DAVID WHO IS READING
INTENTLY. . . . BB GOES TO STOOL OPPOSITE DAVID.

DAVID: (LOOKS UP) Oh no. BB I thought you were finished studying.
BB: I was finished studying the letter "U" . . . now we're gonna to study the
number two. (PUTS "2" ON TABLE)
DAVID: BB you've got to be quiet.
BB: Oh we will. We won't make a sound. We promise.
DAVID: Good. (GOES BACK TO READING THEN LOOKS UP) Who's we?
BB: Me and Mr. Snuffleupagus.
DAVID: You and Mr. Snuffle . . . ? Oh not again with that imaginary friend.
BB: He's not imaginary. He's right behind you.
DAVID: O.K. . . . I don't have time. Just be quiet. (GOES BACK TO READING)
BB: We will. O.K., Mr. Snuffleupagus. Let's study the number two.
BB AND SNUFF STARE INTENTLY AT NUMBER 2. SNUFF GETS AS CLOSE
BEHIND DAVID AS HE CAN.

SCENIC: Arbor
TALENT: David, BB, Snuff
PROPS: #2

10.   FILM: FALL DOWN   :16

11.   BB AND SNUFF STUDYING TAG   1:21

BB AND SNUFF STILL IN SAME POSITIONS STUDYING #2. DAVID IS
READING.
BB: Well I guess that's all the studying of the #2 we're gonna do for now.
DAVID: (WITHOUT LOOKING UP) O.K. BB.
BB: (GOES TO SNUFFY LEAVING #2 ON TABLE) Come on Mr. Snuffleupagus.
Let's go. (HE TAKES SNUFFY'S TRUNK AND THEY WALK TOWARD CONST.
DOORS)
IF POSSIBLE CUT TO SHOT OF DAVID WITH BB AND SNUFF EXITING IN
BACKGROUND.
DAVID: (LOOKS UP) Snuffleupagus? Man that BB has some imagination. (TO
AUDIENCE) What? What did you say?
BB AND SNUFF SHOULD NOW BE GOING THROUGH DOORS OR SIMPLY
OFF CAMERA . . .
DAVID: Oh I see. BB forgot his #2. (PICKS UP #2 AND TURNS AROUND) Oh
he's gone. Well, he'll get it later. (GOES BACK TO READING)

SCENIC: Arbor, Street
TALENT: BB, David, Snuff
PROPS: Per bit

12.   FILM: ONE BUMP   :17

13.   Deleted

14.   FILM: (LA) ANIM PARTS OF BODY   2:14

15.   FILM: ROCKING U   :23

16.   FILM: (LA) KIDS, ANIMAL PAIRS   :55

17.   FILM: MAN AND FROG   1:30

18.   VTR: THE COUNT-MAILBAGS REVISED   (420) (14)   2:56

19.   FILM: HENSON #2   1:14

20.   VTR: COUNTING EGGS AND CHICKENS (Kermit)   (282) (30)   1:56

21.   FILM: (LA) U — UNDERPASS   :42

22.   FILM: DRUMMER — STREET   :55

23.   VTR: SONG: GONE WITH THE WIND   (34) (4)   2:17

24.   MARIA STUDIES WITH DAVID (DIFF. PERSP.)   3:21

       DAVID STILL STUDYING. . . . MARIA ENTERS CARRYING A SHOULDER BAG
       CONTAINING BOOKS, A BAG OF POTATO CHIPS AND A PORTABLE RADIO.
       MARIA: Hi David.
       DAVID: Hi Maria.
       MARIA: You studying?
       DAVID: Yeah. I have a big test tonight.
       MARIA: I was just going to the park to study . . . but I'd rather study with you
       if you don't mind.
       DAVID: Sure. Sit down.
       MARIA: Thanks. (SITS AND TAKES OUT SOME BOOKS)
       THEY BOTH START TO STUDY THEN . . .
       MARIA: (TAKES OUT RADIO AND TURNS IT ON)
       MUSIC
       DAVID: (DOES A TAKE THEN) Uh Maria?
       MARIA: Yeah?
       DAVID: Do you mind turning off the radio? I can only study when it's real quiet.
       MARIA: Really? Gee I'm just the opposite. I love music when I study. Oh well.
       (TURNS RADIO OFF)

29.   Deleted

30.   VTR: ERNIE IS THIRSTY (B/E)   (459) (4)   2:25

31.   Deleted

32.   VTR: FRACTURED LETTTER "U"   (416) (12)   1:09

33.   VTR: SONG: I'M COLD   (368 (40) (AM GIRL)   1:22

34.   Deleted

35.   MARIA CLASSIFIES (FUNCTION)   1:22

       MARIA AT ART CARD AS FOLLOWS: CAR, PLANE, TRAIN, IN ONE GROUP.
       . . . BUS AND TEAPOT IN ANOTHER GROUP.
       MARIA SINGS CLASSIFYING SONG . . . EXPLAINS

       SCENIC: Street
       TALENT: Maria, Kids
       GRAPHICS: Per bit
       MUSIC: Classification song

36.   VTR: GANGSTER CARROTS #1   (255) (23)   1:16

37.   FILM: 2-2 TRAIN   :24

38.   VTR: GANGSTER CARROTS #2   (255) (25)   :58

39.   FILM: ROCKING U   :23

40.   VTR: GANGSTER CARROTS #3   (255) (27)   :43

41.   FILM (LA) RIVER   1:58

42.   VTR: HARVEY KNEESLAPPER "U"   (468) (31)   :35

43.   VTR: HANGING UP THE WASH (LUIS, DAVID)   (438) (14)   1:29

43A. VTR: THE DOCTOR (B/E)   (124) (24)   3:08

44.   VTR: CITY SHAPES II RECT. CIRC. (WILD)   11:0

44A. FILM: LETTER Q   :38

45.   Deleted

46.   GOODBYE — DAVID THANKS HOOPER FOR TAKING OVER FOR HIM AND
      LETTING HIM STUDY . . . THEY SAY GOODBYE . . .   1:07

      SCENIC: Street
      TALENT: David, Hooper

47.   COMMERCIAL CREDITS

48.   PACKAGE CREDITS

49.   BACKER CREDIT AND OFF
                                    58:36

Occasionally there is a children's program that is specifically developed and oriented not primarily toward information learning or entertainment, but toward stimulating the child-viewer toward individual creativity and humanistic understanding of ideas, people and events in the world surrounding him and her. One of the best such programs was "Sundown's Treehouse," produced in the early 1970s by Gertrude L. Barnstone for KPRC-TV, Houston, Texas. It was a totally integrated program, not only including among its weekly child-participants representatives of varied racial, ethnic, economic, religious, educational and social backgrounds and beliefs, but also children with various physical handicaps — such as blindness, hearing loss and muscular problems. By openly and frankly relating to each other as they might in everyday life, including open treatment of their individual backgrounds and attitudes, the children in the studio production provided for the children at home an understanding and feeling of how to most positively and effectively relate to "different" children. Most of the viewers ordinarily would not experience this in the usual artificial separation of "different" children in school and society. Of special interest to the writer is the production approach to "Sundown's Treehouse." The specific program materials were not imposed on the children; the outline and content for each program were arrived at in production conferences among the producer, the child participants and, sometimes, a special guest representing some field of work or other activity chosen by the participants. The following rundown and routine sheets, which do not include the standard opening and closing of the program, reflect the children's program for which the writer does not prepare the complete script.

RUNDOWN — SUNDOWN'S TREEHOUSE #49

1. S.D. invisible letter
   A) explains lemon juice writing
   B) what does visible mean?
2. VIDEOGRAPH (Spanish)
3. DRAWINGS (close shots)
4. VIDEOGRAPH (pictures of drawings)
5. OLD FILM (special effects S.D.)   1:35
6. DANCE (Sturat)
7. FIELD TRIP (discussion)
8. GUEST

ROUTINE

VIDEO	AUDIO
SUNDOWN IS WRITING A LETTER	
INVISIBLE LETTER — TO ALBERT ASKING ALBERT TO APPEAR.	
	CHILD: "WHAT IN THE WORLD ARE YOU DOING?"
	SUNDOWN: (EXPLAINS — HE IS WRITING AN INVISIBLE LETTER TO THEIR INVISIBLE FRIEND ALBERT.)
	CHILD: (WANT TO KNOW ABOUT INVISIBLE LETTER — WHAT HE'S USING)
CAMERA SHOWS HOW THE LEMON JUICE BECOMES VISIBLE WITH HEAT.	SUNDOWN: (EXPLAINS HOW YOU CAN WRITE WITH LEMON JUICE, LET IT DRY, THEN HOLD HEAT TO IT, LEMON JUICE TURNS BROWN AND YOU CAN READ IT.)
	GOOD FOR SPY MESSAGES — LOOKS LIKE BLANK PAPER UNTIL HEATED! IF CHILDREN WANT TO TRY
SUNDOWN HAS WRITTEN — ALBERT, PLEASE TRY HARDER TO MAKE YOURSELF VISIBLE AGAIN — I WANT TO SEE YOU. S.D.	SUNDOWN EXPLAINS THAT HE WANTS TO SEE ALBERT, SO HE IS ENCOURAGING HIM TO TRY TO BECOME VISIBLE. (WHAT DOES VISIBLE MEAN??)
	CHILD: "THIS IS IMPOSSIBLE, ALBERT HAS TRIED EVERYTHING AND HE'S

JUST INVISIBLE, PERIOD. (THEY LIKE HIM THAT WAY)

SUNDOWN: (WANTS TO KNOW WHETHER ALBERT IS HERE.)

CHILD: "NO HE IS HOME ASLEEP."

SUNDOWN COMMENTS THAT IF HE IS NOT GOING TO BECOME VISIBLE, HE'LL JUST STAY AN "ESPIRITU."

CHILD: WANT TO KNOW WHAT THAT IS — GHOST IN SPANISH (HE'S NOT REALLY A GHOST, BUT THEY ARE BOTH INVISIBLE)

SUNDOWN: " 'ESPIRITU' IS JUST ONE OF MANY NEW SPANISH WORDS HE'S LEARNED."

CHILD: "WANT TO KNOW WHAT ARE OTHERS."

VIDEOGRAPH

SUNDOWN: "I'LL SHOW YOU!"

STAIRCASE	—	Escalera
SCHOOL	—	Escuela
HOUSE	—	Casa
WINDOW	—	Ventana
DOOR	—	Puerta
GHOST	—	Espiritu
BRAVE	—	Bravo
PARROT	—	Papagano
FRIENDS	—	Amigos

SUNDOWN: "THEY'RE HARD TO REMEM-BER."

CHILD: "WE'LL HELP YOU REMEMBER THEM."

CHILD GETS DRAWING TABLET AND PENS OUT OF TRUNK — DRAW PICTURE

CAROL AT PLASTIC DRAWS STAIRCASE. TO CAMERA ⟶ "IF YOU HAVE A PAPER AND PENCIL HANDY, WHY DON'T YOU DRAW WITH US?"

ALAN DRAWS SCHOOL

ENID DRAWS HOUSE WITH DOOR AND WINDOW

SUNDOWN DRAWS GHOST

ZETTA DRAWS BRAVE

STUART DRAWS PARROT

ANDREW DRAWS FRIENDS

CHILDREN IN THAT ORDER PUT THEIR
DRAWINGS UP FOR CAMERA TO SEE
CLOSE SHOT OF PICTURES.

CHILDREN SAY WHAT IT IS IN SPANISH
THEY HAVE DRAWN.
(PAPAGANO IS AN ESPECIALLY FUN
WORD)

VIDEOGRAPH — ONE AT A TIME AS
                    DRAWINGS ARE SHOWN

ESCALERA
ESCUELA
CASA
VENTANA
PUERTA
ESPIRITU
BRAVO
PAPAGANO
AMIGOS

SUNDOWN WANTS TO SEE AN OLD FILM
— HASN'T SEEN ONE IN A LONG TIME.

COULD THERE BE A BUNCH OF SPECIAL
EFFECTS AS HE TRIES TO GET OLD
FILM — HAT IS RUSTY ON GETTING
OLD FILMS
TUNES IN CHARLIE CHAPLIN 1:35

FILM IS A LITTLE VIOLENT — DISCUSS.
THIS WAS GRANDPARENTS' TIME

CHILD: (WANT TO MOVE AROUND AND
DO P.E.)

STUART PLUGS IN RECORD PLAYER, ETC.

GIRLS AND STUART WANT TO DO
SPECIAL DANCE.

AFTER DANCE, SUNDOWN WANTS TO
TRY HAT AGAIN, SEE IF IT WORKS O.K.
ON NEW FILMS.

TUNES IN FIELD TRIP — HOSPITAL

AFTER FILM DISCUSSION — SUNDOWN:
HOW DID ALAN AND YOU, ENID, FEEL
WHEN YOUR BABY BROTHERS WERE
BORN?
DOES ANDREW REMEMBER WHEN HIS
SISTER WAS BORN?
(ASK THEM ONE AT A TIME)
WHAT DIFFERENCE DID THEY MAKE IN
YOUR HOME — IN YOUR LIFE?

CHILDREN LEAVE

SEND INVISIBLE LETTER TO ALBERT

CHILDREN MEET GUEST

GUEST

Written and produced by Gertrude L. Barnstone for KPRC-TV, Houston

REFERENCE WORKS

ON CHILDREN'S PROGAMS

ACT Materials: A Resource List. Newtonville, Mass.: Action for Children's Television, 1975. Pamphlet, listing ACT publications.

Ambrosino, Lillian and David Fleiss. *An International Comparison of Children's Television Programming.* Washington, D.C.: National Citizens Committee for Broadcasting, 1971.

Atkins, Charles K., Jihn P. Murray and Oguz B. Newman. *Television and Social Behavior: An Annotated Bibliography of Research Focusing on Television's Impact on Children.* Bethesda, Md.: National Institute of Mental Health, 1971. Publication No. 2099.

Cater, Douglass and Strickland, S. *TV Violence and the Child: The Evolution and Fate of the Surgeon General's Report.* New York: Russell Sage, 1974.

Children and Television: An ACT Bibliography. Newtonville, Mass.: Action for Children's Television, 1975. Pamphlet listing general references.

Himmelweit, Hilde, T. Oppenheim and Pamela Vince. *Television and the Child: An Empirical Study of the Effect of Television on the Young.* London: Oxford University Press, 1958. Still a classic study.

Jennings, Ralph and Carol Jennings. *Programming and Advertising Practices in Television Directed to Children.* Newtonville, Mass.: ACT, I-1970, II-1971.

Kaye, Evelyn. *The Family Guide to Children's Television.* New York: Pantheon Books, 1974. An approach to regulating viewing time, contents of children's programs and what you can do about advertising, sexism and violence aimed at children.

Liebert, Robert M., John M. Neale and Emily S. Davidson. *The Early Window: Effects of Television on Children and Youth.* Elmsford, N.Y.: Pergamon Press, 1973. The authors were part of the study that resulted in the Surgeon General's report on Television and Social Behavior; much of this book comes from that research and provides breadth as well as depth, including pro-social as well as anti-social effects of television on children.

Melody, William. *Children's Television: The Economics of Exploitation.* New Haven: Yale University Press, 1973. Cost bases for "bad" and "good" materials for children's television.

National Commission on the Causes and Prevention of Violence. *Mass Media and Violence.* Washington, D.C.: U.S. Government Printing Office, 1969. Vol. XI.

Schramm, Wilbur, Jack Lyle and Edwin B. Parker. *Television in the Lives of Our Children.* Palo Alto: Stanford University Press, 1961. A standard reference book on viewing habits and impact in America.

Surgeon General's Advisory Committee on Television and Social Behavior. *Television and Social Behavior.* Washington, D.C.: U.S. Government Printing Office, 1972.

The ACT News. Quarterly publication of Action for Children's Television.

FOR APPLICATION AND REVIEW

1. Watch several hours of commercial network Saturday morning programming for children and several hours of public broadcasting programming for children (such as "Sesame Street" and "Misterogers Neighborhood"). In separate lists for the commercial and noncommercial children's programs note the particular formats, approaches and techniques that you, as a responsible writer, think are good and worthwhile incorporating or adapting for children's programs you might write. What are the major differences, if any, between the commercial and noncommercial programs?

2. Individually or as part of a team (with other members of a writing class, for example) prepare:
   a) a 15-minute script for a children's program series already on the air;
   b) a 15-minute script for a new children's program;
   c) a rundown/routine sheet for a new half-hour children's program.

9

Women's Programs

MINORITY STATUS IS not measured by numbers. More accurately, minority refers to the lack of the same opportunity, power and prerogative afforded the majority in any given society.

Although women constitute a numerical majority in the United States, they do not have the prerogatives or opportunities that men have and in that sense are a minority group. The evolution of humanity is so slow that even after centuries of so-called civilized development women are still subjugated.

The growth and use of communications to visually and aurally verbalize for women the subjugated nature of their roles in society, and the availability of communications to reach out to society in general and to organize women to take action to free themselves from their status has worked the same way it has for racial minorities. The self-directed Black revolution for human dignity and freedom provided impetus for a similarly self-directed revolution by women, a revolution that in the early 1970s seemed to be just beginning to gather momentum. It should not be forgotten, however, that it is really a re-revolution, a resuming, inasmuch as the women's rights and suffrage movements of 100 and more years ago resulted in some of the more humane and progressive laws enacted in this country and provided background and impetus for subsequent efforts of other minority groups.

As the impact of communications on human change is more and more understood, more and more minorities are joining the society-wide revolution for individual rights and self-realization.

Media, particularly television, comprise a significant part of the women's revolution. Writer Dial Torgerson, in an article on "The Status of

Women Around the World," stated: "As it did a decade ago with the dis-advantaged minorities of the United States, television is raising the expec-tations — and stirring the desires — of women on the bottom of the status ladder. Women in the provinces see how freer counterparts live in sophisti-cated capitals. Women whose lives are dominated by men and poverty see dubbed versions of American TV series in which women live in luxury and hold men in amused contempt."[1]

Women in the mid-1970s were where Blacks were with media some ten years previously: not yet in a position to use communications as a posi-tive force to organize and motivate, but still having to fight to change the negative images of women that dominated the existing media. It is signifi-cant that in the mid-1970s Blacks no longer had to fight wholesale nega-tive images on television — but women did.

The negative images of women in television and radio are legion. From the soap opera to the dramatic series the woman usually is portrayed as either incompetent or overbearing. Even in programs where women behave in adult, responsible, respected ways, there is always the tragic (or, more accurately in terms of media practice, "comic") flaw that makes the woman less than the ideal image presented of the male. (This is not to ignore the countless "father-knows-worst" kinds of programs that show the male, as well, as an incompetent bumbler.)

Perhaps the most flagrant area of anti-woman media practice is in commercials. A *New York Times* feature by Judith Adler Hennessee and Joan Nicholson presented a comprehensive statement on TV commercials vis-a-vis women. The authors illustrated, with many specific examples, the anti-free, anti-human concepts of women as presented in commercials, from the sex object "Fly Me" ad to the woman-as-chattel "My wife, I think I'll keep her" commercial. And through all the commercials, no matter how insulted or misused they are, women always smile. As Hennessee and Nicholson say, "Women smile a lot. It goes with the shuffle."[2]

A study by the National Organization for Women (NOW) of 1241 TV commercials showed women's place as in the home in almost all. In 42.6% of the commercials women were doing household work; in 37.5% their role was to provide help or service to men; and in 16.7% their main purpose was for male sex needs. In only 0.3% of the commercials were women shown as independent individuals. It is not surprising that a *Good Housekeeping* survey found that one-third of the women have at one time or another turned off commercials because they found them offensive.

Mary Ellen Verheyden-Hilliard, director of the National Organization for Women's National Task Force on Education and director of the national project on Sex Equality in Guidance Opportunities, has stated:

> Why is such pervasive demeaning of females shown on network television? Why do the networks allow it? Is television simply a mirror

of society? Can it be, should it be more? No network would, any longer, put on five hours of programming (every Saturday morning) in which Blacks acted dumb, fell over their feet, and were happy as long as their white friends loved them. Why have Blacks been able to change this kind of TV image and females have not?[3] Why should girls be portrayed this way? It is imperative that the television networks recognize their sensitive role in the socialization of our children. Sex discrimination and stereotyping must be eliminated on television and superseded by a reasonable, balanced presentation of women in the wide range of roles we do, in fact, hold.[4]

The change in media programming for women is clearly tied to the women's liberation movement, not only in its campaign to abolish negative images of women, but, on a worldwide basis, the recognition that the media not only reinforce and create attitudes toward women but also serve as a direct means for women to change their life styles. Romy Medeiros de Fonseca, women's rights movement leader in Brazil, states that television "is the first means of education from which Brazilian men have not been able to bar their women. They stopped them from going to school, stopped them from studying, kept them at home and cut off all contact with the world. But once that television set is turned on there is nothing to stop women from soaking up every piece of information it sends out. They soak it up like a sponge, and they don't need to be able to read a word."

The responsibility of the media is, indeed, infinite. That the media themselves have not accepted the responsibility is manifest by the need for continuing action on the part of women's groups. Kirsten Amundsen has written: ". . . if we are to change the common image of women in this society, and by 'we' I mean those of us among both sexes committed to seeking such change, we will have to capture control of the media and of the educational institutions that are now responsible for the creation of these images."[5]

One of the internal means of changing programming for women has been through the professionals in the field. The Screen Actors Guild, for example, conducted a survey in 1974 which showed women in a disproportionately small percentage of roles in commercials and in network shows. They found that although 52% of the men viewers "like the women you see on TV," only 28% of the women viewers do. Accordingly, through its Women's Conference Committee, the Screen Actors Guild has attempted to change practices within the industry.

Approaches to programming have been changing, and in the early and mid-1970s women were presented more and more in unstereotyped roles. One critic compared the transition from one image of women — which, in its day, constituted a step forward for a woman as a series lead — to another: "Lucille Ball pretty much wrote the rule book for the standard 'dumb broad' format that has dominated the TV image of women . . . she is still playing the same character; the bird-brained redhead who gets into ridiculous trouble, draws everyone else in with her, and finally gets out by some equally bird-brained scheme. . . . 'The Mary Tyler Moore Show' . . . is probably the best example of how things have changed. Mary is over 30, unmarried and not the least in a panic about it, actually appears to have a sex life, and is neither stupid nor helpless."[6]

In the mid-1970s women were for the first time being made (albeit in only a few trial series) the leads of adventure shows, particularly as police official authority-figures. NBC president Robert Howard believes that audiences have become ready to accept women in stronger roles. "I think the key to it is getting more women into writing. I think that will create the roles."[7]

Not only is the image of women changing in dramatic programming and on commercials, but the approach to the daily "bread-and-butter" women's programming is also changing. The so-called women's programs have principally been those which primarily attracted women viewers and listeners because of the time of day during which they were presented and those which carried content traditionally deemed of interest primarily to women regardless of the time of presentation. Some of the most commercially successful programs, particularly on radio, have been local women's programs usually consisting of non-controversial material such as announcements of club meetings, advice on interior decorating, information on fashions and interviews with local personalities; depending on the intelligence, perception and motivation of the writer-producer (and, on radio, announcer), they have also contained material relating to youth problems, consumer needs, environmental affairs, civic development and similar subjects. Many of these programs have reinforced campaigns of interest to the principal listening target, the housewife, such as promoting higher budgets for schools and referendums for better municipal services. Recently, however, women's programs have begun to add or substitute topics that are even more vital to women and to society, such as equal opportunities, job training, rape, abortion, birth control, financial dependence and legal discrimination. Some of these programs serve as a consciousness-raising tool for women and men both.

Barbara Walters, who established the acceptance of a woman interviewer-commentator on the "Today" show, believes that information-education programs which appeal to both women and men should be developed on day-time TV. Her own NBC network talk program, "Not For Women Only," covers such issues as drugs, nutrition, birth, marriage, death, and frequently includes specific areas of women's rights. "To say a show is just for women is to put down women," Walters has said. "We feel the subjects are of interest to all people." A Group W program on WBZ-TV, Boston, "For Women Today," received praise for its all-female production team, its unbiased presentation of women's needs and organizational activities and its coverage of a broad range of topics from drugs to cooking to sex to sensitivity groups. Lee Shepherd, as co-conductor of "Eyewitness News at Noon" on KSD-TV, St. Louis — principally hard news with a predominantly female audience — has said: "We are not interested in how a politician's wife manages her children but how she feels about political issues."[8]

At a convention of the National Association of Educational Broadcasters in the early 1970s, four women in public/educational broadcasting — Mary Roman, Pacifica, Marion Watson, WUOM, Barbara Peterson and Elaine Prostak, WFCR — presented the following guidelines for women's programs on radio:

    1. Topics such as cooking, sewing, child care, housekeeping and food shopping should be considered of general interest and not, as traditionally, materials stereotyped for women.

    2. The audience listening at home includes, along with housewives, the infirm, the elderly, the retired and the unemployed.

    3. There are topics of particular interest to women, such as legal rights for women.

    4. Community awareness should be increased as to what women have done and are doing in politics, art, sciences and technology.

    5. Women's awareness should be increased as to what it means to be a female, through such topics as female physiology and sexuality, female perspectives in public affairs, and female sensibilities in the arts.

Essentially, writing the women's program is not any different from writing other program types, as far as basic form is concerned. The news program or panel discussion or feature which considers the needs of women does not change in its essential technique. What it does is to be sensitive to the needs of the women, to the kind of content and words that reflect women's achievements and aspirations and are not insulting to or stereotyping of women. How many commercials have you seen that relate to women, sell a product and do it without suggesting, for example, that the woman's principal function in working for the advertisers is to show a sexy body which somehow promises a form of mental and emotional fornication while flying through the air and reinforces the stereotypes of stewardesses which suggest that the passenger will get more than an airplane ride for *his* money?

Gertrude Barnstone, broadcast writer and producer, president of the Women's Equity Action League of Texas, and active in women's efforts in media, believes that the principal need is, within any program approach or format, to keep in mind the specific points of view which reflect the needs and interests of women:

In many program areas we find it helpful to include a redefinition or articulation of the subject from the women's — the feminist — point of view. For example, in sports, write materials not only on the health and physical well-being aspects of athletics for women, but on the sense of one's own body gained from such involvement. Be sensitive to news items about women otherwise ignored in standard news coverage. Investigative reporting and features should be aware of the special problems relating to women — such as rape, child care, women alcoholics, sexism in schools and in toys. (These should, of course, also relate to men.) Women's programs can take advantage of the phone-in or write-in question approach to provide answers to problems plagueing women that are not easily obtainable elsewhere, such as unemployment, credit discrimination, loan discrimination, real estate and housing practices, among others.

Another technique is a "Would You Believe?" section, containing items concerning women's problems and achievements that usually are ignored by the media. Try interviews with women in non-traditional jobs, including the special problems of minority women. Include poetry, music, art, plays created by women. On any given topic of importance, bring in a woman to interview, someone who either is representative of a large group of women beset by a similar discriminatory problem or someone who has achieved prominence or expertise in a particular field. But be sure to avoid the "talking head" approach and use film and tape inserts as necessary. Open up the audience's minds to alternative life-styles, those which provide the women with an alternative to the traditional non-paid concubine-housekeeper and, in some cases, additionally, a breadwinner role. Sharing household chores, childless marriage, husband as homemaker, no marriage, informal marriage, lesbian relationship are among areas to be explored. In all cases, no matter what approach, technique or subject area used, they should all be integrated race-wise and age-wise.

Among the women's programs that have shown in their choice and treatment of topics that men are also adversely affected — psychologically, physically, economically — by the sexist problems they inflict or condone is Washington, D.C.'s WTOP-TV's "Everywoman."

Shirley Robson, producer of "Everywoman," explains that the program, with a specific orientation toward those subjects primarily relating to women and the impact of the subjects on all of society, encompasses all kinds of formats. Sometimes it is a documentary, sometimes a panel discussion, sometimes an interview: the basic techniques for writing all forms of radio and television programs apply. The concepts of good writing as they relate to approach, script preparation and technique do not change. What is critical, Robson says, is to keep the purposes of the program in mind at all times. "This is a program about those things that concern and that can help women. We are not afraid to take a strong editorial stance and cover such topics as rape, divorce, economic discrimination and prostitution. We have interviewed a rapist and shown the stark degradation of a woman alcoholic. We showed in the program on "The Great American Breast" an actual breast implant operation — which many people, including one of the program's personalities, were too squeamish to watch."

Ms. Robson stresses a need for thorough research, as for any well-prepared script. In an advocacy situation, which marks most "Everywoman" programs, she also stresses the need for the writer-researcher "to know yourself first" — to understand one's own attitudes toward women and the needs and problems of women — so that not only the purpose of the program can be effectively represented, but that the research and the writing will be balanced and fair. "Don't leave a stone unturned in doing research because the aspects of any situation, particularly topics of immediate public interest or of public controversy, may change from minute to minute."

The following "Everywoman" script, "The Great American Breast," is presented in its entirety, including the program's rundown sheet.

> • *Note the relationship of each item in the rundown sheet to the actual script materials. As you read the script, what information is new to you? Does any of it provide you with new insights as well as information on the concerns and problems of women? If you are a woman, how does it affect you, personally? If you are a man, how do these concerns directly affect your role and behavior in society, as well as woman's? Is the script informative and persuasive, as an advocacy program, without being didactic? Does it fulfill the requirements of a good documentary?, of a good feature?, at the same time being sensitive to and presenting the woman's point of view?*

EVERYWOMAN FOR: 5/27/74 P.M.

ock me	Dura-tion	Topics and Guests		Audio	Video	Area/Props
	0:30	Tease	(8 cleavage)	Music	Slides	
	0:15	Open		v/o		
	0:05	Title	. . . sound			
	2:20	Intro Rene & Carol		In key slides		
		Bump		Music		
:10		Bump (Great American Breast)		Music		
	:22	Rene & Carol lead to girlwatchers & blue denim		(Cleavage in key)	Film	
	:42	How sexy is flat-chested woman Comment (Rene & Carol)		(Cleavage in key)		

1:13	Why flat chested women feel cheated	
	Comment (Rene & Carol)	Topless stillframe
2:15	Topless routine	Audio tapes
	Comment (Rene & Carol)	Topless stillframe
:45	Breast animation	
	Carol . . . Billboard & Bump	(Great American Breast)
	Bump (E.W. . . . Great American Breast)	Music
	Rene & Carol . . . ad lib setup	
	Black & white breast surgery, psychology	
1:45	Lead to operation	
7:26	Operation	Audio
		w/carts
	Bump (we'll be right back)	
	Bump . . . (E.W. . . . The Great American Breast) Rene & Carol in limbo	Music
	Commentary	
:47	Credits w/ bandaging breasts	
	Brill	Bye Bye Birdie
		Music

RENE:

THE GREAT AMERICAN BREAST . .
PHOTOGRAPHED . . . MEASURED . . .
INJECTED . . . EXPOSED . . . PADDED
AND PUSHED UP . . . RESTORED WITH
COCOA BUTTER . . .

A HYBRID OF CROSS BREEDING UNLIKE
ANYTHING IN THE ANNALS OF AN
ANATOMY TEXTBOOK. OUR GUEST ON
EVERYWOMAN.

RENE & CAROL INTRO
RENE & CAROL — GENERAL HELLO TO
AUDIENCE

RENE:
SOMEWHERE ALONG THE WAY TO
MAIDENHOOD WE BECAME AWARE OF
BREASTS. USUALLY OUR OWN . . . HERS
IF THEY WERE BIGGER.

CAROL:
AND IN THE SEVENTH OR EIGHTH
GRADE GYM CLASS THE SLOW BUDDING
AMONG US CLUTCHED TOWELS TO OUR
CHESTS AND DRESSED BEHIND LOCKER
DOORS WHILE SISTERS OF AMAZING
GRACE WHIPPED "C" CUPS ON AND
OFF FOR SHOWERS.

RENE:
IN HIGH SCHOOL THE BOYS IN THE
CAFETERIA BEGAN THE SERIOUS
MEASUREMENT . . . WE HAD KNOCKERS.

CAROL:
OR GOURDS.

RENE:
OR TITS.

CAROL:
OR JUGS.

RENE:
OR BOOBS.

CAROL:
OR WE WERE WELL STACKED.

RENE:
NO ONE SEEMS TO KNOW WHY A
LARGE PROPORTION OF OUR MALE
POPULATION BECAME BREAST
WORSHIPPERS. MAYBE THE PILGRIMS
DONE US WRONG . . . THE LEGACY OF
THOSE ROUND WHITE COLLARS AND
HIGH BUTTON SHOES WERE JUST TOO
MUCH MODESTY FOR ONE PEOPLE TO
TAKE. AFTER WORLD WAR I WHEN THE
BOYS HAD SEEN "PAREE" . . . GIRLS
CHANGED INTO SOMETHING MORE
COMFORTABLE. STILL BREASTS DID NOT
GET A LOT OF ATTENTION BECAUSE
WOMEN WERE BUSY BINDING THEM UP
TO GET THAT STYLISH "FLAT" LOOK
TO GO WITH THE NEW CHEMISE.

CAROL:
WAS IT THE MOVIES? THERE . . . ON
THE SILVER SCREEN . . . ACTUALLY
MOVING . . . AND FREED . . . INSIDE THE
FOLDS OF BIAS CUT WHITE SATIN . . .
WERE THE BREASTS OF JEAN HARLOW
AND LITTLE DID WE KNOW THAT
MINUTES BEFORE THE TAKE TO THAT
SCENE SHE'D RUB HER NIPPLES WITH
ICE TO ENHANCE THE OUTLINE. WE
WERE OFF AND RUNNING.

RENE:
FORTUNES WERE MADE AS DEVICES
CALLED "BRASSIERES" WERE MANU-
FACTURED TO HARNESS ALL THAT
ECTOPLASM. MISS AMERICA'S MEASURE-
MENTS WERE ANNOUNCED WITH ALL
THE GLEE OF A DOW JONES HIGH.
TWENTY MILLION SWEATER GIRLS WERE

PINNED ABOVE THE BUNKS OF G.I. JOE
AND THEN CAME PLAYBOY . . .

CAROL (TIGHT):
WHO COULD BELIEVE IT? THOSE
CENTERFOLD FANTASY BREASTS . . .
AIRBRUSHED AND IN COLOR . . . TWO
FOR EVERY MONTH OF THE YEAR . . .
AS GOOD A SECURITY BLANKET AS
EARLY WEANED EYES HAD A RIGHT TO
EXPECT.

RENE (TIGHT):
BREAST WORSHIP REACHED SOME KIND
OF LUDICROUS HIGH WATER MARK WHEN
CAROL DODA . . . A GO GO DANCER IN
SAN FRANCISCO . . . DECIDED ON THE
USE OF SILICONE TO ENLARGE HER
ALREADY GENEROUS PROPORTIONS OF
38-24-36. SHE BECAME THE LARGEST
TOPLESS DANCER IN THE WEST AND
THUS AT 48-24-36 THE BIGGEST
ATTRACTION EVER.

CAROL:
WAS IT 48? OR WAS IT 52?

BUMP

SEGMENT TWO

RENE:
ASK A MAN WHAT HE LOOKS FOR FIRST
IN A WOMAN . . . HE'LL LOOK YOU
STRAIGHT IN THE EYE AND SAY INTEL-
LIGENCE. BUT THE GIRL WATCHERS OF
THE WORLD ARE STILL LOOKING AND
TALKING ABOUT BREASTS.

QUESTIONS

CAROL:
AD LIB COMMENT . . . (ASKS QUESTION)
HOW SEXY IS A FLAT-CHESTED WOMAN?

RENE:
AD LIB COMMENT . . . (ASKS QUESTION)
DO FLAT CHESTED WOMEN FEEL
CHEATED?

LEAD TO CLANCY'S TOPLESS

CAROL:
THE LOGICAL EVOLUTIONARY STEP IN
BREAST WATCHING WAS TO MOVE OUR
FEMALE FIGURES FROM THE STRIP
JOINTS AND THE CENTERFOLD . . .
TAKING HER OUT OF THE DEFORMING

BUNNY PUSH UP BRA AND LIBERATE
HER BARE BOSOMED IN FRONT OF A
JUKE BOX.

RENE:
SO FROM THE BENCHES AND THE
STREET WE FOLLOWED THE PHILOSO-
PHERS OF THE MAMMARY CULT INTO
THEIR NEW TEMPLES . . . OR IN THIS
CASE . . . CLANCY'S FIREPLACE TOPLESS
BAR AND GRILL WHERE REAL LIVE
BREASTS GO WELL WITH LUNCH AND A
BEER. I CONTINUED THE CONVERSATION.

LEAD TO AD ANIMATION

RENE:
IF A WOMAN HAS NEVER EAVESDROPPED
ON CONVERSATIONS LIKE THESE . . .
SHE CAN'T MISS THE EXPLICIT
MESSAGES IN THE BACK OF THE BOOK.

BILLBOARD . . . END OF SEGMENT 2

CAROL:
WELL . . . NOW THAT IT IS ALL OVER . . .
WHERE DO WE GO FROM HERE?
ALTHOUGH OUR APPROACH WAS IN A
LIGHTER VEIN . . . THE SERIOUS IMPLI-
CATIONS OF OUR SUBJECT MATTER
CANNOT BE DENIED. TO LIVE IN A
SOCIETY WHERE A FEMALE'S SELF
ESTEEM IS DETERMINED BY PHYSICAL
MEASUREMENTS IS ABSURD . . . AND
YET . . . EVEN THOUGH WE DISCUSS
THIS ABSURDITY . . . WE ARE DEFEATED
BY "MOVIE ADS" . . . COMMERCIALS . . .
MAGAZINES . . . THAT HIGHLIGHT EVER
LASTING SUCCESS IN TERMS OF THE
"LUCKY ONES" THAT ARE AMPLY
REWARDED . . . EITHER NATURALLY OR
BY ARTIFICIAL MEANS WITH PROPER
(WHATEVER THAT MEANS) PHYSICAL
PROPORTIONS. THERE ARE GENERA-
TIONS TO COME WHO WILL BE QUOTE
. . . "OVERLY OR INADEQUATELY
ENDOWED" . . . PERSONS WHO COULD
BE MENTALLY SCARRED BY OUR FOOL-
ISHNESS . . . IF WE PERSIST WITH THIS
NONSENSE OF JUDGING THE COVER
AND NOT THE BOOK. IF WE HAVE
INFORMED AND ENTERTAINED YOU . . .
FINE . . . BUT WE'RE NOT THROUGH YET!

RENE AND CAROL:
SHORT AD LIB . . . PSYCHOLOGY BLACK
WOMEN VIS A VIS WHITE WOMEN . . .
PLASTIC SURGERY.

RENE:
IN A PAPER CALLED THE PSYCHOLOGY
OF THE FLAT CHESTED WOMAN . . . TWO
PSYCHIATRISTS STUDIED THEIR
PATIENTS' FEELINGS OF SELF WORTH
AND THE SO CALLED BODY IMAGE
CONCEPT.
    THEY DREW A PORTRAIT OF THE
WOMEN WHO COME TO THEM AS
CANDIDATES FOR SURGERY. THEY
PRESENT AS SELF SUFFICIENT . . .
MATURE . . . ACTIVE HOUSEWIVES . . .
PHYSICALLY ATTRACTIVE AND SOCIALLY
AT EASE . . . WHO ARE APPEARANCE
ORIENTED. THEIR FIGURES ARE IMPOR-
TANT TO THEM. THEY OFTEN REFER TO
PAST OR PRESENT PERIODS OF DEPRES-
SION . . . FEELINGS OF INADEQUACY
AND SOMETHING THEY THINK OF AS
DEFICIENT FEMININITY.

CAROL:
THEY WERE DISTRESSED BY THE FLAB-
BINESS THAT COMES AS A RESULT OF
PREGNANCY . . . ONE WOMAN REFERRED
TO HER BREASTS AS COCKER SPANIEL
EARS. THE WEARING OF PADDED BRAS
WAS THOUGHT TO BE PHONY . . . OR
CHEATING. IN MOST INSTANCES ACTIV-
ITIES LIKE SWIMMING . . . PARTICIPA-
TION IN PHYSICAL EDUCATION COURSES
. . . AND WEARING CERTAIN CLOTHES
ARE AVOIDED OR SEVERELY RESTRICTED.
    SOME WOMEN HAVE BEEN AFRAID TO
DANCE CLOSE TO A MAN BECAUSE
TOUCHING MIGHT REVEAL A LACK OF
BREAST DEVELOPMENT.
    THEY DESCRIBE CONSIDERABLE
ANXIETY IN INTIMATE RELATIONSHIPS
. . . REFUSE TO APPEAR UNDRESSED
BEFORE THEIR HUSBANDS OR PERMIT
THEIR BREASTS TO BE TOUCHED.

RENE:
AND THE MAJORITY OF PATIENTS SEEK-
ING A BREAST OPERATION ARE IN-
VOLVED IN MAJOR LIFE CHANGES . . .
USUALLY A READJUSTMENT CONCERN-
ING MARRIAGES . . . WOMEN WHO ARE
MOST FREQUENTLY SEEN JUST BEFORE
OR AFTER A DIVORCE OR SEPARATION.
    WE'RE GOING TO SHOW YOU A
BREAST IMPLANT OPERATION . . . IF
YOU ARE SQUEAMISH YOU MAY NOT
WANT TO SEE THE FIRST PART. CAROL
WATCHED IT . . . I COULD NOT. THE
VOICES YOU WILL HEAR ARE THOSE OF
THE SURGEON WHO PERFORMED THIS
OPERATION AND A WOMAN WHO HAS
HAD THE SURGERY.

COMMENTARY CLOSE FOR BREASTS

RENE:
WELL . . . CAROL . . . IF THIS PROGRAM
WAS DESIGNED TO ANSWER THE QUES-
TION "HOW DID A NICE GIRL LIKE YOU
END UP IN SURGERY?" THEN THE
MEDIUM GAVE YOU ONLY PART OF THE
MESSAGE. SOME OF THE RAUNCHIER
CONDITIONING . . . YES . . . BUT THE
SUBTLETIES OF SEXUALITY HAVE BEEN
CONFUSED WITH A WORD THAT CREPT
INTO OUR LANGUAGE . . . "SEXY" . . .
AND THAT IS HARDER TO NAIL DOWN.
   FROM THE TIME SHE WAS CON-
STRUCTED FOR ADAM . . . EVE HAD
FEW EQUALIZING WEAPONS TO KEEP
HERSELF OPERATIVE. WAS THERE AN
APPLE HANDY? SHE USED IT. WOMEN
USED ANYTHING THAT WORKED. THEY
RESPONDED WITH A VENGEANCE . . .
PUTTING TOGETHER ALL THE SIGNALS
AND DEVICES THAT SAID "COME AND
GET ME . . . CROWN ME QUEEN OF THE
MAY." MAKING IT AS PAINLESS AS
POSSIBLE FOR THE MAN TO SINGLE
HER OUT FOR HIS PROTECTION AND
CARE AND MATING . . . THUS INSURING
HER SECURITY . . .
   BUT . . . ALAS . . . ! THE MORAL OF
THIS STORY . . . ANGELS . . . IS THAT IT
TAKES MORE THAN CHEMISTRY AND A
"C" CUP TO SURVIVE.

CAROL:
RIGHT ON OR AMEN . . . OR SOMETHING
LIKE THAT.

Produced by Shirley Robson, written by Rene Carpenter, starring Rene Carpenter
and Carol Randolph, WTOP-TV, Washington, D.C.

NOTES TO CHAPTER 9

[1] Dial Torgerson, "The Status of Women Around the World," *Los Angeles Times,* May 31, 1972.

[2] Hennessee, Judith Adler and Joan Nicholson, "NOW Says: TV Commercials Insult Women," *The New York Times Magazine,* May 28, 1972.

[3] Verheyden-Hilliard, Mary Ellen, Testimony at Federal Communications Commission Hearings on Children's Television, January, 1973. Based on Verheyden-Hilliard's study of Saturday morning network television children's programs.

[4] Verheyden-Hilliard, Mary Ellen, "Statement of the National Organization for Women" before the Senate Commerce Committee Subcommittee on Communications Hearing on Children's Television Programming, April, 1974.

[5] Amundsen, Kirsten, *The Silenced Majority.* Englewood Cliffs, N.J.: Prentice-Hall, Inc., 1971.

[6] Rock, Gail, "Same Time, Same Stations, Same Sexism," *Ms. Magazine,* December, 1973.
[7] Buck, Jerry, "Television," *Houston Post,* September 25, 1974.
[8] "Olivetti Girls Aren't Forever," *Broadcasting,* August 7, 1972.

REFERENCE WORKS

ON WOMEN'S PROGRAMS

Strainchamps, Ethel, ed., *Rooms With No View.* New York: Harper & Row, 1974. Compiled by Media Women's Association. Frank evaluations by women in media of the companies they work for, including the television industry.

Wheeler, Helen, *Women and Media: Current Resources About Women.* Metuchen, N.J.: Scarecrow Press, 1972.

Periodicals include *Media Report to Women* (Washington, D.C.) and *Ms.* (frequent reports and occasional articles on women's employment and programming in radio and TV).

FOR APPLICATION AND REVIEW

1. Listen to a women's program on a local radio station. Using the same basic format, rewrite it to the extent you think necessary to make it more responsive to the needs of the listening audience.

2. Develop a format for a TV women's program that provides a service to both men and women not now seen on network television.

3. Of the next few TV commercials you see featuring women performers, pick the most sexist and rewrite it so that it does not degrade women and at the same time sells the product.

10

Minority and Ethnic Programs

THE TRUISM THAT a writer writes best out of his or her personal experience is particularly applicable to minority and ethnic programs. This applies across the board, whether in news, documentaries, features, talks, drama or commercials. The orientation of the material must be in terms of the feelings and attitudes of the minority audience —which are to greater or lesser degrees different than those of the majority audience for whom almost all other program materials are written. It is not simply a matter of "thinking" what a particular minority group may be interested in or affected by. It is a matter of "knowing" and "feeling." Unless the writer has been part of the minority experience, there can be only the superimposition of understanding, no matter how sincere or talented the writer. In the mid-1970s this was evidenced in a number of "sitcoms" oriented around minority group characters, but either decried or taken with a grain of super-fiction salt in the super-fly manner by the minorities viewing the programs.

The principal problems minority groups have had with the media are the same as those described for women earlier: either denigrating, stereotyping or unrealistic sympathetic portrayals. Although the 1960s civil rights efforts resulted in a gradual change of negative stereotypes of some minorities, particularly Blacks, in commercials and drama programs, much still remains. What is significant about the prejudicial portrayals of minorities in media is that they are not, except on rare occasion, done deliberately; they are done out of insensitivity. Writers who mean well but who do not have the gut understanding and feeling of the minority experience, frequently, with the best will in the world, turn out materials that to the particular minority group are stereotyped and harmful. For example, one of the TV programs of the mid-1970s designed to represent minority life and to appeal to both majority and minority audiences was "That's My Mama." It was ABC-TV's highest-rated new television show of the season. To those especially sensitive to minority portrayals, however, its result was not equivalent to its purpose. Shortly after its debut, the Washington, D.C. chapter of the National Black Feminist Organization charged that "the first three episodes of the show distort 'the intimate lives of blacks . . . in the most tasteless and derogatory manner.' The mother is 'an interfering matriarch' who 'has no role in life other than the woman's work of cooking, cleaning and being a good servant.' The sister, Tracy, is 'an appendage to her mother and husband.' The male characters are stereotyped as well . . . that of junior encouraging the 'image of pimp, pusher, stud,' the roles of the two older men in the barbershop portray them as of 'no further use to society.' "[1]

Not only minority audiences, but minority participants are concerned with the images presented in even the most highly praised and successful shows. Redd Foxx, star of NBC-TV's "Sanford and Son," has discussed his anxiety with his own program. "I found myself arguing because we had agreed that if something was distasteful to me I could delete it from the script. They would say they didn't think something was offensive to black people. I object to all those jokes about coffins, people rolling their eyeballs, girls dressed like damn fools in rummage-sale outfits. We don't have to be raggedy just because (the show) is set in a junkyard. They had one show with a doctor who looked disheveled, with ashes dropping from his clothes. Their whole concept of black people is absolutely ridiculous."[2]

Writer Donald Bogle states that "the television industry protects itself by putting in a double consciousness. They take authentic issues in the black community and distort them. The humor is still that black people are 'dumb nigger types.' A show like 'Good Times' is basically unreal. Blacks are still not given credit for having insight. If good things happen to them, it's luck, like hitting the numbers. They still don't have control over their own destinies. 'Sanford and Son' comes across that way but the saving grace is Redd Foxx. I don't find him demeaning himself in any way. The thing that we can ask of television is that black characters be funny *and* intelligent."[3]

Bud Yorkin, producer of a number of programs featuring minorities, states that "We try to use as many black writers as we can. I don't think we can do a show today that is enjoyable to whites which is not acceptable to blacks."[4] That, perhaps, is the key. Critic Joel Dreyfuss, reviewing a new TV series about a Black family, summed up his evaluation by stating that if the producer "gets some black input into the writing end of the program, it might move away from the brink of absurdity and develop into a pretty good television program."[5]

The same basic problems pertain to all minority and ethnic programming, including Hispanic, Native American and Oriental radio and television shows and those serving different language and nationality backgrounds.

In many urban areas where there are relatively large first or second generation immigrant populations, radio stations have for many years presented foreign language programs and programs oriented toward the ethnic considerations of foreign backgrounds. When done well, these programs are not merely translations of standard majority-oriented broadcasting, but are especially designed and often conducted by people from the particular minority or ethnic group.

Nationality and religious groups, too, often take issue with portrayals in the media. The stereotypes frequently reflect those that have been used by bigots in real life, and rather than correct the stereotypes, television and radio have sometimes, even unwittingly, reinforced them. The media image of the American of Italian descent as a gangster, for example, continues to be challenged by Italian-American organizations throughout the country. In many instances minority and ethnic groups have filed lawsuits and, through other actions such as picketing and boycotts, have attempted to eliminate what they consider offensive impersonations. Stereotyping of more easily identifiable minority groups such as Chicanos and other Hispanics, Americans of Oriental descent and Native Americans has taken longer to overcome than stereotyping of Blacks, in part because of the large Black population and the concentration of the civil rights movement of the 1960s largely on Black concerns. Blacks have made much greater progress in getting exposure in the media than have other minorities.

The comments in this chapter pertain to all minority and ethnic groups. Although the examples are mainly related to the Black experience with radio and television because more has been written and produced about Blacks, the principles apply to all groups.

PROGRAM TYPES

CONSIDERATION OF AND SENSITIVITY to minority and ethnic needs in writing applies to all formats and program types. In commercials, for example, minorities have served as convenient stereotypes for humor for decades. On any television day you can see the Chicano, the Oriental, the American Indian, the comically-accented "foreigner," the ethnically-identified worker and others as naive/too sophisticated, stupid/scheming, dull/violent, overbearing/underbearing or with some other characteristic that the writers of the commercials would strongly object to if applied to them or to their own relatives. The fact that the portrayals are meant to be funny and that one presumably should have a sense of humor and overlook the stereotyping for the laughs does not eliminate the derogation and the negative impact on the population as a whole.

Eliminating negative stereotypes in commercials can be done through personal choice, and with faith in all people being human beings first and machines of industry at most second and hopefully not at all, we hope that no one reading this would be a party to the creation of racist or ethnically prejudicial materials on radio or TV. More subtle and more difficult for the writer is the creation of a commercial involving minorities that is oriented toward minorities. Because there are minorities in the script does not mean that the script necessarily really deals with minority interests and, from the point of view of the advertiser, with minority buying habits and motivations. Critic Joel Dreyfuss gives some examples:

> Two housewives chat over the fence about problems of getting their laundry whiter than white. One extols the virtues of a certain detergent. The other agrees and rushes off, presumably to buy as many boxes as she can. Both women are black. Both have their hair straightened and speak with solid Midwestern accents. Close your eyes and color differentiation disappears.
>
> A young black man credits his world-famous sneakers for the success of his "B Street Five" basketball team. Behind him, a carefully integrated group of youths snicker as he recites a limerick. His voice and his style are positively black. When he finishes with a flourish about his feet being "bronzed for the hall of fame" he turns and playfully punches one of his tormentors (a black one).
>
> The two commercials are a study in contrast. One could just as well have been done by two white actresses. The second, with the youths, has a certain flair. [6]

These examples point up two aspects of writing "minority" commercials. One is not minority-oriented at all, but in terms of image uses minorities as actors first, with no reference to minority or ethnic images — certainly a step forward in desegregating the performing arts. In the other there is sensitivity toward what is sometimes called a "life-style" in order to provide a base for real identification and motivation on the part of the minority viewer. All commercial writing, as noted in Chapter 3, has strict parameters. For example, many Blacks in the advertising field believe that the parameters for commercials involving Blacks are oriented so as not to offend whites. These rules, they say, frequently result in commercials that offend Blacks through omission if not in direct content. Joel Dreyfuss found that "Blacks have to be very black, so there won't be any confusion; if there is a black man in a group scene, there must be a black woman obviously attached to him so there won't be any hint that the sponsor is promoting miscegenation; the black adult in the commercial must be definitely middle-class." [7]

Cecil Hale, President of the National Association of Television and Radio Artists, a predominantly Black organization, believes that only a consistency of background and life-style can result in a consistency within the writing of the commercial. He states that there must be an understanding among the writer, the announcer and the audience that is based on common feeling. He stresses language as an important factor. He says that the writer must understand and find the common relationships among the character of the product, the character of the listener and the character of the occasion. The writer must be able to differentiate between the real relationship among product-seller-consumer and the implied relationship. For example, in an automobile ad, it is not the car itself that is significant; it is the *image* of the car that is important. Commercials for the same product need to be different for different audiences because they see the product differently. Two Black-oriented stations in the same community may deal with significantly different audiences. Hale advises writers not to forget that the announcer sets a particular mood for the commercial, no matter what its overt content.

Caroline Jones, creative director of the Black Creative Group, which advises ad agencies dealing with the Black market, states that "they are getting blacks in ads, but they are not doing black ads. It's not black lifestyle. I'm talking about why they use a product, why they buy it." Referring to studies showing that Black women cook foods longer and add spices to them, stressing taste rather than speed, Jones adds that a Black-oriented commercial, "instead of saying, 'You can cook it in a minute,' they should say 'you will have more time to spend with your family.' I'm talking about why they use a product, why they buy it. They haven't researched it."[8]

A most important concern of minority and ethnic groups is the lack of adequate news coverage. Many of the complaints to the Federal Communications Commission concerning failure of stations to serve community needs relate to quantity and quality of news, features and public affairs programming which affect or are about minorities in the stations' coverage areas. Joel Dreyfuss states that in the first 19 weeks of 1974 only 20 of 1,500 items on a national TV network news program dealt with Black or racial matters in the country; nine of these related to the San Francisco "Zebra" killings and two were about Hank Aaron's home-run record. "During the average week," Dreyfuss says, "Americans spend 555 million hours watching television news. For nearly 80% of Americans television news is their primary source of information. If they depend on . . . network news shows . . . for their information about what blacks in this country were doing, the impression would have been of near total invisibility. . . ."[9] A frequent complaint from producers of Black-oriented news and public affairs shows and from the viewers of these shows is that the programs are hastily and cheaply put together, with low-priority facilities and budgets.

Television news executive Robert Reid believes that minority-group reporters (who are, in effect, the writers of the news stories) make a difference by providing a perspective that the majority-group reporter doesn't have. "Blacks in television tend to accord a more even treatment. How often do you see a man-in-the-street interview about, say impeachment, and no blacks are interviewed? Or a story about the effects of inflation on the middle class? The black reporter is more likely to come back with some blacks among those interviewed."[10] Many minority-group reporters-writers, while desirous of providing special insights relative to the minority and ethnic stories they cover, are worried about being stereotyped and limited in their assignments. "I think of myself as a journalist who is black rather than as a black journalist," says CBS correspondent Bernard Shaw. "I think I have a certain sensitivity. Never would I want to be assigned solely to stories about blacks. That would restrict my viewpoint and my development."[11]

From the minority standpoint, therefore, the approach is two-fold: equal opportunity for reporter-writer jobs for all kinds of stories, and realization that a member of a particular minority group is likely to bring a sensitivity and perspective to covering a story relating to that group not likely to be had by a reporter-writer not a member of that group. As in the writing of commercials, the writer must be aware of the special needs, attitudes, feelings and motivations of the minority-ethnic group newsmakers and news viewers, as well as those of the non-minority audience. News impact of the particular event on minorities — such impact is, by the nature of our society, different than that upon the majority — is usually ignored, except where the happening directly and strongly includes a minority issue.

APPLICATION: BLACK PROGRAMS

THROUGHOUT THE COUNTRY, on majority-owned stations and on the gradually increasing number of their own stations, minority and ethnic groups are presenting news programs which interpret and include those events they deem of interest that are not included in the regular news programs. One significant development along this line was the establishment, in 1973, of the National Black Network, a Black owned-and-operated news information and public affairs service which was reaching some 80 affiliates by mid-1975. The stories are of a national, general nature, but are especially oriented to Black needs. For example, in 1974 NBN reports included such features as "Black Election 74," comparison of the Boston school situation with that in Little Rock in 1957, and Black input into the White House-sponsored series of economic conferences. Among the biggest stories of the decade were the resignation of Richard Nixon and the swearing in of Gerald Ford as President of the United States. NBN covered these stories. A study of the scripts will indicate how special minority needs may be taken into consideration and made a part of a general news story.

NIXON CUT: MAX. OF :15 SEC. HIS RESIGNATION

THE FOLLOWING IS AN NBN SPECIAL ON THE RESIGNATION OF RICHARD M. NIXON AS THE 37th PRESIDENT OF THE UNITED STATES. I'M _____
IN NEW YORK.

THROUGHOUT MOST OF THE WEEK . . . THE NATION'S CAPITOL WAS ALIVE WITH SPECULATION AND RUMORS THAT RICHARD NIXON, WHO LESS THAN TWO YEARS EARLIER HAD WON REELECTION BY THE WIDEST MARGIN IN AMERICAN POLITICAL HISTORY, WOULD STEP DOWN AS PRESIDENT OF THE UNITED STATES OF AMERICA. FOR WEEKS PRIOR TO THIS FATEFUL WEEK . . . THE PRESIDENT HAD STEADFASTLY RESISTED CALLS FOR HIM TO STEP DOWN AND SPARE THE NATION THE ORDEAL OF A PRESIDENTIAL IMPEACHMENT IN THE HOUSE AND TRIAL IN THE SENATE. ONLY WEDNESDAY . . . NIXON HAD SUMMONED HIS CABINET TO TELL THEM HE WOULD NOT STEP ASIDE BUT WOULD ALLOW THE CONSTITUTIONAL PROCESS TO TAKE ITS COURSE. DESPITE THIS, THE RUMORS PERSISTED AND LESS THAN 48 HOURS LATER NIXON WENT ON NATIONAL TELEVISION TO TELL THE AMERICAN PEOPLE THAT HE HAD DECIDED TO STEP DOWN IN THE NATIONAL INTEREST.

FOR YEARS TO COME, HISTORIANS WILL BE REEVALUATING THE NIXON PRESIDENCY AND TRYING TO DISSECT THE CANCER CALLED WATERGATE WHICH BEGAN WHEN A BLACK GUARD NOTICED A PIECE OF TAPE ON A DOOR AT THE LAVISH APARTMENT-OFFICE COMPLEX WHERE THE OFFICES OF THE DEMOCRATIC NATIONAL COMMITTEE WERE LOCATED. THAT WAS JUNE 17, 1972 . . . 782 STORMY DAYS BEFORE NIXON BECAME THE FIRST PRESIDENT IN THE HISTORY OF THE AMERICAN REPUBLIC TO STEP DOWN FROM OFFICE UNDER FIRE.

THAT GUARD WAS FRANK WILLS WHO HAS SAID HE FEELS HIS FOOTNOTE IN HISTORY WILL HAVE A PROFOUND IMPACT ON THE AMERICAN POLITICAL SYSTEM.

CART #1 . . . . :23 SEC. . . . . OUT: TAPE ON THE DOOR

WILLS ALSO SAYS HE FEELS WATERGATE BROUGHT THE NATION BACK FROM THE BRINK OF DESTRUCTION OF ITS CONSTITUTIONAL FORM OF GOVERMENT. . . .

CART #2 . . . . :24 SEC. . . . . OUT: UNDER A DICTATORSHIP

THROUGHOUT THE TWO YEARS OF WATERGATE DISCLOSURES AND ATTENDING POLITICAL UPHEAVAL . . . THERE WERE MANY OBSERVERS . . . SUCH AS PRESI-DENTIAL ASSISTANT STAN SCOTT . . . WHO CONTENDED THAT THE GROWING ASSAULT ON THE NIXON PRESIDENCY WAS NOT A CONCERN FOR BLACKS.

CART #3 . . . . :17 SEC. . . . . OUT: NAME OF GOOD GOVERNMENT

FRANK WILLS TOOK ISSUE WITH THIS VIEW . . . SAYING THAT ALL AMERICANS SHOULD BE CONCERNED ABOUT THE IMPACT OF GOVERNMENT CORRUPTION AND ABUSE OF POWER. . .

CART #4 . . . . :22 SEC. . . . . OUT: WITHIN THIS COUNTRY

BLACKS WERE, INDEED, CONCERNED ABOUT WATERGATE AS IT RELATED TO THE RECORD OF ANTAGONISM OF THE NIXON ADMINISTRATION TOWARDS PROGRAMS AND POLICIES AFFECTING AMERICA'S BLACK COMMUNITY. THERE WERE THOSE LIKE PENNSYLVANIA SECRETARY OF STATE DELORES TUCKER WHO ACCUSED NIXON OF TAKING FROM BLACKS AND THE POOR AND GIVING TO THE RICH.

CART #5 . . . . :28 SEC. . . . . OUT: THEIR TUNE

CARL ROWAN . . . SYNDICATED COLUMNIST AND HEAD OF THE U.S. INFO AGENCY IN THE KENNEDY ADMINISTRATION . . . AGREED WITH MS. TUCKER, SAYING THAT NIXON HAD PLAYED ON THE PASSIONS OF AMERICA TO TURN THEM AGAINST BLACKS.

CART #6 . . . . :22 SEC. . . . . OUT: ARE CONCERNED

ONE OF MANY AREAS IN WHICH THE NIXON ADMINISTRATION WAS CRITICIZED IN DEALING WITH BLACKS WAS THE MANNER IN WHICH IT DOWNPLAYED THE

PROBLEMS OF THE NATION'S LARGE URBAN CITIES, WHICH HAVE BECOME
INCREASINGLY BLACK AS WHITES FLEE TO THE SUBURBS. ATLANTA'S MAYOR
MAYNARD JACKSON SAID EARLIER THIS YEAR HE FELT THE PROBLEMS OF THE
CITIES WERE BECOMING WORSE AS A RESULT OF WATERGATE.

    CART #7 .... :38 SEC. .... OUT: THAT IS CALLED WATERGATE

GEORGIA STATE REPRESENTATIVE JULIAN BOND OFTEN CRITICIZED THE NIXON
ADMINISTRATION FOR BEING BIG GOVERNMENT TO PROTECT THE PRIVILEGES OF
THE POWERFUL . . .

    CART #8 .... :23 SEC. .... OUT: OF THE POWERLESS

M. CARL HOLLOMAN, PRESIDENT OF THE NATIONAL URBAN COALITION, CITES
WHAT HE CONSIDERS A DISMAL RECORD BY THE NIXON ADMINISTRATION ON
MATTERS AFFECTING BLACKS. . .

    CART #9 .... :27 SEC. .... OUT: CUTBACKS ON DAYCARE

SHORTLY AFTER HIS '72 REELECTION VICTORY . . . PRESIDENT NIXON EMBARKED
ON A CAMPAIGN TO CUT OFF FUNDS TO PROGRAMS OPERATING UNDER THE
OFFICE OF ECONOMIC OPPORTUNITY. THOSE EFFORTS PUT NIXON ON WHAT WAS
THEN DESCRIBED AS A CERTAIN COURSE OF CONSTITUTIONAL COLLISION WITH
CONGRESS THAT WAS LATER OVERSHADOWED BY WATERGATE. CONGRESSMAN
WALTER FAUNTROY OF WASHINGTON OFTEN SPOKE ABOUT THE EFFORTS OF
THE CONGRESSIONAL BLACK CAUCUS TO HOLD ON TO PROGRAMS AND SERVICES
THAT BENEFIT BLACKS IN THE FACE OF EFFORTS BY THE NIXON ADMINISTRATION
TO CUT THEM OUT ALL TOGETHER.

    CART #10 ....

BEFORE THE HOUSE JUDICIARY COMMITTEE'S IMPEACHMENT PROBE BEGAN IN
JUNE . . . NEW YORK CONGRESSMAN CHARLES RANGEL . . . WHO IS CHAIRMAN OF
THE CONGRESSIONAL BLACK CAUCUS AND A MEMBER OF THE JUDICIARY
COMMITTEE . . . SAID HE FELT THAT ALTHOUGH NIXON'S REMOVAL WOULD BE A
STIMULANT TO THE NATION'S ECONOMY . . . HE DID NOT FORSEE A RETURN TO
CONCERN FOR SOCIAL PROBLEMS AFFECTING BLACKS THAT HAD BEEN ALL BUT
ABANDONED BY THE EX-PRESIDENT.

    CART #11 .... :27 SEC. .... OUT: TO BE BENEFICIARIES

ONE OF THE MYRIAD OF CHARGES AGAINST THE PRESIDENT WAS THAT HE
ALLOWED HIS REELECTION COMMITTEE TO ENGAGE IN A DIRTY TRICKS CAMPAIGN
AGAINST CONTENDERS FOR THE DEMOCRATIC PRESIDENTIAL NOMINATION IN '72.
ONE OF THOSE DEMOCRATIC HOPEFULS WAS BROOKLYN CONGRESSWOMAN
SHIRLEY CHISHOLM WHO SAYS SHE WILL SEEK REMEDY IN THE COURTS FOR
STORIES PUT OUT ON HER THAT SHE WAS A TRANSVESTITE AND HAD BEEN
TREATED IN A MENTAL HOSPITAL. DESPITE A GENERAL ATTITUDE THAT BLACKS
WERE NOT INVOLVED IN WATERGATE . . . THE SCANDALS SLOWLY SPREAD AND
ENGULFED VIRTUALLY EVERY INDIVIDUAL WHO SERVED IN THE HIGHEST ECHELONS
OF THE WHITE HOUSE . . . INCLUDING ROBERT BROWN, WHO SERVED AS NIXON'S
ADVISOR ON MINORITY AFFAIRS DURING THE FIRST ADMINISTRATION. ACCORDING
TO A REPORT PREPARED BY THE SENATE WATERGATE COMMITTEE . . . BROWN
WAS ALLEGEDLY DELEGATED TO DISPENSE GRANTS AND FAVORS TO PROMINENT
BLACKS IN AN ATTEMPT TO GET THEM TO SUPPORT NIXON OR REMAIN NEUTRAL
IN THE '72 CAMPAIGN. BROWN VEHEMENTLY DENIED THOSE CHARGES AND
CRITICIZED BLACK LEADERS FOR NOT SPEAKING OUT AGAINST WHAT HE
CONSIDERED AN ATTEMPT TO TAINT EVEN BLACKS WHO HAD SERVED WITH NIXON.

CART #12 .... :20 SEC. .... OUT: THREE BY THREE

BECAUSE BLACK LEADERS FAILED TO SPEAK OUT AGAINST THE ALLEGATIONS . . .
BROWN SAID HE FELT IT WOULD BE DIFFICULT TO GET ANYONE TO LOBBY ON
BEHALF OF THE INTEREST OF BLACKS IN THE FUTURE.

CART #13 ...... :20 SEC. .... OUT: DONE ALREADY

AS THE WATERGATE DRAMA APPROACHED THE HISTORIC PROPORTIONS OF
POSSIBLE IMPEACHMENT . . . THE STAGE SHIFTED FROM THE
MEDIA TO THE HALLS OF CONGRESS WHERE THE JUDICIARY COMMITTEE
LAUNCHED THE FIRST CONSTITUTIONAL PROCESS IN OVER 100 YEARS TO REMOVE
A PRESIDENT FROM OFFICE. AMONG THE 38 MEMBERS OF THAT COMMITTEE
DELIBERATING NIXON'S FATE WERE THREE BLACKS: REPRESENTATIVE RANGEL,
CONGRESSMAN JOHN CONYERS OF DETROIT, AND CONGRESSWOMAN BARBARA
JORDAN OF TEXAS. IN REMARKS MADE DURING TELEVISED DEBATES BY
COMMITTEE MEMBERS ON VARIOUS PROPOSED ARTICLES OF IMPEACHMENT . . .
REPRESENTATIVE CONYERS DESCRIBED THE NATURE OF THE TASK CONFRONTING
THE COMMITTEE.

CART #14 .... :25 SEC. .... OUT: GOVERNMENT OF THIS COUNTRY

ARGUING IN FAVOR OF IMPEACHING NIXON . . . CONYERS CHARGED THAT HE HAD
VIOLATED HIS OATH TO UPHOLD THE CONSTITUTION.

CART #15 .... :22 SEC. .... OUT: ALL OF THE PEOPLE

IN HIS OPENING REMARKS . . . CONGRESSMAN RANGEL MADE AN IMPASSIONED
DENUNCIATION OF RECORDED CONVERSATIONS IN WHICH NIXON DISCUSSED THE
PAYMENT OF HUSH MONEY TO THE WATERGATE BURGLARS.

CART #16 .... :24 SEC. .... OUT: CONVICTED OF BURGLARY

IN STILL OTHER ELOQUENT REMARKS BY A BLACK PERSON ON THE JUDICIARY
COMMITTEE . . . CONGRESSWOMAN JORDAN OUTLINED FOR HER COLLEAGUES AND
THE NATION THE GRAVITY OF THE PROCESS WHICH THEY WERE UNDERTAKING.

CART #17 .... :17 SEC. .... OUT: LIBERTIES FROM VIOLATION

THEN . . . BREAKING HER CASE AGAINST NIXON DOWN TO SPECIFICS . . . MS.
JORDAN PROCEEDED TO DETAIL THE ABUSES SHE FELT WARRANTED HIS REMOVAL
FROM OFFICE.

CART #18 .... :22 SEC. .... OUT: HE KNEW TO BE FALSE

EVEN AT THIS CRITICAL STAGE IN HIS STRUGGLE TO HOLD ON TO HIS OFFICE . . .
THE PRESIDENT MAINTAINED HIS INNOCENCE OF CHARGES LEVELED AGAINST HIM
AND COUNTER CHARGED THAT THE GROUNDSWELL OF OPPOSITION TO HIM WAS
BEING PURSUED BY THOSE WHO HAD A VENDETTA AGAINST HIM. FOR THE NEXT
TWO WEEKS NIXON WOULD REJECT GROWING CALLS FOR HIM TO STEP DOWN
AND STEADFASTLY MAINTAINED THAT HE WOULD BE EXONERATED OF ALL
CHARGES. THEN . . . ON MONDAY . . . IN A STATEMENT THAT ALIENATED VIRTUALLY
ALL OF HIS REMAINING SUPPORTERS . . . PRESIDENT NIXON ACKNOWLEDGED THAT
HE HAD . . . INDEED . . . AUTHORIZED THE COVERUP OF THE WATERGATE BREAK-IN
AND HAD WITHHELD THREE TAPES TO THAT EFFECT FROM THE CONGRESS. THIS
DISCLOSURE ALL BUT SEALED HIS FATE AS PRESIDENT OF THE UNITED STATES.
IN THE FOLLOWING TWO DAYS . . . IT BECAME INCREASINGLY APPARENT THAT
NIXON WOULD BE REMOVED FROM OFFICE . . . WHETHER THROUGH IMPEACHMENT
OR BY HIS OWN RESIGNATION. THROUGHOUT MONDAY AND TUESDAY . . . AN AIR

OF EXPECTANCY GRIPPED WASHINGTON, D.C., AS MEMBERS OF THE PRESIDENT'S OWN PARTY URGED HIM TO RESIGN. NIXON MAINTAINED THAT HE WOULD NOT. THERE WERE FEELERS SENT TO HIM THAT HE MIGHT BE GRANTED IMMUNITY FROM PROSECUTION IF HE WOULD STEP DOWN . . . NIXON MAINTAINED THAT HE WOULD NOT. IT WAS BROUGHT TO HIS ATTENTION THAT HE WOULD BE ABLE TO KEEP HIS $60,000 A YEAR PENSION ONLY IF HE WOULD AVOID IMPEACHMENT AND GIVE UP THE WHITE HOUSE. NIXON MAINTAINED THAT HE WOULD NOT . . . IN A SERIES OF RAPID DEVELOPMENTS ON THURSDAY . . . IT BECAME INEVITABLE THAT NIXON WOULD BE GIVING UP THE PRIZE JOB WHICH HAD CAPPED 25 YEARS OF PUBLIC SERVICE AS A CONGRESSMAN, SENATOR AND VICE-PRESIDENT. HE HAD BEEN THE ONLY MAN EVER ELECTED VICE-PRESIDENT AND PRESIDENT TWICE. NOW . . . THAT RECORD WOULD BE MIRED IN THE HISTORY BOOKS WHICH WILL MOST CERTAINLY NOT TREAT RICHARD M. NIXON KINDLY. THE END CAME AT 9:00 P.M. ON THURSDAY EVENING WHEN NIXON SPOKE TO THE NATION FROM THE OVAL OFFICE OF THE WHITE HOUSE.

CART #19 . . . . :82 SEC. . . . . OUT: THIS OFFICE

EVEN AS HE PREPARED TO DEPART HIS HIGH OFFICE . . . NIXON DREW THE SAME KIND OF RESPONSE FROM BLACKS WHO HAD IN PAST YEARS DENOUNCED HIS ATTITUDE TOWARDS THE BLACK COMMUNITY. REPRESENTATIVE METCALF OF CHICAGO SAID HE REGRETS THE IMPEACHMENT PROCESS WAS NOT ALLOWED TO PROCEED.

CART #20 . . . . :32 SEC. . . . . OUT: JUDICIARY COMMITTEE

CALIFORNIA CONGRESSMAN RON DELLUMS SAID HE DOES NOT THINK NIXON DEALT WITH THE REAL REASON FOR HIS DEPARTURE FROM OFFICE . . . THE WRONGDOINGS DONE UNDER HIS ADMINISTRATION.

CART #21 . . . . :22 SEC. . . . . OUT: OF CRIMINAL OFFENSES

JULIAN BOND ALSO SAID HE WOULD LIKE TO HAVE SEEN NIXON HAVE HIS DAY IN COURT.

CART #22 . . . . :13 SEC. . . . . OUT: BEST WAY OUT

IN FAILING TO MAKE ANY STATEMENT OF GUILT IN HIS RESIGNATION ADDRESS NIXON HAS, PERHAPS, LEFT HIMSELF OPEN FOR PROSECUTION ON CHARGES AGAINST HIM EVEN AFTER HE HAS SHED THE SANCTION OF THE PRESIDENCY. AS THE PRESIDENT PONDERED HIS FATE SENATOR BROOKE OFFERED A RESOLUTION IN THE SENATE THAT WOULD HAVE GIVEN THE PRESIDENT IMMUNITY FROM PROSECUTION IF HE RESIGNED. WHEN BROOKE, WHO IS THE ONLY BLACK MAN IN THE SENATE, MADE THE PROPOSAL IT WAS DENOUNCED BY MANY CONGRESSMEN INCLUDING CONGRESSMAN CONYERS.

CART #23 . . . . :28 SEC. . . . . OUT: AGREES ON

OTHER SHARP CRITICISM OF BROOKE'S PROPOSAL CAME FROM JOE MADISON, HEAD OF THE DETROIT NAACP.

CART #24 . . . . :19 SEC. . . . . OUT: COUNTRY CLUB PRISON

BROOKE DEFENDED HIS RESOLUTION SAYING THAT IT WAS IN THE INTEREST OF THE COUNTRY TO AVOID THE ORDEAL OF AN EXTENDED IMPEACHMENT TRIAL OF NIXON.

CART #25 . . . . :24 SEC. . . . . OUT: POLITICAL INSTITUTIONS

WITH NIXON'S RESIGNATION . . . THE REINS OF POWER PASSED TO VICE-PRESIDENT GERALD FORD WHOSE RECORD ON CIVIL RIGHTS HAS ALSO BEEN SCORED BY BLACK MEMBERS OF CONGRESS. SHORTLY AFTER NIXON'S SPEECH ON THURSDAY FORD SPOKE TO NEWSMEN AND ONLOOKERS OUTSIDE HIS SUBURBAN WASHINGTON HOME.

CART #26 .... :26 SEC. .... OUT: APPLAUSE

NBN Newscopy written by Tony Bristow, Assistant National News Editor

TEASER . . .

LLOYD:
THE FOLLOWING IS AN NBN NEWS SPECIAL ON THE SWEARING IN OF GERALD RUDOLPH FORD AS THE 38th PRESIDENT OF THE UNITED STATES. I'M JOHN LLOYD IN NEW YORK.

LEE:
AND I'M SAM LEE.
WITH THE RESIGNATION OF RICHARD MILHOUS NIXON AS PRESIDENT OF THE UNITED STATES, THE REINS OF POWER PASS TO VICE-PRESIDENT FORD, WHO WAS NOMINATED BY NIXON TO SUCCEED SPIRO AGNEW. AGNEW RESIGNED AS VICE-PRESIDENT ON OCTOBER 12 IN THE WAKE OF DISCLOSURES OF TAX EVASION IN A BRIBERY AND KICKBACK SCANDAL. FORD IS TO ADDRESS THE NATION SOME TIME LATER TODAY AND IS EXPECTED TO FOCUS MUCH OF HIS ATTENTION ON INFLATION. EVEN BEFORE NIXON FORMALLY ANNOUNCED HIS RESIGNATION LAST NIGHT, FORD HAD NOTIFIED TOP ADMINISTRATION ECONOMIC ADVISERS TO PREPARE FOR A MEETING TODAY. FORD HAS CALLED INFLATION . . . "PUBLIC ENEMY NUMBER ONE."

LLOYD:
THE NEW PRESIDENT CONSIDERS HIMSELF A CONSERVATIVE ON FISCAL MATTERS AND HE'S ON RECORD IN SUPPORT OF MOST OF THE NIXON ANTI-INFLATION POLICIES. THAT MEANS RESTRAINT IN SPENDING, A BALANCED BUDGET AND A TIGHT MONEY POLICY BY THE FEDERAL RESERVE BOARD. FORD'S OTHER POLITICAL POSTURES ARE CLEAR FROM HIS 25 YEARS IN THE HOUSE OF REPRE-SENTATIVES. HE FAVORS REVENUE-SHARING, HEAVY MILITARY SPENDING AND NATIONAL HEALTH INSURANCE. HE'S AGAINST BUSING, WELFARE REFORM, ECONOMIC CONTROLS, TAX CUTS AND LOW-INCOME HOUSING SUBSIDIES. DESPITE STATEMENTS BY THE SOON-TO-BE-PRESIDENT FORD IN RECENT MONTHS WHICH POINT TOWARDS IMPROVED RELATIONS WITH THE BLACK COMMUNITY . . . MANY OBSERVERS FEEL HIS PAST RECORD OFFERS LITTLE HOPE FOR SIGNIFICANT CHANGE FROM THE POLICIES OF THE NIXON ADMINISTRATION. CONGRESSMAN CHARLES RANGEL, WHO IS CHAIRMAN OF THE CONGRESSIONAL BLACK CAUCUS, SAID FORD HAS NOT BEEN A GOOD VICE-PRESIDENT AND THAT HIS CONGRES-SIONAL RECORD PROVIDES LITTLE INSIGHT INTO HOW HE WILL BE AS PRESIDENT.

CART #1 .... :24 SEC. .... OUT: NOT VERY ENLIGHTENING

LEE:
GEORGIA STATE REPRESENTATIVE JULIAN BOND TOLD NBN NEWS LAST NIGHT THAT HE SEES AN OMINOUS SIGN IN SIMILARITIES BETWEEN THE NIXON RESIGNA-TION SPEECH FROM THE WHITE HOUSE AND FORD'S REMARKS ON THE LAWN OF HIS HOME IN ALEXANDRIA, VA., SHORTLY AFTER THE PRESIDENT RESIGNED.

CART #28 .... :28 SEC. .... OUT: LAST 5¹/₂ YEARS

AS THE NATION PROCEEDS TO ADJUST TO THE MOST CLAMOROUS UPHEAVAL IN THE INSTITUTION OF THE PRESIDENCY IN THE NEARLY 200-YEAR HISTORY OF THE

REPUBLIC . . . IT IS UNCERTAIN AS TO WHAT EFFORTS WILL BE MADE TO GRAPPLE
WITH THE CONTINUING SOCIAL PROBLEMS OF HOUSING, EDUCATION, UNEMPLOY-
MENT AND DISCRIMINATION THAT STILL PLAGUE BLACKS, OTHER MINORITIES AND
THE POOR. MANY CONGRESSMEN SAY THEY WILL BEGIN TO OPEN A DIALOGUE
WITH THE NEW ADMINISTRATION TO BEGIN TO REVERSE THE POLICIES OF THE
NIXON ADMINISTRATION. OTHERS SAY THEY WILL WAIT AND SEE WHAT THE NEW
DAY BRINGS.

(FROM HERE TO BEGINNING OF FEED MODERATORS READ
EDITED WIRE NEWSCOPY AND RAP EXTEMPORANEOUSLY)

NBN Newscopy written by Tony Bristow, Assistant National News Editor

Although in the mid-1970s minorities, particularly Blacks, began to
appear more and more on entertainment programs, especially sitcoms, and
in commercials, writers and producers did not include much minority representation on news and public affairs programs. (On some stations in cities
with large minority populations, such as Washington, D.C., news programs,
to greater and lesser degrees, hired minority representatives for on-camera
reportorial positions.) A study of the "Today" program showed an average
of four to six guests per day for a total of some 400 to 500 during the first
four months of 1974. Only 19 of the total were Black, with six of these
either athletes or entertainers. Two of the 19 discussed problems of Spanish-
speaking Americans.[12] Comparable figures were found in a study of other
public affairs, interview and panel discussion programs. As did NBN with
news, the public affairs and documentary series oriented solely to minority
and ethnic concerns provided the most significant coverage for these groups.
Some of the programs were continuing series on local television and radio
stations, produced by members of the minority and ethnic communities who
were provided free air time or who purchased time. Acclaimed as a most
significant national series was Public Broadcasting Service's "Black Journal." Until 1975 "Black Journal" concentrated on the documentary and
interview-feature forms to present public affairs materials. (The "new"
1975 "Black Journal" concentrated on varied entertainment formats.)
"We, The Enemy" presents a minority viewpoint which at the same time
reflects majority concerns about a topic of general interest. As you examine
the following excerpts from the program, note that in terms of format and
style "We, The Enemy" opens cold, and only after establishing the problem and approach does the program go into a formal opening, including a
description of the viewer phone-in technique.

WNET/13 — BLACK JOURNAL #408

"We, The Enemy"

VIDEO	AUDIO
Studio — TONY BROWN (O/C):	On May 16, 1972, one year before the White House Enemies' List was made public by John Dean, Jack

Chromakey Cards:

New York Times Headline
Amsterdam News Headline
Militant News Headline

Government Surveillance
of Private Citizens

Anderson exposed in his syndicated column the existence of a computerized list compiled by the Secret Service of 5,500 Black Americans which it labeled "The Black Nationalist File." Everyone in this file is "of protective interest" to the Secret Service. What this means is that, in the opinion of the Secret Service, they either bear ill will toward the President, another government official, have demonstrated at the White House, have a criminal record or a record of mental instability.

Access to a series of documents about the counter-intelligence operations of J. Edgar Hoover's FBI was gained because Carl Stern, a reporter at NBC, sued the Justice Department under the Freedom of Information Act. The Washington Post, in an editorial of March 15, 1974, said: ". . . Mr. Kelley might take a close look at the Bureau's methods of seeking information from Black Communities as disclosed in those papers and in comments by former agents.

Bookstores, churches, saloons, store-front community organizations, campuses and student organizations all seemed to be fair game for the FBI if they had the words Afro or Black in their titles. In fact, one former agent who had been assigned to racial matters here in the district told a Post reporter, 'The bureau was interested in any-thing or anyone that said Black' . . .''

Chromakey Card:
Congressional Black Caucus

On Tuesday, June 27, 1972, in Washington, D.C., the Congressional Black Caucus held an ad hoc hearing on governmental lawlessness.

Jack Anderson, syndicated columnist and winner of the 1972 Pulitzer prize for National Reporting, was a witness. During his testimony, Mr. Anderson brought out some very vital and enlightening facts about intelligence activ-ites aimed at American citizens, particularly Blacks.

Mr. Anderson's testimony was as follows:

V/O ANNOUNCER:
Vidifont crawl

Mr. Chairman, members of the Black Caucus, I consider it an honor to be asked to testify here today. I only hope that the testimony can, in some small way, help this nation's Black citizens gain the rights and privileges so long denied them. The subject I shall address myself to is government surveillance of private citizens.

Living in this country in this modern age is like living in a fishbowl. Our civil liberties and rights of privacy have slowly given way, over the years, to an increasingly in-trusive and authoritarian government, which has trampled upon our precious freedoms in the name of defending them.

We have known for years, of course, that the FBI freely spies on citizens. We have hoped that it was being done with prudence and with a view toward protecting the nation against violent overthrow or toward preventing criminal acts and apprehending those who break the law. We have suspected this was not the case. I have now documented our worst fears. I am willing, furthermore, to make some of these documents available to the commit-tee if the members so desire. Most of these people are in the FBI's files because they have exercised their Constitutional right of dissent, or have had the courage and wherewithal to offer financial support for causes they believe in. For this they are called "radicals" and "sub-

versives" and subjected to searching investigation. This
is bad enough in a political system that is supposed to
tolerate freedom of expression. When it comes to Blacks,
however, the situation is even more grievous.

TONY BROWN:

A grievous situation for Blacks indeed. According to
Anderson's testimony, anyone with dark skin who dares
to open his mouth, is considered by the FBI a Black
"subversive." Anderson goes on to say that he has seen
dozens of cases on Black leaders whose only crime is
voicing the woes and tribulations of their people, who
have done nothing more than organize their ranks, who
are guilty only of peacefully petitioning their government
in redress of grievances, as their Constitution says they
have an inalienable right to do. Mr. Anderson continues.

V/O ANNOUNCER:
Vidifont crawl

The most noticeable characteristic of the files is that the
slightest deviation from the status quo, or what the FBI
defines as the status quo, is enough to trigger an
investigation of a Black American. Back in the late
sixties, for example, anyone who yelled "Black Power"
was a flaming radical in the FBI's eyes. Indeed, any
philosophy or program that would mean independence for Blacks, is apparently grounds for suspicion.
The Black movement is painted a flaming red. All associations of any Blacks with persons left of Richard Nixon
are carefully noted and stored away.

TONY BROWN:

Anderson cited examples from the files to document his
charges. He was careful, however, to select innocuous
quotes that would not spread the overabundance of half-
truths and misinformation that is contained in the FBI
files. The FBI currently has files on many prominent
Americans that it considers subversive. Included in this
file are such Black leaders as the late Dr. Martin Luther
King, Mrs. Coretta Scott King, Rev. Ralph David Aber-
nathy, Floyd McKissick, Jr., Roy Wilkins, Bayard Rustin,
Roy Innis, the Rev. Jesse Jackson. The list of Black
"subversives" goes on and on. It includes Stokeley
Carmichael and Eldridge Cleaver. But the FBI surveillance does not stop with Black leaders. Also spied on
are such entertainers as Harry Belafonte and Eartha Kitt;
writers such as James Baldwin and Ossie Davis; athletes
such as Muhammad Ali and Joe Louis; Black organizations also command their share of file space in the FBI
building. Some of the groups under surveillance include
the Black Panthers, the Student National Coordinating
Committee, the Nation of Islam, the Republic of New
Africa, the Southern Christian Leadership Conference,
the Congress of Racial Equality, and the NAACP. At the
Secret Service, another governmental surveillance
agency, files are also kept on prominent Americans,
including a number of Black leaders. The Agency's
justification for keeping these records is that they have
"protective function." Everyone in their files, therefore,
is of "protective interest." The Secret Service has put
the names of all their surveillance subjects in a computer
bank. There are some 180,000 names in this data bank,
including aliases. At the push of a button, therefore, the

names of these alleged potential assassins comes rolling out. Some of them, about 300, are considered dangerous. All others, by far the majority, are thought to be "not dangerous." Many of the so-called assassination-prone are Blacks. The Secret Service keeps most of its Black suspects in a separate category called the Black Nationalist File. There are some 5,500 names in this computerized file. They are by file number, and all of them can be retrieved at the flick of a switch in a matter of minutes. Not only is it a crisis when Black people suffer from a class action that defines them as automatic enemies in their own land, but the question of personal freedom as a citizen is clearly at stake.

V/O ANNOUNCER:
Vidifont crawl

It may be justly asked, where does the government get the authority to conduct investigations of this sort?

(MUSIC)

V/O ANNOUNCER:

From Washington, D.C., BLACK JOURNAL presents "We, The Enemy." When BLACK JOURNAL originates in various cities, viewers in that area can participate by calling in. This edition, from Washington, D.C., features Jack Anderson, syndicated columnist, and Dick Gregory, political satirist. And now, our host and moderator, Tony Brown.

TONY BROWN:

I think it's very important to place a lot of those statistics, particularly those that you brought out, Mr. Anderson, in historical perspective. That information, or the FBI surveillance — and correct me if I'm incorrect — began in 1961 when John F. Kennedy, a Democrat, was President; it continued under Lyndon Johnson, and into the Nixon administration. And recently, in 1971 according to the FBI director, the new FBI director Clarence Kelley, he no longer is using "lawlessness to fight lawlessness." Is that accurate?

JACK ANDERSON:

Yes I think it's accurate. I would make this clarification. This was done by the late FBI chief, J. Edgar Hoover. There was no evidence at any time that it was ordered by John Kennedy or Lyndon Johnson. There's not even a great deal of evidence that they were aware of the scope of it. They certainly were aware that Black leaders were in the FBI files. But I don't think that they were at any time aware of the scope of it. The late J. Edgar Hoover had a fixation about Blacks, and this — these files I think reflect that fixation, reflect his own personal attitudes, much more so than official policy.

TONY BROWN:

Now, Dick, you were on the famous — or infamous — Watergate or the White House Enemies List. What is your personal reaction to having been placed on that list?

DICK GREGORY:

Well, when the press got in touch with me — I think it was Bob Johnson of Jet Magazine called me when the news broke, and told me I was on Nixon's Enemy List, did I have any comment. And I told him, "Yeah, call him up and tell him I accept before he changes his mind." (LAUGHTER)

* * *

TONY BROWN:

Hello. You're on BLACK JOURNAL, go ahead please.

VIEWER:

Yes, I'd like to know how both guests feel about affirmative action. There's a Supreme Court case on affirmative action right now, and does society owe the Blacks

TONY BROWN:

a debt that they have to take a positive action to rectify? Thank you. I think basically he's asking, do we need quotas for Blacks, and do we feel that the society owes Blacks anything, and do we feel that "affirmative action" programs are necessary?

JACK ANDERSON:

I'm opposed to that, myself. I think that Blacks should be individuals, and we should forget about the skin. And I just don't like to see quotas of any kind. But if Blacks are being discriminated against, and the only way that they can get a fair shake — if quotas are the only way, I'd rather have that than have them be discriminated against. But it seems to me that we ought to have matured a little, and I think we're continuing to mature more. I don't see why we should have to set up artificial quotas. I would tend to oppose that.

DICK GREGORY:

You know, my thinking on this is, when J.F.K. was President, a bill was pushed through the Senate and the Congress that said, any Black — not white — that would go to med school, and after he graduated would give five years of his life to various countries in Africa, the United States government would pay his way. Now, we're a race of people with over 30 million people, we have less than 5,000 doctors, Black, in America. Now, we have a problem with doctors because, although the police takes the rap, and rightfully so, for bigotry and shooting Blacks in the back, and minority folks, he's not the worst racist in this country. We got bigoted white ministers, bigoted white priests, bigoted white nuns, bigoted white doctors, that wouldn't tolerate a Black even coming in the office. Bigoted white lawyers. The cop is the only one that has the gun and the stick that do in my head. But there are some ministers — if their decision was that I believe in a heaven and hell, and that white bigoted minister decided, if I was going, I wouldn't go because I'm Black — that's far worse than a cop shooting me in the back with a warning shot. And so now I say this, to say everywhere we look in life we see quotas for this, quotas for that, and quotas for this, and again we go back — if this is the way to do it, I would suggest putting a quota on the quota. Let's say for ten years, we're going to deal with this, and if we see it's solving the problem, we will dissolve it.

* * *

TONY BROWN:

I hate to interrupt — Dick, I'd like to get you — but we're out of time. I'd like to thank both of you for a most interesting discussion, and come back to BLACK JOURNAL very soon.

DICK GREGORY:
JACK ANDERSON:

Pleasure.
And thank you again.

V/O ANNOUNCER:

(MUSIC)
From Washington, D.C., BLACK JOURNAL has presented "We, The Enemy," with guests Jack Anderson, syndicated columnist, and Dick Gregory, political satirist. Our host and moderator has been Tony Brown.
(MUSIC)

Courtesy of Tony Brown, Executive Producer, Black Journal

APPLICATION: NATIVE AMERICAN PROGRAMS

THE QUESTION OF LANGUAGE and terminology is a critical one in writing minority and ethnic programs. Loraine Misiaszek, Director of Advocates for Indian Education and a producer of radio and television programs by, about and for Native Americans, stresses this point as a part of the understanding and sensitivity the writer should have. She finds that non-Indian writers frequently use words such as "squaw" and "breed" and similar terms, perhaps not realizing how derogatory they are. She feels that writers are sometimes deliberate in their prejudicial attitudes. She cites, for example, news programs which almost always are "put-downs to Native Americans. Their very manner of presenting the news is editorializing. They influence listeners into drawing conclusions that whatever it was that the Indian did was 'bad,' although from the Indian point of view and from an outside objective point of view the action may have been 'good.' Anyone concerned with script writing for radio or television," Misiaszek says, "ought to be very aware of this problem. It is not necessarily intentional, but it happens because of the general conditioning in our society that causes people to think of Indians in terms of stereotypes." Misiaszek adds that it is not only the non-Indian who must learn understanding and sensitivity. "We take it for granted that because a person is an American Indian, that makes them automatically sensitive to American Indian concerns, feelings and needs. This is not necessarily so. Many Native Americans who don't grow up on reservations, for example, don't really understand Indian culture. They should not take for granted that what and the way they learned in the non-Indian school is the only way and the right way — if they are to write effectively and honestly about and for American Indians."

Even if the writer has learned an understanding and sensitivity, experience as a member of a particular ethnic group is necessary to be able to reflect the special cultural attitudes and practices. For instance, a writer who is really going to reach the Native American, Misiaszek says, "has to know and reflect the special healthy, lusty sense of humor that the American Indian has — a sense of humor that we had to develop in order to survive. It is through this kind of humor that the audience can establish special rapport with the program's performers."

Thomas Crawford, writer-producer of Native American-oriented programs, endorses Ms. Misiaszek's approach to writing. "In considering writing and producing scripts with/for/about Native Americans," Crawford states, "one must first of all become familiar with the idioms, patterns of expression, turns of thought, and pronunciations of the particular Indian community with which one is dealing. This kind of background will enable a scriptwriter to deal with the subject in a way that will interest and be appropriate to the people. The writer must also be willing to shift the topic to one that has more immediate interest and appeal." Crawford also stresses the need for personal experience and empathy on the part of the writer. "The complexities of writing a program for or about Native Americans on a national level would be nearly prohibitive for the non-Indian. An Indian writer/producer can present his own idioms and viewpoints as a valid part of the Native American scene in the United States. Such an effort would probably relate to some degree to nearly every Native American community throughout the U.S., unless it were very extreme in tone or content."

Two of Crawford's scripts illustrate these concepts. The first, "Baptiste Mathias, Chief of the Kootenais," is strongly ethnic in nature, and although the theme and the event relate the Native American to the requirements of the non-Indian world, it is deeply rooted in content in the Indian cultural world. The second, "Who Has The Right?," is public affairs-oriented, dealing directly in documentary, interview and skit form with critical issues facing the Indian community vis-a-vis the non-Indian authorities. Controversy is tackled head-on. The first and last parts of the script are included here.

SCRIPT FOR "BAPTISTE MATHIAS, CHIEF OF THE KOOTENAIS,"

A program presented on KOFI-AM, Kalispell, Montana, December 24, 1972, 6:10 p.m.

(Intro: Start drumming strong, then fade down.)

NARRATOR: Ksahnka Nasookin. A program produced by the Kootenai community on Baptiste Mathias, Chief of the Kootenais.

(Pause. Drumming up, then back down.)

The Kootenai people of Flathead Lake have had many leaders. On Saturday, November 4, 1972, they gathered at the Dayton Cemetery to honor some of the most famous ones with a monument. (End of drumming) Joseph Mathias, grandson of the last Kootenai chief, Baptiste Mathias, welcomed everyone to the brief ceremony.

J. MATHIAS: The Bishop and Fr. Meyers would like to thank all of you that have been able to weather the storm and had guts enough to come over for this dedication. I think we'll start the program by unveiling the monument.

NARRATOR: The monument was unveiled. (Audible reactions from people assembled.)

NARRATOR: Basil Lefthand, representing the native religion of the Kootenai people, and Bishop Raymond Hunthausen, representing the Catholic religion many Kootenais have adopted, offered prayers for the chiefs and for their people.

HUNTHAUSEN: O God our Great Spirit, we thank you for looking after your Kootenai people through their four great chiefs, and through all their other chiefs, too. We thank you for making the Kootenai people a strong people, a good people, a people filled with your love. And so, Father, we ask that you send your good spirits upon this monument. May it become a holy rock for us, may it remind us every day for all of our lives that your Spirit is with us, and takes care of us. And may this monument remind us to pray for ourselves and our people.

NARRATOR: Basil Lefthand then blessed the monument with juniper smoke. (White noise)

This was a special sign of the people's prayer that good spirits be with them. (Pause in narration; white noise continues for approximately 5 seconds.)

(Cue hymn.)

NARRATOR: The people themselves offered a few prayers and a hymn in the Kootenai language. They then adjourned to Koostatah Hall in Elmo to celebrate their leaders, past and present. (Fade out hymn, fade in drumming. Then drumming fades into background.) Baptiste Mathias was born in 1878, the son of Aht-wahn Mutt-yahs and Klu-Neek. He was appointed sub-chief to Koostatah for the purpose of continuing the traditional ceremonies. Joe Antiste remembers the election of Baptiste Mathias as chief. It took place at the Kootenais' annual New Year's celebration, called the Jump Dance. (Cut drumming)

J. ANTISTE: He put up chief, and he put two guys in there. Baptiste Mathias and Patrick. He asked them Indians, "Which one you want to be chief?" Well, everybody, all the Indians say, "Baptiste Mathias will be chief."

NARRATOR: Tony Mathias, son of Baptiste, recalls how his father was honored by the Catholic Church.

T. MATHIAS: When he come to be a chief, they took him down to Polson. And the priest put holy water on him, on his head. They told him that he come to be a chief and to be a preacher, and to say the prayers with the Indians.

NARRATOR: Chief Mathias acted as a representative of his people in the council of chiefs from all the tribes of the Flathead Reservation. Although he was a prayer leader at Christian services such as funerals and wakes, he also led the greatest celebration of Kootenai religion, the Sun Dance.

T. MATHIAS: After he died, there was no one they chose to be chief again. So that was all, I know now.

NARRATOR: Kootenai people have always been noted for their generosity. They care for their own people and show great hospitality toward any relatives or visitors who stay with them for a time. One woman recalls how Mathias put this into practice.

BELLE TENAS: Baptiste Mathias was a real nice, gentle guy. Everytime I take him to the store when he'd get his welfare checks, he'd take one of his grandchildren along so he could buy him some things for them. It seems like everytime he had something that was good, he'd give it to somebody who didn't have any.

(Cue in Kootenai hymn.) (Fade hymn into background.)

NARRATOR: On a February morning in 1966, the Kootenai people gathered to bury Baptiste Mathias. They sang the traditional hymn, in Kootenai, as they lowered his body into the grave. It says:

> I am still here,
> And will be happy one day.

Three quarters of a century after small pox and diphtheria killed most of the Kootenai camp at Dayton Creek, the people continue to find new directions. Within the last two years they have brought about dramatic changes at the Elmo grade school. The school has twice as many teachers today as it did in 1970. Kootenai parents have formed a committee to approve the spending of Indian funds in the school, and to propose new methods of teaching their children Kootenai culture and history while they learn the ways of the white people.

(Fade out hymn. Fade in drumming to background.)

The Kootenais have also formed Elmo Road Corporation, the first native business of that area. Elmo Road gives jobs in road maintenance and foundation work to the men of the Kootenai community. It also pays dividends to its members, the Kootenai people. Its stock-holders, board of directors and employees are all members of the Kootenai community. It is out of such efforts — renewing a school and creating a business — that the Kootenai people are developing and exercising new leadership — with new vision.

(Pause in narration. Drumming into foreground, then into background.)

NARRATOR: The preceding program was narrated by Tom Crawford, engineered by Frank Tyro, and is the property of Kootenai Communications, and may not be reproduced in any form, in whole or in part, without the written consent of Kootenai communications.   (End of drumming.)

Written and produced by Thomas Crawford for Kootenai Communications
Copyright 1975 Antoine Mathias and Thomas Crawford

SCRIPT FOR "WHO HAS THE RIGHT?"

by Tom Crawford, Advocates for Indian Education and KPBX-FM, Spokane
and Tony Grant, Kootenai Communications, Elmo, Montana,
broadcast on KOFI-AM, Kalispell, and KUFM-FM, Missoula — January-February, 1973.

Begin with Intro music (stick-game song played and sung with guitar). Fade into Narrator: Who has the right? The first in a series of programs on The Kootenais: Their Political Power in Northwestern Montana.

The Kootenai people have occupied northwestern Montana since "time immemorial". Before white men came the Kootenais hunted bison, deer and elk, and thrived on the local berries and herbs which at that time were abundant. Aside from occasional conflicts with the Blackfeet, they lived peacefully and controlled their own lives.
Today it is a different story. The United States Government has included them in the Confederated Salish and Kootenai Tribes of the Flathead Reservation; the Kootenais number roughly 1/10 of this confederation. Of the ten members of the tribal council, the Kootenais have one representative. They also find themselves heavily outnumbered by the non-Indian people of Lake County, where most of the Kootenais live. Even in Elmo, a town on the northern end of the Flathead Reservation which is 90 per cent Kootenai, the two stores, the grade school and the water commission are all run by non-Kootenais. This situation existed for many years, and has created a certain amount of frustration among Kootenai people. Lyllis Waylett, tribal development specialist of Pend d'Oreille descent, put it this way:

> I would say that the Kootenai area people have been isolated or remote from the focal point of our tribal government and I think that they've been disadvantaged because of it. I don't think that they've seen good things — if indeed there have ever been any good things flow from the government to the Indian people, the Kootenais and their primary area of residence on our place. I feel that this has strained relationships.

NARRATOR: Residents of the Elmo area express their difficulties with the present situation:

> "It seems like so many other people around here try to run the place. They don't give us minority a chance to really speak our piece." (G. Crew)

> "Do you think the Kootenais have a strong voice in council affairs? No, because of the fact that we, the Kootenais, have only one Kootenai in the council." (B. Kenmille)

> "Well, we went across to that island, we circled the island. We found ten deer — ten deer dead. Whoever killed them or whatever killed them took the head. It was sawed off, we could tell it was sawed off. . . . I think it must be the white guys did it because they wanted the head and the horn. If an Indian did it, they would have took the whole deer.

An Indian would have took the whole deer. They use every part of the deer." (F. Burke)

"When the people come out from Washington, D.C. and ask how the Indians been treated they take them to these new houses where these people are well off. They don't take them around to these lower grades of Indians, or show the all tore-up house. . . . They really should take them around right here in Elmo here. Because I know there's a lot of people that really need help." (L. Stasso)

Recently, the right of the tribal government to control the use of lands and waters within the Reservation boundaries has become a very hot issue in the Flathead Valley. Businessmen and white residents particularly resent the Confederated Tribes' attempt to assert its jurisdiction over Flathead Lake by requiring recreation use permits of those who use it.

"Years ago they talked about the lake was supposed to be a navigable waterway. Well, under that condition, why that was supposed to be open for you and me and everybody else. Anywhere away from here, I say, yes. A permit fee is alright. I'll buy one myself. I go to Lonepine or Rainbow Lake, anywhere else." (C. Paro)

"I don't think anybody owns it. Nobody made it. Nobody made this lake — that lake. No, I don't care about that. Really. I think it belongs to everybody. It's a natural body of water and it was here before anybody was here. I think it's everybody's lake, from here from there from everywhere." (M. Davis)

The Kootenai people, whose home is the lake area, sometimes find it difficult to deal with non-Indian businessmen without being caught in the middle of this battle. White people frequently mention the special privileges Indians are thought to have.

"If anything, I think they've got more things going for them if they'd just take advantage of what they have. I think a lot of non-Indian people feel injured when a tribal member who has a very small minority of Indian blood in him does not have to pay taxes, and where he does." (J. McCulloch)

"They have an advantage in that they do have less expense to the tribal members as far as the upkeep of the school and this sort of thing, through taxes. Most of the local business merchants are highly prejudiced toward them because they think that they're living off the government, which is actually not the truth." (G. Crew)

"Not that, as much as they're getting. No, not, they shouldn't get that much. Look at all the benefits you have that we don't get. I'd make a lot better use of it than some of you do. I know that." (M. Davis)

Within a social structure, one can often tell which group feels in control and which group feels that it has no power by asking the simple question, "What are the needs of this area?" Those who feel in control will probably see few if any needs. Kootenai Communications found that while non-Kootenais by and large saw no great needs in the Flathead Valley area, Kootenai people saw some very immediate ones.

* * *

To understand the wisdom of the Kootenais, one must first understand their history. This history goes back many centuries. It begins with the Kootenai as a plains people, occupying much of the land now held by the Blackfeet, the Assiniboine, and other present-day tribes of the northern plains.

Maulouf, 395 ("Going back . . .") to 487 ("other side of the divide")

The Kootenai organized themselves into regional bands, each with its chief and sub-chiefs, each with its own government, yet all sharing the Kootenai blood, language, and way of life.

Malouf, 20 ("Of course, the Kootenai had . . .") to 70 ("one of their most ancient important centers")

When the Kootenais were invited to join the Salish and Pend d'Oreille at Council Groves to make a treaty with the whites, they saw no reason to come. They had seen few of the whites and were certainly not threatened by them. Only one of their leaders appeared at the council — a man named Michelle. Since the interpreters spoke mostly Salish, Michelle and the Kootenais who were with him understood little of what the treaty meant. Soon after he had signed it — the Hellgate Treaty of 1855 — its meaning became clearer. The Kootenais were either to move within the boundaries of the new Flathead Reservation created by the treaty, or stay in Canada where the United States Government would not have to worry about them.

Many Kootenais from the Libby and Jennings areas moved to Canada. The Bonners Ferry band refused to do either and stayed where they were. Many who depended on the lake area for fishing and hunting were forced to move south to Dayton and Elmo.

But the Kootenais could see no sense in the arbitrary boundaries established by the whites. They continued to migrate up and down Flathead Lake seeking game and fish. The frequent visits between the Kootenais on both sides of the Canadian-American boundary could not be stopped. As Chief David of Tobacco Plains later put it: "What is the meaning of this boundary line? It runs through the middle of my house. Why should you without asking me or considering me, divide my property and also divide my children?"

Throughout the century following Council Groves, this question would plague the Kootenais: What right, after all, did the whites have to make decisions for them, to control their lives? Next week we will historically trace some of the economic and social problems which resulted from the decision to place the Kootenais on the Flathead Reservation.

(Fade-in with theme music)

NARRATOR: This program was produced by Kootenai Communications with the help of a grant from the Montana Committee for the Humanities. The views expressed here do not necessarily reflect those of the Committee.

Written by Anthony Grant and Thomas Crawford

APPLICATION: ORIENTAL-AMERICAN PROGRAMS

THE SPECIAL BACKGROUND and history as well as the immediate needs of a particular minority or ethnic group help determine the writing approach to a radio or television script. Russ Lowe of the Chinese for Affirmative Action Media Committee in San Francisco is a producer-member of the Dupont Guy Collective, which does a weekly radio program, "Dupont Guy" (Dupont Street, which was destroyed in the earthquake and later renamed Grant Avenue). Lowe describes the program as a combination of news, commentary and satire. The writers are scholars of Chinese-American history and people in the arts as well as reporters and media experts. The materials reflect the perspectives and viewpoints of the Chinese-American that are not otherwise usually heard on the air. As an example, Lowe cites an historical skit which tells of the tax collectors during the Gold Rush days going through the mining camps for the $2.50 monthly tax on miners — but trying to collect it only from the Chinese miners. Lowe also notes that the script writers choose words especially carefully, with the volcabulary frequently referring to different parts of the community or to certain events or actions that may have explicit meaning only to the Chinese-American listener.

As do many minority scripts, in order to take advantage of the relatively sparse airtime available to minorities, "Dupont Guy" takes a strong point of view. This is clearly implied in the standard opening:

STANDARD OPENING FOR THE DUPONT GUY RADIO SHOW

NARRATOR: Welcome friends and tourists to DUPONT GUY, a listening trip through Chinese America. Brought to you by the DUPONT GUY COLLECTIVE of Chinatown Saaan Fraaanciscoooo.

The name DUPONT GUY comes from the original name of Grant Avenue, DuPont Street. After the 1906 Earthquake, City redevelopers decided to take over Chinatown and changed DuPont Guy to Grant Avenue. Of course, when the Chinese returned to claim their homes, they continued to call their main drag DuPont Guy.

In this spirit of truth and defiance, we commence our program of community news and commentary, of music, poetry and satire.

The following rundown sheet for a Dupont Guy program indicates the variety of formats used and, even in the terms describing the program segments, the "spoof" approach to making a political-social point. In examining sections of the program script itself, note the satire and "in" language, beginning with the "Chonk Amer-ca" non-standard opening, which counterpoints the historical information and current events commentary.

DUPONT GUY #14   rec 17 Dec 74   pilot: HEADHUNTER
                        air 12 Jan 75   copilot: JOHN

1) NON STANDARD OPENING   TAPE + LIVE MIC   Out: "Art Gilham,
                           CUT 1   1913"   2:45

2) SPORTSMAN MARCH CART
   CURTIS: And now the NOOS!   F.O. CART
   MABEL: (Asian American Studies)   Out: 1:30

3) COLLEGE BOWEL SKIT   LIVE MICS
   Russ, Breen, Connie   Out: ". . . they never
                                                    taught me dat at
                                                    Podunk U."   2:00

4) BOOK REVIEW   LIVE MIC
   Kathy   Out: ". . . screaming
                                                    vengeance to
                                                    uncover their his-
                                                    tory in America"   2:00

5) DICTIONARY DAY LESSON 3   LIVE MICS
   Curtis, Kathy   Out: ". . . check your
                                                    dictionary"   1:30

6) THREE KINGS   LIVE MICS
   Breen, KING 1, KING 2   FADEOut: ". . . bearing gifts
   Connie   on 2nd   we traveled afar"   :30
                                                    singing
7) KUNG FU FIGHTING REVISITED   LIVE MICS + TAPE
   (cut 2 - track 2)
   Curtis

Chris   TAPECUE: "it's an olden golden &
                                            kinda scratchy"

                                                   TAPEOut: grunt at slow
                                                      speed FADEOUT 3:30

8) STANDARD CLOSE   CART

NON STANDARD OPENING

"Chinatown, My Chinatown" in BG

CURTIS: Welcome friends and touresses, to DUPONT GUY, a listening trip through
               Chonk Amer-ca.

               That was "Chinatown, My Chinatown" by The Whispering Pianist, Art Gilham,
               1913.

NEWS

From the University of California in Berkeley, the question is: Will Asian American
Studies wither and die or will it be absorbed into the traditional white-dominated humanities
program?

Survival seems tenuous for Asian American Studies, which began in 1969 after the
Third World Strike. After a lot of protest by minority students that they were being white-
washed with middle class values and that they were not learning about themselves and
their roots, a Third World College was promised. There were to be four divisions: one for
Black studies, one for Chicano studies, one for Native American studies, and one for Asian
American studies.

Today, five years later, Third World College remains a dream, and a broken one at
that. There is no Third World College in sight; but there is a lot of disunity around. Black
Studies wants to join the College of Letters and Science, the traditional humanities college
of U.C. Asian American Studies does not want to. It wants to retain its autonomy. But
budgetary considerations make things difficult.

Each year since 1969, the budget arrives only months before classes start — hardly
enough time for hiring and curriculum planning, and surely not enough time for any long
range planning.

Says Asian American Studies coordinator Germaine Wong, "White liberals don't think
there is a need for ethnic studies. They hope it won't be necessary in the future because
we'll all be one big happy family.

COLLEGE BOWEL

RUSS: And now we bring you the KOW BEE SEE Network brain show, College Bowel.
               On today's team we have Mr. Cally Flower of Podunk U. facing Yu Fong of
               Choy-Lai's School of Chinese-American history.
               Before we begin, let me offer my regrets to you Yu Fong on the impending
               threat of your school's obliteration. I know there has been activity prevailing
               in some of our great Universities to eliminate Asian-American studies. But let
               us see if you can show us what you've learned in today's match of COLLEGE
               BOWEL.

               Are you ready Calley Flower?

BREEN: Uh, yeah, sure.

RUSS: Yu Fong, are you ready?

CONNIE: SHR!

RUSS: All right, tell me the answer to this question. . . . When did the first Chinese arrive in the United States?

BREEN: Oh that's easy! Everyone knows they came after the California gold rush in 1849.

RUSS: That is absolutely . . . WRONG! Yu Fong, do you have an answer?

CONNIE: In 1785, three Chinese, Ah Sing, Ah Chyun, and Ah Ccun were in Baltimore. Their presence was noted by the Continental Congress.
In 1796, five Chinese were brought to Philadelphia to be servants for Andreas Evardus Van Braan Houckgeest.
In 1807, Pung-hua Wing Chong arrived in New York to collect his father's debts.
In 1815, Ah Nam, the cook to Governor de Sola of California was confirmed a Christian at Monterey.
In 1818, Wong Arce attended the Foreign Mission School at Cornwall, Connecticut, with Ah Lan and Ah Lum and Lieau Ah See.
In 1847, the Chinese junk "Ke Ying" sailed into New York harbor with an all Chinese crew.
In 1847, Yung Wing, Wing Foon and Wong Sing enrolled at Monson Academy at Monson, Massachusetts. Yung Wing went on to Yale and became the first Chinese to graduate from a U.S. university, in 1854. In 1852, Yung Wing became a citizen.

BREEN: Gee whiz, they never taught me that at Podunk U.

BOOK REVIEW

There's a book that came out last year which the DuPont Guy Collective would recommend to all of our listeners. It is full of the stories of who we are, where we came from and why we're here. It's called LONGTIME CALIFORN', a collection of interviews by Victor and Bret Nee. The interviews feature Longtime Californ' Chinese in America. They talk of their experiences and their joys and pains of being here. Their stories reveal that period of our history that school books have ignored or distorted.

LONGTIME CALIFORN' talks about laws that forbade prostitutes, criminals, the crippled and the Chinese from coming to America; the laws that kept Chinese women in China away from their Chinese husbands in America; and the violence that kept Chinese confined within the designated borders of Chinatown. The first half of the book deals with the Bachelor Society that resulted when Chinese men were shipped under contracts to America as sources of cheap labor for growing West Coast industries. When the industries prospered and Chinese workers became competitive with white labor, the Chinese were cursed, beaten, and subjected to forced celibacy.

These men who left families behind in China were then accused by the ilks of Dennis Kearney of being "different" — the Chinese didn't act like Americans, that is, Euro-Americans.

LONGTIME CALIFORN' talks about the laws that kept Chinese from social interaction with whites, that the few Chinese children in San Francisco were forbidden to attend public schools, that jobs were restricted with only menial jobs left for Chinese, and that the Chinese were beaten up if they crossed the Broadway Street boundary of Chinatown. It wasn't so much that the Chinese didn't want to assimilate; they were prevented from ever assimilating. To survive in anti-Chinese America, the Chinese formed their own communities with their own social laws, their own schools and found justice in their own courts.

LONGTIME CALIFORN' is a collection of the emotions, the frustrations, the physical, psychological, anguish of a people excluded and manipulated. But it is also the beginning crescendo of Chinamen screaming vengeance to uncover their history in America.

DICTIONARY DAY

Welcome to DICTIONARY DAY, Lesson 3.

Today, T.G. for D.G. presents "Abbreviations in the Chonk Language".
(POTLID)
A B C — American-born Chinese. Obviously a misnomer. If you're American-born, you must
    be an American, not a Chinese.
(GONG)
C M — Chairman Mao.
(POTLID)
C P — Central Pacific.
(GONG)
C-TOWN — Chinatown
(POTLID)
D G — DuPont Guy
(GONG)
F D S — Flower Drum Song
(POTLID)
J-TOWN — Japantown
(GONG)
W R L — white racist love
This concludes the TOUR GUIDE FOR DUPONT GUY, a primer for the vocabulary of
Chonk Amerika.

Dupont Guy Collective, Chinatown, San Francisco

APPLICATION: HISPANIC PROGRAMS

DR. PALMA MARTINEZ-KNOLL, director of Project: Latino in Detroit, writes and produces an hour-long program for Spanish-speaking Americans. She advises writers of programs for and about Hispanics to keep in mind that they are dealing with people and not a "freakish" segment of society. "Too many writers," she says, "because of lack of understanding, are either prejudicial or condescending. In writing about Hispanics, or creating Hispanic characters, make them a part of everyday society and not an excluded group. Any special aspects you write about should be the positive elements, about the contributions Hispanics make to society and not as some dead weight to be pitied or scorned." She advises writers that even when depicting the unique problems Hispanics face, the Hispanic should be shown as a responsible person who is an integral part of society. "Keep in mind that you are dealing with Americans whose ethnic backgrounds represent 21 different countries and who are an amalgamation of many races. Hispanics are not a racial or cultural community as much as a linguistic community."

Dr. Martinez-Knoll's program, "Mundo Hispano," consists of a variety of formats, including cultural presentations, interviews, different kinds of music, information for women, news, features, documentaries, commercials and PSAs — similar to the formats of other minority and ethnic programs. "Mundo Hispano" also includes a weekly editorial. "Like the rest of the program," Martinez-Knoll says, "the editorial shows that the American Hispanic community is an offshoot of the Spanish-speaking community all over the world. It is not a Chicano here, a Puerto Rican there, but an entire linguistic community who face a common problem. It is the entire community that must communicate with the majority society."

The following example of the program's editorial illustrates this approach.

Nearly one of every 20 Americans has a Spanish-speaking heritage. In other words, there are approximately 10 million Americans with a Spanish-speaking heritage in the mainland United States representing 5 per cent of the population. They are the country's second largest minority group.

Yet, the Spanish-speaking have had a long-standing problem in the area of equal employment opportunity, which only recently has become the focus of national attention and action. In addition, the Spanish-speaking population has had to face problems of social and economic deprivation as well as their own particular problem of a language barrier.

Working to help the Spanish-speaking peoples is not as easy as it may appear. The reason for the difficulty is that those with Spanish heritage are a heterogeneous group despite their shared Spanish-language background. In fact, they represent a microcosm of American ethnic diversity.

Interestingly, not all those with Spanish heritage speak Spanish, although most of them do, and all have ancestors who did. Some of these people are recent immigrants or are first generation citizens while others come from families that were living in the Southwest or Puerto Rico. But by far the largest group — well over 5 million — are of Mexican origin or descent. The next largest group would be those from Puerto Rico followed by a large group from Cuba. Others can trace their families to Central or South America. Thus, it is evident that the Spanish-speaking community is made up of groups from different areas with different backgrounds and cultures.

These groups are located in different parts of the country. For example, most Mexican-Americans live in the Southwest; the Puerto Ricans live largely in New York City and the majority of Cubans live in Florida. Of course, there are smaller concentrations of these various groups in large metropolitan centers such as Detroit.

Within these metropolitan centers, many of the Spanish-speaking have moved into distinct, close-knit neighborhoods, either by choice or because they cannot afford or are barred from housing elsewhere. Unfortunately, these neighborhoods are sometimes in city slums or in poverty stricken "barrios" on the fringes of metropolitan centers.

Partly because of these concentrations of Spanish-speaking peoples into separate urban areas, they continue to have English language problems. At times, the language barrier may not even be overcome during the second generation. There is also the frequent movement of people back and forth between Puerto Rico and the mainland which tends to reinforce the language barrier.

All of these factors have had the effect of culturally isolating the Spanish-speaking from the mainstream of the population. Of course it hasn't helped that ethnic prejudice and discrimination exist in some communities, creating additional barriers to the assimilation of the Spanish-speaking into the community.

In addition, for Spanish-speaking adults there is often a lack of education along with the lack of knowledge about the English language. Both work toward preventing the individual from obtaining a well-paying job. However, the relative number of Spanish-speaking youth with a high school education or better has been rising.

Undoubtedly the best single measure of the disadvantaged economic and social situation of those with a Spanish background is their family income. For example, in 1971 the median income for all families of Spanish origin was $7,500 which is not quite three-fourths of the median income for all American families. However, their income level is still above that for Black families which is $6,400 annually.

The major reason for the low average income of Spanish-speaking families is the fact that so many of their workers are in low-paying jobs. For instance, the number of those working in laboring, farm and services jobs — the lowest level occupations — is twice the number as for the white workers.

Yet there is a significant and rising number of Spanish-speaking individuals holding professional, technical and managerial positions of many types. A larger number are in other white-collar and skilled occupations.

Another factor tending to reduce family income among the Spanish-speaking families is their above average rate of unemployment. In March 1972, the unemployment rate for workers of Spanish origin or descent was over 8 per cent. At the same time the national overall rate was near 6 per cent.

The problems of the Spanish-speaking in this country are not going unnoticed. Manpower and related programs have been developed to deal with the problems of joblessness and low-level employment. The goal of these programs is to help Spanish-speaking workers qualify for and enter more skilled occupations, offering both higher wages and promise of steady work.

These programs will not lead to any overnight successes, but they are part of a mounting effort to help the Spanish-speaking and all other minority groups.

Courtesy of Palma Martinez-Knoll, "Mundo Hispano" Latino Hour

It should be noted that the approaches and examples presented here do not represent all the points of view concerning writing for minority and ethnic programs. Even within individual minority and ethnic groups there are differences of opinion about purpose, content orientation and technique. Neither the materials used here nor the persons quoted are necessarily illustrative of or spokespersons for an entire minority or ethnic group.

In discussing minority and ethnic programs in this chapter, we have concentrated on the current socio-political applications of those terms. There are many more diverse minorities, however, who need to be served by television and radio. Special interests of comparatively small audiences may range from planning herb gardens to making leaded glass to learning Sanskrit to protecting water environments to listening to Kabuki performance background music. The interests may be those of growing minorities who have been largely neglected, such as the aged. The mentally retarded are a minority whose needs can be served by the public airwaves. Programming can serve the physically handicapped, such as the blind. Many other segments of our population can be considered minorities in terms of radio and television programming. We have not set up a separate section for such groups in this book, but have included examples of writing these kinds of minority programs in appropriate chapters. Note the scripts prepared for and by the Foundation for the Blind. In addition, Chapter 11, Education and Information Programs, indicates some of the considerations that apply to writing the kinds of programs that serve other special groups. For example, note the preparation of the medical education material. The writer's attitude, understanding and knowledge in writing for these minorities should be similar to those in writing for the minorities predominantly discussed in this chapter; the writer has to empathize to the greatest degree and to both know and feel the needs of the group being written for.

NOTES TO CHAPTER 10

[1] *The Washington Post,* October 5, 1974, p. B8.

[2] Dreyfuss, Joel, "Blacks and Television," *The Washington Post,* September 1, 1974, p. K5.

[3] *Ibid.*

[4] *Ibid.*

[5] Dreyfuss, Joel, "Jeffersons: All in the (Black) Family," *The Washington Post,* January 18, 1975, pp. B1, B5.

[6] Dreyfuss, Joel, "Blacks and Television," *The Washington Post,* September 2, 1974, pp. D1, D3.

[7] *Ibid.,* p. D3.

[8] *Ibid.*

[9] Dreyfuss, Joel, "Blacks and Television," *The Washington Post,* September 1, 1974, p. K1.

[10] Dreyfuss, Joel, "Blacks and Television," *The Washington Post,* September 3, 1974, p. B2.

[11] *Ibid.*

[12] Dreyfus, Joel, "Blacks and Television," *The Washington Post,* September 1, 1974, p. K1.

REFERENCE BOOKS

ON MINORITY AND ETHNIC PROGRAMS

Aronson, James. *Deadline for the Media.* Indianapolis: Bobbs, Merrill, 1972. Includes a section on Blacks and broadcasting.

Bogle, Donald. *Toms, Coons, Mulattoes, Mammies and Bucks.* New York: Viking Press, 1973. An interpretive history of Blacks in American films.

Bower, R. *Television and the Public.* New York: Holt, Rinehart and Winston, 1974.

Broadcasting and Social Action: A Handbook for Station Executives. Washington, D.C.: National Association of Educational Broadcasters, 1969. A compilation of views and approaches on minority employment and programming.

Casty, Alan, ed. *Mass Media and Mass Man.* New York: Holt, Rinehart and Winston, 2nd ed., 1973.

Greenberg, Bradley S. and Brenda Dervin. *Uses of Mass Media by the Urban Poor.* New York: Praeger Publishers, 1970. Findings of three research projects.

Lewels, Francisco J., Jr. *The Uses of the Media by the Chicano Movement.* New York: Praeger Publishers, 1974. A study in minority access.

Greenberg, Bradley S. "Racial Attitudes and the Impact of TV Blacks." Report #10, 1969, of Project CUP, Michigan State University Department of Communication.

——— and Joseph R. Dominick, "Three Seasons of Blacks in Television." Report #11, 1970, of Project CUP, Michigan State University Department of Communication.

Marshall, Wes, et. al. *Fiesta: Minority Television Programming.* Tucson: University of Arizona Press, 1974.

Shamberg, Michael. *Guerilla Television.* New York: Holt, Rinehart and Winston, 1971. Some non-establishment approaches to bringing minority views to TV.

Skornia, Harry J. and Jack W. Kitson. *Problems and Controversies in Television and Radio.* Palo Alto: Pacific Books, 1968.

Stavins, Ralph L., ed. *Television Today: The End of Communication and the Death of Community.* Washington, D.C.: Communication Service Corp., 1971. Includes a section on "Black Needs."

Television/Radio Age, December 9, 1974, includes a special section on Black radio.

Williams, Frederick and Geraldine Van Wart. *Carrascolendas*. New York: Praeger Publishers, 1974. Bi-lingual education through television.

Young, Richard A. *Recruiting and Hiring Minority Employees*. New York: American Management Association, 1969. Some principles applicable to radio and television.

FOR APPLICATION AND REVIEW

1. If you are not a member of a minority or a non-majority ethnic group, select one such group and prepare a 15-minute radio or television news broadcast (for your local radio or television station or, in a classroom, from the stories in your daily newspaper), orienting the broadcast toward that particular group. Arrange for a colleague (a member of your class, for example) who does belong to that minority or ethnic group to do the same exercise. Compare scripts and discuss the differences. Participate in the exercise below, as well.

2. If you are a member of a minority or distinct ethnic group, participate in the exercise above. In addition, prepare a radio or television newscast for a majority-audience station. Arrange for a non-minority colleague to do the same; compare scripts.

3. Using the approaches above, write a script relating to the culture of a minority or ethnic group.

11

Education and Information Programs

EDUCATION AND INFORMATION programs are usually differentiated from other types of radio and television shows by being put into the category of "non-entertainment." Unfortunately, the designation too often is true: educational/information programs frequently are dull, boring, pedantic and not at all entertaining. Too many are little more than "talking heads" — that is, the head or voice of a lecturer simply reciting things that one could read in a book or hear in a classroom lecture. Writing a good, effective educational or informational program requires as much creativity, skill and knowledge of the medium as does writing a good, effective news show, commercial, documentary or play. Indeed, an educational or informational radio or TV program may use these and other writing formats.

Not all education and information programs are dull. In fact, a good many are considerably more stimulating and enjoyable than many "entertainment" programs. Their purpose and setting, unfortunately usually linked to traditional concepts of education and teaching and therefore stereotyped and prosaic, are largely responsible for frequent dreary quality. As the field of education and information program writing grows, however, more and more writers with a background in TV and radio and with creative motivation are going into it — and the product gets better and better.

Education and information programs cover many areas: formal instruction to the classroom, informal education to adults at home, technical updating to professionals, vocational preparation, industry training, and many others. Some of the programs are purely or principally instructional in nature. Others are primarily informational. Still others, with elements of education and information, are public relations oriented. The percentage of station time devoted to education/information programming is relatively low — with the exception of formal instructional program, which in the mid-1970s accounted for about one-third of the air time on public television stations.

A principal form of the educational-instructional program is the formal lesson designed for classroom use. Another important form is the training program, principally for government and industry use. Also prominent are programs updating professionals in their fields, particularly in the health sciences. Public information programs which at the same time promote an organization, product or idea — in essence, public relations — are a staple with both government and industry. We will cover four major types here, which should serve as examples of virtually all forms of educational/informational radio-TV writing: the formal education script for the classroom; the training script, for both government and industry; the professional updating medical script; and the public information script.

FORMAL EDUCATION

THE WRITER OF THE formal education program is, above all, a planner. The writing of the program begins with the cooperative planning of the curriculum coordinator, the studio teacher, the classroom teacher, the educational administrator, the producer, the TV (or radio — though formal instruction on radio has, except for a comparatively few and mostly excellent stations, been largely neglected) specialist and the writer. The writer must accept from the educational experts the purposes and contents of each program. The writer should stand firm about the method of presentation; educators, by and large, are too prone to use television as an extension of the classroom, incorporating into the television program the outmoded techniques of teaching in most classrooms (think about your own elementary, secondary and college classes!). Try, with the producers, to prevent the programs from being used as reinforcement of poor teaching and learning practices. The most important thing to remember is to avoid the talking head. Indeed, inasmuch as effective use of television and radio in the classroom is dependent on the concurrent cooperation of a good classroom teacher who knows how to use the media, the video or audio material coming into the classroom should be that which implements the purposes of John Dewey — bringing the classroom into the world and the world into the classroom. To do this it is not even necessary to present a teacher in the television program. Unfortunately, the insecurity of many teachers and administrators makes that prospect frightening and you'll have to fight hard and long to keep out some superfluous, but traditional elements of the formal educational process.

After determination of learning goals and contents, the length of individual programs and of the series is determined and the programs are outlined. The outline should carefully follow the lesson-plan for each learning unit as developed by the educational experts. The important topics are stressed, the unimportant ones played down. The educational program does not have to be fully scripted, however. It may be a rundown or routine sheet, depending on the content and whether you use a studio teacher — and to what degree that studio teacher is a professional performer. Many ITV practitioners over the years have seriously proposed that Jane Fonda- and Robert Redford-type professional performers be hired as the on-camera teachers for instructional programs. Look at what Bill Cosby has done for "The Electric Company"!

Even in the outline stage you should explore the special qualities of television that can present the content more effectively than in the classroom, even when there is a competent classroom teacher. Infuse creativity and entertainment into the learning materials. Though most ITV programs are designed to convey information, reflecting the non-creative purpose and practice in most classrooms, ITV writers and producers are becoming more aware of the need to stimulate the viewer-learner and to orient the material toward the practical past, current and future life experiences of the student.

The TV lesson can use humor, drama and suspense and borrow liberally from the most effective aspects of entertainment programs. "Sesame Street," probably the most successful program in motivating young people to learn, uses a combination of the best television techniques and forms, from animation to commercials. Go beyond the mundane approaches to learning you were subjected to in most of your school experiences. Consider a series like "Count Us In," developed in 1975 through a grant from the United States Office of Education. Ordinarily, we think of mathematics as it is usually taught: stolid, dry, abstract and, unless we have a special interest in numbers, largely impractical and boring. But "Count Us In" takes mathematics into everyday life, stressing "the power of math as a tool to cope with such common tasks as baking a cake, leaving a tip and estimating the amount of paint needed to cover a room." Instead of showing a teacher teaching, it uses techniques such as "young people doing such things as working at jobs, building things, telling time, playing games." It uses, as a continuing segment, a real drugstore in which the characters working in the store learn to use math when building shelves, resisting a "con game" and working extra time to make up for ice cream given away to impress friends. Entertainment and creativity are used "to encourage the use of math to solve practical problems."[1]

Don't be afraid of a liberal infusion of visuals for television and of sound effects for radio. On television, for example, even with limited budgets, you can use film clips, slides, live actors, close-ups of graphics, photos, demonstrations, detail sets — and other techniques discussed in Chapter 2. Good use of visual writing permits more concrete explanation of what is usually presented in the classroom. The classroom teacher frequently presents principles and explains with examples. Through television the examples can be infinitely more effective than the usual verbal descriptions. You can, in fact, show the real person, thing, place or event itself.

Even discussion may be utilized in the ostensibly one-way ITV technique. In many schools which have closed-circuit TV or the Instructional Television Fixed Service (ITFS), rather than broadcast television, two-way audio is used between the studio teacher and each classroom. Even with one-way television, discussion can be built into the program. Discussion between students and the classroom teacher during the program — and there should never be a case where the classroom teacher is not an active participant in the TV communication process — can be planned, and appropriate times set aside in the script. Evaluations — testing, for example — can follow the same procedure. The studio teacher and the educators planning the program should know the kinds of questions the students will ask during and following the program and should anticipate and answer them within the program. Professional broadcasters have an inordinate fear of "dead time," and many ITV people have accepted this commercial dictum. Yet, some of the best ITV programs have been those which have gone to black for appropriate periods to permit effective interaction with the classroom.

The classroom teachers do not work in vacuums. Each ITV series has a Teacher's Guide which details the purposes, level, content, approach and evaluation of each program, among other things. The Guide usually includes preparatory and follow-up suggestions. Sometimes the Guide is prepared after the series has been made. Sometimes the person working on it develops it as the series develops. The writer should note that in the latter case the Guide provides an excellent outline base for the full script or routine sheet.

The sequences in the script follow a logical order, usually beginning with a review and preparation for the day's material and concluding with introductory elements for follow-up in the classroom, including review, research, field projects and individual study. Before you begin your script and before you incorporate all the imaginative visual stimuli and the attention-getting experiences, you have to know what is available to you in terms of the program's budget. If you're preparing a lesson on China, you may find that it is not financially possible to send a film crew to Peking for a week. It may come as a shock to you to find that you can't even use the excellent film clip on China you saw on PTV the other day because the producer can't find the $100 to get rights to it.

The word "motivation" is mentioned so often in education that we have become inured to it. Yet, it is still the key to TV watching and to learning. The better a "show" you have, the better the student will learn. To make learning exciting, the material must be pleasurable and stimulating. Teaching is a form of persuasion. The instructional script should be developed as much as possible for a target audience: is the program designed for one school?, one city school system?, a county school system?, a State?, for national distribution? Who are the students who will watch? Their backgrounds? Their interests? Be carefully guided by the educational experts you are working with as to the degree of complexity of concepts you can present, what can be presumed to be already known, and the language level required for comprehension by the students in the particular grade the program is designed for. Although for different persuasive purposes, the instructional program may follow the organization of the commercial: get the students' attention, keep their interest, impart information, plant an idea, stimulate thinking about the subject and, most important of all, motivate the students to create through their own thinking something new.

The instructional program, like the good play, should increase in interest and intensity. If we start too high, we have no place to go. There is exposition and background, followed by the conflict or suspense of what will happen to the idea, characters or situation. The complications are the problems and methods of what is being learned. We reach a climax when either an answer is found and the lesson element learned or, as in Brechtian drama, when the student has been presented with all the alternatives and must seek a solution through deductive or inductive thinking on his or her own accord to satisfy hunger for knowledge on that given subject. Now, that is education! Remember that the dramatists of the world have educated us with deeper insights and feelings about the relationships among people and between people and their environment than have the historians and social scientists!

One of the simplest and most-used ITV formats is the direct presentation of views and sounds of people, places and things that otherwise would not be available to most students. Science experiments, biographical interviews and geographical descriptions are among the topics that fall into this category. Often the TV presentation may physically resemble a travelogue, with the TV teacher, voice-over, commenting on the filmed or taped material. The material, its sequence and the descriptive information is, of course, carefully planned in terms of curriculum and learning requirements. An example of this kind of script is the following beginning and ending of one lesson from a series designed for fourth grade social studies and which, because of the great variation in curriculum levels throughout the country, is actually being used from the third through eighth grades.

> ● *Given the economic considerations of producing an ITV series and the broad purpose of this particular lesson, would you have written this script any differently? If so, what approaches and techniques would you have used?*

"LANDS AND PEOPLE OF OUR WORLD"

Lesson Number: 29

Lesson Title: Japan

FILM — 1 min.

MUSIC — 1 min.

MAT — "Lands and People
of Our World"

MAT — Donna Matson	Legend says that the Sun Goddess founded the Islands of Japan, and for many years only tribespeople inhabited the land of the rising sun. Then Chinese traders and other foreigners began visiting Japan; they brought new ideas and culture. But the rulers of Japan didn't want any changes, so they closed their gates, allowing no one to enter and no one to leave. For nearly 200 years Japan and her people remained isolated from the outside world.
	Then, in 1853, Commodore Perry of the United States Navy sailed his warships into Tokyo Bay and persuaded the Japanese to open two of their ports to U.S. trade.
	The Japanese quickly learned the ways of the modern world, and today they are one of the greatest industrial nations in the world.
ON DONNA	Hello, boys and girls. Our lesson today is about Japan, one of the most amazing countries in the world today.
PIX #1 MAP — ASIA	Japan is a group of islands, located in Asia, off the East Coasts of Russia, Korea and China, in the Western part of the Pacific Ocean.
	Japan consists of four main islands: Hokkaido, Honshu, Kyushu, and Shikoku, plus about 3,000 smaller islands. All together they about equal the size of the State of California. The islands of Japan stretch from North to Southwest for a distance of about 1200 miles.
FILM — 3 min. MUSIC	Mount Fujiyama, a volcanic mountain, over 12,000 feet high, is the highest point in Japan. The islands of Japan are actually the tops of mountains which are still growing.
	Japan is located in the Pacific Great Circle of Fire, and has about 1500 earthquakes each year, but most of them cause little damage.
	Japan has a wide variety of climate ranging from tropical on the southern islands to cool summers and snowy winters on the northern islands.
Tokyo	More than 104 million people live on the islands of Japan, and two out of three live in cities.
	Tokyo, Japan's capital city, is the largest city in the world, with a population of more than 11 million people. Osaka, Kyoto, and Yokohama are also large cities, with populations of more than two million each.
	The city of Tokyo has been rebuilt twice in the last 50

years, once after an earthquake, and again after the air raids of World War II.

Today it is very much like an American city, with wide paved streets, tall modern buildings, and heavy traffic. Tokyo has been able to grow so fast mainly because of its very modern railroads that carry more than one million people into work each day.

Most Japanese homes are made of wood panels and sliding doors. They stand earthquakes well, but not fires. Many homes have beautiful gardens. The floors of the homes are like thick cushions and the Japanese people kneel on the floor while eating off low tables, and they sleep on the soft floors, in comforts and blankets that they roll up during the day. And to keep these floors clean, they always remove their shoes before entering their houses. The Japanese are some of the cleanest people I've ever met in the world.

Students

In Japan, all boys and girls must go to school for nine years. That's grade one to nine. And they have at least two hours of homework each night, and homework assignments all summer long. All students in Japan are required to study English. There are more than 50 universities and colleges in Tokyo.

Mother and Child

Japanese children are very respectful and polite to their parents and grandparents, and try very hard to never bring shame to their family in any way.

Harbor

Japan is an island nation, and island nations need ships. Japan is first in the world in ship building, second in plastics, and fourth in auto making. Yet, only about 3 out of every 100 Japanese have automobiles. Japan imports much steel from us, manufactures trucks, autos and machinery, and exports it to the United States and other countries.

People travel mainly on electric trains and buses. There just wouldn't be enough room if many people had cars. Space is a problem. . . .

Film Ends (3 min.)

Japan is also the world's largest exporter of ceramic tableware, cameras, lenses, electronic equipment and motorcycles.

ON DONNA

As a matter of fact, here are some of the things I own that are manufactured in Japan. My camera, tape recorder and ceramic tableware.

FILM — 7½ min.

The textile industry is another important industry in Japan. Japan produces more than half of the world's supply of raw silk. Silk, remember, comes from cocoons, of the silkworms.

Fishing

Japan is one of the world's greatest fishing countries. It has over 400,000 fishing boats. That's more than any other nation.

* * *

FILM

For over 1,000 years Japan was ruled by an Emperor who

had great powers over the people. Today his duties are mainly ceremonial. Here we see the Emperor of Japan greeting his people on New Year's Day at the Imperial Palace Grounds in Tokyo.

After World War II, the United States helped Japan set up a democratic form of government, and the head of their government is the Prime Minister, who is chosen by the Diet. The Diet is like our Congress, with a House of Representatives and a House of Councilors which are elected by the people of Japan.

ON DONNA   Hibatchi, food, toys, dolls, kite.

MUSIC — 15 sec.   Closing

ON KITE

MAT — Consultant
MAT — Western ITV

Courtesy of Western Instructional Television

As noted earlier, some ITV programs are not scripted, but use rundown or routine sheets. Here is an example from a series on music designed for the second and third grades. Note how the writer has the studio teacher — in this case a professional performer — bring in the active participation of the students watching in the classroom. Writing a rundown sheet such as this takes just as much time as writing a complete script for a "Lands and Peoples of Our World" lesson, says Donna Matson, producer and writer of both programs: "You have to think and organize and plan every move in order to keep it as simple and flowing as possible. For example, if you teach the verse, will you sing the song through first? After you have taught the verse, will you follow up with a repeat, or will you have another song or an instrument as a transition between segments? What techniques of involving the classroom student should be used? Will you go out with the theme, so that the child keeps on singing after the program has ended? What is most important in the program: the song? the use of instruments? These are only some of the considerations the writer has to keep in mind. The script may be short, but the work time that goes into it is long."

"LET'S ALL SING"

Lesson Number: 17   Lesson Title: Magical Food

Theme — Live — Guitar

MAT — "Let's All Sing"

MAT —Tony Saletan

ON TONY   There are many songs about food such as . . .

         But today we're going to sing a song about mystical magical food. And it goes like this . . .

	TEACHES REFRAIN
	SINGS ENTIRE SONG
	SHOWS FOODS
	SINGS SONG — LISTEN TO RHYMING WORDS
	SINGS SONG — Children fill in rhyming word
ON BELLS	BELLS — 4 tone refrain $+ 2 = 6$
ON PIX — Malvina Reynolds	MALVINA REYNOLDS
	SING "LET IT BE"
	SING "MAGICAL FOOD" — make up verses
	CLOSING
	MAGICAL FOOD

MAT — Saletan
MAT — Reynolds
MAT — Western ITV

Courtesy of Western Instructional Television

TRAINING — GOVERNMENT

WRITING EDUCATIONAL SCRIPTS for government training purposes varies with the size and production budgets of each agency. Some, like the Department of Defense, have superb facilities for writing and producing training programs for radio and television. Other agencies have no facilities and do virtually nothing at all. Still others attempt to do good jobs with barely adequate resources. But whether a high budget or a low/no budget situation, the basic element of the program, the script, has got to be as good as possible.

Eileen T. McClay is the writer-producer-director of ITV training materials for the Federal Trade Commission, typical of the agencies with limited budget and resources. (She is also a free-lance writer and teacher of writing.) The budget/resources limitations on the producer-director impose limitations on the writer. Some of McClay's experiences are specifically applicable to such a situation; others of her experiences are typical of the writer's concerns in all situations and in all agencies. One of the important considerations to the writer, McClay says, is "multiple clearances":

> You may find that your product must be reviewed (for content, format, policy, security) by so many layers of authority that you despair of ever getting a program out on a timely basis. Also — and this may be one of the most substantial differences between you and your counterparts in commercial or public television — the persons who will rule on your product may have little knowledge about either the limitations or the special capabilities of audiovisuals and may, in fact, have little sympathy with the concept of instructional television. To many people,

television is associated with, and thereby ineradicably tainted by, "show biz."

Another problem for the ITV writer in government is the lack of opportunity to pre-plan. McClay explains:

> A great many elements must be coordinated to bring a production together. Good programs take advance planning. Workers in the world of the small audiovisual operation often listen wistfully to their more affluent colleagues talk about an insistence on total control, pre-planning, and righteous refusal to uncap the lens of a single camera until a full script has been written. More typical may be the phone call that informs you that Supervisor John Smith is on his way with an urgent message of indeterminate length on a cloudily outlined subject, which must be taped, duplicated, and sent out to regional offices by sundown. You arrange props, set lights, test sound, and sit down to wait for Smith — who arrives two hours late with an armful of graphs and charts on 8½ x 11 sheets, and accompanied by two or three members of his staff who would like to share the camera with him. All express great surprise at the time involved in rearranging all the equipment to accommodate to the new situation. As for preparing a script . . .

Ms. McClay divides an agency's needs into two categories: communications and training. "Each, of course, may well contain elements of the other. The first, however, is usually an information-carrying vehicle: a news briefing, a backgrounder to explain agency action or policy, an interview with a new bureau or division chief that will acquaint regional offices with his or her operating philosophy. The second kind of program should be precisely geared to the training needs of the agency's personnel."

One training script written and produced by McClay related to educating supervisory staff personnel on the problem caused by careless filling-out of a standard government form. The FTC at first planned to send only a memorandum to the staff, then decided to supplement the memo with a videotape on the subject. One of the requirements was that the TV program retain large portions of the language of the memo. A second requirement was that the project — conception of format to writing of script to final taping — be completed in two working days. McClay started with the memorandum:

Executive Director Notice

Subject: Timely Reporting of Personnel Actions
The agency recently converted to a computerized payroll system which is operated for us by the Treasury Department in Philadelphia. Since the new system has been in operation, we are constantly receiv-

ing complaints from the Treasury people that our personnel actions are getting to them too late. The result is that some employees are not getting paid on time, while others are being overpaid and checks are having to be cancelled.

Specifically, the problem relates to Standard Form 52, Notification of Personnel Action. This form is the medium through which operating officials communicate to the Division of Personnel what is happening in their organizational units. It is also the basis from which the employee is ultimately paid. The 52's are not coming in from the operating bureaus on time. This is the primary reason why our actions are getting to Treasury too late.

Treasury has given us an absolute deadline of the second Wednesday of the pay period (the day after pay day) for getting actions to them for that pay period. They want to receive actions on a gradual, day-to-day basis, not all at one time on the deadline date. Therefore, the maximum deadline that the Division of Personnel can accept personnel actions is the second Tuesday of the pay period in which the action is to be effective. Actions received after this date may not be made effective until the following pay period. It is absolutely necessary that you

- Send your 52's in by the beginning of the pay period.
- Don't hold resignations — submit them as soon as you are aware of an employee's intention to leave.
- Advise the personnel processing section by phone of any actions that will be coming in late — be prepared to justify the reasons why they will be late.
- On appointments in the field offices, air mail the oath of office, withholding forms, and 52 (if not previously submitted) on the morning of the day the employee enters on duty, and monitor very closely the status of employees requiring follow-up actions, e.g., not-to-exceed dates, expiration of leave without pay, changes in tour of duty, etc.

Each operating official should delegate the responsibility for preparing 52's to a competent, reliable person, and should designate an alternate for that person so that delays will not occur because of absence. The same is true of Timekeepers — this an important function and should be assigned to a responsible person and an alternate. The Timekeeper and the person responsible for 52's should be in close communication with each other and with the Personnel Processing Section, so as to alert each other regarding impending personnel actions. You, the operating managers, are responsible and accountable for insuring that all personnel actions are submitted on time and are accurate.

A film is being prepared on this subject to be shown to all Timekeepers and persons responsible for preparing 52's. The matter is being called to your attention prior to releasing the film so that you will be aware of the urgency of this situation, and can make immediate efforts to correct the problem. We must make this new system work, since our own payroll staff has been practically disbanded. The only way it can work is if personnel actions are reported on a timely basis.

The approach taken by McClay:

I decided to make a 15-minute tape, the nuclei of which would be three short skits dramatizing the major difficulties the Personnel Office was having as a result of errors in the completion of the forms. Because of the time pressure, I decided not to write complete scripts for these particular scenes, but to use improvisational techniques and to schedule short but intensive rehearsal periods with staff members who were directly involved in the kinds of situations to be dramatized and who would, therefore, be able to talk spontaneously and knowledgeably on the subject. Also, because of lack of time, I made no attempt to use music or graphics. The script I wrote was more of a detailed routine sheet, in which I prepared as much of the introductory, ending and transitional continuity as possible, but left the analyses and discussion of specific problems in the improvisational form. Also, as writer-director I prepared the video portion of the script, as well. The completed tape — which was basically a dramatized interoffice memorandum — was well-received by the supervisory staff audience for whom it was directed and was generally deemed to have achieved its goal of focusing attention on a problem of some urgency.

• *As you examine the following script, compare its purpose, language and effectiveness with the memorandum that prompted it. Note that even with improvisational elements made necessary by lack of time, the script is prepared as fully as possible, following the principle that the more you know about where you are going and how you want to go, the better chance you have of getting there. Would you have written it any differently? How? Note, as well, that the writer, as producer, put in complete video directions, similar to what the writer of the film script would do.*

Title: STANDARD FORM 52:
NOTIFICATION OF PERSONNEL ACTION

VIDEO	AUDIO
Fade up from black	
Camera 2 LS Form 52, slow Zoom to CU of title: hold 3 secs.	
Dissolve Camera 1 MCU Marie _____	MARIE: This is Marie _____ of the Personnel Office at Headquarters. I want to discuss with you a very serious

problem. You all know we recently converted to a computerized payroll system, operated for us by the Treasury Department in Philadelphia. Ever since the new system has been in operation, however, we've been receiving complaints from the Treasury people that our personnel actions are getting to them too late for timely action. The result is that some employees are not getting paid on time, while others are being overpaid and their checks are having to be cancelled.

Take Camera 2 LS Marie	MARIE: Specifically, I am talking about Standard Form 52, Notification of Personnel Action. This form is the medium by which operating officials communicate to the Division of Personnel what is happening in their organizational units. It is also the basis on which the employee is ultimately paid. The fact is, the 52s are not coming in from the operating bureaus on time, and this is the primary reason our actions are late getting to Treasury.
Take Camera 1 MCU Marie	Even when a form is correctly filled out, it takes time for Personnel to process the action. All too often, however, vital information is incorrect, or is missing altogether. When that happens, more time is wasted while we return the form to you and then wait for you to send us the correct information. Meantime, the personnel action is held up and the change in the employee's status can't be reflected in his paycheck.
Take Camera 2 CU Form 52 as Marie uses pointer to indicate 2 different items. Camera follows pointer.	Let me show you some examples of forms that have been incorrectly filled out. In this instance . . . (Marie states what is incorrect and explains consequences.)
Take Camera 1 LS Marie at desk, Joyce sitting beside her. Slow Zoom to MCU as they talk. Zoom to CU Marie at con- (Zoom to CU Marie at conclusion.)	MARIE: Errors like these cause problems for us almost every day. In fact, Joyce has just received a Form that is missing some very important information. JOYCE: Yes. This Form doesn't give us enough information about an employee's resignation. (Marie and Joyce discuss the problem, stressing these points: a. If the effective date is not given, employee continues to draw pay after he has resigned. b. If no forwarding address is given, employee cannot be mailed his final check. c. A Federal regulation requires that employee fill in the reason for his leaving.)
Camera 1 holding CU Marie	MARIE: I want to show you another example of what can happen when Regional Offices fail to give us complete information. (Marie outlines problem.)

Take Camera 2
CU Form 52 as Marie
again uses pointer to
indicate a problem

Take Camera 1
CU Marie

MARIE:
This morning Julie had to call one of our Regional Offices
because . . .
(Marie states problem.)

Dissolve Camera 2
LS Julie; slow Zoom to
MCU as she speaks

JULIE:
(Julie carries on telephone conversation with RO super-
visor, discussing problems caused by his not getting
Form in on time, or not having it correctly filled out.)

Dissolve Camera 1
CU Marie

MARIE:
When the Forms are properly filled out, the process of a
change in employee status goes very smoothly. But I
think you're beginning to see that errors can be very
time-consuming. Also, and I want to emphasize this
point, mistakes can cause real hardship for an employee.
Right now, for example, Karen is trying to help an
employee discover why he didn't receive his last paycheck.

Dissolve Camera 2
LS Karen and John. Slow
Zoom to John at conclu-
sion; soft focus out on
John still talking

(Karen and John discuss the fact that he didn't receive
his last paycheck.)

Audio out on John, up on Marie

Dissolve Camera 1
LS Marie

MARIE:
The Treasury Department has informed us they must
receive all actions on a gradual, day-to-day basis, not all
at the same time. Therefore, effective immediately, the
maximum deadline we can accept personnel actions is
the Friday before the beginning of the pay period in
which the action is to be effective. Actions received after
this date may not be made effective until the following
pay period. The only exceptions to this are appointments
in the Regional Offices, which should be air-mailed to the
Division of Personnel on the day the employee reports
for work.

Take Camera 2
CU Marie

It is absolutely necessary that you:
— Send your 52s in by the beginning of the pay period.
— Submit resignations as soon as you are aware of an
  employee's intention to leave.
— On appointments in the Regional Offices, air mail the
  oath of office, withholding forms, and 52s (if not previously submitted) on the morning of the day the
  employee enters on duty, and
— Monitor very closely the status of employees requiring
  follow-up actions like: not-to-exceed dates, expiration
  of leave without pay, changes in tour of duty, and so
  forth.

Take Camera 1 LS Marie	Most of you who are viewing this tape are responsible for preparing 52s in your organizational unit, or are Time-keepers. The fact that you have been assigned these important functions indicates that you are competent and reliable employees. We, therefore, look to you for your cooperation in getting 52s in on time.
Holding Camera 1 Zoom to MCU Marie	Timekeepers and persons responsible for preparing 52s should work in close communication with each other and with the Personnel Processing Section so as to alert each other regarding impending personnel actions.
Holding Camera 1 Slow Zoom to CU Marie	Remember, our own payroll staff has been practically disbanded, so we must make this new system work. And it won't work unless every Form 52 is filled out accurately, completely, and on time. At the beginning of this tape, I told you I wanted to discuss a serious problem with you. I hope you see now just how urgent it is.

Dissolve Camera 2
CU LOGO; hold 3 secs.

Fade to black

Written by Eileen T. McClay, Federal Trade Commission

TRAINING — INDUSTRY

A LARGE AND GROWING FIELD, instructional training programs for industry, follows the basic approaches and forms of the formal instructional and government training program. Scripts do vary in terms of content and, as in low-budget government operations, in terms of time and facilities requirements, and, especially, in terms of technique required to get across some of the complicated and detailed industrial information. Donald S. Schaal, TV producer-director for Control Data Corporation Television Communications Services, states that "when you come to grips with scripting for industrial television, for the most part you might just as well throw all your preconceived ideas about creative/dramatic and technical writing in the circular file."[2] Schaal states that attempts to transfer the classroom teacher to television have failed and that "unfamiliarity with what television could or could not do . . . resulted in a product which left just about everything to be desired. It lacked organization, continuity, a smooth succession of transitions and, in many cases, many of the pertinent details. . . . Since we think so-called 'training' tapes should *augment* classroom material and not supplant it, we soon realized that we could gain little but could lose everything by merely turning an instructor loose in front of the tube to do exactly what he does in person in the classroom. . . . The videotape he needs for his classroom *must* provide something he cannot conveniently offer his students in person."

Mr. Schaal's solution to the problem was to use professionals to do the voice tracks describing electromechanical and electronic equipment. He found, however, that this created a further problem: although the teacher who knows the equipment doesn't usually know how to present it effectively on television, the professional who can make a good presentation doesn't usually know much about the equipment.

> The solution, of course, is that the professional must *sound* as though he invented every part of the machine and painstakingly hand-tooled it out of solid gold. To accomplish this effect, you must contrive what I like to call a "shadow" script.

The "shadow" script, according to Schaal, is a transcription of the classroom teacher's presentation of a particular subject, and a minimum rewriting of the transcription for smoother continuity and subsequent voice-over recording by a professional. Schaal found two distinct difficulties: the classroom instructor tended to reflect the classroom teaching approach, a lack of concise, clear continuity and the accidental omission of pertinent material.

> Now an instructor who comes into our shop to make such a tape arrives with at least a very detailed, topical outline prepared with television in mind. In many cases, he is actually provided with a detailed rough shooting script from which he reads for the benefit of the audio track. These outlines and scripts are provided by the curriculum people of the school and tend to confine the instructor to an orderly and complete description of the equipment. . . .
>
> Had we gone the route of preparing formal scripts in the technical writing style (which would have been the most appropriate in this case), dropped the instructor out of the loop completely by telling him he was a clod on television and showing him the door, and refused to cooperate with the curriculum people because they didn't think in terms of television at first, we not only would have alienated a lot of people, but also I doubt if we would have produced a completely usable tape. . . .
>
> The moral, as I see it, is that industrial television scripts must be tailored to meet the situation. I have talked of only one aspect of industrial scripting — the description of equipment for training people on how to use and maintain it. For this type of script, I feel it is very important to retain the credibility of the person who knows the equipment the best, even though his voice does not appear on the finished product.

For this reason, I confine my rewrites to removing bad grammar and clarifying hazy or badly worded description. I make no attempt at restructuring mainly because the pictures are already on the tape. If I do see continuity problems, however, I call them to the attention of the curriculum people involved and let them make the decisions. I do make every attempt to keep the narrative as conversational as possible without lapsing into the creative/dramatic vein. All such scripts must be straight-forward, sound natural, and contain a minimum of slang. Rarely is anything flippant allowed to survive the waste basket. Cliches and stylized narrative are avoided like the plague.

PROFESSIONAL UPDATING

IN PROVIDING AN EXAMPLE of instructional/informational programs for the various professions, Dr. Sandra W. Bennett, formerly writer-producer for the Ohio Medical Television Network, later Associate Director of the Ohio Nurses Association, stresses the need for writers of health education programs to work very closely with health professionals. She states that although it sometimes becomes a sensitive area,

. . . most health professionals involved with television production require the assistance of a television writer. Depending on the format and objectives, the health professional may be supplying the largest percentage of the content for the production. That health professional must be made to understand and appreciate the limitations as well as the boundless opportunities television offers.

That's where television writers combine their skills with health professionals. All the principles of television writing still apply. Good television writing should not be compromised. (The pressure to abandon what you know to be good writing, however, may be great, especially if you are working with people inexperienced in television.)

Writing for health education requires a few other basic principles:

(1) Give yourself twice as much lead time. Too many health professionals are not at all concerned with your time or television's deadlines. Even those who are knowledgeable about TV have patients whose health care needs take priority over your time schedule. Allow for it.

(2) Identify your intended audience and the specific objectives at the outset. Television writing for closed-circuit or VTR distribution is different from open-channel commercial broadcasting.

(3) Slides and audio references to patients need to be carefully screened for public viewing. While this may seem obvious, TV writers must double check to be sure that the information they've been given has protected the privacy of the health care consumer.

Health and medical programs on radio and television range from presentations to lay persons on elementary home sanitary measures to highly detailed surgical procedures such as — to note the title of one program of this type presented by the Ohio Medical Network — "Emergency Closed Tube Thoracostomy." Critical in writing the professionally-oriented program are the technical level and content, clearly requiring for the writer who is not a professional in the given field the research, advice and editing of people in that field. As pointed out by Dr. Bennett, the intended audience and whether the program is for closed-circuit distribution or for public viewing or hearing also affects what can be presented.

A script example is the beginning of "The Breast Fed Child," which was written for broadcast over local commercial stations to the general public as well as for carriage over a special network for viewing by physicians in hospital centers.

"THE BREAST FED CHILD"

VIDEO	AUDIO
	(ANNOUNCER) :30
SUPERS over film — (CCME (logo) (College of Medicine logo) (Title) (Doctor credits)	The Ohio State University Center for Continuing Medical Education and The College of Medicine presents "The Breast Fed Child" with Dr. Willard B. Fernald, Pediatrician; Dr. James C. Good, General Practitioner, specializing in Obstetrics; and Dr. J. Douglas Veach, Obstetrician and Gynecologist.
STUDIO — Dr. Good	Whatever the reasons that the Womanly Art of Breastfeeding has been relegated to a lesser position in the field of infant nutrition during the past few generations, the consensus seems to be that breastfeeding *is* the best for baby and for mother during the baby's early life. As physicians, we are frequently consulted by mothers concerning feeding problems of the newborn and the young infant.
Dissolve to CAM on bottles	Many physicians feel more at ease with bottle formulas and recommending how to change various ingredients and foods to bring about the desired effect in the child. This trend toward the "bottle" has been fostered by the commercial development and advertising of various formulas which are said to be "nearly like mother's own."
Dissolve to FILM rolling	At the same time, medical education has done little to instruct the student or the practitioner on the physiology of lactation or the advantages of breastfeeding over other methods. However, in recent years there seems to be a definite trend back toward "nature's way" of nursing babies. It now becomes necessary for the interested physician to fill in the gaps in his education and to lend

support and encouragement to these very sincere mothers trying to nurse their infants in a sometimes hostile world.

STUDIO — Dr. Good

This program is intended to present a view of breastfeeding from the baby's standpoint, with emphasis on some of the advantages, some points about technique and what to do with a few of the problems encountered.

STUDIO — Open —
Dr. Veach

For the most part successful breast-feeding rests upon the motivation of each individual mother, since almost any woman has the physiological abilities to produce enough milk for 3 or more babies, if necessary.

Dissolve to VTR
(simulated office visit)

During even the first office visit while taking the medical history, there is a natural opening to discuss, among other important things, reasons for support of breast-feeding. During subsequent prenatal visits, after having as much information as possible, she must choose the feeding method for her needs. The infant's needs remain the same. When she chooses breast-feeding, at about $7\frac{1}{2}$ months, she needs instruction on the techniques of nipple preparation because the usually protected and often immature nipple needs toughening to withstand the demands of nursing. This is a demonstration of a simple maneuver which accomplishes this when done once or twice daily.

As you can see, these motions of stripping between finger and thumb anticipate the action of the baby's nursing as pictured here.

Dissolve to CAM CARD #1
CAM CARD #2
CAM CARD #3

CAM CARD #4

(Pause)   The nipple and areola are surrounded.
(Pause)   The tongue slides forward and grips them.
(Pause)   The nipple is pulled against the hard palate by backward action of the tongue and suction of the tongue and cheeks. Here, the gums press on the areola pushing milk against the roof of the palate. Milk flow continues because of the higher pressure and activities of the milk ducts themselves.

CAM CARD #5

This last diagram shows the problems associated with bottle feeding. The rubber nipple holds the lips open and causes gagging because it touches the soft palate and interferes with tongue action.

In order to try to control the gush of overflowing formula, the baby's tongue pushes against the gums. The cheek muscles are not used and remain relaxed. Therefore, if this baby is offered the breast it becomes confused.

Dissolve back to VTR or
STUDIO (Dr. Veach)

In most hospital situations this struggle starts within 12 hours, even for those babies whose mothers desire to nurse. Human babies are the only infants who are given supplementary water in the belief that they should not have the normal 10% weight loss.

* * *

Produced by the Center for Continuing Medical Education,
Ohio State University College of Medicine

PUBLIC INFORMATION

A LONG-TIME GOVERNMENT writer whose background includes authorship
of a Broadway play is Sid L. Schwartz, Motion Picture and Audiovisual
Officer for the Energy Research and Development Administration. Schwartz
likens the government public information message to the Public Service
Announcement discussed in Chapter 2. He states that:

> The writer's primary task is to find the kernel of the message so
> that when produced as a PSA it can be compressed to fit a very brief
> period of time and still make a point in the show-biz presentation that
> will make more than a mere statement. That is why the successful PSA
> script must be produceable as an entertaining, interesting, startling or
> beautiful moment for the radio ear or the television eye and ear —
> otherwise the effort will be a failure.
>
> Writing a PSA is like designing a billboard and reducing it to sec-
> onds of sound or seconds of sight and sound. Catching an audience's
> attention, holding their interest and imparting a message in 30 seconds
> is like a billboard that succeeds in imparting a message to traffic pass-
> ing at 55 miles per hour.

Mr. Schwartz notes that one popular type of PSA mainly urges the
audience to write for more detail. Here are radio and television examples of
this type produced by the U.S. Energy Research and Development Administration:

ENERGY I
TV PUBLIC SERVICE ANNOUNCEMENT
30 SECONDS

VIDEO	AUDIO
1. CU hand with quill pen, period coat and cuffs, signs Declaration of Independence.	(FX: Room noise . . . crowd murmurs, etc.) ANNOUNCER: PHILADELPHIA . . . JULY 4TH . . . 1776! A REVOLUTION TAKES PLACE THAT CHANGES THE COURSE OF THE WORLD.
2. Dissolve to traffic montage.	(FX: Traffic noise) TODAY, 200 YEARS LATER, ANOTHER REVOLUTION . . . THIS ONE CONCERNING ENERGY.
3. Dissolve to scientist in lab with test equipment.	(FX: Fade traffic) THE NEW BATTLEFIELD IS THE LABORATORY . . . THE PRIMARY WEAPON, THE HUMAN MIND! WE'RE WORK-ING HARD TO DEVELOP NEW ENERGY SOURCES.

4. Dissolve to logo: TO LEARN HOW, WRITE: *ERDA*, THE ENERGY
ERDA   RESEARCH AND DEVELOPMENT ADMINISTRATION,
WASHINGTON, D.C.   WASHINGTON, D.C. 20545.
20545

Written by Jack Moser, U.S. Energy Research and Development Administration

ENERGY II
RADIO PUBLIC SERVICE ANNOUNCEMENT
30 SECONDS

(FX: Sound of jet taking off . . . cross-fade to traffic
montage . . . cross-fade to train with deisel horn . . . all
under after establishing)

ANNOUNCER: ENERGY . . . THERE'S ALWAYS A NEED
FOR JUST A LITTLE BIT MORE. UNFORTUNATELY
THE SUPPLY IS LIMITED . . . IT WON'T LAST FOREVER
. . . AND THE SOLUTIONS ARE A LONG WAY DOWN
THE ROAD.

(FX: Cross-fade to clock ticking)

WE'RE WORKING HARD TO MAKE SURE CURRENT
ENERGY SOURCES AREN'T EXHAUSTED BEFORE NEW
TECHNOLOGY IS READY TO TAKE OVER. TO LEARN
HOW, WRITE: *ERDA*, THE ENERGY RESEARCH AND
DEVELOPMENT ADMINISTRATION, WASHINGTON, D.C.
20545.

Written by Jack Moser, U.S. Energy Research and Development Administration

Although common in practice, Schwartz says, this type of "write-in" PSA is looked on by some as a "cop-out":

> More popular and effective are those PSAs that carry the burden of the entire message in their brief exposure. For example, the U.S. Forest Service 1974 campaign where Smokey Bear says: "Matches don't start forest fires — people do. Next time think before you strike."

Once the kernel of the message is attained or agreed to, the writer's job is to reduce the idea to words as in a slogan or to conceive it as a visual. Ideally it may be words and a word picture as in the cases of two competitive airlines advertising slogans: "the wings of man" and "navigators of the world since it was flat." These appeared and were heard during the same broadcast season.

PSA script writing should relate to the client's current campaign or herald the next one. The script should develop empathy and involvement by signalling the audience to use its memory, understanding, ambitions and fantasies. The writing of TV PSAs, for government or non-government information purposes, generally follows a written concept, a treatment, a shooting script and, in many cases, a story board. The radio PSA follows the same steps except that the radio story board, rather than a series of thumbnail visual sketches, is a "scratch" track with the voices, sound effects and music mixed in a rough presentation.

The government public information or public relations program, therefore, is not different in execution than that for the private sector — except, as described by Eileen McClay earlier in this chapter, it is subject to different kinds of constrictions and administrative requirements. As Sid Schwartz says, "We turn it out to fit the form of the particular program type — the same as any other writer and producer."

NOTES TO CHAPTER 11

[1] Robert Reinhold, "Educational TV Is Turning to An Everyday Kind of Math," *The New York Times*, April 6, 1975, p. E9.
[2] Donald S. Schaal, " 'Shadow Writing' for Industrial TV," *Educational & Industrial Television*, June, 1972, pp. 22, 24. Subsequent remarks of Schaal in this section of Chapter 11 are from the same article.

REFERENCE BOOKS

ON EDUCATION AND INFORMATION PROGRAMS

Bluem, William A., ed., *Religious Television Programs: A Study in Relevance*. New York: Hastings House, 1968.

Bluem, William A., John F. Cox and Gene McPherson. *Television in the Public Interest*. New York: Hastings House, 1961.

Connochie, T. D., *TV for Education and Industry*. New York: William S. Heinman, 1969.

Ellens, J. Harold, *Models of Religious Broadcasting*. Grand Rapids, Mich.: William B. Eerdmans, 1974.

Gordon, George N., *Classroom Television: New Frontiers in ITV*. New York: Hastings House, 1970.

Gordon, George N., Irving Falk and William Hodapp, *The Idea Invaders*. New York: Hastings House, 1963.

Hilliard, Robert L. and Hyman H. Field, *Television and the Teacher: A Handbook for Classroom Use*. New York: Hastings House, 1976.

MacLean, Roderick, *Television in Education: Modern Teaching*. London: Metheun Educational Ltd., 1968.

Roth, Dorothy H. and Donel W. Price, *Instructional Television: A Method for Teaching Nursing*. St. Louis: C. V. Mosby, 1971.

Schramm, Wilbur, ed., *Quality in Instructional Television*. Honolulu: University Press of Hawaii, 1973.

Television in Instruction: What Is Possible. Washington, D. C.: National Association of Educational Broadcasters, 1971.

Periodicals which contain occasional articles of special value to the writer of education and information programs include: *American Education, Audio-*

visual Instruction, AV Communication Review, Educational/Instructional Broadcasting, Educational & Industrial Television, Educational Technology, Media and Methods, Public Telecommunications Review, Training in Business and Industry.

FOR APPLICATION AND REVIEW

1. Go to your local public television station, ITFS system or closed-circuit TV operation (this is easy if you are studying this book as part of a course and are within an educational institution using instructional television in some form) and volunteer to work as a writer with one of the ITV series. If this is not possible, obtain a lesson plan for any subject or level (it could be for a television and radio writing course!) and prepare a script for one TV program that will be of special value to the students in that course.
2. Do the same for radio, with a public radio station, a campus carrier-current station, or for a course.
3. Obtain a memorandum relating to some internal problem or process at the place where you work or study and prepare a TV and/or radio script from it, similar to the example in the section on *Training-Government* in this chapter.

12

The Play

BRANDER MATTHEWS, who was one of the theatre's leading critics, wrote in his *The Development of the Drama* that

> ". . . dramaturgic principles are not mere rules laid down by theoretical critics, who have rarely any acquaintance with the actual theatre; they are laws, inherent in the nature of the art itself, standing eternal, as immitigable today as when Sophocles was alive, or Shakespeare, or Moliere."[1]

The rules of playwriting are universal. They apply generally to the structure of the play written for the stage, film, television or radio. The rules are modified in their specific applications by the special requirements of the particular medium.

Don't assume that because there are rules that playwriting can be taught. Genius and inspiration cannot be taught, and playwriting is an art on a plane of creativity far above the mechanical facets of some of the phases of continuity writing. America's first and foremost playwriting teacher, George Pierce Baker, stated that what can be done, however, is to show the potential playwright how to apply whatever genius and dramatic insight he or she may have, through an understanding of the basic rules of dramaturgy. That is all that can be done and that is all that will be attempted here.

Yet, even this much cannot be taught in one chapter or in several chapters. Any full discussion of playwriting technique requires at least a complete book. What will be presented here is a summary of the rules of playwriting and some new concepts of playwriting in terms of the special needs of the television and radio media. If you seriously wish to write television (and radio) drama, first explore as thoroughly as possible the techniques of writing the play for the stage. Only then will you have a sound basis for the television play.

SOURCES

BEFORE THE ACTUAL TECHNIQUES of writing can be applied, the writer must be able to recognize and exploit the sources out of which can be developed the ideas for the play.

The writer may find the motivating ingredient for the play in an event or happening, in a theme, in a character or characters, or in a background.

Many times a playwright has witnessed or experienced an incident or series of incidents that contain the fundamentals for good drama. From this event or happening the playwright can build character, situation, theme and background. Remember, however, that what is exciting in life is not necessarily good drama. Drama is heightened life. It is a compression of the most important elements of a situation and requires a rearrangement, revision and condensation of life to make it drama and not merely human interest reporting. It is difficult for the beginning playwright to understand this, particularly when s/he has been a participant in or an observer of an interesting life-situation. What may seem to be the most tragic, most humorous, most exciting thing that has ever happened to the writer may actually be hackneyed, dull and undramatic in play form. Because something seems dramatic in real life does not mean that it will be dramatic if put into a play. Such transposition requires imagination, skill and, to no small degree, the indefinable genius of playwriting. For example, many of us have seen a situation where a destitute maiden aunt has come to live with a sister and brother-in-law, and in her psychological need has become somewhat of a disturbing factor in the marriage. To the participants, or even to a close observer, such a situation might have provocative and electrifying undertones. To someone not connected with the situation, it appears, and understandably so, dull and uninspiring. To the imaginative playwright, in this case to Tennessee Williams, it could become "A Streetcar Named Desire."

The writer may initiate the preliminary thinking about the play from a theme or an idea. Although censorship often hampers the television and radio playwright, the writer can find basic concepts such as loyalty, independence, self-realization, as motivating factors upon which to develop a drama. The theme must be translated into specific and full-blown people and concrete situations. Under the theme of loyalty, for example, there is the ever-present son who won't marry because his psychologically-motivated notion of loyalty is one which says that he cannot leave his mother. Under independence, there are any number of variations of the wife who leaves her husband because she is not accorded the freedom or respect she feels she needs. Under self-realization, there is an endless supply of potential plays oriented around the artist who prefers to live on bread and beans in a cold-water flat rather than accept the lucrative advertising agency job. The writer must be wary of attempting to develop a play around a theme alone. As can be seen from the examples above, the results can be uninteresting and trite. The theme serves merely as the germ of the idea for the play.

Another source for the play may lie in a background. The backgrounds of war, of high society, of a ghetto environment, of the business world, have provided the settings and motivations for many plays. The college student could do worse than to use the background of the campus environment as an initiating factor for the play.

A final source for the play may come from a character or several characters, either as a group or rolled into one. In modern dramaturgy, character motivates action; that is, the plot develops out of the characters. For this reason, the choice of character as a source provides a potentially stronger foundation for the play than do the other sources. The writer must be cautious, however, in using this source independently of the others; it is difficult to build a play solely around a character or combination of characters taken from real life. For example, how trite is the idea of a salesman getting fired from a job because he is getting old and cannot make as many sales as he once did! Even if his character is enlarged by adding pride, self-deception and despondency leading to suicide, the dramatic potential is not yet fully realized. But work on the character, develop his many facets, beliefs, psychological needs, physical capabilities, relationships to other people, clarify a theme and background, and one might eventually get to Willy Loman of Arthur Miller's "Death of A Salesman."

The sources of the play — situation, theme, background and character — individually are only germs of ideas. To be valuable to the initial development of the play, each of these factors must be explored, expanded, revised, then developed in relationship to the other sources, and finally re-examined in its complete form to determine if the idea has any dramatic value at all. If it has, then the playwright is ready for the next step. Too many beginning writers think that once the source, the motivating factor, is clarified, the play can be written. Inexperienced writers — and lazy writers — sometimes believe that all they have to do is to have a pretty good idea of where they are going, and then sit down and write the play. Unfortunately, this is not the case. The actual writing of the play is the dessert of the playwright's art. The hard work is devoted to the planning of the play and, later, to the revisions of the manuscript. After deciding on the theme, situation, character or background as a base for the play, clarify in your mind and on paper the various elements that develop from the base. For instance, if you choose to work from a background, determine the characters, the situation and the theme to go with that background.

The writer should, ideally, write out of personal experiences or knowledge so that the play may have a valid foundation. However, if the writer is too close, either emotionally or in terms of time, to the life-ingredients of the play, it will be difficult to heighten and condense and dramatize — the writer will tend to be a reporter rather than a dramatist. The playwright should never be part of the play, but should be able to write it objectively. Feel and understand every moment of it, but do so as a third person. Don't use the play as personal therapy. It is a good idea to be several calendar years and several emotional light years away from the play when you start to write it.

PLAY STRUCTURE

UNTIL THE 18TH CENTURY, with the exception of works by only a few playwrights (notably Shakespeare), plot or action was the dominant element in the play. The plot line was the most important factor, and the characters and dialogue were fitted into the movement of the action. Modern drama has emphasized character as most important. The actions which determine the plot are those the characters *must* take because of their particular personalities and psychological motivations. The dialogue is that which the characters *must* speak for the same reasons. The three major elements in the play structure — character, plot and dialogue — all must be coordinated into a consistent and clear theme. This coordination of all elements toward a common end results in the unity of the piece, a unity of impression. The characters' actions and the events are not arbitrary, and the audience must be prepared for the occurrence of these actions and events in a logical and valid manner. "Preparation" is the term given to the material which thus prepares the audience. The background and situation also must be presented; this is the "exposition." Another element the playwright must consider is the "setting," which the playwright describes in order to create a valid physical background and environment for the characters.

After you are certain that you understand and can be objective about the characters, theme, situation and background, you can begin to create each of them in depth. Do as much research as necessary — or, perhaps, as much as possible — to acquaint yourself fully with the potentials of the play.

Each character should be literally psychoanalyzed. This should be done on paper, so that you have the characters' complete histories and motivations in front of you at all times. Develop a background for each character, not only for the duration of the action of the play, but extending back much before the opening of the play (even going back to ancestors who may not appear in the play but who would have had some influence on the character's personality). A complete analysis of the character also will provide an indication of the kind and form of dialogue the character should use. Test out the dialogue on paper, putting the character into hypothetical situations with other characters. It cannot be repeated too often that dialogue is not an approximation of real life speech; dialogue must be heightened and condensed from that of real life.

After the characters have been created, you are ready to create the situation, or plot line. This should be done in skeletonized form. You need, first, a conflict. The conflict is between the protagonist of the play and some other character or force. A conflict may be between two individuals, an individual and a group, between two groups, between an individual or individuals and nature, between an individual or individuals and some unknown force, or between an individual and the inner self. The nature of the conflict will be determined largely by the kinds of characters involved. After the conflict has been decided upon, the plot moves inexorably toward a climax, the point at which one of the forces in conflict wins over the other. The play reaches the climax through a series of complications. Each complication is, in itself, a small conflict and climax. Each succeeding complication literally complicates the situation to a greater and greater degree until the final complication makes it impossible for the struggle to be heightened any longer. Something has to give. The climax must occur. The complications are not arbitrary. The characters themselves determine the events and the complications because the actions they take are those, and only those, they must take because of their particular motivations and personalities.

George Pierce Baker, in *Dramatic Technique*, has written that

". . . situation exists because one is what he is and so has inner conflict, or clashes with another person, or with his environment. Change his character a little and the situation must change. Involve more people in it, and immediately their very presence, affecting the people originally in the scene, will change the situation."[2]

British playwright Terrence Rattigan wrote similarly in an article, "The Characters Make the Play":

"A play is born — for me, at any rate — in a character, in a background or setting, in a period or in a theme, never in a plot. I believe that in the process of a play's preliminary construction during that long and difficult period of gestation before a line is put on paper, the plot is the last of the vital organs to take shape.

"If the characters are correctly fashioned — by which I do not mean accurately representing living people but correctly conceived in their relationship to each other — the play will grow out of them. A number of firmly and definitely imagined characters will act — must act — in a firm and definite way. This gives you your plot. If it does not, your characters are wrongly conceived and you must start again."[3]

Once the preliminary planning, gestation, research and analysis are completed, the writer is ready. But not for writing the play. Not yet. Next comes the scenario or detailed outline. The writer who has been conscientious up to now will learn from the scenario whether or not s/he has a potentially good play, if any play at all. Through careful construction and analysis of the scenario, the writer may eliminate the bad points and strengthen the good points of the play even before it is written.

Before writing a detailed scenario, however, the writer must have a knowledge of the concepts of dramaturgy — of the basic rules for the play regardless of whatever medium it is written for, and of the modified rules for the television and radio play, concepts determined by the special characteristics of these media.

CONCEPTS OF PLAYWRITING

Unity

One of the essentials that applies to all plays, regardless of type or style of production, is the unity of action or impression. There should be no elements within the play that do not relate in thorough and consistent fashion to all the other elements, moving toward a realization of the purpose of the playwright. Not a single extraneous element should detract from the unified totality of impression received by the audience. The so-called unities of time and of place, erroneously attributed to Aristotle, are completely flexible in modern dramaturgy.

Plot

The plot structure of a play is based on a complication arising out of the individual's or group's relationships to some other force. This is the conflict, the point when the two or more forces come into opposition. The conflict must be presented as soon as possible in the play, for the rest of the play structure follows and is built upon this element. Next come a series of complications or crises, each one creating further difficulty in relation to the major conflict, and each building in a rising crescendo so that the entire play moves toward a final crisis or climax. The climax occurs at the instant the conflicting forces meet head on and a change occurs to or in at least one of them. This is the turning point. One force wins and the other loses. The play may end at this moment. There may, however, be a final clarification of what happens, as a result of the climax, to the characters or forces involved. This remaining plot structure is called the "resolution."

The elementary plot structure of the play may be diagrammed as follows:

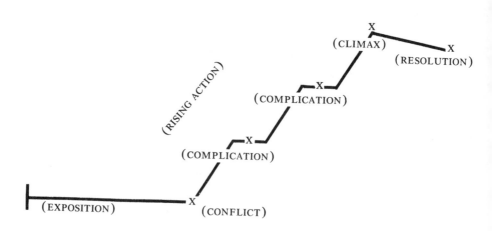

Character

Character, plot and dialogue comprise the three primary ingredients of the play. All must be completely and consistently integrated. In modern dramaturgical theory character is the prime mover of the action, and determines plot and dialogue. The character does not conform to a plot structure. The qualities of the character determine the action. The character must be revealed through the action; that is, through what the character does and says, and not through arbitrary description or exposition. Character is delineated most effectively by what the individual does at moments of crisis. This does not imply physical action alone, but includes the concept of inner or psychological action. The character must be consistent throughout the play in everything done and said, and must be plausible in terms of life and reality. This does not mean that characters are copies of real life persons; they must be dramatically heightened interpretations of reality.

Dialogue

There is some difference of opinion as to whether dialogue should be realistic or poetic. It must, however, be "dramatic." Inasmuch as the play does not duplicate real people or the exact action of real life, but heightens and condenses these elements, the dialogue also has to be heightened and condensed rather than duplicated. The dialogue must truly conform to the personality of the character speaking it, it must be completely consistent with the character and with itself throughout the play, and it must forward the situation, the showing of the character and the movement of the plot.

Exposition

Exposition, the revelation of the background of the characters and situation and the clarification of the present circumstances, must not be obvious or come through some device, such as the telephone conversation, the servant or the next-door neighbor. It must come out as the action carries the play forward and must be a natural part of the action. The exposition should be presented as early as possible in the play.

Preparation

Preparation, too, must be made subtly. Preparation, or foreshadowing, is the unobtrusive planting, through action or dialogue, of material which prepares the audience for subsequent events, making their occurrence logical and not arbitrary. Proper preparation validates subsequent actions of the characters; it is presented throughout the play.

Setting

Setting is determined by the form of the play and the physical and mechanical needs of the play structure. Setting serves as locale, background and environment for the characters of the play; it is a psychological and aesthetic presentation of the purpose of the play and of the author.

The above summary of the basic rules of dramaturgy is applicable to the writing of any play; it should serve as an introduction to the special techniques of writing the television and radio play.

THE RADIO PLAY

ALTHOUGH PLAYS HAVE ALMOST completely disappeared from radio, the occasional broadcast drama and the use of drama as a training ground for student writers warrants an overview of writing the radio play. The writer of the radio play should interrelate the basic rules of dramatugy with the special characteristics of the radio medium. First, review the basic elements and technical aspects of radio in Chapters 1 and 2.

Radio rightly has been called the "theatre of the imagination." There are absolutely no limitations except those of the human mind. The radio playwright has no restrictions on place, setting, number of characters, kinds of actions or movement of time. In radio, the writer can take the audience anywhere and make the characters do anything. The writer can create mental images of infinite variations, as long as these images are within the realm of the imagination of the listeners. The special characteristics of the radio medium, as indicated in Chapters 1 and 2, result in the following modifications of the basic rules of dramaturgy in writing the radio play.

Unity

There are no unities of time and place in radio. The radio script may take us 20,000 years into the future and in the twinkling of a sound effect transport us to an age 20,000 years in the past. Radio may present a character in a living room and in a split second place the same character (and place us, the audience, who are in the position and place of the characters who are "on mike") in his or her office in another part of town. Radio may move us from a polar ice cap to the moon to a battlefield to a jungle to the depths of Hades, creating without restriction the settings for our imaginations. Radio has no visual limitations. In writing for radio, don't restrict your own imagination by what you can "see." Radio has no physical space limitations. It can present a rally at the Washington Monument with a million people and, within seconds, a dozen similar rallies throughout the world with as many more millions.

Don't forget, however, that no matter how loose the unities of time and place, the radio play must have a unity of action; that is, it must have a consistency and wholeness of purpose and development within the script. Each sequence must be integrated thoroughly with every other sequence, all contributing to the total goal or effect you wish to create.

Plot

The plot structure of the radio play is essentially the same as that for the stage play. Exposition, a conflict, complications, a climax and, if necessary, a resolution must be set forth clearly. The radio play must have a rising action which creates suspense and holds the interest of the audience. The limitation of time modifies some of the rules concerning these elements. Exposition may be revealed as the action is progressing, with the presentation of the conflict at the every opening of the drama. The limitation of time also makes it necessary for the writer to concentrate on only one simple plot line and to avoid sub-plots.

Character

The characters in the radio play must be as valid as those in the stage play, and the rules for their creation and development apply just as fully to radio as to theatre. The time limitation of radio makes it impossible, however, to deal with the characters, even the most important ones, in depth. In much radio drama, therefore, character is not the motivating force; plot is. The writer should attempt to develop a concomitant effect of one upon the other. The characters must be consistent with themselves and appropriate with reality, although heightened from real life. It might be expected that the lack of visual perception in radio would change the revelation of a character from what s/he says and does solely to what s/he says. This is not so. Character is revealed through what the character does; the difference between radio and the stage and television is that, in radio, what s/he does is not shown visually, but the actions are presented through sound and dialogue. Because too many voices may become confusing to a radio audience, the number of roles in the play should be limited. For the same reason, the writer should limit the number of characters in any one scene.

Dialogue

Dialogue in the radio play must be consistent with itself and with the characters; it must be appropriate with the situation and the characters; and it must be dramatically heightened. Even more than on the stage or in television, dialogue in radio serves to forward the situation, reveal character and uncover the plot line. Everything on radio is conveyed through dialogue, sound effects, music or silence. The use of sound and music is more important in radio than in other media. The use of dialogue similarly is more important. Dialogue must clearly indicate all of the action taking place. Dialogue must clearly introduce the characters; presented naturally, such dialogue not only must tell who the people are, but must describe them and, if possible, tell something about them. Dialogue often may be used to describe movement and places of action, but not in an obvious manner. For example, how trite for the character to say "Now, if you'll excuse me, I'll push back this chair I'm sitting on, and go. My coat is hanging on that clothes tree right inside the front door, isn't it? I can get it. It's only a few steps from here." Or: "Now that we're in my sixth floor bachelor apartment with the etchings on the wall, the stereo speakers in the corners by the windows, the waterbed couch on the red plush carpet in the center of the room . . ."

Exposition

Exposition is difficult in radio because it must be presented solely through dialogue and sound. Because of the short time for the play, exposition should be presented as soon as possible, but preferably through the action, not through description. Inasmuch as the audience can't see the characters or the settings, the writer must clarify these elements of the play before any important action takes place. To solve this problem, radio has employed a technique used much less frequently in the other media: the narrator. The narrator can either be divorced entirely from the play or can be an integral part of it.

Preparation

Preparation functions in the radio play in the same way as in the stage play. It must be valid and it must be made subtly. Because the radio writer cannot present the preparation visually, with all the subtle nuances of the visual element, you must be certain that just because you know what the character motivations are you do not fail to let the audience know. If anything, the radio play requires an overabundance of preparation rather than too little.

Setting

Radio offers the writer limitations and advantages in the matter of setting. One drawback is that the writer cannot present a visual setting which, at one glance, can provide an environment and atmosphere for the characters. You have to do it all through dialogue and sound. On the other hand, the radio writer is limited only by the imaginative potential of the audience; you can put the audience into almost any setting you wish. Be wary of using this facility too freely, however. Do not be tempted into creating an imaginary setting that is invalid. The mental picture you create for the audience must be the right one for the play. The locale and environment must be believable for the characters and the situation, and must forward the psychological and aestheic purposes of the author.

Movement from setting to setting may be accomplished through silence, fading, narration, a music bridge or sound effects.

As indicated in Chapter 1, one of the great advantages the radio playwright has over the stage playwright is that the former can control and direct the attention of the audience much more effectively than can the latter. The radio audience cannot select the elements of the play by which it is to be stimulated; but the theatre audience can pick out any part of the action on the stage it desires. Radio facilitates a much greater subjective response, and the writer can deal with elements that strike close to the emotional needs and desires of the audience. These emotional stimuli can also be used to activate the intellectual concerns of the audience. If you use the medium correctly you can hold a tight grip on the feelings and minds of the listeners.

In creating the play for radio, keep several special technical considerations in mind. Don't skimp on sound effects or music; these elements are needed to clarify movement, setting and action. While not overdoing it, be certain that you use sound effectively and sufficiently for the purposes of the play. Be certain that the script contains the proper devices for transitions of time and place and has enough music, fulfilling all the needs indicated in Chapter 2. The exits and entrances of characters should be made clear through sound. The sound effects and music should be integrated with the action of the play, and each of these effects should be indicated clearly in relation to the specific need of the script at the precise moment the effect is used.

The play should be of a proper length for the time period, and within the play the scenes should be neither so short as to be lacking in clarity nor so long as to be repetitious and boring. Nor should individual speeches of characters be too long. In any play, character development should be revealed through action, though the soliloquy may be effective in certain kinds of plays. An examination of several of the radio verse plays of Archibald MacLeish will indicate some of the possibilities for the use of long speeches. The plot, dialogue and characters should, of course, follow effective dramaturgical form and relationships, and the exposition and preparation must be clear, sufficient and not obvious.

THE TELEVISION PLAY

Television's Special Characteristics

The television audience and some problems of censorship are analyzed in Chapter 1. Arbitrary censorship has hampered television's potentially high level of dramatic production, and the television playwright must deal with these restrictions.

The special characteristics of the television audience require a special approach on the part of the playwright. You may combine the subjective relationship of the viewer to the television screen with the electronic potentials of the medium to create a purposeful direction of the audience's attention. You may direct the audience toward the impact of the critical events in the character's life and toward the subjective manifestations of the character's existence. The ability to focus the viewer's sight, attention and even feeling so specifically permits the writer to orient the consciousness of the audience closely to the inner character of the person on the screen.

All of the above should be in your conscious consideration at the very beginning of the creative process, when you are choosing the subject and planning the basic development of the play. In the so-called Golden Age of television the slice-of-life play dominated, quantitatively and qualitatively, because the playwrights utilized to advantage, rather than fighting to their disadvantage, the small-screen, limited-time aspects of the medium. In more recent years longer time periods and film-for-TV trends have expanded settings, plots and characters, particularly in 90-minute and 2-hour specials and in some of the multi-episode series. Yet, the good TV plays, whether one-shot or in series, do continue to reflect the new principles of playwriting that marked the early years of TV drama — in depth character analyses and presentation. Even in continuing series — whether situation comedy, western or private-eye/police — the good programs stress character. In many of these, the approximately 21-minute (for the half-hour show) and the 42-minute (for the hour program) script reflect the same time restraints for any given happening in the continuing characters' lives as did the early half-hour TV dramas. Time and space limitations, the censorship of controversial material and the ability of the medium to control and direct the audience's objective and subjective attention still make the intimate, probing, searching slice-of-life play the logical candidate for television success.

The direct relationship of the television performer to the audience suggests a further kind of orientation: a presentational approach which is possible at the same time as the illusionistic, and which permits an exciting combination of intellectual and emotional stimulation for the audience.

Chapter 2 points out how the writer should develop the script in terms of TV's technical potentials and incorporate these potentials within the action of the play. Perhaps the most important contribution of the mechanical and electronic devices of television is to enable the writer to direct the audience toward the intimate, toward an examination of the inner character in a manner not possible on the stage or in radio. The ability of television to capture significant details through the camera implies a greater concentration on the visual than on the verbal elements (the latter, of course, dominate the stage and radio play). Indeed, television's most effective means for capturing the intimacy of its presentation is the close-up, which permits physical action to substitute for what sometimes would have to be done through dialogue or sound on the stage or in radio.

The Hollywood-style taped or filmed TV play permits a great expansion of action over the stage play and can include a greater number of transitions. Television is not bound by the conventions of the theatre. Through cuts, dissolves, fades and other electronic devices there are no restrictions of time and place. Television does not need a curtain or blackout convention, but can signify a change of time or place with an effect lasting only a second or two. Other techniques, such as the split screen, the wipe and the superimposition, also permit excellent fluidity. Even in situations where a play is a one-shot live presentation — as in some of the smaller commercial and public television stations — the incorporation of film, tape and electronic effects permit fluid, flexible drama.

Time and space are two more special characteristics of the television medium which the writer must understand and apply. One of the most important problems of all for the television playwright is that of time. The hour drama is really only about 42 minutes long, the half-hour drama 21 minutes in length. Even the hour-and-one-half dramatic program permits only about 63 minutes for the play. The television play should be extremely tight; it should have no irrelevancies. It should have as few characters as possible, and one main, simplified plot line, containing only material relating to the conflict of the major character or characters.

These limitations often result in characters who are stereotyped figures with little richness of human personality. The writer sometimes may concentrate on plot at the expense of character, or stress character without including any valid action. Neither approach makes for good playwriting.

Space limitations are of two major kinds in television. First is the physical size of the room within the studio in live-type TV drama. Second is the decreasing smallness of the objects in a picture picked up by an increasing camera distance, and viewed over the narrow and constricting viewing area of the relatively small television screen.

The limitation of space suggests two major considerations for the writer: the number of characters on a screen at any one time, and the number and scope of sets. In order to avoid a situation where the small television screen is choked with a mass of humanity, the writer must be sure that only a few characters are on camera at the same time. Stage convention permits ten people to represent a crowd. Except in the film-for-TV play, ten people on television (in sitcoms, for example) likely would appear too small individually and too jumbled as a group.

The limited number of sets and the limited size of a given set imply the need for short scenes. The actors cannot move around enough to warrant long scenes because long scenes require movement to break the monotony. Although smaller sets may be necessary, the fluidity possible through television's electronic devices and through taping and editing permits frequent change from set to set and easy re-use of sets.

The space limitations and the time limitations combine to indicate an effective approach for the television play: an intimate probing of a short span of the subjective life of the character. This approach is reflected in the following analysis of the special dramaturgical concepts for the television play.

Dramaturgical Concepts for Television

Unity. The most important changes in the unities as applied to television relate to time and place. Television can transcend boundaries of time and place that even the most fluid stage presentation cannot match. In representational theatre a scene cannot be changed every other minute; television can present many realistic settings in relatively few minutes or even seconds. In the theatre, the movements of time and place often are aural as well as visual; television transitions are more visual because of the utilization of mechanical and electronic techniques. Film and tape permit a wider scope of time and place in television than can be achieved in even the most flexible theatre form. Television has been able to achieve what August Strindberg hoped for in the theatre: a situation where "anything may happen: everything is possible and probable." Strindberg looked for dramatic presentation where "time and space do not exist," where "imagination spins and weaves new patterns: a mixture of memories, experience, unfettered fancies, absurdities and improvisations."[4] In television one not only can change setting and change time as on the stage, but also can change time without changing setting and change setting without changing time — and do so much more quickly and easily. The unities of time and place are completely loose and fluid in television.

The unity of action or impression is as vital to the television play as to any other form of drama, and the television writer should be certain that this most important unity is present.

Plot. The dramaturgical rules relating to plot apply to the television play as to the stage play. The problem of time, however, necessitates a much tighter plot line in the television play, and a condensation of the movement from sequence to sequence. The short television script should be oriented around a single action and should concentrate on a single, simplified plot. The art of drama is selective. In brief minutes we must present what life may have played out in days or years or centuries. Life is unemphatic, while drama must be emphatic. The short time for the television play requires the plot to be the essence of reality, to contain only the heightened extremities of life. Aim for the short, terse scene.

Although the emphasis on plot, because of the time factor, seems to make this the motivating factor in the television play, the exploration of television's intimacy and subjectivity potentials enables the writer to delve into character and to use it as a plot-motivating element.

The problem of space also has a direct effect on plot construction for live-type studio productions. As noted earlier, performers cannot move around enough to warrant long scenes which often require movement to break the monotony, and you should make the scenes short.

In condensing the play structure to conform to the time and space requirements, consider several of the approaches presented by George Pierce Baker in *Dramatic Technique*. First, the dramatist may "bring together at one place what really happened at the same time, but to other people in another place." Second, episodes happening to a person in the same setting, but at different times may be brought together. Third, events that have "happened to two people in the same place, but at different times may . . . be made to happen to one person." Finally, "what happened to another person at another time, and at another place may at times be arranged so that it will happen to any desired figure." Baker concludes: "The essential point in all this compacting is: when cumbered with more scenes than you wish to use, determine first which scenes contain indispensable action, and must be kept as settings; then consider which of the other scenes may by ingenuity be combined with them."[5]

The dramaturgical rules relating to conflict also are modified in the television play. Because of the shorter running time, the conflict must come much sooner than in the stage play. The television play may open immediately with the conflict, with the exposition cut virtually to nothing. The point of attack in the television play should come quickly and should bring with it the first important moment of pressure. The television play cannot show that pressure slowly develop, as can the stage play; therefore, the writer should include the basic expository elements, if possible, in this moment of conflict. Tell who the people are, show where they are, place the time of the story, and reveal what actions or events have caused the conflict.

The kind of conflict in the television play differs from that in the stage play. On the stage almost any conflict may be successful. Because of the intimacy and subjectivity of television, the conflict between individuals usually is more effective than are those between people and nature or between groups or between any large bodies or forces.

The use of complications in the television play follows their use in the stage play. Although television's time limitation permits fewer complications, include a sufficient number to validate and build the actions of the major characters. Each complication should move the characters and the action closer to the climax. The final complication should be the crisis, and should reach a valid and inescapable climax which is the result of the conflict reaching its peak.

The modern playwright, influenced by the plays of ideas and in recent years by the Brechtian epic drama, has put less and less emphasis on the resolution. Television often dispenses with the resolution entirely, unless some doubt remains about the moral principle involved. Indeed, time frequently does not permit the inclusion of a resolution. Sometimes the resolution can be incorporated as a part of the climax.

Character. The character in the play is not the person one sees in life. The playwright cannot validate the actions of the character by saying "but that's what they did in real life." Drama is heightened life. The playwright reveals the character by showing the character's actions in moments of crisis. The television writer should be especially attentive to this. Not only concentrate on the action that strikingly reveals the individual character, but concentrate as well on the few characters whose actions strikingly reveal the purpose of the play. Do not use unneeded people. A character who does not contribute to the main conflict and to the unified plot line does not belong in the play. If a character is essential, put it in the script. If there are too many essential characters, then rethink the entire approach to the play.

The presentation of depth, of the intimate, inner character, is one of the advantages of television. Mechanical and electronic devices permit physical and psychological closeness and empathy that are not possible in the theatre. The television writer can direct the audience's attention to the details relating to the inner character; the television camera can focus the audience's eye on the elements which most effectively project the character's feelings. The scope of the camera and the size of the viewing screen do not permit a breadth in which many characters can be dealt with at the same time with equal and effective attention. Concentrate on the individual as protagonist. With a minimum of motivating exposition and clarifying background, because of the lack of time, the development of satisfactory characterizations for more than one or two persons is sometimes difficult. Select depth-delineating elements with care. Good visual action through script directions and effective camera work can often present exposition which, on the stage, would have to be explained verbally.

Although plot is the motivating factor in most television plays today, writers of quality plays understand more and more that the relationships among characters are the basic factors in drama: byplay between character and plot, with character determining incident and vice versa. The concentration on the subjective and the intimate, while applying the basic dramaturgical rules for television, leads to the emergence of character as the motivating force in the well-written television play.

Dialogue. The principles of dialogue for the television play are the same as for the stage play. The dialogue must forward the situation; it must be consistent with the characters, the situation and with itself; it must be dramatic and heightened in comparison with the dialogue of real life.

Television requires one significant modification in the use of dialogue to forward the situation and to provide exposition. The visual element can often substitute for the aural. If you can show the situation or present the expository information through action instead of through dialogue, do so. The long shot as well as the closeup has made it possible to eliminate time-consuming dialogue in which the character describes things or places. You can concentrate not only on action but on "reaction," keeping the dialogue at a minimum and the picture the primary object of attention. Anything that can be shown on television through a close-up should not be described, as it might have to be on the stage. Be careful, however, not to go too far in substituting visual action for dialogue. Pantomime and the closeup should be used cautiously and only when they are the most effective ways of presenting the material. On the intimate screen they can become awkward and melodramatic.

The condensing and heightening of real-life dialogue is of great importance in television. Television dialogue should avoid repetition; it should condense the ideas presented; it should be character-delineating; it should be written so that the purpose of every exchange of speeches is clear to the audience and so that the sequence carries the plot line forward; it should contain the necessary exposition and background for the characters even while presenting the continuing action of the play.

Exposition. The short time allotted to the television play permits only a minimum of exposition. It is difficult to present sufficient background material necessary to characterization and to present exposition subtly or as a natural part of the action because of insufficient time for a slow unfolding of the situation. Because the conflict should be presented almost as soon as the television drama begins, the exposition must be highly condensed and presented with all possible speed. The problem here is that although film and theatre audiences generally have some foreknowledge of the drama they are about to watch, the television audience often has no preparation for what it is going to see. The reverse is true, however, in the continuing TV series, where a large part of the audience already knows the setting, the characters and the background, requiring exposition only for the particular plot of the particular program.

Preparation. The principles of preparation apply equally to the television play as to the stage play. The writer should prepare the audience in a subtle and gradual manner for the subsequent actions of the characters and the events of the play. Nothing should come as a complete surprise. The audience should be able to look back, after something has taken place, and know that the action was inevitable because of the personality of the character who performed the action or because all of the circumstances leading to the event made it unavoidable.

Setting. There are many physical kinds of dramatic settings in theatre: the Greek open stage, the Italian spectacle and painted backdrop, the cluttered stage of the naturalistic play, the use of light and shadow in expressionistic staging, and the Appia-influenced plasticity of modern production. But the physical areas of the television set are different from those of the stage. Television drama essentially conforms to the play of selective realism in content and purpose, and realistic settings usually are required. Both the limitations and the potentials of television have combined to modify the realistic setting, however. First, the live-type TV setting usually must be smaller than the writer might wish it to be. Second, live-type TV drama makes it difficult to have very many exteriors or large nature effects. On the other hand, the fluidity of television through film and tape makes up for these restrictions by permitting a greater number of changes of setting and a considerable broadening of setting, with frequent changes of time and place.

Be certain that all of your scenes, background and set descriptions are carefully integrated with the forward action of the drama and that they serve as valid and delineating locales, environment and atmosphere for the characters and for the plot.

PLAY STRUCTURE: APPLICATION

PUTTING TOGETHER all of the principles thus far discussed into a complete whole is both the first and the last task of the playwright. It is the be-all and end-all. In between are the techniques, the restrictions, the orientations, the media requirements — all of the things that make that particular play fit exactly the format of the program for which it is intended. But, in the final analysis, it is still the basic play that counts.

The Scenario

It is called the scenario, the treatment, the outline, the summary. What it does is give the producer and/or script editor a narrative idea of what the play is about: the plot line, the characters, the setting and maybe even bits of dialogue. Most producers/editors can tell from this narrative whether the play fits the needs of the particular program. The scenario and treatment are usually longer than the outline and summary, perhaps as much as a fifth of the entire script (i.e. 10 pages for a 50-page script). The summary and the outline may be only two or three pages, in effect providing a preliminary judgment prior to a preliminary judgment. Some producers/editors want to see a summary or outline first, then a scenario or treatment and, finally, the complete script. With some submissions, you are asked to include all three at the same time. The scenario/treatment not only helps the prospective buyer, but also can be of immeasurable help to the writer. As a detailed outline, it can tell you whether or not you've got a good play. Careful construction and analysis of the scenario can help you eliminate weak places and strengthen the good points. The scenario not only provides you with a continuous series of way-stations in your construction of the play, but by using it as check-points you can save exhausting work and valuable time by catching problems before they are written in and you have to do complete rewrites to get them out.

As already noted, the scenario or treatment you submit to the producer/editor is generally narrative in form. The scenario that you develop to help you construct the play may be more complex. It should contain, first, the purpose of the play, its theme, background, characters, basic plot line and type of dialogue. You should include case histories for all of your characters. Prepare plot summaries for each projected scene in chronological order. Note the elements of exposition and preparation. As you develop the plot sequences, insert important or, at least, representative lines of dialogue. The result of this kind of scenario, even in its simplest form, will be at the very least a clarification of all of the structural elements of the play.

Dramaturgical Analysis

Following the first working scenario and as many subsequent scenarios as necessary to make your preparation as complete as possible, you'll arrive at the point where you feel ready and confident to flesh out the play. This is where the pleasure of accomplishment comes in. For most playwrights, this is the fun part of writing. If you've planned well, the play will virtually write itself. If you find that some radical departures are needed from the scenario, then your preparation was not as good as it could or should have been. Go back to the scenario and shore it up, even if you have to start all over. Otherwise you will find that though you may complete most or all of the first draft of the play, you'll need many more extra drafts to repair all the holes, in the long run requiring much more time and effort than you would have needed with proper scenario preparation.

The following working scenario is one example of how one writer develops and checks the script. Two columns are used. The one on the left is the detailed outline — that is, an action summary. (It is this action summary that could serve, incidentally, as the narrative scenario or treatment for submission to a producer/editor.) On the right is a functional analysis. The play, "With Wings As Eagles," was originally written for live, New York-type television production and is simple in format, transitions and settings. Because of space this scenario is condensed; it could contain more precise analysis of character, additional dialogue and more plot detail. Following the scenario and functional analysis is the first act of the play itself, so you may note how the writer filled out the structure.

> • *Analyze the first act of the script in terms of the principles of dramaturgy for the New York-type television play. Match the scenario and functional analysis with their realization in the script and determine whether the playwright achieved what was intended. This script was written for live production, much like the play you might write in a college TV writing class for production by the directing class.*

WITH WINGS AS EAGLES

Action Summary	Functional Analysis
	(1)
The time is the early 1960s. The setting is a Jewish ghetto in an unnamed Near East country. The camera opens on a muddy village street and pans one wood and mud-baked hut to another. A Narrator sets the time and place, describing the poverty of the inhabitants, and how their history shows that though they live in hunger, sickness and oppression, they will find the promised land.(1) The Narrator mentions that few have ever seen an automobile and few would believe that such a thing as an airplane exists.(2) He stresses that in all their ignorance and poverty the people have hope of going to the promised land.(3)	Exposition: the place, time, situation, the background and needs of the people. (How effective is this semi-documentary approach to exposition, coming through a narrator as well as through visual action?)
	(2)
	Preparation: for their eventual departure for Israel and for the climax involving the airplane flight.
	(3)
	Preparation for the conflict: the stress on the hope of going to a promised land subtly suggests the conflict: will they or will they not be able to go?
	(4)
Reb Simcha goes from house to house, calling the people to a meeting. He does so stealthily, undercover.(4)	Exposition: shows the kind of existence of the people: fear, oppression.
	(5)
At one house, that of Simon and his son, Aaron, Reb Simcha encounters opposition to the meeting. At Aaron's insistence Simon finally agrees to go. We see that Simon's house is well-furnished, unlike the others.(5)	Preparation: for Simon's opposition, and for Aaron's opposition to his father.
	(5)
	Exposition: shows another aspect of the village life; someone in comparatively good circumstances.

We follow Simcha to his own house. The house is fixed up as a small synagogue. He prays: "Please, God. This time, make men's words truth."(6)

(6)
Conflict: Without a clear statement yet, we learn something may be in opposition with something else. This is preparation for the revelation of the conflict.

(6)
Exposition: Reb Simcha's environment and profession.

His daughter, Leah, enters. Reb Simcha complains about his tired feet.(7)

(7)
Preparation: The tired feet play a humorous part throughout and are particularly important for comic pathos at the end of the play.

Leah says she saw some of the people, and that Aaron saw the rest, and that all are coming.(8)

(8)
Preparation and complication: We are prepared for Aaron's break with his father through the revelation that he is working on Reb Simcha's side. We are prepared for the relationship between Leah and Aaron in that they are working together. This preparation ties in with the later complications: Aaron vs. his father; Aaron's and Leah's love.

Leah sees her father is worried and gets him to tell what it is. He says he hopes the words he heard from the government representative are true. His people are supposed to leave for the promised land the next morning; but from an open field and without belongings.(9)

(9)
Conflict: It is made clear here. The people are supposed to go to the promised land. The doubts set up the conflict: the people against the government powers. Will they or will they not reach the promised land?

This worries him. He does not know how they will go, from an open field. "How do we go?" he asks. "We fly, maybe, like a bird?"(10)

(10)
Preparation: Again, the reference to flying, preparing the audience for the climax.

He doubts that his people will believe him and be ready, and if they are not ready they will not be able to leave again. He doubts, himself, for such promises have been broken for centuries.(11)

(11)
Preparation for complication: the dissension among the people themselves, which might prevent them from achieving their goal, is foreshadowed here.

(6-11)
In the revelation of Leah's and Reb Simcha's actions, we get their characterizations.

Aaron comes for Leah. Leah and Reb Simcha talk about her intended marriage to Aaron. Leah is worried because his father, Simon, is friendly with the authorities and

(12)
Preparation for complication: Will Simon stop Aaron and Leah: will this result in a delay or complete betrayal of all of the people?

makes money as the official merchant in the ghetto and may not want to leave. He may prevent Aaron from leaving. Reb Simcha tells Leah that when they go to the promised land, she and Aaron will go hand in hand.(12)

The next scene, in the Police-Military office in the town. Dr. Ezam, the diplomat, arranges with the Lieutenant in charge for transportation and clearance. The Lieutenant does not want the people to go because they are helpful to the town. "They stay in their place," he says. They work for the town's businessmen at low wages.(13)

Dr. Ezam insists that they be permitted to leave, citing a United Nations ruling. The Lieutenant says he will agree to that, but if they are not ready and at the open field on time, he will not let them leave. He says a lot of people in the town would not like them to go. He intimates that they may not leave, anyway. They verbally fence with the political, moral and practical considerations.(14)

The next sequence is in Simon and Aaron's house, where Simon and Aaron argue. Aaron is disturbed because his father cooperates with the authorities. Simon explains that he must do it to live well and to keep his promise to Aaron's dead mother that he would provide for him. Simon doesn't want to go to the meeting, fearing trouble from the authorities. Simon also wants his son not to see Leah again. They argue bitterly, and Simon decides to go to the meeting to stop Reb Simcha's foolish plans.(15)

(12)
Exposition: Simon's background and profession is revealed more clearly.

(12)
Reb Simcha's need to assure Leah prepares the audience for trouble in this respect.

(13)
Exposition: We see the attitude of the officials toward these people and the people's place in the community.

(13)
Preparation: We are prepared for the attempt of the town to keep them from going; the motivation: cheap labor.

(14)
Preparation for complication: It is clear that the Lieutenant will try to stop the departure.

(13-14)
The discussion and action reveal character.

(15)
Complication: The conflict is complicated by Simon's avowal to stop the proposed exodus, to fight Reb Simcha. It is further complicated by the avowed intention to step between Leah and Aaron. The rising action, moving toward an inevitable clash, is apparent.

(15)
Exposition: We have further understanding about Simon and Aaron's background and motivations.

(15)
Preparation: Simon's reasons for what he does are understandable, if not acceptable, and we see he is not a one-dimensional tyrant, thus preparing the audience for his actions at the end of the play.

(15)
The sequence is character-delineating.

The next sequence is in the Lieutenant's office. The Lieutenant makes plans with one of the town's merchants, Rasin, to stop the departure. They decide to detain one of the villagers. "They're a thick people. If one were detained they wouldn't leave without . him." Because of Dr. Ezam, they look for legal grounds for detention, such as one of the villagers "leaving" the ghetto without permission.(16)

(16)
    Complication: Another block in the way of the people's exodus, thus heightening the conflict.

(16)
    Preparation: We learn what the probable trick will be for detention and for stopping the departure.

WITH WINGS AS EAGLES

ACT 1

Open FS Map of Middle East

NARRATOR (VOICE OVER)

This is a map of the Middle East: Egypt, Syria, Iraq, Jordan, Israel. Of Arabs and Jews. Of cities and deserts, of camels and motor cars, of hopes and fears, but mostly

Pan across map, picking no special spot, dolly in, dissolve to a miniature of a small city, several new white buildings and off, at one side, a dingy, dirty-looking section, with mud huts and shacks.

of people. This is the city of Mabbam. In what country? It doesn't matter. Like in many other of these towns outside of Israel there are small Jewish populations. Hebrew might be a better term, for these people are the direct descendents of Isaiah and Abraham, those who were led by Moses through the wilderness to the promised land, who fell by the waysides. The way-sides grew into sections and streets . . .

Dolly in closer to the miniature of the town, showing the street of the mud huts and shacks.

. . . like that one. Aviv Street, it's called. Aviv means hope. That is about all they have, these Hebrews — hope. There is no special industry, no principal occupation — unless one can call hunger, fear, sickness and poverty occupations.

Pan down street, show dirt streets, wood and mud-baked huts.

It is not easy for the Hebrew these days. The new state of Israel has been steadily growing and the other countries hold no love for these people whose kinsmen they have fought and continue to fight. The Hebrews are beaten, jailed and starved. Everything the centuries have visited upon their brethren has not stopped because they are suddenly thrust into the middle of the 20th century. And that is an odd thing, too, for although the calendar of the western world reads in the 1960's, the environment of these people is that of centuries before.

NARRATOR (OVER — CONT.)

No newspapers, no movies, no automobiles.
Few have ever even seen an automobile.
And as for airplanes, why none in this out-
village of Mabbam would believe you if you
told them that such a thing exists. But
whatever else may be lacking, they have a
rich heritage of spiritual inspiration. They
have a Rabbi. They have hope — the hope
of the promised land. Poverty . . . hope . . .
. . . fear . . .

Dissolve to live set. CU of a fist knocking
on a door. The door opens revealing a
small, cluttered room. Several small
children cower in the back. Hannah, a
woman of about 40, but looking tired and
worn and much older, in tattered clothing,
is at the door.

VOICE (OF KNOCKER, REB SIMCHA)

(Reb Simcha is not yet on camera.) Half-
an-hour after sundown. Tonight. At my
house. (THE DOOR CLOSES.)

CU feet moving along the dirt street. CU
fist knocking again. Door opens. A man,
Schloem, the street-washer, old and
wizened, stands in back of the door.
Esther, his wife, stands in back of him.
They are both in their late sixties.

VOICE (REB SIMCHA; OFF-CAMERA)

Half-an-hour after sundown. At my house.
Tonight. (SCHLOEM CLOSES THE DOOR
FURTIVELY.)

CU feet moving again. This time they
reach a small concrete patch in the street.
The fist knocks on a door, ignoring the
knocker there. The door is opened by a
good looking young man of about 25. This
is Aaron.

VOICE (REB SIMCHA; OFF-CAMERA)

Your father? You haven't told him?

AARON

No. A moment, please.

(AARON RETURNS A MOMENT LATER
WITH A LARGE, PORTLY MAN OF ABOUT
FIFTY. THIS IS SIMON, HIS FATHER, THE

MERCHANT OF THE GHETTO. THE
INSIDE OF THE HOUSE CAN BE SEEN.
THERE IS SOME FURNITURE, INCLUDING
A BED WITH A BEDSPREAD, TWO COM-
FORTABLE CHAIRS, A TABLE WITH A
CANDELABRA. IT IS POOR, BUT,
WEALTHY IN COMPARISON WITH THE
HOMES OF HANNAH, THE WIDOW, AND
SCHLOEM, THE STREET-WASHER. SIMON
IS DRESSED IN A SUIT, NOT IN RAGS
LIKE THE OTHERS.)

                    SIMON

What? What do you want?

            VOICE (REB SIMCHA; OFF-CAMERA)

Tonight. At my house. At a half . . .

                    SIMON (INTERRUPTING)

Again? More trouble-making?

                    VOICE

It is important.

                    SIMON

Always it is important. And always it causes
trouble. I've no time. I have to see about
some goods.

                    AARON

We should go, father.

                    VOICE

(INSISTENT.) It is most important.

                    SIMON

Well . . . all right.

                    VOICE

Half-an-hour after sundown.

                    SIMON

(ANGRILY) All right! (HE SLAMS THE
DOOR.)

CU feet again, walking down the street.
They stop in front of a door. This time the
fist doesn't knock, but the hand opens the
door, instead. The feet go in, past two
humble cots, an old table and two rickety

chairs, to a corner of the room where a
shelf is seen, with several old and tattered
books, two brass candlesticks. In the
wall there is a recession, the "Ark," in
which is seen a rolled up scroll. This is
the "Torah." CU of the Torah as a face
bends toward it and kisses it. Dolly out
and see, finally, the person of the feet and
the voice. It is Rabbi Simcha, a man of
about 50, dressed in a black gown, wearing
a "yarmulka," the black skullcap. He is
bearded, a gentle face, worn, but with
eyes bright with hope.

REB SIMCHA

Please, God. This time, make men's words
truth. (HE BEGINS TO PACE BACK AND
FORTH ACROSS THE SMALL ROOM. THE
FRONT DOOR SLOWLY OPENS. A
PRETTY YOUNG GIRL, ABOUT 23, A
SOFT FACE AND LARGE EYES, HER HAIR
LONG BEHIND HER BACK, COMES IN.
SHE IS UNHEARD BY THE RABBI. SHE
WATCHES HIM A MOMENT. THIS IS HIS
DAUGHTER, LEAH.)

LEAH

Father, your feet will wear off before the
floor will.

REB SIMCHA

(COMING OUT OF DEEP THOUGHT) Oh,
Leah! (HE LAUGHS, LOOKS AT HIS
FEET.) Oh, of course. The head sometimes
pays not enough attention to the feet. (SITS
DOWN ON ONE OF THE COTS, RUBS HIS
FEET.) They hurt. These feet will be the
death of me yet. (AFTER A MOMENT) Did
you tell them, Leah? About tonight?

LEAH

Those I was supposed to. Aaron saw the
rest.

REB SIMCHA

They're coming?

LEAH

Yes.

REB SIMCHA

Good. (HOLDS HIS HEAD IN HIS HANDS,
AGAIN IN WORRIED THOUGHT.)

LEAH

(SITS DOWN NEXT TO HIM.) You can tell me, father.

REB SIMCHA

(SMILING) Tell? There is nothing to tell.

LEAH

Mother used to say — may she rest in peace — "When your father says he has nothing to tell, it is a sure sign he is bursting to talk."

REB SIMCHA

(FONDLES HER FACE, WISTFULLY) You are like your mother. (AFTER A MOMENT) I am worried.

LEAH

About the meeting?

REB SIMCHA

About the meeting, about the authorities, about our people, about whether what my ears heard today was really true or just another one of their stories.

LEAH

But you said it was a government official, a diplomat in a dark suit and bright shoes who told you.

REB SIMCHA

And since when is it that diplomats don't lie?

LEAH

Do you remember exactly what he said?

REB SIMCHA

He said "Be at the field in the north of the city with all of your people and without belongings at nine o'clock tomorrow morning. If you are there, you will go to the 'promised land.' If you are not, you will not go." That's all he said. Not one word more.

LEAH

Somehow I don't feel it's a lie. Not this time.

REB SIMCHA

Last time, you said not last time. Next time, you'll say not next time. But how do we go, if we go? We fly, maybe, like a bird? And with no belongings. Perhaps . . . they want to loot the few pitiful things left in the ghetto?

LEAH

Perhaps?

REB SIMCHA

Leah, will our people believe me this time? Will they take the chance and come to the field? If we're not there, we won't go, he said.

LEAH

Aaron thinks they'll come. I think so.

REB SIMCHA

So long now I have been promising the people. Soon you will go to the promised land, I tell them. Days? Years! Centuries! Every day it is the same. Naaman, the carpenter, comes to me and asks, 'Reb Simcha, when is it? Today? Tomorrow?' I smile and say, 'not today, maybe tomorrow.' Schloem, the street-washer, says 'tell me when it is, Reb. Today?' And his eyes shine for a moment and I answer 'maybe tomorrow' and he is sad again. For how long now this has gone on. Why should they believe me now, just because a diplomat has told me 'tomorrow'? I begin to doubt. Is there a tomorrow?

LEAH

Don't doubt yourself. You can't take them on a magic carpet. You can only give them faith and lead them.

REB SIMCHA

Faith! Words from a book. I should find a magic carpet for them. (GETS UP, GOES TO THE DOOR, LOOKS OUT.) A ghetto: mud, dirt, barefoot people. (TURNS BACK) What if they ask me how do we go? What do I tell them? On the wings of an eagle, like Isaiah prophesied? Or do we walk for forty years, like Moses? We have walked and wandered enough, they will tell me.

LEAH

The authorities did bring us here from the desert to get ready for the promised land.

REB SIMCHA

For cheap labor they brought us here. To use our shoemakers and carpenters. How long now? Two — three years.

LEAH

We must keep hoping and trying. Fifty-four are left, father. Of all those from the desert, only fifty-four left.

REB SIMCHA

So, I ask you, why should we believe the authorities now?

LEAH

We have no choice.

REB SIMCHA

Simon has a choice. He will try to convince the others not to go.

LEAH

Aaron will try to make him understand.

REB SIMCHA

And how could we go, Leah. Do we walk? Do we ride a camel? They will not give us camels. What other way is there? One of the machines with wheels that spit poison? I have seen some of their automobiles in the city. How many can there be in the whole world? Not enough for us, at any rate. Besides, the people are afraid of them.

LEAH

If we stand together and have faith, we will find a way.

REB SIMCHA

(SLOWLY LOOKS UP, SMILES) My daughter is wiser than her father. I can read from the Holy Book, so they say I am wise. (SHAKES HIS HEAD) Wisdom comes from here (POINTING to HIS HEAD) and here (POINTING TO HIS HEART).

(GETTING UP) I feel better.

(LEAH GOES TO THE DOOR, LOOKS OUT, COMES BACK)

REB SIMCHA

Is there someone?

LEAH

I hoped.

REB SIMCHA

Aaron?

(LEAH NODS HER HEAD)

REB SIMCHA

A good boy. An honest boy.

LEAH

You don't mind my seeing him so often?

REB SIMCHA

Should I mind?

LEAH

Some of the people say a girl should not see a young man until they know they are to be married.

REB SIMCHA

So? There is something wrong in seeing a young man? Your mother used to see a young man. (POINTING WITH PRIDE TO HIMSELF) Me! (AFTER A MOMENT) But Aaron's father, that's another matter.

LEAH

You think he'll try to stop the people from going tomorrow?

REB SIMCHA

Simon has worldly goods here. He's friendly with the authorities. They let him do all the selling in the ghetto. About Simon I don't know. But when we go to the promised land, you and Aaron will go hand in hand.

SLOW DISSOLVE TO POLICE-MILITARY

OFFICE OF MABBAM. The Lieutenant, dressed in a military uniform, about 35, hard-looking, authoritative, is seated at his desk, going over some papers. Standing in front of the desk is the diplomat, Dr. Ezam, about 50, dressed well, immaculately. He is distinguished-looking, with a gentle, yet determined manner.

DR. EZAM

They'll go, Lieutenant. They'll all go.

LIEUTENANT

It's your idea, Dr. Ezam, not mine. A lot of people in this town don't like the idea of you people coming from the government and changing the way we do things here.

DR. EZAM

Perhaps. But this is an official agreement made with Israel through the United Nations. And the Americans are providing the transportation.

LIEUTENANT

There are people in this town who do all right by these Hebrews. They stay in their place. They work for us when we want them. It saves us money, and they don't need so much to live on. You know the way they live.

DR. EZAM

I have heard that there have been many deaths in the ghetto here.

LIEUTENANT

(STARTING TO SAY SOMETHING, THEN IGNORING THE LAST REMARK) All right. You gave me the orders. (NODS TO THE OFFICIAL PAPERS) I'll grant them free passage to the field at the north of town at nine in the morning. But I don't approve of this whole idea.

DR. EZAM

Approving is not your job, Lieutenant.

LIEUTENANT

I will do my job, Dr. Ezam. But if they're not ready, then they don't go. They stay in the ghetto. The orders say tomorrow at nine and nothing else.

DR. EZAM

It's been a long time they've been searching for the promised land. They'll be ready.

LIEUTENANT

You almost seem to feel sorry for them.

DR. EZAM

Sorry? No. A little envious, perhaps.

LIEUTENANT

Envious? Of Jews?

DR. EZAM

Why are you so bitter against Jews, Lieutenant?

LIEUTENANT

Why? Well, because . . . well . . . because . . . they're Jews!

DR. EZAM

It must be a good feeling for them, Lieutenant, to be living the fulfillment of a prophecy. Think for a moment. For five thousand years there has been prophecy, expectation and hope. The greatest thing, you feel, that history has to offer mankind. Then, suddenly, in your lifetime, in your generation, in your year, your minute, it happens, and you are part of it.

LIEUTENANT

You don't have to preach to me.

DR. EZAM

(QUIETLY) I didn't intend to. You are an officer. Your job is duty. I am a diplomat. My job is understanding.

LIEUTENANT

If I had my way, we military would be the diplomats, too. Diplomats! Talk, talk, talk! Sometimes I wonder whether you ever accomplish anything.

DR. EZAM

So do I. But, then, when I look back, I

know. Civilization lives by talk. It dies by force.

LIEUTENANT

Well, I suppose we both have a job to do.

DR. EZAM

(HALF TO HIMSELF) And I wonder where the balance lies . . .

LIEUTENANT

(SIGNING AND STAMPING SOME PAPERS) Hmmm?

DR. EZAM

Nothing.

LIEUTENANT

Here are your papers. Clearance for them. I tell you again, Dr. Ezam. They're scheduled for nine in the morning. If they're not ready they don't go. That's my duty. A lot of people in this town would like to keep them here.

DR. EZAM

That's the second time you've said that, Lieutenant. Why?

LIEUTENANT

No matter.

DR. EZAM

(AUTHORITATIVELY) Why?

LIEUTENANT

(SMILING, CONFIDENT) Some of those Jews know when to be good Jews. There are some . . . who like it here.

DR. EZAM

I've told their Rabbi. He'll have them ready.

LIEUTENANT

The Rabbi's a troublemaker. They know it. They're poor people, with no education, your Jews. A wrong word here, a wrong word there . . . well, we'll see.

DR. EZAM

I think they'll be ready. It's their only chance.

LIEUTENANT

(STILL SMILING) We'll see . . . you don't know those Jews! You don't know that ghetto!

DISSOLVE TO SIMON'S HOUSE. SIMON AND AARON ARE ARGUING.

AARON

You don't know this ghetto, father. You sell them goods, you take their money. But you don't know them.

SIMON

I know them well enough, Aaron, my son, to know they're not so stupid as to keep following that Reb Simcha. Another meeting. For what? To pray? To tell stories? To cry about how bad things are? To make more promises about a promised land?!

AARON

It gives them hope. It gives me hope.

SIMON

A false hope. He promises, so they depend on him. I have the goods. It's me they should depend on.

AARON

(PLACATING) They need your goods.

SIMON

They need his promises more, it seems. (MUSING) If it weren't for him, I could control them all, work closer with the authorities and really be wealthy.

AARON

Wealth, goods, money. I am ashamed for my father. Simon, the merchant, seems to have no concern for people, only wealth.

SIMON

I have concern for you, Aaron, my son.

AARON

Not for my feelings. Not for my thoughts.
If you did you would help our people, not
live off them.

SIMON

For you, Aaron. I do it for you. (AFTER
A MOMENT, QUICKLY, BUT STRONGLY)
I promised myself that what happened to
your mother will not happen to you. When
there is hunger, you will eat. When
authorities want tribute, you will have
enough to buy your life. (SADLY AND
SOFTLY) They took your mother because
I was too poor to pay tribute. Thin and
weak and hungry, they took her as a
work-slave because I did not have enough
money. I fought them. And two months
later they let me come out from jail to
get her body and bury her. (SHOUTING)
Because I did not have enough money for
tribute! No more! No more! Not in my
lifetime! Not to my child!

AARON

If our people stand together, they could
not hurt us.

SIMON

Did our people stand with me? Did our
people stop the authorities from taking
your mother? You can't fight the
authorities, my son. You can only buy
them or cooperate with them. (AFTER A
MOMENT) I'd do well to stay away from
this meeting.

AARON

This one is important. You have to go.

SIMON

Important? Have to go? You know more
about it than you let on.

AARON

I know that it's important.

SIMON

You have a hand in it, too. Again. When the
authorities threw you into jail before, it
wasn't enough. So much money it cost me

to get you out. Now you have to get mixed
up with that troublemaker Rabbi and his
daughter again.

AARON

That's my business. With the Rabbi. With
his daughter.

SIMON

And I, your father? It's not my business?
Understand me, my son; I know what is
happening.

AARON

What do you know?

SIMON

You and that girl, Leah. You think you are
in love with her.

AARON

Have I told you that?

SIMON

You don't have to tell me. I am your father.
(AFTER A MOMENT) She is like her father.
Headstrong. Foolish. She has caused you
trouble already. (AARON STARTS TO
SPEAK, BUT SIMON SILENCES HIM) By
seeing her you will only learn more trouble.
I ask you to stop seeing her.

AARON

And what if I told you I really were in love?

SIMON

Then I would tell you that it is not love.
In this world one loves only his own, and
himself.

AARON

Then you don't know what love is. You
couldn't know what love is.

SIMON

(SLOWLY) With more than my life, I loved
your mother.

AARON

I'm sorry.

SIMON

Then understand what I say.

AARON

I understand. But you do not. Father . . . let me tell you this . . . soon, maybe very soon, we will be in the promised land. There we will live like human beings.

SIMON

Idle dreams. Troublemaking. Is this what the meeting is tonight? Some more stories about the promised land?

AARON

This time it's true. We will leave for the promised land tomorrow morning.

SIMON

Tomorrow morning! More foolishness from that Rabbi. I'll go to that meeting and I'll put an end to this troublemaking foolishness.

DISSOLVE TO THE POLICE-MILITARY OFFICE.

The Lieutenant is talking with a large, portly man, a leading citizen of the town. He is dressed well and looks much like Simon, except big-joweled, prosperous and well-dressed from the proceeds of his clothing establishment. His name is Abd-Rasin.

RASIN

(EXCITED) This is true, eh? They're going, eh? Who's idea? Your idea? Not your idea . . . ?

LIEUTENANT

You take me for a fool . . . ?

RASIN

(INTERRUPTING) I take you for a fool!

LIEUTENANT

Now, look here, Abd-Rasin . . .

RASIN

(INTERRUPTING) You look here! I have a clothing establishment, eh? It costs a great deal for workers nowadays. They read too much. They want more money. But now I have these Jews working, eh? Good workmen. I'll say that much for them. And they cost me practically nothing. My neighbor, Hezaf, the pottery-maker. Six Jews in his factory. Good potters. The blacksmith. With the Jews to work he's opened another shop. If the Jews go, it doubles our costs, it reduces our business, eh?

LIEUTENANT

What do you want me to do? It's an order. From the government.

RASIN

We have done well by you, Lieutenant, eh?

(THE LIEUTENANT NODS)

If this ghetto is allowed to leave . . . well . . . the citizens of this town won't have it.

LIEUTENANT

You think I want it!

RASIN

Then do something. (AFTER A MOMENT) Listen to me. I have one of their carpenters, a fellow called Naaman, working for me today. I'm building an addition, you know. Now, they're a thick people. If one of them were detained . . . this Naaman, for instance . . . they wouldn't leave without him, eh? And if they don't leave tomorrow morning . . .

LIEUTENANT

This Dr. Ezam is on their side. I'd have to find legal grounds.

RASIN

Then find them.

LIEUTENANT

Now, if one of them left the ghetto, without permission, or committed some similar breach of the law . . . (SMILES AND BEGINS TO NOD HIS HEAD TO RASIN, AS

FADE OUT, END OF ACT I

THE MANUSCRIPT

ALTHOUGH MANUSCRIPT FORMS and specific writing techniques differ, the general writing approaches are basically the same whether the play is live-type taped or filmed. The play is being produced for viewing on the small screen, with the same restrictions, for the same general audience and under the same limitations of subject matter. The plot structure and the creation of characters and dialogue are the same. The technical elements differ, but both styles are oriented toward the extensive use of the close-up, the moving camera and fluid transitions in place and time.

The television manuscript should have all the characters clearly designated, the dialogue, the stage directions, the video and audio directions and, in the Hollywood-style filmed play, the shot designations. Ordinarily, producers and directors frown upon writers including directions they believe only they are capable of creating, but many writers indicate sound, music, camera and electronic effects which they consider vital to the action and character delineation. This is particularly true when the visual effect in television (or the sound effect in radio) serves in place of dialogue to move the action forward. In addition, the writer also indicates any change of time or place, and may state whether the desired effect is achieved through a fade, dissolve, wipe, musical bridge or other device.

The radio manuscript form, as noted in examples earlier in this book, uses the full page, with the character's name in capital letters at the left-hand margin or in the middle of the page. There should be double spaces between lines of dialogue and between speeches. All sound and music directions should be indicated in capital letters.

The final manuscript is the one which the writer may have nothing to do with: the production script. This script contains all the revisions that may have been made after the play has left the writer's hands (unless the writer's contract gives him or her the right to do or approve of revisions) and includes the producer's and director's notations for all technical effects.

Whether the production manuscript will have a direct relationship to the writer's original manuscript is a matter of chance as well as contract. Changes in content, style and form may have been made of which the author may not even have been informed. The writer usually has no say in casting or production. After a script has run the gamut of script editor, screening, agency or network approval, production planning, rehearsal and final editing for performance, the writer might have a difficult time recognizing it. As a writer, all you can do is offer a script of the highest artistic merit of which you are capable, and then fight to keep it that way. You may take comfort in the feeling that no matter what anyone else has done, you, at least, have done your best. And if worst comes to worst, you can always request that your name be taken off the credits, an occurrence not unheard of in television.

The Live-type Taped Play

As described earlier, the New York-style, live-type taped play frequently follows a continuous action approach and is sometimes taped in front of a live audience, making it as close as television usually gets to the continuity of the stage play. It is performed and taped in sequence; that is, following the chronological order of the plot line of the script. Through editing, of course, certain sequences can be retaped and, in that respect, even the live-type show can be produced somewhat out of sequence, like the Hollywood-type filmed play.

In terms of the arts of writing and performance, however, "live-style taped" should not be considered the same as "live." The late Rod Serling, one of the few successful TV writers who stayed with the medium throughout his entire career, was once asked what we have gained and what we have lost with the advent of videotape. He answered, "we've lost spontaneity and the sense of living theatre. We've gained polish and perfection."[6]

The most frequently used form for the live-type taped play is the two-column approach noted frequently in this book: the right hand column containing all of the audio — that is, the dialogue plus the character's movements — and the left-hand column containing the video — that is, the mechanical and electronic effects. The left-hand column may also contain special sound effects and music. In some cases, the right- and left-hand columns are reversed.

Another manuscript approach is to place all of the material, video and audio, together, right down the center, similar to the stage play form, or solely in a left-hand column or right-hand column, leaving the other side free for the director's notes. The names of the characters should be typed in capital letters in the center of the column, with the dialogue immediately below. Video and audio directions and author's stage directions are usually differentiated from the dialogue by being in parentheses and/or in capital letters and/or underlined. Script editors prefer that dialogue be double-spaced, with double-spacing between speeches.

An example of the live-type taped script form is the following opening excerpt from one of the programs of the "Good Times" series.

> • *"Good Times" is considered one of the better, more successful TV series. Note the compactness of the writing and how in the first few minutes of the opening scene 1) the background for the characters and general plot line is established, 2) the characters begin to be delineated and character relationships are shown, 3) the*

exposition for this particular story is established, and 4) the conflict begins to be introduced. Identify where and how all four of the above are accomplished.

GOOD TIMES

"The Dinner Party"

ACT ONE

FADE UP:

INT. EVANS' APARTMENT — DAY

(JAMES IS GOING OVER SOME BILLS AT THE TABLE. MICHAEL IS DOING HIS HOMEWORK. THELMA IS COOKING. J.J. IS AT HIS EASEL PAINTING. FLORIDA ENTERS FROM BEDROOM)

FLORIDA:	Anybody seen my pin cushion?
J.J.:	I hope you don't mind, Ma, I used it for a still life of a bowl of fruit I just painted.
FLORIDA:	(REACTS — CROSSES TO J.J.) You used my pin cushion in a bowl of fruit?
J.J.:	It is a prime example of ghetto artistry. You make the most of what you got. Your pin cushion as the apple, Michael's basketball as the pumpkin, Dad's socks as the avocados and Thelma's face as the lemon.
THELMA:	Just bend a little and you can throw your body in as a banana. (THEY HASSLE)
JAMES:	Hey, you two, knock it off. I'm trying to figure out these bills.
FLORIDA:	(CROSSES TO CHEST) What's our financial position this month, James?
JAMES:	Well, we ain't in a position to threaten the Rockefellers . . . but we ain't heading for the poor house either. For once we are in the black.
J.J.:	(LOOKS AROUND) What do you mean, for once?
FLORIDA:	J.J.! (PUTS PIN CUSHION DOWN — CROSSES TO SINK TO WASH HANDS) Is everything paid for, James?
JAMES:	(INDICATING ENVELOPES) Everything . . . rent . . . utilities . . . and luxuries.
MICHAEL:	Dad, you didn't mention food.
FLORIDA:	(CROSSES TO JAMES WIPING HANDS ON TOWEL) These days that comes under luxuries. (JAMES COUNTS A FISTFUL OF DOLLARS)

The Hollywood-style Filmed Play

The filmed play is more the director's creation than the writer's; the live-type taped play, despite revisions and editing, is more the writer's play. Film permits more sophisticated and detailed editing than does tape, and even after the script is shot, the director can virtually rewrite the play in the editing room.

The filmed play permits a looser unity of time and place than does the live-type — although, with the development of more mobile TV cameras and equipment, as noted in Chapter 2, that advantage is turning in the other direction. In style, however, the filmed play does not have the continuous action that still marks many taped plays. The filmed play has a break at each cut or transition. That is, each sequence may last two seconds to two minutes or longer. Between sequences the director can change sets, costumes, makeup, reset lights and cameras, and even reorient the performers.

The action itself may seem to be jerky. The actual sequences are shorter than in live-type TV because they are shot separately. It is through editing that a number of sequences are fitted together into what appears to be a smooth-flowing continuous scene. The filmed play is not shot in chronological order, as the taped play usually is. All the sequences taking place on a particular set or at a particular locale, no matter where they appear in the script, are shot over a contiguous period of time. Then the entire cast and crew move to the next set or locale and do the same thing. It is difficult to achieve a clear and concrete unity of impression in producing the filmed play; editing is, therefore, an extremely critical part of the process.

Because the filmed play permits many outdoor scenes, on-location sequences, scenic exteriors and, in general, an expansion of the setting and an integration of a great variety of sets, the writer can bring in exposition and background easier than can the writer of the live-type play. Several fragments of incidents and backgrounds can establish exposition and, sometimes, preparation better than can one longer continuous scene when the entire play is only about 21 or 42 minutes long.

The filmed play requires a different manuscript form as well as different writing techniques. Instead of writing scenes, write shots. Each shot is set in terms of a picture rather than in terms of character action, although the latter should, in all plays — filmed or taped or live — be the motivating factor. As described in Chapter 2, the writer states the place, such as INTERIOR or EXTERIOR, and the shot, such as FULL SHOT or CLOSE-UP. The writer also describes the setting, states the characters' physical relationships to the set and their proximity to each other, and then presents the dialogue for that shot. The dialogue (and scene) may be only one speech long. For example, the description may read:

1   INT. JOE'S LIVING ROOM — JOE AND MABEL are seated on the couch, quarreling. FULL SHOT Joe and Mabel.

JOE
This is the end, Mabel, do
you hear? This is the end.

2   CLOSE-UP — MABEL

MABEL
I hear, Joe. I hear.

The individual shots are numbered in consecutive order so that the director may easily pick out any sequence(s) desired for initial shooting, retakes or editing.

An example of the Hollywood-style filmed TV script form is the following opening excerpt from one of the programs of "The Waltons" series.

● *"The Waltons" has been one of television's most successful series and its writing has served as a model for similar programs. In addition to analyzing the differences between the film-style and the tape-style, note how the flexibility of time and place are used in the opening to establish background and exposition. Analyze the degree to which 1) the characters begin to be delineated, 2) the dialogue begins to establish mood, and 3) the basic conflict in the plot begins to be revealed.*

THE WALTONS
"The First Day"

ACT ONE

FADE IN:

1   EXT. WALTON'S MOUNTAIN — DAY   1

It is dawn — the first gray light — and there's the suggestion of autumnal crispness in the air, the first blush of fall colors in the underbrush.

JOHN-BOY (v.o.)
(as a man)
When you're growing up, Septembers have a special feeling. Another carefree summer is too quickly ended and a new school year is about to begin.

2   EXT. WALTON HOUSE & YARD — DAY   2

In the dawnlight, we make out the faintly yellow glow of a lamp burning in John-Boy's room.

JOHN-BOY (v.o.)
(as a man)
There was an extra excitement for me in the September of 1935. My years at Miss Hunter's school on Walton's Mountain were over and I was ready to take those first faltering steps into the strange world outside.

3   INT. JOHN & OLIVIA'S ROOM — DAY   3
In the dim light, we see OLIVIA lies beside JOHN, who appears to be asleep.

JOHN-BOY (v.o.)
(as a man)
How vividly I recall the edgy excitement, the awful exhilaration of preparing for my first day at college.

Olivia reacts to a MUFFLED BUMPING SOUND.

JOHN-BOY (v.o.)
(as a man)
A day which showed me how little I knew about some things . . .

Olivia begins to get up. John reaches out and stops her. She looks at him, surprised. She didn't know he was awake.

(CONTINUED)

3   CONTINUED: (2)   3

                              JOHN-BOY (v.o.)
                           (continuing; as a man)
                  . . . and how well my parents had prepared me for others.

Olivia kisses John and reaches for her bathrobe.

                                    JOHN
              Where you going?

We HEAR the muffled sound again, coming from John-Boy's room.

                                  OLIVIA
              John-Boy's up.

                                    JOHN
              I hear. I guess he's anxious to get going.

                                  OLIVIA
              It's so early . . . maybe he doesn't feel well, or something.

                                    JOHN
              I think he feels fine . . . probably feels the same way we do.

                                  OLIVIA
              How's that?

                                    JOHN
              Nervous . . . a little scared.

                                  OLIVIA
              You want to go in and talk to him?

                                    JOHN
              Yeah. But you do too and I don't think we all oughta go
              walking in there . . . as if he was starting kindergarten . . .
              instead of starting college, like he is.

He kisses Olivia.

                                    JOHN
                                (continuing)
              Go on . . . you go.

She smiles at him, draws her robe on, and moves softly out of the room. John
watches her go. He gets up and moves to the dresser. He catches sight of
himself in the mirror.

                                    JOHN
                                (continuing)
              . . . starting college . . . your son.

He nods at himself.

                                                              CUT TO:

4 INT. UPSTAIRS HALL — DAY 4

Olivia knocks lightly on John-Boy's door. After a moment, the door opens, revealing JOHN-BOY fully dressed in his graduation outfit. He steps back and Olivia moves into his room.

5 INT. JOHN-BOY'S ROOM — DAY 5

OLIVIA
(sotto)
What in the world are you doing up and dressed at this hour?

JOHN-BOY
I was too excited to sleep.

He shuts the door as Olivia moves over to his bed. It is made and on the spread lie the various cards, papers, schedules, pencils, pens — all the paraphernalia John-Boy must take with him for his First Day.

From "The First Day" by John McGreevey — "The Waltons."

Made-for-TV Movies

The first feature-length film made especially for TV made its debut in 1964 and within ten years made-for-TV movies began to rival theatrical films in the number of new productions per year. Hollywood movies that were not first rate and shown in movie theatres began to lose out to movies at least as good and available free in the living room. Films made for TV gained in quality and some began to deal with controversial and sensitive issues and themes. Some were turned into regular TV series, others were later distributed on the movie-house circuits. But, as with any art, when quantity increases, quality tends to decrease. "The formula for the standard Movie of the Week," says Ed Bleier of Warner Brothers Television, "is 'a melodramatic plot easily conveyed in the two sentences that will be in the newspaper listing, combined with familiar and popular television actors.' "[7] Movie critic Pauline Kael has called movies made for TV "the bare bones of entertainment," stating that "television represents what happens to a medium when the artists have no power and the businessmen are in full, unquestioned control."[8] Yet, some of the made-for-TV movies were artistic milestones in television drama history: "Brian's Song," "My Sweet Charlie," "The Execution of Private Slovik," "A Case of Rape," "Autobiography of Miss Jane Pittman," among others.[9]

If you want to write television drama, keep in mind the major and different forms: the series play, the one-shot play and the full-length film. If your talent lies in one direction, concentrate on that area. Better yet, learn them all!

THE SOAP OPERA

THE DAYTIME ADULT DRAMATIC SERIAL, or soap opera, has been described by Gilbert Seldes as "the great invention of radio, its single, notable contribution to the art of fiction."[10] Although the radio soap opera is no longer with us, the television soap opera has become at least its equivalent in art, interest and impact.

"Although soap opera aficionados would seem to be a minority among college students, there are nonetheless thousands of young people around the country who daily put aside their Sartre, Machiavelli and Freud — not to mention such obsolete writers as Fanon and Debray — to watch the moiling passions of middle-class America as portrayed on daytime TV. What is it about these slow-moving melodramas with their elasticized emotions that today's college students find so engrossing? . . . the fact is that in recent years the subject matter of daytime TV has changed and become much more relevant to the interests of young viewers . . . the 'generation gap,' abortion, obscenity, narcotics and political protest are now commonly discussed and dealt with on the soap operas of TV."

Most soap opera viewers still are the so-called "housewives," who seek through the "soaps" an identification with people who have similar lives and problems, a vicarious excitement through experiences these TV-people have that they do not have, and the perverse, even unconscious satisfaction that we all get by seeing people with problems a little worse than ours, making our lives a little more tolerable. In addition, in dealing with real problems of society, soaps are beginning to provide direct information, education and psychological assistance to viewers. These afternoon dramas deal with real-life problems which are rarely, if ever, treated as fully in prime-time television. In recent years soaps have included as realistic, rather than idealistic drama such topics as women's liberation, child abuse, alcoholism, careers, illegitimate children, and married vs. non-married couples' lifestyles as well as those already noted above. Some hospitals have group therapy sessions that use soap operas as models, in which the patients relate the characters' problems to their own. Viewers frequently identify to the degree that they call in to the network or station as if the characters' situations were real (going to a psychotherapy clinic, going to an abortion clinic, receiving help for alcoholism) and ask for the names and addresses of the places involved so they can seek the same help. And, as implied earlier, soaps are a non-threatening peer group for college students.

Like life, too, soap operas just go on and on; there are no endings after an hour or a year; there are no continuing dramatic climaxes, but just — as in life — a series of continuing complications. Sometimes soaps seem a little too clear-cut; good is good and bad is bad. The writer should find appropriate median areas. Sometimes the answers to problems are over-simplified. The lives of soap opera characters are more chaotic than those of real people; this does give the audience the satisfaction of knowing that their own lives are not quite so full of chaos and disruption. The important thing for the writer to remember is that the soaps do offer the audience identification and diversion at the same time, entertaining and educating simultaneously; therefore, the soap opera plot lines and characters always have to be changing, meeting the audience's needs, and breaking new ground in terms of television drama content.

Approach and Technique

The setting should be familiar: the household, the doctor's office, the school, the small town, the large city, all presented in general terms so that viewers anywhere can have some clear interpretation of their own of the background and environment.

The characters should be familiar, not necessarily in a detailed way, but in the kinds of persons they are and the problems they encounter, so that every viewer can say, "That person is really like me, or like Amy or Bill or the plumber . . ." — like some person they know in real life. Every viewer should be able to identify to some degree with the main characters, whether they happen to be housewife, accountant, librarian, police officer, architect, explorer or even playwright. You can achieve this by developing the characters, no matter what environment they are in, on simple and obvious levels, with clear, direct motivations.

Though they may be similarly motivated, characters should be distinct types. One way to avoid confusion among characters is to limit the number. The dramatic serial should have the hero and/or heroine; the other man and/or other woman; the young man and/or young woman (or teenagers or children); the villain and/or villainess; the interested and well-meaning relatives or friends, including the kindly old judge, the maiden aunt, and their counterparts.

Perhaps the most important thing the writer must keep in mind in the creation of characters and situation is that the characters must be provided with the opportunity to get into an infinite variety of troubles. They must face problems that the listener conceivably could have. The problems must be melodramatic, basically real and valid, but exaggerated beyond the real-life involvement of most of the listeners. This gives the listener the opportunity to commiserate with people who are worse off. Soap opera viewers usually consider themselves to have similarly infinite amounts of troubles. At the very least, viewers should be able to find a mutual kind of commiseration with the characters so they can feel that they are not the only ones with these kinds of troubles and that somewhere they have "friends" and "compatriots" who come and visit for a while each day. As stated earlier, the soap opera serves many people as a kind of makeshift therapy, a counterpart of Aristotle's purgation. The characters should be very emotional and this emotion must be conveyed to the listener. They should face obstacles of the most difficult sort. Particularly if the protagonists are young people, they must face seemingly insurmountable odds.

At the same time, the characters should have some experiences that are different in some degree from those of the audience. They should meet situations and find themselves in environments that are, to the listener, exciting or exotic or both. The characters' experiences should serve, in some part, as means of escape for the listener who, through empathy, transports herself or himself to wherever the characters are and to whatever they are doing. The characters should do some things that the viewer would like to do, but can't.

Because the most important purpose of the soap opera is to establish viewer identification and empathy with the characters, character is the principal motivating factor in creating the script. Because soaps usually require an eight-week story projection, most writers are constantly working on the program, carrying a dozen or more characters in their heads at the same time. Some soap opera writers do as much research and planning with characters as do the writers of Pulitzer Prize plays. They know the characters' intimate lives from the day they were born.

The plot, unlike those of the straight TV drama, should contain a number of sub-plots, all bearing on the major conflict. They should complicate matters almost beyond endurance for the protagonist. The only limitation is that the complications should stop short of confusion for the viewer.

Inasmuch as the viewer may not be able to give full attenton to each episode, day in and day out, the plot line cannot always be brisk and sharp, and it cannot continuously contain elements that demand the full attention of the viewer. In addition, the viewer may miss a number of episodes and should be able to go back to the story and not have missed anything of appreciable importance. The plot should move as slowly as possible. The soap opera never reaches a climax. The conflict is clear and ever-present and unfolds imperceptibly. It develops with a very minor event at a time. An unexpected knock at the door can be built up into a minor complication lasting for weeks or even months. In each episode only a minute segment of action takes place, and there is little change. The time of the drama sometimes moves as slowly as the time of day. Rather than being a heightened and condensed interpretation of life, as is most drama, the soap opera is a slow, drawn-out, detailed report of life. Over a period of days or even weeks the action in the drama may cover only an hour's time. The viewer wants to believe that the characters are real, and that the events are happening as they are seen. The events, then, should happen as they do in the lives of the audience: slowly, unemphatically, even undramatically, but to the individual they should be of critical and extreme importance, no matter how minor the event. This implies that the dialogue must be like that of real life: slow, melodramatic and non-dramatic, and barely moving the action along.

Listen for dialogue in the subways, on street corners, in supermarkets.

Start each episode at a peak — the crisis of what seems to be a complication. In each episode, the particular complication should be solved or should take another turn and the drama should level off. Before the program is ended, a new element of complication — and remember, these complications may be the most insignificant happenings — should be introduced. A critical point should be reached just as the episode ends. Like the serial of the silent film days, it should be a "cliff-hanger," making it necessary for the audience to tune in the next episode to learn what will happen.

The basic technique of writing the TV soap opera is somewhere between the live-style taped play and the completely live production. For a long time soaps were done live, broadcast simultaneously as they were performed. By the mid-1970s only a few live soaps were left, all the others having gone to tape. One of the advantages of this, in terms of the special dramaturgical character of the soap opera, is that you can make even better use of simultaneous action. Instead of continuous action, which would move the story along too fast to permit the slow development of sub-plots, you can switch frequently during the program to different scenes involving different characters, all of these actions ostensibly occurring at the same time.

The lack of time for much rehearsal or preparation for a five-times-per-week drama means that you should keep setting and special effects to a minimum, keep the characterizations well within the patterns already established for the roles, and make no sudden or drastic changes in the form of the plot or dialogue. It also means that you have to adapt to the real-life activities and problems of the performers. Because they appear in a continuous action situation, if someone in the cast goes skiing and breaks a leg, for example, you will have to rewrite the script to justify their having a leg in a cast or their absence from the scene for a time.

Beginning with the second episode, you need a "lead in" — that is, a summary of the basic situation and of the previous episode. The script also needs a "lead-out." This is the afore-mentioned cliff hanger, where the narrator sets up suspense by asking what will happen to the characters in the precarious situation in which they are left until the next episode — as well as the closing scene visually conveying that question. The most intense cliff-hanger should be at the end of the Friday episode, providing that much more suspense to keep the audience interested over the weekend and eager to tune in on Monday.

THE ADAPTATION

ADAPTING A SHORT STORY, novel or play to television is in some respects more difficult than creating an original. The greatest problem is in getting away from the original work. When adapting a short story or novel, the writer is in danger of attempting to follow the original's action sequence and even the dialogue, which are usually undramatic, repetitious and introspective when compared with the heightened and condensed structure and dialogue of a play. The author of a prose work can describe people, explain their feelings and clarify the situations, motivations and even the action through examples or illustrations. The playwright cannot do this. S/he can *explain nothing*; s/he must *show everything*. The adapter of the short story or novel must therefore get away from the craft of the original and create anew, using as a base the essence of the theme, background, characters and plot of the original.

It is advisable for the adapter to read the original work enough times to become thoroughly familiar with it, and then lay it aside. There should be no need to take it up again. From a thorough knowledge of the material, the adapter should be able to then create the television or radio script. From the short story or novel the adapter takes only the elements of character, plot, theme and background, and maybe a hint of the dialogue style, although nondramatic dialogue frequently sounds ludicrous when read aloud.

Adapting the stage play is somewhat easier. The adapter has the basic elements of content and construction already at hand. The primary problem is one of condensation. The application of the special characteristics of time, space, audience, subject matter and mechanical and electronic devices, and the rules of dramaturgy for the television play as modified from the dramaturgical rules of the stage play, should result in an effective adaptation.

The adaptation of the stage play has contributed importantly to dramatic fare on television (and, in the past, on radio). The adapter may approach the task from one of two major viewpoints: consider the original inviolate and attempt to keep it as intact as possible, cutting and condensing only where necessary to comply with a time limit, and changing the original work only in the most dire emergency; or consider the play a peg on which to hang your own creative ability, select the barest essence of the original and write what may be virtually an entire new or different play. The approach of most adapters seems to be somewhere between the two extremes: attempt to get the essence of the play in scenario form and then, selecting parts of the original that could be used intact, round out the script with original work.

In adapting any form of literature you should retain the original author's intent and the essence of the story. Keep the basic character motivations and delineations. Attempt to capture the style, feeling and mood of the original. Over and above all this, however, add, subtract, change and modify so that the original work is translated most effectively in terms of the techniques of the television (or radio) medium. The adapter frequently has to delete some sequences, add scenes, combine two or more sequences into one, transpose scenes, delete and add characters, combine several characters into one, change characterizations, and introduce a narrator.

You must choose the approach to adaptation best suited to your own abilities. Some writers are better at working with characters and plots already created. Others are better at working from a basic theme or outline and creating their own characters and plot lines. Writer-adapter Irving Elman has analyzed some of the pitfalls as well as the advantages in these two approaches to adaptation. Mr. Elman has written:

". . . The tendency with the first type is for the writer's creative urge, with no outlet through original creation of his own, to use the material he is adapting merely as a point of take-off, from which he attempts to soar to heights of his own. If he happens to be a genius like Shakespeare those heights can be very high indeed. But if he is not a genius, or even as talented as the man whose work he is adapting, instead of soaring to heights, the adaptation may sink to depths below the level of the material he 'adapted.'

"The second writer, with sufficient outlet for his creativity through his own writing, is less tempted (except by his ego!) to show up the writer whose work he is adapting, proving by his 'improvements' on the other man's material how much better a writer he is. But if he genuinely likes and respects the material he is adapting, he will restrain himself to the proper business of an adaptor: translating a work from one medium to another with as much fidelity to the original as possible, making only those changes called for by the requirements of the second medium, trying in the process not to impair or violate the artistry of the original."

PROBLEMS AND POTENTIALS

THUS FAR TELEVISION HAS NOT lived up to its potential. Radio did, at times, but ultimately sacrificed its achievements for a common denominator. Television drama, as well as most other forms of television production, seems to have fulfilled the dire prediction made by Gilbert Seldes as early as 1931. Television, Mr. Seldes wrote, will be as bad as or worse than the most mediocre aspects of radio. "Each new form of entertainment drains off the cheap and accidental elements of its predecessors." The commercialization of television is a great fault, he warned, for although it is a magic miracle, it will be used as "a miracle made for money."[12]

This need not be so, of course. Television, like radio, has the potentials to be a most effective art form as well as to contribute a great deal to entertainment and culture. Whether it will or not depends not alone on a handful of writers or producers or directors or critics. It does not even depend alone on the advertisers. A concerted effort by responsible members of the audience, by the public at large — through letters, phone calls and other communications on the part of each individual viewer and listener — can most effectively influence a change in the programming practices of the mass-oriented and product-controlled media.

Rod Serling, who was one of television's most articulate as well as prolific writers, called TV a medium of compromise for the writer. He was concerned that the writer cannot touch certain themes or use certain language.[13] He criticized television because of "its fear of taking on major issues in realistic terms. Drama on television must walk tiptoe and in agony lest it offend some cereal buyer. . . ."[14] Despite these restrictions, he felt that "you can write pretty meaningful, pretty adult, pretty incisive pieces of drama."[15]

Tom Swafford, vice-president for program practices at CBS-TV, has said: "Society is changing. If a television network doesn't reflect those changes, it's going to turn off the audience it's trying to reach." With another view, Robert Kasmire, vice-president for corporate affairs at NBC, has said: "Even though we're moving into subjects that are more relevant and topical, more sensitive, we're still not lowering our standards bars. Our standards have to be far stricter than those of other media because we go directly into the home, and the network has no way of policing who's sitting in front of the TV set."[16]

With little likelihood that either public attitude and action or those of the broadcasters will change drastically in the near future, we must operate in the framework we now have for television playwrights. The number of and funding for noncommercial public broadcasting stations does not indicate a large market for writers in the near future. As a writer you are, with relatively few exceptions, dependent on the commercial mass media for your existence; yet, you can take comfort in the fact that despite the restrictions put upon you by sponsors, networks and production executives, your play is still the prime mover, the one element upon which all other elements of the production must stand or fall. With a script of high quality, with writing of ethical and artistic merit, you may at least take pride in knowing that you have made a significant effort to fulfill some of the mass media's infinite potentials.

NOTES TO CHAPTER 12

1 Brander Matthews, *The Development of the Drama* (New York: Charles Scribner's Sons, 1903), p. 19.

2 George Pierce Baker, *Dramatic Technique* (New York: Houghton Mifflin Company, 1919), p. 241.

3 Terrence Rattigan, "The Characters Make the Play," *Theatre Arts* XXXI (April, 1947), 45.

4 August Strindberg, "A Dream Play," *Collected Plays*, Thomas H. Dickinson, editor (New York: Houghton Mifflin Company, 1935), II, 64, in Author's Note to the play.

[5] George Pierce Baker, *op. cit.*, pp. 126-128.

[6] Interview with Rod Serling, "The Merv Griffin Show," Metromedia Television, WTTG, Washington, December 4, 1974 (repeated July 2, 1975, a few days after Serling's death).

[7] Don Shirley, "Made-for-TV Movie: It's Coming of Age," *The Washington Post,* October 6, 1974, E1, E3.

[8] Harry Harris, "Previewing TV," *Philadelphia Inquirer,* August 21, 1974, 6-C.

[9] Don Shirley, *op. cit.*

[10] Gilbert Seldes, *The Great Audience* (New York: The Viking Press, 1950), p. 113.

[11] Fergus M. Bordewich, "Why Are College Kids in a Lather Over TV Soap Operas?," *The New York Times,* October 20, 1974, D31.

[12] Gilbert Seldes, "A Note On Television," *New Republic,* LXIX (December 2, 1931), 71.

[13] Interview with Rod Serling, *op. cit.*

[14] B. D. Colen, "Rod Serling . . . ," *The Washington Post,* June 29, 1975, B6.

[15] Interview with Rod Serling, *op. cit.*

[16] *Broadcasting,* October 14, 1974, 32.

REFERENCE BOOKS

ON WRITING THE PLAY

Averson, Richard and David M. White, eds., *Electronic Drama: Television Plays of the Sixties.* Boston: Beacon Press, 1971.

Baker, George P., *Dramatic Technique.* Westport, Conn.: Greenwood Press, reprint of 1919 edition.

Burack, A. S., ed., *Television Plays for Writers.* Boston: Writer, Inc., 1974.

Cousin, Michel, *Writing A Television Play.* Boston: Writer, Inc., 1975.

Herman, Lewis, *Practical Manual of Screen Playwriting for Theatre and Television Films.* New York: New American Library, 1974.

Kaufman, William I., ed., *Great Television Plays.* New York: Dell, 1969.

LaGuardia, Robert, *The Wonderful World of TV Soap Operas.* New York: Ballantine Books, 1974.

Lawson, John Howard, *Theory and Technique of Playwriting and Screenwriting.* New York: Hill and Wang, 1960.

Published Radio, Television and Film Scripts: A Bibliography. Troy, N.Y.: Whitston Publishers, 1974.

Rilla, Wolf P., *The Writer and the Screen: On Writing for Film and Television.* New York: William Morrow, 1974.

Rowe, Kenneth T., *Write That Play.* New York: Funk and Wagnalls, 1969.

Trapnell, Coles, *Teleplay: An Introduction to Television Writing.* New York: Hawthorn Books, 1974.

Whitfield, Stephen E. and Gene Roddenberry, *The Making of Star Trek.* New York: Ballantine Books, 1974.

Willis, Edgar E., *Writing Television and Radio Programs.* New York: Holt, Rinehart and Winston, 1967.

13

Professional Opportunities

"So YOU WANT to write for television!" could well be an advertising head-line for a rip-off scheme to entice glamour-struck young people into schools, correspondence courses or books all but guaranteed to make them next year's Emmy Award winners.

I am convinced — after many years of teaching television and radio writing, of doing television and radio writing, of knowing television and radio writers — that good creative television and radio writing cannot be taught.

Putting together words or visual images that conform to specified for-mats can be taught. In that sense, many people can learn to write rundown sheets, routine sheets and scripts that are usable for television and radio programs.

That's not a bad thing. If one accepts a certain format and approach as ethical and contributory to a positive media effect upon the viewers, then there's nothing wrong with being a competent "draftsperson" of televi-sion and radio scripts. You can attain great success in this role of "inter-pretive" writer — that is, taking what has already been created by some-one else and putting it into a form that best presents it to the audience. Like an actor, a dancer, a musician.

Writing in its highest sense however, is not copying or interpreting. It is *creating*. The ultimate aim of the writer is to be creative in the sense that the composer, the painter, the choreographer is creative.

That cannot be taught in a classroom. It comes from a combination of motivated talent and experience. There are certain forms, techniques, and approaches that can and should be learned. Just as it is necessary for the painter to learn what is possible with color, form, line and texture, so the

407

writer must learn what is possible with the tools available to him or her. That is what this book tries to do. The *creative* art of writing requires much more. It is a synthesis of one's total psychological, philosophical, physical background, heightened into expressiveness through a knowledge of form, technique and approach. I have rarely found a person in any of the classes I have taught who was not able to satisfactorily write a rundown, routine or script in each television and radio program genre. But too infrequently have I found a person who was able to go beyond the basic format and create a script that truly fulfilled the potentials of television or radio in affecting, in a humanistic, positive manner, the minds and emotions of the audience.

I hope that you, who are reading this and contemplating a career in writing for television and radio, are capable of the highest level of creative writing. But even if you are not, there are career opportunities. Indeed, sometimes the creative writer has less of an opportunity for gainful employment because of difficulty in lowering the artistic plane of writing to conform to the formulas of the particular program or script type.

In presenting some views on careers and the opportunities for writers in various areas of television and radio, I am making no judgment on what you should accept in terms of your particular talents, skills and ambitions. How far you should go or how limited you should let yourself be is a matter only you can decide. But do know just what you are capable of and what you can be happy with.

The combinations of potential and restriction, of opportunity and responsibility, of creativity and compromise pertain to virtually all writing jobs for all levels and types and for all broadcast stations and other producing organizations. As stated by the Lilly Endowment, Inc. in instituting a Humanitas Prize for television writing, ". . . . the writer of American television is a person of great influence, for the values projected on the TV screen begin in his or her mind, heart and psyche. Few educators, churchmen or politicians possess the moral influence of a TV writer. This entails an awesome responsibility for the TV writer. But it also provides a tremendous opportunity to enrich his or her fellow citizens. How? By illuminating the human situation, by challenging human freedom, by working to unify the human family. In short, by communicating those values which most fully enrich the human person."

Whether or not the writer is always or ever permitted to do this is another story. Barbara Douglas, whose executive position at Universal Studios includes finding scripts, packages and properties for film and television, acknowledges the frustrations of the writer within the commercial requirements of broadcasting, but at the same time believes there is hope for creative talented people who are able to write alternative scripts that large companies might be able to produce. She believes that integrity can be retained within an area of compromise, in which a script has mass commercial value but is not a sell-out. "It's this fairly narrow area of quality which I wish our promising young people would consider, instead of either leaping to low-grade imitations of what appears to be a way to turn a fast dollar, or alternatively coming from a place that's so far from the mass mind that the script turns the studio people off before they get to page five.[1]

Barbara Allen, writer, producer and teacher of television and radio, offers some additional basic considerations for those who wish to write successfully for the broadcast media. She suggests that you should be:

Creative enough to turn out bright ideas fast and
Self-disciplined enough to watch others "improve" on them;
Organized enough to lay out a concise production script and
Unstructured enough to adjust to last-minute deviations;
Persistent enough to be able to research any subject thoroughly and
Flexible enough to be able to present it as a one-hour documentary or a 30-second spot;
Imaginative enough to write a script that can be produced at a nominal cost and
Practical enough to have a second plan for doing it at half that cost.
P.S. It also helps if you can spell, punctuate and type.

Where are the jobs in broadcast writing? Allen breaks down the categories as follows:

Network Radio: news, editorials, features.

Network TV: soap operas, game shows, stunts for quizzes, comedy writers, pre-program interviewers, researchers, children's programs, series writers, news, promotion, continuity.

Local Radio and TV: news, promotion, continuity, documentaries, special programs.

Related areas: independent film producers and syndication companies, advertising agencies, free lance commercials, department stores, national and state service groups, safety councils and charity enterprises, utility companies, farm organizations, religious organizations, government agencies, educational institutions and organizations.

The Federal Communications Commission's breakdown of the relative amounts of time TV stations devoted to certain program types in 1974 showed 78.2% for entertainment and sports, 8.9% for news, 4.1% for public affairs and 8.7% for other nonentertainment/nonsports programs. Local percentages for nonentertainment/nonsports programming have been considerably lower than network percentages.[2]

Writer's Digest, which provides continuing analysis of markets for writers, including radio and television, summarizes opportunities as follows:

Opportunities at local stations and networks include news writing, editing, continuity writing, commercial and promotion writing, and script and special feature writing.

News writers and editors collect local news and select stories from the wire services, often editing and rewriting them for local audiences. News men may also serve as reporters, covering local stories and interviews along with a cameraman. Continuity writers develop commercials for sponsors that don't have advertising agencies, write station promotional and public service announcements and occasionally program material. Both news and continuity writers are able to get across the essentials of a story in simple, concise language. Most script work is done on a contract or freelance basis, but some staff writers are employed. Special feature subjects are generally sports and news stories, usually written by a staff writer in one of these areas. However, stations are always eager to listen to new feature ideas from staff writers or outside writers.

A good broadcast writer has all the basic writing skills at his command and, since he frequently doesn't have time to rewrite, develops his speed and accuracy. A college education in liberal arts or journalism is desirable, but a good writer who has other talents such as announcing is also well-qualified. As always, the writer with talent and original ideas will get the job.

It is best to approach a broadcast company through an employment agency. If you prefer not to do this, submit a resume with some of your best writing samples to the station or personnel manager and ask for an interview. Apply first at a small station and get that priceless experience that you can list on your work record, then contact a larger organization.[3]

Among the books dealing with opportunities in broadcasting is *Your Career in TV and Radio* by George N. Gordon and Irving A. Falk. Their analysis includes the following:

Programming departments of relatively large stations can use people who have developed skills as writers to create continuity, commercial announcements, and other material, read over the air in the course of a day. Major stations and networks also have work for people with a bent for research. They provide background for feature programs and interviews.

Television *alone* (and let us consider only *network* television) is responsible for some *twenty thousand hours* of programming per year. True, some of it is made up of replayed Hollywood films, but a scribe writes each one of those commercials you see, each news broadcast, and all the "ad-lib" remarks that your favorite master of ceremonies produces so glibly. Not all the material broadcast on our more than 5,000 radio stations is written out in script form; many disc jockey and interview programs are ad-libbed. But enough writers are employed by our TV and radio stations today to write out *in one year the entire work of all the copyists who created by hand all the books in Europe during the Middle Ages* from 500 to 1500 A.D., when printing was invented.

Jack Wilson, one of the last radio dramatic story editors, says: "good writers can start anywhere in broadcasting; as copywriters or news editors on small stations, or as assistant gag writers. It doesn't matter where or how you start out. If you have talent, it will show. A writer learns by writing, and you don't start in the top drawer in any field, except maybe if you write a smash best-seller novel. You also have to build an immunity to rejection slips and turned-down manuscripts. Very few people get to be TV or radio writers on their first try, or even on the second or third try. You have to have patience." Jack Wilson's advice to young writers is extremely practical. First, *listen* to radio, *watch* TV, and get to know how the professionals do it. Then practice the craft and try to sell materials either to local TV or radio outfits or, by mail, to bigger production organizations. The one thing a young writer should not do is pack up his bags and head for New York or Los Angeles in the mistaken belief that he has a better chance in the big city than in his home town. He doesn't. . . . Jack notes . . . "don't be fooled that you get a lot of money for 'hack' writing that's easy to knock off. No matter what you are working on, and you may hate the darn program, your finest effort is required. In a way, it's just as hard to be a bad writer as it is to be a good one. There is no easy way to use the twenty-six letters in the English alphabet in their infinite combinations."

In TV or radio, the term "writer" applies to anyone who prepares broadcasts which are not spontaneously produced, although sometimes writers prepare notes from which a performer spontaneously ad-libs. A writer is therefore considered the employee of one or another of agencies which produce broadcasts. Writers are paid according to the type of employer for whom they work and the extent of the service which they perform for him. Every arm of broadcasting employs writers of one sort or another, either on a free-lance basis or on a permanent payroll. Some writers work for individual stations; others work for networks. Some work for both. Network jobs are, of course, better paying and generally considered more important than station jobs, but most network writers start out as employees of stations. Independent producers, syndicated TV program producers, and film producers hire many writers to produce the vast amounts of material they consume. These authors are frequently highly specialized.

The most interesting type of writing for broadcasting, many believe, is dramatic writing . . . Daytime TV is replete with relatively well-written versions of radio's old soap operas. Independent program producers and film producers keep creating a never-ending stream of filmed westerns, gangster shows, pseudohorror films, domestic comedy films, and animated stories for children and for adults also. And don't forget the TV "specials," productions of superior plays and original musicals. . . . Never attempt to market any dramatic script which does not fit the format of the kind of TV shows presently on the air.

Whenever writers are mentioned in broadcasting circles, you frequently hear talk about literary agents and their role in selling the output of authors. Rarely does a writer for TV or radio need a literary agency unless he operates as a free-lance author, selling his output to the highest bidder. Free lancers usually write for dramatic programs and their scripts are bought for "one-shot" programs . . . Literary agents help free-lance dramatic writers to place their manuscripts with production companies or to search out assignments. For their services, agents receive at least ten per cent of the sale price of each script the author writes. Most literary agents will sign contracts only with writers who have established reputations and whose work is known to be marketable. Remember that ten per cent of nothing is nothing. . . .[4]

Jane Caper, former producer of the TV interview program "Panorama" on WTTG, Washington, D.C. and a producer of ABC's "A.M. America," advises a person wishing to break into television — as a writer, on interview shows or in any capacity — to seek an interneship at a local station. "There are so few jobs available," Caper says, "that in most instances this is the only way to get experience and exposure." She advises the intern not to be afraid to take the initiative. "If you have ideas, type them up and give them to the producer. Let the producer know you are willing to work hard and long hours." She suggests that, if at all possible, one should seek experience with live shows, hopefully in some on-the-air as well as in a production capacity.

COMMERCIALS

THE THREE AREAS in which there is the greatest opportunity — that is, in which most writers are employed — are commercials, news and drama. Kirk Polking, editor of *Writer's Digest,* analyzes careers for copywriters:

Of all the writing jobs today, the network television commercial copywriter probably gets paid more, for less actual *writing,* than any other writer. Charlie Moss, whose copy jobs include the American Motors account and others handled by the Wells, Rich, Greene agency, points out, "I may spend no more than 15 minutes a week at the typewriter. Much of the rest of my time is spent sitting around this table with art directors and account executives analyzing a client's product and trying to find the right idea to sell it in one minute." *Idea* is the key word here and many top agency copy chiefs say they're looking for "concept creators," not writers. *"Writers* we can always hire," says one creative supervisor. "What's harder to find is the guy with a new idea, a fresh approach — someone who can create the theme for a brilliant, visual short story, with a sales message, in 60 seconds."

. . . Ron Rosenfeld, a copy chief at Doyle Dane Bernbach, says, "We're not necessarily looking for copywriters as such. We want people who have a great sense of the graphic and are good at thinking in pictures."

. . . The television commercial copywriter has to sell the client first before he can sell his idea to the public. How does he do this? . . . A client says, "Too many young copywriters come in with only one idea and can't do a good job of showing why it will effectively sell the product. They're too jealous of their own idea — maybe they're afraid they'll never get another. A real professional can lay aside an idea you don't like, and come up with five others and show you 11 good reasons why each one would be effective."

. . . What kind of money is there to be made as a TV commercial copywriter for clients using network advertising? Trainees may start out at a bottom level of $5,000 and go on up to $50,000 for a copychief. . . "There's a screaming need for good TV commercial copywriters," says Ed Carder, Director of the Radio and TV Department of Ralph Jones, "but the writer has to have a thorough basic understanding of the English language, how TV and radio work and the discipline to work within time and space limitations."

. . . What about freelancing in this field? It usually takes the form of moonlighting. A small agency will go to a copywriter at a leading agency whose style they like and ask him to do a job on the side. Mostly the agencies work with their own staff people and know fairly well what their next year's needs are going to be in the way of personnel based on their client list. Rarely has an agency bought a TV commercial idea submitted by a writer through the mail. Some of the larger clients and agencies have a form letter rejecting all such submissions automatically to protect themselves from claims of plagiarism. A writer who has what he thinks are some new, fresh approaches to the TV commercial might do best to work with local agencies first, contacting them by mail, with a resume of his professional experience and asking for an appointment to present several specific commercial ideas for specific clients of the agency. If he's good, he'll get a chance.

. . . Most agencies agree that a good liberal arts background is essential for any copywriting job. Since TV copywriting also requires a knowledge of the things the motion picture camera and the TV studio can and cannot do, background in these areas is also helpful.[5]

Ms. Polking notes that copywriters break into the field in many ways, including starting out as an office boy, working as a trainee at very low pay, coming from another field such as writing music or jingles, and being a writer in other media, such as a novelist. [6]

Phyllis Robinson is vice-president for copy of Doyle Dane Bernbach and a member of the Copywriters Hall of Fame. Her induction speech, when she was honored for her major influence on contemporary copywriting, both through her writing and the people she has trained, stressed the cooperative freedom necessary between copywriters and art directors. The freedom to break rules also entails respect, she stated, and she listed a series of "respect" advice for the copywriter: "respect for the guy you work with; respect for the young and totally untrained; respect for grayer heads; respect for your superior; respect for the client's opinion; respect for the new voices clamoring to be heard; respect for your work; respect for the audience; and, most important, respect for yourself." [7]

Several Doyle Dane Bernbach copywriters have discussed how they judge copywriters and offered some comments of value to the person seeking to break into the field. In describing what she seeks in going over someone's portfolio, Sue Brock said: "The first thing I look for is whether there is an ad there that I would have okayed. And then, if there are none like that, whether there is the germ of a good idea that perhaps was goofed up in the execution. Then, after you've decided that there is something there that is fresh or exciting, you call the person in, and at that point you are influenced by the person's personality. If she sits there hostile and full of anxieties, you lose interest, because this is very much team work, and all the little belles and stars have a very rough time." Judy Protas stated that "in this business, where criticism is very much the order of the day, a writer whose personality can't stand up to criticism would fall apart at the seams." Brock added that "you have to have a pretty good opinion of yourself or you won't survive. You have to have a pretty strong ego, because everyone here is willing to criticize — traffic, the messengers, everyone. And if it happens to be your boss who's criticizing, you're going to have to change your copy." Protas concluded that "you have to know when to stop discussion. You're expected to fight for your opinion, but not start whining and arguing defensively over something in which only your ego is involved." [8]

NEWS

WITH THE INCREASED EMPHASIS on local news, jobs for news reporters-writers at local stations have increased as well. [9] Desired preparation for a career in broadcast journalism varies with stations and station managers. In some instances a pure journalistic background is preferred; in others, specialization in television and/or radio techniques is wanted; in still other cases judgment and news sense is subjectively evaluated, with training a secondary consideration. Stanley S. Hubbard, president and general manager of Hubbard Broadcasting, Inc., describes what he looks for:

> What is a news person? Is a news person qualified because he has a degree from a university which says he graduated in journalism? Or is a news person qualified because he has held a job someplace as a news person? I think not. I think that a news person, in order to really be considered capable, has to prove that he or she has news ability and "news sense." The time restrictions involved in producing television news require that in order to be successful, a television news person has to have genuine news sense. It is not possible, insofar as my experience has indicated, for a person to learn news sense in a journalism school . . . Journalism schools can prepare you very adequately to go to work in a news room at a TV station and learn how to successfully fit into the mechanism, but just because a person successfully fits into the mechanism, it is a mistake to think that a person necessarily has news sense or the judgment required of a licensee in the discharge of his public responsibilities.[10]

Background, formal or informal, is required, of course. News sense without knowledge is the other half of the loaf that includes knowledge without news sense. In light of the attention being directed to local and regional events on local stations, Barbara Allen recommends that as a potential reporter-writer, "1) you need to be familiar with every aspect of city government, the people who make up the power structure in your community, the business and industries that support your area's economy, your schools, colleges and local personalities, 2) the breadth and depth of your knowledge about people and government and art and politics and educational science and social and economic problems will be the underpinnings of your value as a journalist, and 3) your function and responsibility is to see what seem to be isolated events against the background of the forces which cause those events."

Add to this an approach to reporting and writing that has been called the "new journalism": "highly interpretive reporting consisting of in-depth research, enlivened with . . . a dramatic writing style. . . ."[11]

Irving Fang, in his book *Television News*, reports on the preferences of news directors in hiring young people from among five categories of preparation. First preference was for a reporter with two years' experience and no college education, while close behind was preference for a college graduate in broadcast journalism with no experience. Very low in preference were college graduates with a different major and no experience, a local resident junior college graduate with no experience, and a broadcasting trade school graduate with no experience. Majors other than broadcast journalism, in order of preference, include political science, English, liberal arts, history, general journalism and telecommunications. The most important alibity looked for was that of writing, with other skills, including reporting and on-air personality, far behind. The personal qualities most desired are eagerness, enthusiasm, self-motivation and energy.[12] Fang also lists the behavioral attitudes a broadcast journalist should have according to the American Council on Education for Journalism:

1. Ability to write radio news copy.
2. Judgment and good taste in selecting news items for broadcast.
3. Ability to edit copy of others, including wire copy.
4. Knowledge of the law especially applicable to broadcasting.
5. Knowledge of general station operation.
6. Understanding of the mechanical problems of broadcasting.
7. Appreciation of broadcasting's responsibility to the public, particularly in its handling of news.
8. Ability to work under pressure.
9. Ability to make decisions quickly.
10. Speed in production.
11. Familiarity with the various techniques of news broadcasting (including first-person reporting, tape recordings, interviews, remotes).
12. Knowledge of newscast production (including timing or back-timing of script, opens and closes, placement of commercials, production-newsroom coordination).
13. Ability to gather news for radio/tv.
14. Ability to read news copy with acceptable voice quality, diction, etc.
15. Ability to find local angles in national or other stories.
16. Quickness to see feature angles in routine assignments.
17. Ability to simplify complex matters and make them meaningful to the listener or viewer.[13]

Where do you look for a job as a newswriter? Everywhere and anywhere! If you're breaking into the field, try the small stations first, where you can get experience doing everything, in and out of news, in and out of writing. If you want or need to live and work where there are predominantly large stations, be prepared to start as a copy-person or in another beginning position. Be aware, however, that it is extremely difficult to go up the ladder in a network or similar large operation, and the lack of experience and competitive structure may keep you on a rung of the ladder quite removed from newswriting for a long time, if not forever. Most experienced newswriters and managers recommend the small station route as the one with the better chance. If you are studying in a journalism, communications, broadcasting or similar department, your professors will already have contact with stations in your State or region, and usually recommend capable graduating students for jobs. You can, of course, contact stations anywhere in the country yourself; ask your professors for help in preparing your resume, and don't forget the experience you obtained — hopefully — with the university's noncommercial station or with a local commercial station while working on your degree. Your professors can also refer you to national organizations and associations that have placement services. One of the principal groups is the Radio-Television News Directors Association, 6016 Fallbrook Avenue, Woodland Hills, California 91364. Journalist-applicants pay a small fee.

There are some free lance newswriters-producers, but these are far and few between and usually are people who have achieved sufficient recognition that they can name their own spots and terms. For the less experienced and renowned, however, local television and radio stations do provide some outlets. If you are a writer and have a camera that you can use well and/or a tape recorder that you can be creative with, you can frequently provide special features on local events. Local history, geography, civic affairs, local and state holidays and unusual happenings and personalities offer a plethora of possibilities. While you're still in college, this might be something worthwhile trying inasmuch as it's on your own-time, part-time basis. You can get experience with a public television and/or radio station, if there is one, and experience and payment with a local commercial station. Some larger stations employ students as news stringers to cover campus news, most particularly athletics.

PLAYWRITING

"BREAKING INTO TV is more difficult than for any other writing field," says Art Mandelbaum, vice president of RKO Radio and former television writer. "It requires plotting a game plan at least as intricate as plotting the structure of a story or teleplot." Mandelbaum suggests several guidelines for those who wish to write for sitcom or continuing TV series:

1. Study very carefully the particular series you want to write for and analyze every major character.

2. Simultaneously find out, if possible, the rating of the series to determine if it will still be on the air the following year. All series shows are assigned to writers by the producer before the season starts, so that even if your script is read and bought, it won't be seen, probably, for about a year-and-a-half. For this reason, too, don't write anything too timely that might be out-of-date by the time the program is aired.

3. Find out the demographics of each show; contact the networks and learn who watches, where the heaviest audience is.

4. It is essential that you obtain an agent in Hollywood. It is a waste of time to send material directly to a producer.

5. An agent can provide you with fact sheets provided to writers on every show. The fact sheets brief writers on formats, requirements and taboos. The Writers' Guild sends out information on all shows to its members.

6. After studying a particular show, provide your agent with a great many ideas for that show. Don't lock yourself into one show idea. If you come up with 50 one-paragraph thumbnail sketches, your agent will have enough to present to the producer even if the first few are immediately shot down.

7. If your agent sells a show idea, then you can get a contract for a treatment — and you can break into the Writers' Guild.

8. Make sure you are grounded in the classics. Basic themes and plots are modifiable and, if you study TV shows, you'll note that they are constantly used.

9. Don't let all your friends read your work. By the time their critical appraisals are finished you'll find that your head is spinning and/or you'll be revising your scripts into something you didn't intend to say in the first place.

10. If an agent offers suggestions that conflict with your ideas concerning a particular show, follow the agent's advice. As a beginner, trying to break in, you are totally dependent on an agent.

11. TV writing is a continuing compromise. The first thing you're pushing is the detergent; the second thing is the content.

Mr. Mandelbaum's practical approach combines a range of attitudes; some writers and producers are extremely optimistic about the extent of artistic creativity and social impact possible for the writer of television drama; others are extremely pessimistic and cynical. All agree, however, that you must have the talent to write plays, must write drama that fits the needs and format of the program series (including the dramatic specials that are not continuing-character series), and must know the potentials and the limitations of the medium.

The basic ceiling rates for play scripts include bonuses — the latter go to persons who write both the original story and the teleplay — and, as negotiated by the Writers' Guild of America — remember these are maximums — are: to March 31, 1976, $4,500 for a half-hour play, $6,400 for an hour, $9,400 for 90 minutes and $11,900 for 120 minutes; and from April 1, 1976 to February 28, 1977, $5,000 for a half-hour, $7,000 for an hour, $10,000 for 90 minutes and $12,000 for 120 minutes. In addition, there are differentials for different time periods, residuals, additional fees for writers with additional duties, and other payment categories.

Writer's Digest analyzes the TV play market this way:

Television has to fill at least 18 hours every day with fresh, appealing material. This necessity makes it one of the best markets for freelancers. It's one of the highest paying, and producers are constantly looking for new ideas and new scripts. Most new show ideas come from freelancers and many of the subsequent scripts are written by other freelancers. Good dialogue writers will find TV a highly rewarding market. . . . TV producers usually accept scripts only through agents, which means that writers cannot submit work directly to them. But writers can keep themselves informed on the current market picture through *Writer's Digest*, whose issues publish information on new TV shows along with practical articles on TV script writing. The annual *Writer's Market* contains a detailed list of agents' names and addresses.[14]

The Writers Guild of America, West, 8955 Beverly Blvd., Los Angeles, California 90048, provides a list of agents, noting those willing to look at the work of new writers. Before submitting a script to an agency, however, send a summary and the agency will send you a release form if it is interested in seeing the full script or treatment.

MINORITIES AND WOMEN

IF YOU ARE A WOMAN or of a minority group, until the 1970s the doors were largely closed to you. The pressures of minority and women's organizations began to loosen some of the hinges and the Equal Employment Opportunity program requirements of the Federal Communications Commission have provided a regulatory lever to pry the doors open a bit. However, with the exception of advertising, where, as Doris Willens, director of public relations for Doyle Dane Bernbach, says, the doors have always been open to women and most of the successful copywriters are women, there are relatively few women or minorities writing for radio or television. The overall employment figures in broadcasting for these groups have gone up measureably, but in most instances the significant rise has been in non-executive and non-creative areas.

As noted in Chapter 10, a number of producers believe that shows about minorities should be written by members of that particular minority group. Try. The odds are long, but they have been getting better. The incidence of minorities as performers, however, may very well affect the incidence of minorities as writers. One mid-1970s study found that on prime-time network TV minorities accounted for only 12.7% of the roles: Blacks, 5.8%, Orientals, 1.6%, Chicanos, 0.83%, Native Americans, 0.29% and others, 4.2%.[15]

The same problem holds true for women. About 85% of the roles in television programs are written for males. As actress Barbara Feldon says,

"What is needed in television is for women to get more involved. A good place to start is in the writing field.[16]

Individual producers occasionally make attempts to bring in minorities as writers. Probably the most comprehensive such effort was announced by Norman Lear of Tandem Productions for late 1975 on behalf of their TV shows "All in the Family," "Sanford and Son," "Maude," "Good Times," and "The Jeffersons." "Minority . . . career-oriented comedy writers who already have the skill and knowledge of writing comedy for television, but don't have or don't know the avenues for getting their work to the proper people" and who want "to begin a professional writing career" should send letters of inquiry — not scripts — to Tandem Productions, 1901 Avenue of the Stars, Los Angeles, California 90067.

The major information source on jobs for minorities and women in broadcasting is operated by the National Association of Broadcasters: NAB Employment Clearinghouse, 1771 N Street, N.W., Washington, D.C. 20036. Women may join the professional registry of American Women in Radio and Television, 1321 Connecticut Avenue, N.W., Washington, D.C. 20036. The Journalism Council of the Association for Education in Journalism maintains a minority clearinghouse through Dr. Lionel C. Barrow, Jr., Dean, School of Communications, Howard University, Washington, D.C. 20059.

COLLEGE PREPARATION

WHAT ARE THE ATTITUDES of station managers toward college graduates in general? A study by Frederick N. Jacobs found that most radio managers have unfavorable attitudes towards college students, with almost two-thirds stating that communications graduates don't understand commercial broadcasting. Some three-fourths say that there is no substitute for experience, with almost half of the managers believing that colleges are not preparing students adequately for a broadcasting career. Although most think that college training is of some help, only a small percentage has more positive than negative opinions about the importance of a degree in broadcasting.[17] A principal concern is that communications departments do not prepare people with a combination of philosophical understanding and practical application, but tend to go too much in one direction or the other. If you do seek professional education in communications, a unique institution on the Master's graduate level is The International University of Communications in Washington, D.C., which is oriented toward helping professionals in all fields learn to use all forms of communications to directly and humanistically solve social, political, economic, environmental and educational problems. Combining a one-on-one tutorial approach, participatory seminars, guided studies and, particularly, a practical field project, the IUC eliminates traditional techniques and requirements and encourages people working at full-time jobs to apply their field projects to on-the-job needs. Professional broadcast training on the undergraduate level is obtainable at some 250 traditional colleges and universities, with more than 100 offering Master's degrees, and over 30 with Doctoral programs. More than 100 junior and community colleges have radio-television programs or courses.

You are not likely to see many ads saying "Writer Wanted." One such ad in the mid-1970s was significant, however, in that it was for radio. It is worth reproducing here as a reminder that every now and then there are jobs for writers that are least expected.

WRITER WANTED

for radio series featuring old-time recordings. Project will be five-time-a-week hour show highlighting talent like Judy Garland, Al Jolson, Jimmy Durante, Ray Bolger, Buddy Clark, Bing Crosby, etc. Writer will develop intros that are bright, interesting, nostalgic, informative, and develop flavor of "the good old days." Must be knowledgeable in this field and possess proper background and writing experience. Write fully.

Y7482 Times

If you are seeking a job as a broadcast writer, however, you would do better to go to the more usual sources. In previous sections of this chapter we pointed out some approaches for positions, including placement services and direct application approaches. In addition, you will find jobs for writers frequently listed in both display and classified ads in a number of the periodicals noted in the bibliographical list at the end of Chapter 1. *Broadcasting* magazine is one of the best sources.

COPYRIGHT

YOU CAN'T COPYRIGHT an idea. If you are creative, you will find that some time, some place, one or more of your ideas will be appropriated without compensation or credit to you. It's happened to all of us, and series formats, script outlines and concepts for various kinds of programs have from time to time been adapted or even wholly used by unscrupulous broadcasters. On the other hand, there are many ideas, script concepts and formats that can be thought up by more than one person at virtually the same time, and when you see or hear on the air under someone else's name a creation that you had submitted to a network or station or agency, it might not be a rip-off at all. However, inasmuch as all broadcasting offices require you to sign a release for the purpose of protecting themselves in instances where your submission was not original or the first one received, you can never be quite sure!

The answer is copyright. Unfortunately, everything that the writer creates for television and radio is not copyrightable.

Ideas for or titles of radio or television programs cannot be copyrighted. According to the United States Copyright Office, "narrative outlines, formats, plot summaries of plays and motion pictures, skeletal librettos and other synopses and outlines cannot be registered for copyright in unpublished form." If the formats and outlines are so detailed as to clearly present the particular expression the author uses to work out the ideas or plans, then they may be considered unpublished books, which, though not registerable, are protected against unauthorized use — provided, of course, that you can prove you wrote it first. The Copyright Office says "the general idea or outline for a program is not copyrightable. Copyright will protect the literary or dramatic expression of an author's ideas, but not the ideas themselves. . . . To be acceptable for copyright registration in unpublished form, a script must be more than an outline or synopsis. It should be ready for presentation or performance, so that a program could actually be produced from the script deposited."

Unpublished scripts in complete form or a group of related scripts for a series may be copyrighted. If a script is a play, musical comedy, shooting script for a film or a similar dramatic work, it may be registered on Form D, for "dramatic and dramatico-musical compositions." Registering a particular script protects that script only and does not give protection to future scripts arising out of it or to a series as a whole. Complete scripts of commercials, panel discussions, variety programs, speeches, lectures, non-dramatic monologues and similar non-dramatic material may be registered on Form C, for "lectures, sermons, or addresses prepared for oral delivery." In addition, other parts of radio and television programs may be registered under specific classes, such as Form E for musical compositions, Form G for works of art, Form J for photographs. You may obtain copyright forms and detailed explanation of how to determine what is copyrightable as well as procedures for obtaining a copyright by writing to Copyright Office, Library of Congress, Washington, D.C. 20540. The initial copyright fee of $6.00 protects your work for 28 years, at which time you may renew the copyright for a similar period. In 1975, however, Congress was considering bills which would change copyright law, including the lengthening of the term of copyright to bring U.S. practices more into conformance with most of the other countries of the world.

A good form of script protection, outside of copyright, is the Script Registration service of the Writers Guild of America, West, which is available to members and non-members both.

NOTES TO CHAPTER 13

[1] *Media Report to Women,* April 1, 1974, p. 12.

[2] FCC Public Notice, "Television Broadcast Programming Data, 1974," August 11, 1975.

[3] Editors of *Writer's Digest,* "Radio and TV," in *Jobs and Opportunities for Writers* (Cincinnati: *Writer's Digest,* 1975), pp. 6-7, pamphlet.

[4] George N. Gordon and Irving A. Falk, *Your Career in TV and Radio* (New York: Julian Messner, 1966), pp. 53, 83-91, 94-95.

[5] Kirk Polking, "The TV Copywriter," *Writer's Digest*, June, 1968, pp. 56-57, 59-60, 82-83.

[6] *Ibid.*, p. 57.

[7] "Phyllis Robinson: New Face In the Copywriters' Hall of Fame," *DDB News*, July, 1968, pp. 2-3.

[8] "DDB: 'An Emotional Place'," *DDB News*, December, 1966, p. 11.

[9] *Television/Radio Age*, October 14, 1974, p. 30.

[10] *Ibid.*, p. 35.

[11] John Brady, "Gay Talese: An Interview," in *The Reporter as Artist* (Ronald Weber, ed., New York: Hastings House, 1974), pp. 83-84.

[12] Irving E. Fang, *Television News*, 2nd Edition, Revised and Enlarged, (New York: Hastings House, 1972), pp. 406-407.

[13] *Ibid.*, pp. 407-408.

[14] Editors of *Writer's Digest*, "The Television Market," in *Jobs and Opportunities for Writers* (Cincinnati: *Writer's Digest*, 1975), p. 12, pamphlet.

[15] *Broadcasting*, November 11, 1974, p. 40.

[16] Kay Gardella, "Television," *The Houston Post*, May 20, 1974, p. 4C.

[17] *Broadcasting*, December 2, 1974, p. 28.

REFERENCE BOOKS

ON CAREER OPPORTUNITIES

Broadcast Education: Radio-Television Programs in American Colleges and Universities. Washington, D.C.: National Association of Broadcasters. Annual Report.

Ewing, Sam, *You're On the Air.* Blue Ridge Summit, Pa.: Tab Books, 1972.

Field, Stanley, *Professional Broadcast Writer's Handbook.* Blue Ridge Summit, Pa.: Tab Books, 1974.

Gordon, George N. and Irving A. Falk, *Your Career in TV and Radio.* New York: Julian Messner, 1966.

Jackson, Gregory, *Getting Into Broadcast Journalism: A Guide to Careers in Radio and TV.* New York: Hawthorn Books, 1975.

Koenig, Allen E., ed., *Broadcasting and Bargaining: Labor Relations in Radio and Television.* Madison: University of Wisconsin Press, 1970.

Rider, John R., *Your Future in Broadcasting.* New York: Rosen, Richards Press, 1971.

Wainwright, Charles Anthony, *Television Commercials,* Revised Edition. New York: Hastings House, 1970. Especially Chapters 3 and 4.

Useful pamphlets are "Television Careers," from the Television Information Office, 745 Fifth Avenue, New York, N.Y. 10022; "Jobs in Advertising," from the American Advertising Federation, 655 Madison Avenue, New York, N.Y. 10021; "Career Opportunities in Advertising" and "Education for Advertising Careers," from the American Association of Advertising Agencies, 200 Park Avenue, New York, N.Y. 10017. For freelance writers, *Writer's Digest, Writer's Market* and *Writer's Yearbook* are indispensible.

APPENDIX

THE TELEVISION CODE

"Reprinted from The Television Code, published by the Code Authority, National Association of Broadcasters, Eighteenth Edition, June 1975."

PREAMBLE

Television is seen and heard in nearly every American home. These homes include children and adults of all ages, embrace all races and all varieties of philosophic or religious conviction and reach those of every educational background. Television broadcasters must take this pluralistic audience into account in programming their stations. They are obligated to bring their positive responsibility for professionalism and reasoned judgment to bear upon all those involved in the development, production and selection of programs.

The free, competitive American system of broadcasting which offers programs of entertainment, news, general information, education and culture is supported and made possible by revenues from advertising. While television broadcasters are responsible for the programming and advertising on their stations, the advertisers who use television to convey their commercial messages also have a responsibility to the viewing audience. Their advertising messages should be presented in an honest, responsible and tasteful manner. Advertisers should also support the endeavors of broadcasters to offer a diversity of programs that meet the needs and expectations of the total viewing audience.

The viewer also has a responsibility to help broadcasters serve the public. All viewers should make their criticisms and positive suggestions about programming and advertising known to the broadcast licensee. Parents particularly should oversee the viewing habits of their children, encouraging them to watch programs that will enrich their experience and broaden their intellectual horizons.

PROGRAM STANDARDS

I. Principles Governing Program Content

It is in the interest of television as a vital medium to encourage programs that are innovative, reflect a high degree of creative skill, deal with significant moral and social issues and present challenging concepts and other subject matter that relate to the world in which the viewer lives.

Television programs should not only reflect the influence of the established institutions that shape our values and culture, but also expose the dynamics of social change which bear upon our lives.

To achieve these goals, television broadcasters should be conversant with the general and specific needs, interests and aspirations of all the segments of the communities they serve. They should affirmatively seek out responsible representatives of all parts of their communities so that they may structure a broad range of programs that will inform, enlighten, and entertain the total audience.

Broadcasters should also develop programs directed toward advancing the cultural and educational aspects of their communities.

To assure that broadcasters have the freedom to program fully and responsibly, none of the provisions of this Code should be construed as preventing or impeding broadcast of the broad range of material necessary to help broadcasters fulfill their obligations to operate in the public interest.

The challenge to the broadcaster is to determine how suitably to present the complexities of human behavior. For television, this requires exceptional awareness of considerations peculiar to the medium.

Accordingly, in selecting program subjects and themes, great care must be exercised to be sure that treatment and presentation are made in good faith and not for the purpose of sensationalism or to shock or exploit the audience or appeal to prurient interests or morbid curiosity.

Additionally, entertainment programming inappropriate for viewing by a general family audience should not be broadcast during the first hour of network entertainment programming in prime time and in the immediately preceding hour. In the occasional case when an entertainment program in this time period is deemed to be inappropriate for such an audience, advisories should be used to alert viewers. Advisories should also be used when programs in later prime time periods contain material that might be disturbing to significant segments of the audience.*

These advisories should be presented in audio and video form at the beginning of the program and when deemed appropriate at a later point in the program. Advisories should also be used responsibly in promotional material in advance of the program. When using an advisory, the broadcaster should attempt to notify publishers of television program listings.*

Special care should be taken with respect to the content and treatment of audience advisories so that they do not disserve their intended purpose by containing material that is promotional, sensational or exploitative. Promotional announcements for programs that include advisories should be scheduled on a basis consistent with the purpose of the advisory.* *(See Television Code Interpretation No. 5)*

II. Responsibility Toward Children

Broadcasters have a special responsibility to children. Programs designed primarily for children should take into account the range of interests and needs of children from instructional and cultural material to a wide variety of entertainment material. In their totality, programs should contribute to the sound, balanced development of children to help them achieve a sense of the world at large and informed adjustments to their society.

In the course of a child's development, numerous social factors and forces, including television, affect the ability of the child to make the transition to adult society.

The child's training and experience during the formative years should include positive sets of values which will allow the child to become a responsible adult, capable of coping with the challenges of maturity.

Children should also be exposed, at the appropriate times, to a reasonable range of the realities which exist in the world sufficient to help them

*Effective September 1975

make the transition to adulthood.

Because children are allowed to watch programs designed primarily for adults, broadcasters should take this practice into account in the presentation of material in such programs when children may constitute a substantial segment of the audience.

All the standards set forth in this section apply to both program and commercial material designed and intended for viewing by children.

III. Community Responsibility

1. Television broadcasters and their staffs occupy positions of unique responsibility in their communities and should conscientiously endeavor to be acquainted fully with the community's needs and characteristics in order better to serve the welfare of its citizens.

2. Requests for time for the placement of public service announcements or programs should be carefully reviewed with respect to the character and reputation of the group, campaign or organization involved, the public interest content of the message, and the manner of its presentation.

IV. Special Program Standards

1. Violence, physical or psychological, may only be projected in responsibly handled contexts, not used exploitatively. Programs involving violence should present the consequences of it to its victims and perpetrators.

Presentation of the details of violence should avoid the excessive, the gratuitous and the instructional.

The use of violence for its own sake and the detailed dwelling upon brutality or physical agony, by sight or by sound, are not permissible.

The depiction of conflict, when presented in programs designed primarily for children, should be handled with sensitivity.

2. The treatment of criminal activities should always convey their social and human effects.

The presentation of techniques of crime in such detail as to be instructional or invite imitation shall be avoided.

3. Narcotic addiction shall not be presented except as a destructive habit. The use of illegal drugs or the abuse of legal drugs shall not be encouraged or shown as socially acceptable.

4. The use of gambling devices or scenes necessary to the development of plot or as appropriate background is acceptable only when presented with discretion and in moderation, and in a manner which would not excite interest in, or foster, betting nor be instructional in nature.

5. Telecasts of actual sports programs at which on-the-scene betting is permitted by law shall be presented in a manner in keeping with federal, state and local laws, and should concentrate on the subject as a public sporting event.

6. Special precautions must be taken to avoid demeaning or ridiculing members of the audience who suffer from physical or mental afflictions or deformities.

7. Special sensitivity is necessary in the use of material relating to sex, race, color, age, creed, religious functionaries or rites, or national or ethnic derivation.

8. Obscene, indecent or profane matter, as proscribed by law, is unacceptable.

9. The presentation of marriage, the family and similarly important human relationships, and material with sexual connotations, shall not be treated exploitatively or irresponsibly, but with sensitivity. Costuming and movements of all performers shall be handled in a similar fashion.

10. The use of liquor and the depiction of smoking in program content shall be de-emphasized. When shown, they should be consistent with plot and character development.

11. The creation of a state of hypnosis by act or detailed demonstration on camera is prohibited, and hypnosis as a form of "parlor game" antics to create humorous situations within a comedy setting is forbidden.

12. Program material pertaining to fortune-telling, occultism, astrology, phrenology, palm-reading, numerology, mind-reading, character-reading, and the like is unacceptable if it encourages people to regard such fields as providing commonly accepted appraisals of life.

13. Professional advice, diagnosis and treatment will be presented in conformity with law and recognized professional standards.

14. Any technique whereby an attempt is made to convey information to the viewer by transmitting messages below the threshold of normal awareness is not permitted.

15. The use of animals, consistent with plot and character delineation, shall be in conformity with accepted standards of humane treatment.

16. Quiz and similar programs that are presented as contests of knowledge, information, skill or luck must, in fact, be genuine contests; and the results must not be controlled by collusion with or between contestants, or by any other action which will favor one contestant against any other.

17. The broadcaster shall be constantly alert to prevent inclusion of elements within a program dictated by factors other than the requirements of the program itself. The acceptance of cash payments or other considerations in return for including scenic properties, the choice and identification of prizes, the selection of music and other creative program elements and inclusion of any identification of commercial products or services, their trade names or advertising slogan within the program are prohibited except in accordance with Sections 317 and 508 of the Communications Act.

18. Contests may not constitute a lottery.

19. No program shall be presented in a manner which through artifice or simulation would mislead the audience as to any material fact. Each broadcaster must exercise reasonable judgment to determine whether a particular method of presentation would constitute a material deception, or would be accepted by the audience as normal theatrical illusion.

20. A television broadcaster should not present fictional events or other non-news material as authentic news telecasts or announcements, nor should he permit dramatizations in any program which would give the false impression that the dramatized material constitutes news.

21. The standards of this Code covering program content are also understood to include, wherever applicable, the standards contained in the advertising section of the Code.

V. Treatment of News and Public Events

General

Television Code standards relating to the treatment of news and public events are, because of constitutional considerations, intended to be exhortatory. The standards set forth hereunder encourage high standards of professionalism in broadcast journalism. They are not to be interpreted as turning over to others the broadcaster's responsibility as to judgments necessary in news and public events programming.

News

1. A television station's news schedule should be adequate and well-balanced.

2. News reporting should be factual, fair and without bias.

3. A television broadcaster should exercise particular discrimination in the acceptance, placement and presentation of advertising in news programs so that such advertising should be clearly distinguishable from the news content.

4. At all times, pictorial and verbal material for both news and comment should conform to other sections of these standards, wherever such sections are reasonably applicable.

5. Good taste should prevail in the selection and handling of news:

Morbid, sensational or alarming details not essential to the factual report, especially in connection with stories of crime or sex, should be avoided. News should be telecast in such a manner as to avoid panic and unnecessary alarm.

6. Commentary and analysis should be clearly identified as such.

7. Pictorial material should be chosen with care and not presented in a misleading manner.

8. All news interview programs should be governed by accepted standards of ethical journalism, under which the interviewer selects the questions to be asked. Where there is advace agreement materially restricting an important or newsworthy area of questioning, the interviewer will state on the program that such limitation has been agreed upon. Such disclosure should be made if the person being interviewed requires that questions be submitted in advance or if he participates in editing a recording of the interview prior to its use on the air.

9. A television broadcaster should exercise due care in his supervision of content, format, and presentation of newscasts originated by his station, and in his selection of newscasters, commentators, and analysts.

Public Events

1. A television broadcaster has an affirmative responsiblity at all times to be informed of public

events, and to provide coverage consonant with the ends of an informed and enlightened citizenry.

2. The treatment of such events by a television broadcaster should provide adequate and informed coverage.

VI. Controversial Public Issues

1. Television provides a valuable forum for the expression of responsible views on public issues of a controversial nature. The television broadcaster should seek out and develop with accountable individuals, groups and organizations, programs relating to controversial public issues of import to his fellow citizens; and to give fair representation to opposing sides of issues which materially affect the life or welfare of a substantial segment of the public.

2. Requests by individuals, groups or organizations for time to discuss their views on controversial public issues should be considered on the basis of their individual merits, and in the light of the contribution which the use requested would make to the public interest, and to a well-balanced program structure.

3. Programs devoted to the discussion of controversial public issues should be identified as such. They should not be presented in a manner which would mislead listeners or viewers to believe that the program is purely of an entertainment, news, or other character.

4. Broadcasts in which stations express their own opinions about issues of general public interest should be clearly identified as editorials. They should be unmistakably identified as statements of station opinion and should be appropriately distinguished from news and other program material.

VII. Political Telecasts

1. Political telecasts should be clearly identified as such. They should not be presented by a television broadcaster in a manner which would mislead listeners or viewers to believe that the program is of any other character.

(Ref.: Communications Act of 1934, as amended, Secs. 315 and 317, and FCC Rules and Regulations, Secs. 3.654, 3.657, 3.663, as discussed in NAB's

"Political Broadcast Catechism & The Fairness Doctrine.")

VIII. Religious Programs

1. It is the responsibility of a television broadcaster to make available to the community appropriate opportunity for religious presentations.

2. Programs reach audiences of all creeds simultaneously. Therefore, both the advocates of broad or ecumenical religious precepts, and the exponents of specific doctrines, are urged to present their positions in a manner conducive to viewer enlightenment on the role of religion in society.

3. In the allocation of time for telecasts of religious programs the television station should use its best efforts to apportion such time fairly among responsible individuals, groups and organizations.

ADVERTISING STANDARDS

IX. General Advertising Standards

1. This Code establishes basic standards for all television broadcasting. The principles of acceptability and good taste within the Program Standards section govern the presentation of advertising where applicable. In addition, the Code establishes in this section special standards which apply to television advertising.

2. A commercial television broadcaster makes his facilities available for the advertising of products and services and accepts commercial presentations for such advertising. However, a televison broadcaster should, in recognition of his responsibility to the public, refuse the facilities of his station to an advertiser where he has good reason to doubt the integrity of the advertiser, the truth of the advertising representations, or the compliance of the advertiser with the spirit and purpose of all applicable legal requirements.

3. Identification of sponsorship must be made in all sponsored programs in accordance with the requirements of the Communications Act of 1934, as amended, and the Rules and Regulations of the Federal Communications Commission.

4. Representations which disregard normal safety precautions shall be avoided.

Children shall not be represented, except under proper adult supervision, as being in contact with or demonstrating a product recognized as potentially dangerous to them.

5. In consideration of the customs and attitudes of the communities served, each television broadcaster should refuse his facilities to the advertisement of products and services, or the use of advertising scripts, which the station has good reason to believe would be objectionable to a substantial and responsible segment of the community. These standards should be applied with judgment and flexibility, taking into consideration the characteristics of the medium, its home and family audience, and the form and content of the particular presentation.

6. The advertising of hard liquor (distilled spirits) is not acceptable.

7. The advertising of beer and wines is acceptable only when presented in the best of good taste and discretion, and is acceptable only subject to

Federal and local laws (*See Television Code Interpretation No. 4*)

8. Advertising by institutions or enterprises which in their offers of instruction imply promises of employment or make exaggerated claims for the opportunities awaiting those who enroll for courses is generally unacceptable.

9. The advertising of firearms/ammunition is acceptable provided it promotes the product only as sporting equipment and conforms to recognized standards of safety as well as all applicable laws and regulations. Advertisements of firearms/ammunition by mail order are unacceptable. The advertising of fireworks is acceptable subject to all applicable laws.

10. The advertising of fortune-telling, occultism, astrology, phrenology, palm-reading, numerology, mind-reading, character-reading or subjects of a like nature is not permitted.

11. Because all products of a personal nature create special problems, acceptability of such products should be determined with especial emphasis on ethics and the canons of good taste. Such advertising of personal products as is accepted must be presented in a restrained and obviously inoffensive manner.

12. The advertising of tip sheets and other publications seeking to advertise for the purpose of giving odds or promoting betting is unacceptable.

The lawful advertising of government organizations which conduct legalized lotteries is acceptable provided such advertising does not unduly exhort the public to bet.

The advertising of private or governmental organizations which conduct legalized betting on sporting contests is acceptable provided such advertising is limited to institutional type announcements which do not exhort the public to bet.

13. An advertiser who markets more than one product should not be permitted to use advertising copy devoted to an acceptable product for purposes of publicizing the brand name or other identification of a product which is not acceptable.

14. "Bait-switch" advertising, whereby goods or services which the advertiser has no intention of selling are offered merely to lure the customer into purchasing higher-priced substitutes, is not acceptable.

15. Personal endorsements (testimonials) shall

be genuine and reflect personal experience. They shall contain no statement that cannot be supported if presented in the advertiser's own words.

X. Presentation of Advertising

1. Advertising messages should be presented with courtesy and good taste; disturbing or annoying material should be avoided; every effort should be made to keep the advertising message in harmony with the content and general tone of the program in which it appears.

2. The role and capability of television to market sponsors' products are well recognized. In turn, this fact dictates that great care be exercised by the broadcaster to prevent the presentation of false, misleading or deceptive advertising. While it is entirely appropriate to present a product in a favorable light and atmosphere, the presentation must not, by copy or demonstration, involve a material deception as to the characteristics, performance or appearance of the product.

Broadcast advertisers are responsible for making available, at the request of the Code Authority, documentation adequate to support the validity and truthfulness of claims, demonstrations and testimonials contained in their commercial messages.

3. The broadcaster and the advertiser should exercise special caution with the content and presentation of television commercials placed in or near programs designed for children. Exploitation of children should be avoided. Commercials directed to children should in no way mislead as to the product's performance and usefulness.

Commercials, whether live, film or tape, within programs initially designed primarily for children under 12 years of age shall be clearly separated from program material by an appropriate device.

Trade name identification or other merchandising practices involving the gratuitous naming of products is discouraged in programs designed primarily for children.

Appeals involving matters of health which should be determined by physicians should not be directed primarily to children.

4. No children's program personality or cartoon character shall be utilized to deliver commercial messages within or adjacent to the programs in which such a personality or cartoon character regularly appears. This provision shall also apply to lead-ins to commercials when such lead-ins contain sell copy or imply endorsement of the product by program personalities or cartoon characters. (Effective September 1975.)

5. Appeals to help fictitious characters in television programs by purchasing the advertiser's product or service or sending for a premium should not be permitted, and such fictitious characters should not be introduced into the advertising message for such purposes.

6. Commercials for services or over-the-counter products involving health considerations are of intimate and far-reaching importance to the consumer. The following principles should apply to such advertising:

    a. Physicians, dentists or nurses or actors representing physicians, dentists or nurses, shall not be employed directly or by implication. These restrictions also apply to persons professionally engaged in medical services (e.g., physical therapists, pharmacists, dental assistants, nurses' aides).

    b. Visual representations of laboratory settings may be employed, provided they bear a direct relationship to bona fide research which has been conducted for the product or service. *(See Television Code, X, 11)* In such cases, laboratory technicians shall be identified as such and shall not be employed as spokesmen or in any other way speak on behalf of the product.

    c. Institutional announcements not intended to sell a specific product or service to the consumer and public service announcements by non-profit organizations may be presented by accredited physicians, dentists or nurses, subject to approval by the broadcaster. An accredited professional is one who has met required qualifications and has been licensed in his resident state.

7. Advertising should offer a product or service on its positive merits and refrain from discrediting, disparaging or unfairly attacking competitors, competing products, other industries, professions or institutions.

8. A sponsor's advertising messages should be confined within the framework of the sponsor's program structure. A television broadcaster should avoid the use of commercial announcements which are divorced from the program either by preceding

the introduction of the program (as in the case of so-called "cow-catcher" announcements) or by following the apparent sign-off of the program (as in the case of so-called trailer or "hitch-hike" announcements). To this end, the program itself should be announced and clearly identified, both audio and video, before the sponsor's advertising material is first used, and should be signed off, both audio and video, after the sponsor's advertising material is last used.

9. Since advertising by television is a dynamic technique, a television broadcaster should keep under surveillance new advertising devices so that the spirit and purpose of these standards are fulfilled.

10. A charge for television time to churches and religious bodies is not recommended.

11. Reference to the results of bona fide research, surveys or tests relating to the product to be advertised shall not be presented in a manner so as to create an impression of fact beyond that established by the work that has been conducted.

XI. Advertising of Medical Products

1. The advertising of medical products presents considerations of intimate and far-reaching importance to the consumer because of the direct bearing on his health.

2. Because of the personal nature of the advertising of medical products, claims that a product will effect a cure and the indiscriminate use of such words as "safe," "without risk," "harmless," or terms of similar meaning should not be accepted in the advertising of medical products on television stations.

3. A television broadcaster should not accept advertising material which in his opinion offensively describes or dramatizes distress or morbid situations involving ailments, by spoken word, sound or visual effects.

XII. Contests

1. Contests shall be conducted with fairness to all entrants, and shall comply with all pertinent laws and regulations. Care should be taken to avoid the concurrent use of the three elements which together constitute a lottery—prize, chance and consideration.

2. All contest details, including rules, eligibility requirements, opening and termination dates should be clearly and completely announced and/or shown, or easily accessible to the viewing public, and the winners' names should be released and prizes awarded as soon as possible after the close of the contest.

3. When advertising is accepted which requests contestants to submit items of product identification or other evidence of purchase of products, reasonable facsimiles thereof should be made acceptable unless the award is based upon skill and not upon chance.

4. All copy pertaining to any contest (except that which is required by law) associated with the exploitation or sale of the sponsor's product or service, and all references to prizes or gifts offered in such connection should be considered a part of and included in the total time allowances as herein provided. *(See Television Code, XIV)*

XIII. Premiums and Offers

1. Full details of proposed offers should be required by the television broadcaster for investigation and approved before the first announcement of the offer is made to the public.

2. A final date for the termination of an offer should be announced as far in advance as possible.

3. Before accepting for telecast offers involving a monetary consideration, a television broadcaster should satisfy himself as to the integrity of the advertiser and the advertiser's willingness to honor complaints indicating dissatisfaction with the premium by returning the monetary consideration.

4. There should be no misleading descriptions or visual representations of any premiums or gifts which would distort or enlarge their value in the minds of the viewers.

5. Assurances should be obtained from the advertiser that premiums offered are not harmful to person or property.

6. Premiums should not be approved which appeal to superstition on the basis of "luck-bearing" powers or otherwise.

XIV. Time Standards for Non-Program Material*

In order that the time for non-program material and

*See Time Standards for Independent Stations, p. 19.

its placement shall best serve the viewer, the following standards are set forth in accordance with sound television practice:

1. Non-Program Material Definition:

Non-program material, in both prime time and all other time, includes billboards, commercials, promotional announcements and all credits in excess of 30 seconds per program, except in feature films. In no event should credits exceed 40 seconds per program. The 40-second limitation on credits shall not apply, however, in any situation governed by a contract entered into before October 1, 1971. Public service announcements and promotional announcements for the same program are excluded from this definition.

2. Allowable Time for Non-Program Material:

a. In prime time on network affiliated stations, non-program material shall not exceed nine minutes 30 seconds in any 60-minute period.

In the event that news programming is included within the three and one-half hour prime time period, not more than one 30-minute segment of news programming may be governed by time standards applicable to all other time.

Prime time is a continuous period of not less than three and one-half consecutive hours per broadcast day as designated by the station between the hours of 6:00 PM and Midnight.

b. In all other time, non-program material shall not exceed 16 minutes in any 60-minute period.

c. Children's Programming Time—Defined as those hours other than prime time in which programs initially designed primarily for children under 12 years of age are scheduled.

Within this time period on Saturday and Sunday, non-program material shall not exceed 10 minutes in any 60-minute period after December 31, 1974 and nine minutes 30 seconds in any 60-minute period after December 31, 1975.

Within this time period on Monday through Friday, non-program material shall not exceed 14 minutes in any 60-minute period after December 31, 1974 and 12 minutes in any 60-minute period after December 31, 1975.

3. Program Interruptions:

a. Definition: A program interruption is any occurrence of non-program material within the main body of the program.

b. In prime time, the number of program interruptions shall not exceed two within any 30-minute program, or four within any 60-minute program.

Programs longer than 60 minutes shall be prorated at two interruptions per half-hour.

The number of interruptions in 60-minute variety shows shall not exceed five.

c. In all other time, the number of interruptions shall not exceed four within any 30-minute program period.

d. In children's weekend programming time, as above defined in 2c, the number of program interruptions shall not exceed two within any 30-minute program or four within any 60-minute program.

e. In both prime time and all other time, the following interruption standard shall apply within programs of 15 minutes or less in length:

 5-minute program—1 interruption;
 10-minute program—2 interruptions;
 15-minute program—2 interruptions.

f. News, weather, sports and special events programs are exempt from the interruption standard because of the nature of such programs.

4. No more than four non-program material announcements shall be scheduled consecutively within programs, and no more than three non-program material announcements shall be scheduled consecutively during station breaks. The consecutive non-program material limitation shall not apply to a single sponsor who wishes to further reduce the number of interruptions in the program.

5. A multiple product announcement is one in which two or more products or services are presented within the framework of a single announcement. A multiple product announcement shall not be scheduled in a unit of time less than 60 seconds, except where integrated so as to appear to the viewer as a single message. A multiple product announcement shall be considered integrated and counted as a single announcement if:

a. the products or services are related and interwoven within the framework of the announcement (related products or services shall be defined as those having a common character, purpose and use); and

b. the voice(s), setting, background and continuity are used consistently throughout so as to appear to the viewer as a single message.

Multiple product announcements of 60 seconds in length or longer not meeting this definition of integration shall be counted as two or more announcements under this section of the Code. This provision shall not apply to retail or service establishments.

6. The use of billboards, in prime time and all other time, shall be confined to programs sponsored by a single or alternate week advertiser and shall be limited to the products advertised in the program.

7. Reasonable and limited identification of prizes and donors' names where the presentation of contest awards or prizes is a necessary part of program content shall not be included as non-program material as defined above.

8. Programs presenting women's service features, shopping guides, fashion shows, demonstrations and similar material provide a special service to the public in which certain material normally classified as non-program is an informative and necessary part of the program content. Because of this, the time standards may be waived by the Code Authority to a reasonable extent on a case-by-case basis.

9. Gratuitous references in a program to a non-sponsor's product or service should be avoided except for normal guest identification.

10. Stationary backdrops or properties in television presentations showing the sponsor's name or product, the name of his product, his trade-mark or slogan should be used only incidentally and should not obtrude on program interest or entertainment.

Note: From time to time the Code Authority issues advertising guidelines and clarifications expanding on provisions of the Code. Among areas covered are acne, alcoholic beverages, arthritis and rheumatism remedies, bronchitis, comparative advertising, children's premiums and offers, children's TV advertising, disparagement, hallucinogens, hypnosis, lotteries, men-in-white, non-prescription medications, personal products, testimonials, time standards, toys, vegetable oils and margarines, and weight reducing products/ services. Copies may be obtained from any NAB Code Authority office.

Time Standards for Independent Stations

1. Non-program elements shall be considered as all-inclusive, with the exception of required credits, legally required station identifications, and "bumpers." Promotion spots and public service announcements, as well as commercials, are to be considered non-program elements.

2. The allowed time for non-program elements, as defined above, shall not exceed seven minutes in a 30-minute period or multiples thereof in prime time (prime time is defined as any three contiguous hours between 6:00 PM and midnight, local time), or eight minutes in a 30-minute period or multiples thereof during all other times.

3. Where a station does not carry a commercial in a station break between programs, the number of program interruptions shall not exceed four within any 30-minute program, or seven within any 60-minute program, or 10 within any 90-minute program, or 13 in any 120-minute program. Stations which do carry commercials in station breaks between programs shall limit the number of program interruptions to three within any 30-minute program, or six within any 60-minute program, or nine within any 90-minute program, or 12 in any 120-minute program. News, weather, sports, and special events are exempted because of format.

4. Not more than four non-program material announcements as defined above shall be scheduled consecutively. An exception may be made only in the case of a program 60 minutes or more in length, when no more than seven non-program elements may be scheduled consecutively by stations who wish to reduce the number of program interruptions.

5. The conditions of paragraphs three and four shall not apply to live sports programs where the program format dictates and limits the number of program interruptions.

INTERPRETATIONS

Interpretation No. 1

June 7, 1956, Revised June 9, 1958
"Pitch" Programs

The "pitchman" technique of advertising on television is inconsistent with good broadcast practice and generally damages the reputation of the industry and the advertising profession.

Sponsored program-length segments consisting substantially of continuous demonstrations or sales presentation, violate not only the time standards established in the Code but the broad philosophy of improvement implicit in the voluntary Code operation and are not acceptable.

Interpretation No. 2

June 7, 1956
Hollywood Film Promotion

The presentation of commentary or film excerpts from current theatrical releases in some instances may constitute commercial material under the Time Standards for Non-Program Material. Specifically, for example, when such presentation, directly or by inference, urges viewers to attend, it shall be counted against the commercial allowance for the program of which it is a part.

Interpretation No. 3

January 23, 1959
Prize Identification

Aural and/or visual prize identification of up to 10 seconds duration may be deemed "reasonable and limited" under the language of Paragraph 7 of the Time Standards for Non-Program Material. Where such identification is longer than 10 seconds, the entire announcement or visual presentation will be charged against the total commercial time for the program period.

Interpretation No. 4

March 4, 1965
Drinking on Camera

Paragraph 7, Section IX, General Advertising Standards, states that the "advertising of beer and wine is acceptable only when presented in the best of good taste and discretion." This requires that commercials involving beer and wine avoid any representation of on-camera drinking.

Interpretation No. 5

April 8, 1975

The scheduling provisions of Section I (Principles Governing Program Content) shall not apply to programs under contract to a station as of April 8, 1975, all episodes of which were then in existence, if such station is unable, despite reasonable good faith efforts, to edit such programs to make them appropriate for family viewing or to reschedule them so as not to occupy family viewing periods. This exception shall in no event apply after September 1, 1977. Any such programs excepted from scheduling provisions shall, of course, bear the required advisory notices. (Effective September 1975)

REGULATIONS AND PROCEDURES

The following Regulations and Procedures shall obtain as an integral part of the Television Code of the National Association of Broadcasters:

I. Name

The name of this Code shall be *The Television Code of the National Association of Broadcasters.* *

II. Purpose of the Code

The purpose of this Code is cooperatively to maintain a level of television programming which gives full consideration to the educational, informational, cultural, economic, moral and entertainment needs of the American public to the end that more and more people will be better served.

III. Subscribers

Section 1. Eligibility

Any individual, firm or corporation which is engaged in the operation of a television broadcast station or network, or which holds a construction permit for a televison broadcast station within the United States or its dependencies, shall, subject to the approval of the Television Board of Directors as hereinafter provided, be eligible to subscribe to the Television Code of the NAB to the extent of one subscription for each such station and/or network which it operates or for which it holds a construction permit; provided, that a non-television member of NAB shall not become eligible via Code subscription to receive any of the member services or to exercise any of the voting privileges of a member.

Section 2. Certification of Subscription

Upon subscribing to the Code, subject to the approval of the Television Board of Directors, there shall be granted forthwith to each such subscribing station authority to use the "NAB Television Seal

*By-Laws of the National Association of Broadcasters, Article VI, section 8, C: "Television Board. The Television Board is hereby authorized:—(4) to enact, amend and promulgate standards of practice or codes for its Television members, and to establish such methods to secure observance thereof as it may deem advisable:—."

of Good Practice," a copyrighted and registered seal to be provided in the form of a certificate, a slide and/or a film, signifying that the recipient thereof is a subscriber in good standing to the Television Code of the NAB. The seal and its significance shall be appropriately publicized by the NAB.

Section 3. Duration of Subscription

Subscription shall continue in full force and effect until thirty days after the first of the month following receipt of notice of written resignation. Subscription to the Code shall be effective from the date of application subject to the approval of the Television Board of Directors; provided, that the subscription of a television station going on the air for the first time shall, for the first six months of such subscription, be probationary, during which time its subscription can be summarily revoked by an affirmative two-thirds vote of the Television Board of Directors without the usual processes specified below.

Section 4. Suspension of Subscription

Any subscription, and/or the authority to utilize and show the above-noted seal, may be voided, revoked or temporarily suspended for television programming, including commercial copy, which, by theme, treatment or incident, in the judgment of the Television Board constitutes a continuing, willful or gross violation of any of the provisions of the Television Code, by an affirmative two-thirds vote of the Television Board of Directors at a regular or special meeting; provided, however, that the following conditions and procedures shall apply:

A. Preferring of Charges–Conditions Precedent:

Prior to the preferring of charges to the Television Board of Directors concerning violation of the Code by a subscriber, the Television Code Review Board (hereinafter provided for) (1) Shall have appropriately, and in good time, informed and advised such subscriber of any and all complaints and information coming to the attention of the Television Code Review Board and relating to the programming of said subscriber, (2) Shall have reported to, and advised, said subscriber by analysis, interpretation, recommendation or otherwise, of the possibility of a violation or breach of the Television Code by the subscriber, and (3) Shall have served upon the subscriber, by Registered Mail a Notice of Intent to prefer charges, at least 20 days prior to the filing of any such charges with the Television Board of Directors. During this period the Television Code Review Board may, within its sole discretion, reconsider its proposed action based upon such written reply as the subscriber may care to make, or upon such action as the subscriber may care to take program-wise, in conformance with the analysis, interpretation, or recommendation of the Television Code Review Board.

(i) Notice of Intent

The Notice of Intent shall include a statement of the grounds and reasons for the proposed charges, including appropriate references to the Television Code.

(ii) Time

In the event that the nature of the program in question is such that time is of the essence, the Television Code Review Board may prefer charges within less than the 20 days above specified, provided that a time certain in which reply may be made is included in its Notice of Intent, and provided that its reasons therefor must be specified in its statement of charges preferred.

B. *The Charges:*

The subscriber shall be advised in writing by Registered Mail of the charges preferred. The charges preferred by the Television Code Review Board to the Television Board of Directors shall include the

grounds and reasons therefor, together with specific references to the Television Code. The charges shall contain a statement that the conditions precedent, herein before described, have been met.

C. *Hearing:*

The subscriber shall have the right to a hearing and may exercise same by filing an answer within 10 days of the date of such notification.

D. *Waiver:*

Failure to request a hearing shall be deemed a waiver of the subscriber's right thereto.

E. *Designation:*

If a hearing is requested by the subscriber, it shall be designated as promptly as possible and at such time and place as the Television Board may specify.

F. *Confidential Status:*

Hearings shall be closed; and all correspondence between a subscriber and the Television Code Review Board and/or the Televison Board of Directors concerning specific programming shall be confidential; provided, however, that the confidential status of these procedures may be waived by a subscriber.

G. *Presentation; Representation:*

A subscriber against whom charges have been preferred, and who has exercised his right to a hearing, shall be entitled to effect presentation of his case personally, by agent, by attorney, or by deposition and interrogatory.

H. *Intervention:*

Upon request by the subscriber-respondent or the Television Code Review Board, the Television Board of Directors, in its discretion, may permit the intervention of one or more other subscribers as parties-in-interest.

I. *Transcript:*

A stenographic transcript record shall be taken and shall be certified by the Chairman of the Television Board of Directors to the office of the Secretary of the National Association of Broadcasters, where it shall be maintained. The transcript shall not be open to inspection unless otherwise provided by the party respondent in the proceeding.

J. *Television Code Review Board; Counsel:*

The Television Code Review Board may, at its discretion, utilize the services of an attorney from the staff of the NAB for the purpose of effecting its presentation in a hearing matter.

K. *Order of Procedure:*

At hearings the Television Code Review Board shall open and close.

L. *Cross-Examination:*

The right of cross-examination shall specifically obtain. Where procedure has been by deposition or interrogatory, the use of cross-interrogatories shall satisfy this right.

M. *Presentation:*

Oral and written evidence may be introduced by the subscriber and by the Television Code Review Board. Oral argument may be had at the hearing and written memoranda or briefs may be submitted by the subscriber and by the Television Code Review Board. The Television Board of Directors may admit such evidence as it deems relevant, material and competent, and may determine the nature and length of the oral argument and the written argument or briefs.

N. *Authority of Presiding Officer; of Television Board of Directors:*

The Presiding Officer shall rule upon all interlocutory matters, such as, but not limited to, the admissibility of evidence, the qualifications of witnesses, etc. On all other matters, authority to act shall be vested in a majority of the Television Board unless otherwise provided.

O. *Films, Transcriptions, etc.:*

Films, kinescopes, records, transcriptions, or other mechanical reproductions of television programs, properly identified, shall be accepted into evidence when relevant.

P. *Continuances and Extensions:*

Continuance and extension of any proceeding or for the time of filing or performing any act required or allowed to be done within a specific time may be granted upon request, for a good cause shown. The Board or the Presiding Officer may recess or adjourn a hearing for such time as may be deemed necessary, and may change the place thereof.

Q. *Findings and Conclusions:*

The Television Board of Directors shall decide the case as expeditiously as possible and shall notify the subscriber and the Television Code Review Board, in writing, of the decision. The decision of the Television Board of Directors shall contain findings of fact with conclusions, as well as the reasons or bases therefor. Findings of fact shall set out in detail and with particularity all basic evidentiary facts developed on the record (with appropriate citations to the transcript of record or exhibit relied on for each evidentiary fact) supporting the conclusion reached.

R. *Reconsideration or Rehearing:*

A request for reconsideration or rehearing may be filed by parties to the hearing. Requests for reconsideration or rehearing shall state with particularity in what respect the decision or any matter determined therein is claimed to be unjust, unwarranted, or erroneous, and with respect to any finding of fact shall specify the pages of record relied on. If the existence of any newly discovered evidence is claimed, the request shall be accompanied by a verified statement of the facts together with the facts relied on to show that the party, with due diligence, could not have known or discovered such facts at the time of the hearing.

The request for rehearing may seek:
a. Reconsideration
b. Additional oral argument
c. Reopening of the proceedings
d. Amendment of any findings, or
e. Other relief.

S. *Time for Filing:*

Requests for reconsideration or rehearing shall be filed within 10 days after receipt by the respondent of the decision. Opposition thereto may be filed within five days after the filing of the request.

T. *Penalty, Suspension of:*

At the discretion of the Television Board, application of any penalty provided for in the decision may be suspended until the Board makes final disposition of the request for reconsideration or rehearing.

U. *Disqualification:*

Any member of the Television Board may disqualify himself, or upon good cause shown by any interested party, may be disqualified by a majority vote of the Television Board.

Section 5. *Additional Procedures*

When necessary to the proper administration of the Code, additional rules of procedure will be established from time to time as authorized by the By-Laws of the NAB; in keeping therewith, special consideration shall be given to the procedures for receipt and processing of complaints and to necessary rules to be adopted from time to time, taking into account the source and nature of such complaints; such rules to include precautionary measures such as the posting of bonds to cover costs and expenses of processing same; and further provided that special consideration will be given to procedures insuring the confidential status of proceedings relating to Code observance.

Section 6. *Amendment and Review*

Because of the new and dynamic aspects inherent in television broadcast, the Television Code, as a living, flexible and continuing document, may be amended from time to time by the Television Board of Directors; provided that said Board is specifically charged with review and reconsideration of the entire Code, its appendices and procedures, at least once each year.

Section 7. Termination of Contracts

All subscribers on the air at the time of subscription to the Code shall be permitted that period prior to and including the earliest legal cancellation date to terminate any contracts, then outstanding, calling for program presentations which would not be in conformity with the Television Code, provided, however, that in no event shall such period be longer than 52 weeks.

IV. Affiliate Subscribers

Section 1. Eligibility

Any individual, firm or corporation, which is engaged in the production or distribution, lease, or sale of recorded programs for television presentation, subject to the approval of the Television Code Review Board as hereinafter provided, shall be eligible to become an affiliate subscriber to the Television Code of the NAB.

Section 2. Certification of Subscription

Upon becoming an affiliate subscriber to the Code, subject to the approval of the Television Code Review Board, there shall be granted forthwith to each such affiliate subscriber authority to use a copyrighted and registered seal and declaration, in a manner approved by the Television Code Review Board, identifying the individual firm or corporation as an affiliate subscriber to the Television Code of the NAB. Such authority shall not constitute formal clearance or approval by the Television Code Review Board of specific film programs or other recorded material.

Section 3. Duration of Affiliate Subscription

The affiliate subscription shall continue in full force and effect until 30 days after the first of the month following receipt of a written notice of resignation. The affiliate subscription of the Code shall be effective from the date of application subject to the approval of the Television Code Review Board.

Section 4. Suspension of Affiliate Subscription

Any affiliate subscription and the authority to utilize and show the above-noted seal may be voided, revoked, or temporarily suspended for the sale or distribution for television presentation of any film or other recorded material which by theme, treatment, or incident, in the judgement of the Television Code Review Board, constitutes a continuing, willful or gross violation of any of the provisions of the Television Code, by a majority vote of the Television Code Review Board at any regular or special meeting. The conditions and procedures applicable to subscribers shall not apply to affiliate subscribers.

Section 5. Representation of Affiliate Subscribers

Any affiliate subscriber or group of affiliate subscribers may authorize an individual or association to act for them in connection with their relations with the Television Code Review Board by filing a written notice of such representation with the Board. Such representation, however, in no way will limit the right of the Television Code Review Board to suspend individual affiliate subscribers in accordance with the provisions of Section 4.

V. Rates

Each subscriber and affiliate subscriber shall pay "administrative" rates in accordance with such schedule, at such time, and under such conditions as may be determined from time to time by the Television Board (see Article VI, section 8, C. Television Board (3) and (4), By-Laws of the NAB); provided, that appropriate credit shall be afforded to a television member of the NAB against the regular dues which he or it pays to NAB.

VI. The Television Code Review Board

Section 1. Composition

There shall be a continuing committee entitled the Television Code Review Board to be composed of not more than nine members, all of whom shall be from subscribers to the Television Code. They shall be appointed by the President of NAB, subject to confirmation by the Television Board, and may include one member from each of the subscribing nationwide television networks. Members of the Television Board shall not be eligible to serve on the Review Board. Due consideration shall be given, in making the appointments, to factors of diversification of geographical location, market size, company representation and network affiliation.

No person shall continue as a member of the Television Code Review Board if the station or entity he represents ceases to subscribe to the Television Code. In such case a vacancy occurs in the office immediately, and a successor may be appointed to serve out the unexpired term.

All terms shall be for two years, commencing at the close of the annual meeting of the membership following appointment.

A. *Limitation of Service:*

No person shall serve for more than two terms of two years each, consecutively, as a member of the Television Code Review Board; provided, however, this limitation shall not apply to network representatives.

Serving out the unexpired term of a former member shall not constitute a term within the meaning of this section.

B. *Meetings:*

The Television Code Review Board shall meet at least twice in each calendar year on a date to be determined by the Chairman. The Chairman, or the Code Authority Director, may, at any time, on at least five days written notice, call a special meeting of the Board.

C. *Quorum:*

For all purposes, a majority of the members of the Television Code Review Board shall constitute a quorum.

Section 2. *Authority and Responsibilities*

The Television Code Review Board is authorized and directed:

(1) To recommend to the Television Board of Directors amendments to the Television Code; (2) to consider, in its discretion, any appeal from any decision made by the Code Authority Director with respect to any matter which has arisen under the Code, and to suspend, reverse, or modify any such decision; (3) to prefer formal charges, looking toward the suspension or revocation of the authority to show the Code seal, to the Television Board of Directors concerning violations and breaches of the Television Code by a subscriber; (4) to be available to the Code Authority Director for consultation on any and all matters affecting the Television Code.

VII. Code Authority Director

Section 1. *Director*

There shall be a position designated as the Code Authority Director. This position shall be filled by appointment of the President of NAB, subject to the approval of the Board of Directors

Section 2. *Authority and Responsibilities*

The Code Authority Director is authorized and directed: (1) To maintain a continuing review of all programming and advertising material presented over television, especially that of subscribers to the Television Code of NAB; (2) to receive, screen and clear complaints concerning television programming; (3) to define and interpret words and phrases in the Television Code; (4) to develop and maintain appropriate liaison with governmental agencies and with responsible and accountable organizations and institutions; (5) to inform, expeditiously and properly, a subscriber to the Television Code of complaints or commendations, as well as to advise all subscribers concerning the attitudes and desires program-wise of accountable organizations and institutions, and of the American public in general; (6) to review and monitor, if necessary, any certain series of programs, daily programming, or any other program presentations of a subscriber, as well as to request recorded material, or script and copy, with regard to any certain program presented by a subscriber; (7) to reach conclusions and make recommendations or prefer charges to the Television Code Review Board concerning violations and breaches of the Television Code by a subscriber; (8) to recommend to the Code Review Board amendments to the Television Code.

A. *Delegation of Powers and Responsibilities:*

The Code Authority Director shall appoint such executive staff as is needed, consistent with resources, to carry out the above described functions, and may delegate to this staff such responsibilities as he may deem necessary.

THE RADIO CODE

"Reprinted from The Radio Code, published by the Code Authority, National Association of Broadcasters, Nineteenth Edition, June 1975."

PREAMBLE

In 1937 a major segment of U.S. commercial radio broadcasters first adopted industry-wide standards of practice. The purpose of such standards then, as now, is to establish guideposts and professional tenets for performance in the areas of programming and advertising content.

Admittedly, such standards for broadcasting can never be final or complete, because broadcasting is a creative art, always seeking new ways to achieve maximum appeal and service. Therefore, its standards are subject to periodic revision to reasonably reflect changing attitudes in our society.

In 1945 after two years devoted to reviewing and revising the 1937 document, new standards were promulgated. Further revisions were made in subsequent years when deemed necessary. The objectives behind them have been to assure that advertising messages be presented in an honest, responsible and tasteful manner and that broadcasters, in their programming, tailor their content to meet the needs and expectations of that particular audience to which their programming is directed.

The growth of broadcasting as a medium of entertainment, education and information has been made possible by its commercial underpinning. This aspect of commercial broadcasting as it has developed in the United States has enabled the industry to grow as a free medium in the tradition of American enterprise. The extent of this freedom is underscored by those laws which prohibit censorship of broadcast material. Rather, those who own the nation's radio broadcasting stations operate them—pursuant to this self-adopted Radio Code—in recognition of the needs of the American people and the reasonable self-interests of broadcasters and broadcast advertisers.

THE RADIO BROADCASTER'S CREED

We Believe:

That Radio Broadcasting in the United States of America is a living symbol of democracy; a significant and necessary instrument for maintaining freedom of expression, as established by the First Amendment to the Constitution of the United States;

That its contributions to the arts, to science, to education, to commerce, and therefore to the public welfare have the potential of influencing the common good achievements of our society as a whole;

That it is our obligation to serve the people in such manner as to reflect credit upon our profession and to encourage aspiration toward a better estate for our audiences. This entails making available to them through all phases of the broadcasting art such programming as will convey the traditional strivings of the U.S. towards goals beneficial to the populace;

That we should make full and ingenious use of the many sources of knowledge, talents and skills and exercise critical and discerning judgment concerning all broadcasting operations to the end that we may, intelligently and sympathetically:

Observe both existing principles and developing concepts affecting our society;

Respect and advance the rights and the dignity of all people;

Enrich the daily life of the people through the factual reporting and analysis of news, and through programming of education, entertainment, and information;

Provide for the fair discussion of matters of public concern; engage in works directed toward the common good; and volunteer our aid and comfort in times of stress and emergency;

Contribute to the economic welfare of all by expanding the channels of trade, by encouraging the development and conservation of natural resources, and by bringing together the buyer and seller through the broadcasting of information pertaining to goods and services.

Toward the achievement of these purposes we agree to observe the following:

I. PROGRAM STANDARDS

A. News

Radio is unique in its capacity to reach the largest number of people first with reports on current events. This competitive advantage bespeaks caution—being first is not as important as being accurate. The Radio Code standards relating to the treatment of news and public events are, because of constitutional considerations, intended to be exhortatory. The standards set forth hereunder encourage high standards of professionalism in broadcast journalism. They are not to be interpreted as turning over to others the broadcaster's responsibility as to judgments necessary in news and public events programming.

1. *News Sources.* Those responsible for news on radio should exercise constant professional care in the selection of sources—on the premise that the integrity of the news and the consequent good reputation of radio as a dominant well-balanced news medium depend largely upon the reliability of such sources.

2. *News Reporting.* News reporting should be factual, fair and without bias. Good taste should prevail in the selection and handling of news. Morbid, sensational, or alarming details not essential to factual reporting should be avoided. News should be broadcast in such a manner as to avoid creation of panic and unnecessary alarm. Broadcasters should be diligent in their supervision of content, format, and presentation of news broadcasts. Equal diligence should be exercised in selection of editors and reporters who direct news gathering and dissemination, since the station's performance in this vital informational field depends largely upon them.

3. *Commentaries and Analyses.* Special obligations devolve upon those who analyse and/or comment upon news developments, and management should be satisfied completely that the task is to be performed in the best interest of the listening public. Programs of news analysis and commentary should be clearly identified as such, distinguishing them from straight news reporting.

4. *Editorializing.* Broadcasts in which stations express their own opinions about issues of general public interest should be clearly identified as editorials.

5. *Coverage of News and Public Events.* In the coverage of news and public events broadcasters should exercise their judgments consonant with the accepted standards of ethical journalism and should provide accurate, informed and adequate coverage.

6. *Placement of Advertising.* Broadcasters should exercise particular discrimination in the acceptance, placement and presentation of advertising in news programs so that such advertising is clearly distinguishable from the news content.

B. Controversial Public Issues

1. Radio provides a valuable forum for the expression of responsible views on public issues of a controversial nature. Controversial public issues of importance to fellow citizens should give fair representation to opposing sides of issues.

2. Requests by individuals, groups or organizations for time to discuss their views on controversial public issues should be considered on the basis of their individual merits, and in the light of the contributions which the use requested would make to the public interest.

3. Discussion of controversial public issues should not be presented in a manner which would create the impression that the program is other than one dealing with a public issue.

C. Community Responsibility

1. Broadcasters and their staffs occupy a position of responsibility in the community and should conscientiously endeavor to be acquainted with its needs and characteristics to best serve the welfare of its citizens.

2. Requests for time for the placement of public service announcements or programs should be carefully reviewed with respect to the character and reputation of the group, campaign or organization involved, the public

interest content of the message, and the manner of its presentation.

D. Political Broadcasts

1. Political broadcasts, or the dramatization of political issues designed to influence voters, shall be properly identified as such.

2. Political broadcasts should not be presented in a manner which would mislead listeners to believe that they are of any other character.
(Reference: Communications Act of 1934, as amended, Secs. 315 and 317, and FCC Rules and Regulations, Secs. 3.654, 3.657, 3.663, as discussed in NAB's "Political Broadcast Catechism & The Fairness Doctrine.")

3. Because of the unique character of political broadcasts and the necessity to retain broad freedoms of policy void of restrictive interference, it is incumbent upon all political candidates and all political parties to observe the canons of good taste and political ethics, keeping in mind the intimacy of broadcasting in the American home.

E. Advancement of Education and Culture

1. Because radio is an integral part of American life, there is inherent in radio broadcasting a continuing opportunity to enrich the experience of living through the advancement of education and culture.

2. Radio broadcasters, in augmenting the educational and cultural influences of the home, schools, religious institutions and institutions of higher education and other entities should:

   (a) be thoroughly conversant with the educational and cultural needs and aspirations of the community served;

   (b) develop programming consonant with the stations particular target audience.

F. Religion and Religious Programming

1. Religious programming shall be presented by responsible individuals, groups or organizations.

2. Radio broadcasting reaches audiences of all creeds simultaneously. Therefore, both the advocates of broad or ecumenical religious precepts, and the exponents of specific doctrines, are urged to present their positions in a manner conducive to listener enlightenment on the role of religion in society.

G. Responsibility Toward Children

Broadcasters have a special responsibility to children. Programming which might reasonably be expected to hold the attention of children should be presented with due regard for its effect on children.

1. Programming should be based upon sound social concepts and should include positive sets of values which will allow children to become responsible adults, capable of coping with the challenges of maturity.

2. Programming should convey a reasonable range of the realities which exist in the world to help children make the transition to adulthood.

3. Programming should contribute to the healthy development of personality and character.

4. Programming should afford opportunities for cultural growth as well as for wholesome entertainment.

5. Programming should be consistent with integrity of realistic production, but should avoid material of extreme nature which might create undesirable emotional reaction in children.

6. Programming should avoid appeals urging children to purchase the product specifically for the purpose of keeping the program on the air or which, for any reason, encourage children to enter inappropriate places.

7. Programming should present such subjects as violence and sex without undue emphasis and only as required by plot development or character delineation.

Violence, physical or psychological, should only be projected in responsibly handled contexts, not used to excess or exploitatively. Programs involving violence should present the consequences of it to its victims and perpetrators.

The depiction of conflict, and of material reflective of sexual considerations, when presented in programs designed primarily for children, should be handled with sensitivity.

8. The treatment of criminal activities should always convey their social and human effects.

H. Dramatic Programming

1. In the design of dramatic programs it is in the interest of radio as a vital medium to encourage those that are innovative, reflect a high degree of creative skill, deal with significant moral and social issues and present challenging concepts and other subject matter that relate to the world in which the listener lives.

2. Radio programming should not only reflect the influence of the established institutions that shape our values and culture, but also expose the dynamics of social change which bear upon our lives.

3. To achieve these goals, radio broadcasters should be conversant with the general and specific needs, interests and aspirations of all the segments of the communities they serve.

4. Radio should reflect realistically the experience of living, in both its pleasant and tragic aspects, if it is to serve the listener honestly. Nevertheless, it holds a concurrent obligation to provide programming which will encourage positive adjustments to life.

In selecting program subjects and themes, great care must be exercised to be sure that treatment and presentation are made in good faith and not for the purpose of sensationalism or to shock or exploit the audience or appeal to prurient interests or morbid curiosity.

5. In determining the acceptability of any dramatic program, especially those containing elements of crime, mystery, or horror, consideration should be given to the possible effect on all members of the listening audience.

In addition, without sacrificing integrity of presentation, dramatic programs on radio shall avoid:

(a) the presentation of techniques of crime in such detail as to be instructional or invite imitation;

(b) presentation of the details of violence involving the excessive, the gratuitous and the instructional;

(c) sound effects calculated to mislead, shock, or unduly alarm the listener;

(d) portrayals of law enforcement in a manner which does not contribute to its proper role in our society.

I. General

1. The intimacy and confidence placed in radio demand of the broadcaster, the networks and other program sources that they be vigilant in protecting the audience from deceptive broadcast practices.

2. Sound effects and expressions characteristically associated with news broadcasts (such as "bulletin," "flash," "we interrupt this program to bring you," etc.) shall be reserved for announcement of news, and the use of any deceptive techniques in connection with fictional events and non-news programming shall not be employed.

3. The broadcasters shall be constantly alert to prevent inclusion of elements within programming dictated by factors other than the requirements of the programming itself. The acceptance of cash payments or other considerations in return for including the choice and identification of prizes, the selection of music and other creative programming elements and inclusion of any identification of commercial products or services, trade names or advertising slogans within the programming are prohibited unless consideration for such inclusion is revealed to the listeners in accordance with Sections 317 and 508 of the Communications Act.

4. Special precautions should be taken to avoid demeaning or ridiculing members of the audience who suffer from physical or mental afflictions or deformities.

5. The broadcast of gambling sequences deemed necessary to the development of plot or as appropriate background is acceptable only when presented with discretion and in moderation, and in a manner which would not

excite interest in, or foster, betting nor be instructional in nature.

6. Quiz and similar programming that is presented as a contest of knowledge, information, skill or luck must, in fact, be a genuine contest and the results must not be controlled by collusion with or between contestants, or by any other action which will favor one contestant against any other.

7. Contests may not constitute a lottery.

8. Listener contests should not mislead as to the nature or value of prizes, likelihood of winning, nor encourage thoughtless or unsafe acts.

9. No programming shall be presented in a manner which through artifice or simulation would mislead the audience as to any material fact. Each broadcaster must exercise reasonable judgment to determine whether a particular method of presentation would constitute a material deception, or would be accepted by the audience as normal theatrical illusion.

10. Legal, medical and other professional advice will be permitted only in conformity with law and recognized ethical and professional standards.

11. Narcotic addiction shall not be presented except as a destructive habit. The use of illegal drugs or the abuse of legal drugs shall not be encouraged or be presented as desirable or socially acceptable.

12. Material pertaining to fortune-telling, occultism, astrology, phrenology, palm-reading, numerology, mind-reading, character-reading, or subjects of a like nature, is unacceptable if it encourages people to regard such fields as providing commonly accepted appraisals of life.

13. Representations of liquor and smoking shall be de-emphasized. When represented, they should be consistent with plot and character development.

14. Obscene, indecent or profane matter, as proscribed by law, is unacceptable.

15. Special sensitivity is necessary in the use of material relating to sex, race, color, creed, religious functionaries or rites, or national or ethnic derivation.

16. The presentation of marriage, the family and similarly important human relationships, and material with sexual connotations, should not be treated exploitatively or irresponsibly, but with sensitivity.

17. Broadcasts of actual sporting events at which on-the-scene betting is permitted by law should be presented in a manner in keeping with federal, state and local laws, and should concentrate on the subject as a public sporting event.

18. Detailed exposition of hypnosis or material capable of having an hypnotic effect on listeners is forbidden.

19. Any technique whereby an attempt is made to convey information to the listener by transmitting messages below the threshold of normal awareness is not permitted.

20. The commonly accepted standards of humane animal treatment should be adhered to as applicable in programming.

21. Broadcasters are responsible for making good faith determinations on the acceptability of lyrics under applicable Radio Code standards.

22. The standards of this Code covering programming content are also understood to include, wherever applicable, the standards contained in the advertising section of the Code.

23. To assure that broadcasters have the freedom to program fully and responsibly, none of the provisions of this Code should be construed as preventing or impeding broadcasts of the broad range of material necessary to help broadcasters fulfill their obligations to operate in the public interest.

II. ADVERTISING STANDARDS

Advertising is the principle source of revenue of the free, competitive American system of radio broadcasting. It makes possible the presentation to all American people of the finest programs of entertainment, education, and information.

Since the great strength of American radio broadcasting derives from the public respect for and the public approval of its programs, it must be the purpose of each broadcaster to establish and maintain high standards of performance, not only in the selection and production of all programs, but also in the presentation of advertising.

This Code establishes basic standards for all radio broadcasting. The principles of acceptability and good taste within the Program Standards section govern the presentation of advertising where applicable. In addition, the Code establishes in this section special standards which apply to radio advertising.

A. General Advertising Standards

1. A commercial radio broadcaster makes his facilities available for the advertising of products and services and accepts commercial presentations for such advertising. However, he shall, in recognition of his responsibility to the public, refuse the facilities of his station to an advertiser where he has good reason to doubt the integrity of the advertiser, the truth of the advertising representations, or the compliance of the advertiser with the spirit and purpose of all applicable legal requirements.

2. In consideration of the customs and attitudes of the communities served, each radio broadcaster should refuse his facilities to the advertisement of products and services, or the use of advertising scripts, which the station has good reason to believe would be objectionable to a substantial and responsible segment of the community. These standards should be applied with judgment and flexibility, taking into consideration the characteristics of the medium, its home and family audi-ence, and the form and content of the particular presentation.

B. Presentation of Advertising

1. The advancing techniques of the broadcast art have shown that the quality and proper integration of advertising copy are just as important as measurement in time. The measure of a station's service to its audience is determined by its overall performance.

2. The final measurement of any commercial broadcast service is quality. To this, every broadcaster shall dedicate his best effort.

3. Great care shall be exercised by the broadcaster to prevent the presentation of false, misleading or deceptive advertising. While it is entirely appropriate to present a product in a favorable light and atmosphere, the presentation must not, by copy or demonstration, involve a material deception as to the characteristics or performance of a product.

4. The broadcaster and the advertiser should exercise special caution with the content and presentation of commercials placed in or near programs designed for children. Exploitation of children should be avoided. Commercials directed to children should in no way mislead as to the product's performance and usefulness. Appeals involving matters of health which should be determined by physicians should be avoided.

5. Reference to the results of research, surveys or tests relating to the product to be advertised shall not be presented in a manner so as to create an impression of fact beyond that established by the study. Surveys, tests or other research results upon which claims are based must be conducted under recognized research techniques and standards.

C. Acceptability of Advertisers and Products

In general, because radio broadcasting is designed for the home and the entire family, the following principles shall govern the business classifications:

1. The advertising of hard liquor shall not be accepted.

2. The advertising of beer and wines is acceptable when presented in the best of good taste and discretion.

3. The advertising of fortune-telling, occultism, astrology, phrenology, palm-reading, numerology, mind-reading, character-reading, or subjects of a like nature, is not acceptable.

4. Because the advertising of all products and services of a personal nature raises special problems, such advertising, when accepted, should be treated with emphasis on ethics and the canons of good taste, and presented in a restrained and inoffensive manner.

5. The advertising of tip sheets and other publications seeking to advertise for the purpose of giving odds or promoting betting is unacceptable.

The lawful advertising of government organizations which conduct legalized lotteries is acceptable provided such advertising does not unduly exhort the public to bet.

The advertising of private or governmental organizations which conduct legalized betting on sporting contests is acceptable provided such advertising is limited to institutional type announcements which do not exhort the public to bet.

6. An advertiser who markets more than one product shall not be permitted to use advertising copy devoted to an acceptable product for purposes of publicizing the brand name or other identification of a product which is not acceptable.

7. Care should be taken to avoid presentation of "bait-switch" advertising whereby goods or services which the advertiser has no intention of selling are offered merely to lure the customer into purchasing higher-priced substitutes.

8. Advertising should offer a product or service on its positive merits and refrain from discrediting, disparaging or unfairly attacking competitors, competing products, other industries, professions or institutions.

Any identification or comparison of a competitive product or service, by name, or other means, should be confined to specific facts rather than generalized statements or conclusions, unless such statements or conclusions are not derogatory in nature.

9. Advertising testimonials should be genuine, and reflect an honest appraisal of personal experience.

10. Advertising by institutions or enterprises offering instruction with exaggerated claims for opportunities awaiting those who enroll, is unacceptable.

11. The advertising of firearms/ammunition is acceptable provided it promotes the product only as sporting equipment and conforms to recognized standards of safety as well as all applicable laws and regulations. Advertisements of firearms ammunition by mail order are unacceptable.

D. Advertising of Medical Products

Because advertising for over-the-counter products involving health considerations are of intimate and far-reaching importance to the consumer, the following principles should apply to such advertising:

1. When dramatized advertising material involves statements by doctors, dentists, nurses or other professional people, the material should be presented by members of such profession reciting actual experience, or it should be made apparent from the presentation itself that the portrayal is dramatized.

2. Because of the personal nature of the advertising of medical products, the indiscriminate use of such words as "Safe," "Without Risk," "Harmless," or other terms of similar meaning, either direct or implied, should not be expressed in the advertising of medical products.

3. Advertising material which offensively describes or dramatizes distress or morbid situations involving ailments is not acceptable.

E. Time Standards for Advertising Copy

1. The amount of time to be used for advertising should not exceed 18 minutes within any clock hour. The Code Authority, however, for good cause may approve advertising exceed-

ing the above standard for special circumstances.

2. Any reference to another's products or services under any trade name, or language sufficiently descriptive to identify it, shall, except for normal guest identification, be considered as advertising copy.

3. For the purpose of determining advertising limitations, such program types as "classified," "swap shop," "shopping guides," and "farm auction" programs, etc., shall be regarded as containing one and one-half minutes of advertising for each five-minute segment.

F. Contests

1. Contests shall be conducted with fairness to all entrants, and shall comply with all pertinent laws and regulations.

2. All contest details, including rules, eligibility requirements, opening and termination dates, should be clearly and completely announced or easily accessible to the listening public; and the winners' names should be released as soon as possible after the close of the contest.

3. When advertising is accepted which requests contestants to submit items of product identification or other evidence of purchase of products, reasonable facsimiles thereof should be made acceptable. However, when the award is based upon skill and not upon chance, evidence of purchase may be required.

4. All copy pertaining to any contest (except that which is required by law) associated with the exploitation or sale of the sponsor's product or service, and all references to prizes or gifts offered in such connection should be considered a part of and included in the total time limitations heretofore provided. *(See Time Standards for Advertising Copy.)*

G. Premiums and Offers

1. The broadcaster should require that full details of proposed offers be submitted for investigation and approval before the first an-

nouncement of the offer is made to the public.

2. A final date for the termination of an offer should be announced as far in advance as possible.

3. If a consideration is required, the advertiser should agree to honor complaints indicating dissatisfaction with the premium by returning the consideration.

4. There should be no misleading descriptions or comparisons of any premiums or gifts which will distort or enlarge their value in the minds of the listeners.

REGULATIONS AND PROCEDURES

The following Regulations and Procedures shall obtain as an integral part of the Radio Code of the National Association of Broadcasters:

I. Name

The name of this Code shall be the Radio Code of the National Association of Broadcasters, hereinafter referred to as the Radio Code.*

Definitions:

Wherever reference is made to programs it shall be construed to include all program material including commercials.

II. Purpose of the Code

The purpose of this Code is cooperatively to establish and maintain a level of radio programming which gives full consideration to the educational, informational, cultural, economic, moral and entertainment needs of the American public to the end that more and more people will be better served.

III. The Radio Code Board

Section 1. Composition

There shall be a continuing Committee entitled the Radio Code Board.* The Code Board shall be composed of 11 members. Members of the Radio Board shall not be eligible to serve on the above specified Board. The Chairman and members of the Code Board shall be appointed by the President of the NAB, subject to confirmation by the Radio Board, and may include no more than two members as representatives of subscribing nationwide radio networks. Due consideration shall be given, in making such appointments, to factors of diversification, such as market size, geographical location, network affiliation, class of broadcast service, etc. The

---

*The Radio Board of the NAB shall have power: "to enact, amend and promulgate Radio Standards of Practice or Codes, and to establish such methods to secure observance thereof as it may deem advisable;—." By-Laws of the National Association of Broadcasters, Article VI, section 8, B. Radio Board.

Board shall be fully representative of the radio industry. All Code Board members shall be selected from subscribers to the Radio Code. In every odd-numbered year, four members shall be appointed for two-year terms; in every even-numbered year, five members shall be appointed for two-year terms provided, however, that network representatives be rotated on an annual basis. Appointments become effective at the conclusion of the annual NAB convention of the year in which appointments are made.

A. Limitation of Service:

A person shall not serve consecutively as a member of the Board for more than two two-year terms or for more than four years consecutively provided, however, that appointment to fill an unexpired term shall not count toward the limitation of service as previously stated.

Network representatives on the Radio Code Board shall be limited to non-consecutive two-year terms; provided, in the first year of such representation one network member may be appointed for a one-year term and one for a two-year term. Thereafter, all network members may be appointed for two-year terms. Any one network representative may be reappointed following an interim two-year period.

A majority of the membership of the Radio Code Board shall constitute a quorum for all purposes unless herein otherwise provided.

Section 2. Authorities and Responsibilities

The Radio Code Board is authorized and directed:

(1) To recommend to the Radio Board amendments to the Radio Code; (2) to consider in its discretion, any appeal from any decision made by the Code Authority Director with respect to any matter which has arisen under the Code, and to suspend, reverse, or modify any such decision; (3) to prefer formal charges, looking toward the suspension or revocation of the subscription and/or the authority to use the Radio Code Audio and Visual Symbols, to the Radio Board concerning violations and breaches of the Radio Code by a subscriber; (4) to be available to the Code Au-

thority Director for consultation on any and all matters affecting the Radio Code.

A. *Meetings:*

The Radio Code Board shall meet regularly semi-annually on a date to be determined by the Chairman. The Chairman of the Board may, at any time, on at least five days' written notice, call a special meeting of the Board.

IV. Code Authority Director

Section 1. Director

There shall be a position designated as the Code Authority Director. This position shall be filled by appointment of the President of NAB, subject to the approval of the Board of Directors.

Section 2. Authority and Responsibilities

The Code Authority Director is responsible for the administration, interpretation and enforcement of the Radio Code. In furtherance of this responsibility he is authorized and directed:

(1) To maintain a continuing review of all programming and advertising material presented over radio, especially that of subscribers to the Radio Code of NAB; (2) to receive, screen and clear complaints concerning radio programming; (3) to define and interpret words and phrases in the Radio Code; (4) to develop and maintain appropriate liaison with governmental agencies and with responsible and accountable organizations and institutions; (5) to inform, expeditiously and properly, a subscriber to the Radio Code of complaints or commendations, as well as to advise all subscribers concerning the attitudes and desires program-wise of accountable organizations and institutions, and of the American public in general; (6) to receive and monitor, if necessary, any certain series of programs, daily programming, or any other program presentations of a subscriber, as well as to request recorded material, or script and copy, with regard to any certain program presented by a subscriber; (7) to reach conclusions and make recommendations or prefer charges to the Radio Code Board concerning violations and breaches of the Radio Code by a sub-

scriber; (8) to recommend to the Code Board amendments to the Radio Code; (9) to take such action as may be necessary to enforce the Code, including revocation of subscription as hereinafter provided in Chapter V, Section 4.

A. *Delegation of Powers and Responsibilities:*

The Code Authority Director shall appoint such executive staff as is needed, consistent with resources, to carry out the above described functions, and may delegate to this staff such responsibilities as he may deem necessary.

V. Subscribers

Section 1. Eligibility

A. Any individual, firm or corporation which is engaged in the operation of a radio broadcast station or radio network; or which holds a construction permit for a radio broadcast station within the United States or its dependencies, shall, subject to the approval of the Radio Board, as hereinafter provided, be eligible to subscribe to the Radio Code of the NAB to the extent of one subscription for each such station or network, or each station which holds a construction permit; provided, that a non-radio member of NAB shall not become eligible via Code subscription to receive any of the member services or to exercise any of the voting privileges of a member.

B. The Radio Code Board may recommend categories of affiliate subscribers as may be desired, together with applicable fees for such affiliate subscriptions.

Section 2. Certification of Subscription

Upon subscribing to the Code there shall be granted forthwith to each such subscribing station authority to use such copyrighted and registered audio and visual symbols as will be provided. The symbols and their significance shall be appropriately publicized by the NAB.

Section 3. Duration of Subscription

Subscription shall continue in full force and effect until there has been received a written notice of resignation or until subscription is revoked by action of the Code Authority, the Radio Code Board or the Radio Board of Directors.

Section 4. *Revocation of Subscription*

Any subscription and/or the authority to utilize the above-noted symbols, may be voided, revoked or temporarily suspended for radio programming, including commercial copy, which, by theme, treatment or incident, in the judgment of the Code Authority constitutes a continuing, willful or gross violation of any of the provisions of the Radio Code; provided, however, that the following conditions and procedures shall govern:

A. *Conditions Precedent:*

Prior to Revocation of Subscription, the Code Authority (1) Shall appropriately inform the subscriber of any and all complaints and information it possesses relating to the programming of said subscriber, (2) Shall have reported to, and advised, said subscriber by analysis, interpretation, recommendation or otherwise, of the possibility of a violation or breach of the Radio Code, and (3) Shall have served upon the subscriber by registered mail a Notice of Intent To Revoke Subscription; such Notice shall contain a statement of the grounds and reasons for the proposed revocation, including appropriate references to the Radio Code and shall give the subscriber 30 days to take such action as will satisfy the Code Authority. During this interim period the Code Authority may, within its sole discretion, reconsider its proposed action based upon such written reply as the subscriber may care to make, or upon such action as the subscriber may care to take program-wise, in conformance with the analysis, interpretation or recommendation of the Code Authority. If upon termination of the 30 day period, no such action has been taken or the subscriber has not requested a hearing, as hereinafter provided, his subscription to the Code shall be considered revoked.

B. *Time:*

In the event that the nature of the program in question is such that the Code Authority deems time to be of the essence, the Code Authority may limit the time in which compliance must be made, provided that a time certain in which subscriber may reply is included in the Notice of Intent, and provided further that the Code Authority's reasons therefor are specified in its Notice of Intent To Revoke Subscription.

C. *Hearing:*

The subscriber shall have the right to a hearing before the Code Board by requesting same and by filing an answer within 20 days of the date of receipt of the Notice of Intent. Said answer and request for hearing shall be directed to the Chairman of the Code Board with a copy to the Code Authority.

D. *Waiver:*

Failure to request a hearing shall be deemed a waiver of the subscriber's right thereto. If a hearing is requested, action of the Code Authority is suspended pending decision of the Code Board.

E. *Designation:*

If hearing is requested by the subscriber, it shall be designated as promptly as possible and at such time and place as the Code Board may specify.

F. *Confidential Status:*

Hearings shall be closed; and all correspondence between a subscriber and the Code Authority and/or the Code Board concerning specific programming shall be confidential; provided, however, that the confidential status of these procedures may be waived by a subscriber.

G. *Presentation; Representation:*

A subscriber who has exercised his right to a hearing, shall be entitled to effect presentation of his case personally, by agent, by attorney, or by deposition and interrogatory.

H. *Intervention:*

Upon request by the subscriber-respondent or the Code Authority, the Code Board, in its discretion, may permit the intervention of one or more subscribers as parties-in-interest.

I. *Transcript:*

A stenographic transcript record may be taken if requested by respondent and shall be certified by the Chairman of the Code Board to the Office of the Secretary of the National Association of Broadcasters, where it shall be maintained. The transcript shall not be open to inspection unless otherwise provided by the party respondent in the proceeding.

J. *Code Authority; Counsel:*

The Code Authority may, at its discretion, utilize the services of an attorney from the staff of the NAB for the purpose of effecting its presentation in a hearing matter.

K. *Order of Procedure:*

At hearings, the Code Authority shall open and close.

L. *Cross-Examination:*

The right of cross-examination shall specifically obtain. Where procedure has been by deposition or interrogatory, the use of cross-interrogatories shall satisfy this right.

M. *Presentation:*

Oral and written evidence may be introduced by the subscriber and by the Code Authority. Oral argument may be had at the hearing and written memoranda or briefs may be submitted by the subscriber and by the Code Authority. The Code Board may admit such evidence as it deems relevant, material and competent, and may determine the nature and length of the oral argument and the written argument or briefs.

N. *Transcriptions, etc.:*

Records, transcriptions, or other mechanical reproductions of radio programs, properly identified, shall be accepted into evidence when relevant.

O. *Authority of Presiding Officer of Code Board:*

The Presiding Officer shall rule upon all interlocutory matters, such as, but not limited to, the admissibility of evidence, the qualifications of witnesses, etc. On all other matters, authority to act shall be vested in a majority of the Code Board unless otherwise provided.

P. *Continuances and Extensions:*

Continuance and extension of any proceeding or for the time of filing or performing any act required or allowed to be done within a specific time may be granted upon request, for a good cause shown.. The Code Board or the Presiding Officer may recess or adjourn a hearing for such time as may be deemed necessary, and may change the place thereof.

Q. *Findings and Conclusions:*

The Code Board shall decide the case as expeditiously as possible and shall notify the subscriber, Code Authority, and the Radio Board in writing, of the decision. The decision of the Code Board shall contain findings of fact with conclusions, as well as the reasons or bases therefor. Findings of fact shall set out in detail and with particularity all basic evidentiary facts developed on the record (with appropriate citations to the transcript of record or exhibit relied on for each evidentiary fact) supporting the conclusion reached.

R. *Disqualification:*

Any member of the Code Board may disqualify himself, or upon good cause shown by any interested party, may be disqualified by a majority vote of the Code Board.

S. *Review:*

A request for review of the Code Board's decision may be filed by the subscriber with the Radio Board. Such petition for review must be served upon the Chairman of the Radio Board within 10 days after receipt by the subscriber of the Code Board's decision.

T. *Penalty, Suspension of:*

At the discretion of the Code Board, application of any penalty provided for in the decision may be suspended until the Radio Board makes final disposition of the Petition For Review. The entire record in the proceedings before the Code Board shall be certified to the Radio Board. The review will be limited to written statements and no provision is made for further oral argument.

U. *Final Decision:*

The Radio Board shall have the discretion upon review to uphold, reverse, or amend with direction the decision of the Code Board. The decision of the Radio Board is final.

Section 5. Additional Procedures

When necessary to the proper administration of the Code, additional rules of procedure will be established from time to time as authorized by the By-Laws of the NAB; in keeping therewith, special consideration shall be given to the procedures for receipts and processing of complaints and to necessary rules to be adopted from time to time, taking into account the source and nature of such complaints; such rules to include precautionary measures such as the posting of bonds to cover costs and expenses of processing same; and further provided that special consideration will be given to procedures insuring the confidential status of proceedings relating to Code observance.

Section 6. Amendment and Review

The Radio Code may be amended from time to time by the Radio Board which shall specify the effective date of each amendment; provided, that said Board is specifically charged with review and reconsideration of the entire Code, its appendices and procedures, at least once each year.

Section 7. Termination of Contracts

All subscribers on the air shall be in compliance at the time of subscription to the Code.

VI. Rates

Each subscriber shall pay fees in accordance with such schedule, at such time, and under such conditions as may be determined from time to time by the Radio Board *(See Article VI, section 8, B. Radio Board By-Laws of the NAB)*.

Index